GOVERNMENTAL INSTITUTIONS AND PROCESSES

HANDBOOK OF POLITICAL SCIENCE

Volume 5

GOVERNMENTAL INSTITUTIONS AND PROCESSES

Edited by
FRED I. GREENSTEIN Princeton University
NELSON W. POLSBY University of California, Berkeley

 **ADDISON-WESLEY PUBLISHING COMPANY**

Reading, Massachusetts
Menlo Park, California • London • Amsterdam • Don Mills, Ontario • Sydney

This book is in the
ADDISON-WESLEY SERIES IN POLITICAL SCIENCE

Copyright © 1975 by Addison-Wesley Publishing Company, Inc. Philippines copyright 1975
by Addison-Wesley Publishing Company, Inc.

ISBN 0-201-02605-8
ABCDEFGHIJ-HA-798765

PREFACE

Early in his career, the fledgling political scientist learns that his discipline is ill-defined, amorphous, and heterogeneous. This perception will in no way be rebutted by the appearance of a presumably encyclopedic eight-volume work entitled *The Handbook of Political Science*. Indeed, the persistent amorphousness of our discipline has constituted a central challenge to the editors of the *Handbook* and has brought to its creation both hazards and opportunities. The opportunities were apparent enough to us when we took on the editorial duties of the *Handbook;* the hazards became clearer later on.

At the outset, it seemed to us a rare occasion when a publisher opens quite so large a canvas and invites a pair of editors to paint on it as they will—or can. We immediately saw that in order to do the job at all we would have to cajole a goodly number of our colleagues into the belief that our canvas was in reality Tom Sawyer's fence. We did not set out at the beginning, however, with a precise vision of the final product—i.e., a work that would be composed of these particular eight volumes, dealing with the present array and number of contributions and enlisting all the present contributors. Rather, the *Handbook* is the product of a long and in some ways accidental process. An account of this process is in order if only because, by describing the necessarily adventitious character of the "decisions" that produced this work, we can help the reader to see that the *Handbook* is not an attempt to make a collective pronouncement of Truth chiseled in stone, but rather an assembly of contributions, each an individual scholarly effort, whose overall purpose is to give a warts-and-all portrait of a discipline that is still in a process of becoming.

We first became involved in discussions about the project in 1965. Addison-Wesley had already discussed the possibility of a handbook with a number of other political scientists, encouraged by their happy experience with a two-volume compendium of highly respected review essays in social psychology (Lindzey, 1954), which has since been revised and expanded into a five-volume work (Lindzey and Aronson, 1968–69).

Of the various people to whom Addison-Wesley aired the handbook idea, we evidently were among the most persistent in encouraging such a project. No doubt the reason was that we were still close to our own graduate work in a department where a careful reading of many of the chapters in *The Handbook of Social Psychology* was in some ways more fundamental to learning our trade than a comparable exposure to many of the more conspicuous intellectual edifices of the political science of the time. Gardner Lindzey, in writing his introductory statement to the first edition of *The Handbook of Social Psychology* (reprinted in the second edition), described *our* needs as well as those of budding social psychologists in saying that

> the accelerating expansion of social psychology in the past two decades has led to an acute need for a source book more advanced than the ordinary textbook in the field but yet more focused than scattered periodical literature. . . . It was this state of affairs that led us to assemble a book that would represent the major areas of social psychology at a level of difficulty appropriate for graduate students. In addition to serving the needs of graduate instruction, we anticipate that the volumes will be useful in advanced undergraduate courses and as a reference book for professional psychologists.

With the substitution of "political science" in the appropriate places, Lindzey's description of his own purposes and audiences reflects precisely what we thought Addison-Wesley might most usefully seek to accomplish with a political science handbook.

In choosing a pair of editors, the publisher might well have followed a balancing strategy, looking for two political scientists who were poles apart in their background, training, and views of the discipline. The publisher might then have sought divine intervention, praying for the miracle that would bring the editors into sufficient agreement to make the planning of the *Handbook*—or *any* handbook—possible at all. Instead they found a pair of editors with complementary but basically similar and congenial perspectives. We were then both teaching at Wesleyan University and had been to graduate school together at Yale, at a time when the political science department there was making its widely recognized contribution to the modernization of the discipline. Each had recently spent a year in the interdisciplinary ambience of the Center for Advanced Study in the Behavioral Sciences. Moreover, we were both specialists in American politics, the "field" which in 1973 still accounted for three-quarters of the contributions to *The American Political Science Review*. There were also complementary divergencies. Within political science, Polsby's work and interests had been in national politics and policy-making, whereas Greenstein's were more in mass, extragovernmental aspects of political behavior. Outside political science, Polsby's interests were directed more toward sociology and law, and Greenstein's tended toward psychiatry and clinical and social psychology.

To begin with, neither we nor the publisher could be sure without first gathering evidence that the discipline of political science was "ready" for a handbook comparable to the Lindzey work. We were sure that, if it was at all possible for us to bring such a handbook into being, we would have to employ the Aristotelian tack of working within and building upon existing categories of endeavor, rather than the Platonic (or Procrustean) mode of inventing a coherent set of master categories and persuading contributors to use them. First, at our request the publisher inquired of a number of distinguished political scientists whether they felt a need would be served by a handbook of political science similar to *The Handbook of Social Psychology*. This inquiry went to political scientists who had themselves been involved in extensive editorial activities or who were especially known for their attention to political science as a discipline. The responses were quite uniform in favoring such a handbook. The particular suggestions about how such a handbook might be *organized*, however, were exceptionally varied. But fortunately we had asked one further question: What half-dozen or so individuals were so authoritative or original in their contributions on some topic as to make them prime candidates for inclusion in any political science handbook, no matter what its final overall shape? Here agreement reemerged; the consultants were remarkably unanimous in the individuals named.

Seizing the advantage provided by that consensus, we reached the following agreement with the publisher. We would write the individuals who constituted what we now saw as a prime list of candidates for inclusion as authors and ask whether they would be willing to contribute to a handbook of political science, given a long lead time and freedom to choose the topic of their essay. (We did suggest possible topics to each.) It was agreed that unless we were able to enlist most of those with whom we were corresponding as a core group of contributors, we would not proceed with a handbook. Since all but one of that group indicated willingness to contribute, we signed a publishing agreement (in September 1967) and proceeded to expand our core group to a full set of contributors to what we then envisaged as a three-volume handbook, drawing on our core contributors for advice. Our queries to the core contributors were a search not so much for structural and organizational suggestions as for concrete topics and specific contributors to add to the initial list.

The well-worn term "incremental" suggests itself as a summary of how the table of contents of *The Handbook of Political Science* then took shape. As the number of contributors increased, and as contributors themselves continued to make suggestions about possible rearrangements in the division of labor and to remark on gaps, the planned three volumes expanded to eight, most of which, however, were shorter than the originally intended three. Throughout, Addison-Wesley left it to us and the contributors, within the very broadest of boundaries, to define the overall length of the project and of the individual contributions. And throughout, we urged the contributors not to seek intellectual anonymity in the guise of being "merely" summarizers—or embalmers—of their fields but rather to endeavor to place a distinctive intellectual stamp on their contributions.

A necessary condition of enlisting the initial group of contributors was a production deadline so far in the future as to dissolve the concern of rational individuals about adding to their intellectual encumbrances. As it turned out, our "safely remote" initial deadline (1970) was in fact a drastic underestimation of the number of postponements and delays.* Along with delays there have been occasional withdrawals, as individual contributors recognized that even with a long fuse the task of preparing a handbook article would be a major one and would inevitably preempt time from other projects and interests. Departing contributors were often helpful in suggesting alternatives. Both through the late enlistment of such substitutes and through the addition of collaborators taken on by invited contributors, we feel we have been spared a table of contents that anachronistically represents only the cohort of those individuals who were responsible for the shape of political science circa 1967.

Whether one builds a handbook table of contents a priori or ex post facto, *some* basis of organization emerges. We might have organized a handbook around:

1. *"political things"* (e.g., the French bureaucracy, the U.S. Constitution, political parties);

2. *nodes or clusters in the literature* (community power, group theory, issue voting);

3. *subdisciplines* (public administration, public law, comparative government, political theory, international relations);

4. *functions* (planning, law-making, adjudication);

5. *geography* (the American Congress, the British Cabinet, the politicoeconomic institutions of the U.S.S.R.);

6. or any combination of the above and further possibilities.

Any of our colleagues who have tried to construct a curriculum in political science will sympathize with our dilemma. There is, quite simply, no

---

* For the comparable experience of *Handbook of Social Psychology* editors with delays, see Lindzey, 1954, p. vii, Lindzey and Aronson, 1968–69, p. ix.

sovereign way to organize our discipline. Although much of our knowledge is cumulative, there is no set beginning or end to political science. Apart from certain quite restricted subdisciplinary areas (notably the mathematical and statistical), political scientists do not have to learn a particular bit of information or master a particular technique at a particular stage as a prerequisite to further study. And the discipline lacks a single widely accepted frame of reference or principle of organization. Consequently, we evolved a table of contents that to some extent adopted nearly *all* the approaches above. (None of our chapter titles contains a geographical reference, but many of the chapters employ one or more explicitly specified political systems as data sources.)

The protean classifications of subspecialization within political science and the ups and downs in subspecialty interests over the years are extensively reviewed by Dwight Waldo in his essay in Volume 1 on political science as discipline and profession. A further way to recognize the diversity and change in our discipline—as well as the persisting elements—is to note the divisions of disciplinary interests used by the directories of the American Political Science Association, the membership of which constitutes the great bulk of all political scientists. A glance at the three successive directories which have been current during our editorial activities is instructive.

The 1961 *Biographical Directory of the American Political Science Association* (APSA, 1961) represents a last glimpse at a parsimonious, staid set of subdisciplinary categories that would have been readily recognizable at the 1930 Annual Meeting of the Association.

1. American National Government

2. Comparative Government

3. International Law and Relations

4. Political Parties

5. Political Theory

6. Public Administration

7. Public Law

8. State and Local Government

In the next *Biographical Directory* (APSA, 1968), there appeared a categorization that was at once pared down and much expanded from the 1961 classification. A mere three "general fields" were listed. The first was "Contemporary Political Systems." Members electing this general field were asked to specify the country or countries in which they were interested, and those countries were listed parenthetically after the members' names in the subdisciplinary listing, presumably out of a desire to play down the importance of "area studies" as an intellectual focus and to accentuate the importance of functional or analytic bases of intellectual endeavor. "International Law, Organization, and Politics" was the second general field, and "Political Theory and Philosophy" was the third. But the 26 categories in Table 1 were provided for the listing of "specialized fields." They included some venerable subdivisions, perhaps in slightly more fashionable phrasing, and other distinctly nonvenerable subdivisions, at least one of which (political socialization) did not even exist in the general vocabulary of political scientists ten years earlier. In this *Handbook*, the 1968 categories have many parallels, including the general principle of organization that excludes geography as a specialized field criterion while at the same time recognizing that political scientists can and should study and compare diverse political settings. Diplomatically avoiding the presentation of a structured classification, the editors of the 1968 *Directory* relied on the alphabet for their sequence of specialized fields.

TABLE 1 Subdisciplinary categories used in *Biographical Directory* of the American Political Science Association, 1968

1. Administrative law
2. Administration: organization, processes, behavior
3. Budget and fiscal management
4. Constitutional law
5. Executive: organization, processes, behavior
6. Foreign policy
7. Government regulation of business
8. International law
9. International organization and administration
10. International politics
11. Judiciary: organization, processes, behavior
12. Legislature: organization, processes, behavior
13. Methodology
14. Metropolitan and urban government and politics
15. National security policy
16. Personnel administration
17. Political and constitutional history
18. Political parties and elections: organizations and processes
19. Political psychology
20. Political socialization
21. Political theory and philosophy (empirical)
22. Political theory and philosophy (historical)
23. Political theory and philosophy (normative)
24. Public opinion
25. Revolutions and political violence
26. State and local government and politics
27. Voting behavior

Even with this burgeoning of options, many members of the discipline evidently felt that their interests were not adequately covered. Goodly numbers took advantage of an opportunity provided in the questionnaire to the APSA membership to list "other" specialties, referring, for example, to "political sociology," "political behavior," "political development," "policy studies," "communication," "federalism," and "interest groups."

The 1973 *Biographical Directory* (APSA, 1973) attempted still another basis of classification, a revised version of the classification used in the 1970 *National Science Foundation Register of Scientific and Technical Personnel.* Braving a structured rather than alphabetic classification, the authors of this taxonomy divided the discipline into nine major classes and a total of 60 specialized classifications, with a return to the antique dichotomy of foreign versus U.S. politics. The specifics of the 1973 listing are given in Table 2.

TABLE 2 Subdisciplinary categories used in *Biographical Directory* of the American Political Science Association, 1973

I	Foreign and Cross-National Political Institutions and Behavior
1.	Analyses of particular systems or subsystems
2.	Decision-making processes
3.	Elites and their oppositions
4.	Mass participation and communications
5.	Parties, mass movements, secondary associations
6.	Political development and modernization
7.	Politics of planning
8.	Values, ideologies, belief systems, political culture
II	International Law, Organization, and Politics
9.	International law
10.	International organization and administration
11.	International politics
III	Methodology
12.	Computer techniques
13.	Content analysis
14.	Epistemology and philosophy of science
15.	Experimental design
16.	Field data collection
17.	Measurement and index construction
18.	Model building
19.	Statistical analysis
20.	Survey design and analysis
IV	Political Stability, Instability, and Change
21.	Cultural modification and diffusion
22.	Personality and motivation
23.	Political leadership and recruitment
24.	Political socialization
25.	Revolution and violence
26.	Schools and political education
27.	Social and economic stratification

(continued)

As will be evident, the present *Handbook* contains articles on topics that appear on neither of the two recent differentiated lists and omits topics on each. Some "omissions" were inadvertent. Others were deliberate, resulting from our conclusion either that the work on a particular topic did not appear ripe for review at this time or that the topic overlapped sufficiently with others already commissioned so that we might leave it out in the interests of preventing our rapidly expanding project from becoming hopelessly large. There also were instances in which we failed to find (or keep) authors on topics that we might otherwise have included. Hence readers should be forewarned about a feature of the *Handbook* that they should know without forewarning is bound to exist: incompleteness. Each reviewer will note "strange omissions." For us it is more extraordinary that so many able people were willing to invest so much effort in this enterprise.

It should be evident from our history of the project that we consider the rubrics under which scholarly work is classified to be less important than the caliber of the scholarship and that we recognize the incorrigible tendency of inquiry to overflow the pigeonholes to which it has been assigned, as well as the desirability that scholars rather than editors (or other administrators) define the boundaries of their endeavors. Therefore we have used rather simple principles for aggregating essays into their respective volumes and given them straightforward titles.

The essays in Volume 1 on the nature of political theory which follow Waldo's extensive discussion of the scope of political science are far from innocent of reference to empirical matters. This comports with the common observation that matters of theoretical interest are by no means removed from the concerns of the real world. And although we have used the titles *Micropolitical Theory* and *Macropolitical Theory* for Volumes 2 and 3, we have meant no more thereby than to identify the scale and mode of conceptualization typical of the topics in these volumes. Here again the reader will find selections that extensively review empirical findings.

Similarly, although the titles of Volumes 4, 5, and 6 on extragovernmental, governmental, and policy-output aspects of government and politics may appear to imply mere data compilations, the contents of these volumes are far from atheoretical. This is also emphatically true of Volume 8, which carries the title *International Politics*, a field that in recent decades has continuously raised difficult theoretical issues, including issues about the proper nature of theory. Volume 7 carries the title *Strategies of Inquiry* rather than *Methodology* to call attention to the fact that contributors to that volume have emphasized linking techniques of inquiry to substantive issues. In short, contributions to the eight volumes connect in many ways that can be only imperfectly suggested by the editors' table of contents or even by the comprehensive index at the end of Volume 8.

It can scarcely surprise readers of a multiple-authored work to learn that what is before them is a collective effort. It gives us pleasure to acknowledge obligations to five groups of people who helped to lighten our part of the load. First of all, to our contributors we owe a debt of gratitude for their patience, cooperation, and willingness to find the time in their exceedingly busy schedules to produce the essays that make up this *Handbook*. Second, we thank the many helpful Addison-Wesley staff members with whom we have worked for their good cheer toward us and for their optimism about this project. Third, the senior scholars who initially advised Addison-Wesley to undertake the project, and who may even have pointed the publishers in our direction, know who they are. We believe it would add still another burden to the things they must answer for in our profession if we named them publicly, but we want to record our rueful, belated appreciation to them. Fourth, Kathleen Peters and Barbara Kelly in Berkeley and Lee L. Messina, Catherine Smith, and Frances C. Root in Middletown kept the paper flowing back and forth across the country and helped us immeasurably in getting the job done. Finally, our love and gratitude to Barbara Greenstein and Linda Polsby. And we are happy to report to Michael, Amy, and Jessica Greenstein, and to Lisa, Emily, and Daniel Polsby that at long last their fathers are off the long-distance telephone.

Princeton, New Jersey   F.I.G.
Berkeley, California   N.W.P.

REFERENCES

American Political Science Association (1961). *Biographical Directory of The American Political Science Association,* fourth edition. (Franklin L. Burdette, ed.) Washington, D.C.

American Political Science Association (1968). *Biographical Directory,* fifth edition. Washington, D.C.

American Political Science Association (1973). *Biographical Directory,* sixth edition. Washington, D.C.

Lindzey, Gardner, ed. (1954). *Handbook of Social Psychology,* 2 volumes. Cambridge, Mass.: Addison-Wesley.

Lindzey, Gardner, and Elliot Aronson, eds. (1968–69). *The Handbook of Social Psychology,* second edition, 5 volumes. Reading, Mass.: Addison-Wesley.

CONTENTS

CONTENTS OF OTHER VOLUMES IN THIS SERIES

1
CONSTITUTIONALISM

HARVEY WHEELER

INTRODUCTION: THE MYSTIQUE OF CONSTITUTIONALISM

There is something mysterious about government, and even more so about law: government, because it furnishes a practical exemplification of the philosophic proposition that the whole is greater than the sum of its parts; law, because its effort, and sometimes its result, is to bring social order and political stability out of chaos. But constitutionalism stands for an even greater mystery. It purports to guarantee that these attributes of law and government will be directed to the realization of the common good and that this will be achieved through the collective efforts of ordinary people, even though as individuals they might act only from selfish and private motives. On one level this mystique derives from the belief that the rule of law—a direct descendant of medieval natural law—can be made supreme in human affairs. A second doctrine derives from the eighteenth century expositors of constitutionalism. They tended to convey the impression that constitution making was a branch of science, not unlike Newtonian celestial mechanics, and that if one utilized the proper structural principles in making a constitution it would, almost automatically, produce freedom and justice (Lovejoy, 1966, pp. 37–65). This was the political counterpart of the self-regulating mechanism that was then thought to govern the price system in free markets even if people abandoned themselves to private vices. This latter constitutional mystique inhered in special institutional devices for harnessing human power drives to the production of the public good.

In recent times constitutionalism appears to have lost its mysterious self-regulative powers, and the family of its adherents has suffered a grievous decline. As the number of constitutional democracies diminished, the departing members seemed to abandon it roughly in the order of their initial adoption. France had virtually discarded constitutional democracy under de Gaulle. Italy was close behind. Only a few of Britain's imperial progeny remain among the faithful, and even with them the picture is spotty. South Africa has had a quasi-fascist regime for some time. Pakistan has a dictatorship. India is a doubtful member of the family. The prospects for the two Irelands are not bright. Only Canada, Australia, New Zealand, and the United States seem steadfast, and even for this latter group, as with Britain herself, the situation is becoming ever more precarious.

Outside the English-speaking world there are West Germany and the European marcher states, such as Switzerland, Holland, and Belgium. Beyond these lie Scandinavia, and possibly Israel, where the situation is something like that of India. On the periphery are Japan, Tanzania, and a scattering of others such as Malta, followed by a few potential converts like Yugoslavia and Mexico. This list is not exhaustive, but it does give an idea of the range of the various regimes that can still in some way be associated with constitutional democracy. The list is also instructive, for a rapid perusal suffices to underscore the perilous position constitutional democracy now occupies in the world.

While the low point does not yet appear to have been reached, the zenith can be located during the 1920s in the democratic reconstruction period that followed World War I. That was also the finest hour for the political philosophy of constitutionalism. Constitutionalism was thought of as the structural theory scholars abstracted from the working principles of the most effective of the constitutional democracies then existing. Leading contributors were men such as Alexander D. Lindsay, Charles H. McIlwain, Walter Lippmann, Harold Laski, Herman Finer, Carl J. Friedrich, Friedrich A. Hayek, and Francis D. Wormuth.

Constitutionalism was an embattled doctrine from the start. Lindsay, Lippmann, and McIlwain wrote during the early New Deal, when the Western positive state was just arising. The question then was whether or not the freedoms attributed to the negative state of classical liberalism could be preserved under the expansion of government that followed the Great Depression.

The debate of the thirties was no innovation. The American political tradition has always been characterized by a predilection for discussions of the nature of constitutionalism, though there was never solid agreement about just what constitutionalism meant. However, in spite of this uncertainty, Americans have always in the past been certain that, regardless what constitutionalism meant, they possessed it. Indeed, the institutional genius Americans have habitually attributed to their own political tradition has even led them to assume that constitutionalism is the exclusive property of the Anglo-American nations or, alternatively, that constitutionalism may be simply whatever the Anglo-American political systems happen to be at any given time. As crisis has spread through the democracies all over the world, the search into the essential nature of constitutionalism has been resumed with a special intensity. Following Watergate, and the close brush with dictatorship it revealed, however, there is little basis for confidence about the chances of its preservation.

Ancient constitutionalism dealt with an all-embracing state. Modern constitutionalism, however, had, from its birth, been associated with limited government. This was so, said Charles H. McIlwain, "by definition." It was usually concluded, during the eighteenth and nineteenth centuries, that limited government required keeping government small and inactive. If that were the case the new type of positive government that succeded the Great Depression was incompatible with the principles of constitutionalism. The critics of positive government claimed that it and constitutional government were contradictions in terms. It was over this issue that many of the great theoretical debates that began in the thirties were waged.

Constitutionalism also had to accommodate the changed view of humanity that began to emerge in the late nineteenth century as individualistic rationalism lost credibility. The human being was no longer regarded as the atomistic political agent our traditional constitutional morality had assumed. Immersed in functional groups and doubtful of personal capacity and political potency, the contemporary person finds the credibility of individualistic rationalism undermined but nonetheless demands that constitutionalism guarantee the individual political values that were associated with the former inner-directed status.

The component groups that are indigenous to contemporary society are qualitatively different from the social groups prevalent in 1789. The conditions of political activity have almost reversed themselves from the time of James Madison, when the politically significant components of the nation were the states. Virginia and Massachusetts were prime examples. They were territorially, socially, and economically autonomous. Possessed of such coherence, they produced, on the national level, "factions" whose members were convinced that the values they saw confirmed in their own regional environments should be generalized for all of society.

Early America's state-born factions were not single-purpose pressure groups occupying a restricted segment of society, such as we now think of when we consider contemporary political forces such as unions and corporations. Rather, they were a series of general-purpose units. The two most powerful ones were the nascent manufacturing society of the North and the planter society of the South. Each made exclusive bids for total power. Under such conditions the problem of politics, as James Madison saw, was to politically disassociate their indigenous components through a system of atomizing representative devices that, after breaking through the homogeneity of the individual states, might facilitate the achievement of general, societywide decisions in Congress.

Our times face a different problem. It is to devise a politics for a society that has witnessed the disintegration of the wholistic territorial groupings that worried Madison. First came the development of groupings such as unions, corporations, and professions, and then followed their informal amalgamation into a techno-organizational establishment. The component parts can see no further than the politics of self-interest; the informal amalgam—Dwight Eisenhower christened it the military-industrial complex—sees politics as the struggle for power and control. To have claimed in the late nineteenth century that what was good for Virginia was good for the nation might have been untrue, but it was plausible. To claim in the mid-twentieth century that what is good for General Motors is good for the nation is patently false.

The conceptions associated with constitutionalism have remained constant, but their referents have shifted to such an extent that the old constitutionalizing techniques no longer suffice. Politics is eternally concerned with the achievement of unity from diversity, but the elements of diversity are now qualitatively different from those of the eighteenth century and the elements of unity much more noxious. The nineteenth century German sociologist Ferdinand Tonnines foresaw something like what has happened in America when he described the transition from *Gesellschaft* ("community") to *Gemeinschaft* ("society; associations") (see Gardiner, 1893; Vann Dicey, 1905). Under such conditions constitutionalism must also change. Madison's theory that salvation lies in the numerousness of "factions" is no longer applicable. On the contrary, we are progressively persuaded that it is rather our destruction that is implied by the numerousness of our modern indigenous techno-organizational associations. One problem facing twentieth century constitutionalism is to adjust its aims to cope with a society in which the individual has little political significance except as the member of a monstrous techno-organizational group, a society which in the process of pressing its characteristic drive for power and control on its members has left them desensitized with regard to the common aims and general interests that a proper constitutional order ought to elicit from its citizens.

Even dictatorships possess some characteristics of constitutionalism on a restrictive scale. Indeed, when the sphere of politics is restricted to the relationships among the members of a ruling class, all regimes are to some extent constitutional. This is little more than a tautology, a generalization from the fact that one way of describing the members of a ruling class is as those whose exercise of political power cannot easily be withdrawn from them without threatening the stability of the society as a whole. Mosca (1939) described how this happens when ruling classes surround themselves with self-protective "juridical defenses." In order to defend their prerogatives, ruling classes institute rule of law protections and in order to stabilize their regimes such protections are extended to a broadening social base. From this point of view a study of comparative constitutionalism would begin with a sociological description of the ruling establishments of the societies in question. Constitutional *democracy* would judge these societies on the basis of two criteria: (1) the numerousness of the people who could be said to participate in political power and (2) the extent to which these people were truly representative of the society's indigenous power groupings. And this is, in fact, the way scholars typically study comparative constitutionalism.

We know that the constitution of each country reflects in some sense the broad sociological configurations of its people, but beyond this it also seems true that in some countries the constitution is able to serve as a kind of democratic magnifier of civic wisdom, able somehow to produce the actual effects of greater democracy and deeper wisdom than seems practically possible in modern society. The formal properties of the democratic constitution of the French Third Republic were not markedly different from those of English democracy, yet English democracy always seemed able to maintain a larger degree of political wisdom than was possible in France. Political scientists lamely attributed this to the superior constitutional morality of the English, as if a constitutional multiplier effect was somehow able to operate in England. But when we try to come closer to understanding just how this magnifying action works and when it does so, we find constitutionalism to be an extremely elusive concept. Usually the attempt to identify how this so-called magnification of democratic civic wisdom is brought about by some constitutions and not by others has been a taxonomic effort, like that applied by Aristotle to the study of governmental forms. Such a study might yield a general theory of governmental forms, and upon completing such a study one might be able to give an abstract answer to the question, What is a constitution? But this would not be the same as answering the question, What is constitutionalism? A taxonomic analysis of the constitutions of England, France, Germany, and Italy of the mid-1920s reveals only minuscule constitutional differences among them. But scholars nonetheless are almost unanimous in judging that only England exhibited the principles of constitutionalism.

Again, to speak of constitutionalizing something—the military, the secret police, education, or science—means more than merely providing for them through supportive governmental agencies: to nationalize and to constitutionalize are not synonymous. On the contrary, the military, the secret police, or the presidency may be "nationalized" and still function as a despotic threat in society. Such a threat leads to the demand for constitutionalization—seeing that they function according to the principles of constitutionalism. Constitutionalism, among other things, attempts to elicit, protect, and magnify the application of democratic civic wisdom to the problems of government.

This feature distinguishes the general theory of governmental forms from the special theory of constitutionalism. The former has been the staple of political philosophy since Plato. The latter comes into its own only after the democratic revolutions that began in the seventeenth century. The democratic feature made the basic difference and also complicated the problem. Modern constitutionalism had to solve the problem of making government at once popular and proper. The task is better stated in reverse: to prevent despotism and inhibit corruption, while at the same time governing effectively. Of course, this was easier for the first liberal constitutional democracies to accomplish than it is for today's bureaucratic monoliths. They were able to reduce to a minimum what government did. The Americans then devised an intricate governmental mechanism that was powered by the forces of democracy and yet controlled by a series of self-activating inhibitory governmental mechanisms. The design specifications for the 1789 Constitution in effect called for an automatic peace, freedom, justice, and order machine. After a few minor adjustments of the feedback mechanisms, it very nearly—or at least more nearly than any other—came up to the design specifications. Its near automaticity made it the marvel of the world, and this feature, which so stubbornly eluded other constitutional designers, became the distinguishing mark of modern constitutionalism. It is also the feature that no longer works.

The designers of the 1789 Constitution were talented, almost to a man, but they were also lucky, and this is not always given its proper due. They were not working from scratch and they were not spinning gossamer institutions out of airy theories. They were essentially writing into fundamental law functional principles derived from the British constitution, after correcting it for abuses here and there. They substituted republican for monarchical authority; they invented federalism to supplant the unifying authority of the imperial crown, and then added quickly the judicial review they had pled for when oppressed by what James Wilson earlier called "unconstitutional" parliamentary decrees. There was more to the story—how they converted British parliamentary supremacy into the separation of powers, checks and balances principle. But even here, though the doctrinal steps in the process are intricate to unravel, the resulting mechanism fell out quite naturally from the effort to republicanize the concentrated imperial authority of the sovereign British king-in-Parliament. The balances of powers, checks and balances conversion was an enormously successful tour de force, but the maneuver was not cost-free. For what was sacrificed, along with ministerial responsibility to parliament, was the ready ability to dislodge a corrupt, incompetent, or unpopular adminstration. Impeachment, to be sure, was written into the Constitution, but it was a ponderous procedure, at once so complex and so grave as to virtually foreclose its availability for less than catastrophic crises of confidence. But a government unable to make emergency alterations short of a catastrophy is, in a sense, dependent on catastrophy —or revolution—for meeting extraordinary crises. This was the essential structural weakness of the 1789 Constitution as it was written. It assumed, in effect, that governmental crises would cooperatively arrange their appearances so as to coincide with the preordained quadrennial periodicity of national presidential elections. It was a fateful error, though its commission is easy to account for.

British constitutionalism, as the writings of Charles H. McIlwain illustrate, was little more than the institutionalization of civil disobedience. Ministerial responsibility in Britain meant that crown officials could be deposed through a parliamentary vote of no confidence. Parliamentary votes of no confidence were but the institutionalization of impeachment proceedings, and impeachment proceedings were but the constitutionalization of the bloody baronial tradition of civil disobedience that began at Runnymede and culminated in the execution of Charles I. It was this very tradition on which colonial civil disobedience had based itself shortly before the Revolution. It was the one principle on which all the victorious revolutionaries agreed. They can be forgiven for having assumed that future Americans would never forget the maxim by which their forefathers had lived: constitutionalism is the institutionalization of civil disobedience. Jefferson, who certainly hadn't forgotten it by 1800—his "political revolution of 1800" was, or rather could have become, the institutionalization of civil disobedience—casually assumed that Americans were just naturally the sort of liberty-loving creatures who would pull off a revolution every generation or so. Jackson, Calhoun, and all patriots up to the end of the Civil War made the same assumption, and they were right. But the Civil War ended more than Confederate state sovereignty. It also stilled the congenital American impulse to rebellion, the civil disobedience safety valve our Founding Fathers had not deigned to write into the Constitution. The imperative need for unity at all costs and the centralizing (federalizing) arrangement that served this need deprived the Constitution and its adherents of the leverage the Founding Fathers thought they had deposited for all times in the hands of the people. America has never really recovered from the Civil War, and there were many aspects of it she very well should *not* recover from. But she also, in shedding the bad, sacrificed along the way her only built-in provision for the constitutionalization of civil disobedience. If Watergate, in its deeper meaning, teaches us no more than the need to reconstitutionalize an appropriate contemporary form of civil disobedience, it will have a *felix culpa*—a fortunate fall.

These are matters to be returned to later. First, however, we need to know more about the nature of constitutionalism. There are some ready shorthand phrases for describing it. We have seen some of them and shall encounter more. But constitutionalism, like other words referring collectively to massive institutional forces—capitalism is one—is a complex phenomenon. An intuitive grasp of its inner meaning may be facilitated by an exploration of the anthropological roots from which it emerged.

THE INVENTION OF THE HIGHER LAW:
AN ANTHROPOLOGY OF CONSTITUTIONALISM

A law of physical nature purports to state an invariable relationship between material components of the environment. An example is the law of the rate of acceleration of falling bodies. But *natural law* refers to human beings. It purports to state a relationship that ought to hold between human beings if they are to provide themselves with optimum benefits and enjoyments. According to natural-law doctrine, a natural law may not "exist" or actually ever have been followed by any human being, but nonetheless it may be called "true." It is said to be "true"and applicable to all human beings because it can be discovered by human reason and wherever it is followed its alleged benefits will be enjoyed.

A famous example of a natural law is the maxim *pacta servanda sunt,* contracts must be kept. This natural-law proposition can be read as stating that implicit in the existence of human society at however primitive a level is the keeping of agreements and contracts. It is impossible to imagine human society without this principle, though the principle may be more or less extensively applied and it may be well or ill kept. The members of a society may not realize that the keeping of contracts is implicit in their having a society at all: it is not necessary that a society know it is following a natural law in order to benefit from it. It is not necessary to the theoretical existence of natural law that anyone ever discover it. Natural law "exists" in the form of rules implicit in the natures of persons individually and collectively. Natural law is like an axiom of geometry in one sense: it cannot be repealed, but it can be ignored.

Natural law is not an ethic. An ethic tells us the nature of good and bad. Natural law is often given ethical content, but this is not a necessary part of natural law. *Pacta servanda sunt* can be interpreted as carrying moral obligation, but it also can be interpreted as carrying no more than functional obligation, as one of the minimum functional prerequisites to having human society. Hans Kelsen used this principle as the basis for working out a general theory of law that carried only nonethical obligation (1945; see also 1967).

Natural law is not a folkway. A society may have many customs and folkways that carry only local or temporal significance. It may be the custom that whenever a man fails to keep an agreement he may be challenged to a duel by the aggrieved party. The folkway providing for private enforcement through dueling is a local arrangement, but enforcement of the obligation of contract is a feature applicable to human society in general.

The suggestion that there is such a thing as functional, as distinct from ethical, obligation raises some serious philosophical problems. Since the time of Hume and Kant it has been generally assumed that there can be no valid way of deriving obligation from facts. Hume concluded there is no obligation implicit in any facts. This famous argument by Hume appeared to completely discredit teleology and natural law. Nor was such a demonstration unexpected. Teleological approaches to physical and social events had been under devastating attack from scientists and empiricists for over a hundred years. Hume's demonstrations merely rationalized what might be called the "ideology" of the physical science approach to the interpretation of empirical data. Kantian phenomenology appeared to clothe Hume's propositions with logical unassailability.

The interesting thing is that when Hume himself wrote about political theory he ignored the strictures about fact, value, and reason contained in his philosophical writings, and properly so. Moral duties, said Hume, carry obligation because of the "necessities of human society" and of the impossibility of having human society

> if these duties were neglected. A small degree of experience and observation suffices to teach us, that society cannot possibly be maintained without the authority of the magistrates, and that this authority must soon fall into contempt where exact obedience is not paid to it. The observation of these general and obvious interests is the source of all allegiance, and of that moral obligation which we attribute to it. If the reason be asked of that obedience, which we are bound to pay to government, I readily answer. Because society could not otherwise subsist. (Hume, 1971)

Humean ethics is clearly functional. Its authority derives from the nature of things—Montesquieu's "necessary relations of things." In short, Hume used logic to derive value from fact, and he did so with considerable validity. But it was possible for his conclusions to be valid only because human beings had also done in practice what he had done in theory. Both human beings and Hume could do this because cultural "facts" are qualitatively different from physical "facts"; they contain certain types of values at their core. This will be made clearer through an exploration of the way human beings invented natural law.

Anthropologists have taught us that primitives are not childlike adults and that primitive cultures do not contain built-in teleological developmental or evolutionary patterns that determine their growth from simple to more complex cultural forms. Moreover, if cultural transitions do take place in primitive cultures, there is no basis for assuming that one specific new cultural form must always develop out of a given simpler form. In particular, there is no reason for assuming that because primitive Greek culture developed into a quite sophisticated civilization in a specific evolutionary pattern, any other primitive culture would ever experience the same development. We may use evidence drawn from Greek experience, but we may not imply that human nature in general or any other social system in particular must follow the same pattern. However, the fact that the Greeks did exhibit their own specific developmental pattern holds important lessons for us. It happened that in the case of the Greeks we are able to discover a structural explanation of their development of natural law and idealism.

An animistic world view is found in many sophisticated as well as many primitive cultures. In such a view all things exhibit principles of life and will. Each thing in the world, including the world itself, contains a "soul," even though there may be distinctions between the sacred and the profane. Nothing is inanimate, or lifeless. There is no death in the world in the modern Western sense of death, for that notion of death meant the conversion of something animate into something inanimate. In an animistic culture death may be terrifying, but it is also a transition to another form of "life," because nothing is "dead" in the modern sense.

Until the seventeenth century the official world view of the West was animistic. It was only with the ascendency of modern physical science that animism was excluded from specified realms of existence and material things were no longer regarded as containing souls within themselves. The physical universe as described by science no longer exhibited will, either its own or God's. It was regarded as being explainable without regard to any spiritual or external principle of causation. Causation could be explained on the basis of relationships intrinsic to the system under observation. However, the development of inanimate scientific relationships took place in a direct progression out of animate, quasi-magical relationships. Astrology was a very sophisticated way of studying and measuring the motions of heavenly bodies. It attained great mathematical sophistication and great predictive power while still within the realm of magical explanation and magical assumptions about the connection between happenings in the macrocosmos and the microcosmos. The transition from astrology to astronomy, from alchemy to chemistry, and from Paracelsian magical medicine to scientific medicine are only three of the most prominent instances of transitions from magical animistic systems to scientific inanimate systems.

But animism itself was already a sophisticated approach and it developed out of anthropomorphic precursors in much the same way that it gave way to scientific successors. Anthropomorphism is a form of animism in which the things of the world are visualized and thought about as if they had not only souls but also humanlike personalities. The religions and the cosmologies of Greece and Rome were anthropomorphic. Their gods and goddesses symbolized departments of nature such as rivers, forests, agriculture, and heavenly bodies as well as the arts, sciences, and virtues. Anthropomorphism is itself a highly rationalized and "scientific" approach, for it permits connecting together observed occurrences from some area of experience into a coherent narrative with great explanatory power.

The moon in a nonanthropomorphic culture may be the object of mystery and fetishistic magic, but little can be made of it unless there is some symbolic idiom through which its phases and motions can be connected together and also connected to other events that seem to be related to the moon. But once the moon is "seen" in anthropomorphic terms, a very complex "science" of the moon can be developed. The story of the moon can be told in terms of human and superhuman biographical events. The Greeks and Romans developed a marvelously intricate myth-science for all departments of human experience on the basis of anthropomorphic myths.

Although anthropomorphic "science" has very low efficacy when compared to the inanimate sciences of the modern West, it is nonetheless extremely efficacious. Quite complex and sophisticated civilizations can be built on anthropomorphic foundations. However, there is one great difference between anthropomorphic and inanimate sciences. Anthropomorphic sciences are basically "political" sciences. The relationships between humans and the universe and the relationships between parts of the universe are seen and interpreted in the same terms as are the relationships that people have with each other.

Inanimate science can be used to *manipulate* "things" that have no wills of their own and are unable to prevent the manipulation from taking place. Anthropomorphic science can be used to *influence* living, humanlike gods who have wills of their own and might, but for system of power relationships and influences in which they exist, do something quite different and willful. We may guess some of the reasons that preurban Greeks came to visualize the events they experienced in political terms.

Preurban Greeks were highly integrated into their cultural order. Even though with them, as with many primitive peoples, various cults were monopolized by different families and secret societies, there was very little that was kept from each member of the society. Religion was an elaborately social process, requiring the participation of every member. The fundamental myths belonged to the society as a whole and were shared by every member. The system of rules and roles followed by the society was assimilated thoroughly by all members as they were ritually initiated through their various life stages.

Though there was specialization of labor, even at very primitive levels, no technology was so completely intellectualized that it could not be understood by each member. Others might have been more skilled at house making, boat making, weapon making, or hunting than any ordinary member; nonetheless, each member understood all of these other functions, saw how they fitted into the function of the society, and thereby was integrated into the culture and felt at one with it. In preurban Greek society the members, in maturing, participated in almost every phase of their culture, appreciated the significance of its "science," and through their own participation in it assimilated their culture, integrating it as they integrated themselves with its goals.

It is slightly different, however, with the area that we in modern times have distinguished as the inanimate physical environment. What we call the physical environment seemed more chaotic and terroristic to preurban people than it does to Westerners. In their anthropomorphic and demonological myths and in their animistic magic, preurban people in general pictured the physical universe as a vast and frightening animated arena featuring the willful struggles of titanic forces, making what we rigidly separate as cultural and physical into different manifestations of the same governing forces. What appears in modern science as an ordered physical universe appeared to preurban people as a multiform and even chaotic struggle whose outcome is in doubt from moment to moment.

Being highly integrated into their social order but disoriented toward the physical universe, primitive people often reacted with a kind of reverse positivism and projected into the terroristic and hostile physical environment "political" and "lawful" elements similar to those they saw at work in their social system.[1] The resulting anthropomorphic, or demonological, cosmology accounts for otherwise ununderstandable events. Preurban Greek cosmology "politicized" the physical universe through a mythology that explained how original cosmic rulers brought order out of chaos.

Such anthropomorphic cosmic rulers were approached in the same way as were earthly rulers. One had to learn how to earn their favor, how to propitiate the great demons who wielded power throughout the universe:

> The structure and behavior of the world were held to be continuous with—a mere extension or projection of—the structure and behavior of human society. The human group and the departments of Nature surrounding it were unified in one solid fabric of moirai—one comprehensive system of custom and taboo. The divisions of Nature were limited by moral boundaries, because they were actually the same as the divisions of society. (Cornford, 1957, p. 55)

Politicized cosmic demonology may occur when people are well oriented toward their social system but disoriented toward their physical universe.

It is by no means the case that the process being described here occurred only in ancient Athens. On the contrary, Mircea Eliade (1971) has documented its universality. Paul Wheatley has found remarkable evidence of a similar process at work in ancient China.

> The collective memory of traditional society is by no means unresponsive to happenings in the past but, unable to retain individual persons and specific events, transforms them respectively into archetypes and categories, heroes and heroic situations. And because myth is the ultimate, not the primal stage in the creation of these archetypes, it is often hazardous to reverse the process and to isolate the paradigm at the core of the legend. (Wheatley, 1971, p. xv)

Wheatley argues that ancient Chinese cities, like those of the ancient Mediterranean world, were constructed as a sacred precinct, a residence of the gods, and an *axis mundi* (1971, p. 481).

Anthropomorphism is the name we give to man's tendency to "create" nature, God, and heaven in his own image, and the evidence for this tendency is copious, especially in the case of the Greeks. Durkheim (1947) had treated all religion as an expression of man's collective needs, and following his suggestion many brilliant interpretations of primitive cosmologies and religions have been made. But the collective representations of cultural needs are not made in any rigid fashion. The world of Odysseus, according to M. I. Finley (1954), portrayed the functional ethic of eighth century Greece, but it portrayed that ethic in heroic models whose actions were also shaped by the fact that they were derived from more primitive rituals. Moreover, the heavenly images were constructed in a special way. Olympianism, as William James said, was monarchial deism, but it was not a simple mirror image of the everyday institutions and practices of the Greeks reflected into the heavens. It is not possible to tell the story of heaven in earthly terms maintaining in the story all of the variability randomness and accident that actually occur daily in the culture. Merely to retell the story of some event requires the storyteller to eliminate some of the multifarious happenings that were contemporaneous with that event in order to portray the particular event in question rather than several others. The storyteller must abstract a certain sequence of happenings out of their web of cultural connectedness, whether or not he or she is aware of going through an abstraction process. This abstraction process is even more evident when a culture builds itself a heaven. Longfellow, in the *Song of Hiawatha,* provides us with a quaint illustration of the process involved.

> Hiawatha:
>
> Saw the moon rise from the water
> Rippling, rounding from the water,
> Saw the flecks and shadows on it,
> Whispered, 'What is that, Nokomis?:'
> And the good Nokomis answered:
> 'Once a warrior, very angry,
> Seized his grandmother, and threw her;
> Up into the sky at midnight;
> Right against the moon he threw her;
> 'Tis her body that you see there.'

This poetic description illustrates the human abstraction process at its most elementary level. The moon may have previously "existed" as something mysterious and magical. But so long as it "existed" unqualified and undifferentiated, the culture could make little of it. However, the angry warrior "projects" his grandmother into the heavens, superimposing her on the "moon." The moon is now no longer merely something anonymously magical and mysterious. Now it is alive in the sense that a woman is alive. Now the moon "is" a woman —a white goddess, perhaps. Now the "story" of the moon can be told, for the story of the moon is the biography of a womanlike heavenly person. Movements of the moon, which were previously unintelligible, now become events in the life of a person. Relationships between the moon goddess and the sun god can be told in human terms. The moon's phases, its connection with the tides, its connection with the seasons, with fertility, and with the female menstrual cycle can all be woven together into a novelistic tale: the myth of the moon goddess. As more and more heavenly events are incorporated into the anthropomorphic biography of the moon goddess and her reign, the result is a more and more complex "science." This science may be meticulously accurate from a mathematical standpoint and yet retain its portion of magic. This was true of astrology. As the study of heavenly relationships becomes more and more exact it may find itself depending less and less on the anthropomophic and magical framework through which the science was given birth. The transition to astronomy as the study of self-contained relationships becomes possible. Each of the stages in the transition from fetishism to science was accomplished through successive abstraction maneuvers. But the ability to make the abstractions depended upon the original projection of an anthropomorphic rationale onto heavenly occurrences. The moon and its motions and relationships could not be "seen" until "she" could be seen in the imagery of a white goddess. This projected imagery enabled us to rationalize and systematize lunar events. These events could only then be separated from—abstracted from—the imagery (white goddess) that made them possible. Myth, astrology, and astronomy proceed from each other in successive abstraction operations. Myths are to this extent cultural mirrors or projection machines that reflect into the heavens features and relationships familiar on earth. Once the projection has taken place the resulting picture can be seen and analyzed as a picture.

Something similar is involved in the way an artist projects an image from his subject matter. Having projected an image—onto canvas, in marble, or in written imagery—the artist can then concentrate on the properties of the projected imagery rather than on the original subject matter from which the image was projected. The original projection maneuver is an aesthetic achievement. But once a gifted artist has made such a projection his or her process can be analyzed. The steps followed can be studied and explained. The whole process can be "scientized." And even though the "scientific" or "academic" imitators who follow a great artist may not produce great art, they can produce comparable images in a comparable fashion.

Much of the myth content of a culture is produced in the same way that artists produce their images. Homely, everyday features of the culture are projected into the heavens. This process of making the heavenly projections automatically and unconsciously achieves an "abstraction" of cultural forms in the same way that an artist's image is an abstraction from his or her subject matter. But as with the artist, cultural projections "utopianize" (in Karl Mannheim's sense) the cultural elements that are projected. It is not possible for the projection process to work any other way. One cannot make a myth of all of the diverse events of the culture. If the myth is to tell the story of the marriage between the moon goddess and the sun god, the courtship and family system used for the myth will be one that is "typical" for the culture, not one that is atypical. It will be a type of marriage that is possible and believable for the members of the culture that develops the myth. As it involves wondrous and magical personages, it may also be a type of marriage that is "ideal." There can also be stories of "typical" failures in a culture, and these will have their place in some of that culture's myths, but for the chief cosmological actors in the myth system it will be "ideal-typical" (in Max Weber's sense) success patterns that are chosen.

Another example of unconscious ideal-typical images is often found in dreams. There is copious evidence of this not only in psychoanalytic literature but also in ancient literature. In Homer the evidence is strong that poets of his day treated dreams as if they were objective fact, without making a rigid qualitative distinction between experiences of the waking and the sleeping worlds. Eric R. Dodds suggests that early Greeks were conscious of living in two worlds —the dream and the sensible worlds—without attributing unreality to the dream world (1951; see also 1963). Freud had long ago noted the similarities between dream imagery and myth imagery (1956). Hence, the Greeks were richly endowed with sources from which ideal-typical patterns could be drawn. But it is not necessary to account precisely for how ideal-typical patterns may have become unconsciously projected into heaven. It is enough to remark on the fact of the projection. And on this fact the evidence is incontrovertible. It is also undeniable that the ideal-typical features that are projected into the heavens are taken from behavioral norms and cultural forms. The order of the universe is pictured as if it operated on the same principles as the cultural order.

Behind the Olympian gods stands "a remote power, which is both primary —older than the gods themselves—and moral. It is called Moira, Destiny" (Rose, p. 12). Moira stands for "the provincial ordering of the world . . . a representation of Necessity and Justice (Must and Ought)" (Cornford, 1957, p. 12). Moira is the first stage of the projection process—an unqualified realm of obligation and necessity. Zeus is but a thinly veiled Homeric paterfamilias—a supernatural, ideal-typical head of the household. "It was natural," said Dodds, "to project onto the Heavenly Father those curious mixed feelings about the human one which the child dared not acknowledge even to himself" (Dodds, 1951, p. 48).

Jane Harrison allows us to make an extended picture of the degree of cultural projection. "Behind Gaia the Mother, and above even Zeus the Father, stands always the figure of Themis" (Harrison, 1962, p. xxii). Themis is conventional law, moral norm. It is what will later become natural law. Dike is closely related, the "way," or the order of the cosmos. Greek Dike to us carries some of the feeling of behavioral norm rather than scientific law, but this is because it describes the behavioral norms of an animistic universe. Dike has to do with the succession of seasons, the course of the heavens: the behavioral instincts of nature. Themis is Olympian, Dike is chthonian. Harrison made the reasonable suggestion that Themis is mother of Dike for the same reason that God is the lawgiver of the universe: man wants to control events; he wants right conduct to bring prosperity (pp. 516, 17–31). Accordingly he makes "science" the daughter of "politics." No Greek philosopher reversed this order. In making the order of the physical universe dependent upon the order of the cultural universe the Greeks merely confirmed the overall pattern of their scientific imagery, which consisted of a projection into the heavens of myth-encased abstractions drawn from their own cultural order.

Hesiod, at the close of his story of Zeus, related the foundation of the heavenly order with anthropological accuracy. Hesiod tells of the "institution of a social order ... symbolized by the obviously allegorical marriage of Zeus with Themis (law) and the birth of their children, the Seasons, whose names are Good Government, Justice, and Peace, and the Fates (Moira), who gave to mortal men their portions of good and evil. . . . It will hardly be denied," comments Cornford, "that we have there the divine counterpart of the installation of a new earthly king, or the annual renewal of his authority over his people and of his power over nature" (Cornford, 1952, p. 248). In another connection Cornford had argued that philosophy inherited its notions of God and soul from primitive religion. Philosophy also got from religion (in this projection process) the "governing conception of a certain order of nature, variously regarded as a dominion of Destiny, of Justice, or of Law. . . ." For this reason the reign of necessity in the universe "is also and equally a moral rule, a kingdom of Justice" (Cornford, 1957, p. 5).

Quite simply, what has happened is that the Greeks projected an order into the universe that was an analogue of their own cultural order. Two things followed from this. It was an order of obligation and morality administered by gods in the same way that the earthly order of obligation and morality was administered by the earthly priest-king-paterfamilias; the order of the universe was a reflection of the only kind of order that was conceivable. This meant that the universe automatically became what we would call a natural-law universe rather than a physical science universe. Secondly, and what is more important at the moment, having projected a natural law order into the universe, the nature of that kind of order could be pictured, it could be "seen," and it could be analyzed. Natural law became visible in the heavens. This permitted and indeed made inevitable a second stage in the process. This second stage was the counterprojection of natural law from the heavens back to the very earthly institutions from which it had been drawn in the first place.

The original projection process had automatically produced ideal-typical norms for the heavens. These were abstractions from the quasi-symbolic behavioral norms of the culture. The abstractions existed in the form of narrative myths relating the characteristics of Themis and Dike. The characteristics of Themis and Dike could be seen and analyzed in these myth containers and their behavioral implications could be converted into authoritative rules applicable to human relations. Coherent with this is Cornford's admonition that the ancient philosophers were always nonscientific. They did not seek to explain things but sought rather for "that knowledge which must direct the conduct of human life" (Cornford, 1952, p. 46).

Behind philosophy there is law and religion.

> behind religion lies social custom, the structure and institutions of the human groups. . . . Moira, the supreme power in the universe, was very closely allied to Nomos, the sense of constitutional order. Now it appears that Moira is simply a projection or extension of Nomos from the tribal group to the elemental grouping of the cosmos. We can read a new sense into the apothegm ascribed to Pythagoras, that "Themis in the realm of Zeus, and Dike in the world below, hold the same place and rank as Nomos in the cities of men; so that he who does not justly perform his appointed duty, may appear as a violator of the whole order of the universe" (Cornford, 1952, p. 54)

Both Cornford and Pythagoras are talking about the process described above as projection and counterprojection, the process through which natural law was invented. A philosopher like Anaximander then moves on to a further step. For what Anaximander did was to take the old Homeric personalized controls and remove their supernatural character, eliminating Zeus and his fellow Olympians. There is still a moral order in which justice prevails, but the will of a personal god has disappeared, giving place to natural causes and eternal motion (Cornford, 1952, p. 41). Plato moves a step further when he rationalizes the entire system of order into an ideal-typical constitution that carries the authority of an absolute ethic and also the standard by which human affairs can be judged and ruled. Aristotle's "final cause" was a further extension of this process and one that led to the formal enunciation of natural law as an explicit doctrine.

The point of this discussion has been to illustrate the way in which human beings, merely as they go about the business of producing human culture, also produce natural law as a direct consequence. Natural law *can* be produced because human culture is quasi-symbolic, because myth systems projected from quasi-symbolic behavioral norms exist in the form of ideal-typical abstractions from behavioral norms and in this form provide standards of value for the judgment of behavioral norms. The process is similar to that of the engineer who produces standards for evaluating production workers by abstracting ideal-typical norms from observation of actual production behavior. This is a naturalistic view of natural law, but it is possible to take such a view because human beings produce natural law "naturally."

Natural law carries the implication of obligation, and it has a factual foundation. The process through which human beings produce natural law disproves Hume's proposition that values cannot be derived from facts. Cultural facts simply do not exist without norms—values—built into them. This provides the foundation for the ancient view of political science as well as of constitutionalism and the "higher law." For one way of stating the conclusion of this analysis is to say that a sound political science yields policy recommendations that possess a form similar to natural-law propositions. Something like this has frequently turned up in jurisprudence. Moreover, an investigation of the theoretical implications of the common-law procedures, the traditions, the rule of law, and constitutionalism involve a problem related to natural law—the problem of the validity of law.

Natural law, as we have seen, is not only produced naturally, it is also self-validating. This is so because although it was projected from functioning cultural institutions, its derivation from those institutions is not apparent to the members of the culture. Natural law and related ethical rules appear to derive their validity from God or some other transcendent principle. Because the actual political order is seen to be aiming at the realization of these God-oriented rules, the question of the validity of the political order does not arise. This raises the problem of freedom under law.

There are two basic ways in which to interpret freedom. The first and more obvious is freedom from restraint; the second and more obscure way is systemic. The first way is the view of freedom that most accords with immediate impressions. It is the absence of anything that inhibits the individual's desire to do anything he or she wishes.

Systemic freedom is the result of the more sophisticated reflection that in order to be able to do anything it is necessary to follow or submit to the functional prerequisites for the achievement of that desire. This becomes extended in two ways. Viewing humans as creatures capable of employing tools and developing powers, it is possible to describe the systemic conditions under which their tools may be employed and under which their powers may be developed. A social system in which people can realize the maximum potentiality of tools and develop their powers to a maximum point obviously provides more freedom than would occur if each merely gratified his or her wants freely and without restraint. Throughout most of Western history natural law has been the rubric under which systemic freedom has been discussed. However, a problem arose because natural law had no greater claim to people's allegiance than did the abstract properties of systemic analyses of freedom. Indeed, natural law usually appealed to a higher authority for its source of obligation. The ancient Stoics were confronted with the impossible task of demonstrating the operational validity of natural law for a society in which God was dead. The Stoic quest led ultimately to attempts to provide naturalistic or scientific foundations for natural law. This failed for two reasons. In the first place was the reason pointed out by Hume. If cultural events are regarded as facts similar in nature to physical or material facts, we can easily prove that it is invalid to derive values from such facts. Here natural law is confronted with the dilemma of being forced to choose between making its dictates matters of faith or rejecting the attempt to provide law with a higher ground of validity. The second reason for failure derives from the collective nature of systemic freedom. This involves the problem discussed by Plato in the first part of *The Republic.*

We distinguished the two forms of freedom on the individual level. The same distinction applies with even more force on the collective level. When systemic freedom is extended to collective rather than individual problems, it appears demonstrably true to those who "see" far into the problem of collective behavior that each individual in a social system may receive greater freedom if all people adopt the imperatives of the system seen as a whole.

There is a simple logic by which this becomes apparent. If one makes a theoretical extension of the spacial, long-run (in time), functional (in "social space"), and structural (organizational) consequences of any projected collective act, one sees the projected act in different ways than if the act is considered from a static, isolated, or individualistic viewpoint. The classic example of this has to do with capital formation. A given group in a corporation has the problem of deciding whether to distribute or to reinvest its profits. At first thought it appears that each member of the group will be better off if the profits are distributed. However, on further reflection it becomes clear that only a small portion of the share of profits from each member, reinvested in capital development, will shortly make available to each member much larger profits than would ever be possible if all profits were distributed as they were earned. The collective acceptance of present restraints on profit enjoyment as a precondition to the greater future enjoyments of profits is a collective dimension of systemic freedom.

Natural law had the virtue of revealing some of the elusive systemic dimensions of freedom. For, as we have seen, natural law projects the general, the long-run (in time, function, structure, and space), and the collective implications of different types of human behavior. For when a society produces ideal-typical patterns of behavior for its gods and heroes, what it does is speculate on the collective implications of various patterns of behavior when they are generalized for all persons, when the long-run consequences of such patterns are projected, and when such patterns are considered from the standpoint of how well or ill they fit with the other patterns of behavior that go to make up a concatenous social system. In addition, a myth system—as a social system in operation—contains the revelation, the authoritative assurance that the system will work. That is, it contains the lesson that a social system is more than the sum of its individuals. This "more than" element, which is the "profit" accruing to individuals for making their social system work, would not otherwise be intelligible to individuals. It would be "utopian" and impractical if it were simply described speculatively, or in a treatise on political theory. Few who looked only at the literary description of the hypothetical system could perceive that it might work. But seeing it at work in a myth system induces confidence in its workability as well as, or because of, faith in its validity.

All of these achievements, which are nonrationally illustrated in myth systems, are abstractly and theoretically described in the natural-law systems derived from them. But being tied to their mythical foundations, natural-law systems, in common with the theological and philosophical systems that are also derived from myth systems, carry implications of universality, absoluteness, and infinity. That is, the obligation possessed by natural law is dogmatic rather than functional, infinite rather than finite. A finite behavioral norm made universal and infinite is an absolute ethic. But there is no valid way of proceeding from finite particulars to infinite universals. This is the basic fallacy toward which natural law tends. Natural law hides from itself its mundane cultural origins in an effort to preserve its claim to normative validity, but in doing so it sacrifices its claim to logical and theoretical validity. It is not possible to relate cultural facts into a logically valid theoretical system that will have absolute normative validity. The only validity that can be given a norm of behavior is to prove that it is the logically necessary "efficient cause" for a given "final cause." Prescriptive norms of behavior may have only formal, instrumental validity. This may be a sufficient ground of validity for the social theorist, but social systems are not made up of social theorists. And no social system will work unless the lowliest and least speculative members of the system are as fully persuaded of the necessity and validity of the system's behavioral norms as are the most astute social theorists.

This is not a problem in simple social systems. Under extremely simple conditions there is an immediate and transparent connection between the individualistic and systemic implications of every decision-making problem. The extended implications of even such serious problems as deciding for or against war or peace can be portrayed to all in tribal councils and assemblies. Such institutions effectively reveal the alternative goals that are possible and the individual behavioral implications of each competing proposal or goal. The means that must be willed in order to will ends are observable and understandable to all. Primitive politics is self-validating in this operational sense as well as because it partakes of the overall validity of the universe. But once social conditions and political problems become so complex that decisions affecting all must be resolved in remote and intricate institutions, an unbridgeable gap appears between the individualist and systemic implications of an action. People are deprived of any basis for perceiving the systemic validity of the prescriptive norms required of them. Ultimately they must simply have faith in the validity of their social system. They are presented by their society with a task that must be made to appear to them to be morally right inasmuch as its systemic validity cannot be perceived. The English common law is an example of how this process may work.

Historians of the English common law and of English constitutionalism often refer to medieval English law as "folk" law. Such discussions leave the impression that there was some mystical spirit, or *Geist,* controlling and directing English culture. Any such notion is obviously reminiscent of natural-law and "higher-law" doctrines and repugnant to those of a materialist or positivist bent. Already in the seventeenth century the opposition between Francis Bacon and Sir Edward Coke turned upon this issue. Coke's theories of the common law and of the "artificial reason of the law" implied a principle of sovereignty and a source of authority that was higher than that of the king. Bacon gave a positivist defense of the established legal and monarchial order. Bacon's jurisprudence was thoroughly naturalistic; he was the first of the legal realists. Hobbes, who began his career as Bacon's secretary, extended this approach from law to the entire political order. This debate has continued down to the present day.

There is no doubt that the main outlines of the English common-law system were formed during the early Middle Ages. England was then a primitive culture and the common law retains yet today many marks of its primitive origins. It is called a system of "unwritten" law. As they search for "the law" applicable to cases and disputes arising before them, judges study precedents ferreted out of the opinions of other judges. On this basis they announce their "opinion" of how "the law" applies to the new case. Judges hand down "opinions" of the implications of the law and this permits them to render "decisions" in particular cases. But their opinion of the law was formed from earlier opinions, and these, in their turn, were of the same sort as their own—earlier "opinions" of how "the law" applied to earlier cases. Where, then, is "the law"? The answer is that it is "unwritten." No common-law judge has ever written down "the law" concretely. Every common-law judge who has ever existed has only written down opinions of how "the law" applied to particular cases. "The law" doesn't "exist" in any concrete sense and never has. It is almost inconceivable that anyone starting out to invent a legal system would have invented this one. And yet it developed in a perfectly intelligible way.

From the earliest times two of the distinctive features of the common law have been its jury system and its rules of evidence. Both of these developed from primitive legal practices. In preliterate England, law was customary and "heroic." It was heroic in a sense common to many primitive cultures. It was best expressed by certain "cultural paragons." These were revered older men who best expressed, remembered, and preserved the culture's ethic and customs. The law was preserved in their memories and it was expressed in their actions. They did not "own" the law personally; everyone owned it equally and in common. But there often arose disputes over the law and over what was right. Two parties in conflict with each other would each claim to have right on their side. That is, each would claim to be following the law. The problem was to decide which law was "the law," which law was right. Litigants entered court, all bringing their own law, and the problem was to "try" the law. For this purpose jurors—culture paragons—were called to say (swear) what the law was. The general principle was that "old law breaks new law," and this was another reason for having the jury composed of the older culture paragons. The problem was to find out—to "discover"—what was the "good old law" by asking the most prominent elders to say how such problems were dealt with in the old days. Although there were many distinct types of jury trial, one prominent type was devoted to resolving conflicting hypotheses about what the law was. An implicit assumption of the process was that "the law" inhered in the culture and could be discovered and applied to individual disputes by following the appropriate law-discovery method. Law was not "invented" or considered to be manmade until the seventeenth century. Even then, Lord Coke, the "father of the common law," gave strength to the anti-Stuart faction with his historical researchers purporting to prove that the old law supported its claims against the king and hence "broke" the new decrees of James I.

During the sixteenth century a revolution occurred in the rules of evidence. This happened in conjunction with the transformation of the jury from a repository of knowledge about the good old laws into judges of the facts about a given dispute. For after law records and books had been in continuous existence for several generations they were obviously more reliable repositories of information about what the old law was than were the memories of old men. At the same time the law clerks and magistrates began to acquire the status of a guild whose field of expertise was the old law. They "engrossed" and monopolized the law and its "artificial reason," in Coke's happy phrase. They began to be able to state unaided and with confidence what previous opinions about the good old law had been.

Gradually the differences that arose among conflicting parties centered legally on what facts should be used by the law clerks and magistrates in discovering which one of the previous opinions about the good old laws was applicable to the case at hand. The reliable determination of the facts of the case was a precondition to the selection of the appropriate precedents to resolve the dispute. By helping make this determination the jury was converted from judge of the law into judge of fact. The judge took to himself the old function of saying what law applied to the facts at issue. In doing this he searched back through the records of opinions of previous judges, comparing the facts of earlier opinions with those of the dispute at hand. He knew that there would not be an exact match between the two sets of facts. But applying the assumption that earlier opinions were not instances of the law given concretely but rather applications of the law to earlier conditions, he was able to guess how the law would apply to the present facts. The law was never concrete. The law was never written and never fully "discovered." Rather, each judge from case to case attempted a restatement of the implications of the law for the facts at hand. The function of the common-law judge was similar to that of an anthropologist studying the legal structure of a primitive culture.

The crucial maneuver lay in the implied hypothesis made by the judge and by both parties to the dispute. For they implicitly assumed that there was a "law" whose principles were discoverable through the evidences of it that lay embedded in the earlier precedents. However, as the resolution they sought would apply only to a specific dispute, when that resolution was found, the opinion that stated it would no more state "the law" than had the earlier opinions. It would merely resolve the dispute at hand in accordance with the dictates of the unwritten law. The fundamental law remained elusive, persisting in back of the culture, holding it up, but evading conceptual capture by any given judge.

The implicit functional theory of the common law is that it is possible to analyze any human institution, such as a property system or a family system and finally even a constitution, into the principles according to which it functions. These functional principles will exist in the form of abstract hypotheses as to what must be the behavioral norms—the common laws—of the institution, the "constitution" implicit in the institution. This was the way the ancients invented natural law, and it was how the English invented, first, common law and, later, constitutionalism. Any conflict arising over a society's implicit constitution can be resolved in the form of a hypothetical new behavioral norm (a judicial decision) that states the proposition (the opinion) that the functional principles underlying the society logically entail that the rule of the instant decision be followed whenever a situation like that presently at dispute might arise. Few common-law judges may have been aware of going through this rational process, but this process reveals the constitutional logic implied in their derivation of opinions from precedents. It is the juridical counterpart of the projection and counterprojection process that was described earlier.

The logical stages in the production of common law and ultimately of constitutionalism can now be seen to be very similar to the logical stages previously described for the production of natural law. First comes the projection of the abstract functional principles of institutions through a deliberative law-trying process. Then there is the counterprojection, or reflection, of the derived principles back on society in the form of authoritative standards of behavior. The standards of behavior, as the common law of the constitution, carry the obligation of a functional ethic stating the behavioral norms that are the logically entailed operating principles of the social system. But the true functional source of the ethic that validates the laws announced by judges is not perceived. Moreover, that ethic, though it is enforced by the state, does not appear to have been produced by either the state or its officials. Rather, the force of constitutional law appears to derive from an ethic that, though announced by, was not invented by human beings. Constitutional law appears to express an autonomous ethic that exists as a higher law apart from politics, and being a higher law it can furnish the source of the validity of the derivative common law opinions that are announced from time to time by judges sitting on minor cases. Common-law judges, especially the most creative and speculative ones, like justices Coke, Marshall, and Cardoza, frequently identified their most fundamental constitutional opinions with the higher law. Numerous scholars— C. H. McIlwain and E. H. Corwin are recent examples—have followed this judicial lead. F. W. Maitland avoided higher law assumptions by refusing to talk about constitutionalism at all. Instead, he borrowed a surrogate from Gierke: the concept of the "real personality of the group." This permitted him to adopt a sociological rather than a jurisprudential stance when he dealt with the trust, the corporation, the corporation sole (an office possessing the status of a corporation but consisting of one person), and the crown. As we shall see, Gierke's notion was a good lead, up to a point. It helped account for many of the historical facts about collective legal action and many arcane features of the medieval English constitution. But this advantage was purchased at the price of incorporating the mystical notions of *Geist* and real personality into the mundane functional problems of English law. Legal persons such as corporations and states can be given empirical juridical existence, that is, a "real" personality, more simply through the process previously outlined. Here we are speaking of nonindividual rules of actions attributable to legal persons. This introduces a further facet of constitutionalism: the "rule of law."

The rule of law has been always closely allied to the notion of natural law. It has a very hallowed usage, reaching back beyond the Middle Ages into classical times. Plato expressed in *The Laws* one of man's eternal political quests when he wrote of the search for a "sacred and golden cord of reason . . . the common law of the State" (Plato, *Laws*, Bk. I, p. 211). The rule of law is not the same as natural law, for the rule of law is said to obtain among human beings on earth, while natural law is said to provide a higher foundation for the validity of the rules of human conduct. A natural-law interpretation of the rule of law might be to say that the rule of law is what natural law would become if it were translated into positive law. Plato's summary was:

> When I call the rulers servants or ministers of the law, I give them this name not for the sake of novelty, but because I certainly believe that upon such service or ministry depends the well- or ill-being of the states. For that state in which the law is subject and has no authority, I perceive to be on the highway to ruin; but I see that the state in which the law is above the rulers, and the rulers are the inferiors of the law, has salvation and every blessing which the Gods can confer. (Plato, *Laws*, Bk. IV, p. 285)

Aristotle added the characteristic amendment that it was not enough for the state to be merely law abiding. It was not just following the laws that provided for the rule of law, but following *good* laws. This became his basis for distinguishing between the three virtuous forms of government and their corrupt forms (Wormuth, 1949, pp. 10–25).

Plato's notion was really more naturalistic than was Aristotle's, and in this matter, as in many others, the modern naturalist Francis Bacon reverted to the Platonic concept in describing the rule of law. To Bacon the rule of law is simply the opposite of the rule of violence and terror. With Bacon the rule of law begins to approach the modern Anglo-American notion of due process of law: the traditional procedures and forms that must be followed when actions are taken in the name of government. The sociologist Gaetano Mosca gave a naturalistic interpretation. This was the basis for his notion of "juridical defense." Mosca (1939) argued that regardless of the formal structure of the state —monarchy, aristocracy, or democracy—any state that had existed over a long period of time found it necessary to regularize the relationships between the rulers and the ruled. The ruled had to know what was expected of them and the rulers had to know what they could count on. This was not because of any altruism but merely so that the business of a political community could get done and so that the rulers could count on holding their positions with security. In this sociological view the rule of law is the deep structure of the state. It expresses a conservative structural principle that must ultimately develop in every stable political organization. Here conservatism is used in the same sense as when the biologist states that the gene structure of an organism represents a conservative principle. A similar notion is held by those who suggest that in order to survive, the modern corporation must develop rule-of-law relationships between managers and employees: this is the application of the principles of constitutionalism to internal corporate affairs. Albert Vann Dicey (1889), who carried on the classical liberal idea of constitutionalism, was the most eloquent of those who identified the rule of law with constitutionalism. A more recent expression of this position is found in Friedrich A. Hayek's *The Constitution of Liberty* (1960).

In all of these instances there is implied a viewpoint similar to that of medieval English folk law. It is assumed that the substance and the content of what will be done is intrinsically just and all that is required is to regularize the procedures through which authorities act.

If a preexisting social organization is assumed to be valid, or if the principles of valid social organization are assumed to be preexistent, like the rate of acceleration of falling bodies, these principles need only be discovered and applied, they need not be validated. All that is required is a process of discovery that can be shown to be procedurally valid. There is no fundamental difference between the higher-law tradition of medieval English common law and the rule-of-law tradition of neoclassical liberalism. Both were attempts to spell out the functional ethic implicit in a given social system, and both were equally accurate and scientific, from a structuralist point of view. Both approaches revealed the systemic juridical implications of social orders that were taken as "given." Professor Hayek's impressive book probably should have been called "The Constitution of Liberalism," for what he did, with great theoretical elegance, was to construct an abstract model of a liberal culture and then trace out its implicit ethical norms, stating them abstractly in the form of the functional juridical principles that comprise the constitutional prerequisites for such a culture: he constructed an abstraction of the constitutional implications of a given (liberal) social system. Similarly, the twelfth century jurist Ranulf de Glanvill, in writing the first textbook of English law, produced an abstraction of the constitutional implications of the way his own society worked (1965). Both resulted in abstract legal models of a social system. Each model, in turn, could be subjected to a functional analysis; each juridical model could be inspected to find out what were its implicit prescriptive norms. The result—the prescriptive norms implicit, for example in Glanvill's model—could be called "medieval constitutionalism." This, in effect, was the task to which Professor McIlwain devoted much of his life and which he summarized in the book *Constitutionalism, Ancient and Modern* (1958b). Constitutional theory requires just this sort of work. It consists of deriving the functional prescriptions implicit in abstract models derived from social systems. The models may also be prospective as in the constitution making done by the founders of the American Constitution. Constitutionalism amounts to the implicit final causes of a social system, the constitutional behavior that must take place in order for it to function properly.

Hence, as in Philadelphia in 1787, it is possible to invent rather than merely to discover constitutional principles. Natural law discovered the prescriptive implications of going institutions. Although it involved a rational process, the institutions from which it worked had developed nonrationally. We may paraphrase Aristotle's criticism of Plato's notion of the rule of law in this connection. Aristotle had said that the rule of law was not merely following the law, but rather following good laws. And we may add that it is not merely deriving the prescriptive implications of going institutions that provides sound projections, but also deriving the prescriptive implications of more rational possible institutions. The greater validity of such invented prescriptions does not rest on the ethical fiat attached to them but on the fact that they better describe the "necessary relations arising from the nature" of the society. Ethical fiat and natural law are constitutionalism in its utopian stage, as it has been said that medieval astrology and alchemy were astronomy and chemistry in their utopian stages. Ethical fiat is attached to a functional prescription when it cannot be proved, as was attempted in the *Federalist Papers,* to be a necessary final cause. It is an attempt to short-circuit the process of proving the necessary implications of a given system of relationships, much as magic short-circuited the process of uncovering causal relationships. The only validity constitutionalism can have is functional validity. Each of the conventions of the "unwritten" British constitution can be shown to be derived in the same way that the ordinary English judge derived the everyday principles of the "unwritten" common law. Both are instances of the rule of law and both are instances of efforts to describe the prescriptive implications of the necessary relations arising from the nature of the social institutions specific to England at a given time. As we shall see shortly, the same process was at work in the "invention" of the American Constitution.

One of the most important conventions of the British constitution is the principle that the opposition party does not precipitate a government crisis unless it is able and prepared to accept the responsibility of forming a government. This convention is stated in the form of a prescription. But it is not an ethical prescription, it is a functional prescription. British parliamentary institutions would not work if this prescription were not observed. After World War II the West Germans were so persuaded of the functional necessity of this prescription that they wrote it into their new constitution. Its importance to German constitutionalism derives not from its being in their Basic Law but in the fact that it is a sound functional prescription implicit in the operation of a specific political system.

There are several modes of projection that aid in deriving functional prescriptions that are subject to analytical verification. For any proposed rule of action, its long-run implications may be different from its short-run implications. The long-run qualification of the proposed rule of action may be revealed by projecting it through time, space, function, and structure. For any given rule of action, its universal implications may be different from its particular implications. These, as Kant indicated, may be seen by generalizing it for all people. For any given action, its intrinsic implications may be different from its extrinsic implications. These may be seen by measuring its degree of concatenation with other actions also required by the social system.

Systemic functional prescriptions are like the conventions of the British constitution. They are properties of the overall social system rather than of its individual components. Certain types of actions will be functional requirements of the system.

These modes of projection are the formal procedures out of which constitutional theory is derived. Constitutional theory exists in the form of hypothetical quasi-symbolic behavioral norms. On the theoretical level its validity may be formal, but the test of validity will be the extent to which functional necessity can be proved in theory, the extent to which its norms are the axiomatic properties of projected social system. This is a shorthand expression of what occurred, or what was summarized, in the Philadelphia Constitutional Convention and in the *Federalist Papers* that followed. A later discussion will attempt to show how this came about, how American constitutionalism was invented.

THE RECENT DEBATE OVER CONSTITUTIONALISM

A constitution, at Roman law, was merely an enactment by the emperor. That usage was consistent with the etymology of the word—"to make, set up, or put in place"—and also with the meaning it had during the Middle Ages, as for example in the Constitutions of Clarendon (1164), drawn up during the reign of Henry II to define the limits of civil and ecclesiastical jurisdiction (McIlwain, 1958b, p. 23). With minor exceptions (McIlwain, 1958b, p. 25) the term did not, until the seventeenth century, convey the idea of the fundamental frame of government, for the primary meaning of constitution referred to man-made positive, rather than declarative, law. Hence, after the fifteenth century, as man-made plans of church and civil government began to appear, it was appropriate to refer to them as constitutions and only after that could the term constitution come to mean the structural forms and limits set up by people for government.

Of course one did not create constitutions out of nothing or from whim. They had to possess validity of some sort, and this typically derived from a more fundamental law of God, reason, or nature. Hence, constitutional government, a phrase that appeared in England in the seventeenth century, referred both to the actual frame of government and also to a mode of conducting government that would accord with the principles of some fundamental source of validity lying outside the constitution itself. For some time during the seventeenth and eighteenth centuries the principles of kingship announced by the defenders of the Stuart monarchs stood in opposition to those announced by the proponents of constitutional government. Each rested its claim to authority on higher but different sources of validity.[2] During the eighteenth century the authority of kingship was undermined and the ensuing regimes were known as constitutional monarchies.

Constitutional*ism,* which first appeared in the early nineteenth century, was initially a term of approbrium. In 1832 Robert Southey, then England's poet laureate, used it in disparagement of the radical reformers of his times. Gradually constitutionalism came to refer to the principles underlying that form of state in which kingship had been rendered subordinate to either constitutional principles or, in some cases, to an actual written constitution. Republican regimes, most prominently those of America and France, originally resulted from the application of the principles of constitutional monarchy to a regime with an elected executive standing in place of a king.[3] Although this substitution soon produced a new stage of constitutional thought, its assimilation took several decades. Mosca, writing well into the twentieth century, underscored the traditional meaning by distinguishing between constitutional and parliamentary government. The term constitutional was restricted to constitutional monarchy. Mosca's distinction was between governments in which the executive ministers resigned not when they were defeated in the legislature but only through the action of the head of state (constitutional), and those in which the ministers were appointed by the head of state but had to resign whenever they lost their majority in the legislature (parliamentary). He described America as a presidential form of government and appeared to classify it by analogy along with constitutional monarchies rather than with parliamentary governments (1939, pp. 262–63). Mosca argued that in parliamentary regimes specific constitutional safeguards might be eliminated, while in constitutional monarchies preservation of the king requires preservation of the chartered limitations on his authority and also of constitutionalism. Hence, constitutionalism might be sacrificed if royal authority is completely eliminated. Perhaps he was reflecting the view of Sir Roger Twysden, who in the seventeenth century wrote, "The world, now above 5,500 years old, hath found means to limit kings, but never yet any republique" (quoted in McIlwain, 1958b, p. 138). What Mosca called the "liberal" state came closest to the contemporary meaning of constitutionalism (Mosca, 1939, pp. 409–10).

The pivotal figure for twentieth century doctrines of constitutionalism is Otto Gierke, the great historian of medieval natural-law doctrines. Gierke flourished during the latter half of the nineteenth century. Romanticism was at its apex. Sociology—and socialism—were brash and lusty. Democracy was overtaking both constitutional monarchy and republicanism. Nationalism and imperialism were triumphant. Industrialization had grown into an institutional juggernaut. Science as well as the fine arts were laying foundations for spectacular achievements. And with all this came a magnificent explosion of historical scholarship without equal either before or after. Some of the most spectacular achievements were in medieval history, and in England, at least, one result was, in effect, a second "reception" of the Roman law. Savigny's history of Roman law (1815–31) had paved the way. Sir Paul Vinogradoff's legal histories (1892, 1929) later helped bring this home to a wider English audience, but it struck with special force because of the earlier work of Otto Gierke, whose *Das Deutsche Genossenschaftsrecht* was published in 1881. Gierke's work had an enormous effect on a brilliant group of English medievalists, the most prominent of whom was F. W. Maitland. In 1900 he had published an English translation of part of the third volume of Gierke's work under the title *Political Theories of the Middle Ages* (see Maitland, 1957).

Maitland, though he never wrote explicitly about constitutionalism, was impatient equally with the narrow legalism that led from Bishop William Stubbs (whom he admired) to John Austin and with the political empiricism that led from William Hallam (the first to employ the term constitutional history) to Samuel Rawson Gardiner. Maitland's own researches had led him to plumb the mysteries of such things as the *Corporation Sole* (1936) and *The Crown as a Corporation* (1911). However, Maitland's underlying concern with corporate institutions was motivated by an interest in what we now call constitutionalism. He believed, from historical research as well as constitutional conviction, that the Roman law "concession" theory of the authority of the corporation was wrong. This doctrine held that the corporation was a legal fiction and existed only by virtue of its legal creation by the state. The concession theory portrayed the corporation as an artificial contractual association rather than a natural, self-validating fellowship. Only the latter doctrine, in Maitland's view, furnished an autonomous foundation for the liberties, franchises, and rights necessary to safeguard self-government. Gierke, employing the distinction between fellowship (*Gesellschaft*) and association (*Gemeinschaft*), had argued that while an association could result from a legal and contractual relationship between individuals, a proper self-validating fellowship, tracing to Germanic rather than Roman institutions, was a "real" collective person. Gierke developed the theory of the real personality of the group, an organismic idea that accorded both with Maitland's own constitutional convictions as well as with what Maitland was discovering about English medieval institutions, especially the corporate form known as the trust (Stoljar, 1958, pp. 20–44; Cameron, 1961). Following Gierke part way, Maitland argued that groups could be self-validating and were almost as real as a human being. Gierke provided him with a theoretical basis for the group realism he felt essential to constitutional theory.

Constitutionalism, the idea as well as the term, was central to Gierke's work. He was at pains to discredit the positive-law theory of the modern state, chief responsibility for which he visited upon Thomas Hobbes, and to resurrect a principle of constitutionalism whose validity could be given a foundation independent of the authority of the state. Searching back through the then obscure doctrines of the medieval jurists, he discovered that they had developed a dualistic theory of the state, which Gierke christened "double majesty." This was the doctrine that the people, as an organic entity, had always, during the Middle Ages, stood alongside the king as an equal, if occasionally ineffective, participant in majesty (not sovereignty). While the medieval schoolmen had grounded these doctrines on a natural law grounded in theology, Gierke saw behind that conception a prescriptive natural law that expressed the same sociological reality Maitland was to discover at the heart of medieval English institutions.[4] The explication, in one way or another, of the nature of this abiding institutional juristic substance became the quest of the succeeding theorists of constitutionalism.

J. N. Figgis, Maitland's prize student, at pains to demonstrate an autonomous ground for the authority of the institutional Church, also drew heavily upon Gierke. Figgis' classic study of medieval constitutionalism was a description of how its leading doctrines emerged when the opponents of papal absolutism developed their theories of Church government during the fifteenth century Conciliar Controversy (Figgis, 1960, pp. 41–71). Several of Figgis' contemporaries in England found his analysis applicable to other groups besides the Church. This sociological-historical impulse stimulated the thinking that led to the great upwelling of constitutional theory that appeared in England after the 1920s. Figgis had argued that the Church was not subject to domination by the state; the socialist intellectuals wanted to do the same thing for labor unions and other indigenous collectivities. In their hands the semisociological juristic tradition that derived from Gierke was joined with an idealistic strand of political philosophy drawn from T. H. Green's ethical philosophy of the state (1907) to issue in the theories of guild socialism that acquired vogue in England prior to the rise of facism.

The problem had come to a head over the advent of what by then had come to be called the positive, social welfare state. Its proponents were confronted with the necessity of accomplishing a delicate theoretical maneuver. The hallowed English constitutional tradition of the negative state that stemmed from Locke and later from the utilitarians had been individualistic, positivistic, economistic (if not materialistic), and somewhat anarchistic. As a result, the accepted theory of English constitutionalism seemed to be totally incompatible with the positive state required to institute collectivism. Constitutionalism had been born from the struggle against the Stuart mercantilists, and their doctrines had been in some ways similar to the collectivist ideas of England's twentieth century socialists. Moreover, the Lockean tradition had been chaperoned through the nineteenth century by liberal individualists such as Lord Acton and Albert Vann Dicey, who held fast to the central liberal political dogma of the limited state. They argued that the political core of constitutionalism was to be found in the rule of law restrictions of governmental action. Anything that undermined this central tenet—such as collectivism, the positive state, and even administrative law—was anathema. In the United States, somewhat later, these issues came to a head in a famous series of constitutional law cases fought out before the Supreme Court during the 1920s and 30s. But this resolution was impossible in England. Anything an English Parliament might decree was, from a legal standpoint, constitutional, and no appeal lay to the courts. Hence, English opponents of the new socialist proposals could not charge that they were unconstitutional at English law. The absence in England of judicial review of the constitutionality of legislative enactments forced the argument out of the technical realm of constitutional law and into that of general constitutional theory. This specific characteristic of the English constitution ultimately forced both sides of the argument to enunciate the underlying principles of constitutionalism. This lot fell to the contending academic polemicists of the day and as a result of their writings constitutionalism became the central concept in political theory for more than a generation.

The neoliberal collectivists such as T. H. Green and Maitland countered the orthodox liberal individualists by reaching beyond Locke and the seventeenth and eighteenth century English empiricists into Continental idealism on the one hand and medieval constitutionalism on the other, attempting thereby to undermine the enormous authority and prestige of the solid English constitutional tradition upon which the orthodox liberals drew. Gierke, with his unrelenting attack on individualism, as well as his doctrine of the reality of the corporate group-person, was perfectly suited to their needs. If Gierke had not existed, Maitland and Figgis would have been hard pressed to invent something comparable solely out of indigenous English materials. Gierke permitted the neoliberal socialists to ignore the august tradition that stemmed from Locke and to answer the standpat rule of law orthodox liberals by resurrecting a hallowed and immemorially constitutionalist English law that derived from ancient charters and constitutions. Hence, they argued, the positive state and even socialism were demonstrably compatible with the deeper meaning of English constitutionalism.

Ernest Barker (1958), another Maitland disciple, and A. D. Lindsay (1962) consolidated the tenets of the requisite political theory. Harold Laski (1967) leveled a devastating attack against orthodox individualistic liberalism. W. Y. Elliott (1928), writing under a heavy indebtedness to Green and Lindsay, attempted to Americanize the philosophic side of the argument, translating the English academic war against empiricism into one against utilitarianism, the American counterpart of which was then, under John Dewey, running at high tide. Elliott's *Pragmatic Revolt in Politics* contains more copious references to constitutionalism than had previously appeared in print anywhere.

Benjamin F. Wright (1962), Elliott's colleague at Harvard, completed the Americanizing maneuver. Starting with the early New England divines and relying heavily on John Adams, he attempted, with only partial success, to demonstrate the existence of an ongoing natural-law theme lying at the heart of the American constitutional tradition. C. H. McIlwain (1910), scion of a distinguished Harvard tradition that had long advocated the adoption in America of a version of England's parliamentary system, was also a medievalist in the Maitland mold. McIlwain did not publicly enter the debate over constitutionalism until the 1930s. By that time the appearance of fascism had shifted the argument over constitutionalism to a new plane. Fascism relied on organismic theories of the state, and this fact alone went far in discrediting Gierke's theory of the real personality of the group.

The recent appalling effects of tribal particularism have served to heighten the suspicion held by some of us a good while before, that after all the impressive apparatus of Gierke's *Genossenschaftsrecht* sometimes merely conceals the weakness of some of its principal historical conclusions instead of really strengthening them. The too ready acceptance of these conclusions by F. W. Maitland, the greatest of all our modern historians of English medieval institutions, unfortunately created a vogue in England and America for these views which a careful examination of them seems hardly to justify. (McIlwain, 1958b, p. 42; see also p. 91)

Early studies of fascism had indicated that in Italy and Germany constitutionalism had been undermined by the creation of a "second state," which was anticonstitutionalist and which, while leaving the formal structure of the old state standing, subverted it by creating a second, totalitarian regime, which, when superimposed on the old state, was able to substitute its anticonstitutionalist "people's law" for the traditional constitutional law, rendering the latter unable to forestall the spread of Nazi terror (Fraenkel, 1941).

Fascism directed the attention of the neoliberal constitutional theorists back to the rule of law tradition. The problem now was to incorporate it into a doctrine of constitutionalism for a positive, social welfare state freed from organismic foundations without, however, capitulating to orthodox individualistic rule of law liberalism. McIlwain's solution was to identify constitutionalism with the higher-law and vox-populi traditions. The latter could then be distinguished from the noxious *Volksgeist,* which had come into such disrepute in Nazi Germany. He ignored Greek analysis of formal constitutional structures, concentrating instead on fragmentary statements about the higher law drawn from Plato's *Statesman.* McIlwain argued that "modern" constitutionalism had originated in Rome, but not in the familiar mixed-state doctrines of Polybius and Plutarch, rather, in the stoic doctrines of law found in Cicero, Seneca, and the *Institutes* of Justinian.

In the final pages of his impressive study McIlwain made his own stand clear even though he denied that the preceding survey permitted him to "deduce any strict definition of constitutionalism" (1958b, p. 135). It turned out that medieval Englishmen had been on the right track. Constitutionalism, said McIlwain, rests on the medieval distinction between *jurisdictio* (an "independent judiciary") and *gubernaculum* ("government"), and this distinction is applicable to modern constitutionalism. "The reconciliation of these two remains probably our most serious practical problem. . . . There is the same necessity now, as in ages past, to preserve these two sides of political institutions intact . . . and to guard against the overwhelming of one of them by the other" (1958b, p. 139). However, modern Englishmen had done better than their medieval forebearers by two maneuvers. In the first place they brought most of *gubernaculum* under *jurisdictio,* under, that is, the rule of law. In the second place they lodged the source of the validity of what was left in the people, acting through democratic processes. The maintenance of constitutionalism requires that democracy be kept vital and that the rule of law, through the independence of the judiciary, be kept vigilant. That is about the size of it, except that one must avoid a typical American pitfall. Separation of powers and other such appurtenances of the American Constitution are irrelevant to constitutionalism: "Among all the fallacies that have obscured the true teachings of constitutional history, few are worse than the extreme doctrine of the separation of powers and the indiscriminate use of the phrase 'checks and balances'" (McIlwain, 1958b, p. 141). These are irrelevant to ensuring an independent judiciary. Indeed, "the doctrine of the separation of powers," he pronounced, "has no true application to judicial matters," despite the contrary opinions of certain "closest philosophers like Montesquieu" (pp. 141, 142).

McIlwain performed an astounding tour de force. Laying down what was to become the bible of future theories of constitutionalism, he purported to display the essence of the topic and did so while scarcely mentioning the classical liberals such as Locke and Montesquieu and without carrying his essential story beyond the England of 1630. The time-honored staples of constitutional theory such as the mixed state, separation of powers, and checks and balances dropped completely from sight and with them any special American claim to having contributed to modern constitutionalism.

Francis Wormuth (1949) shortly redressed the balance in a brilliant study that, while not ignoring the medieval materials, reestablished the more familiar linkages between constitutionalism and the structuralist tradition, which reached from the mixed state of antiquity to the separation of powers doctrines of modern times. In order to put these two back together again, it was necessary to resume the story where McIlwain had left off, namely, with the mid-seventeenth century civil wars. That was where most of the devices and ideas of modern constitutionalism found expression: the written constitution, separation of powers, bicameralism, and judicial review. However, these were not without their own resonances in ancient and medieval times. So once the ancient origins and the seventeenth century inventions were placed in what Wormuth believed to be the proper perspective, it was possible for him to supply the connective tissue for a juncture between the general theory of constitutionalism and the more special tradition of American constitutionalism (Wormuth, 1949, p. ix).

The central problem of constitutionalism, said Wormuth, was that stated by Hamilton in *The Federalist*: " 'First enable the government to control the governed; and in the next place to oblige it to control itself. A dependence on the people is, no doubt, the primary control on government; but experience has taught mankind the necessity of auxiliary precautions'" (quoted in Wormuth, 1949, p. 3). "To these auxiliary precautions," Wormuth continues, "we give the name constitutionalism" (p. 3). Hence, one of the essentials McIlwain relied on in describing the modernization of medieval constitutionalism, namely, the bringing of *gubernaculum* under popular control, is separated from the more specific problem of constitutionalism. Instead, two kinds of devices are concentrated upon. One is the protection of "substantial interests from governmental encroachment" (p. 3). This referred not only to the protection of property but also the protection of the civil rights so prominent in American constitutionalism. This provides the basis for doctrines of toleration and pluralism that have occupied the attention of so many American political scientists (see Hanson, 1970, pp. 336–73). Prominent here are the checks and balances so repugnant to McIlwain. The other feature in Wormuth's analysis is a "persistently recurring idea of the character of law: generality and prospectivity" (Wormuth, 1949, p. 4).

Wormuth's summary was:

> If law is to be general and prospective in character, it is improper for the legislative power to deal with particular cases. The temptation to improvise a special rule may prove too strong. Likewise, it is improper for the executive power, which applies rules to individuals, to possess legislative power, for once again persons may be deprived of the advantage of known and settled rules. Among arguments for separating the legislative and executive functions these were perhaps the most cogent.
>
> The doctrine of separation of powers was immediately assimilated to the mixed monarchy, with the king in the role of independent executive; a second balance, that of legislature against executive, was added to the conventional balance of king, lords and commons. Here we have most of the elements of modern constitutional thought. (pp. 8–9)

Wormuth, it is clear, is poles apart from McIlwain. His is a structural analysis. It suggests that constitutionalism rests upon certain formal institutional arrangements and procedures, which, if instituted and maintained, can go a long way toward guaranteeing the protection of certain crucial interests and the safeguarding of procedural due process of law.

For Wormuth, medieval double majesty is the pivotal factor. During the seventeenth century the stress between its two partners became intolerable and finally the dualistic medieval constitution was overthrown in favor of something more akin to ancient conceptions of jurisprudence and mixed monarchy. Here again Wormuth challenges McIlwain, who was at pains to disavow Gierke. To Wormuth, the *dominium politicium et regale* of Fortescue, as well as the other English texts seized on by McIlwain, were all evidences of the medieval double majesty, which pertained to kingship narrowly conceived rather than to the modern state. This was precisely what was overthrown by modern constitutionalism, and the crucial maneuver came in the mid-seventeenth century, when "commonwealth," or national civic consciousness (citizenship), supplanted "kingdom," or personal loyalty to the king (allegiance) (Hanson, 1970, pp. 30–40).[5]

Wormuth's work revalidated the authenticity of the early seventeenth century protoliberals who had drawn up the Cromwellian constitutions. Especially prominent in his story is James Harrington, who was so deeply admired by John Adams as well as by many other architects of the American Constitution. But it also resurrected Hobbes, Locke, and the classical liberals who had labored so arduously over the structural principles of constitutional government. This was the tradition McIlwain ignored. We cannot avoid seeking for the truth of the matter. It is not merely a question of resolving the intricate issues of historical interpretation at issue in these two doctrines of constitutionalism, though this is a matter not to be dismissed lightly. But the more pressing problem arises because of the American constitutional crisis that arose during the Nixon administration. For the scholars who offered remedies for those evils found themselves, unwittingly, coming to opposition over issues that were contemporary counterparts of the opposing historical traditions represented by McIlwain and Wormuth. On the one hand are the "Anglican" constitutional theorists like Sam Beer. Beer, following McIlwain, argues that we should not tamper with the basic governing structure that has evolved in recent years. Specifically, we should not whittle away at the structure of the presidency and we should not succumb to the dangerous delusion that somehow Congress can be made to reassert a nostalgically imagined congressional activism designed to reassert a separation of powers mechanism fallen out of balance through the growth of executive power. On the contrary, argues Beer (1973), the solution must be sought in the strengthening of the party institutions, which will permit the resurgence of the political side of the dualistic balance between people and government.

On the other hand are the "Americanists" like Arthur Schlesinger, Jr. (1973) and Arthur S. Miller (1973), who concentrate on the structural imbalances that have grown up between Congress and the presidency and advocate novel arrangements capable of mediating between the two. Of course, numerous other structural innovations, usually designed to strengthen Congress, became the common currency of the debate unleashed by Watergate. However, it is apparent that the issue cannot be resolved until a more accurate conception of the essence of constitutionalism can be achieved. For this, we must turn to a reconsideration of the emergence of constitutionalism in America.

Suppose we restate the issue. On the one hand constitutionalism is viewed in the context of an ongoing dialectic between people and power. Power is expressed through government (*gubernaculum*) and popular control of government is expressed through the rule of law (*jurisdictio*). The problem of constitutionalism is to facilitate the expression of popular will through electoral institutions so that government will always be forced to function in accord with the precepts of the rule of law. The primary focus of popular concern is to maintain the independence of the judiciary.

An independent judiciary will be capable of subjecting issues arising from the exercise of governmental authority to the rule of law. At its highest expression this will result in a jurisprudence akin to natural law and hence appropriately called the rule of law.

Those on the other side take up the argument at precisely this point. Popular institutions are necessary but not sufficient. They were essential to the creation of the modern state but something more than an independent judiciary is required to tame it. On the contrary, it is incompatible with the requirements of constitutionalism to leave the people and the government standing side by side, as had been the case prior to the introduction of constitutions with formal mechanisms to control the exercise of governmental authority. Both doctrines rely on an implicit automaticity; one is rationalistic and the other mechanistic. Both lodge the underlying validity of the state with the people; they differ on how that source of validity is to be expressed through government. In the first it is to be achieved through the rule of law, discovered and applied by the judiciary; in the second it is to be guaranteed through formal devices and procedures protected against governmental encroachment by the judiciary. The two doctrines are opposed, especially on the level of historical scholarship, but they are not contradictory. Constitutionalism does rely on an assumption that something like a secularized version of natural law can be discovered and applied to the problems of government, and it also relies on an assumption that certain formal structures will optimize the possibilities for doing so.

THE CLASSICAL BACKGROUND

Separation of powers; checks and balances; federalism; these are the central doctrines associated with American constitutionalism. Where do they come from? What is the source of their validity? What gives them significance today? Does their present-day significance spring from the same source that gave them validity in the past? If not, what *ought* to be their significance today?

In the past it was customary to say that Americans bestowed on their Constitution the devotion that Europeans once gave to their monarchs. Today the prestige of the Constitution has been seriously eroded. The Constitution as surrogate monarch is under seige by one of its children grown monstrous: the monarchial presidency. This points up the paradox of our constitutional tradition. The Constitution has been modified and reinterpreted almost beyond recognition from one generation to the next and yet our veneration for the Constitution has, until recently, continued unabated. But if transformation has been the order of the day in our constitutional history, how far can the practice reach? Are there any constitutional principles immune from evolutionary erosion and interpretive transformation? Specifically, what is, or ought to be, the status of the distinctive principles on which the American Constitution was based? Two of these are federalism and separation of powers. Do they represent the distillation of history's best wisdom about universal constitutional principles? If so, how did Americans find out about them and why have so many other peoples remained ignorant of their virtues? Answers to these questions, if indeed they can be answered, can only be sought from the history of constitutional theory. Doctrines concerning separation of powers, for example, reach back to the earliest beginnings of political speculation. Federal theory is of the most recent birth.

Federalism concerns sovereignty; its understanding requires us to delve into the deepest issues concerning allegiance. What do Americans mean by allegiance? To whom or to what do they owe allegiance? Americans swear an oath of allegiance that reads: "I pledge allegiance to the flag and to the republic for which it stands . . . ." What are the other dimensions of allegiance? At one time, prior to the great intersectional feud that occupied Americans during the middle of the nineteenth century, we had something we called dual citizenship. Each American owed allegiance to his state as well as to the nation. State allegiance was often quite strong. It still is in places like Minnesota and Virginia. But in addition to its spiritual force, state allegiance was originally a constitutional principle. Until the Civil War it stood on an equal footing with national citizenship. And of course, those who held the doctrine of secession maintained that loyalty to one's state took precedence over loyalty to the nation. Today, state citizenship has only minor technical significance. What does allegiance mean in other countries? To whom or to what does a Russian owe allegiance? To the nation? To the party? To the Revolution?

But what difference will it make even if we do succeed in ferreting out the analytical and historical significance of the problems surrounding governmental functions and allegiance? Assume that we might indeed uncover the various strands of thought and custom that led to the constitutional doctrines Americans now revere. Assume that we could uncover and evaluate all the local, temporal, and parochial forces and traditions that at a precise moment in 1789 came together to produce a time-bound constitution with specific application for the people of those days. Would this undermine the Constitution's more general significance?

Suppose it is true, as Woodrow Wilson and others have alleged, that the 1789 Constitution embodies a self-harmonizing balance of power mechanism analogous to those Isaac Newton found in the heavens and Adam Smith found in free markets? Suppose we find that federalism was merely the way our Founding Fathers preserved the remnants of the Gothic institutions they brought with them to the new world in the seventeenth century?

All this, like the fully ornamented Bach being rediscovered today, might be revealed as a richly ornamented baroque constitution, but what difference would it make if we proved all this to be true? Every deep-seated tradition is that way, is it not? There are no universal events: all events are finite historical happenings with unique causes. All events are local and particular; that is the only way they can happen. Every historian is always proving some version of this fact, wittingly or not. Indeed, one can't even *be* an historian without constantly proving that whatever happened did so as a result of, or followed in sequence from, an earlier series of very special forces and causes.

Nonetheless, human beings *do* create things with universal significance: the Roman law, Buddhism, constitutionalism, etc. And while these universal creations were always the products of their unique historical foundations, that fact can never qualify or detract from the legitimacy of any claim they may have to universality. This applies also to American federalism and the separation of powers system. The mere fact that historical investigation may explain away their reputed novelty cannot of itself detract from whatever universality they may possess. The historian merely helps to remove some of the aura of inviolability or sanctity our institutions and doctrines have acquired. But if one begins by believing something embodies the essence of universal truth, how is this belief affected by historical demythologizing?

Possibly the answer is not at all. But this is one of the things we wish to find out. For if after all of its historical foundations are revealed, a treasured doctrine still appears to possess universal validity, then we are much more secure in our initial belief. If, on the other hand, the historical investigation leads us to perceive the parochial in what was originally taken to be the universal, we are that much ahead for having done our history. We are then in a position to purify and make more truly universal the partial truth with which we began. So at least we have nothing to lose from making the historical excursion; either way, we are better off than before.

As with most investigations in political theory, the first place to start is with Plato and Aristotle. There have been many efforts to uncover American-type separation of power schemes in their writings, and it is possible to find many suggestive references. However, ultimately the effort must fail. The reason goes to the heart of political philosophy. Nineteenth century separation of powers doctrine depended on a mechanistic view of the political order. Applying this approach led to the construction of constitutions out of autonomous component parts the way children make toy buildings with erector sets. Whatever virtues result, they are the product of the elemental autonomous forces, just as one builds machines using the principles physics tells us about the forces of nature. Separation of powers mechanisms are intrinsically atomistic. Their composite properties are quantitative and additive rather than qualitative and organic.

Plato and Aristotle always viewed the political order qualitatively. Today they might even be called systems analysts, for the functions they describe are systemic rather than mechanistic, as Plato made clear at the start of the *Republic*. But even though we cannot find true separation of powers schemes among the writings of the ancients, a brief survey of their doctrines will be useful to illustrate the differences between their doctrines and those of the nineteenth century political theorists. Moreover, despite the basic incompatibility between separation of powers and the doctrines of Plato and Aristotle, several features of their writings *were* found useful by eighteenth and nineteenth century mechanistic constitution makers.

Plato had several different ways of analyzing states. The maintenance of the Republic required exactly the right social classes, and they had to be harmonized in precisely the right way in order for the political order to function properly. Three social classes were distinguished, each possessing its characteristic virtues. All were blended into an integral system under justice. This system prevented each from giving vent to its characteristic vice. Overall harmony was maintained by the ruling guardians, who alone possessed deliberative and legislative powers. The auxiliaries provided protection and administration; the craftsmen, sustenance. Plato called the Republic an aristocracy, a government of the virtuous (whether by one man or a few.) But even so, the Republic might fall subject to the cycle of growth, maturity, and decline found everywhere throughout nature (Plato *Republic,* 1945, p. 269 ff.). This could happen if a generation of rulers failed to arrange marriages according to the principles of eugenics. The educational system, and after that the population, would become debased. Purebred citizens (gold, silver, iron, etc.) would give way to people of the baser alloys. Genetic degeneration would cause dissension to break out and this would lead to a cycle of constitutional degeneration. First would come timocracy, then oligarchy, then democracy, and finally, despotism. Despotism, in which vice reigned supreme, was at the opposite pole from the Republic. So the Republic was a countercyclical organic polity in which classes, functions, and virtues were harmonized. The unharmonious forces of government issued in chaos.

The *Statesman* also contained what today would be called a systems approach to politics. First, the dialectical approach was used to distinguish quantitative from qualitative analysis; only the latter was said to be appropriate for the analysis of political systems, because it alone permitted their analysis "in relation to the fixed norm to which they must approximate if they are to exist at all." The degree to which constitutions attained "the due measure which marks off good . . . from bad" provided the basis for evaluating them. Qualitative analysis was appropriate for analyzing what we might now call "software"—constitutions. This differed from the analysis of things with concrete existence in that its findings are derived from "imperative" rather than "critical" knowledge (Plato, *The Sophist and the Statesman,* p. 258).

Building on this foundation, the *Statesman* goes on to prove that a political system possesses certain necessary properties. It followed that decision making (statesmanship) had to be conceived of as being architectonic and therefore to some degree functionally autonomous, for it was what activated, integrated, and preserved a political order. This was no more a separation of powers than is found in the nervous system of the human body.

SEPARATION OF POWERS AND THE CLASSICAL MIXED STATE

Next, states were classified on the basis of the proportion of the population holding sovereign power: one (monarchy), the few (aristocracy), and all (democracy). However, each one had a pure and a corrupt form. The distinction rested on the idea of the public interest and on what Plato called law-abidingness. The formal structure of each type of government looked the same in both pure and corrupt cases. One could distinguish a pure from a corrupt monarchy only by the political substance of what was done rather than by the forms through which authority was exercised. A corrupt monarchy (tyranny) was one in which the ruler governed to his own interest. A proper monarchy was one in which the ruler governed in the public interest.

So the classification scheme rested on two principles: one of form and one of essence. The first was determined by the proportion of the population sharing in the political process: government by the one, the few, and the many; the second was based on whether authority was exercised selfishly or in the public interest. There is a little trouble with the latter notion when we come to consider democracy. The idea of rule according to private interests seems a little strained and artificial when it is applied to democracy. How is it possible for the people as a whole to govern themselves in their selfish, as distinct from their public, interests? The apparent difficulty disappears if one resorts to Rousseau's distinction between the will of all and the general will. The will of all was what resulted when each person voted on the basis of his selfish interests. The general will was produced when each person voted for what was in the common interest. So the classical distinction is applicable to democracy after all. Plato's term for a proper democracy is sometimes translated as "constitutional government." The terms *demagoguery* and *mobocracy* are often used to describe its corrupt form. According to Plato, each pure form of government tended to degenerate into its corrupt form. This in turn led to revolution and the installation of a new pure form of government in its place. It was a theory of revolutionary political cycles analogous to the theories of business cycles produced by modern economists.

Remembering the balancing and harmonizing scheme of the *Republic,* we might now expect *The Statesman* to present us with a mixed government designed to incorporate the best features of all three virtuous archetypal forms. It is easy to imagine what such a separation of powers scheme would be like. If all three virtuous forms were mixed together at once, the virtue of each might inhibit the appearance of the vices of the others and thereby produce a kind of checks and balances system for the moral order. But while a moral mechanics such as that would fit well with Newtonian ideas and with the style of thought of the Founding Fathers of the American Constitution, it would be decidedly un-Platonic.

Plato shows this in *The Statesman* when he refuses to devise a combination form of government and turns instead to his seventh form, which is "genuine" while the other six are all "imitative." The seventh form is that of the statesman and it runs according to principles that are above the law.

In the *Laws* (Plato *Dialogues,* 1953, Vol. 4, p. 262) this same basic approach is carried further, and what appears to be a mixture of democracy with monarchy is really systemic analysis in which the decision-making function is made abstract, like a self-programming computer, and is installed as the ruling rational faculty of the political order.

Aristotle, always more of an empiricist, gave these ideas a special twist. He made a few additions and changes but he was primarily noteworthy for having made some careful empirical tests of the theory. The result of his study of over 150 constitutions was the conclusion that in actual fact the pure forms of government rarely exist. When they do, they tend to be unstable. This was because of an additional factor, the tendency of states to founder over the opposition between the rich and the poor. Aristotle's arresting statement was that the typical polis is not one city but two: a city of the rich and a city of the poor (Aristotle *Basic Works,* 1941, p. 1209). This was the birth of a rudimentary type of class analysis and, together with it, a class theory of revolution. But of course we should not read Aristotle through the eyes of Marx. Both Plato and Aristotle were more like John Maynard Keynes than Karl Marx. They tried to describe countercyclical governmental systems for avoiding chaos and maintaining equilibrium. Aristotle's proposal was that property should be distributed so that the polarization of rich and poor would not occur. Then the opposing interests of rich and poor would be moderated by the presence of a large and influential middle class. Political harmony would be the result. Aristotle did not leave us very many concrete details about the form of government he had in mind, but what he did say was destined to bear rich speculative fruit throughout the succeeding centuries. His "mean" form of government, which translators normally call simply "polity" or "constitutional government," was a synthesis of oligarchy and democracy.

Aristotle also distinguished the fundamentally different activities that he claimed are present in all constitutions: those activities relating to deliberation and those relating to the magistracies. Then he went on to distinguish eight types of judicial power (*Basic Works,* 1941, p. 1231). It is not clear to what extent each of these latter are thought of as being autonomous. Moreover, Aristotle's three basic categories of governmental activity were never identified with the three pure forms of government found in Plato. For like Plato, Aristotle assumed that of necessity each pure form contained all of the activities intrinsically characteristic of any political system. However, each of the different pure forms transmuted all of the basic governmental activities in a characteristic manner. Deliberation was not the same function in an oligarchy it was in a democracy, etc.

All this speculation about pure forms, mixed forms, and cycles of revolutions may seem a bit fanciful to the modern mind. But it is only fair to point out that the ancient political philosophers had considerable empirical evidence in support of their theories of governmental forms and cycles—more evidence, perhaps, than contemporary economists have for the existence of different economic forms and the recurrence of business cycles. Moreover, when one tries to get inside such crucial concepts of modern economics as profit, rent, interest, labor, property, and capital, the atmosphere becomes quite rarified. By comparison, the governmental forms and cycles of the ancients seem plainly verified by experience. But who has ever seen a concrete example of any of the basic economic concepts the modern world has identified with the essence of materialism? Perhaps people will someday come to look upon economic theory with much the same skepticism that some now affect regarding ancient theories of the cycles of governmental revolution.

The next important contribution came from Polybius, the famous Greek political theorist who lived at the time of the Roman Republic. He praised the Roman Republic much the way our own political theorists have been accustomed to praising the British constitution. Polybius believed that· history had verified Plato's theory of the six-stage cyclical degeneration and revolution of constitutions, adding the conclusion that the doctrine deserves to be called a "natural law" (Polybius *Histories,* 1966, p. 220). However, it was a law whose agency of realization was the people. Kings and aristocracies held power at the pleasure of the people. When they became corrupt it was the people who displaced them. And when democracy turned into ochlocracy (mobocracy) it was also the people who decided it was time to put everything in the charge of one man, reverting to monarchy.

Polybius would certainly have called Stalin's Russia and de Gaulle's France monarchies (though not kingdoms). Probably he would have regarded contemporary American presidential government and English ministerial government in the same way. However, he saw Rome as an example of mixed government. His explanation is probably the first true theory of mixed government. The mixture was not of function but of general constitutional types: monarchy, aristocracy, and democracy. 'These elements were expressed through the consuls, the Senate, and the people. Moreover, Polybius theorized that equilibrium would be maintained between the three governmental types because of their being mixed together. To explain this he developed an explicit theory of checks and balances out of which harmony was produced between the three departments of the Roman Constitution (*Histories,* p. 221). But this was not the same kind of checks and balances later found in the American Constitution, unless one insists that the functions described in the American Constitution are properly interpreted as surrogates for the classic pure types of government rather than as governmental functions, a position John Adams came close to adopting.

It is with Cicero that we find the jurisprudential essentials of constitutionalism brought together for the first time. Writing at the end of the Republic, he continued the scheme of Polybius. However, he also explained something about which Polybius, a Greek, was strangely silent. This was the rule of law. With this addition to the stream of political theory, the juristic components of constitutionalism are born. It led Cicero to propose a new kind of dualism between the politically organized concert of institutional forces and the officially established legal authority of the ruler. Cicero's phrase for this dualistic principle was *consensus iuris.* He went on to explain that in a government of laws rather than of men, the laws govern the officials and the officials govern the people. "The magistrate is a speaking law and the law a silent magistrate." This was a combination of the principle of the mixed state with that of the rule of law: namely, the jurisprudential maneuvers whereby the laws of various nations had yielded the *ius gentium,* the law of peoples, and this in turn had yielded the principles of *ius naturale.* If one makes this natural process into a self-conscious jurisprudential endeavor, it is obvious that the rule of law, in the definition Cicero gave to it, can be the result. But then one must ask how such a process for reducing the operating principles of disparate institutions to general legal principles can be conducted validly. The answer was provided by Stoicism. Its principles of equality, universality, and public service were philosophic guidelines for discovering from operating institutions the "natural laws" that were applicable to practical human affairs. Then it was only necessary for the people and the Senate, in constant deliberation, to establish the basic guidelines for the political order, resolving the dualism of the mixed state and the rule of law. All these elements together make up the first coherent juridical theory of constitutionalism. All that is lacking, though it is hinted at in the formula "the Senate and the Roman people," is the democratic component.

THE MEDIEVAL BACKGROUND

All those who have been nurtured on the jurisprudence of John Austin—and most of us have, whether or not we know it—naturally assume that there must be a single sovereign source of ultimate legal authority and competence in every proper state. Because of this often-unconscious assumption, most of us have a great deal of difficulty in understanding the workings of medieval political institutions. The Austinian system of political and legal theory was a fixture of the intellectual outlook of the early nineteenth century. It migrated to America along with the utilitarianism out of which it had developed in England. As the nineteenth century progressed, the Austinian tradition was reinforced among American intellectuals (in part because of the high repute of philosophers of sovereignty and the state produced by German scholarship and philosophy) until it acquired the status of dogma for several generations of American political theorists. This happened despite the fact that Austinian legal sovereignty was completely inapplicable to the sovereignty-fracturing foundations on which the American Constitution rested. For the American Constitution, like the medieval polity, embodied an essentially dualistic principle of organization reminiscent of that exhibited in the Roman state.

An important by-product of the Austinian doctrine was the conclusion that the state had, and of necessity ought to have, a monolithic structure. This is necessarily the case if one must always be able to locate one place within the state where the final disposition of legal omnicompetence resides, an ultimate pinnacle of authority where all conflicts are finally resolved. This is required because in the hierarchical juridical world of John Austin, nothing can be left at loose ends. Pluralism is anathema to legal sovereignty. Every legal issue must have a final resting place, and it must be the same place for all (see Austin, 1954). This is what is taken in if one imbibes the doctrine that the state must possess a monolithic structure. Of course, this idea went down fairly easily in England, where there was a centralized governmental system that left no constitutional autonomy to cities or provinces. More important was the supremacy of the legislative function that had been established by the Whig Revolution. Even so, the more discerning adherents of the Austinian doctrine had a little trouble with their creed because they lived in a democratic era. The role of the people, as Cicero had observed, required that room be made for what was called "political," as distinguished from legal, sovereignty. In England political sovereignty referred to the rational exercise of the judgment of the people at the polls. One could say that it was concerned with the substance of politics rather than its legal form. Thus the state could be legally authoritarian while its political substance remained democratic. This is reminiscent of what Cicero might have meant by *consensus iuris*. Later, Lenin was to put these same two principles in his theory of democratic centralism. But such reflections need not detain us now, for in truth, Austin and his followers were aware of the problem; they were no more successful than was Lenin in really making room in their theory of the state for the political sovereignty of the people. The Austinian state was an entity sufficient to itself. Its legal structure assumed a political society and then provided for positive law to descend from on high. There was no built-in procedure for it to accommodate itself to democracy's contrary principle of authority. That would have required an explicitly dualistic theory of the state, which was explicitly denied by Austinian jurisprudence.

It was denied in theory, but it could not be denied in fact, especially in America. And in spite of the fact that generations of American scholars grew up under the spell of Austinian legal sovereignty, there always was hanging in the background another sovereign principle. Though scholars like Maitland, Lindsay, and Dewey called our attention to this second principle, it was largely ignored by jurisprudence and by constitutional theory, despite the fact that it lingered constantly at the edge of political thought.

We have seen that if one tries to account for both legal sovereignty and popular sovereignty at once, the very effort makes "sovereignty" dissolve into something that is incorrigibly dualistic. The first reaction is that this is self-contradictory. Of course, the Romans didn't think so, and possibly we wouldn't either if we had never learned about Austinian legal sovereignty. Does not such a conclusion rest entirely on the validity of the theory of the monolithic state? Moreover, the doctrine of the monolithic state is an historical rarity.

Sovereignty in the Middle Ages was in no sense monolithic. It was riven at its core, completely dualistic. Many scholars have tried to explain the dualistic nature of the medieval constitution. Harrington (1747; see also Andrews, 1937) called it "the Gothic balance." Usually it has been labeled *double majesty,* a term first employed by Otto Gierke (1957, p. 60; see generally Wormuth, 1949). Double majesty is a confusing notion. It calls to our minds the picture of a two-headed, Januslike sovereign. And despite the intrinsic unbelievableness of such an image, it is exactly what medieval monarchy was like.

Those who have tried to uncover the historical origins of medieval double majesty have detected many possible sources. Recall that in early Rome there had been two kings. Even later, when the Senate and the people shared in the political process, there was a sharp distinction between the war-making imperium of the consuls and authority over domestic affairs. Something similar obtained in the Germanic tribes to the north. They provided for one leader to rule in normal times and another to rule in the event of war. The war leader was completely sovereign for the duration of the military operation. The authority of the peacetime ruler was then held in abeyance, and after the conclusion of hostilities he resumed the exercise of his accustomed prerogatives. This notion of dual kingship was so firmly implanted in Germanic tribal institutions that, as the late medieval literary sources show, it was gradually transmuted into the later dualism of the sovereign people on the one hand and the sovereign monarch on the other. The people took the place of the older domestic sovereign and the functions of the medieval war leader came under the personal prerogatives of the king. Medieval theories of kingship, especially those found in the so-called mirror-of-princes literature, quite often distinguish between these two different principles of monarchial authority.

The dualistic tradition inside medieval regimes was repeated on the level of Christendom as a whole. The theory of the two cities issued in that of the two swords: separate authority for sacred and secular jurisdictions. And inside the Church itself the Conciliar Controversy duplicated the secular dispute between king and barons.

Here a warning is in order. The modern issue of democracy against monarchy did not arise. Rather, the problem was to discover the proper role of popular authority in a monarchy. The king's authority was held to be absolute. Yet, kings and their apologists together repeatedly proclaimed that the voice of the people was the voice of God, a formula they considered did not derogate from their own authority by one whit. Medieval England had its own special counterpart of this dualistic tradition. There the popular aspect of monarchy was assimilated into what is sometimes called the folk spirit, but more often the common law; for the common law was thought of as the common possession of the entire people. This dualistic Anglican tradition became institutionalized in a series of conflicts between various English kings and their chief barons. One of these gave us the Magna Charta. It is but the most famous of a whole series of such confrontations. In these intermittent uprisings the barons were trying, as they sometimes phrased it, to set metes and bounds to the king's authority. The more rash sometimes threatened to put a bridle upon the kings, but this latter statement really went too far. It verged on treason. However, even in the ordinary formulation of the dualism of law and king there was always a hidden seed of treason. When the barons won, as at Runnymede, treason was never mentioned. Only unsuccessful rebels got hanged. And of course when the baronial faction lost out, as it did from time to time, its leaders were regularly executed for treason. However, the centuries-long struggle in which successive kings and their baronial opponents traded ascendancy back and forth produced a profound constitutional formula that accommodated both sides at once—the realm of settled law and the sphere of royal absolutism —and this was expressed and reinforced in a long series of English legal cases.

These disputes were much like those that arise today between labor and management—or between students and university authorities. If a conflict between king and barons could not be settled by negotiation, the only recourse open to the barons was to strike against the king, which they frequently did. But attack on the principle of royalty was hazardous, even when done in the name of the law, for the authority of the barons toward their own vassals rested on the same principles of allegiance as did the king's authority over the barons. To threaten the higher jeopardized the lower. Accordingly, it became a maxim among the barons that their disobedience was not a violation of their personal loyalty to the king, that their allegiance was not more owing to the laws than to the king—a doctrine incompatible with kingship. Instead they developed the doctrine of the king's wicked advisers. According to this doctrine, it was not the king himself who was wrong; rather, the king was the victim of wicked advisers. The barons could then oppose the policies of evil counsellors without seeming to challenge the principle of kingly authority itself. Wicked advisers could be purged to ensure that the king's proper will could find expression. Gradually, over many centuries, this form of baronial civil disobedience became institutionalized in Parliament through impeachment proceedings against errant ministers of the crown. This in turn led to the emergence of the working principles of the British constitution: the king acts only on the advice of his ministers; the ministers of the king's cabinet are responsible to Parliament for acts done in the name of the crown; and a cabinet must resign if it loses the confidence of Parliament. In a sense then the British contribution to constitutionalism is the institutionalization of civil disobedience.

This, however, was not to emerge for many centuries. In the meantime a workable formula was achieved by distinguishing between the king's body-politic (the area of common-law authority) and the king's body-personal (the area of the king's absolute prerogative.) The ruler was a sovereign king and his polity was a sovereign kingdom. Each could be distinguished from the other. In later times, by the mid-sixteenth century, this formula came to be expressed as two separate royal prerogatives: the prerogative ordinary and the prerogative absolute (Wormuth, 1972, p. 54). Finally, to add to the complexity—and it even tried the genius of a mind so subtle as Maitland's (1936)—the ambiguous term *crown* was sometimes used to refer to the prerogative ordinary. The confusion here resulted from the fact that the strongest of the kings, those who tended to swallow up or ignore the prerogative ordinary, naturally insisted that their crown included both.

Now, in the first area, the area of the crown (or the body-politic, or the prerogative ordinary), there was the realm of settled law. This consisted of the common-law arrangement that had grown up by and large out of feudal relationships, mainly from principles of land tenure. This growth of English common law occurred in much the same way the ancient Roman common law had developed. England's king had his place in the common law and it was a most, or rather *the* most, exalted one. He was literally the kingpin of the pyramid of fealty arrangements that reached from the lowest serf up to the lordly apex of the kingdom. (It is well to remember that this was a network of mutual oaths—sworn allegiances providing for reciprocal rights and duties.) These allegiances, or bonds, were, in effect, individual contracts of law or government. One of the duties the contract imposed on the landlord was the obligation to provide his liege with government, that is, to provide security and protection, to hold court, to administer its rulings, and in general to guarantee enjoyment of the blessings of law and order. In this realm, and we need not hesitate to conceive of it as a complete and autonomous realm of government, the king had his place just as did every other liege lord. Moreover, the king's behavior was "regulated." He was a lawful and a law-abiding king. He was constrained not only by the force of custom and the binding power of his own solemn oath, but also by the reciprocal nature of all those relationships not nationalized by the king's military force. Any abrogation of a duty to his subjects by the king might be answered by a comparable abrogation of duties to their sovereign on the part of his subjects. Of course, in the event of an irreconcilable dispute over the lawfulness of a king's acts, the only possible way to resolve the issue was through a resort to arms. But this was not necessary as often as the modern mind might imagine. For everyone knew that the breaking of customs and sworn oaths would rupture the entire fabric of society. The forces of what Carl Friedrich (1941, p. 26) called the "rule of anticipated reactions" operated quite effectively. One can see its operation pictured in Shakespeare's kings, who measured every action by a careful calculation of the reaction it was likely to bring.

England was ruled by a king, but he was a common-law king. At the same time, however, he was an absolute king. For there was not only the politics of the constituent parts of the monarchy—the politics of village and town, manor and estate—there was also the politics of the realm as a whole—the politics of the federal level, so to speak. This involved such things as conducting diplomacy and commanding the armed forces. Moreover, the king had a special sovereignty over the outlying provinces, the colonies, the separate realms (such as Ireland, Scotland, and Wales), the royal manors, and the cities with independently chartered freedoms. These all had to be linked together in some way, and this was provided for under the king's prerogative absolute. All these coordinative and systemic needs grew enormously after the thirteenth century. At the same time, commercial relationships were expanding at a rapid pace. In order to provide for the common defense, to maintain commerce and communication, and to see to the administration of the law, all the land's separate components had to be linked together by highways, a stage postal service, a navy, a coinage system, a court system, crown officers, etc.

The degree of authority to be exercised had to be sufficient to support the new requirements of peace and order, which operated on principles different from those that had characterized the network of liege-seignior contracts which had grown out of the law of the fief. This latter was the law of the land. The other was the law of the king's peace. As the modern era approached, the king's law began to expand at a rapid rate and the older law of the land underwent a profound commercial transformation. Neither one of the prerogatives of double majesty could accommodate these new changes without themselves undergoing considerable change and expansion. This is exactly what both of them did, and as they did so, conflicts between the two inevitably increased in number and intensity. For example, there was no way to provide for expanded intermanorial, interprovincial (or interstate, one might say) needs out of the pluralistic network of feudal contractual relationships that pyramided up to the king under the common law. Maintaining the king's peace was always regarded as a function the monarch provided out of his prerogative absolute. He defrayed part of the cost of charging turnpike tolls and imposts. His justices charged fees for the services they rendered, etc. But most of the cost of government was paid for out of the personal income produced by the manorial, provincial, and colonial possessions of the crown. Unfortunately, these sources of income did not suffice when it became necessary to expand the king's highways, to create and maintain a vast bureaucracy, to facilitate the expansion of trade, and to maintain the conditions of commercial exchange through the regulation of coinage. All these functions came under the king's absolute prerogative, as did also the function of defending the realm in war.

At first, war had been almost a private venture of the king in cooperation with his chief barons. Later it became a vast national undertaking, and one that was extremely expensive. But because it was an engagement of the realm acting as one person, it too resided in the king's absolute prerogative. Obviously no one else could be entrusted with the war-making function. But after the sixteenth century, no king had sufficient ordinary resources to exercise it. His sources of monarchial revenue were simply too small to maintain a large national army.

Diplomacy, the power to receive and recognize foreign ambassadors as well as to appoint diplomats to go abroad, was another of those functions that grew up outside of the common-law tradition and under the king's prerogative absolute, for here again the king stood for the realm, acting as a whole, integral person.

A moment's reflection will show that the powers described above under the medieval English king's prerogative absolute are strongly reminiscent of the powers that the American Constitution specifically allotted to the federal government in 1789. This curiosity is matched by another: that same Constitution reserved the nation's common-law jurisdiction to the states. Both arrangements are in perfect accord with the principles of medieval double majesty. Nor was this an accident. And to see why it was not, we must briefly trace out what finally happened to double majesty in England. For the constitutional crisis that arose between the colonies and England in 1776 derived from the fact that the political order of the New World had been set in motion in the early seventeenth century, a time when the English constitution from which it sprang still operated according to medieval double-majesty principles.

THE UNION OF THE CROWNS OF ENGLAND AND SCOTLAND

The opening of the seventeenth century in England brought with it the close of the Tudor dynasty. And it was generally expected that profound political changes would also ensue. The gothic prerogatives had gotten out of balance. Accordingly, there grew up a weighty debate over the principles of the English constitution.

Already, under Elizabeth I, England's great mercantilist explosion had begun. Today's historians call the Elizabethans the Americans of the seventeenth century. This commercial revolution alone was enough to force a reconsideration of the nature and the limits of the powers in the two traditional departments of double majesty, as well as of the increasingly vexatious problem of locating the boundaries between them. Elizabeth's death gave a strengthened stimulus to constitutional speculation because of the special situation surrounding the advent of her successor, James I, the king of England. Previously this same man had reigned in Scotland as King James VI. There had been one or two other claimants who possibly might have succeeded Elizabeth instead of James VI, but it was this Stuart king of Scotland who won out. His succession actually occurred in more or less the same way new corporation presidents succeed to office today. So James VI of Scotland became also James I of England, two kings at once, a thing by no means uncommon during the nation-building era of Europe. Probably if he had been king of some land other than Scotland, say, a remote land whose people didn't speak a related tongue, few if any perplexing constitutional issues would have been raised by his succession to the crown of England. But then, of course, it would have been unlikely at that time for a remote foreigner to occupy England's throne, except by conquest.

The issues created by the accession of James sprang directly from the nature of the dualistic medieval constitution already described, and it is easy to see why perplexities had to arise. Political union is one of mankind's most mysterious processes, as witness our contemporary quandry over how to unify nation-states into a world order. Then, as now, the problem of union raised the deepest questions of both sovereignty and allegiance. We now assume that the two are virtually inseparable, and this is consistent with John Austin's jurisprudential doctrine of legal sovereignty. But where there is an actual human sovereign instead of an abstract principle of legal sovereignty, the identity between sovereignty and allegiance is not so clear as it first appears to be. Seventeenth century Britons were confronted with the problem of determining the constitutional effect produced when a man who held the crown of the one country added to it the crown of another. We need not concern ourselves at this point over what happens to the king himself as a result of his acquisitions of two crowns. Rather, we want to find out what happens to the two countries that come under a single ruler and thereby change from a condition of mutual autonomy to one of partnership, from a unitary to a pluralistic realm. What would be the constitutional result if this happened today in a monarchy or a dictatorship or even in a constitutional democracy? Perhaps a better way of dramatizing the issue is to ask what would have happened to the separate industrial empires of Henry Ford II and Howard Hughes if either acquired rulership over both. For anyone who has difficulty comprehending medieval double majesty, these examples should make it a little easier to understand. In a fancied union of the "crowns" of Ford and Hughes, it is obvious that the new ruler of the combined realms would be able to achieve considerable personal control over the operation of each component of the union. However, there would also be extensive areas from which his personal prerogatives would be positively excluded. There would be, in short, two principles of control operating simultaneously in the new combination of industrial firms. But finding out just what belonged in each area and how to draw the line between the two would require a long and tedious process of trial and error, of negotiation and even adjudication. America's great family corporations have operated on a principle quite like the medieval principle of double majesty. They have had to do so in order to accommodate their two essential features: personal rule combined with bureaucratization. When we speak of the more recent corporations, after the so-called managerial revolution, we describe how the once-great family magnates have been either deposed or made into constitutional monarchs. The "managerial revolution" in the industrial firm is the corporate counterpart of the Whig revolution that constitutionalized the English monarchy.

King James has the reputation among historians of being an apostle of absolutism. It is doubtful that he really was. But James did believe that the mere fact of his becoming king of the two separate countries, Scotland and England, wrought a fundamental political change in the relationships between the two realms. He felt that it unified them into a single new nation and he proposed that it be called Britain. The reasoning James gave was simple: everyone in each of the two countries now owed allegiance to him. Allegiance, reasoned James, was the primary factor in determining the political and legal relationships between citizens, that is, their citizenship. He concluded that all citizens had been unified, one to another, Scottish and English together, the very instant they fell under the rule of the same king. Looking at matters from where King James sat, this seems to be an unexceptionable argument. One can imagine that a Howard Hughes might have made exactly the same argument to the "citizens" of Ford upon his succession to the joint presidency. However, to those Englishmen who resided far below the crown, James' argument didn't seem quite so persuasive. A furor of dissent was immediately unleashed. After all, the two countries had quite different cultural and political traditions. Scotland had grown up under the sway of the Roman-law tradition, and this was as alien to the proper common law of the Englishman as was haggis to pease porridge. Moreover, recently there had been a series of Catholic rulers in Scotland, somewhat more recently, that is, than in England. But Scottish Catholicism had given way to a strident Calvinism that threatened to swell the streams of English sectarianism into a Protestant flood that might wash away the English ecclesiastical establishment. Finally, there was good reason, on a practical basis, in support of the more or less conservative opposition of the English parliamentarians. They balked at admitting that merely because they had acquired a foreign king, a mysterious monarchial alchemy had unified them with a foreign land. But this was an argument that could not be pressed too far, because if it were, it verged on the hazardous topic referred to above, namely, the limits of the subject's loyalty to the king's person. To open this question was not only dangerous, it was also explosive. And what it threatened to explode was nothing less than the entire constitution itself: the traditional, dualistic, medieval constitution. This was what James Harrington meant when he later described double majesty as a form of gunpowder rather than government.

But what did allegiance to the person of the king mean if not that all who owed allegiance to him were related to each other as his subjects? To deny that a genuine union had really been wrought between Englishmen and Scotsmen when James became their common king seemed to be saying that allegiance was more owing to the separate laws and institutions of the individual nations than it was to their king. The union of the two crowns under James created the need to make a choice. Before James brought the Stuart dynasty to the throne of England, the need for making this choice could be avoided, even though the crucial feature of the medieval constitution was its dualistic foundation for allegiance and sovereignty. The only previous Englishmen who had asserted that allegiance was more owing to the laws than to the kings were the notorious Despensers, Hugh the Elder and his son. The fourteenth century *Case of the Despensers (Statutes of the Realm,* Vol. 1) is famous among English legal antiquarians. Hugh and his son had been high royal advisers between the kings and their barons. It was normal for the barons to celebrate their intermittent victories by expelling the king's top officials and putting their own men in office. The charge against the deposed officials was often treason, though it was hard to make such a case against those who had been the king's most loyal supporters. In the *Case of the Despensers* the victorious baronial faction defended its paradoxical position with the somewhat whimsical explanation that the Despensers had maintained the treasonable doctrine that allegiance was more owing to the law than to the king. It seems to have been a kind of a joke—a power joke—a majestic irony. But this curious irony aside, the *Case of the Despensers* established a clear precedent at English law. Anyone who later dared question the nature of allegiance was quickly throttled with an ominous reference to the Despensers.

James, the wearer of an uneasy new crown, was understandably touchy on the subject of allegiance. A seventeenth century palace wag called it James' "neuralgic thread." After all, medieval kingship had rested on the principle of the subject's personal allegiance to the king—to the king's body-personal, not his body-politic. So the Englishmen who greeted Scotland's James VI as a successor to Elizabeth I could not deny their direct allegiance to the person of their new king. But they balked at affirming that the fact of their allegiance alone was sufficient to cause a thorough political and juridical union between England and Scotland. Their problem was to find a way to make this point without denying their unqualified allegiance to the king, thereby avoiding the treasonable position of claiming that allegiance was more owing to the laws than to the king. Every Englishman knew it was worth as much as his head to affirm *that belief.*

Looking somewhat ahead we know that it was exactly the reversal of this priority of allegiances that would mark the emergence of the modern English constitution a few furious decades later, in 1688. The modern industrial state made loyalty and allegiance due to the state as a corporation—a proprietor of land and a fountain of authority—rather than to a principle of association. The modern Western state dissolved the network of personal allegiances that had always before linked person to person in society. The struggle to consummate this reversal—the substitution of the principles of government in the estate (state) for the politics of association—expresses the juridical difference between medieval and modern politics. But this puts us ahead of our story, and we must return for a moment to the time when allegiance was still ambiguous, owing both to king *and* law, incorporating both association and state.

CALVIN'S CASE AND THE ENGLISH CONSTITUTION

Toward the end of the sixteenth century a series of legal cases began to arise involving the juridical nature of the crown. These cases permit us to trace the development of the double-majesty doctrine, for the judges were forced to decide exactly what fell within the prerogative absolute on the one hand and what was proper to the prerogative ordinary on the other. In doing so, it became customary for the successive judges summarily to denounce the subversive doctrine of the Despensers, especially in cases involving the law of the prerogative ordinary. In effect, the judges surreptitiously assimilated kingship to law in one breath and with the next piously denounced those who, in earlier times, had championed that principle. So, as the seventeenth century approached, more and more judges went out of their way to denounce the "execrable" doctrine of the Despensers, while effectively making it part of the law of the land. This juristic fermentation had been long at work when, in all innocence, James thrashed his way onto the constitutional scene and proposed that Parliament ratify the organic union he believed had been produced by his personal union of the two crowns of England and Scotland. But Parliament balked. It even refused to give him the title "King of Britain," and he adopted the style by proclamation, an act that further angered the parliamentary faction.

Next, in some umbrage himself, James turned to the courts. Of course, they were "his" courts, the king's courts. The judges were his personal appointees. "Lions," but "lions under the throne," had written Bacon (1905) and no one missed the point. Thinking he had the votes of the judges well under control, James contrived to institute a legal case that he felt would resolve the issue of union the way he wanted it. This was to become the famous *Case of the Postnati,* commonly known as *Calvin's Case (Howell's State Trials,* Vol. 2, p. 559; on James see James, 1918, pp. 296–97). It is to this case that the whole prior discussion has been pointing.

Calvin's Case is as Janus-faced as the doctrine it confirms and restates. It stands in baroque splendor astride the boundary between the medieval and the modern world, commanding the confluent streams of constitutional law that come together at that great historic divide. Yet, if there is such a thing as one leading case for both British and American constitutional law, it is *Calvin's Case*. It leads to both Locke and Madison, to parliamentary sovereignty, as well as to federalism and the separation of powers. This more than warrants our giving some serious attention to the problem of the allegiance of the infant Scot, Robert Calvin and of the meaning of allegiance for all postnati, or persons who, like young Calvin, were born after the death of Elizabeth, when separate monarchs no longer ruled the two realms of England and Scotland.

There were altogether fourteen judges sitting at that time in the three high courts. And to try *Calvin's Case*, as was the custom for very significant cases, all the high judges were convoked in joint session in the Exchequer-Chamber. The case, which was technically a dispute over a land-title, was argued elaborately before them all. The way in which a land title case could present the larger issue of political union and constitutional structure was beautifully simple. Land had been bought in England in the name of the newly born child Robert Calvin—that is, he had been born in Scotland *after* James became king of England as well as of Scotland. The traditional English law held that no alien (and therefore no Scot) could hold title to English land. This followed from the principle of feudal law, according to which land ownership carried with it the obligation to serve in the king's armies in the event of war. This was an obligation no foreigner could accept or discharge without the risk of becoming treasonous in his own land should the king ruling over his alien property wage war against his native king. But what about young Robert Calvin and all such post-Elizabethan Scots? How could they be regarded as aliens at law when they owed allegiance to the same king as did the English? Immediately this brought to a head the issue previously referred to, namely, the potential conflict between one's loyalty to the person of the king and to the law. And the constitutionally quick-witted will quickly perceive that something very akin to this same issue was raised 150 years later by a group of New Englanders as they grew restive under the colonial regulations passed by England's parliamentary Whigs.

But return now to our fourteen Stuart judges pondering the constitutional significance of young Robert Calvin's title to English land. If they decided he could own land in England this would amount to deciding that he was a citizen of England. This in turn would make citizenship, and all it implied, rest on personal ties of loyalty to the king. But if that were the case, how could one distinguish between the post- and the antenati? Older Scots also owed allegiance to the man who was king of England. Why did they not automatically become "naturalized" English citizens with James' accession to the English throne? There had to be some difference between them because of the selective effects on them of the mysterious force that was activated the instant of James' succession to the throne of England.

In those days the extraordinary convocation of all the chief judges did not constitute a proper court. That is, the convocation did not produce its own rulings. Rather, each judge announced his own opinion, and something like an informal consensus usually resulted. Moreover, the convocation did not preserve an official record of the opinions announced by the individual judges. Only when individual judges preserved or published their own notes or opinions privately do we have any record of the cases argued. In *Calvin's Case* the judges were almost unanimous. Twelve of them agreed that Robert Calvin could hold title to land in England. It followed, in the logic of the law, that Robert Calvin was not an alien. Obviously this legal effect was produced by the accession of James. But the strict rule of the decision tells us little of the larger issue that exercised James, namely, to achieve by judicial decision what had been withheld him by Parliament: the organic union of England and Scotland. This was the issue everybody wanted to know more about. Accordingly, all the leading judges were shortly in print with their opinions about the case. Sir Edward Coke, whom tradition accords the title "father of the common law," was one of the judges, and his opinion is usually taken as the most authoritative statement of the law (*Howell's State Trials,* Vol. 2, p. 629). However, Francis Bacon was the attorney who argued the case for the crown and his published brief, which is much fuller, is an indispensable supplement to the opinions of the judges (Bacon, *Works,* Vol. 15, pp. 189–248). But the most important thing about the case is that when we put all these documents together piece by piece they permit us to reconstruct (like a jigsaw puzzle) an intelligible account of the English constitution at the opening of the seventeenth century. For in order to resolve the case, each judge found it necessary to announce an explicit theory of kingship. It is the first time English constitutional law is laid out for our minute inspection. Moreover, with Bacon and Coke as the chief expositors—two of the most formidable legal minds of all time—the authenticity of the result is fully vouchsafed. What they tell us is that as the seventeenth century opened, England possessed a fundamentally dualistic constitution.

There were two principles of allegiance and two principles of sovereignty. On one side was the arena of the law. Here, as we already know, the king was a common-law king. The other side, of course, involved the arena of the prerogative absolute, also familiar from above. But the special effect of *Calvin's Case* was to leave England and Scotland completely separate on the institutional level of the dualistic constitution and unified only on the level of the prerogative absolute. That is, the formula produced by *Calvin's Case* provided a constitutional principle whereby two polities could be regarded as unified for some joint purposes and yet autonomous for all others. This is a stunning moment in constitutional history, for it lays down the foundation for the invention Americans will later bequeath to the world under the name of federalism.

The path from *Calvin's Case* to *McCulloch* v. *Maryland* (1819) leads first into the constitutional theory of the British Empire and quickly thereafter into dominion theory. *Calvin's Case* starts us off by explaining the legal theory of how the parts of Great Britain and the colonies were linked together in the crown, and it is to the precise nature of this linkage that we now must turn. Of course, all this did not fall together neatly with transparent deductive clarity. Rather, the arguments tumbled out in a tangled cascade of juridical ingenuity. However, if we keep in mind the nature of medieval double majesty and the process whereby England's two great seventeenth century jurists laid the constitutional groundwork for modern federalism, it is somewhat easier to unravel.

The prerogative ordinary was the realm of particularity, pluralism, and of settled social, institutional, and legal ties. The prerogative absolute was the realm of the universal, the unified, and the contingent; of personal loyalties and bonds. Prior to the death of Elizabeth I both realms existed in each of the two countries. What the succession of James did was to unify the two nations on the second level only. The previously separate realms of the prerogative absolute were coalesced into one, and this was the only place union occurred. The other realm, that of the prerogative ordinary, remained separate for each nation, with each one maintaining its own autonomous domestic legal system just as before. This meant that King James possessed one prerogative absolute but two (and more) separate bodies-politic, one called England, another called Scotland, and as many other domestically autonomous bodies-politic as there were crown colonies and territories. The empire was unified, but its parts were, or could be, autonomous. It was merely that each autonomous body-politic had the same king, and in theory his kingship over the most powerful body-politic, England, did not imply that England as a king-country amalgam could exercise hegemony over any of the others, though in actual practice England's supremacy was tacitly admitted. Under the doctrine of *Calvin's Case* each crown possession was confirmed in its constitutional right to its own legal system. The king had many different bodies-politic but he had only one crown. By virtue of his crown, James was sovereign over all the people in their capacities as individuals rather than as members of a given polity. There was, however, a second allegiance. Although it was not stated in so many words at the time, the effect of *Calvin's Case* was to match the double majesty of the king with a corresponding double citizenship of the subject. The people, in effect, were citizens of the larger, imperial union and also citizens of their respective component polities. This, of course, is one of the essentials of the condition we call federalism. With a few deft juridical injections, the medieval tradition of double majesty was made pregnant with one of the most important institutional inventions in the history of politics.

Calvin's Case lay embedded deep in the center of the stream of English constitutional history. The Cromwellians tried to supersede it, but the victorious Whigs, once they had neutralized their citizen king, speedily returned to its principles. None of the leading features of *Calvin's Case* was ever overruled, and it remains today in England and also in America the leading case on questions of sovereignty, allegiance, and union. Invariably, when disputes later arose over these issues, *Calvin's Case* was the leading authority to which the disputants on both sides appealed in defending their positions.

It is easy to visualize how disputes might come about and what the opposing positions would be. One obvious question would be, Could the prerogative absolute overrule actions or statutes that otherwise would be perfectly lawful under the prerogative ordinary? There are different ways of resolving this problem, and they lead down separate paths to the different ways England and America resolved the problem of constitutionalizing the arbitrary exercise of authority.

What are the possible alternatives? If we reject dictatorship, they are legislative sovereignty on the one hand or some kind of distributive authority, as was to emerge in the New World, on the other. But, of course, this latter requires that an explicit provision be made for some way of arbitrating conflicts between those among whom authority is distributed. We cannot yet properly call this principle of adjudication by the name of judicial review, even though the single English instance of judicial review, *Dr. Bonham's Case* (1610), arose just after the time of *Calvin's Case*. All three possible successors to double majesty were tried. Dictatorship was suppressed in seventeenth century England; its suppression is still an issue in contemporary America. Legislative supremacy then emerged in England. Following the revolution, distributed authority won out in America. But this merely leads to the next question: Why was it that England chose the path of legislative sovereignty in a centralized nation and why did America opt for distributive authority—federalism, checks and balances, and judicial review?

To answer this we must remind ourselves of one overriding characteristic of the medieval tradition of double majesty from which both attempted resolutions sprang. This is that *both* of the two realms of medieval double majesty were monarchial. It is *not* the case that the realm of the medieval prerogative ordinary could be identified with what later became the House of Commons, or even with both Commons and Lords considered together as an embryonic legislature. Those two houses never comprised a legislature, not either one separately or both together. The two together were not even described as "parliament." Parliament—remember its full title is "The High *Court* of Parliament" (McIlwain, 1910)—was the central institution of English *kingship,* and the role and presence of the king was always central to its work. Parliament consisted of the *three* orders, or "estates": *King,* Lords, and Commons. So the constitutional puzzle we are trying to unravel does not arise initially as the issue of republicanism versus monarchy. Rather, it is born of the effort to extend the rule-of-law principles of the king's prerogative ordinary to encompass the traditionally uncontrolled authority of the king's prerogative absolute. Both original ingredients are medieval. What is not medieval is the supersession of monarchial dualism by subordinating one of its branches to the other.

We must think of early Europe's governments as having been ruled by two kings at once (Kantorowics, 1957). Then, when one ruler acquires the right to exercise both kingships, double majesty is born. This is probably the true historical origin of double majesty, but even if it is not, it is an aid to understanding. And we recall that ancient states often had two kings, one for war and another for peace, and that contemporary socialist regimes sometimes have two dictators ruling side by side: a party head governing in conjunction with the head bureaucrat. Both dualisms are very much like the dualistic structure of medieval kingship. Moreover, some of the people's democracies appear today to be experiencing constitutional tribulations similar to those that beset Stuart England's regimes during the seventeenth century.

In fact, one can read the political problems of Renaissance and Reformation times in terms of those of the present. Late Renaissance Europe went through what can be called a Stalinist period before it came to its constitutional period. Moreover, the function of Renaissance and baroque absolutism—Tudor and Bourbon—was much the same as the function of Stanlinism and Maoism: to lay the foundation for a mercantilist economy capable of initiating the capital-accumulation process. Of course, the initial mercantilists were interested only in maximizing the treasures of the "crown," but the result was the same as that achieved by the later "people's" mercantilists, who ran their economies so that all net profits accrued to the government. The fact that the latter government was described as the collective manifestation of the people does not, except rhetorically, distinguish the Stalinists from the "enlightened" despots of old. They also claimed to rule in the interest of the people. We can even push the comparison further. Many economists, John Simons and Paul Sweezy are examples (1964), have suggested that contemporary Yugoslavia is an example of the way a Whig revolution may occur in a modern "people's" mercantilism.

But to return to our seventeenth century English prototype, it may be helpful if we try to visualize the organization chart of double majesty. A few such charts actually were drawn by seventeenth century constitutional theorists. The most useful one is that attributed to Francis Bacon (*Works*, Vol. 15, p. 377). From it we can see graphically what has been described above: a dualistic English constitution. Its two autonomous principles were law and the king. They were separate but they were not opposed to each other. Moreover, each twin was internally dualistic. Within the law there was a rule-of-law area. There the king was under the law. But equally a part of the law was a second area, in which the law itself acknowledged the king's superiority as well as the law's own inability to correct the king for any alleged offense within the area of sanctioned absolutism.

Note that this was not the same thing as saying that there was an area in which the king was lawless or despotic. On the contrary, this absolutism was explicitly defined by law. It was rather that the king and his ministers (and these included many sworn magistrates and judges) possessed *lawful* prerogatives whose exercise could not be called into account by any writ or process of adjudication. This only *seems* mysterious. Actually, there is a similar legally endowed area of absolutism in all governments. For example, in America today the Supreme Court exercises a power of judicial review that the law recognizes and authorizes but is powerless to correct. The American president possesses several legally absolute powers, most of them pertaining to war, diplomacy, national security, executive privilege, and executive appointments. The legislative branch also possesses a lawful absolutism whose abuses, if they occur, cannot be corrected by law. Most familiar is the legislator's exemption from being sued for statements made in Congress. These are all examples of exemptions from the law that are established and protected by law. They illustrate precisely what Bacon meant (*Works,* Vol. 15, p. 377) when he said England's constitution provided for a twofold power of the law, one that controlled the king and one in which the law protected the king's uncontrollability.

The second branch of Bacon's constitution described kingship per se. The king, like the law, also possessed a twofold power. In one the king was absolute. Remember, the law did not provide for an arbitrary power but rather for a power over which it disclaimed control. The difference is important. A modern parallel is found in the laws that preserve a free market from being controlled but do not thereby condone irresponsible market activities. Similarly, seventeenth century royal apologists often argue that the only guarantor of a free society was a "free" king, just as twentieth century apologists for capitalism speak of a free market as the guarantor of a free society. So even though the second side of the Tudor constitution described an area of absolute authority, this did not mean that the king possessed the right to rule in an arbitrary fashion. Of course, individual kings might commit arbitrary acts, and of course some that did so might go scot free. But this is like saying that an American senator, Senator Joseph McCarthy, for example, could use his authority in an arbitrary manner and those he injured would have no recourse at law. And yet American constitutional lawyers, like their Tudor counterparts, were still correct in denying that any senator possessed a right to the exercise of arbitrary authority.

Bacon's seventeenth century constitutional chart tells us that the king's second branch of authority was "limited." If we think of the other absolute prerogative as referring chiefly to war powers and diplomacy, this "limited" prerogative can be thought of as including those administrative powers granted the king by law.

The career of a later seventeenth century judge, Sir Matthew Hale, bridges the span between the Stuarts and the Restoration. Moreover, he served as judge under Cromwell and Charles II alike, maintaining his neutrality and independence throughout. At the time, extremists on both sides charged Hale with cowardice and lack of principle, charges that find no support in his official behavior. On the contrary, Justice Hale was merely attempting to preserve the dualistic principles of double majesty as he understood them. Confirmation of this is found in Hale's *Analysis of the Crown*. This contains an organization chart of the British constitution much like that attributed to Bacon. His two constitutional pinnacles are called "government" and "the prince." Government in turn possessed two subdivisions of authority, general and particular. Each of these was further divided in two. The same doubly dualistic scheme was applied to the prince, who possessed one category of prerogatives by virtue of his title and another as a result of his "natural and political capacities." Each of these was further divided into two parts. It should be pointed out that these were times during which the Ramist dialectical method held sway (Ong, 1958). That method, which possessed a close affinity with the ecclesiastical and constitutional struggles of the day, consisted primarily of dividing each issue into two, a process that was repeated indefinitely until a resolution of the initial issue was discovered. Ramist dualistic dialectical method was popular not only in England but also in the American colonies, where it had become the generally accepted mode of analysis by the time of the revolution.

CALVIN'S CASE AND THE IMPERIAL CONSTITUTION

The first American colonies were founded under England's seventeenth century constitution, an England that was a monarchy whose organic political essence was expressed in a high court of Parliament consisting of King, Lords, and Commons. The governmental authority expressed in Parliament flowed through two channels: the law and the king. That which flowed through the law controlled and also freed the king, just as we say today that acquiring a charter of incorporation frees but also controls a business enterprise. The authority that flowed through the king was initiated from laws as well as from royal acts and commissions. As a result there were four areas, or rather, four modes, through which authority moved. But taken together they amounted merely to a fuller articulation of the traditional pair familiar from our earlier discussion of medieval double majesty.

Bacon's seventeenth century constitution was obviously based on the old prerogative-ordinary and prerogative-absolute dualism. However, the change he made was substantial, for his scheme was applicable to a king like James, who was king over two realms, each with its own separate legal and administrative order but both of which were also united by virtue of their allegiance to the same king. That is, Bacon's constitutional chart in effect adjusts the traditional conception of double majesty to account for the ruling in *Calvin's Case*. For after *Calvin's Case* we must imagine not only two orders of majesty in a single monarchy but, beyond this, an imperial mode, for it is at this time that the meaning of empire assumes constitutional significance.

Suppose we now try to delineate the British constitution as of 1608 (*Calvin's Case*) so as to account for the governance of the empire as well as of each component part. No simple chart of hierarchical relationships will do. We need a different scheme, one that is three dimensional and organic. A large petalled flower is a helpful image. For what we must account for is not only the royal constitution of the component colonial petals but also the separate constitution, the way their union and coordination are provided for in a central core—a royal pestle, so to speak—with the whole organism dominated by a lofty regal stamen: that part of the king that is in some respects independent of, but in most respects organically related to, both separate petals and central pestle. Thus we account for the crown as the seminal repository of the king's prerogative absolute and the area through which the personal allegiances of the subjects achieve the union of the crowns that was officially recognized in *Calvin's Case*. At the same time we also account for the territorial and legal autonomy retained by the separate lands over which the king reigns. In doing both we account as well for the germ of federalism.

Now it is time to recall that this constitution was not solely applicable to the British Isles. For the king, under the exercise of the prerogative absolute, chartered companies to found new colonies. And those colonies ultimately acquired a constitutional position comparable to that of Ireland and Scotland in the imperial constitution. The colonial lieutenant governor was the surrogate for the king. He acted in the name of the king for colonial affairs, much as did the lord chancellor inside England proper. The governor's colonial council was drawn from the colonial elite and was the counterpart of the home government's House of Lords. The colonial assembly, or House of Burgesses, was the counterpart of England's own Commons. Together, lieutenant governor, council, and Burgesses comprised the counterpart of the homeland Parliament. Within a colony there were certain matters pertaining primarily to domestic affairs. These were customarily left to the colonial parliament's own self-governing processes. These were matters of the prerogative ordinary, so to speak. However, there were also some matters that were customarily determined by the executive fiat of the lieutenant governor (or the crown as represented by the lieutenant governor). This was the colonial counterpart of the prerogative absolute. The lines dividing these two were no sharper in the colonies than they were at home, but in general, domestic autonomy held sway over matters concerning the public health, safety, morals, and general welfare of the colony as a separate community; the prerogative absolute applied to matters of common defense, foreign trade, coinage, diplomacy, international relations, armed forces, and all problems concerning intercolonial or interimperial relationships.

These were the federative problems of the empire—the king's dominions, as they were called.

This was the constitutional theory of the first British Empire, the one that ended with the American Revolution. One can see that its constitutional principles were direct derivatives of medieval double majesty. And in fact, so long as medieval constitutionalism remained vital in the homeland, there were relatively few problems in the other parts of the empire. But remember Harrington's witticism about the Gothic balance being a form of gunpowder rather than government. Gothic balance indeed, and it was just during Harrington's lifetime that it became unbalanced and began to blow apart in England. That explosion, triggered by the civil wars, was to reverberate throughout the English homeland for fifty years and more, until new principles of constitutional order were finally instituted. The consummation was celebrated in the event we know by the name of the Glorious Revolution of 1688.

So Harrington was right. Double majesty did turn into a form of gunpowder. The English civil wars were not sectional. They were not even class wars. They were the two Gothic prerogatives at war against each other. And in the end the prerogative ordinary won out, assimilating to itself the prerogative absolute. Royal discretion was neutralized, or put into commission. Every governmental act was still done in the name of the king, but by a monarch who was king in name only. The old prerogative absolute was assimilated to the consultative and deliberative principle traditionally associated with the rule of law.

In theory the Whig Revolution preserved the regality of every governmental act, but it insisted that in practice the king act only through ministers accountable to the houses of Parliament. John Locke was the first to try to explain the deeper significance of what the Whigs had done. Then Montesquieu, keeping always a weather eye on the special constitutional needs of France, gave a Gallic reading of Locke and his Glorious Revolution. As the eighteenth century revolutions broke out, Edmund Burke cast about a discriminating eye, giving benediction to the infant American Revolution but anathematizing the un-English one across the channel. Whig historicism, forging the remote past into a forced march on 1688, was well under way. After the Burkean eulogy came Bishop Stubbs and then Sir Albert Vann Dicey. This is the tradition best represented in America by Walter Lippmann and Fredrick von Hayek. But to smoke out the inner constitutional logic of the Whig Revolution we had best seek tutelage from John Locke, the political theorist who was closest to it in spirit as well as in time.

Locke, as all political scientists recall, wrote *Two Treaties of Government*. What is not so well remembered is that the two treatises were successive commentaries on the two principles of double majesty. The first treatise, written in refutation of the monarchist Filmer, was intended to prove that the prerogative absolute could not swallow up the prerogative ordinary. The second, more famous treatise was intended to prove that the prerogative ordinary could (and should) swallow up the prerogative absolute. In his effort to make this demonstration Locke was forced to devise a new organizational chart for this revolutionary type of monarchy that was to be no longer dualistic. For remember, Locke's purpose was to develop a theoretical underpinning for the Whig effort to eliminate the shreds of absolutism from the old constitution. The device Locke chose was to supersede institutional double majesty with a conceptual variant. He made the political order rest on two contracts. Theories of social contract had been long familiar, but not *two* of them. Locke saw that two were needed in order to supersede double majesty, specifically, the balanced parity between law and the king that had been described by Bacon. First Locke had the people covenant to create a society, establishing in that act their own monolithic sovereignty. Then as sovereigns they could negotiate a second contract with a king (William III, for example) to provide them with certain necessary governmental services. This fixed matters so that the king was always subordinate rather than absolute, because the prior authority created by the first contract held him always an agent and never a principal. So it followed in constitutional logic as well as in actual practice that sovereignty could reside only in a popular assembly—in the legislative function, so to speak. This is how the doctrine of legislative sovereignty first arose. The legislative function acquired sovereignty in much the same way monarchs had previously acquired sovereignty from their predecessors in a coronation, contract-confirming ceremony. The legislative functions took the place of kingship as well as of the king. If one merely takes the formula of England's dualistic medieval constitution and reverses the signs, so to speak, and gives precedence to law rather than the king (the damned and damnable opinion of the Despensers), parliamentary sovereignty is the result, and the constitutional structure of Locke's *Second Treatise* follows logically (1947, p. 194 ff.).

Subordinate to Parliament, said Locke, are two governmental functions: the executive (the administrative offices that previously answered only to the king) and the federative. In theory this brought the old prerogative absolute completely under the rule of law, that is, the supreme Parliament. In a passing reference Locke also mentioned the judicial function. But instead of exalting it, he placed it way down on the third level of authority, subordinate to the already-subordinated executive. So, the once-coequal partners of the old constitution were reshuffled and made to fall out in a new, unified way. If one now draws an organization chart of the English constitution it is seen to bear no resemblance to the schemes of mixed government devised by the ancients. For the Whig conversion of double majesty did not result in a mixture of three equal, autonomous forms of government, much less of governmental functions. Its aim was just the opposite: to subordinate all governmental functions to one sovereign institution. Even more important is the fact that the Lockean scheme explicitly denies what Americans assume to be the essence of the constitutional wisdom of all times, namely, that every government is naturally divided into three distinct and autonomous functions: administering, policy forming, and judging. Neither Locke, nor his Whigs, nor any succeeding Englishmen ever discovered this natural law (though it *had* been discovered earlier by Harrington, the republican!). When the British constitution entered modern times it merely revised the medieval formula and deposited in a Parliament that had bridled the king all his sovereign powers. Parliament's sovereign legislative umbrella took in all the possible subdivisions of government. John Locke's executive and federative functions included the king's old prerogative-absolute authority over the coinage, the maintenance of the king's peace, authority over the royal highways, control of the armed forces and of diplomacy, authority over international and imperial relations, and so on. Generally speaking the executive functions Locke describes are those that concern domestic affairs in their collective aspects; the federative functions are those that concern the nation in its external collective manifestation, as in diplomacy, foreign affairs, defense, and warfare. The judiciary naturally occupied a still lower plane because it had been on a plane subordinate to the king in the old scheme. It needed to be independent, in the sense of being free from arbitrary political influence, but not autonomous. A judiciary coequal with the legislative function was unthinkable to any proper Whig.

Take a modern example of the same point. Within General Motors Corporation the Chevrolet division may possess independence but is by no means autonomous. This is something like the way the Whigs thought of the judiciary. Its independence was to be carefully maintained, but so was its constitutional subordination.

The foregoing redistribution of prerogatives is the constitutional meaning of the Whig Revolution. It is easy to see that this reorganization could work well enough *inside* a country that had lived under double majesty. But what about its extended constitutional implications? Specifically, what about the empire? What about Scotland, Ireland, and Wales? Recall from *Calvin's Case* that double majesty had served as a constitution not only for the domestic affairs of the English homeland but also for the empire. So if one transforms the principles of double majesty *within* the empire's homeland, must a similar transformation be extended to the constitution of the empire itself? When the domestic Parliament of England neutralized the king's prerogative absolute it struck at the very life principle of the imperial tie. According to the constitutional theory of the empire announced in *Calvin's Case,* the crown possessions —and this even included England herself, for England was, at least in part, a crown possession—all stood in exactly the same legal relation to the crown. Moreover, this very doctrine had been insisted on by the seventeenth century leaders of the English Parliament in order to underscore England's legal autonomy vis-à-vis Scotland. This was the principle that had prevented the complete unification of England and Scotland when James' accession united the two crowns. Recall also that English parliamentarians claimed that James wrought a unification only of the two crowns, that is, a union only of the separate prerogatives absolute of the two previously independent kingdoms. In stating their case, the English parliamentarians had taken great pains to show that acts of the English Parliament traditionally had not been enforceable inside other crown possessions such as Ireland and the channel islands.

THE AMERICAN CONSTITUTION:
DOUBLE MAJESTY REPUBLICANIZED

But then came the Whig constitutional revolution. We understand its effects inside England, but what about its effects inside the other crown possessions? These had come under the "federative" (which included the imperial) department of the old consitution. Did the consummation of a Whig revolution by England's own domestic Parliament automatically consummate a comparable revolution inside the component parts of the rest of the empire? It is a perplexing question, however one looks at it, and not the least curious of its aspects is that it poses just the opposite question from that posed by King James in *Calvin's Case.* There it was the quention of how deeply domestic institutions could be affected by changes in the crown's federative sphere. Here it was the question of how deeply the separate federative components of the empire could be affected by a revolution performed inside the homeland. If the federative function was neutralized at home, what happened to the federative power in the other territorial components of the constitution? Previously each one had been related to all the others in exactly the same way they were related to England. We must repeat, did the consummation of a Whig revolution inside England's Parliament automatically consummate a comparable revolution inside the other parts of the empire? Specifically, and this is where the rub came, did the Whig Revolution at home establish the legal title of the English Parliament as heir to all previous royal prerogatives, even those under which the colonies had been governed? Put most plainly, was England's Parliament henceforth to stand in relation to colonial governing councils exactly as the king had done previously? (see McIlwain, 1958a; Schuyler, 1929; Wheeler, 1956). Or, as was to come to the fore later in the colonies, did the opposite occur? Did the consummation of a Whig revolution in the homeland accomplish a similar revolution inside all the components of the empire?

If the answer to this question had been a clear yes, there might have been some chance of preserving the old imperial system, constitutionalized. But then another perplexing issue would have required resolution. If the effects of the Whig Revolution in England were to be applied throughout the empire, how was that result to be achieved in the domestic constitutions of the separate colonies? Did they automatically become duplicate Whig regimes? If not automatically, did they have a right equal to England's to reorganize their politics so as to domesticate for themselves the principles of the Whig Revolution? These were the constitutional issues posed throughout the empire by the Glorious Revolution inside the motherland. They would have arisen in vexatious forms even had the mother Parliament behaved with strict constitutional propriety. But she did not. And that fact effectively guaranteed there would come a new explosion; the "form of gunpowder" that had been detonated at home was, with varying time intervals, to explode over and over again throughout the overseas dominions of the crown.

The colonial detonators were remarkably like those that had ignited the first explosion at home. In England the Stuart kings, claiming authority under the prerogative absolute, had levied a series of novel taxes on trade. Parliament protested that these were not matters for prerogative fiat but rather for parliamentary determination. Who was right—and a good legal case can be made on both sides—is not so important for our purposes as the fact that 170 years and a Whig revolution later, Parliament was doing to the colonies exactly what had earlier moved Parliament to rebellion when it was done at home by the Stuarts. But as a result of the earlier struggle the American colonists had at their disposal all the patriotic documents of the Whig Revolution when they prepared their case against Parliament's authority to levy taxes on the colonies.

Colonial polemicists quickly became legal antiquaries—not too difficult a transition for chapter-and-verse New World Calvinists to make. And as they rummaged back through the great law cases that had preceded the English civil wars—*Bate's Case* (1606), the *Five Knights' Case* (1627), the *Ship Money Case* (1638), and not ignoring the juridical time bomb hidden away in *Dr. Bonham's Case* (1610)—with a sure hand they selected *Calvin's Case* as the foundation for their plea. We already know why. *Calvin's Case* had erected double majesty as the crowning (literally) principle of domestic and imperial constitutional law, and double majesty stood for the legal—and parliamentary —autonomy of each of the several crown possessions.

Previously we looked at Britain's Whig Revolution from the inside. But when seen from the outside, through the eyes of the colonists in the New World, the English constitution appeared quite different. From inside Britain the king was seen always to be close at hand, an omnipresent king, with an ever-ready seal to be affixed only with the advice of ministerial factions who shifted in and out of parliamentary ascendency. Englishmen had changed their monarchy in a fundamental way, but there was no doubt at all about its still being a monarchy.

From the outside all this looked quite different. From the New World, all one saw was that Parliament had interposed its own authority between king and colony. Thus while the king's function remained essential inside Britain, the opposite was true inside the colonies. The victory of Whigs over king transformed the colonies into satellites that, in effect, were republics (not constitutional democracies) in all but name. Had there been no king inside England it would have made a monumental domestic difference: the difference between the Cromwellian constitution and the Whig constitution. But in the view from Salem, Massachusetts, it would have made no essential difference had England been a republic instead of a monarchy. Indeed, one way of restating the colonial complaint is to say that Parliament had violated the constitutional principles necessary to maintain a monarchial constitution for the empire. This was actually said. In effect, argued the colonists, they were living under a de facto republic but one that was despotic because there was no check on Parliament's legislative sovereignty over them; this complaint was similar to that leveled in the mid-twentieth century by the East European satellites against the arbitrary controls of the Russian Communist party. So when the colonists came later to take the daring step of introducing republicanism into the modern world it was not really so daring at all, for they were doing little more than giving formal constitutional expression to the de facto republicanism already forced on them by the English Parliament, albeit corrected to inhibit the legislative despotism they had experienced from the mother of parliaments.

At first, however, the colonists were much more conservative. They opposed the acts of what on the plane of the empire was virtually a republican legislature acting in the name of and claiming the imperial prerogatives of the old monarchial imperial constitution described in *Calvin's Case*. That is—and this represented a monumental shift in consciousness—the de facto republicanism of Parliament led the colonists into evaluating English legislation on the basis of its constitutionality, declaring some to be unconstitutional and therefore null and void. Now, of course, the idea of unconstitutionality was completely inconceivable within the assumptions of the Whig Constitution of domestic England: Parliament embodied the crown, the monarchy, and sovereignty. No other institution, not the judiciary and certainly not the subject colonies, could declare its sovereign acts to be unconstitutional. The whole idea of unconstitutionality was constitutionally irrational from the English standpoint, and so it has remained. It's invention by the Americans—one of the great inventions of constitutional theory—flows directly out of their attempt to apply the logic of *Calvin's Case* to changes in the imperial constitution wrought by the Glorious Revolution.

The English position made sense only if one could fairly claim that the legislative function, no matter who exercised it, was sovereign. That is why the colonists had to question the very principle of legislative sovereignty itself under the double majesty doctrine of *Calvin's Case*. There, sovereignty had been proclaimed to be intrinsically dualistic, if not divisible, with some parts of it appropriate to the king as executive and some parts appropriate to Parliament as legislature. But these were *not* the same as John Locke's later executive and legislative functions; just the contrary. Inevitably this meant that a transformation was in store for the judicial function as viewed from inside the colonies. We've already observed the subordinate status of the judiciary in

England, but what of the New World? There we can observe its necessary emergence as an autonomous partner in the constellation of constitutional powers. This happened when the colonists exercised, in effect, judicial review when they declared certain parliamentary acts were void under the English constitution. In order for such colonial judgments to be valid there had to be an autonomous, coequal judicial function, and in order for the colonies to survive that function had to be able to rule on the constitutionality of executive and legislative acts. Judicial review was a structural necessity of the constitutional situation in which the colonists found themselves placed after the Glorious Revolution.

James Wilson was among the many colonists who had searched meticulously through the British constitutional precedents in an effort to find a basis for colonial opposition to parliamentary impositions. That basis was found in *Calvin's Case,* and the British Parliament was forthwith informed. That is, James Wilson notified Parliament that its own acts were unconstitutional. Wilson introduced a resolution before the Pennsylvania Convention of 1775 to proclaim "that the act of the British parliament for altering the charter and constitution of the colony of Massachusetts Bay . . . [is] unconstitutional and void; . . . it is the right of the British subjects to resist such force; that this right is founded both on the letter and the spirit of the British Constitution" (Wilson, 1967, p. 752). Note, in passing, that a formal constitution is here hypostatized, un-British as that may seem. Wilson proceeded to defend his resolution with arguments that any legislative or executive acts contrary to the constitution are "unconstitutional and void." Finally, Wilson buttressed his case by drawing on the medieval baronial doctrine of the king's wicked advisers:

> The king can do no wrong. To do wrong is the property, not of power, but of weakness. We feel oppression and will oppose it; but we know— for our constitution tells us—that oppression can never spring from the throne. We must, therefore, search elsewhere for its source. . . . Our constitution tells us that all oppression springs from the ministers of the throne. The attributes of perfection, ascribed to the king are, neither by the constitution, nor in fact, communicable to his ministers. . . . Can anyone hesitate to say that to resist such force is lawful: and that both the letter and the spirit of the British constitution justify such resistance? (p. 758)

Earlier we saw how the opponents of monarchial despotism in England laid the groundwork whereby this same doctrine of civil disobedience ultimately produced the conventions of the modern British constitution. Here we see how the application of civil disobedience to the eighteenth century American setting lays the groundwork for later doctrines of a constitution as a supreme law, of unconstitutionality, and, ultimately, of the inevitable concomitant: judicial review. The inner structure of the eventual American Constitution had already begun to reveal itself before the first Concord shot was fired, even before rebellion was generally contemplated, a full twenty years before the august architects met surreptitiously in Philadelphia and struck off what they and everybody else truly believed was one of history's greatest political inventions. But the leading doctrines of the Philadelphia document could hardly have turned out otherwise.

DOMINION THEORY AND FEDERALISM

Federalism was another one of the inventions that distinguished the Philadelphia Constitution. The story of its invention requires us to follow the development of James Wilson's constitutional doctrines as the crisis with England worsened. Already in 1774 Wilson had produced the rudiments of a dominion theory for the constitution of the empire. This was in "considerations on the nature and extent of the legislative authority of the British Parliament" (1967, p. 721). There again he returned to the doctrines of *Calvin's Case*. Wilson correctly perceived that the basic principle of the original imperial constitution was that acts of the English Parliament were not enforceable in Ireland because the Irish did not send members to England's Parliament. It followed, argued Wilson, that the territorial limits to the authority that could be exercised by the English Parliament derived from the principles of representation by which it was composed:

> The inhabitants of Ireland were the subjects of the king as of his crown of England; but it is expressly resolved, in the most solemn manner, that the inhabitants of Ireland are not bound by the Statutes of England. Allegiance to the King and obedience to the Parliament are founded on very different principles. The former is founded on protection; the latter on representation. An inattention to this difference has produced, I apprehend, much uncertainty and confusion in our ideas concerning the connection, which ought to subsist between Great Britain and the American Colonies. (p. 736)

Wilson further remarked that appeals from colonial courts were made to the king-in-council, a feature of the old prerogative absolute, not to the regular domestic courts of England.

Did this interpretation remove *all* connection between England and the separate parts of her empire? No, answered Wilson:

> A denial of the legislative authority of the British Parliament over America is by no means inconsistent with that connection .... On the contrary, that connection would be entirely destroyed by the extension of the power of Parliament over the American plantations.

He cites Blackstone, who said that the colonies "are no part of the Mother Country, but distinct (though dependent) dominions." The colonies, concluded Wilson,

> are subjects of the King of Great Britain. They owe him allegiance. They have a right to the benefits which arise from preserving that allegiance inviolate. They are liable to the punishments which await those who break it. This is a dependence which they have always boasted of . . . . From this dependence . . . arises a strict connection between the inhabitants of Great Britain and those of America. They are fellow-subjects; they are under allegiance to the same Prince; and this union of allegiance naturally produces a union of hearts. It is also productive of a union of measures through the whole British dominions. To the King is entrusted the direction and management of the great machine of government. He therefore is fittest to adjust the different wheels, and to regulate their motions in such manner as to co-operate in the same general designs. He makes war: He concludes peace: He forms alliances: He regulates domestic trade by his prerogative, and directs foreign commerce by his treaties with those nations, with whom it is carried on. He names officers of government; so that he can check every jarring movement in the administration. He has a negative on the different legislatures throughout his dominions, so that he can prevent any repugnancy in their different laws. The connection and harmony between Great Britain and us . . . will be better preserved by the operation of the legal prerogatives of the Crown than by the exertion of an unlimited authority by Parliament. (p. 744)

Here is the first full elucidation of the constitutional theory of self-governing dominions unified under the crown into a commonwealth of nations. Wilson's scheme was rejected by the English Parliament without its deigning to even consider it. But a few decades after the American Revolution this very doctrine with little elaboration became acknowledged as the fundamental constitutional law of the British Empire. As recently as 1931, when the British Commonwealth of Nations still existed, it was restated explicitly in the Statute of Westminster IV. What little remains of the British Empire, besieged today by Irish civil disobedience just as it was two centuries earlier by civil disobedience in the New World, still operates on the principles enunciated by James Wilson in 1774.

We are all familiar with the problems that arose during the period of the post-revolutionary confederacy. The autonomy of the states predominated over the rudimentary functions vested in the general government. Something was needed to provide a "more perfect union," while still preserving essential autonomy for the member states. This was the problem the framers faced in Philadelphia, and their maneuvers, debates, and compromises are well known. But the point to be borne in mind here is that from the standpoint of constitutional theory, the basic problem confronting the new republic was not how to make autonomy devolve upon the ex-colonies. That would have been the problem only if they had been *organically* unified before. Rather, it was the problem of finding a substitute for the kind of union previously provided by the English crown. The confederacy failed because it ignored this problem. Indeed, the new confederacy provided *less* unity than had been present before, even though the prior seat of unity had resided in England rather than in the New World. So the problem was how to transplant from the old world to the new a general government for the new republic comparable to the realm of union that had previously existed in the English crown. The method arrived at in Philadelphia was to adopt Wilson's prerevolutionary doctrine of autonomous dominions in a commonwealth of nations and to give it republican form. The result was federalism. If one thinks back on Wilson's description quoted above it is easy to see the origin of the powers of the new federal government in the catalogue of powers he defines as legitimate for the crown to exercise in a commonwealth of nations. Moreover, the "reserved powers" of the new states became just those that Wilson had believed appropriate for the antonomous dominions to exercise in his proposed imperial commonwealth of nations.

Further illustration of this transformation process was given in 1785, two years before Philadelphia, in Wilson's essay entitled "Considerations on the Power to Incorporate the Bank of North America" (1967, p. 824). This essay expounds the principles of the constitution of the confederacy. However, not surprisingly, the logic Wilson develops follows that he initially devised to expound the constitutional principles for a proper imperial commonwealth. At the same time, however, it foreshadows the principles that are to be made explicit in the federal Constitution of 1789. The question addressed is the powers of the confederate Congress. These, he states, derive from the states. But it does not follow that Congress has no other powers than those expressly delegated.

> The United States [i.e., the general government] have general rights, general powers, and general obligations, not derived from any particular states, nor from all the particular states, taken separately; but resulting from the union of the whole. . . . The confederation was not intended to weaken or abridge the powers and rights, to which the United States were *previously entitled* [italics supplied]. It was not intended to transfer any of those powers or rights to the particular states, or any of them. If, therefore, the power now in question [that of incorporating a bank] was vested in the United States before the confederation; it continues vested in them still. The confederation clothed the United States with many, though, perhaps, not with sufficient powers; but of none did it disrobe them. . . .

To charter a corporation, said Wilson, was an "executive" power.

> Before the revolution, charters of incorporation were granted by the proprietaries of Pennsylvania, under a derivative authority from the crown. . . . From analogy, therefore, we may justly infer, that the United States in Congress assembled, possessing the *executive* [italics supplied] powers of the union, may, in virtue of such powers, grant charters of incorporation. . . .

Next Wilson states that "the United States in Congress assembled possess, in many instances, and to many purposes, the legislative as well as the executive powers of the union" (p. 830). That is, the new union automatically inherited all the old powers of the crown. These were in part executive, in part legislative, and in part judicial. The confederate Congress, as the only formal institution established by the new union, inherited and could exercise all these powers. It only remained for the Philadelphia Convention to separate into distinct institutions these three functions that had been inherited in an amalgamated form.

Remarkable evidence about how the old imperial constitution was transformed into the new federal Constitution came in a long footnote at the end of Wilson's 1774 essay on the "Legislative Authority of Parliament." Some persons, said Wilson, might object to his dominion theory, for "how," he asks rhetorically,

> can the trade of the British Empire be carried on, without some power, extending over the whole, to regulate it? The legislative authority of each part . . . is confined within the local bounds of that part: how, then, can so many interfering interests and claims, as must necessarily meet and contend in the commerce of the whole, be decided and adjusted?

Wilson's first answer is to proclaim the virtues of free trade—this two years before *Wealth of Nations*. But then he suggests that a "commerce power" be entrusted to the king "as a part of the royal prerogative." The prescient conclusion is:

> If the power of regulating Trade be vested by the principles of the constitution in the Crown . . . a perpetual distinction will be kept up between that power, and a power of laying impositions on trade. The prerogative will extend to the former: it can, under no pretense, extend to the latter: as it is given, so it is *limited,* by the Law. (p. 746)

Double majesty republicanized led straight from *Calvin's Case* to Philadelphia.

SEPARATION OF POWERS

Francis Wormuth's researches show us that double majesty also died hard inside England. To establish parliamentary sovereignty was not the same thing as establishing at one stroke the complete primacy of the legislative function. On the contrary, all functions of government were concentrated in Parliament, which still included the king. However, this merely converted the old debate about the two royal prerogatives into a new one about parliamentary functions. The two parliamentary functions discussed in the new debate were but thinly disguised surrogates for the old prerogatives. They were the legislative and executive powers. The judiciary was mentioned occasionally, but never as an equal to the others, for it had always been on a lower tier of government. The judicial function was declarative. In the older tradition law was thought of as being "discovered," not fabricated by human beings. And the judiciary merely declared the result of their discovery process. This tradition has continued uninterrupted into the modern British constitution.

The debate over the legislative and executive powers of Parliament persisted as long as kings retained some measure of autonomy. The argument was that the two must be in separate hands to prevent the evils of special legislative and discriminatory administration. If the king, under his executive power, could influence legislation, he could pass special laws against individuals. If his executive power was unchecked he could apply the laws arbitrarily. The problem was to see that the executive power was permanently subordinated to the legislative power: to ratify and constitutionalize the victory of the prerogative ordinary over the prerogative absolute. The full solution, in fact, was not to appear until the nineteenth century, when the principle became established that the king acts only through his ministers and the ministers are responsible to Parliament. In theory, however, the solution was provided already in the seventeenth century by John Locke.

First, as we have seen, was Locke's theory of the two contracts: double majesty constitutionalized. For the first contract, the contract of society, was the old prerogative ordinary made primary and supreme. After society had contracted itself into being, it could then execute a second contract of government with an executive authority: a king. With this order of priorities, or prerogatives, established, it was possible to ensure the ascendancy of the legislative over the executive function. In this way the popularization of double majesty yielded the modern British constitution with its principle of legislative supremacy.

But if the British had suffered only from the despotism of monarchs, the American colonies had experienced that of an English legislative body. They would not, as they would later prove, countenance a king with absolute prerogatives, not even one masquerading as a republicanized president. But neither would they institute over themselves another supreme legislature able to treat the states as the English Parliament had treated the colonies. So much did these experiences dominate their fears that the first constitution, that of the confederacy, placed Locke's theory of the two contracts on a territorial basis. It provided first for the primacy of the states, as if they had contracted together to establish a society. Then they executed, in effect, a second contract of government, establishing the confederate Congress. However, the confederate Congress, as Wilson made clear, was not to be thought of merely as a legislature. It was a New World parliament with the same parentage and potentially the same functions as those of the "mother of parliaments." This was so, as Wilson argued in discussing the charter of the bank as an "executive" function, even though the powers of the Congress, legislative as well as executive, were severely restricted and even though the exercise of those powers, as Locke had argued, was subordinated to the true sovereign, namely the states. So the fundamental constitutional principle on which the Americans rested their frame of government was to convert double majesty into federalism, giving most of the old prerogative ordinary to the states. They then deposited not only general legislative powers but also severely restricted elements of the old prerogative absolute in the Continental Congress. When this proved insufficient they drafted a new constitution for a "more perfect union." This meant creating a "more energetic" general government. That in turn required giving it more extensive legislative and executive powers.

The primary model the colonists had for this was Britain's Whig constitution, in which the king still retained considerable authority; witness George III. In order to prevent just such excesses they relied on many of the conceptions that had been explored during England's interregnum experiments with republicanism. Francis Wormuth has ferreted them out with considerable ingenuity (Wormuth, 1949, p. 9; see also Northrop, 1960). If we inspect his evidence carefully we find an important theme emerging. It was the feature that gave modern constitutionalism its distinguishing mark. This was what Woodrow Wilson called the "Newtonian" quest for a self-harmonizing mechanism. One conceived of a constitution as if it were a mechanism. One talked of authority as being susceptible to power analysis. The various powers could be divided, separated, and interconnected, like the reciprocating parts of an internal combustion engine. The result would be a self-harmonizing mechanism. The natural-law foundation that had predominated since the time of Cicero was replaced by a principle of mechanics. Mechanics took the place of natural law in constitutionalism, economics, politics, and so on.

Even so, some of the Founding Fathers believed the new Constitution would operate basically according to the English model. George Washington interpreted the presidency as a ceremonial office. Hamilton, he thought, would be a British-model secretary of the treasury and function as prime minister, implementing administration policies through his ability to influence Congress. This was the way things were done in England, where the full establishment of the principles of the responsibility of the king's ministers to Parliament was still far in the future.

In effect, Americans converted the two old partners of double majesty into legislative and executive branches, with the medieval autonomy of each branch carefully preserved. The result was, as of old, separation of powers.

BAROQUE CONSTITUTIONAL MECHANICS

Thomas Kuhn (1962) has pointed out that the history of science has been characterized by the succession of a series of distinct thought styles, or paradigms, and that these have a considerable influence on the kinds of problems scientists will select for investigation as well as on the intelligibility and acceptability of various competing contributions and theories. Lord Kelvin's self-confessed inability to understand Clark Maxwell's propositions because he could not picture them in terms of a concrete model is a well-known illustration. The same thing has been true of political science. Plato and Aristotle pictured the political order as an organism. Various political organisms were classified into different species, which were related to each other through cycles of development and degeneration. It followed that political science was similar to medicine and the statesman was comparable to the physician. Justice was like health. It was a condition of the system as a whole and could not be analytically subdivided into constituent parts with their own autonomous characteristics. A political constitution was real, and existed, but like a human being's constitution it was not something for which there was a concrete referent capable of quantitative measurement. Rather, it required qualitative measurement according to a rational standard, like the standards of good and bad behavior. Thus, one made judgments of good and bad about political constitutions, just as one did about human behavior. These could be made through dialectical rather than analytical methods. Dialectics revealed the norms to which political orders ought to conform, as well as the functions required for their accomplishment. The Romans cast these approaches in terms of jurisprudence rather than medicine, with natural law as a teleological principle toward which all constitutions must strive if they are to realize their optimum potentialities. Christendom pictured natural law as the principles of a heavenly political order which could best be approximated in sacred rather than secular organizations. With the Renaissance and its loss of faith in sacred institutions came the acceptance of the mundane and the human, expressed in naturalistic rather than natural-law terms, and the discreditation of the applicability of ideal or ethical standards to the conduct of political affairs. In modern times this secularizing development merged with the principles of science, especially Newtonian mechanics, and constitutional theory along with economic theory discarded ancient conceptions of qualitative analysis and justice. Constitutions were pictured on the model of a machine rather than an organism. Modern political science took people as they were rather than as they ought to be and relied on their self-interested tendencies to build political mechanisms, the way physics relied on the forces of nature to build smoothly working industrial machines.

The structural foundations for the American Constitution came from the Middle Ages, but its political science came from the age of Newton. The result was a curious combination of the Gothic and the mechanistic: a baroque constitution. This, indeed, is no more than we would have expected. It was the typical pattern found throughout the age of the Baroque. This is not to argue that everything produced by the Founding Fathers was so tainted with Gothic and mechanistic elements as to be thoroughly discreditable. On the contrary, both contained nuggets of validity. There is something immemorially true, as well as being intrinsic to the realization of justice, about the medieval (and the ancient) proposition that a political order cannot ignore the dialectic between the higher law and the positive law. Moreover, the mechanistic separation of law making from law administering not only commends itself to reason but also guards against the evil of special legislation and arbitrary administration. An independent judiciary, if not one coequal with the other branches of government, is logically required to avoid having people be judges in their own cause. But this does not mean that these constitutional paradigms are adequate to cope with the complexity of contemporary political problems. Beyond this it is apparent that the mechanistic framework in which these principles were conceived by the men of the eighteenth century is painfully inadequate for the more complexly intertwined constitutional and political problems arising in our time.

In short, the adequacy of the American Constitution must be challenged on several grounds. Its Gothic territorial federalism no longer conforms to the associational realities and the community needs of our times. Its tripartite provision for governmental powers is woefully inadequate and its mechanistic paradigm has become self-contradictory. We know that equilibrium cannot be produced out of automatically counterbalancing powers. Moreover, government is now being charged with responsibility for the complete inventory of man's social problems rather than merely a few rudimentary functions of the negative state. This requires a constitution with a much fuller complement of functions than the eighteenth century allowed. But more important, it requires the application of a systemic approach to the political order, like that espoused by the ancient political philosophers as well as by contemporary systems theory. This is not only because we must now deal with a fuller range of political problems than ever before but also because we must now address ourselves to the qualitative element in politics rather than relying on unseen-hand types of constitutional mechanisms. It is no accident that these pressing needs should come to light at the same time our contemporaries are busily applying systemic approaches to every type of organizational and administrative problem under the aegis of systems theory. From every hand there come urgent calls for new ecological approaches to political problems. In short, what we require is a new theory of constitutionalism, one that is in tune with the scope of political problems confronting us. We must discover the systemic properties of our needed constitutional functions. This demands that we rebuild starting from constitutionalism's twin foundations, the rule of law and civil disobedience institutionalized; not by attempting to repair the torn fabric that remains from 1789.

EPILOGUE: THE MYTH OF CONSTITUTIONALISM

The founders of modern constitutionalism were rationalists who held the belief that rational processes are relevant in some discoverable way to the problems arising from nature as well as from mankind; that people are rational creatures able to discover what these relevancies are; that they are able to know what actions are in their own and society's best interests; and that they are able to realize these best interests through the use of reason in human institutions. Rationalism holds that people are somehow able to submit the world to the rule of reason.

Scientific technology and constitutionalism represent two prominent areas of rationalist effort. Scientific technology refers to a special class of rationalist efforts whereby people attempt to control their material environment. Constitutionalism refers to a special class of rationalist efforts by people to control their social environment. Although the total number of societies that have produced rationalism is very small, almost every society that became highly articulated produced it in some form.

One precondition of rationalism is the capability of manipulating the environment self-consciously. All human beings have assumed that their environment could be *influenced,* but there is a difference between manipulation and influence. One influences something that has its own will and could do otherwise but for the influence exerted. One manipulates something that is not aware of or not able to perceive that it is being manipulated. One manipulates other things in a relationship that is basically scientific. However, when one influences other things the relationship is basically "political." Most human beings have approached their environment in a political relationship. Primitives often attempt to influence their material environment politically through contracts with gods, demons, anthropomorphic spirits, and animistic nature forces. A universe of political relationships and influences is an animistic universe in which everything is alive and willful. Even culture "lives," and law "lives" (the "living law" of familiar Anglo-Saxon tradition) in such a universe.

In a culture that assumes that everything in the environment is alive, there is no such thing as "death" in the modern sense of absolute nothingness. Primitive worlds are peopled with the spirits of winds and forests and also with the spirits of departed members. People "die"; they are aware they are mortal; their death is terrible; but it is also a transition to another mode of life. So long as this is assumed to be true, the persistence of life after death appears to be an observable fact of nature. Life after death is what might be called in animistic cultures a datum of empirical "science," and not a matter of faith.

The change occurred with the development of rationalism. Rationalism exhausted "life" from nature and from "science." It created a new form of death, a death that was a final nothingness. Rationalism scientifically "disproved" the possibility of life after death. The sympathetic reception accorded the writings of Carlos Castañeda derived from their appeal to an ineradicable human nostalgia for animism. The nostalgia is ineradicable because the human being is an animal who with maturation becomes aware of being mortal and hence has a built-in childhood foundation for this regressive nostalgia. But Castañeda's writings were especially appealing because of their implicit rationalism: the author was a properly credentialed Ph.D. in anthropology and was merely reporting the facts of social science as he discovered them—a compelling illustration of the paradox of rationalism. A similar line of argument was one of the central points in the philosophy of Unamuno. His conclusion was that rationalist man, having created life as a short interlude between two nothingnesses, had in fact become the author of a life that was both meaningless and absurd. The absurdity of life may not have been apparent for all societies that have possessed rationalism, but the sense of absurdity has had an especially acute impact on the people of modern Western society, with their lingering nostalgia for the primitive spiritual tranquility of prior animistic beliefs. The result was that rationalism in its Western form resurrected as a matter of faith the immortality it had disproved as a matter of science. Faith, despite its absurdities, was the only thing that could make life in a rationalist universe meaningful.

Even though rationalistic Westerners could never positively convince themselves of the validity of a faith in immortality, and even though they always suspected that the belief was unwarranted by the facts, Westerners collectively held to this faith and even created a special God whose primary function was to ensure immortality, a novel obligation foisted upon the godhead as a result of Hellenic rationalism.

This necessity to believe, in the face of overwhelming improbabilities, is what Unamuno called the "tragic sense of life." He drove these thoughts to their logical conclusions. One of these conclusions was that even though faith in immortality and in God appears untenable, the need for this faith is observable in all sorts of ways.

For one thing, faith in immortality is logically necessary to most people if they are to follow a rationalistic life. This is so because life must hold some ultimate meaning in order to warrant meeting the rigorous demands made on people by rationalism. It is so because people who have faith in immortality and God will behave differently because of that faith. They will engage confidently in projects that cannot bear fruit until long after their deaths. The more complex Western culture has become, the more immediately fruitless have become the functions of each person. Each worker in a huge rationalized enterprise must engage in functions that are pointless unless the indefinite success and survival of the enterprise (as distinguished from the people in it) appear to be important to all workers. Moreover, as all life functions become more routinized and more drab, people are increasingly dependent on elements apart from their own life functions to make a routinized life seem valid. The conclusion follows that faith in some form of transcendence or immortality and in some form of immortality-ensuring God or transcendental principle becomes a functional necessity for rationalistic industrial people in an even deeper sense than for other types of human beings. Though such faith might be intrinsically indefensible to the rationalistic intellect, it is socially and functionally necessary to the rationalistic intellect; it is a "myth" without which the belief in rationalism would be irrational.

Unamuno's tortured cry echoed that of Senancour's Obermann: "If it be that nothingness is the fate which awaits us, we must not so act that it shall be a just fate." Each person must, according to Unamuno, play throughout life a grim and cheerless dare to a probably nonexistent God, proving by the excellence of that life (or the intensity of the sense of guilt) that human beings do not deserve the nothingness that probably awaits them.

As one looks at such people from above, so to speak—from the philosopher's lonely and farseeing vantage point—it is clear that although it is necessary for rationalistic people to play out this role, the role is nonetheless absurd, ludicrous, and quixotic. People must tilt against sins that do not really "exist" except in the sense that the quixotic tilting is what creates them and validates them as sins. Because this act of "creation" is necessary to the modern rationalist human being, Unamuno rescues the quixotic role from its traditional position as atypical, insane, and hallucinatory ludicrousness and identifies it with the fundamental absurdity of rationalism in a life leading to nothingness. The quixotic thus becomes the noblest and most "rational" heroic model for rationalistic bureaucratic human beings in constitutional societies.

Oedipus had revealed the form of tragedy appropriate to the classical Greeks; Sisyphus, as the archetypal Quixote, reveals the form of tragedy appropriate to Western rationalists. It follows that for people in general, rationalism and faith—or naturalism and supernaturalism—are not opposed but are mutually interdependent. Supernaturalism cannot exist without rationalistic naturalism. Supernaturalism, immortality, and God were "created" by rationalism and depend for their continuing vitality on the maintenance of rationalism. However, rationalism in its turn is dependent for its validity and its functional applicability to the problems of life, on the vitality of supernaturalism. Science as a social institution considered in its "collective" sense, if not in the case of each individual scientist, demands supernaturalism. This is the conclusion to which contemporary existentialism arrived—Christian and non-Christian alike.

Existentialism said: let us assume that God is dead. But this makes a rational life absurd and meaningless. What can make a rational life meaningful and valid? The answer is to live *as if* there were a just God and immortality. For such beliefs validate actions that otherwise would be absurd but that are necessary to the enhancement of life even if there is neither God nor immortality. This resulted from a projection and reflection process similar to the one Eliade found in all religious phenomena. Human beings project their functional necessities into the heavens from whence they are reflected back to them as the divinely sanctioned norms to which they must adhere. "God" becomes the guarantor and validator of rationalism. "God" becomes the projection of the functional and structural necessities of the culture. "God" becomes the far-sighted Copernican (as distinguished from the short-sighted Ptolemaic) principle in human relations. "God," finally, becomes the ultimate Platonic Noble Lie: the functional necessities people in general must be induced to observe even though they cannot perceive the sociological necessity that validates them.

This is an enormous maneuver. Moreover, it is the social counterpart of the maneuver by which the modern physical sciences developed their theoretical integrity. An existentialist approach to the social sciences would be comparable to the Baconian-Cartesian approach to the physical sciences, but in the opposite sense to what is usually understood by positivism. For the theoretical foundation of the physical sciences was the expulsion of animism ("God" as well as "life") as a principle of causation external to the relationships under investigation. "God" was supplanted by a theoretically autonomous independent variable intrinsic to the system of relationships. Though often incapable of being perfectly understood, such principles—gravity and evolution are examples—made possible the solution of theoretical problems not previously solvable.

A parallel to this paradox from the physical sciences applies to the rationalistic social sciences. For a rationalistic, or "scientific," approach to society leads to the expulsion of animism, better known from the foregoing discussion as natural law, from social processes as a principle of causation external to the relationships under investigation. The usual way of stating this is that social, especially behavioral, sciences must separate values from facts à la Hume: they must exclude the former and deal only with the latter. A value-free social science must "create" a value-less social system. A value-less social system is one devoid of natural law validity, for a social system devoid of validity cannot possess valid fundamental laws. But we have seen previously that constitutionalism stands for the rational establishment of the validity of the fundamental law. Hence the philosophical paradox at the heart of modern constitutionalism.

Unamuno, citing A. J. Balfour, states the proposition as follows: although each society must of necessity re-create in all its members the ethic essential to its preservation, the characteristic side effect of a highly rationalistic culture is the creation of conditions making it inevitable that the denial of ethical validity in general will become widespread. In becoming widespread it destroys the foundations necessary to maintain a high culture. Balfour and Unamuno call the anomic destroyers of ethics "parasites":

> ... people sheltered by convictions which belong, not to them, but to the society of which they form a part; ... nourished by a process in which they take no share. And when those convictions decay, and those processes come to an end, the alien life which they have maintained can scarce be expected to outlast them. (Unamuno, 1954, p. 27)

This paradox of the rationalistic social and behavioral sciences applies with cruel irony to the Heavenly City on earth: the world of rationalist constitutionalism. Rationalism has come into such ill repute during the twentieth century that discussions concerning it have acquired a slightly archaic aura. Belief in rationalism, like belief in supernaturalism, has been scientifically undermined. Since the nineteenth century there has developed an entire family of social sciences that proceed from assumptions of irrational or nonrational behavior. These behavioral sciences are rationalistic and scientific in themselves, so they are not opposed to science as such. They are opposed only to the older rationalistic social sciences that were founded on the assumption that people tend to behave rationally and scientifically. Democracy and constitutionalism, which were founded on rationalistic assumptions about human behavior, appear to be discredited by discoveries that people are predominantly irrational, or nonrational, animals.

In the wake of the behavioral sciences another development occurred. Not only was there the empirical demonstration of the existence of a substratum of human irrationality, there was also a considerable redefinition of rational behavior, for example, when one looks at human behavior from the assumption of irrational and even compulsive. All behavior can in theory be traced back to some stimulus response on the individual level and/or a conformity-or-aggression response to cultural norms on the social level. Behavior that once would have been deemed eminently rational and logical becomes converted into individually or culturally determined behavior that is then rationalized by the human mind.

Classical economic theory contained the famous "economic man" assumption. It was held that people in general strove rationally to better themselves economically. Even in the beginning this was recognized as being a distortion and an oversimplification, but it was believed to be sufficiently true of empirical behavior to be valid as a tenet of operational theory.

There are two points to be made here. In the first place, it seems true that during the eighteenth and nineteenth centuries people actually did behave more in accordance with the economic man assumption than they did before or after; the empirical situation is different in the twentieth century from what it was in the eighteenth and the nineteenth. One need only compare the nineteenth century Horatio Alger literature with the twentieth century "organization man" literature to get a quick illustration of the empirical differences in behavior between the two periods.

Secondly, the same behavior is interpreted and evaluated differently in the two periods. The industrial moguls of the nineteenth century—men like Andrew Carnegie, Jay Gould, John D. Rockefeller, J. P. Morgan, and Henry Ford —appeared in their times to be eminently rational economic men. But twentieth century biographies of these men usually portray them as compulsively psychopathic and culturally determined illustrations of the behavioral determinism characteristic of their times. A person who in the twentieth century behaves like a nineteenth century economic man tends to be regarded as sick and needful of psychiatric care. Such a person, told he is sick at every hand, comes to believe himself to be sick and goes dutifully to a psychiatrist seeking a cure for his strange and compulsive economic behavior.

The same thing is true in politics. The greatest twentieth century biographies of eighteenth and nineteenth century political leaders "explain" their strange and compulsive behavior according to the "psychopathology of politics." Such are the conclusions of prominent studies of Napoleon, Alexander Hamilton, Abraham Lincoln, William Jennings Bryan, and Woodrow Wilson.

In the twentieth century we apply the same approach to mass behavior. Studies in the behavioral sciences reveal that when the same commodity is packaged in several different colors supermarket shoppers will uniformly choose one color over the others. When asked why, they reply that they prefer the product chosen and think it is "better" than its differently colored competitors. Students in the behavioral sciences conclude that this consumer behavior is "irrational," even though the consumers are obviously making preferential choices on the basis of the only distinctions available to them—behaving in a perfectly rational manner, from another point of view. Yet, so widespread is the conviction that consumer behavior is fundamentally irrational that consumers in general come also to believe that they behave irrationally.

A comparable development has occurred in mass politics. Modern constitutionalism was founded on the assumption that the average person would behave rationally in politics: people would study the issues presented by candidates and participate actively in political affairs. There appears to have been considerable validity for these assumptions during parts of the eighteenth and nineteenth centuries. However, the twentieth century has brought almost complete disillusionment to students of political behavior. Political apathy is widespread. Interest in and knowledge about political candidates and issues is minimal. Voters, like consumers, tend to choose candidates on the basis of their positions on the ballot or the ethnic connotations of their names. Voters tend to behave conservatively during good times and radically during bad times. If a crisis occurs, whoever is in office is likely to be deposed regardless of any direct connection with the crisis. If the weather is dismal on election day the "ins" will fare worse than if the day is bright and cheerful. People in general know that politics is often controlled by bosses who short-circuit the functioning of democratic institutions. Yet voters rarely exhibit any dissatisfaction with boss control, and they seldom display any real devotion to democratic principles. In the twentieth century rationalist constitutionalism appears to have lost all foundation in theory and practice.

However, this too is partly a matter of appearances rather than of reality. In most elections the difference between the candidates is like the difference between boxes of soap on a grocery shelf. The general cultural homogeneity of the people and the selection and filtration system at work in political parties have seen to that. To become fanatically aroused over the normal American election would be quite irrational. The fact that most voters answer "don't know" to public opinion polls about issues such as inflation and foreign policy is as much a testament to their integrity as it is a revelation of political apathy. All educators know that even their brightest scholars will forget important facts and specific analyses shortly after their examinations are over. To expect average voters to keep complex public issues in the forefront of their minds is in itself irrational.

Nor does the fact that voters appear uninformed according to public opinion polls mean necessarily that they will behave irrationally on election day. For in some cases mass information will become sharpened just before election day, as does the information of scholars just before an examination. But in most cases this is not what happens. For the voter tends to realize that no matter how much study is devoted to a complex political issue it will still defy the average person's ability to master it. As a result the individual voter's choice will be decided on other criteria. Voters may "anthropomorphize" the issues presented to them, interpreting them on the basis of personal reactions to the personalities and the characters of the antagonists on both sides of the question. But usually voters do neither. Usually the characters and personalities of the competing candidates are not markedly different. In such a case ordinary citizens either stay at home on election day or vote as they have in the past. Their judgment is that either way it will not make a great deal of difference, and so they engage in a form of "coin flipping" by staying at home; or they follow the only attraction the process offers: "betting" on the "team" they have grown to identify with personally.

Nonetheless, it is clear that rationalistic constitutionalism expected too much of the human being. People are incapable of and uninterested in living up to the requirements demanded of them in theory. And even if this were not true, constitutionalism still would not work according to theory, for constitutional systems do not any longer present people with the operating conditions most conducive to the mass exercise of rationality in politics.

Developments comparable to this had also occurred in the democracies of Athens and Rome. In these, as in twentieth century constitutionalism, the conviction that constitutionalism was unworkable became widespread. Political, economic, and military emergencies contributed to the success of anticonstitutional movements. The conditions that had been devised to foster activist political rationalism failed in that task and instead permitted the growth of irrationalist and anticonstitutionalist movements. However, it is doubtful that any complex culture can long survive that abandonment.

One reason for this is that complex, highly articulated cultures must elicit the rational and creative participation and coordination of a large number of people in order to function well. The most efficient modern device for achieving this has been some form of constitutionalism. The only alternatives are the dictatorial application of police terror and the maintenance of aggressive militarism. Terror and militarism are functional over long periods of time only if they can provide material progress for the culture. However, in those mass cultures that had previously developed highly articulated and rationalized conditions under constitutional institutions, this has proved almost impossible to achieve because of the inordinate investment that must be made in maintaining large terrorist and military organizations. There is some evidence that twentieth century innovations in the behavioral sciences and behavioral drugs may render the manipulation of masses of people in a bureaucratic society more economic, but this has yet to be demonstrated. In the present state of the arts of organizing and controlling large numbers of people in highly complex societies it still seems to be true that anticonstitutionalist institutions are dysfunctional. Yet, as we have seen, constitutional societies contain conditions that tend to produce anticonstitutionalist forces. There is in this a political paradox analogous to the ethical paradox previously attributed to Balfour and Unamuno.

The survival of a highly complex rationalistic culture requires that it maintain the vitality of constitutionalism, and yet constitutionalism produces an environment conducive to the discreditation of constitutionalism and the development and success of anticonstitutionalist movements. This raises a final question. Is it possible that in such societies belief in constitutional rationality must be maintained as a myth, if nothing else, in order for them to flourish and to be preserved?

We are familiar with the Sorelian argument about myth. It was based on the assumption that collectively people do not engage in rational behavior. After analyzing the Christian revolution Sorel concluded that its appeal had been irrational rather than rational. And yet, because people in general came to believe in the irrational tenets of Christianity, the Christian revolution succeeded. Sorel applied this same line of reasoning to the socialist revolution and argued that the workers would not respond to rationalistic revolutionary programs of the sort being devised by the socialist intellectuals of his day but instead would respond to an irrational program—a secular-socialist counterpart to the Christian myth. The myth of the general strike was to take the place of the chiliastic Christian paradise. The general strike was irrational and empirically unrealizable, but in Sorelian theory this was the source of its mass efficacy. Masses could be galvanized into revolutionary action by faith in an unrealizable irrational creed, not by conviction of the practicability of a rational program. Mannheim's analysis of the creative function of utopian theory had a similar foundation. A variation of these approaches seems applicable to constitutionalism.

Actual practices in constitutional democracies appear to demonstrate that masses are incapable of behaving according to the "myth" of rational constitutionalism. In fact, seen from a deterministic, behaviorist viewpoint, all rational action tends to dissolve into irrational behavior. However, much the same behavior may also be interpreted from a rationalist point of view. We have already considered examples of this for economic and political behavior.

Moreover, it makes a difference in the behavior of individuals in a society how their society interprets their behavior. In a slave society with a slave morality, individuals tend to behave like slaves. In a free society with a rationalist morality, individuals tend to behave like free and rational persons. Human beings are often capable of doing "impossible" tasks if they believe that they can and should do them. This is the basis on which morale is engendered in all organizations.

There seems little doubt that in eighteenth century America—the America that made the *Federalist Papers* into best-sellers—there was a much higher level of mass rational political participation than there is in twentieth century America. People were little different then, save for their belief in rational constitutionalism. We now claim that the rationalism they believed in was a myth. But as with myths in general, it was a self-fulfilling myth. The belief tended to elicit the behavior it described.

When science and religion are viewed from Unamuno's standpoint their opposition disappears and they become mutually interdependent. Similarly, deterministic behaviorism and rational constitutionalism are also mutually interdependent.

The conclusion that seems to follow is that mass societies cannot persist except through some form of constitutionalism, and social and behavioral science cannot persist except in some form of constitutional order. Though from one aspect the social sciences concerned with irrational behavior tell us that constitutionalism is empirically unrealizable, yet they depend on its maintenance in order to be able to tell us it is a chimera. Moreover, when they look at constitutionalism from another point of view they teach us that constitutionalism is a functional necessity of rationalist social orders and that it can find approximate realization as a vital myth.

We may call this the "utopian" sense of constitutionalism: constitutionalism as a self-fulfilling myth that can be approximated if it is believed in and is, to that extent, "scientifically" valid. Constitutionalism and the rationalistic tradition of the higher law have a relationship to the social and behavioral sciences comparable to that of God to the physical sciences before Bacon and Descartes. Scientifically we can prove that they do not "exist." Yet the social and behavioral sciences also teach us the existential and functional validity of such principles as myths. To believe in and to follow the tenets of constitutionalism is as quixotic as to believe in God, immortality, and transcendence. But it is equally necessary, especially when considered collectively. This is not the same as saying that one must believe in constitutionalism "because it is impossible." On the contrary, as with belief in sin, believing and acting on beliefs "create" the objects of belief. Even if there were no such thing as rational constitutionalism, the contemporary social sciences would have to invent it in order to make our complex societies work.

NOTES

1.   "On first looking upon the external world, man pictured it to himself as a sort of confused republic, where rival forces made war upon each other" (de Coulanges, 1956, p. 121).

2.   Francis Bacon was an exception (see Wheeler, 1956), as was James I on occasion (McIlwain, 1958b, p. 13).

3.   Marshal MacMahon, on accepting the presidency of France, made it clear that he regarded the Constitution of the French Third Republic as prolegomenon to the restoration of a constitutional monarchy; Maitland (1908) referred to "those kingless monarchies on the other side of the Atlantic."

4.   Of course, Edmund Burke had previously written of England's "prescriptive" constitution, but Burke's natural law conception stands out in stark isolation in the late eighteenth century parliamentary debates. See Burke *Works* (1861, Vol. 6, p. 146 ff.).

5.   Civic consciousness is Hanson's terms for what Locke and others dealt with under the rubric of a social contract.

REFERENCES

Althusius, Johannes (1932). *Politica Methodice Digesta of Johannes Althusius (Althaus)*. Reprint of 1614, 3rd ed. Introduction by Carl Joachim Friedrich. Cambridge, Mass.: Harvard University Press.

Andrews, Charles M., ed. (1937). *Famous Utopias*. New York: Tudor.

Aristotle. *Politics*. In *The Basic Works of Aristotle,* Book 4. Edited by Richard McKeon. New York: Random House, 1941.

Austin, John (1954). *The Province of Jurisprudence Determined and the Uses of the Study of Jurisprudence*. Introduction by H. L. A. Hart. London: Weidenfeld and Nicholson.

Bacon, Francis (1860–64). *Of Judicature*. In *The Works of Francis Bacon,* Vol. 12, pp. 265–71. Edited by J. Spedding, R. L. Ellis, and D. D. Heath. Boston: Brown and Taggard.

_____ (1860–64). *The Works of Francis Bacon*. Edited by J. Spedding, R. L. Ellis, and D. D. Heath. Boston: Brown and Taggard.

_____ (1905). *The Philosophical Works of Francis Bacon*. Edited by J. M. Robertson. Preface and notes by R. L. Ellis and J. Spedding. London: Routledge.

Barker, Ernest (1958). *Reflections on Government*. Paperback ed. (Originally published 1942.) New York: Oxford University Press, Galaxy.

Beer, Sam (1973). "Watergate: the imbalance of government and politics." Paper presented at the Center for the Study of Democratic Institutions, Conference on Constitutional Principles: Their Validity and Vitality Today. Santa Barbara, December 9–13, 1973.

Burke, Edmund (1871). *Reform of Representation in the House of Commons*. In *Works,* Vol. 6. 4th ed. Boston: Little, Brown.

Cameron, James R. (1961). *Frederick William Maitland and the History of English Law*. Norman: University of Oklahoma Press.

Cornford, Francis M. (1952). *Principium Sapientiae*. Cambridge: Cambridge University Press.

_____ (1957). *From Religion to Philosophy: A Study in the Origins of Western Speculation*. New York: Harper Torchbooks.

de Coulanges, Numa Denis Fustel (1956). *The Ancient City*. Garden City, N.Y.: Doubleday.

de Glanvill, Ranulf (1965). *The Treatise on the Laws and Customs of the Realm of England*. Translated by G. D. G. Holl. London: Nelson.

Dodds, Eric R. (1951). *The Greeks and the Irrational*. Berkeley: University of California Press.

_____ (1963). *The Elements of Theology*. Oxford: Clarendon Press.

Durkheim, Emil (1947). *The Elementary Forms of the Religious Life: A Study in Religious Sociology*. Translated by J. W. Swain. Glencoe, Ill.: Free Press.

Eliade, Mircea (1971). *The Myth of the Eternal Return: Cosmos and History*. Princeton: Princeton University Press.

Elliott, W. Y. (1928). *The Pragmatic Revolt in Politics*. New York: Macmillan.

Figgis, J. N. (1960). *Political Thought from Gerson to Grotius, 1414–1625*. (Originally published 1907.) New York: Harper Torchbooks.

Finer, Herman (1949). *Theory and Practice of Modern Government*. New York: Henry Hold.

Finley, Moses I. (1954). *The World of Odysseus*. New York: Viking Press.

Fraenkel, Ernst (1941). *The Dual State*. Translated by E. A. Shils, Edith Lowenstein, and Klaus Knorr. Oxford: Oxford University Press.

Freud, Sigmund (1956). *The Interpretation of Dreams*. Translated by James Strachey. New York: Basic Books.

Friedrich, Carl J. (1941). *Constitutional Government and Democracy.* Boston: Little, Brown.

Gardiner, Samuel Rawson (1893). *The First Two Stuarts and the Puritan Revolution, 1603–1660.* New York: Scribner's.

Gierke, Otto Friedrich von (1868–1913). *Das Deutsche Genossenschaftsrecht.* 4 Vols. Berlin: Weidmann. (5 sections of Vol. 4 trans. by Ernest Barker; see following entry.)

_____ (1957). *Natural Law and the Theory of Society, 1500 to 1800.* Translated by Ernest Barker. (Originally published 1934.) Boston: Beacon Press.

Green, Thomas Hill (1907). *Lectures on the Principles of Political Obligation.* London: Longman, Green.

Hale, Matthew. *Analysis of the Crown.* Hargrave ms. No. 490. London: British Museum.

Hanson, Donald W. (1970). *From Kingdom to Commonwealth: The Development of Political Consciousness in English Political Thought.* Cambridge, Mass.: Harvard University Press.

Harrington, James (1747). *The Oceana and Other Works of James Harrington.* Printed for A. Millar.

Harrison, Jane (1962). *Themis.* New York: World.

Hayek, Friedrich A. (1960). *The Constitution of Liberty.* Chicago: University of Chicago Press.

Howell's State Trials, Vol. 2. (1816). London.

Hume, David (1971). *Essays Moral, Political and Literary.* London: Oxford University Press.

James I. (1918). *The Political Works of James I.* Edited by C. H. McIlwain. Cambridge, Mass.: Harvard University Press.

Kantorowics, E. H. (1957). *The King's Two Bodies: A Study of Medieval Political Theology.* Princeton: Princeton University Press.

Kelsen, Hans (1945). *General Theory of Law and State.* Translated by Anders Wedberg. New York: Russell and Russell.

_____ (1967). *Pure Theory of Law.* Berkeley: University of California Press.

Kuhn, Thomas (1962). *Structure of Scientific Revolutions.* Chicago: University of Chicago Press.

Laski, Harold (1967). *A Grammar of Politics.* New York: Humanities Press.

Lindsay, Alexander D. (1962). *The Modern Democratic State.* Paperback ed. (Originally published 1943.) New York: Oxford University Press.

Locke, John (1947). *Two Treatises of Government.* Reprinted. New York: Hafner.

Lovejoy, Arthur O. (1966). *Reflections on Human Nature.* Baltimore: Johns Hopkins University Press.

Maitland, Frederic William (1908). *The Constitutional History of England.* Cambridge: At the University Press.

_____ (1911). *The Collected Papers of Frederic W. Maitland*. 3 vols. Edited by H. A. L. Fisher. Cambridge: Cambridge University Press.

_____ (1936). *The Corporation Sole*. In *Selected Essays*. Edited by H. D. Hazeltine *et al*. Facs. ed. Essay Index Reprint Service.

_____, trans. (1957). *Political Theories of the Middle Age, 1500 to 1800*, by Otto Gierke. (Originally published 1900.) Boston: Beacon Press.

McIlwain, Charles H. (1910). *The High Court of Parliament and its Supremacy*. New Haven: Yale University Press.

_____ (1958a). *American Revolution: A Constitutional Interpretation*. Paperback ed. (Originally published 1923.) Ithaca: Cornell University Press.

_____ (1958b). *Constitutionalism: Ancient and Modern*. Paperback ed. (Originally published 1940.) Ithaca: Cornell University Press.

Miller, Arthur S. (1973). "Separation of powers: an ancient doctrine under modern challenge." Paper presented at the Center for the Study of Democratic Institutions, Conference on Constitutional Principles: Their Validity and Vitality Today. Santa Barbara, December 9–13, 1973.

Mosca, Gaetano (1939). *The Ruling Class*. Translated by Arthur Livingston. New York: McGraw-Hill.

Northrop, Filmer S. (1960). *Meeting of East and West*. New York: Collier, Macmillan.

Ong, Walter J. (1958). *Ramus' Method and the Decay of Dialogue*. Cambridge, Mass.: Harvard University Press.

Plato, *Laws*. In *The Dialogues of Plato*, Vol. IV. Translated by Benjamin Jowett. New York: Oxford University Press, 1953.

_____. *Statesman*. In *The Dialogues of Plato*, Vol. IV. Translated by Benjamin Jowett. New York: Oxford University Press, 1953.

_____. *The Laws*. In *The Works of Plato*, Vol. 4. Translated by Benjamin Jowett. New York: Modern Library, 1930.

_____. *The Republic of Plato*. Translated with an introduction and notes by F. M. Cornford. New York: Oxford University Press, 1945.

_____. *The Sophist and the Statesman*. Translated by A. E. Taylor. London: Thomas Nelson, 1961.

Polybius. *The Histories*. Edited by E. Badian. Translated by Mortimer Chamber. New York: Washington Square Press, 1966.

Rose, H. J. (1946). *Ancient Greek Religion*. London: Hutchinson's University Library.

Savigny, Friedrich Karl von (1829). *The History of Roman Law during the Middle Ages*. Translated by E. Cathcart. A. Black: Edinburgh.

Schlesinger, Arthur, Jr. (1973). *The Imperial Presidency*. Boston: Houghton Mifflin.

Schuyler, Robert L. (1929). *Parliament and the British Empire*. New York: Columbia University Press.

Simons, John, and Paul Sweezey (1964). "A view of the economy III: from a Marxist." Tape No. 112, Center for the Study of Democratic Institutions. Santa Barbara.

Statutes of the Realm: Great Britain: Laws, Statutes, etc. 1101–1713 (1963). Vol. 1, "Case of the Despensers," pp. 181–84. Reprint ed. (Originally published 1810–28.) London: Dawson's.

Stoljar, S. J. (1958). "The corporate theories of Frederick William Maitland." In L. C. Webb (ed.), *Legal Personality and Political Pluralism.* Melbourne: University Press.

Unamuno, Miguel de (1954). *The Tragic Sense of Life.* Translated by J. E. Crawford Flitch. New York: Dover.

Vann Dicey, Albert (1889). *Introduction to the Study of the Law of the Constitution.* London: Macmillan.

——————— (1905). *Lectures on the Relation between Law and Public Opinion in England During the Nineteenth Century.* London: Macmillan.

Vinogradoff, Sir Paul (1892). *Villeinage in England.* Oxford: Clarendon Press.

——————— (1929). *Roman Law in Medieval Europe.* Oxford: Clarendon Press.

Wheatley, Paul (1971). *The Pivot of the Four Quarters: A Preliminary Inquiry into the Origins and Characters of the Ancient Chinese City.* Chicago: Aldine.

Wheeler, Harvey (1956a). "The constitutional ideas of Francis Bacon." *Western Political Quarterly* 9:927–36.

——————— (1956b). "Calvin's Case (1608) and the McIlwain-Schuyler debate." *American Historical Review* 61:587–97.

Wilson, James (1967). *The Works of James Wilson.* 2 vols. Edited by Robert McCloskey. Cambridge, Mass.: Harvard University Press, Belknap Press.

Wormuth, Francis D. (1972). *The Royal Prerogative, 1603–1649.* (Originally published 1939.) Port Washington, N.Y.: Kennikat Press.

——————— (1949). *The Origins of Modern Constitutionalism.* New York: Harper.

Wright, Benjamin F. (1962). *American Interpretations of Natural Law.* Reprint ed. (Originally published 1931.) New York: Russell.

2

FEDERALISM

WILLIAM H. RIKER

INTRODUCTION: THE MEANING OF FEDERALISM

An initial difficulty in any discussion of federalism is that the meaning of the word has been thoroughly confused by dramatic changes in the institutions to which it refers. Loose alliances have become centralized bureaucracies—going from one extreme to the other—while both have been called federations. Hence, a word that originally referred to institutions with an emphasis on local self-government has come to connote also domination by a gigantic, impersonal concentration of force. Before one can discuss the institutions of federalism, it is, therefore, necessary to explain the word and reconcile its references to what appear to be polar extremes.

The Range of Reference of Federalism

To begin the explanation it is useful to keep in mind the full range of governments to which the word *federalism* has been applied. While each such government is a unique response to local circumstances, I group them here into several categories that many writers have thought literarily convenient.

Primitive leagues. At every stage of world history up to the present, some nations have developed larger governments as it became technically feasible to do so, typically and primarily to exploit the military advantages they offer. Although at the dawn of history the usual method of making big government was conquest, the method of forming a league, or alliance, of tribes or other local units was occasionally used. When the organs of the league had more than military duties—and among primitives they often had religious duties as well—it is not unreasonable to describe them as federations, or confederacies. In the late nineteenth century, after modern federalism had become a well-established political form, historians began to look back on these primitive leagues and to describe them, doubtless anachronistically, by the word customarily used for their modern analogue. The first to make this comparison on a grand scale was E. A. Freeman (1893), who discussed the similarities between ancient Greek and medieval Italian leagues and the United States. This subject has recently been treated with great care (and with no reading back from modern circumstances) in J. A. O. Larsen (1968). Some of these leagues, like those that flourished between the Persian and Roman invasions of Greece, were so weak that the central organization had no power other than to direct troops in battle, while others, like the Athenian Delian League, were actually empires directed from a central city. The one that is best remembered as a true, yet effective league—perhaps because it was extensively discussed by Polybius—is the Achaean League of the third century B.C. Some writers have applied the word *federalism* to the institutions of ancient Israel during the period of the judges and before the league of tribes gave way to Saul's kingship (Elazar 1968; LeFur, 1896; and Mogi, 1938). Detailed analysis of these institutions indicates that it is no more anachronistic to speak of the league of Israel as a federation than it is to speak so of Greek leagues. See Bright (1959, pp. 142–60), where premonarchic Israel is described as an amphictyony, or sacral league. On the basis of the same kind of analogies, the Iroquois league was also a federation, for its central organ had military, religious, and legal duties. Indeed, one suspects that the Iroquois and the Hebrew were remarkably similar, given that they were separated by nearly three thousand years and half a world of miles (see Morgan, 1962; originally published 1851).

The description of these governments as federal may seem anachronistic to some. But had the Philadelphia Convention of 1787, at which modern federalism was invented, never been held, it is likely that the main examples of federalism would continue to be governments like that established by the Articles of Confederation. Were that the case, the classification of Greek, Hebrew, and Indian leagues as federations would not seem anachronistic at all. Hence it would now be a wholly arbitrary restriction on the meaning of the word to limit its application to modern instances.

Early modern leagues. The firstborn of the living instances of federalism is Switzerland, which came into being as a league of three cantons in 1291, grew to nearly its present size in the fifteenth century, survived as a loose confederacy until Napoleon destroyed it, was reformed into a federation on the American model in 1815 and 1848, and survives in that form until today. At the time of its origin, Switzerland was merely one of several Suabian, Alpine, and North Italian leagues created to defend local autonomy against Habsburgs and Holy Roman Emperors (see LeFur, 1896). But of these the Swiss were the only survivors and thus have the credit for being the first of contemporary federations.

Just as the Swiss league was a defense against Austrian Habsburgs, the Dutch Republic was a defense against Spanish Habsburgs. The Union of Utrecht of 1579 provided for federalism that turned out to be far more centralized than any of the true leagues so far mentioned. Although known to Europeans mostly through Montesquieu, who thought it was merely another league, it had in fact an effective central government, owing to the predominance of the province of Holland and its city of Amsterdam. See Janicon (1729), which is the most detailed account of Dutch government, and Temple (1932; originally published 1672), which is the most widely known account. For an evaluation see Riker (1957). Although the Dutch Republic fell before Napoleon and was replaced in 1815 with a still-surviving centralized monarchy, this government was important in the development of federalism, for it served as proof that a nation-state really important in world politics might survive and prosper with the federal form.

The United States of America. The United Colonies of the Second Continental Congress of 1776 and then the United States of the Articles of Confederation of 1781 were merely a league of rebellious provinces, very like the rebellious Dutch provinces of two centuries earlier. This original American confederacy was highly decentralized and probably in greater danger of collapse than the United Provinces of the Netherlands was in its first generation simply because the American revolution had neither the length nor bitterness of the Dutch to bind the rebels together. Then in the Philadelphia Convention of 1787 the delegates worked out a new form of federation, which has, with modification, lasted ever since. This second form of American federation was (or came to be) almost as much a single centralized state as it was an alliance of states; and this fact made it a totally new kind of confederacy. The word *federalism* was developed primarily to describe this new mixture of league and nation. Ever since, the word has referred primarily to governments on the American model, probably because all subsequent federations have been deeply influenced by it.

Latin American federalism. In the generation after the North American revolution, the South American colonies rebelled against Spain and Portugal. Naturally they looked at least in part to the United States for executive, legislative, and territorial institutions appropriate for their new condition. Almost all the new governments were formed as federations on the North American model of territorial organization: Argentina, Mexico, Venezuela, Colombia, Chile, Central American Republic, and Brazil. Within a short time Chile and Colombia abandoned federalism as inappropriate for their conditions and the Central American Republic broke up into its constituent units: Nicaragua, Costa Rica, Honduras, El Salvador, Guatemala. Nevertheless, federalism remains until today an essential feature of at least the Mexican, Brazilian, and Argentinian constitutions. Some writers suggest that Latin federalism is a sham when dictatorial regimes exist, but it is important to observe that these three nations have more often had republican than dictatorial regimes and that federalism is an important component of republicanism. (With respect to republicanism and federalism in Argentina see Sarmiento, 1961; originally published 1845.)

Former English colonies. In the British empire, colonies were typically rather small administrative units that might easily be ruled by one governor. Hence most colonies were too small to be viable national governments when they achieved independence. For the sake of survival, therefore, it has often seemed wise to the colonists to combine former colonies when they separated from the empire. Since the first colonies to separate were those that made the United States, their experience in combining has naturally been looked upon as an example. Furthermore, the British government has itself encouraged federalism in former colonies. Perhaps the British acted out of a genuine sense of parental responsibility to help administrative units with hostile races to live under one government without civil war; perhaps they acted out of an imperial desire to divide and influence even after the colonies separated; but in any event the British colonial office has been one of the main forces for federalism in the modern world. Canada became an independent federation in 1867 and ultimately absorbed Newfoundland. Australia followed in 1901. In 1947 India and Pakistan, both with federal constitutions, became independent. Malaya became a federation early in British occupation; after several years of separate independence, from 1957 to 1961, it absorbed Singapore and Sarawak to become Malaysia, and disgorged Singapore in 1965. Nigeria became an independent federation in 1960; but for all practical purposes its federal form failed to survive the Biafran revolt. Finally, Cameroon became federal and independent in 1961. Besides these now existing federations, several other former British colonies have tried or been forced into the federal form and then abandoned it: New Zealand was a federation from 1852 to the end of the Maori War (1872); the Union of South Africa, although encouraged toward federalism by the London government, consciously rejected the federal form; Burma has what seems to be a federal constitution, but never, apparently, has it had a federal government; Tanzania has a kind of federal structure—left over from the proposed East African Federation—but probably never has had a federal government; Rhodesia and Nyasaland were briefly federated and then broke apart over racial issues; and finally the British West Indian Federation existed for a short time and then dissolved into its many constituent units.

German federalism. In German lands there have been many kinds of associated governments from the Middle Ages onward. Many alliances, for example, the Hanseatic League, have flourished amid the myriad units of local government. Some have argued that the Holy Roman Empire was itself a federation (see Binkley, 1938). Whether it was or not, many kinds of federal government have existed in Germany and Austria in the nineteenth and twentieth centuries. After Napoleon destroyed the Holy Roman Empire, one alternative that followed soon was a customs union. Then in 1866 Prussia drove Austria out of German politics and in 1870 founded the German Empire, which included all the German-speaking lands except Austria. The German empire was federal by almost any standard and was consciously so constructed. An alternative organization, less certainly federal, was the Austro-Hungarian dual monarchy. Most dual monarchies (e.g., Norway-Sweden, England-Scotland) involve the existence of separate governmental bureaucracies for the allied powers, whose only connection is the monarch. In the Austro-Hungarian imperial monarchy there was rather more centralization than in other dual monarchies, however, and hence it may have been something of a federation. Both the German and the Austrian empires were destroyed in 1919 in the aftermath of World War I, and the republics that replaced them were direct adaptations of American federal institutions to Germanic administrative bureaucracies. While these two federations were destroyed by Hitler, they were revived after World War II again on the American model and this time under the direct supervision of American jurists.

Communist federalism. During the period of civil war following the Communist revolution in Russia, some of the main components of the Czarist Empire drifted into independence. In an effort to bring them back into the Russian orbit and to quiet the nationalistic yearnings of linguistic minorities that had not broken off, Lenin developed a unique form of federalism. Although once the federalism was accepted, party domination quickly destroyed local autonomy, federalism became the accepted communist means of dealing with nationalism. For this reason the federal form is retained in the Soviet Union until today. Other communist regimes also face the disruptive force of nationalism, which is hard to understand in terms of communist ideology, and they too have adopted something of the federal form. Yugoslavia has been a federation as long as it has been communist, and Czechoslovakia had federalism imposed on it by the Soviet Union after the Soviet conquest in 1968.

Federalism elsewhere. Africa, which is as balkanized as any geographic area in the world and which has numerous governments that are probably so small as to be doomed to perpetual poverty, apparently seems to its rulers to be in great need of consolidation. Pan-Africanism and a philosophy of negritude are doubtless both ideologies that have meaning primarily as devices to transcend the balkanization. In a similar view, federalism has been much talked about, tried, and even occasionally found successful. Among African federations besides those already mentioned are Ethiopia, Libya, and, briefly, Mali and the Congo (Leopoldville). So strong is the pull of balkanization, however, these have either not lasted long or become dictatorships. One final federation should be mentioned, the Indonesian. As the Dutch left the Indies they imposed a federalism—either out of concern for territorial minorities or out of an intent to subvert the new government. As soon as most of the Dutch were expelled, the Indonesians promptly abolished federalism.

Such is the range of past and present governments commonly referred to as federalisms. Some are centralized dictatorships (e.g., the Soviet Union and some Latin governments sometimes) and others are loose alliances with barely any central institutions at all (e.g., the old Swiss confederation before 1798). Some are successful governments that have survived the test of territorial civil war (e.g., the United States), while others are fragile constructs that have fallen apart almost as soon as they were born (e.g., the British West Indian Federation). Faced with such a wide range of governments described with one word, how can we define the word in a scientifically useful way?

Strategies of Defining Federalism

There are two types of strategies available. One, a strategy of exclusion, involves a restricted definition so that only a small set of quintessential federations qualify for the name. The other, a strategy of inclusion, involves a broad definition so that not only all the previously mentioned federations qualify but also, hopefully, all others to which common usage applies the name in the future. The strategy of exclusion is especially associated with Wheare, who defined federalism so restrictedly that only the United States, Australia, Canada, and Switzerland qualified (1956, although the book was written in the early forties). He specifically excluded even such close imitations as Argentina and the Weimar Republic. The supposed advantage of this procedure is that it limits the objects studied to a set small enough to admit many generalizations that, though limited in application, are readily verifiable. Actually, however, this supposed advantage seldom materializes. When the objects in a set are widely disparate, the limit on generalization is the disparity of objects, not the number of them in the set. As a careful survey of Wheare's book demonstrates, there are very few verified generalizations in it, and none that is verified is particularly impressive. Indeed, it may well be that, by limiting the set of objects studied, one makes generalization all the more difficult because similar but excluded objects cannot be considered. Thus the four governments Wheare studied have quite different cultural contexts and quite different institutions. Hence they have very little in common but federalism.

An adequate comparative study of that feature, moreover, requires reference to the very governments Wheare excluded. Therefore it seems more appropriate to adopt the strategy of inclusion, as have more recent writers than Wheare. These later writers may be reacting to the proliferation of federal governments during the 1940s and 1950s (see Riker, 1964b, and Duchacek, 1970).

The main problem of the inclusive strategy is to define what is the essential element that holds all the particular examples of federalism together under that name. Such a procedure is profoundly different from the exclusive strategy, a lawyer's strategy, which defines more or less by fiat (typically to make it easier to prove a case) and expects the definition to be authoritative because it is enforced by the weight of law or force. The inclusive strategy, on the other hand, is a philosopher's strategy; under it one defines by capturing the spirit of the word, its metaphors and extensions, and expects it to be authoritative because it is assented to. A word gets extended in meaning because people use it to draw analogies and make metaphors. Eventually the metaphorical sense is as much a part of the meaning as the original sense and people have forgotten it is a metaphor at all. So the inclusive strategy involves an analysis of the history of a word, a study of how its metaphorical extensions are made, so that we can understand it in all its uses. Then it is possible to pick out some essential threads of meaning.

The word *federalism* roots in the Latin *foedus*, which according to Lewis's *Latin Dictionary* means "league" or "treaty" or "compact" or "alliance" or "contract" or "marriage contract." *Foedus* is cognate to the Latin *fides* (i.e., trust) and to the English *bind*. Clearly the root meaning of *foedus* is some sort of mutually trusting agreement among parties, a trusting promise. With respect to international politics, the actors or agreeors are of course governments, and the agreement among them is a federation. In that very broad sense, every intergovernmental alliance would be a federation; yet it seems that, certainly by early medieval times, the words for federation had a more restricted sense. They referred to that particular kind of alliance in which the allied governments create an additional government to act for them in at least certain matters. Hereafter I will refer to the mutually trusting allied governments as *constituent governments* and to the government they create as the *central government,* recognizing, of course, that in many historical circumstances these names are somewhat distorting.

With this terminology, the original sense of federalism can be expressed as a political organization with constituent and central governments.

Development of Meaning of Federalism

Building on this original sense, then, one can see how all the examples listed previously have come to be called federations, even though they do not always quite fit the original sense. Medieval leagues (e.g., Switzerland) in which local governments created a central government for the very limited and, indeed, intermittent purpose of military defense fit this original sense perfectly. So does, for example, the Dutch Republic, where feudal units, that is, provinces with parliaments, elected a stadtholder, or executive, and sent delegates to a united parliament in order to carry on a war against the Spanish monarchs. Beginning with the American federations, however, one can see an expansion of the original sense. It is not clear, for example, that constituent governments ever existed in the area of the United States. One view, the states' rightists, would have it that the colonies were constituent governments that delegated authority to the center. The other view, the nationalists, would have it that sovereignty jumped directly from London to the Continental Congress and that the former colonies were simply electoral units for both the imperial and independent governments (see Bennett, 1964). Regardless of which view is correct, it is apparent that the colonies had at least some superficial resemblance to constituent governments, so that the analogy with earlier federalism was not entirely unjustified. In the same way, most modern federalism involves only a fictional creation of the central government by the constituent governments. To take an extreme example, the national (i.e., territorially ethnic) governments in Yugoslavia can be regarded as constituent governments and the government in Belgrade as a central government so that Yugoslavia as a whole is a federation. In this case the notion is certainly fictional that the national governments are constituent governments whose alliance made Yugoslavia exist. Rather Yugoslavia existed for a generation as a highly centralized monarchy before the national (i.e., constituent) governments were created. If there is such a thing as sovereignty, it passed directly from the monarchy to the communist government in Belgrade without any intervention from "constituent" republics, which were, in fact, created only after the central communist government in Belgrade existed. (It is true that federalism had been urged on Yugoslavia earlier [Schlesinger, 1945]; but no constituent governments ever existed as independent entities [Shoup, 1968].) The "constituent" governments that Tito created looked like the genuine constituent governments in other federations, however, because they had certain spheres of activity in which they were supposedly quite separate and independent from the central government. For one thing they were called republics after the fashion of the Soviet republics (some of which did truly exist before the Moscow government controlled them), thus implying at least a semi-independence.

So it is with most other modern federations. What makes these governments look like traditional federations is the division of functions between central and regional governments such that it appears to be the case that the authority was delegated from the independent regional governments to the center. This may be a wholly fictional delegation as in the extreme case of Yugoslavia, or it may have only a tiny historical basis as in the case of Germany, where the Lander bear little resemblance to the feudal units that formed the German Empire of 1871, or it may be true in part and fictional in part as with the Soviet Union and India. In any case, it is the juristic pretense of independence that counts. The regional governments may not in fact be independent. Typically they cannot, for example, secede. (This assertion is, however, to some degree tautological: if federalism succeeds, secession is impossible, for secession may well destroy the federation. One counterexample, however, is Malaysia, which survived the secession of Singapore.) Despite the improbability of secession, the formal division of functions, in which each kind of government assumes a sense of total responsibility for the duties assigned to it, is the essence of federalism.

Definition of Federalism

Thus we can see how contemporary notions of federalism, which emphasize the division of functions, grow out of the earlier notion of federalism as an organization in which constituent units create a central government. It is possible to define federalism so that both emphases are included: *Federalism is a political organization in which the activities of government are divided between regional governments and a central government in such a way that each kind of government has some activities on which it makes final decisions.* In another place I have offered a similar definition, saying that "the essential institutions of federalism are . . . a government of the federation and a set of governments of the member units in which both kinds of governments rule over the same territory and people and each kind has the authority to make some decisions independently of the other" (Riker, 1964b, p. 5).

These definitions allow us to place all governments on a continuum with respect to centralization. At one extreme we place fully centralized governments in which all basic policy is made in the central government, although there may be some or a great deal of administrative decentralization. At the other extreme are alliances in which the central organ of the bureaucracy of the alliance cannot make any policy decisions without first consulting all the member governments. Federalism falls between these two extremes. Something of this situation is depicted in Table 1, where alliances, federations, and

TABLE 1   Degrees of Centralization

Alliances		Federations		Fully centralized governments	
Weak	Close	Peripheralized	Centralized	Regionalized	Dictatorial
Organization of American States	European Economic Union	Switzerland (before 1798)	United States Yugoslavia	Italy	Hitler's Germany

centralized governments are each a range of possibilities on a scale of territorial centralization. Within the range of federalism the extreme possibilities are:

> *minimum:* the rulers of the federation can make decisions in only one narrowly restricted category of action without obtaining the approval of the rulers of constituent units. (The minimum is *one* category of action, not zero, because if the rulers of the federation rule nothing, neither a federation nor even a government can be said to exist.) Some ancient federations were federations in this minimal sense because their rulers were authorized to make decisions independently only about military tactics and then only during the course of battle.

> *maximum:* the rulers of the federation can make decisions without consulting the rulers of the member governments in all but one narrowly restricted category of action. (The maximum number of categories is *all but one,* not simply all, because, if the rulers of the federation rule everything, the government is an empire in the sense that the rulers of the constituent governments have *no* political self-control.) The Soviet Union may be an example of a federation at the maximum. Although the government of this federation is, by its written constitution, one of delegated powers. . . . still the guarantee of independence to constituent units seems only nominal, except, perhaps, in the area of providing for the cultural life of linguistic and ethnic minorities around whom the union republics are constructed. If, in fact, the union republics are fully able to decide about cultural life without consultation with the government of the federation, the Soviet Union is a . . . centralized federalism. If, however, the union republics cannot freely decide even in this area, then the Soviet Union is an empire, not particularly different [in this respect] from the Tsarist empire it succeeds. (Riker, 1964b, pp. 5–6)

Aside from the examples cited in the foregoing quotation, very few governments are at either extreme of federalism. Most lie somewhere in between the extremes. Those that are closer to the maximum than to the minimum we call *centralized;* those that are closer to the minimum than to the maximum we call *peripheralized.* (For a more detailed discussion of the centralized-peripheralized distinction see Riker, 1955.)

Advantages of This Definition of Federalism

This definition, with its emphasis on amounts of activities that governments govern, is to be contrasted with the conventional definition such as that offered by Wheare. His definition is stated as a test:

> Does a system of government embody predominantly a division of powers between general and regional authorities each of which in its own sphere

is coordinate with the others and independent of them? If so, that government is federal. (1956, pp. 32–33)

Lurking behind Wheare's definition is the notion of sovereignty and the necessity for full and formal juristic independence of levels of government. By contrast, the definition offered here avoids the excessive legalism of conventional definitions, while not throwing out the juristic element entirely. Furthermore, it leads to the understanding of federalism as a range of phenomena rather than as a single constitutional thing. In both these respects it is quite different from Wheare's definition, which, following almost all the constitutional lawyers of the previous generation, emphasized not only independence of constituent and central governments but some more or less precise division of functions. Furthermore, Wheare applied his test very strictly. For example, he excluded the Weimar Republic and the USSR because the central governments had potentially full control of fiscal arrangements for the regional governments. He excluded the United Netherlands because, he said, provincial unanimity was required for the union government to act.* To be coordinate, in his mind, the two kinds of governments should be self-sufficient in both fiscal matters and governmental machinery and there should be a precisely divided set of functions.

As may well be observed, no government ever or anywhere, not even the ones Wheare himself accepted, could strictly satisfy such a definition—an exactly coordinate pair of authorities would result in stalemate and disaster. It is always the case that the central government can overawe the constituent governments or the constituent governments can overawe the center. And this is as true of the United States, Australia, Canada, and Switzerland—Wheare's only federal governments—as it is of all the others I have named.

Consequently, most writers since Wheare have directly or indirectly criticized his definition. Livingston, for example (1952), implicitly but sharply criticized it for legalism, pointing out that such a definition consists of demarcating functions and listing a set of legal properties. "We are far too prone," he argues (p. 91), "to say that federal constitutions must contain a certain five or eight or ten characteristics and that all constitutions lacking any of these are not federal"—which was, of course, exactly what Wheare did. Similarly, Friedrich, who defines federalism as a process, is apparently reacting against Wheare's kind of definition. Federalism, Friedrich says, "should not be seen as a static pattern or a design characterized by a particular and precisely fixed division of powers between governmental levels. Federalism is

---

* This assertion, derived from Freeman, is based on a legalistic reading of the Union of Utrecht and no knowledge of actual government. Both Wheare and Freeman are grossly inaccurate. Never once, for example, was the stadtholder elected by all seven provinces. See Janicon (1729).

also and perhaps primarily the process of federalizing" (1968, p. 7). Like Wheare, he believes the "idea of a compact is inherent in federalism," but he also insists that there is much more to it. Unfortunately he is somewhat mystical in describing the additional elements.

The inadequacy of the conventional definition may be difficult to state abstractly, but it is easy to reveal this inadequacy by describing contrary instances, contrary in the sense that they appear to fit the conventional definition, but in fact do not. Two such contrary instances are the United States and Germany. Perhaps the best criticism of the conventional definition in terms of division of functions comes from Grodzins, who, in a famous metaphor, compared American federalism to a marble cake. "The American form of government is often, but erroneously, symbolized by a three-layer cake. A far more accurate image is the rainbow or marble cake, characterized by an inseparable mingling of different colored ingredients, the colors appearing in vertical and diagonal strands and unexpected whirls. As colors are mixed in the marble cake, so functions are mixed in the federal system" (1960b, p. 265). As is always something of a danger with vivid and memorable metaphors like this one, it is possible to take the metaphor itself as a description. Fortunately in this case, the metaphor is based on extensive research. Grodzins' student Elazar (1962) had shown that at least in certain kinds of governmental functions throughout the nineteenth century there was constant cooperation between the states and the nation in accomplishing their tasks. (Further detail on this argument is available in Grodzins, 1966, and Elazar, 1966.) This is not quite so universally true as they asserted. The military function was in fact something the framers of the Constitution had hoped would be cooperatively managed, but it ended up almost entirely in federal hands (Riker, 1958). Similarly, Scheiber (1966) argues that very little sharing of function occurred prior to the Civil War and describes that period of American federalism as "rivalistic state mercantilism." But if there are such exceptions to Elazar's rule in the nineteenth century, they tend entirely to disappear in the twentieth with the rise of "cooperative federalism," grants-in-aid, and the like. Hence, despite the possible exaggeration of Grodzins' and Elazar's position, their main point is probably correct: In function after function there is in fact no division of authority between constituent governments and the center, but rather a mingling. And if this is the case, then the conventional division-of-powers definition of federalism simply is not acceptable for the main example of federal government.

What Grodzins and Elazar pointed out with respect to the United States had long been known of Germany. Brecht distinguished between *vertical* and *horizontal* division of powers.

> The line of demarcation that in the United States separates governmental powers of the nation from those of the states has always been *vertical*.

When power to deal with some subject matter was given to the federal government, it was as a rule full governmental power, including administration and adjudication as well as legislation. This was not so in Germany. The imperial constitution of 1871, while liberally granting the federal government the power to legislate in most fields of general significance, left administrative and judicial functions in almost all matters to the states. While the nation's legislative power was much broader in Germany from the very beginning than it has ever become here, its administrative power was much narrower, at least in the beginning. In other words, the original line of demarcation between powers in Germany was *horizontal* rather than vertical. (Brecht, 1945, p. 47)

While the evidence amassed by Elazar and Grodzins shows that Brecht is not quite correct in describing the United States system as vertical, few would doubt that he is correct about the horizontal, mingling-of-function nature of the German system, with which, as a scholar, he was the better acquainted. Hence his evidence about Germany constitutes a second counterinstance to the conventional division-of-powers definition.

When it has been shown in detail that two important instances of federalism simply do not fit the conventional definition, then it is apparent that there is something radically wrong with it. But matters are even worse, for *no* political system can be an instance of Wheare's definition. If a system displayed the exact balancing between the center and the states on which he insists, it would—in constant stalemate—be unable to act. Real federations are always constructed so that in a crisis one kind of government can and does prevail. Sometimes it takes a civil war to discover where the ultimate strength is; but that there is a stronger side is almost certain. In terms of the formal features of Wheare's definition, it must be rejected on the evidence of all these authors.

Livingston, doubtless in sharp reaction against Wheare's legalism, went very far in an opposite direction. His definition does not depend on governments at all. "Every society," he argues, "is more or less closely integrated. . . . Each is composed of elements that feel themselves to be different. . . . These diversities may turn on all sorts of questions, economic, religious, racial, historical. . . . If they [i.e., those who feel different from the rest] are grouped territorially, . . . then the result may be a society that is federal" (Livingston, 1952, p. 84–85). Unfortunately, this definition goes too far and takes in too much. By it, one makes federations of such unitary governments as the United Kingdom with its Celtic-speaking minorities in Wales and Scotland, France with the Celtic-speaking Britons in Brittany, and Spain with its large Basque-speaking minority in the North. All of these minorities have good reason to feel set apart and put upon. But because the minorities feel different does not make the governments any the less unitary in the sense that all citizens believe any issue may be settled by the central government.

Of course, what Livingston was trying to do was to broaden the definition of federalism from the restrictions Wheare had put on it. But there is another way to do this without throwing out the juristic element entirely. Two writers have shown the way. Davis has argued that "to compress these multiple variations [in the life and structure of federal governments] within these [i.e., Wheare's] concepts is not merely to lose in descriptive reality, but to disfigure reality to serve categories of limited service" (1956, p. 243). He thus suggests, inferentially at least, a recasting of definitions so that more of reality may be considered. Duchacek (1970) takes the same position. After a careful analysis of ten "yardsticks," or standards of federalism—basically of a juristic kind, for example, "Has the central authority exclusive control over diplomacy and defense?" or "Is the federal union constitutionally immune against secession?" —he concludes that none of these yardsticks, either together or separately, can demarcate federalism. Instead he regards it as a space in a continuum.

The trouble with the conventional or exclusive definition is now fully apparent. It is its very exclusiveness that renders it inadequate. The definition offered here in the previous section, because it is an inclusive definition based on the common usage rather than the advocates' usage, is thus more likely to be satisfactory. At least the definition offered here admits as an example of federalism every government that has commonly been called one and extracts from the history of the word the principle that permitted the application. Furthermore, this definition does not fall into Livingston's mistake of throwing out the juristic element entirely. Even in common usage federalism is a juristic concept of sorts, and that fact is retained in our definition by emphasizing the existence of two kinds of governments and their separate ability to make some decisions independently of each other.

To summarize the argument of this introduction, it seems that there is widespread and quite direct dissatisfaction with the legalistic or exclusive definitions as uttered by Wheare. Therefore other writers in the last two decades (Livingston, 1952; Riker, 1964b; Duchacek, 1970) have offered several inclusive definitions of which one has been set forth here in detail. Other interesting discussions of the problem of defining federalism can be found in Birch (1966) and Stein (1968), both of which are review essays.

THE DEVELOPMENT OF FEDERALISM

Looking over the federations mentioned in the introduction, one notes a fairly steady growth in the number of federal governments over the past two centuries, as recorded in Table 2. While there are only 19 currently, these 19 account for well over half the land mass and population of the world. Clearly federalism is a successful form of political organization in the sense that it has

TABLE 2   Growth of number of federal governments

	Federations started in time period	
	Still surviving	Now dissolved
pre–1750	1 (Switzerland)	2 (United Netherlands, Five Nations)
1751–1800	1 (United States)	
1801–1850	4 (Argentina, Brazil, Mexico, Venezuela)	3 (Colombia, Chile, Central American Republic)
1851–1900	3 (Canada, Germany, Austria)	1 (New Zealand)
1901–1950	5 (Australia, India, Pakistan, Soviet Union, Yugoslavia)	2 (Burma, Indonesia)
1951–1970	5 (Malaysia, Nigeria, Czechoslovakia, Cameroon, Tanzania)	8 (Rhodesia, Mali, Congo, British West Indies, Libya, East African Federation, Ethiopia, United Arab Republic)
Number	19	16

survived and proliferated. It is reasonable to ask why this is so. My answer is in three parts.

1. Centralized federalism was invented in the late eighteenth century. Had this invention not occurred, it is doubtful that federalism would have been widely adopted. Almost none of the contemporary federations are or were originally conceived of as peripheralized. It is the centralized form of federalism that the world finds attractive; and, had the notion of this kind of federalism not been available for copying, it is doubtful that many constitution writers would have found federalism itself worthwhile. The invention of centralized federalism is, then, a necessary condition of the contemporary proliferation of federalism.

2. The nineteenth and twentieth centuries have been a period of the buildup and collapse of worldwide empires. As empires have collapsed, many colonials have nevertheless wanted to preserve the one main advantage of empire, namely, large size. Federalism is a convenient means of bringing about sizeable governmental units without the imperial form. All the federations in parts of what once were the British, Spanish, Portuguese, Dutch, and Russian empires have this particular history: the collapsed empire or part of the empire seemed about to become a set of independent former colonies each too small, in the opinion of the dominant politicians, to survive as viable governments. In response to this threat, federal constitutions were devised. The collapse of empire is not a necessary condition of federalism, but it sets one kind of scene in which federalism is appropriate.

3. The nature of the federal bargain is such that, once the bargain is struck, federalism remains. There are good military-diplomatic reasons for making the federal compact, and even if these reasons subsequently evaporate, the bargain itself may remain, possibly because of the special interests the federal relation has itself generated.

In the rest of this section and in the next one I will examine these conditions for the proliferation of federalism in detail.

The Invention of Centralized Federalism

The main practical difference between centralized federalism and peripheralized federalism is that in centralized federalism the central government can force constituent governments to behave as the central government wishes with respect to those functions generally supposed to be vested in the center. On the other hand, in peripheralized federalism it is not possible for the center to discipline a recalcitrant regional government or a recalcitrant group of regional governments. They can be expected to obey an edict from the center only if they agree with it.

To compare the two degrees of federalism in a specific situation we can look at the United States government in the 1780s, when it was peripheralized, and in the 1910s, when it was centralized, with respect to the states' obedience of international treaties. One of the main problems that led to the calling of the Federal Convention of 1787 was the failure of some states to pay England for the property of loyalist colonists confiscated during the Revolution, a repayment mandated by the Treaty of Paris of 1783. Since England refused to hand over forts at Detroit and Mackinac until the payments were made, some American politicians feared the failure to pay would lead to a reopening of the war. There was no way in which the central government or indeed the larger states could force some of the small states to pay their bills. Such was the enforcement on regional governments of treaty obligations in a peripheralized federation. By contrast, 130 years later, the states' willingness to obey was so automatic that it served as a basis for expanding central government authority into yet another sphere. A federal statute regulating the hunting of migratory birds had been ruled *ultra vires* for the central government, thus permitting states to ignore it. As an indirect means of accomplishing the same regulation, therefore, the central government embodied it in a treaty with Canada. This the Supreme Court upheld (*Missouri* v. *Holland*, 252 U.S. 416, 1920) and the states obeyed as a matter of course. The comparison is clear. In both cases diplomatic affairs were a main concern of the central government, but in the former case it could not force states to take action highly relevant to this concern, while in the latter case it could so easily force the states to obey that it used this authority as a trick to expand its influence over what would otherwise have been regarded as an essentially domestic matter.

What makes the difference between these two events is the invention, or more accurately development, of centralized federalism. Where did it come from? It was started at the Philadelphia Convention of 1787, which was called by those who believed the government of the Articles was too weak to fight wars or to keep treaties or to maintain domestic order. The new government, created under the Constitution written at Philadelphia, was not, of course, vastly different. Yet it contained the potential for growth into a centralized federalism. Under the new constitution some great innovations were:

1. Some officials (President and representatives) of the central government were to be chosen, not by the constituent governments or by the central government itself, but by the people of the constituent regions or by special assemblies in the regions. So far as I can discover, this was a genuine innovation for federal government. In all previous cases the officials were chosen by the constituent governments and hence were more likely to be responsible and loyal to them than to the central government. The new arrangements meant that over time these officials might be loyal to the center rather than to a region. This was the essential content of the great compromise by which small states retained their equal representation in one house of the legislature but gave it up to population equality in the other.

2. The central government was given a long list of activities that made it seem almost like a national centralized government, while the constituent governments were forbidden some of these activities.

3. The central government was supposed to be supreme over the regional governments in the event of a conflict about the power of the center. Furthermore, a judiciary was provided that could declare this supremacy and thereby authorize the enforcement of the central government's powers.

(Accounts and interpretations of these innovations are contained in all studies of the Philadelphia Convention, of which a good recent one is Rossiter, 1966. The proceedings of the Convention, so far as they can be reconstructed, are in Farrand, 1911, and, in abbreviated form, in Stolberg, 1958.)

While these constitutional innovations did not immediately transform eighteenth century United States from a loose union of former colonies to the centralized, and highly bureaucratized, leviathan it is today, still they provided the opportunity for the leviathan to grow. The fact that the President is not dependent on the state governments or even on a coalition of state governments for his selection has meant that most Presidents have been loyal to the central government in every conflict with states. The first President was one whose political life was entirely associated with the central government; he set the pattern that even professed believers in states' rights tended to follow. Thus, Jefferson did not hesitate to expand the Union to the advantage of the central government, and Jackson did not hesitate to denounce nullification. Of all the

Presidents only one, James Buchanan, showed consistent partiality for states' rights, and his behavior helped to bring about civil war. The effect of this office on centralizing American federalism can be seen in Corwin (1957), Neustadt (1960), and various essays in Wildavsky (1969).

One organ of the central government, the Senate, was supposed to be entirely dependent on state governments and thus an agency to maintain the peripheralized character of the government of the Articles. But over the course of a hundred years its character changed radically and it too became centralized. (See Riker, 1955, for detail on this transformation.) It is unlikely that any such change would have occurred in the Senate had the Presidency not been constantly centralizing throughout the nineteenth century. The independence of that office from the states is, it appears, the crucial feature of the Constitution in permitting the development of a national orientation of loyalty and political life.

Besides making the national executive independent of the states, the Constitution also gave the legislative and executive a lot more to do than had theretofore been customary in federations. Besides the usual authority in foreign affairs, the central government was given authority to govern interstate commerce (a function that ultimately came to include nearly all regulation of business and industry), to govern territories (which, in the first half of the nineteenth century, contained more land than the states themselves), and to carry through many other nationalizing functions like coining money. The impressive feature of this list of duties is that gradually the central government came to exercise them. For a survey of that process, as adjudicated by the Supreme Court, see Schmidhauser (1958). Most standard constitutional histories describe the process in detail. Unfortunately, most of these works, having been written by lawyers or in the legal tradition, tend to overestimate vastly the importance of utterances by judges.

Assuming, instead, that the socially significant decisions on the allocation of functions are those made by all politicians representing the citizenry, not just those decisions made by judges, it appears that the true relationship of states and nation in administration is that, on all problems of importance, politicians are likely to use both kinds of governments to solve them. This is the point that Elazar (1962) and Grodzins (1966) have made very well by repeated demonstrations. If both kinds of governments appear to be making successful contributions, then the relevant politicians are likely to approve a continued sharing of functions. If the constituent governments appear to fail, however, while the central government succeeds, naturally they turn the function over to the central government. Thus, even though the Constitution specifically divided national defense between the nation and the states, the states performed so poorly in 1812 that the function was fully transferred to the center by the time of the Civil War. Subsequently, the states developed a new defense arm for internal security but they were never able to win back a significant role in national defense. Thus while the Constitution is written as if the framers assumed that the two kinds of government would share the function equally, in fact the states have almost no role (see Riker, 1958, and Derthick, 1965). Most of the centralization of the United States has come about in the same way: activities presumably entirely or largely a function of the state governments have been poorly performed, and the interested politicians and citizens have therefore turned to the central government; when the central government has performed them well, it has gotten credit at the expense of the states. Some typical areas in which this occurred in the nineteenth century were military affairs and regulation of transportation. In the twentieth century some typical areas are aid for the poor and regulation of water resources. In a sense, therefore, one can say that the centralization started in the Constitutional Convention is still going on.

The Significance of Centralized Federalism

Governments combine to form larger ones because the combining governments and their citizens want to gain some advantage that only big governments can bring. To gain the advantage, of course, the big government must be effective enough in operations such as taxing and defense to sustain itself. The peripheralized federalisms of ancient and medieval times lacked just this feature. Typically they were not able to collect taxes effectively. They had to rely on the good faith of constituent governments to pay assessments, since in general they had no way to tax citizens directly. And no government rich or poor is always willing to pay assessments it can evade. For that reason, therefore, federalism—of which only the peripheralized form was known—seldom seemed a feasible method of enlarging government before the nineteenth century. Consequently, most enlargements were by conquest or (rarely) by submission. Beginning with the nineteenth century, however, an example of effective federalism existed in the form of the centralized federalism of the United States. This example doubtless encouraged others to copy it.

That existing federations in the world are partially copied from the United States is one aspect of the history of ideas and of the dissemination of political forms that has been quite well studied. The Latin American revolutionaries of the early nineteenth century had two kinds of intellectual inspiration, American and French revolutionary liberalism. From France came the anti-feudalism component of revolution and from the United States came the liberal components (see Belaunde, 1938). One element of liberalism was federalism, which is why most revolutionary Latin nations tried it, even though in some cases—for example, Chile—it was clearly unneeded because the local governments were not strong enough to hold out against the center. This influence is discussed in detail for Latin America in general in Haring (1938) and Martin (1938); for Mexico in Mecham (1938); for Argentina in Alberdi (1913), a volume comparable to *The Federalist Papers*; and in Sarmiento (1961) and Rowe (1921).

The influence of the American Constitution on the British North America Act (1867) is, of course, strong and immediately apparent. The fathers of the Canadian Constitution constantly compared their situation with that of the United States, about whose politics they were well informed even if they did misinterpret them (see Creighton, 1964; Trotter, 1924; Waite, 1963; and Whitelaw, 1938). Facing as they did a problem of provincial governments wishing to avoid subjugation to a central one, the solution of federalism as expressed next door was obvious. Naturally, however, they improved on it. Since they worked just after (and because of) the American Civil War, they made their federalism somewhat more centralized legally in that residual powers not specifically assigned to one of the two levels were to rest not with the constituent governments as in the United States (see the Tenth Amendment to the U.S. Constitution) but with the central government. In fact, however, the Canadian system has never become as centralized as the system of the United States—possibly because the Canadian system has never had a significant problem of defense.

The American influence was almost equally strong in the Australian case. While half a world away, the American experience was easily accessible because of the absence of language barriers. Furthermore, Australian politicians recognized the similarity of their position with that of the Americans in 1787. Consequently, they adopted many features of American federalism, even using the name Senate for their upper house. They recognized, however, the growing centralization of the American system and tried to avoid getting quite as much of it themselves. (For an exhaustive study of the American influence in Australia see Hunt, 1933; also, the Australian Federal Convention, 1897–98; Deakin, 1944; and Whitelaw, 1938.)

Once the great colonies of Canada and Australia had been successfully launched as federations, the example of these mingled with that of the United States so that its experience is only indirectly relevant to the constitutions of India, Nigeria, etc. Nevertheless, once the influence was established, it continued as part of the British colonial tradition (see Livingston, 1963, and Watts, 1966).

In the continental tradition, American influence entered by way of Switzerland. After a minor civil war in 1847 (the Sonderbund War), Switzerland in 1848 abandoned the peripheralized constitution it had had since the restoration after Napoleon and indeed since medieval times. Quite consciously using American experience as a guide, the drafters of the new constitution gave a grant of all diplomatic power to the central government and provided for bicameralism, which is the American device to allow representation of both the constituent governments and the citizens. (For an elegant description of this constitution and the American influence see Rappard, 1948; see also Hughes, 1954, and Codding, 1961.) While the influence of the American tradition on Switzerland is direct and obvious, it is less so in Germany. About the only clear-cut influence that exists is that German politicians and lawyers knew that centralized federalism worked in the United States. The particular forms of the federal empire of 1871 were, however, uniquely appropriate for German conditions. After the end of the First World War, when the German Empire became the Weimar Republic, the American example was often cited for an increase in centralization (see Holborn, 1938, and Triepel, 1924). The American influence became even stronger in the formation of the fundamental law for the Bonn government because both the American example and the American presence were compelling (see Golay, 1958).

Just as the American influence was most direct on the earlier British federations, so the American influence was most direct on the Swiss (1848) and Weimar constitutions. Other continental federations such as the Soviet, the Yugoslavian, and the Austrian probably owe much more to Germany and Switzerland than to the United States.

As this survey indicates, however, American federalism had a profound impact (either direct or indirect) on the making of most federal constitutions. It is not that these constitutions were copied in detail (although many of the Latin constitutions show verbal similarities), but rather that the American example was proof that a centralized federalism would in fact work. In the United States for nearly two centuries the central government has been reasonably effective—indeed powerful—so that it can govern the military and diplomatic and commercial affairs that the citizens wish it to govern. Yet at the same time in all those two centuries the states have remained in existence and even important in the system. It was the demonstration that an effective central government could be combined with a living and continuing set of constituent governments that so impressed politicians in other nations. Without necessarily copying American institutions in detail they copied the idea of federalism, so that now half the territory of the world is federal.

THE CONDITIONS OF FEDERALISM

One necessary condition for the spread of federalism is thus that there be a highly visible example of effective and viable federal government. Many writers have tried to set forth additional necessary conditions for the adoption of a federal constitution. This literature is elegantly surveyed in Birch (1966). The main issue in that literature, as it is seen by Birch, is whether the necessary conditions are exclusively political or whether they are social and economic as well.

One statement of the exclusively political approach is Riker (1964b, p. 12), where it is argued that federalism is a constitutional bargain among politicians and the motives are military and diplomatic defense or aggression. Riker's sole conditions are:

1. A desire on the part of politicians who offer the bargain to expand their territorial control by peaceful means, usually either to meet an external military or diplomatic threat or to prepare for military or diplomatic aggrandizement.

2. A willingness on the part of politicians who accept the bargain to give up independence for the sake of the union either because they desire protection from an external threat or because they desire to participate in the potential aggression of the federation.

Birch (1966) has revised and expanded these conditions to include the desire to deter internal threats and a willingness to have them deterred. These conditions as revised, which center on the immediate political act of federation, contrast sharply with other sets of conditions that have been offered. Which sets of conditions are most descriptive of reality is the main concern of this section.

A statement of an alternative set of conditions is found in Deutsch (1957, p. 58), where the formation of a constitution is said to depend on the existence of background "forces." This approach appears to be an extreme reductionism in the sense that the relevant features of a political situation are thought to be social and economic, not political. The dispute between the reductionists and the advocates of political conditions centers mainly on the question of whether or not political considerations generate political decisions. In addition, however, since the reductionist conditions are, as in Deutsch's case, usually stated as "forces," there is of course also dispute about how forces can ever be brought to act creatively. In Deutsch's statement the "essential" conditions for an "amalgamated security community," of which class federation is a subset, are:

1. mutual compatibility of main values

2. a distinctive way of life

3. expectations of stronger economic ties or gains

4. marked increase in political and administrative capabilities of at least some participating units

5. superior economic growth on the part of at least some participating units

6. unbroken links of social communication, both geographically between territories and sociologically between different social strata

7. a broadening of the political elite

8. mobility of persons at least among the politically relevant strata

9. a multiplicity of ranges of communications and transactions.

Birch (1966) examines Deutsch's conditions with respect to Nigeria, East Africa, and Malaysia and finds that only 3, 4, 5, and 9 are present in all three federations. Given differential rates of change in the world, conditions 4, 5, and 9 are always present in any randomly selected group of units. Hence to include 4, 5, and 9 in the list is like saying that prices are determined by the existence of people as well, of course, as by supply and demand. Condition 3, expectation of economic gain, is certainly a frequent feature of the situations in which federations are formed. But it does not seem to have been present in the formation of the Soviet Union, as seen in Aspaturian (1950), nor in the formation of the Latin American federalisms, where political independence occupied all the rhetoric of the advocates of federalism. It is thus clear that none of Deutsch's conditions is universal. Hence it is difficult to see that any are essential.

A more commonsensical list of background conditions is found in Wheare (1956, pp. 37–38):

1. a sense of military insecurity and the need for common defense
2. a desire to be independent of foreign powers, for which the union is necessary
3. a hope of economic advantage
4. some previous political association
5. geographical neighborhood
6. similarity of political institutions.

Watts (1966, p. 42), writing only of six new federations in the British Commonwealth, has expanded this list by adding:

7. a need for efficiency
8. community of outlook based on race, religion, language, or culture
9. enterprising character of the leadership
10. existence of models
11. influence of the United Kingdom government in constitution making.

We can eliminate some of these conditions easily. Condition 11, on the United Kingdom, is special to Watts' data and cannot therefore be a general condition. Condition 3, which is similar to Deutsch's condition 3 on the hope of economic gain and which is the only direct overlap with his conditions, can be rejected on the same ground that we have rejected Deutsch's condition 3, namely, that it is not always present. Conditions 7 and 9, on efficiency and enterprise, can be rejected as meaningless, that is, there is always need for efficiency, and successful leadership is always enterprising while unsuccessful leadership is not. Condition 8, on community, can be rejected as false because many federations have been created as federations precisely because they *lacked* community of outlook. There is, of course, always a community of interest, as seen in the desire for a bargain, but there need not be any common racial, religious, linguistic, or cultural basis for agreement. Condition 6, on similarity of institutions, can easily be rejected because India was created out of units, some of which were parliamentary governments and others of which were princely despotisms. Condition 5 can be rejected with the examples of Malaysia and Pakistan, the units of which are not geographically contiguous.

This leaves four conditions, of which Wheare-Watts' conditions 1 and 2 are substantially the same as those that Riker asserts are necessary. Condition 10, on the existence of models, has already been shown to be almost universal in a previous section of this essay. It is possible that condition 4 of Wheare and Watts, the requirement of some previous political association, is also necessary. In this section, therefore, we will examine the validity of these three as yet unexamined conditions that do not seem false on their face.

The rationale of Riker's conditions is that the establishment of a federal government must be a rational bargain among politicians. Some people give up something; for example, the current rulers of the constituent units give up their formally complete autonomy, and in order to justify this loss they must anticipate a substantial gain. The prospective rulers of the federation, though possibly strong enough to unite the nation by force, do not do so and for this they must obtain a reward, namely, peaceful integration. Thus each party to the bargain gains some advantage. The rationale of the Riker-Birch conditions, which are equivalent to the first two of the Wheare-Watts conditions (though Riker and Birch regard them as necessary while Wheare and Watts do not), is that both kinds of rulers gain an advantage from the federal bargain. One expects a bargain to be made when rational advantage is present for both. Indeed the bargain is struck precisely because it is a move in the direction of a Pareto-optimal outcome.

Practically, then, the test is: In every successfully formed federalism it must be the case that a significant external or internal threat or a significant opportunity for aggression is present, where the threat can be forestalled and the aggression carried out only with a bigger government. This is what brings union at all and is the main feature, the prospective gain, in both giving and accepting the bargain. At the same time there must be some provincial loyalty so that the bargain is necessary, that is, it must be necessary to appease provincial rulers. This is what prevents the formation of a full-scale national government and thus brings about federation as an alternative. Furthermore, the case for the necessity of these conditions is stronger if, for all federations that fail, it is the case that

1. for those that break up into constituent units, external or internal threats are not significant; and

2. for those that transform into unitary governments, provincial loyalty is relatively weak.

The rationale for the Wheare-Watts condition that there be some previous political association among units of a federation is not so clear. It may be regarded, however, as a kind of practical surrogate for a portion of the Riker-Birch conditions. That is, previous association may generate a desire on the part of centralizers to integrate by peaceful rather than violent means and a willingness on the part of provincial leaders to accept federation and to trust each other and the prospective leaders of the center. We may think of previous association as one sign of nascent nationalism and one possible affective cement that holds together the rational elements of the bargain. Nevertheless, on this basis one would not expect it to be a necessary condition, merely one that is by chance invariably found. The difference between this condition and those of Riker and Birch is that Riker and Birch predict that *all* future successful federations must display the conditions they lay down, while Wheare and Watts merely say that future federations may exhibit their condition. The test for this latter condition is, however, similar: In every successfully formed federation, there should be some previous association among constituent units.

In the next few pages I will test out the two main propositions (the Wheare-Watts conditions 1 and 2 and the two Riker-Birch necessary conditions) for the 35 federations listed in Table 2. Specifically, it is to be shown that every surviving federation (column 1) originated in a response to a threat or chance for aggrandizement and that, for every dissolved federation, either (1) there was no threat—or it disappeared before the time of dissolution—or (2) there was no significant provincial loyalty.

Switzerland. As the romance of William Tell reminds us, the original confederation of "forest cantons" formed in response to the threat of the tyranny of the Austrian Habsburgs. More to the point, the creation of the modern government of Switzerland with the centralization of 1848 was a response to a threat from the same source. It was an attempt to counter the influence of Metternich in Swiss affairs, which had been conveyed through the Sonderbund, a subfederal league of conservative and Catholic cantons. After the defeat of these cantons in the Sonderbund War and when the Concert of Europe was preoccupied with more threatening revolutions (of 1848) all over Europe, the liberal cantons centralized and Metternich was unable to veto. Thus at both stages of Swiss development the Austrian threat was present. But given the localism of feudalism at the first stage and the existence of the Sonderbund at the second, full nationalization would have been difficult. So both of the conditions for bargaining are fulfilled in the Swiss instance.

United Netherlands. The occasion for the formation of the Dutch federalism was, of course, the revolution against Spain, the first national revolution in the modern world (1570s). Initially the federation expanded and contracted with the fortunes of war, so that federation was a practical demonstration to marginal revolutionaries that local self-government and provincial loyalty could be satisfied on the revolutionary side. Thus both of the conditions for bargaining are satisfied in the Dutch case, when one looks only at the formation. After over two and a quarter centuries of successful federation, why did the Dutch Republic become a monarchy? One answer is that the threat had disappeared: the Spanish threat had long before been beaten back; the English threat, so dangerous to the Netherlands in the seventeenth century, disappeared when William III of Orange became the English king and the Protestant succession was assured in England; and the French threat, a constant menace in the eighteenth century culminating in the Napoleonic conquest (which resulted in a centralized republic in place of the federation), was wiped out at Waterloo. In the restoration, the House of Orange became Dutch royalty in a new kingdom of the Netherlands. Doubtless this was possible because there was no longer an external threat. Furthermore, the relevance of provincial loyalty was much less—owing to the political domination of the province of Holland. So the nationalization of the Dutch federation is characterized by an absence of the conditions that were necessary for the federalism in the first place.

United States. The original formation of the Union was to conduct the war for independence. Since there was no national government initially, merely several colonial local governments, the support of the leaders of revolution in each colony was assured by the prospect of quasi-national governments (i.e., the states) for them to control. Thus, both the conditions for bargaining were present in 1776. The later centralization of 1787, which did not disturb the strengthened and victorious state governments, was essentially a regrouping to improve the ability to resist in the event of a reopening of the war. It has been suggested in Beard (1913) that the motive for the centralization was the material greed of the framers; but this charge cannot be sustained (see Brown, 1956). The traditional view (recently set forth in Riker, 1964b) is that the motive compelling Washington, Franklin, the authors of *The Federalist,* and other outstanding figures about whom we have adequate documentation was that they wanted to strengthen the Union militarily in the face of the danger that the war would be reopened by England and in face of the danger that social revolutionaries (e.g., Shays) would bring about disintegration of the states. Thus both external and internal threats were present and, given the great care the framers took to maintain state governments during the centralization, it is apparent they believed that provincial loyalties were important and needed to be appeased. Thus both conditions that were present in 1776 were still present in 1787.

Spanish American federalism. In the long drawn out revolutionary activity (1810–26) that led to the expulsion of the Spanish power from Latin America, the only strong and continuing political force were the local caudillos. Federalism in Latin America was largely a device to bring these men together in order to fight the wars of independence (see Belaunde, 1938; Mecham, 1938; and Haring, 1938). Both conditions are involved: the threat is Spain and the provincial loyalties exist in the persons of the caudillos. Initially, at least, most of Latin America was contained in federations occasioned by the revolution: Argentina (including Uruguay), Chile, Gran Colombia (later broken up into Venezuela, Ecuador, and New Granada, or Colombia), the Central American Federation (later broken up into Guatemala, El Salvador, Honduras, Costa Rica, and Nicaragua), and Mexico. A good number of these abandoned federalism, leaving only Argentina, Venezuela, and Mexico. Why? The answer seems to be that federalism remained where some kind of serious threat remained and disappeared where the threat disappeared. Chile (wholly isolated), Uruguay (as a break off from Argentina), and Gran Colombia abandoned federalism almost as soon as independence was assured; Central America did so just a little later. Argentina, however, kept the federalism as an incident to the wars between Buenos Aires and the hinterland, and Mexico, of course, suffered subsequently from war with Texas, then the United States, and finally a European invasion. So for those who kept federalism the conditions for bargaining remained, and for those who did not the condition vanished. Furthermore, it is interesting to note that for those that centralized (e.g., Chile) provincial loyalties and caudillos were weak, while for those that dissolved (e.g., Central America) provincial loyalties and caudillos were strong.

Brazil. When the Spanish power collapsed in the rest of Latin America, so did the Portuguese, and the same kind of caudillo government developed as the essential units of power. This structure received formal recognition in the Additional Act of 1834, which reconstituted imperial Brazil along federal lines. This federalism was elaborated in 1889 when the republic replaced the empire. At both the beginning and at the reconstitution the threat was Portugal and Brazilian royalty, an offshoot of Portuguese royalty (see James, 1921). So federalism was a device to unite caudillos in the face of external threat and hence both the bargaining conditions were present.

British Empire federalism of the nineteenth century. Federalism in the United States originated in rebellion; most other British federalisms originated in a more or less friendly separation from Britain, often proceeding no further than independence within the Commonwealth. Consequently, the foreign threat that occasions federalism cannot in these cases be the imperial power, as it was in the case of all the federations so far examined. Nevertheless, the distinction between successful and unsuccessful British federalism is whether or not a foreign threat is present, and in that sense all the enduring British federations are just like the United States.

The first British federation after the United States was New Zealand, which had a federation of two colonies (North Island and South Island) from 1852 to 1876. As New Zealanders became substantially independent from Britain (having shown they could survive the Maori War of 1871–72), they then abandoned federation in favor of a unitary government. It is difficult to say that there ever was a military threat in this case. Even if Maoris constituted a threat initially, they ceased to be a threat after the Maori War of the early seventies. Furthermore, there were no significant provincial loyalties: North Island and South Island were geographic, not emotional, entities. So both bargaining conditions for federalism were absent. Consequently federation lasted only so long as it could be imposed by the imperial authority and disappeared as soon as the country was essentially self-governing.

Canadian federalism, on the other hand, exhibits both conditions very clearly. It was occasioned by what was felt to be a direct military threat from the United States. From the time of the Revolution onward some groups in the United States had sometimes cast covetous eyes on Canada and at the end of the Civil War, when the United States had a large and vigorous army, proposals to invade Canada could seem quite serious, especially when they came from such diverse quarters as a leading abolitionist Republican senator (Charles Sumner) and from Fenian agitators who hoped to free Ireland by involving the United States in a war with England. So for a brief period in the 1860s the United States seemed an immediate threat to Canada, and that was when the Canadian federation was formed. Furthermore, there were intense provincial loyalties, especially in Lower (or French) Canada, so that a truly national government as envisaged by the *Durham Report* (1837) was probably impossible short of civil war. Not only were the French highly provincial, so were the leaders of the Maritimes, who feared absorption into Upper Canada (Ontario). So the second test of the presence of the bargaining conditions is passed.

Australian federalism has often been interpreted as a purely economic bargain to promote intercolonial trade. Such an effect, however, could have been achieved by a customs union. And the Australians rejected that idea and created instead a full-scale national government on top of the states. Why? In the eighties and nineties of the last century three highly aggressive imperialisms were expanding rapidly in the South Pacific: the French in the New Hebrides, the German here and there in Oceania, and the Japanese in Korea. The cumulative impact of these threats, or rather of these actions, which foreclosed similar expansion by the Australian colonies, are what brought the Australian colonies together in 1897–1900 after continued failure to come together from the 1850s. Thus there was an external military threat, but it was probably weaker in the Australian case than in others we have so far examined. Consequently the degree of centralization in the Australian nation as it was initially formed is correspondingly weaker. The long bickering among the colonial governments before they could form a federation at all indicates that the provincial loyalties were considerable. So both of the bargaining conditions are present: a threat and thus a gain in repelling it and provincial loyalties that render federation preferable to unitary government for both sides of the bargain.

German federalism. The 1870 imperial federation in German lands was not occasioned by a threat but was part of Prussian expansion. Aggression, not defense, was the underlying purpose. In 1866 Prussia had eliminated Austria as a power in German affairs and in 1870 Prussia similarly eliminated France. Bismarck intended the momentum thus gained to carry Prussia onward to the status of world power with a great colonial empire just like England and France. For this purpose a united Germany was desired, even by the states that were absorbed. Since, however, provincial loyalties were intense and since Prussia preferred voluntary cooperation to conquest, the obvious solution was the federal empire. Both the bargaining conditions were thus met, a military opportunity in which all wished to engage and sufficient provincial loyalty to render federalism preferable to a unitary state (see Brecht, 1945).

German federalism has been twice reaffirmed, in the Weimar Constitution and in the Fundamental Law of the Bonn government. On both occasions significant threats existed. In 1919, when the imperial forces were expelled, Germany in effect reverted to its constituent units, which separately would have been quite unable to respond in any defensive way at all to the demands of the victorious Allies. The Weimar government was an attempt to keep Germany together and whole in the face of conquest. Much the same threat existed after the Second World War when Germany had been divided among the four conquering armies. In this case the Bonn government was a device to reunite Germany, even, hopefully, Eastern Germany. Since provincial loyalties existed and were identified in 1921 with nonimperial Germany and in 1949 with non-Hitlerian Germany, the constitution writers of both Weimar and Bonn were especially eager to emphasize these provincialisms. Hence at the time of both reaffirmations there was a significant military threat and a significant provincialism, which satisfies the bargaining conditions (see Merkl, 1963, and Golay, 1958). In Dikshit (1971) it is argued supposedly in refutation of the Riker-Birch assertions that other nonmilitary influences (e.g., American domination) were primary. If the necessary conditions are satisfied (as surely they are in this case by reason of the Soviet threat), then there is no point to arguing about degrees of relevance of various influences. The universality of the conditions is proved by their satisfaction in this case, even though they may not be historically the most "important" force.

Austrian federalism has much the same history as German federalism. Whether or not one regards the dual monarchy as a federation, it is apparent that it was created in response to an external threat in the face of provincial loyalties and as a way to engage provincials more deeply in the business of empire. It was announced in 1867 after the Austrian defeat by Prussia in 1866 and was presumably intended to mollify the Hungarian mobility while Franz Joseph continued his competition with Prussia for leadership in the German confederation. When the empire was broken up after the First World War and only "lesser Austria" remained, federalism was adopted for the same reason as in Germany: to unite the provinces in the face of the conquerors. Again, after the Second World War, Austrian federalism served as a way to bring partitioned Austria back together again (see Schlesinger, 1945, and Bluhm, 1968).

Soviet federalism. Soon after Soviet federalism was planned it was contained within a rigid dictatorship of the Bolshevik party. Consequently, most non-Communist commentators are loath to call it a federation at all. Nevertheless, if one looks at the circumstances of its origin it is just like all the other federalisms here discussed, in that both bargaining conditions are clearly present. The external threat was, of course, the memory and expectation of Allied intervention in Soviet affairs, while the internal threat was the memory and expectation of civil war. The demise of imperial Russia had permitted many previously conquered nations on the fringe of Russia proper to break away from Russian control: Finland, Estonia, Latvia, Lithuania, Ukraine, Armenia, Georgia, and the Transcaucasian territories. At the same time, foreign war, first with Germany ending in the disastrous peace of Brest-Litovsk, then incidentally with Allied troops, had made Lenin and the Soviet government fearful of foreign attack. And internal war from 1918 to 1921 had substantially ruined the Russian economy. One way that the Soviet government might meet these threats was, of course, to win back the fringe territories. While the Soviets could not win back those territories with rightist governments except by force, it could hope to win back those with leftist (non-Bolshevik) governments by agreement. And that is what Soviet federalism was initially all about. A set of leftist republics, all with the same military objectives (i.e., to defeat the Whites) but with different social theories, is exactly designed for federalism. There is a universally feared threat and there is a sense of provincial loyalty owing to differences of ideology, so that both the bargaining conditions were satisfied at the time that the Union of Soviet Socialist Republics was planned. That the autonomy of the individual republics had been substantially denied by the time the Constitution was actually adopted in 1924 does not alter the fact that these conditions had existed two years earlier (see Aspaturian, 1950; Yurchenko, 1956; and Schlesinger, 1945).

British federalism after the Second World War. The original intent of federalism in India was to provide some provincial governments with Muslim majorities. Thus the large Muslim minority in the nation would have some local protection. The anticipated threat in this anticipated federalism was religious civil war. But when it came to actual self-government in 1947, most of the Muslims were assigned to Pakistan and the need for federalism appeared to some to be unnecessary. According to this view, federalism is just another trick played by the British on the long-suffering Indian. Just as the British delayed self-government by interminable planning, partial self-government, and vast and meaningless constitutional scholarship, so it is said that Britain fastened federalism on India—even after the fact of Pakistan made it irrelevant—in order to divide and rule. And this argument is made the more plausible by the fact that the main division of India and Pakistan itself was undoubtedly a tactic of divide and rule, not malevolent, as Indians like to think, but merely self-interested. If this view is accepted, then there was no good reason for federalism in India; it is just a British trick that Indians fell for.

There is some truth in this view, for the long British planning for federalism undoubtedly generated some provincial loyalty, making the officers of provincial units think these units were worth saving. But more than this cannot be blamed on the British. Indians took nearly two years to write their own constitution. Its main author was a convinced antifederalist. And yet the consittution is clearly federal. Indian politicians must in that two year period after Pakistan was gone have thought that federalism would serve some purpose. And indeed, they saw two threats. One was the threat of Pakistan itself, which, from the time of troubles and exchange of peoples, Indian politicians recognized as the main potential enemy. The other was the threat of the princely states to refrain from joining India. Had this occurred, the map of India would have looked like a checkerboard and the viability of the new regime would surely have been jeopardized. Sensible men could visualize the situation in which India would have to fight princes and Pakistan simultaneously. So federalism in India was a way to pull the princely states into the Union in order to meet the external threat. And when the question was thus posed the Hindu princes were willing to be drawn in. Thus both the bargaining conditions are fulfilled. (For a complete history of constitution making in India see Bombwall, 1967; see also Pylee, 1960. The actual integration of the princely states into the Union is magnificently described in Menon, 1956. Watts, 1966, and Bombwall, 1967, have good bibliographies.)

What has been said of India is conversely true of Pakistan. Once a Hindu-majority India and a Muslim-majority Pakistan were created by British fiat as they left, it was obvious to both countries who the future enemy would be. Since Pakistan was the smaller of the two, the threat to it was probably the greater. Since the country was geographically divided between Bengal and West Pakistan, provincial loyalties were pronounced. So with the threat from India and the divided nation, the conditions for federalism were clearly fulfilled (see Callard, 1957; Chaudhury, 1959; Watts, 1966; and, for the second constitution, Schuler and Schuler, 1967, and Sharan, 1968).

In Malaya federalism had a long history, having been created as a device for decentralization early in the British rule (see Emerson, 1937). Although federalism was purely an administrative device, it guaranteed the existence of provincial loyalties. In 1948 the loyalties were reinforced in a new constitution to prepare for self-government, which came in 1957. As in the case of India, the main question is: What besides habit and provincial loyalty motivated the Malays to perpetuate the federalism they had had fashioned for them by the colonial office in London? The answer seems to be the existence of two threats: an internal one of Chinese, and an external one of Indonesia. The Malays maintain dominance in Malaysia only by reason of a constitutional gerrymander. Were politics "fairly" structured, there seems little doubt that Chinese would be at least as strong as Malays. The fear of Chinese domination, a fear that led to the exclusion of Singapore from the original Malaya and to the expulsion of Singapore from the new federalism of Malaysia, was thus one threat (see Trager, 1968, and Simandjuntak, 1969). Federalism was thus a device to minimize Chinese influence. Ultimately the acceptance of Singapore was doubtless conditioned by the even greater fear of Indonsia, and the expulsion of Singapore recognized that Indonesia was not as dangerous as it seemed. Hence the variations in size demonstrate the applicability of the bargaining conditions (see Birch, 1966, and Watts, 1966).

Nigeria is perhaps the one possible exception to the conditions here examined. While it had a long history of provincial loyalty—each of the three provinces is dominated by one different tribe—still it is not clear that there was a significant military need for federation. Riker in 1964(b) interpreted Ghana and pan-Africanism as a threat, but Birch (1966) corrected this error by suggesting that pan-Africanism ran the other way and provided a motive of aggrandizement inasmuch as a federal Nigeria would be the most populous country in Africa. Watts (1966) attributed to Nigerians the motive of "the vision of the prestige and power of a United Nigeria" (Watts, 1966, p. 28). Birch (1966) offers, however, the most convincing explanation. The eastern region, later Biafra, saw the diplomatic advantages just mentioned, while the western and northern regions feared to allow an aggressive Nigeria dominated by Ibos without themselves in it. Thus, the threat was substantially internal, a mutual distrust, and safety lay in keeping a close watch on the other fellows. It is this situation that led Birch to revise Riker's conditions to provide for internal as well as external threats. In any event, both the bargaining conditions are, in this interpretation, present in Nigeria. (For good detail on the development of Nigerian federalism see Coleman, 1958; Odumosu, 1963; Awa, 1964; Tilman and Cole, 1962; Schwarz, 1965; Rothchild, 1960; and Mackintosh, 1962.)

Just how one is to interpret the civil war in Nigeria and what backward light it throws on the motive for union is not clear. The history of Biafra seems to support Birch's explanation, however: when the eastern region found it could not dominate the federation, it withdrew. But the west and especially the north, which in Birch's view had entered federation to control the Ibos, would not allow them to secede.

Next door to Nigeria is Cameroon, composed of the former French and British trust territories. It formed for several external diplomatic and military reasons, both a fear of Nigeria, and particularly of Ibos, and an ambition to unite the two parts of the trust territory (see Welch, 1969 and 1966). Unlike the case of most federations, here the existence of these motives is formally known: at the time of independence, British Cameroons were given the choice of joining Nigeria or French Cameroons. They chose the French by a 7:3 margin. What the citizens wanted, so did the main political parties, so both the necessary conditions were fulfilled.

Finally we have several federations that have failed. The three main cases are Rhodesia-Nyasaland, East African Federation, and British West Indies. All of them are characterized by the absence of both of the bargaining conditions. Doubtless the clearest case is the proposed but never implemented East African Federation, which does, however, have a vestigial remainder in Tanzania, the union of what were formerly Tanganyika and Zanzibar. This proposed union was to contain Kenya, Uganda, and what is now Tanzania and was thus to be the most substantial country in Black Africa. But the union was never achieved, although presumably Tanzania is an attempt to start it with two units. The reasons for failure are quite clear. No external threat existed at all and, unlike the case of Nigeria, there was simply no interest in either Tanzania or Kenya and Uganda in internal domination. Hence the leaders of each government were unwilling to give up independence for what each apparently regarded as no gain. Consequently no external or internal threat existed and hence no federation was formed (see Birch, 1966; Franch, 1968; and Nye, 1965). Many observers who took a purely economic and social view of federation assumed that East African Federation was "logical," but it was not logical or necessary exactly because of the absence of a political reason for unity. It is an example like this that most clearly reveals the inadequacy of the reductionist explanation of politics in terms of economic and social factors.

The federation of Rhodesia and Nyasaland existed briefly in the 1950s and 1960s, although it was never a truly independent government. It may, like the East African Federation, be regarded as a stillbirth. That it was so born implies a fatal defect, which in this case was again a complete unwillingness of the several parties to accept union, simply because there was no political threat to be met by union and thus no political gain to be made by union (see Spiro, 1968; Rotberg, 1965; and Watts, 1966).

The West Indian Federation is also a stillborn object. Before it was really free of Britain, Jamaica and then Trinidad withdrew so that the federation collapsed. The reason for the collapse is obvious. At that time there was no possible enemy either externally or internally. Hence, given the insularity and high degree of provincial loyalty, there was nothing to make a bargain about. (For the early development of this federation see Ayearst, 1960; Lowenthal, 1960; Watts, 1966; and for its collapse see Etzioni, 1965, and Flanz, 1968).

Finally, among postwar British federations, one can mention Burma, though it is unclear that it ever was one. Its constitution allows secession and thus appears federal, but its institutions are purely unitary. Since it has no history of any kind of federalism, it is here interpreted as just another stillborn British federation, stillborn because neither bargaining condition for federalism was satisfied.

East European federalisms. Following the example of the Soviet Union, Yugoslavia became a federation after the Second World War. This action, like Nigeria and imperial Germany, was a good example of federation motivated less by a threat and more by the opportunity for aggrandizement. While federalism had often been suggested for Yugoslavia in the prewar period as a solution to its numerous ethnic problems (see Schlesinger, 1945), and while Tito undoubtedly used it this way, the main objective seems to have been a creation of a system that could absorb the rest of Eastern Europe, or at least Bulgaria and Albania (see Frankel, 1955; Shoup, 1968; and Hondius, 1968). That the federalism failed in this objective does not lessen the significance of the motive. So the external military-diplomatic objective was expansion and the willingness of at least the Yugoslav states to accept such a form was attested to by the continuing nationalism of ethnic groups in Yugoslavia. Both the bargaining conditions were thus present.

The case of Czechoslovakia, in which federalism was recently imposed under the influence of Russia, is too new a case to be examined, especially since it was apparently imposed rather than adopted.

Indonesia. Like the British federations that failed, this one too was imposed by a colonial power, presumably to leave behind a viable government, although the Javanese thought it was a policy of divide and rule. In any event, it was a quick failure. Again, one is impressed by the absence of the bargaining conditions in a federation that failed. There was no conceivable external threat in 1948–49, for the Japanese influence had been removed and Indonesia was not yet independent and able to pick its own quarrels with Australia, Philippines, Malaysia, and China. There was, therefore, nothing to be gained by a federal bargain and the Javanese had no reason to offer it. Instead they chose conquest of the outer islands, which, though difficult, was eventually concluded.

Other African federations. A number of other federations in Africa, which have been largely pointless, have existed briefly with no external or internal threat and then either broken up into constituent units or turned into centralized unitary states. Ethiopia, whose federation was simply a sham to absorb the Somaliland trust territory; Congo, where federalism was merely a sham to continue Belgian control of the mineral-rich Katanga province; and Libya, where federalism was simply a convenience of isolated communities, centralized; Mali broke up after years of planning and a few weeks of life, owing largely to the absence of any feeling on the part of provincial leaders that they needed to cooperate. In short, there was no threat (see Foltz, 1965). The United Arab Republic, presumably formed by Egypt and Syria the better to fight Israel, did have a genuine external motive, at least on the part of Egypt. So part of the bargaining conditions were satisfied. But the other part of the condition, a willingness on the part of provincial leaders to subject themselves to the federation, was clearly absent at least on the part of Syria. Its leaders apparently got nothing from the bargain, partly because of the Israeli success. Hence the second condition was absent and Syria withdrew.

The foregoing survey of the governments listed in Table 2 indicates that in every case of a successful federation the two conditions stated by Wheare, Riker, Birch and Watts are present, while these conditions are absent from every one of the federations that failed. This fact certainly confirms the belief of Wheare and Watts that these conditions are especially important (placed by Wheare first and second on his list). Even more significantly, it tends to give one confidence in the theory stated by Riker and Birch. For Wheare and Watts these conditions are inductively arrived-at summations of experience. For Riker and Birch the conditions are deductively arrived-at inferences from the nature of rational political bargaining and the institutions of federalism. As such, these conditions are more than important correlates of federalism. They are instead logically necessary features.

The reader will recall that still another possible correlate was found on the lists offered by Wheare and Watts, namely, that there be some previous association among the constituent units. A brief survey of all the successful federations indicates that most of them had been previously governed together as part of an empire. This is true of the United States, all Latin American federalisms, and all former British colonies. The constituent units of the German empire had a long association in the Holy Roman Empire; the Swiss cantons had a history of Austrian dominion; and the United Netherlands a history of Spanish dominion. The Soviet Union is simply a reformulation of the Russian empire and Yugoslavia is a reformulation of the Kingdom of Yugoslavia. Czechoslovakia, if it is a federalism, is the same as a formerly unitary state. Hence previous association is indeed a perfect correlate of contemporary federalism; but, since there is no theoretical reason for this to be so, it is not possible to say that previous association is a necessary condition.

The foregoing survey has thus yielded four features that are present in every federalism existing since 1787:

1. an example of successful federalism
2. previous association of constituent units
3. and 4. the two necessary political conditions of a desire to expand and a willingness of provincial politicians to accede despite provincial loyalties.

While the first condition is useful and highly contributory, it cannot be said to be necessary. If it were, how could there ever be a first successful one? And indeed the United Netherlands was successful for two hundred years before the United States was developed. The second condition, while heretofore universal, cannot—because of the reasons previously mentioned—certainly be said to be necessary. Finally, the third and fourth conditions above are by this survey shown to be perfect correlates of federalism, existing when federalism survives, not existing when federalism fails. All this renders plausible the suggestion, based on a theory, that these conditions are indeed necessary in a theoretical sense.

Assuming politicians are rational men who attempt to make Pareto-optimal bargains, then one would expect some mutual gain in every formation of a federalism. In terms of the theory of rational political behavior, the Riker-Birch conditions are an effort to spell out precisely what the mutual gains are. If the theory is true, then these conditions are not simply perfect correlates of federalism but are in fact logically necessary conditions of federalism. That is, federalism is not just helped along by these conditions; rather, it cannot come into existence without them.

THE SIGNIFICANCE OF THE NECESSARY CONDITIONS OF FEDERALISM FOR THE INTERPRETATION OF INSTITUTIONS

Presumably one main goal of political science is to describe political institutions. Unfortunately, most political scientists have been content to describe unique events or unique institutions or, at best, to verify hypotheses (which Russell called "guesses") about correlations. Owing possibly to the intractability of the subject, very few have been able to describe political nature scientifically.

Scientific description involves

1. a theoretical statement of the way things move or people behave in a simplified imaginary world; and
2. empirical verification that what is true in the imaginary world is true in the real world.

By the first step, with a theory or a set of assumptions and inferences from them, we learn logically necessary features of the simplified world. By the second step we show that, in relation to the subject under discussion, the real world is very much like the simplified world.

Most attempts at description of politics fail for absence of a theory, so that one simply tells about events, institutions, or correlations as if one were an historian. Seldom do political writers attempt to derive descriptions of behavior from simple axioms. Here, however, we have a scientific description of an institution or at least of a necessary (though not sufficient) condition for the establishment of an institution. There is a theory, namely, that men in politics behave rationally in making bargains. To behave rationally means to strike bargains in which there is a mutual gain. The theory is elaborated by applying it to the situation of constitution making. And two conditions for federal constitutions are inferred. Furthermore, as indicated by the detail of the previous section, there is an empirical demonstration that the theoretically expected behavior actually does occur in every case. (It is not suggested that this verification "proves" the theory; it merely gives one considerable confidence in it.)

One important feature of these conditions is, therefore, that, however restricted the subject matter, some political events are scientifically described. There is another important feature, however, and that is the fact that this verified theory is about politics. The central element of the theory is a rational *political* bargain. So much of what passes as political explanation today is reductionist in the sense that explanation is taken from the political level down to the economic or even the communications level. Of course, after such explanations, nothing political is left. Birch concludes his revision of Riker's theory by remarking that "Riker has succeeded in establishing the importance of certain kinds of political considerations in the formation of federations, and this may be counted a real, if limited, gain in a period in which it seems fashionable to assume that economic and social factors are preeminent" (1966, p. 33).

The significance of these necessary conditions is, then, that they constitute a partially verified *political* theory of the formation of one kind of constitution. It is possible to appreciate the usefulness of this theory by considering two kinds of situations in which people might act (or might have acted) more effectively by reason of having it:

1. at the formation of new national governments

2. at the formation of a federated Europe or world.

All the federations formed prior to the Second World War were *spontaneous,* in the sense that the participants in constitution making themselves turned to federalism to solve their problems. Many, though not all, of the federations formed since the Second World War are *contrived,* in the sense that the plan for federalism came, not from the participants, but from the colonial power engaged in spinning off its colonies. Several motives have been ascribed to colonial officers to account for this fascination with federalism. One is a desire to render the new government viable, a somewhat unbelievable motive because it is too unselfishly benevolent. Another is a desire to weaken the new government by making it easy to divide and rule, also an unbelievable motive because it is so revengefully malevolent. Spiro (1968, p. 86) suggests another motive, self-interested but not malevolent, which seems to accord with reality. These postwar federations were, he suggests, "meant essentially as makeshift arrangements designed to facilitate the transition from colonialism to independence. By 'federating' several colonies at different stages of constitutional advancement toward full independence, the British government was able to affect the average elapsed time before independence, to reduce the overall incidence of violence, and to shape constitutional forms and international alignments of the post-independence period. This pre-manipulation was made all the more effective precisely through employment of all the symbolism of federalism and action based on the false analogy to the older, conventional, 'true' federations." This passage well describes what happened, although Spiro may well be wrong, I suspect, to imply that the colonial office knew what it was doing. Its officials were probably also taken in by the false analogy.

In this motive, as Spiro describes it, the main practical purpose of federalism is served if the imperial power successfully rids itself of its colonies. But all those, including the imperial officers themselves, who did not fully understand this makeshift character of these new African and Asian federalisms were completely misled. Since they were misled, they acted inappropriately and unrealistically long after the main practical goal of the spin-off was achieved. Think of all the political energy futilely spent trying to make a viable constitutional structure for the West Indian Federation or to fit Singapore into Malaysia. Had the local politicians realized that the necessary conditions of successful federalism were absent from their situations, it is likely they would not have wasted much energy on what we can now see was a will-o'-the-wisp. Along with the wasted energy of politicians is the wasted energy of scholars. One cannot help but be saddened by the self-deception of all those who imagine that federalism will occur just because it might alleviate economic problems. (For an example of such perverse idealism see Hicks, 1961; but, perhaps to show that theory is not always necessary to good sense, Mentschikoff begins a discussion of the subject with: "The basic premise of this paper is that there is very little relation between federalism and economic growth" [Mentschikoff, 1964, p. 191]. As a lawyer-economist she recognized what many political scientists cannot: that federalism is a political, not an economic, phenomenon.)

If this theory is correct, as I believe it is, then one of the profound misunderstandings of the last generation is the question of what will engender a European union of federation or, on another level of discourse, a world federalism. For either to appear there must be some significant threat. And in the absence of a threat sufficiently large to render the federal bargain mutually profitable to the participating governments, there is nothing that will bring such unions as these about, no matter how much people *wish* for them to happen. A tremendous amount of propagandizing and even political organizing has been based on the mistaken premise that somehow, if people just work hard enough for it, federation will occur. It is perhaps unkind to disturb such naive faith, but the hope of the scientific enterprise is that the more people know, the more effectively they can act. A particularly unfortunate example of this naivety is to be found in Friedrich (1968), where it is said that federalism is a process of federalizing, as if such a thing comes about by some kind of magic without rational human calculation. (This example is doubly unfortunate if, as the author claims in his preface, this is the frequent advice he has offered to real politicians in the European community.)

THE MEASUREMENT OF FEDERALISM

Davis, in his elegant reassessment (1956) of Wheare's theory of federalism, remarks that the range of life and structure in federal government is much broader than Wheare could allow. So much can happen in federal governments, he says, that "it is no more possible to . . . predict the life which will ensue from the choice of this form of union than one can . . . predict the relationship which will ensue from the form in which the union (for example, a marriage or a constitution) is legally consummated" (p. 242). We have to remember, he suggests, that "at best the federal compact can only be a formalized transaction of a moment in the history of a particular community." His point is well taken. Mature federations are more unlike than alike, having in common only the logically necessary features of the moment of contract. After the contract is made, each develops in its own way, as one would expect of governments for many kinds of societies in many stages of economic development and many levels of political life.

As a consequence of this variety, it is probably impossible to generalize about the operation of federalism. About the origin of federalism it has been possible to construct a partially verified theory. But I am not hopeful of being able to construct a theory about any feature of federations subsequent to their birth. So Davis is correct: the compact is the transaction of a moment and that moment we can generalize about. But what happens later is not easy to describe in general.

Classification of Federalisms

Probably the best one can do is to create typologies of the varieties of federal life around considerations that seem important to the fact of federalism. To that action, then, I turn in this section.

Possibly one of the most remarkable features of federalism is the fact that in some federations there is a substantial degree of centralization over time, while in others the degree of centralization does not significantly change. One question about federalism of considerable interest is: What are the correlates, perhaps even the causes, of this difference?

Of course, given a long enough time, all governments in the modern world have centralized somewhat, regardless of the kind of constitution they have. Easier communication and transportation simply make it possible for agents of the center to place themselves in decisions that might otherwise be local. In the United States a case in point is the development of a national police force, with hundreds of local offices, which it frequently uses to push itself into otherwise local law enforcement problems. The FBI is for the most part doing no more than United States marshals could also have done (but did not do) in the 1790s if they had had the offices and money and the statutory authorization. So that kind of centralization, while genuine enough, does not change the relative authority of the two kinds of governments in any more than a fringe way. Such centralization can be called *technological,* and for the moment I will ignore it.

Rather, I am here interested in what can be called political centralization, when the actual locus of decision making is changed from the governments of the constituent units to the central government. To give an example from the history of the United States, consider the intention of the framers on the division of authority over military decisions. The original intention, as represented by the militia clause in Article I and the Second Amendment, was to guarantee that the states share authority over the military with the central government (Riker, 1958). And indeed as late as the War of 1812 governors could make decisions about deployment of forces in wartime. As late as the First World War a substantial portion of the officers were commissioned by the states. Today the national guard still exists, as by constitutional mandate it must, but in the last two wars it has been barely used and its officers—especially its high officers—almost never used. Indeed for the last two decades its main function has been to provide a way for poor men to avoid the draft. Part of this centralization has been technological, owing, for example, to the expense of weapons and training. But there has been political change too. A major area of political decision that rested as much or more with the states than the nation in 1789 is now almost exclusively a matter for national decision.

Distinguishing, then, between technological and political centralization, I ask: What are the correlates of political centralization? Why do some federations display a lot of political centralization over time and others very little? Why do some swing back and forth between high and low degrees of centralization?

Of course, a big part of the problem in answering these questions is that we have no way of stating categorically which constitutions are politically centralized and which are not. No one would question that the Soviet Union is highly centralized. And, at the other extreme, among the more or less centralized federations of the modern world, most writers would agree that Canada is about as decentralized as one can get. But in between, where does one place a federation like Brazil, which some say is quite centralized and which yet displays a vast amount of local and state initiative in political life? (Kantor, 1968; Peterson, 1970) Or again, what shall we say of India, where constitutional practice allows the center to take over constituent governments under the guise of protecting republican government but where also central planning repeatedly fails, in part because of the very real authority of the states? (Appleby, 1953; Franda, 1968)

With this range of phenomena in mind, we can identify extreme categories.

Fully centralized federalism: wherein, most observers would agree, the vast majority of significant political decisions are made at the center and in which the notion of state or provincial rights is quite meaningless. This category would include the Soviet Union, possibly Yugoslavia, and possibly Mexico.

Partially centralized federalism: wherein, most observers would agree, many significant political decisions are made by constitutent governments and in which the notion of state or provincial rights is meaningful. This category would surely include Canada and Australia and perhaps India and even the United States.

These categories establish a range for political centralization and about this range I reiterate the question: Why are federations spaced the way they are along the scale? This really is a question of what correlates of centralization we can possibly use to measure a location on this range. Thus arises the problem of the measurement of federalism, which I wish to consider in this section.

Decentralized Parties in Partially Centralized Federalism

I approach the problem of measurement with an observation about the two extreme categories. In all the fully centralized federations, the political party system is also fully centralized. (Supporting detail on the Soviet Union is easily available; on Yugoslavia see Shoup, 1968; on Mexico, Stokes, 1961, and Kantor, 1968.) In all the partially centralized federations the political party system is relatively decentralized. A brief survey of 'descriptions of party systems in partially centralized federations indicates that most writers identify the decentralization of parties as a correlate (or in some cases even a consequence) of the federal constitution. Of course, since most of them are not aware of centralized federalism, they speak simply of the relation between decentralized parties and federalism. With our broader interpretation of federalism itself, we can understand them to mean the relation between decentralized parties and only partially centralized federalism.

Probably the first writer to describe in detail the close relation between the structure of parties and the fact of only partially centralized federalism was

Truman (1955). Political scientists have long known that American political parties were undisciplined in the obvious sense that parties cannot be said to have a coherent policy or program or ideology. In sharp contrast to what were once the ideologically coherent parties of Britain and France, American parties contain leaders whose ideologies cover a wide range of the political spectrum. This ideological confusion between the parties, which is apparent enough in their programs, is particularly evident in the behavior of legislators, who cannot typically be relied upon to support a consistent ideological position attributed to the majority party. Standing behind all this ideological and behavioral diversity is the fact that there is no control of personnel by central organs of the party. As Truman emphasized, the process of making nominations is wholly decentralized, with parties organized in each of the states around the nomination and election of governors and in most local governments around the nomination and election of executives. Specifically, parties are diverse because there is no central control of personnel and there is no central control of personnel because there is "separate election of chief executives at both [i.e., national and state] levels, and perhaps all three [i.e., also local]." This separate election "has multiplied and thereby rendered ambiguous the lines of succession within the governmental structure, and ambiguity of this sort seems almost certain to encourage independence and parallelism in party structures rather than coherence and centralization" (1955, p. 130). Other institutions are of course involved in separate elections (see Wechsler, 1955), but the crucial one is federalism. So Truman states: "The basic political fact of federalism is that it creates separate, self-sustaining centers of power, prestige, and profit" (1955, p. 123). Thus, the multiplicity of authorities of an only partially centralized federation is correlated with the decentralization of parties. After a study of the manifestations of party decentralization in Congress and administrative agencies, Grodzins remarked that "the parties function to maintain a division of strength between the central government and the geographical (and other) peripheries. Anything that tightened party control at the top would decrease strength at the bottom" (1960a, p. 996).

Grodzins is careful not to say either that federalism causes the decentralization of parties or that the decentralization of parties maintains an only partial centralization of federalism. Rather he suggests that the two things go along together in a relation of reciprocal reinforcement. This fact is even easier to see if one asks how the partial centralization of federalism might be transcended. In two studies of this question, Riker focussed on efforts of Presidents to control nominations of Congressmen. If such control occurred it would effectively centralize the system, for it would transfer personnel decisions from the periphery to the center. He found that Presidents had by and large been unsuccessful and therefore timid in such efforts (Riker 1964a, Chapter 8; Riker and Bast, 1969). The twin facts (1) that Presidents could perhaps centralize by persuading citizens to vote for Presidentially endorsed candidates and (2) that Presidents either do not try or fail to centralize in this way indicate that popular indifference is the crucial factor in promoting the decentralization of parties. If Presidents could excite the populace sufficiently, they could centralize. But they cannot, so parties remain decentralized and so the federation is only partially centralized. Quite probably this popular indifference or even a popular preference for decentralization is what fundamentally controls both the structure of parties and the structure of the union.

Studies of other federal systems repeatedly emphasize this connection between the only partial centralization of federalism and decentralized party structure. Wildavsky (1961), in a careful study of Australian experience, finds a similar, though less determined decentralization of parties that also is reciprocal with the nature of the federalism. In the Australian case the parties in the states "have developed an interest in perpetuating that [separate] existence, which is defended by a large corps of personnel who benefit from this arrangement. It is this structural fact, rather than underlying differences among the states, which characterizes Australian federalism" (p. 441). Wildavsky analyzes especially the attempts by the federal Labour party executive to control the parliamentary Labour party and concludes: "So long as parties have a federal structure the extra-parliamentary body of the party'cannot aspire to more than occasional intervention in the legislature without seriously antagonizing some large section of the party. In a word, federal structure represents a more intransigent obstacle to the nationalization of political parties than is generally recognized" (p. 458). (See also Greenwood, 1946, and Miller, 1954.)

Of the English-speaking federations, Canada is certainly one of the least centralized. Many federations have dissident minorities whose dissent finds geographic expression in one or more constituent units, for example, southern white racists in the deep South of the United States (although their influence seems largely to have waned), French speakers in western Switzerland, Dravidian-language speakers in the south of India, etc. But none of these dissenters seems at the moment quite so vocal or aggrieved as the French minority in Canada, which centers geographically in Quebec. The main political problem in 1867 was to reconcile Quebec to the formation of Canada, and the main political problem still today is keeping Quebec in the federation (Trudeau, 1968). All of Canadian federalism centers on this issue. Forsey (1965, p. 348) remarks: "The problems of Canadian federalism . . . are not . . . problems of federation at all, but of Canadian Dualism." Naturally, this intense and persistent problem is expressed in the structure of political parties. Muller (1967) argues that there are two layers of national politics in Canada. One is the national parties running the Dominion parliament, the conventional kind of national political function. Beneath this is another layer composed of parties that win power in a province, which may be provincial units of a national party or provincially prominent units of nationally splinter parties (e.g., the New Democratic party and its predecessors; Social Credit; Union Nationale, etc.). The winning provincial parties have three activities: to function in provincial government, to function in the Dominion parliament, and most significant of all, to function in the "second layer of the national party system, which balances central and sectional interests within the federal structure" (p. 145). Muller goes on to point out that the balance of Dominion-provincial relations cannot be maintained by any national institution (like the Senate in the United States) and so it is dependent for maintenance on the bargaining between provincial premiers and the national cabinet and even among provincial premiers themselves. For this purpose the provincial parties are substantially autonomous from the national parties, and indeed Muller points out that Canadian voters often think that arms-length bargaining is better done if the provincial bargainer is of a different party from the central bargainer. Simeon (1972) argues that the essential feature of Canadian federalism is precisely this kind of bargaining. Hence what results from this is a two-party system in each province but a five- or six-party system in the sum of the provinces. While the national parties (the Liberal and, to a lesser degree, the Conservative) are internally centralized, the Canadian party system as a whole is just about as decentralized as it can be to match a federal union that is increasingly decentralized in order to keep Quebec content.

Looking at partially centralized federations other than the English-speaking ones, the same phenomenon is clear. India is decreasingly centralized constitutionally and politically as the state governments and state politicians assert themselves, especially since the death of Nehru. And one finds here, too, that the parties are decentralized. After an exhaustive study of the functioning of the Congress party, Weiner (1967) observes that Congress has been often criticized for not providing unified economic leadership. He defends it by pointing out that necessarily Congress is decentralized: "Realistically, the possibility of a more centralized Congress party . . . is as remote as the possibility of creating more centralized parties in the United States, and for similar reasons. A federal democratic system inhibits the development of highly centralized parties" (p. 486). In a more detailed study of Indian state governmental administration, Franda (1968) concludes that, even though Congress is a dominant single party, the state party units are strong and cohesive and able to resist the central government on administrative decision. "One might even conceive," he says, "of a 'market situation,' in which the degree of state party cohesion and strength, coupled with the willingness and ability of state populations to mobilize for political action, would provide the principal sources of state independence relative to the system's central allocating institutions" (p. 223). This is to say that, in India, partial federal centralization is, in Franda's opinion, perfectly correlated with party decentralization.

The Measurement of Federalism

In a variety of governments, then, the structure of parties parallels the structure of federalism. When parties are fully centralized, so is federalism (e.g., in the Soviet Union and Mexico). When parties are somewhat decentralized, then federalism is only partially centralized. Because of this perfect correlation of, at least, the two extreme categories of federalism with party structure, the inference is immediate: one can measure federalism by measuring parties. The structure of parties is thus a surrogate for the structure of the whole constitution.

Riker has made several efforts to measure federalism (1957, 1964b). One is a classification of party centralization according to two standards:

1. Whether or not the party in control of the national government is in control of constituent governments. If the nationally controlling party cannot win in state and provincial elections (as often happens in the United States and usually happens in Canada), then it can hardly hope to bring about a centralized party structure of a centralized constitution.

2. Whether or not party discipline exists on legislative and executive matters. If party members can act together, then they can hope to centralize; otherwise not.

These two standards can then fit together in a table such as Table 3, taken from Riker (1964b, p. 133), where A represents the highest degree of political centralization in the federation, B the next highest degree . . . , and D the lowest degree. The problem with such a table is, however, that the several measures it contains do not all mean the same thing from system to system. Thus party discipline is a quite different concept in a multiparty system from that in a two-party system. Owing to difficulties such as these, it is not clear that Table 3 really means anything over all federal systems. But there is one measure in Table 3 that does have about the same meaning and clearly is involved with both party and federal structure. That measure is the degree to which the party in control of the central government controls the constituent governments. And a practical way of using that measure has also been devised (see Riker and Schaps, 1957), a so-called index of disharmony, which might just as accurately be called an index of state-party independence.

This index is based on the notion of the power index, which is the percentage chance that a member of a governing body has to be pivotal, or to be the last added member of a minimal winning coalition in the decision-making process (see Shapley and Shubik, 1954). Such an index of the chance to pivot, or to be marginally crucial, can be compiled for single individuals, for all single individuals in a legislature or decision-making system, jointly for the sum of all

TABLE 3   Degree of centralization of federations

			National level disciplined		National level not disciplined	
			Constituent level		Constituent level	
			Disci-plined	Not disci-plined	Disci-plined	Not disci-plined
Chance that party in control of central government will be replaced by another party	Chance that more than half the control of con-stituent governments will be in the hands of parties other than the party in control of the national government	$pr < 0.5$	A—	A	C+	B—
		$pr \geqslant 0.5$	B	B+	C	C
		$pr < 0.5$	B	B+	C	C+
		$pr \geqslant 0.5$	B—	B—	D	D+

(left bracket label: $pr < 0.5$ for top two rows, $pr \geqslant 0.5$ for bottom two rows)

members of a party in a set of legislatures, etc. In short, for various kinds of relevant sets of individuals, averages of power indices can be constructed.

To construct in turn the index of disharmony, one needs the following power indices:

1. The power index of the party (or the coalition of parties) that has a power index greater than 0.5 in the national government taken as a whole and that is identified as the governing party. Name this party (or coalition) A and name all other parties or coalitions with other roman capitals. The power index of this party in the national government is $\Pi(N)_A$.

2. The power index in the sum of the constituent governments for party A. This power index is: $\Pi(C)_A$.

The index of disharmony, D, can be then defined:
$$D = 1 - \Pi(C)_A.$$
This is to say that disharmony is 1 minus the power index in the constituent government of the party that controls the national government. Since all power

indices range from 0 to 1, this index has the same range. If $\Pi(C)_A$ is high, e.g., 0.9, as would be the case when the leading party nationally controls most of the constituent governments, then D, the index of disharmony, would be small, e.g., 0.1. If, on the other hand, $\Pi(C)_A$ is small, e.g., 0.2, as would be the case when the leading party nationally is insignificant in the constituent governments taken together, then D, or disharmony, is large, i.e., 0.8.

As noted, an index so constructed might easily be called an index of state-party independence or, even more directly in point, an index of decentralization. When this latter name is used, the significance is that

> as D rises, the central government is less and less likely to be able to control policy in the constituent governments, simply because there is no informal connection between the levels;

> as D falls, the central government is more and more likely to be able to control policy in the constiuent governments, simply because there is some kind of informal partisan connection between levels.

Thus D, the index of disharmony, can also be regarded as an index of decentralization both of the party system and of the federal constitutional structure. It is apparent that the Soviet Union would have an index of zero, which would indicate a complete absence of decentralization or full centralization. On the other hand a government like Canada would have a fairly high index because many provinces are controlled by national splinter parties. Over time a government like India would in its early years have a very low index rising consistently in recent years and confirming the sense of most observers that India is becoming less centralized.

The index, D, has been calculated for the United States by biennial 1937–55 (see Riker and Schaps, 1957). They find it varies from .31 in 1937, when the centralizing New Deal was at its peak, to .58 in 1955, when Republicans barely controlled the national government and considerably less than half the states. It is no accident that 1955 is regarded as a do-nothing era and one in which great emphasis was put on states' rights. Alexander (1973) has calculated the index from 1837, the earliest date at which there can be said to be a national and local party system in the United States, to 1967. He found a range for D between 0.65 (in 1891) and 0.26 (just after the Civil War, when the Republican victors controlled both the nation and the states). More interestingly, however, he found that D averaged about the same over the very long run and that it apparently varied randomly around and reasonably close to 0.5. Riker and Schaps (1957) also calculated D for Canada and Australia, where its range was quite different. For Canada D varied from 0.10 to 0.90 and furthermore showed a strong tendency to stick at the extremes for considerable periods. For Australia the range was 0.20 to 0.85 and likewise showed a tendency (less strong than in Canada) to stick at the extremes. In both cases it seems clear that a higher degree of decentralization (or disharmony) is indicated than is to be found in the United States.

The Uses of the Index of Decentralization

It is much to be hoped that this index be compiled for a variety of federations, for it will provide a solution to many puzzling problems of federalism and comparative government. Indeed it would make possible a truly comparative study of federalism for the first time. Just as an indication of how much might be gained from the generation of this index, I conclude this section by listing two significant disputes that might be solved by this means.

Scheiber versus Elazar. The traditional view of the development of American federalism is that it has been constantly centralizing. Recently Elazar (1962) and Grodzins (1960b) substituted for that view the notion that the nation and the states had always shared functions, so that no centralization has taken place. Scheiber (1966) has sharply challenged Elazar's evidence. This whole controversy is not much to the point, for it is concerned in its evidence more with the technological than with political centralization. Still, assuming that both sides view technological centralization as an index of political centralization (an assumption that is probably inadequate—see Riker, 1964b, pp. 83, 126), then the controversy remains on the political question. And it is just this question that the index of disharmony is designed to handle. Alexander's evidence indicates that the index has declined very slightly over time, which suggests that in politics at least the amount of centralization is negligible, and this in turn suggests that Grodzins and Elazar are correct. One can easily see how the controversy develops: some centralization may have occurred, but at so glacial a rate that it is not easily visible.

German federalism and other federalism. The nature of German federalism is quite different from federalism in most other places in the world, for most administration of national policy has traditionally been left with the constituent governments. As a consequence, many writers are uncertain how to interpret this fact and how to compare German federalism with others (and even with itself over time). A measure such as D would permit the resolution of such controversy. Thus, for example, Heidenheimer (1958) suggests that federalism is not a particularly significant feature of the German constitution. Merkl (1959), however, emphasizes the existence of a strong federal element in national policy. Pinney (1963) in a study of the Bundesrat, the second chamber in the national government, whose members are selected by the governments of the Lander, concludes that the Bundesrat makes for genuine decentralization, even though the legislative power of the Bundesrat is severely limited. The problem is that these writers are trying to determine a political classification (i.e., whether or not in practice the West German Constitution is decentralized) by means of analyzing constitutional form and legislative behavior. What they should look at is the very essence of politics itself, the distribution of office among parties.

THE ACCIDENTS OF FEDERALISM

The Aristotelian distinction between essence and accident helps to draw the line between what is important and what is not in the interpretation of federalism. Earlier in this review, federalism was defined as a political organization, agreed on by politicians, such that there were both central and regional authorities each able to make some decisions independently of each other. The essence of federalism in this definition is the political feature: (1) the political bargain that creates it and (2) the distribution of power in political parties which shapes the federal structure in its maturity. Everything else about federalism is accident: the demarcation of areas of competence between central and constituent governments, the operation of intergovernmental relations, the division of financial resources. etc. It is true that a vast literature exists on these latter subjects because they have some effect on the immediate details of public policy. But the existence of this literature does not alter the accidental character of these constitutional and administrative features of federalism, to the brief survey of which I now turn.

The Accidental Character of Constitutional and Administrative Arrangements

The absence of a theory of the areal division of powers. If administrative arrangements were essential features of federalism, one would expect a considerable literature on the theory of the areal division of power. There would be practical proposals for remaking federal constitutions according to areal considerations, and behind the practice there would be a body of theory. As a matter of fact, however, I know of very little practical argument on areal division (except the debate and decision on linguistic states in India) and the theory on areal division is minuscule. It is true that there is a vast literature on regions and regionalism, etc. But in this literature it is always assumed that regions exist naturally and that their boundaries are beyond conscious human control. In speaking of the theory of areal division, I refer of course to a theory about the conscious creation of regions and such a theory as that is indeed minuscule.

In Maass (1959) an effort is made to develop a theory of areal division, but only in the essay by Ylvisaker (1959) are there any theoretical sentences. The rest of the volume consists of surveys of practice and of histories of ideology. Furthermore, Ylvisaker's own comments consist mainly of a set of maxims about desirable features of areal division. These maxims reflect only the experience of the author and are not the consequence of an effort to derive inferences from axioms. Several later authors have attempted some conventional theorizing as against the distillation of maxims; in one line of thought the derived inference agrees with Ylvisaker's maxims and in another line directly contradicts them. Since the derivations are not themselves wholly defensible, we are left with a theory that consists of several more or less contradictory essays and no clear way to decide among them.

Modest as this theory is, however, it is worth examining, for it is all we have. One of Ylvisaker's maxims is that constituent units should each have a diversity of interests so that each one is able to have internal debates. Tarlton (1965) describes a federalism with such units as *symmetrical* and remarks: "In a symmetrical model no significant social, economic, or political peculiarities [of units] would exist which might demand special forms of representation or protection" (p. 868). Against this ideal type he sets another, *asymmetrical* unit, which he describes as a unit that "has about it a unique feature or set of features which would separate in important ways, its interests from those of any other state or the system considered as a whole" (p. 869). Applying this distinction, one could say that Australia is symmetric and Canada asymmetric. Tarlton concludes that only symmetrical federalisms are stable. "The higher the level of symmetry, that is, the more each particular section, state, or region partakes of a character general and common to the whole, the greater the likelihood that federalism would be a suitable form of governmental organization. On the other hand, if the system is highly asymmetrical in its components, then a harmonious federal system is unlikely to develop" (pp. 872–73). Thus Ylvisaker and Tarlton reach the same conclusion. Ylvisaker's intuitive perception is that public policy can be more effectively made if there are many voices. Tarlton's argument is that the "secession-potential" is lower if a state is not internally agreed on a policy different from the rest of the nation. Hence the tones of the conclusions are quite different even if the results are similar.

To a certain degree, the Ylvisaker-Tarlton notions have been subjected to empirical tests in Mayer (1970), where, however, neither author is cited. Mayer distinguishes between *congruent* and *formalistic* federations. Congruent federations are like Tarlton's asymmetric units. They have "geographically defined diversities" so that "the political sub-system boundaries are roughly coterminous with cultural or economic sub-system boundaries," as in Canada (pp. 795, 796). Formalistic federations are like Tarlton's symmetric units in that diversities (in, e.g., race, class, etc.) are *not* geographically defined—as in the case of Australia. Mayer hypothesizes that national political parties should be more cohesive in a formalistic federation than in a congruent one. But, upon testing data from Canada and Australia (1958–64), he found *no* significant difference in cohesion in the parliaments of the two governments. One infers that, in this respect at least, Ylvisaker's maxim misses the point because diversities of interests seem not to affect the quality of the internal debate.

A second of Ylvisaker's maxims is directly challenged in Breton (1965). Ylvisaker asserts that each constituent unit should have full power to govern, not just partial authority. Against this Breton develops a general theory of the optimal allocation of public goods. Public goods are those things that once produced cannot be denied to a class of users. Thus, if national defense is produced for one person in the nation, it is necessarily available to everyone else in the class of citizens. As I read his theory, more than an optimal amount of a public good is produced if the governmental unit producing it contains persons not in the class of users. (For example, the highway trust fund contains funds from both heavy and light users of highways; overinvestment in highways occurs because light users are forced to pay for something they could easily do without.) Conversely, less than an optimal amount of a public good is produced if many users of a public good are outside the governmental unit producing it. (For example, if in a metropolitan area only the city has public libraries, but the entire population of the area uses them, then the citizens of the city will not tax themselves to maintain adequate free library service to the suburbs.) The clear inference from this analysis is that optimal production of a public good is achieved when the district producing contains exactly the users, no more and no less. This would in general require a special district for each good and this is just exactly what Ylvisaker wants to prevent because he thinks the special districts have inadequate resources. Breton's analysis has been elaborated in Olson (1969), Rothenberg (1970), and, most elegantly, in Wagner (1971).

I have devoted quite a bit of space to describing these theories—probably more space than they collectively deserve—because I wish to show exactly how slight is the theory of the areal division of powers. One cannot believe that the areal division of powers is either terribly important to federalism or of any particular significance to mankind if this is the only theory that has ever developed about it.

An imaginary experiment. If administrative arrangements do indeed significantly affect the character of federalism, then they should sharply differentiate federal governments from unitary ones. Even a very casual glance at the administrative world should convince one that contemporary federal and unitary governments and their public policy are more like each other than are the federal governments and policy of today like the federal governments and policy of the nineteenth century. This fact strongly suggests that federalism makes no particular difference for public policy. Thus, federalism is said to encourage local cultural autonomy—but was not the one hundred years of persistent and bitter attack (in a federation) by English-speaking Canadians on French culture far more repressive than, say, the general indifference (in a unitary government) of, say, Spanish-speaking Spaniards to Basque culture? Federalism is said to engender difficulties in intergovernmental relations—but may not the resistance of, say, Sicilian officials (in a unitary government) to Roman direction be fully as great as the resistance (in a federation) of, say, Mississippi officials to Washington direction? Again, federalism is said to raise difficulties in industrial regulation by allowing businessmen to play constituent governments and the central government off against each other so that neither one regulates— but was the success of British businessmen any the less than Americans in avoiding regulation in the era of laissez-faire? The most that can be said is that this era lasted just a little longer in the United States.

These examples of the unrelatedness of public policy to federalism have led Riker (1969) to propose an imaginary experiment by which this problem might be examined systematically. To discover whether or not federalism makes any difference for policy, take matched pairs of federal and unitary governments and examine them to discover whether or not there are significant differences in public policy. The matched pairs of governments he suggested were these—all chosen so that they had a similar political culture and public problems: Argentina-Chile, Malaysia-Indonesia, United States-United Kingdom, Australia-New Zealand, Nigeria-Ghana, Yugoslavia-Poland. The actual conduct of such an experiment would be difficult because very few scholars know more than one pair well and probably no one knows all pairs well. Still, the probable outcome of such an experiment is easy to guess at. It is unlikely that there would be any consistent difference in the pairs. Furthermore, public policy within each of the pairs is remarkably similar regardless of the fact of federalism.

It is difficult to escape the conclusion that the accidents of federalism (i.e., the constitutional and administrative detail) do not make any difference at all. They simply provide a standard of style for federal countries that differs somewhat from the standard for unitary ones. In federal countries it is often necessary to go through the form of showing that a government has legal authority to do what it wants to do. But of course if it really wants to do it, the authority is always there. Lawyers, especially constitutional lawyers, have a little more work in a federation than in a unitary system; otherwise there is not much difference.

In the United States, when the central government wants to regulate the pollution in a stream, someone must go through the charming and delicate legal exercise of proving that the stream runs into navigable waters clearly under the jurisdiction of the central government. It adds a bit of expense, the cost of manufacturing a bit of ideology; but the United States is a rich country that can clearly afford this expense. In unitary states like Japan or Britain, when the central government wishes to regulate the pollution in a stream, it merely does so without the elegance of a "constitutional issue." Whether the stream is in fact cleaned up probably depends much more on the political culture than on the style of debate. Indeed, it is more likely that the stream be cleaned up in the United States and England, one federal and one unitary, than in Japan, a unitary government.

I conclude, then, that the constitutional and administrative arrangements of federalism deeply affect the style of public policymaking but do not deeply affect the outcome. Nevertheless, there is a vast literature on the style and some of it is a fascinating literature, so I now turn to a brief survey of it.

Constitutional Problems of Federalism

The standard survey of comparative constitutional structure of federalism is to be found in Bowie and Friedrich (1954). This is useful for the constitutional detail, although it is not concerned with the political realities of federalism. Of the special constitutional features of federalism, two have attracted considerable attention. One is the problem of the second chamber: If one house of the national legislature is popularly elected and one is chosen to represent constituent governments, then the chance is always present that the house chosen by constituent governments frustrates the popularly chosen one. There have been generally two solutions, each of which involves a difficulty. One solution is to eliminate the role of the constituent governments in the selection of the second chamber, as in the United States (see Riker, 1955). The other is to weaken the second chamber to the point of ineffectuality, as in Canada and Australia. West Germany is currently poised between these two extremes, and as a consequence its second chamber has attracted quite a bit of discussion, for which see Pinney (1963) and Cerny (1968).

A second constitutional problem of interest in federalism is the role of a constitutional, or supreme, court. The problem here is of course that a constitutional court seems to be necessary to divide responsibilities between the central government and the constituent governments. Naturally, such divisions always create political resentments, no matter how they are made, and this leads to charges that such courts frustrate the popular will. For a discussion of the development of such a court in the United States see Corwin (1934), Freund (1953 and 1955), and Schmidhauser (1958). For comparative studies of such courts see McWhinney (1960 and 1962a) and Wagner (1959). For a study limited to Germany see McWhinney (1962b). A recent work of a sort now mostly out of style is McKinnon (1964), which is an analysis of the interpretation of the notion of interstate commerce in three federalisms.

Administrative Problems of Federalism

Financial problems: the "perversity hypothesis." Constitutional problems of federalism once loomed large when lawyers had a lot to do with commentaries on the several constitutions. However, now that there exists a generation of political scientists trained in a discipline other than law, we recognize that constitutional problems exist only because people are willing to tolerate them. That is, constitutional difficulties are matters of style, not substance. But when we turn to administrative problems, some of these have appeared to be genuinely matters of substance. One of the problems most likely to involve a matter of substance is that involved in the so-called perversity hypothesis, which suggests that the expected fiscal policies of state and local governments are inherently in conflict with national fiscal policy.

This hypothesis, first set forth in Hansen and Perloff (1944), is based on Keynesian notions of fiscal policy that government should act countercyclically, that is, government should spend heavily in the trough of a cycle in order to stimulate business and should restrict its spending at the crest of a cycle in order to moderate otherwise excessive economic activity. They concluded, after an examination of state and local spending in the 1920s and 1930s, that "the taxing, borrowing and spending activities of the state and local governments have typically run counter to an economically sound fiscal policy. These governmental units have usually followed the swings of the business cycle, from crest to trough, spending and building in prosperity periods and contracting their activity during depression" (p. 49). Hansen and Perloff showed that in the boom of the 1920s state and local governments were large-scale builders and in the depression of the 1930s they followed a deflationary policy. Indeed Hansen and Perloff concluded that states and localities had not only been indifferent to the needs of national fiscal policy but had actually acted perversely, in the sense that they intensified the inflation of the 1920s and the depression of the 1930s.

There is every reason, in Keynesian theory, for states and localities to behave in this way. From the point of view of the larger society these units are in much the same position as private individuals, because they are not, in the expectations of federalism, responsible for the operation of governmental fiscal policy. Since states and localities have the same interests as private persons with respect to the business cycle, and since they have no constitutional or legal responsibility to behave otherwise, one can expect they will in fact behave like private individuals. And if they do, they will most naturally—and most effectively—exacerbate the swings of the business cycle; and if the national government does follow a countercyclical policy, they will negate the national policy. See the model in Baratz and Farr (1959).

This charge, that units in a federation will by acting rationally from the point of view of the unit act contrary to the best interests of the nation, is very disturbing. Because it is so disturbing, it has been intensively investigated. For a bibliography on this investigation see Rafuse (1965). Several writers have reviewed data similar to that of Hansen and Perloff. The most interesting investigations are those based primarily on data after their work. Two works are available: Cohen and Grodzins (1963) and Rafuse (1965). The former, influenced by Grodzins' thesis that the states and the nation act cooperatively, concludes that the sharing hypothesis is justified in relation to fiscal policy as well. Rafuse (1965) finds that any perversity the states might have displayed in the postwar world is thoroughly masked by the very high rate of growth of state and local expenditures. "Through prosperity and recession alike, through periods of inflation and periods of relative price stability . . . the expenditures of states and local governments have risen inexorably" (p. 119). This means that the states have at least acted appropriately in the troughs of cycles. If, as Rafuse suggests, it is inappropriate for states to engage in countercyclical activity and if they should merely meet needs as they arise, then states have done very well because their expenditures have risen at about the same rate as their income. Thus, they have satisfied needs without encouraging inflation.

Of course, Hansen and Perloff were misled into adopting the perversity hypothesis by their assumption that the states could not be made to do what the citizens or the nation wanted. If we understand, however, that states are agents of the society in just the same way as any government, the worst one could expect of them is minor perversities, no matter how pronounced the federalism.

Financial problems: grants-in-aid. In all the contemporary federal unions with a history back to the nineteenth century, the twentieth century has witnessed a similar pattern of change in financial matters. Government in general has grown vastly more expensive, but the costs of the activities of the constituent governments and their subdivisions have grown at a much faster rate than the costs of central government activities. At the same time, central governments have turned out to have the best tax resources. So the functions and costs of constituent governments have risen sharply, while their resources have not risen as much. There are various ways that this might be compensated for: the central government might, for example, turn some of its tax resources over to the constituent units or the constituent units might turn some of their duties over to the central government. In general, neither of these alternatives has seemed attractive. Instead, the central government has kept its tax resources but has turned over some of its receipts to constituent governments. This turnover has been called variously "grants," "grants-in-aid," etc. Two main types of turnover have been involved. One is a grant for a specific purpose so that the central government in a sense controls the budget and the policy of the constituent government. That is, the central government specifies that, regardless of how the constituent unit might like to spend a grant, it must spend it on, say, highways. There is a certain amount of self-delusion here on the part of the central government, of course, for money entering a budget at any single point affects all other allocations. For example, national money given to help the states build highways leaves the states with greater financial resources than they might otherwise have to support schools. But because the specific grant is specific, it involves some control. The national government does in fact control the highway building it finances more than the schoolteaching it does not finance. The other kind of turnover is the unconditional grant, in which the central government simply passes over to the constituent units a specified sum of money. The restricted grant has been especially characteristic of the United

States; the unrestricted grants have, until recently, been more common elsewhere. Three excellent general surveys on this subject are Birch (1955), May (1969), and Oates (1972).

The fundamental rationale of grants-in-aid is that they encourage states to undertake projects that they would not otherwise undertake. The reason for state reluctance, aside from the doubtful possibility that state officials systematically judge benefits differently than do national officials, is that states often do not wish to spend tax money on projects with large spillover effects. That is, they do not wish to spend their resources providing a public good used by citizens of other states. Thus, Kansas might not wish to provide a superhighway used mainly by travellers going right through from East to Far West. The federal grant of highway funds is to compensate Kansas for servicing these "free riders." The economic theory of this action is elegantly set forth in Oates (1972), Wagner (1971), Buchanan and Wagner (1970).

Grants-in-aid, which permit the central government some control over what constituent units do, have usually been interpreted as a kind of centralization. But some kind of intergovernmental fiscal transfer occurs in every system, federal or unitary. It is instructive, therefore, to read the analysis in Philip (1954) of American and Scandinavian intergovernmental fiscal relations as if they were similar things.

American grants-in-aid have been much studied from the period of the 1930s on, when the New Deal policies were supposed to have transformed federalism. Three important studies from that era are Key (1937), a survey, and Clark (1938) and Benson (1941), which are interpretations. The notion that grants-in-aid, however much they multiplied, fundamentally changed federalism has been sharply challenged in Patterson (1969). If the emphasis is correct here that administrative disputes are merely accidental, not essential, to federalism, then this is exactly what one would expect.

Of course, the administrative disputes, while trivial, do marginally affect many important affairs, and so in most federal countries these disputes have been extensively studied. William Anderson and his students produced a series of ten important monographs on intergovernmental relations in Minnesota. These are summarized in Anderson (1955 and 1960). The most impressive of these is Ylvisaker (1956). A more general survey of intergovernmental relations is Graves (1964). An excellent case study is Derthick (1970). But the most detailed surveys are in the publications of government commissions. Ever since the early 1950s, the states have fought back against the presumed centralization of the New Deal by influencing the central government itself to produce committees favoring decentralization. These committees have examined the so-called centralization in exhaustive detail, without, of course, having anything very profound to say about intergovernmental relations. Thus, in the 1950s the *Report* of the Commission on Intergovernmental Relations (1955)—the Kestenbaum Commission—and in the 1960s the annual reports of the Advisory

Commission on Intergovernmental Relations (especially the eleventh report, in 1970) have been vehicles for uttering—even from the central government itself—pious arguments in favor of decentralization. The Advisory Commission has also issued a number of useful reports on special subjects. The most recent detailed report of grants-in-aid is, however, from a private source: Sundquist and Davis (1969).

While the national governmental official attitude toward federalism seems to be that we must make it work, some private scholars despair of the states. See Martin (1965), which is an attack on the states for neglecting the cities. The main attack on the several plans for distributing uncontrolled grants to states has been that they would neglect the cities (see Heller *et al.*, 1968). And even a defense of the states, Sanford (1967), is substantially concerned with documenting their incapacity. Perhaps the best indication of the high degree of distrust with which the American establishment views the state governments is the record of the Ford Foundation in sponsoring research on intergovernmental relations with a view toward improving state and local government. Over the course of the last fifteen years the Foundation has subsidized about seventeen million dollars of such research, more by far than on any other political subject. This research is summarized and discussed in Ford Foundation (1972), in which there is also a good bibliography on Foundation-sponsored publications.

The center of the controversy over grants-in-aid has, however, been money, not power. The plain fact is that states want more money and that is where the rub is. For an early study see Maxwell (1946). More recent detailed studies are to be found in Break (1967 and 1970), Oates (1972) and the report, *Fiscal Balance,* of the Advisory Commission on Intergovernmental Relations (1967). All the spice in the controversy has, however, been provided by the Heller plan and President Nixon's version of it under the name of revenue sharing (see Heller, 1966; Heller *et al.,* 1968; and Regan, 1972). Probably the most sophisticated and useful discussion is Wagner (1971; see also Reuss, 1970). In the halcyon days of John Kennedy, when prosperity produced a big income for the central government without increases in tax rates and there was no war to use up what threatened to be a budget surplus, Walter Heller conceived the bold notion of passing on some of the surplus to the states, which obviously needed it worse than the nation. To a federal bureaucracy steeped in the notion of grants-in-aid, this seemed like the worst sort of heresy, especially since it promised to give them less to do. Naturally there has been a protracted argument over it. Heller's proposal came at one of those rare times when the central government anticipated collecting more taxes than it then had plans to spend. The Vietnamese War increased central expenditures to the point at which not much excess was available; and of course central government bureaucrats have bitterly fought any lessening of their duties by thinking up lots of new things to do with any possible excess of tax income over budgets (e.g., new

weapons systems delayed by the Vietnamese War, "war on poverty," antipollu-
tion measures, etc.). Nevertheless, the Nixon administration did institute revenue sharing on a relatively modest scale, partly, one suspects, in the hope that
it would lead to some diminution of transfer payments made as grants-in-aid
and partly in the vain hope that it might give the White House some weapon
against the bureaucracy. The basic statute for revenue sharing is well described
in Stolz (1974), and the administration of the process is well described in
Nathan, Manvel, and Calkins (1975). It seems truly the case, however, that
expenditure always expands to meet income, and that the current revenue
sharing may be regarded as an aberration of a moment just before another vast
expansion of federal expenditures.

As revenue sharing is adopted, even on a modest scale, it does tend to
change the style of American federalism. It introduces that bargaining among
constituent governments and the center for central-government funds which
characterizes, for example, Canada, Australia, and India. The definitive book
on this bargaining is May (1969) and an elegant description of it is found in
Simeon (1972). Naturally, however, there is also a vast literature for each country, because much bureaucratic prose and pseudoscholarship is written on one
side or the other to win marginal adjustments in the amount of money transferred in the bargains. For India, I cite especially the *Report* of the Administrative Reforms Commission (1968) and two monographs: Venkataraman (1968)
and Sastri (1966). There is, incidentally, a large literature on intergovernmental
relations in India, all of which deals in one way or another with financial
problems (see Haggi, 1967; Chanda, 1965; Roy, 1962; and Aiyar and Mehta,
1965). India is a new federation and a poor country and part of the reason for
the intensive consideration of financial problems lies in these facts. Australia,
on the other hand, is richer and older and yet it too is characterized by an intense concern for financial problems, a concern that is best discussed in the
reports of the Commonwealth Grants Commission. This Commission is charged
with transferring central subsidies to poor ("claimant") states (Tasmania, Western Australia, and usually South Australia). Just how much is transferred and
how the claimant states share it is subject to occasional revision. Naturally,
this revision is the center of much political strategy, bargaining, and the like.

In Canada the process is more formalized, but still very similar to Australia.
The details have often been considered by special government studies, of which
the most outstanding was the *Report* of the Royal Commission on Dominion
Provincial Relations (1940), the Rowell-Sirois *Report*, and its supporting studies. A more recent study is the report of the Royal Commission on Taxation,
Federal-Provincial Fiscal Relations (1967). The volume of readings by Meekison
(1968) has an excellent guide through the literature on financial relations in
Canadian federalism, and the study by Simeon (1972) contains an excellent
description of the bargaining process. For citizens of the United States a good

review of the fiscal problems of Canadian federalism with an excellent bibliography is Advisory Commission on Intergovernmental Relations (1971).

Linguistic adjustments. One of the advantages often alleged to inhere in federalism is the possibility that minority languages can go their own way and develop naturally. This is what federalism is mostly concerned with in the Soviet Union, and surely federalism has not hindered an adequate linguistic adjustment in Switzerland. It is apparent that federalism is not necessary for resolution of language problems, for China, which has always been effectively multilingual, has also often been unitary. Nor is federalism sufficient for the resolution of these problems, as is indicated by the incipient secession of Quebec from Canada, mostly over linguistic problems. Two federal nations have in recent years been wracked with difficulties over language: India and Canada. Good analyses of the Indian case are to be found in the *Report* of the Official Language Commission (1956) and Roy (1962). The Canadian case was elaborately studied by the Royal Commission on Bilingualism and Biculturalism (see also Meekison, 1968).

Regionalism and intergovernmental relations. There is a large literature in the United States on special problems of intergovernmental relations, special, that is, in the sense that there is more complexity to them than the financial problem discussed on page 147. For example, entirely apart from financial considerations, there is a considerable problem of the relation of the actions of the national government on the administration of such supposedly local problems as education. Many of these problems are surveyed in Graves (1964), Ostrom (1969), Ostrom and Ostrom (1965), and Leach (1970). One such problem of special interest in the United States, which has smaller constituent units—and more of them—than other federations, is regionalism, interstate compacts, and the like (see Advisory Commission on Intergovernmental Relations, 1972; Ridgeway, 1970; and Barton, 1965).

THE EVALUATION OF FEDERALISM

I conclude this brief survey by observing that much of the discussion of federalism, like the discussion of all institutions, is moral evaluation. More accurately, it is straightforward ideology in the sense that it is the justification of the advantage of some advantaged interest. Sometimes the moral evaluation or ideology masquerades as science, though of course its nonscientific character is fairly evident, even to the common reader. In a scientific work such as this *Handbook* there is perhaps very little point to the repetition of ideology. Nevertheless as a guide to the reader through that intellectual morass, I offer a brief survey of the ideological issues.

The Beneficiaries of Federalism

Who benefits from federalism? This is the first question one must answer before one can understand the ideology. By its nature, ideology is the justification of an interest served by an institution. To understand an ideology, therefore, it is first necessary to understand who the beneficiary of the institution is. But the identification of who benefits is not easy, largely because the beneficiaries vary over time.

When federations are relatively new, the practical issue in their politics is: Shall the federal system continue to exist or shall it be broken up into the constituent units? When that is the issue, then it is readily apparent that the beneficiaries of the continued existence of the system are those who wanted federalism in the first place. I have earlier argued that those who want it are those who are especially conscious of the need for defense against either external or internal enemies or those who would use the big government of federalism for aggression. For convenience let us call these military beneficiaries "nationalists."

Nationalists are by definition those who put military and police security at the top of their priority list of political goals. Their opponents—for convenience, call them "antinationalists," for they are not necessarily localists—are those who are less concerned about military security and more concerned about other goals such as questions of the distribution of wealth or religious, linguistic, or racial equality.

For example, in the early history of the United States the Federalists were those who first of all wanted to put their house in order against the possible reopening of the war—it was on that basis that Washington could bring together two nationalist politicians like Hamilton and Jefferson whose secondary goals were so diverse. The Antifederalists, on the other hand, were those who were so especially concerned about political democracy and questions of distribution that they were willing to chance weakness in war to achieve these other goals.

Shown in Table 4 is a highly simplified schema of goals just after the Constitutional Convention. The initial success of the Federalist party is owing to

TABLE 4   Priorities of parties in 1789

	Federalists	Antifederalists
Hamiltonians	1. Maintenance of Union 2. Mercantilism	1. Economic and political liberalism 2. Maintenance of Union
Jeffersonians	1. Maintenance of union 2. Economic and political liberalism	

the fact that it could attract both mercantilists and liberals. It lost when Jeffersonians reordered their priorities to be just like the original Antifederalists.

A similar example can be seen in the current politics of India, where the strongest supporters of federal unity are to be found in the north. It is in the north where the danger of war with Pakistan and China have been most consciously felt. Many parties and politicians in the south are, on the other hand, suspicious of federal unity, regarding it as a trap to force the southern speakers of Dravidian languages into linguistic subservience to the Hindi-speaking north, or as a trap to force the non-Brahmanical south into subservience to the Brahmanical north. For many northerners the maintenance of union and the dominance of New Delhi are thus among the most important concerns of politics. For southerners these are typically either neutral or negative goals.

Given this division of politics, at the beginning of a federation, into nationalist and antinationalist impulses, one can say that the initial beneficiaries of federalism are the nationalists, whatever and however contradictory their secondary goals may be.

But the initial circumstances of a federalism do not last forever. In the shifting scene of alliance, both domestic and international, politics make strange bedfellows. Former enemies become friends and former friends become enemies. And these circumstances change the nature of political problems and lead people to reorder their priorities, just as within a couple of years after 1789 Jeffersonians began to become very like the original Antifederalists. On a longer time scale, the circumstances that call forth the original nationalist impulse can even reverse themselves. Thus the United States was formed to fight Great Britain, but in the second century of the American Union it fought two gigantic wars to save England from its political and military mistakes.

With the change in issues, the continued existence of the federation becomes an accepted political premise. It is, of course, possible that the question of existence be reopened, as it was in the United States in 1860 or as it has been recently in Canada or Nigeria. But, aside from such reopening, in mature federations the political issue is no longer whether or not the nation will continue to exist. Rather, political issues are the ordinary nonfederal issues that characterize the politics of any nation: questions of distribution, group influence, racial and religious and linguistic differences, economic policy, etc.

And when these ordinary questions dominate politics, who benefits from federalism then? The answer is, of course, that various minorities benefit. The fact that two levels of government are able to make policy on the same subjects (as is emphasized in Clark, 1938, and Elazar, 1962) means that the government at one level need not behave the same as the government at another level. If they do behave in the same way, with the same values and the same emphasis on instrumentalities, then no one benefits from federalism, for the two levels of government cannot be distinguished. But if they do not behave the same way, then clearly a minority benefits. If nothing but a national policy were made, then the minority that makes a different policy in a province or state would not be able to make that policy. Federalism permits, indeed guarantees, that there will be some subjects on which policy is made locally. Hence it guarantees also the possibility that such policy may differ from national policy. And if it does, then a minority benefits. (An interesting and valiant attempt to prove the contrary is Pennock, 1959, but that author entirely neglects the problem of external costs, which is analyzed on page 157.)

So the question of who benefits from federalism varies with the degree of nationalism and the internal political structure of the federal system. When there is barely enough nationalism to keep the federation going, then the beneficiaries are nationalists, who of course may be of almost any ideological hue. Thus, the victors in the American Civil War contained radical abolitionists and economic conservatives. Or, in Canada, now that the issue of continued existence has been raised to the central position in politics, the beneficiaries of federalism are the English-speaking Canadians and those French-speaking ones who are opposed to a free Quebec. When, however, national feeling is sufficiently strong to guarantee the continued life of the federalism, then the beneficiaries are those who can use constituent governments to enforce minority policies.

Just who these minorities are varies with the political structure of the federalism. In Riker (1964b, pp. 152–55), an effort is made to list some of those minorities for particular systems, but the list is doubtless somewhat inaccurate. Nevertheless, I repeat some of that discussion here if only for its heuristic value.

United States. The United States became sufficiently centralized after the Civil War that the issue of continued existence was no longer raised. In the subsequent century the main beneficiaries of federalism have undoubtedly been southern whites, who could use their power to control state governments to make policy on blacks that negated the national policy. It is possible also that business interests used federalism to evade regulation in the era from 1890 to 1935 (see Corwin, 1934), although it is not clear that a national intention to regulate business in that period ever existed. Clearly, however, in the United States, the main effect of federalism since the Civil War has been to perpetuate racism. Now that race has become a national issue, however, state governments can no longer make policy on race and federalism is irrelevant to racial issues. For the moment the chief significance of federalism in the United States seems to be the protection of some business interests against the juggernaut of the "liberal" bureaucracy in Washington.

Canada. So long as French speakers accepted federation, they have been the main beneficiaries in the sense that Quebec could follow special policies that would not perhaps be admitted in a unitary state. Once the question of free Quebec became a central issue of politics, however, the chains of nationalism rendered those French speakers who are antinationalist into a losing minority.

Until recently, then, the French-speaking minority in Quebec was the beneficiary of federalism, although now some French speakers feel oppressed by it.

India. It was originally intended that federalism would benefit Muslims, who
were expected to be a national minority but a majority in the areas now com-
posing Pakistan and Bangladesh. It turned out, however, that owing to the
formation of Pakistan, the main vocal minority with a geographic base were
Dravidian speakers in the south. These also tend to be non-Brahmans.

Australia. It is not clear that any group has consistently benefitted from Australian federalism. Indeed, as I have previously remarked, it is hard to see why
anyone wishes to keep it, since it mainly has the effect of restraining majorities
of the moment.

Brazil. Given the extreme poverty and political apathy of the bulk of the
population, that bulk can seldom manage to be concerned about any more
than national politics, where occasionally they have a sympathetic government.
In the absence of popular concern the prosperous classes (especially landlords)
manage state governments to their advantage. So in Brazil it has been the
feudal elements that continually benefit from federalism. Lately, however, a
nationalistic capitalism on the North American plan has tended to replace
feudalism with a kind of laissez-faire, and this has apparently neutralized the
landlords' advantages in federalism.

One could go on through a list of all well-established federations, but the
amount learned would hardly justify the space taken. It is sufficient to conclude
with the observation that in every federation there are identifiable beneficiaries
and that one can begin to understand the ideology of federalism by identifying
these beneficiaries.

It is important to note, however, just what the beneficiaries of a mature
federalism get. Since, as I have already shown, the constitutional and administrative features of federalism are accidental rather than essential, it should follow that these do not make a profound difference in political life. And this is
indeed the case. Nothing happens in a federation because of the federal constitutional arrangements that could not happen otherwise in fundamentally
the same way. One can never blame federalism for a political outcome, for outcomes are the consequences of the preferences of the population. One can only
blame federalism for facilitating an emphasis in popular preference. Thus one
does not blame an unlocked window for a burglary; the culprit is the burglar.
The role of the unlocked window is simply to facilitate entry. So it is with
federalism. Federalism itself was never the culprit in American racism, for the
real cause of racist behavior is the preferences of whites. All that federalism

ever did was to facilitate the expression of racist beliefs and the perpetuation of racist acts. As long as whites strongly prefer racist institutions, one can expect institutions to be racist regardless of whether the country is federal or unitary. But when the preference for racist institutions weakens, then federalism helps racism by rendering difficult the enforcement of an antiracist policy on the minority of white racists. So we can say that the beneficiaries of federalism get only marginal benefits on policy, but marginal or not, they are undoubtedly real.

The Ideology of Federalism

The ideologists of federalism do not, of course, utter arguments justifying the benefits that accrue to these beneficiaries. To do so would be to admit that not everyone gets something out of the institution of federalism. Yet it is the nature of ideology to be a claim of universal benefit. Thus the classic ideology, that of bourgeois capitalism, consists of a claim that what is immediately good for capitalists is good for everyone else. This is, of course, true in perfectly free markets. But it is often the case that real markets are not perfectly free. Often markets are rigged to the advantage of some producing group (e.g., farmers, laborers, manufacturers). Thus, somebody has an advantage and this is the fact that ideology obscures. Similarly the ideology of federalism consists of a claim that everyone gets such and such a benefit from it. Since we know, however, from the examination of beneficiaries just completed, that in fact some people, often a majority, do not benefit at all, it is easy enough to spot an ideology, because it is presented as a claim that everybody gets something good from the institutions of federalism. Let us look at some of these claims.

1. *That federalism promotes democratic polity.* It should be abundantly clear, just from looking at the list of federal governments, that not all of them are democracies or even pretend to be democracies, although their claim to be federations is indisputable. Mexico is one example, Yugoslavia is another, Nigeria was a third, before its civil war. To find an association between federalism and democracy is, on the face of it, absurd. Yet there are so many examples of this absurdity in the literature that one hesitates to select a particular one. See, however, American Assembly (1955), Anderson (1955), and Goldwin (1963). A particularly extreme form of this ideological claim is the argument that the process of federalism, by providing opposition, leads to pluralism (Friedrich, 1968). But there does not seem to be much pluralism in the Soviet Union.

2. *That federalism promotes democracy by promoting an interest in state government.* "... local government is more responsive to public opinion and more responsible to the people" (*Federalism as a Democratic Process,* 1942, p. 82) is a typical form of this argument, which has been repeated ad nauseam in the ideological literature. Fortunately this particular claim is subject to direct investigation. One question is whether or not state governments actually are

responsive to democratic control. The recent series of studies initiated by Dawson and Robinson (1963) and brought to a considerable conclusion by Dye (1966) and reviewed by Jacob and Lipsky (1968) generally support the proposition that state governments are more influenced in their actions by the state of their economies than by the demands of their citizens (for a different view see Samberg, 1971). Regardless of the apparent lack of responsiveness of the states, which may be an artifact of measurement, it is clearly the case that governments cannot be democratically controlled if citizens know relatively little about them. And it is clearly the case that citizens know less and care less about state governments than about any other kind: national, local, or international. Jennings and Ziegler (1970) have shown on the basis of survey research that citizens simply do not follow state politics very well. And when people do not know what a government is doing, they cannot hold it responsible. And if they cannot hold it responsible, it can hardly be particularly democratic, especially by comparison with national and local governments, which are more visible.

In general, one would expect that the greatest interest of the citizens would be centered on that level of government that does the most important things. Thus, in a centralized federation one would expect interest to center on the national government, while in a peripheralized federation one would expect the interest to focus on the constituent governments. The evidence from the United States is thus what one would expect from a centralized federalism. Owing to the paucity in the contemporary world of peripheralized federalisms it is difficult to determine if states are more salient in them than is the central government. Perhaps Nigeria before the Biafran revolt is a case of truly peripheralized federation, however. If so, the fact that the main political leaders there preferred state to national office suggests that the states were more salient (see Mackintosh, 1962).

3. *That federalism maintains individual freedom.* This is by far the most popular of the ideological arguments in favor of federalism. Some recent examples of it can be found in Rockefeller (1962), Morley (1959), Kilpatrick (1957 and 1962), and Kirk (1962). The absurdity of this claim was first pointed out by Neumann (1955) and was dealt with at length in Riker (1964b). The substance of that argument is set forth briefly here: Freedom is the right to make rules as one chooses. Rules in turn impose constraints on all those who would not by preference have made exactly those rules. We speak of the person who is constrained by rules as one who has an external cost imposed on him or her. The ideal of freedom is then to minimize the external costs suffered by some person in the society. In an aristocratic society one minimizes the external costs of the well-born; but in the equalitarian society of today, presumably one minimizes the external costs of some representative citizen chosen at random from the whole. The best way to minimize costs for such a citizen is to have policy made by the largest relevant unit of government. For all issues of national con-

cern, then, maximum freedom is attained when policy is made nationally. Conversely, for all issues of local concern, maximum freedom is attained when policy is made locally. See Breton (1965) for a general theory of decentralization based on this notion. Federalism interferes with making policy on national issues nationally. But the converse is not true: nonfederal governments do not necessarily interfere with local policymaking on local issues. Federalism is thus a real barrier to good distribution of the authority to make policy. States' rights guarantee minority governing on national issues, if the minority differs from the majority in significant ways. That is, federalism permits minorities to impose very high external costs on the majority. Thus, for example, in the United States, states' rights from 1890 to 1960 meant that the southern states could develop a tyrannical government that created several generations of poor and uneducated blacks whose maintenance was a charge on the rest of the nation. All this to satisfy the preferences of southern white racists.

In Tarlton (1965) it is argued that federalism works better when the constituent units are alike, "symmetric" is Tarlton's word. The reason for this is that states' rights in an asymmetrical system impose high external costs on national majorities. In general, therefore, in any federal system, but especially in asymmetrical ones like the United States, federalism weakens freedom. So the claim of the ideologists of federalism that the system strengthens freedom is thus false. Indeed federalism, as Riker and Tarlton show, weakens freedom.

(One finds this understanding often set forth in polemical literature, especially where the author argues that national problems must be met nationally. See for example, Jaffa [1963], where, without theoretical understanding, the practical danger of the external costs imposed by minorities on majorities is clearly set forth.)

Moral Evaluation of Federalism

It has so far been shown that the beneficiaries of centralized federalism are those minorities that are permitted to make policy locally on national issues. The contrary assertions of ideologists, that everybody benefits, have been shown to be false. But to show that minorities benefit does not settle the question of moral evaluation. Even if federalism typically hurts a majority, it may well be that a majority might decide to maintain it, especially if the hurt is only marginal.

There are at least two reasons why a majority harmed by federalism might decide to keep it. One reason is that the costs it imposes are relatively low. If, whenever a majority is strongly in favor of a policy, states' rights are overridden, then federalism is only a minor cost on the majority. This well may be the situation in the United States, where in the last generation or so racist states' rights have been fairly consistently denied by a not-very-determined majority in favor of a single national policy on civil liberties. If states' rights can be maintained only when the majority doesn't much care, then the costs of federalism, while greater than the costs of other kinds of government, are not relatively great. In short, then, nations may choose to remain federal simply because federalism doesn't mean very much one way or another. If this is so, then one might well make the moral judgment that federalism is not worth bothering about.

Another reason for keeping a harmful federation is that it might cost too much to get rid of it. To have federalism may be more costly than not having it; yet getting rid of federalism may still be more costly than keeping it. That is, in descending order of cost, the following alternatives may exist for a nation with federal government:

1. dissolving the federation

2. changing (by, e.g., civil war) to a unitary government

3. maintaining the federation

4. maintaining a unitary government.

In such case the *status quo* is preferred, not out of any absolute moral judgment, but out of an instrumental judgment that it is the least expensive of immediate alternatives.

Both these reasons seem to be important in the evaluation of centralized federal governments today. In a federation like Australia the institutions are a minor nuisance and hence not very costly. In a federation like Canada, which may be becoming peripheralized, the costs of transforming to a unitary government may be so great that no one has seriously considered doing so for a generation. In the case of the United States, probably both judgments are relevant.

Both these judgments on federalism are a way of saying that it is not very significant as an institution. Whether or not this statement is factually correct seems to me the most important subject for research on federalism. It would indeed be interesting to know if so much concern for moral evaluation has been wasted on an institution that does not have much effect on political life.

APPENDIX: NOTES ON THE HISTORY OF THE IDEOLOGICAL WRITINGS ON FEDERALISM

In the battle of the books between ancients and moderns, it is possible that, when the subject is morality, the ancients may offer precepts that are of value even today. But when the subject is the interpretation of institutions, especially institutions that did not exist when the ancients wrote, the moderns surely win the battle. It is simply the case that almost everything the ancients wrote is irrelevant because it is not concerned with the subject under discussion.

Federalism in its present forms in the world is largely a twentieth century creation. At the very earliest, modern centralized federalism appears in the first half of the nineteenth century. But this federalism does not really assume its present mature form until the period between the world wars. On that basis, moderns are those who wrote in the 1930s and after, while ancients are all previous writers. That is, the ancients (who are the pre-1930 writers) are the ones who are irrelevant for discussions of contemporary federalism, simply because they cannot then have known what contemporary federalism now is. For this reason, when commenting on the writings about federalism I have confined myself to recent writers.

Nevertheless, in order to guide those who may want to explore the earlier work, this appendix offers some bibliographic remarks on the "ancients." Fortunately most of the bibliographic work has already been done in Mogi (1931). This work is quite sympathetic to federalism, for it was written under the influence of Laski in his pluralist phase. (When Laski turned Marxist he also turned centralist; see Laski, 1939.) Mogi surveyed in remarkable detail the main traditions on federalism up to 1930: (1) German lawyers who interpreted the Imperial and Weimar constitutions, (2) American lawyers who interpreted the United States Constitution, (3) American publicists who engaged in the perennial states' rights debate, and (4) English publicists of the turn of the century whose interest in federalism derived from a vision of a federal commonwealth. The only substantial tradition he ignored was the French, and that gap has recently been filled in a survey by Hoffman (1959); see also LeFur (1896). Since most French writers espoused federalism as a way to attack the centralization of French institutions, however, the usefulness of their work for understanding even the federal states that were contemporary with them is zero.

Althusius is said to have been the first writer to comment on federalism. His main work has been translated in Carney (1964), described in Gierke (1939), and edited by Friedrich in Althusius (1932). Actually, however, Althusius wrote next to nothing on federalism and did not know much about Swiss or Dutch forms, largely because neither was fully developed during his lifetime.

The first ideologues of modern federalism were Alexander Hamilton, James Madison, and John Jay, who produced *The Federalist* as a partisan document in the campaign over ratification. A fine recent edition is by Wright, for which see Hamilton (1961). Excellent recent discussions of *The Federalist* are to be found in Diamond (1961 and 1963). See also Dietze (1961). Many writers have been intrigued with *The Federalist* and have attempted to abstract from it enduring principles of political philosophy. Dahl (1956) is a noteworthy example of such theorizing, but he entirely neglects the federal feature of *The Federalist*. Ostrom (1969b), on the other hand, emphasizes the federal feature, attempting to raise the ideas of *The Federalist* on federalism to the level of general theory.

The nineteenth century American debate on states' rights is well summarized in Bennett (1964). Since much of this literature appeared in opinions of judges, see also Corwin (1934), Corwin (1950), and Schmidhauser (1958).

The current production of ideological literature is enormous. Bachelder and Shaw (1966) contains a bibliography that scratches the surface of the mass for the United States. For Canada see the bibliography in Meekison (1968).

REFERENCES

Administrative Reforms Commission (1968). *Report on Centre-State Relations.* Delhi: Manager of Government of India Press.

Advisory Commission on Intergovernmental Relations (annual, 1959ff.). *Report.* Washington, D. C.: Government Printing Office.

_____ (1967). *Fiscal Balance in the American Federal System,* 2 vols. Washington, D.C.: Government Printing Office.

_____ (1971). *In Search of Balance: Canada's Intergovernmental Experience.* Washington, D.C.: Government Printing Office.

_____ (1972). *Multistate Regionalism.* Washington, D.C.: Government Printing Office.

Aiyar, S. P. (1961). *Federalism and Social Change: A Study in Quasi-Federalism.* New York: Asia Publishing House.

Aiyar, S. P., and Usha Mehta (1965). *Essays on Indian Federalism Presented to Professor M. Venkatarangaiya.* Bombay: Allied.

Alberdi, Juan Bautista, ed. (1913). Alberto Palcos, *Estudios Sobre la Constitucion Argentins de 1853.* Buenos Aires: W. M. Jackson.

Alexander, Paul (1973). "The index of disharmony in the United States." Dissertation, University of Rochester, Rochester, New York.

Althusius, Johannes (1932). *Politica Methodice Digesta.* Edited by C. J. Friedrich. Cambridge: Harvard University Press.

American Assembly (1955). *The Forty-eight States.* New York: Columbia University Press.

Amlund, Curtis (1966). *Federalism in the Southern Confederacy.* Washington, D.C.: Public Affairs Press.

Anderson, William (1955). *The Nation and the States: Rivals or Partners.* Minneapolis: University of Minnesota Press.

_____ (1960). *Intergovernmental Relations in Review.* Minneapolis: University of Minnesota Press.

Appleby, Paul (1953). *Public Administration in India.* Delhi: Manager of Publications.

_____ (1956). *Reexamination of India's Administrative System.* New Delhi: Manager of Publications.

Aspaturian, Vernon (1950). "The theory and practice of Soviet federalism." *Journal of Politics* 12:20–51.

Australian Federal Convention, *Official Report of Debates*. Vol. 1, 1897, Adelaide: C. E. Brestow; Vol. 2, 1897, Sydney: W. A. Gullick; Vols. 3 and 4, 1898, Melbourne: Robert Brain.

Awa, E. O. (1964). *Federal Government in Nigeria*. Berkeley: University of California Press.

Ayearst, Morley (1960). *British West Indies: The Search for Self-Government*. London: Allen and Unwin.

Bachelder, Glen, and Paul C. Shaw (1966). "The literature of federalism: a selected bibliography." Rev. ed. Mimeographed. East Lansing: Institute for Community Development of Michigan State University.

Baratz, Morton S., and Helen T. Farr (1959). "Is municipal finance fiscally perverse?" *National Tax Journal*, 12:276–84.

Barton, Weldon V. (1965). *Interstate Compacts in the Political Process*. Chapel Hill: University of North Carolina Press.

Beard, Charles (1913). *An Economic Interpretation of the Constitution of the United States*. New York: Macmillan.

Belaunde, Victor Andres (1938). *Bolivar and the Political Thought of the Spanish American Revolution*. Baltimore: Johns Hopkins University Press.

Bennett, William H. (1964). *American Theories of Federalism*. University, Ala.: University of Alabama Press.

Benson, George C. S. (1941). *The New Centralization*. New York: Farrar and Rinehart.

—————, ed. (1961). *Essays in Federalism*. Claremont: Institute for Studies in Federalism.

Binkley, Robert F. (1938). "The Holy Roman Empire versus the United States." In Conyers Read (ed.), *The Constitution Reconsidered*. New York: Columbia University Press.

Birch, A. H. (1955). *Federalism, Finance, and Social Legislation in Canada, Australia and the United States*. Oxford: Clarendon Press.

————— (1966). "Approaches to the study of federalism." *Political Studies* 14:15–33.

Bluhm, William T. (1968). "Nation building: the case of Austria." *Polity* 1: 149–77.

Bombwall, K. R. (1967). *The Foundations of Indian Federalism*. New York: Asia Publishing House.

Bowie, R. R., and Carl J. Friedrich, eds. (1954). *Studies in Federalism*. Boston: Little, Brown.

Break, George F. (1967). *Intergovernmental Fiscal Relations in the United States*. Washington: Brookings Institution.

————— (1970). "Changing roles of different levels of government." In Julius Margolis (ed.), *The Analysis of Public Output*. New York: National Bureau of Economic Research.

Brecht, Arnold (1945). *Federalism and Regionalism in Germany: The Division of Prussia*. New York: Oxford University Press.

Breton, Albert (1965). "A theory of government grants." *Canadian Journal of Economics and Political Science* 31:175–87.

Bright, John (1959). *A History of Israel.* Philadelphia: Westminster Press.

Brown, Robert E. (1956). *Charles Beard and the Constitution.* Princeton: Princeton University Press.

Buchanan, James, and Richard E. Wagner (1970). "An efficiency basis for federal fiscal equalization." In Julius Margolis (ed.), *The Analysis of Public Output.* New York: National Bureau of Economic Research.

Callard, Keith (1957). *Pakistan: A Political Study.* New York: Macmillan.

Carney, Fredrick S. (1964). *The Politics of Johannes Althusius.* London: Eyre and Spottiswoode.

Carr, E. H. (1950–64). *A History of Soviet Russia.* London: Macmillan.

Cerny, Karl H. (1968). "Federalism in the West German Republic." In Valerie Earle (ed.), *Federalism: Infinite Variety in Theory and Practice.* Itasca, Ill.: Peacock.

Chanda, Asok (1965). *Federalism in India: A Study of Union-State Relations.* London: Allen and Unwin.

Chaudhury, G. W. (1959). *Constitutional Developments in Pakistan.* London: Longmans.

Clark, Jane Perry (1938). *The Rise of a New Federalism: Federal-State Cooperation in the United States.* New York: Columbia University Press.

Codding, George A. (1961). *The Federal Government of Switzerland.* Boston: Houghton Mifflin.

Cohen, Jacob, and Morton Grodzins (1963). "How much economic sharing in American federalism?" *American Political Science Review* 57:5–23.

Coleman, J. S. (1958). *Nigeria: Background to Nationalism.* Berkeley: University of California Press.

Commission on Intergovernmental Relations (1955). *Report.* Washington, D.C.: Government Printing Office.

Corwin, Edward S. (1934). *The Twilight of the Supreme Court.* New Haven: Yale University Press.

——————— (1950). "The passing of dual federalism." *Virginia Law Review,* 36:1–23.

——————— (1957). *The President: Office and Powers.* New York: New York University Press.

Creighton, D. G. (1964). *The Road to Confederation: The Emergence of Canada 1863–1867.* Toronto: Macmillan.

Currie, David P., ed. (1964). *Federalism and the New Nations of Africa.* Chicago: University of Chicago Press.

Dahl, Robert (1956). *A Preface to Democratic Theory.* Chicago: University of Chicago Press.

Davis, Rufus (1956). "The 'federal principle' reconsidered." *Australian Journal of Politics and History* 1:59–85, 223–44.

Dawson, Richard, and James Robinson (1963). "Inter-party competition, economic variables, and welfare policies in the American states." *Journal of Politics* 25:265–89.

Deakin, Alfred (1944). *The Federal Story: The Inner History of the Federal Cause.* Melbourne: Robertson and Mullins.

Derthick, Martha (1965). *The National Guard in Politics.* Cambridge, Mass.: Harvard University Press.

_____ (1970). *The Influence of Federal Grants.* Cambridge, Mass.: Harvard University Press.

_____ (1974). *Between State and Nation.* Washington, D.C.: Brookings Institution.

Deutsch, Karl, *et al.* (1957). *Political Community in the North Atlantic Area.* Princeton: Princeton University Press.

Diamond, Martin (1961). "The federalist's view of federalism." In George Benson (ed.), *Essays in Federalism.* Claremont: Institute for Studies on Federalism.

_____ (1963). "What the framers meant by federalism." In Robert A. Goldwin (ed.), *A Nation of States.* Chicago: Rand McNally.

Dietze, Gottfried (1961). *The Federalist: A Classic on Federalism and Free Government.* Baltimore: Johns Hopkins University Press.

Dikshit, R. D. (1971). "Military interpretation of federal constitutions: a critique." *The Journal of Politics* 33:180–89.

Duchacek, Ivo O. (1970). *Comparative Federalism.* New York: Holt, Rinehart and Winston.

Dye, Thomas (1968). *Politics, Economics, and the Public: Policy Outcomes in the American States.* Chicago: Rand McNally.

Earle, Valerie, ed. (1968). *Federalism: Infinite Variety in Theory and Practice.* Itasca, Ill.: Peacock.

Elazar, Daniel J. (1962). *The American Partnership: Intergovernmental Partnership in the Nineteenth Century United States.* Chicago: University of Chicago Press.

_____ (1966). *American Federalism: A View from the States.* New York: Crowell.

_____ (1968). "Federalism." In *International Encyclopedia of the Social Sciences,* Vol 5. New York: Macmillan.

Emerson, Rupert (1937). *Malaysia: A Study in Direct and Indirect Rule.* New York: Macmillan.

Etzioni, Amitai (1965). *Political Unification: A Comparative Study of Leaders and Forces.* New York: Holt, Rinehart, and Winston.

Ezera, K. (1964). *Constitutional Developments in Nigeria.* Cambridge: Cambridge University Press.

Farrand, Max (1911, 1938). *The Records of the Federal Convention of 1787,* 4 vols. New Haven: Yale University Press.

Federalism as a Democratic Process: Essays by Roscoe Pound, Charles H. McIlwain, Roy F. Nichols (1942). New Brunswick, N.J.: Rutgers University Press.

Flanz, Gilbert H. (1968). "The West Indies." In Thomas M. Franch (ed.), *Why Federations Fail*. New York: New York University Press.

Foltz, William J. (1965). *From French West Africa to the Mali Federation*. New Haven: Yale University Press.

Ford Foundation (1972). *The Near Side of Federalism: Improving State and Local Government*. New York: Ford Foundation.

Forsey, Eugene (1965). "Concepts of federalism: some Canadian aspects." In Gordon Hawkins (ed.), *Concepts of Federalism*. Toronto: Canadian Institute of Public Affairs. Reprinted in J. Peter Meekison, ed. (1968), *Canadian Federalism*. Toronto: Methuen.

Franch, Thomas M. (1968). "East African Federation." In Thomas M. Franch (ed.), *Why Federations Fail*. New York: New York University Press.

Franda, Marcus F. (1968). *West Bengal and the Federalizing Process in India*. Princeton: Princeton University Press.

Frankel, Joseph (1955). "Federalism in Yugoslavia." *American Political Science Review* 49:416–30.

Freeman, E. A. (1893). *A History of Federal Government in Greece and Italy*. Rev. ed. Edited by J. A. Bury. London: Macmillan.

Freund, Paul A. (1953). "A supreme court in a federalism: some lessons from legal history." *Columbia Law Review* 53:597–619.

——————— (1955). "Umpiring the federal system." In Arthur W. MacMahon (ed.), *Federalism Mature and Emergent*. Garden City: Doubleday.

Friedrich, Carl J. (1968). *Trends of Federalism in Theory and Practice*. New York: Praeger.

Gierke, Otto (1939). *The Development of Political Theory*. New York: Norton.

Golay, John F. (1958). *The Founding of the Federal Republic of Germany*. Chicago: University of Chicago Press.

Goldwin, Robert A. (1963). *A Nation of States*. Chicago: Rand McNally.

Graves, W. Brooke (1964). *American Intergovernmental Relations*. New York: Scribner.

Greenwood, Gordon (1946). *The Future of Australian Federalism*. Melbourne: Melbourne University Press.

Grodzins, Morton (1960a). "American political parties and the American system." *Western Political Quarterly* 13:974–98.

——————— (1960b). "The federal system." In President's Commission on National Goals, *Goals for Americans*. Englewood Cliffs, N.J.: Prentice-Hall.

——————— (1966). *The American System*. Chicago: Rand McNally.

Haggi, S. A. H. (1967). *Union State Relations in India*. Meerut: Meenakshi Prakashan.

Hamilton, Alexander, James Madison, and John Jay (1961). *The Federalist*. Edited by Benjamin F. Wright. Cambridge: Harvard University Press.

Hansen, A. H., and H. S. Perloff (1944). *State and Local Finance in the National Economy*. New York: Norton.

Haring, C. H. (1938). "Federalism in Latin America." In Conyers Read (ed.), *The Constitution Reconsidered*. New York: Columbia University Press.

Heidenheimer, Arnold J. (1958). "Federalism and the party system: the case of West Germany." *American Political Science Review* 52:809–28.

Heller, Walter E. (1966). *New Dimensions of Political Economy*. Cambridge, Mass.: Harvard University Press.

Heller, Walter E., *et al.* (1968). In Harvey S. Perloff and Richard P. Nathan (eds.), *Revenue Sharing and the City*. Baltimore: Johns Hopkins University Press.

Hicks, U. K., *et al.* (1961). *Federalism and Economic Growth in Underdeveloped Countries*. London: Allen and Unwin.

Hoffman, Stanley (1959). "The areal division of powers in the writings of French political thinkers." In Arthur Maass (ed.), *Area and Power*. Glencoe: Free Press.

Holborn, Hajo (1938). "The influence of the American Constitution on the Weimar Constitution." In Conyers Read (ed.), *The Constitution Reconsidered*. New York: Columbia University Press.

Hondius, Fritz W. (1968). *The Yugoslav Community of Nations*. Hague: Mouton.

Hughes, Christopher (1954). *The Federal Constitution of Switzerland*. Oxford: Oxford University Press.

Hunt, E. H. (1930). *American Precedents in Australian Federalism*. New York: Columbia University Press.

Intergovernmental Relations in Review (1960). Minneapolis: University of Minnesota Press.

Jacob, Herbert, and Michael Lipsky (1968). "Outputs, structures, and power: an assessment of changes in the study of state and local politics." *Journal of Politics* 30:510–38.

Jaffa, Harry A. (1963). "The case for a stronger national government." In Robert A. Goldwin (ed.), *A Nation of States*. Chicago: Rand McNally.

James, Herman G. (1923). *The Constitutional System of Brazil*. Washington: Carnegie Institution.

Janicon, F. M. (1729). *État Présent des Provinces—Unies et des Pais Qui en Dépendent*. Hague.

Jennings, M. Kent, and Harmon Ziegler (1970). "The salience of American state politics." *American Political Science Review* 64:523–35.

Kantor, Harry (1968). "Latin American federalism: aspiration or futility?" In Valerie Earle (ed.), *Federalism: Infinite Variety in Theory and Practice*. Itasca, Ill.: Peacock.

Karnes, Thomas L. (1960). *The Failure of Union: Central America 1824–1860*. Chapel Hill: University of North Carolina Press.

Key, V. O. (1937). *The Administration of Federal Grants to States*. Chicago: Public Administration Service.

Kilpatrick, James J. (1957). *The Sovereign States: Notes of a Citizen of Virginia*. Chicago: Henry Regnery.

_____ (1962). "The case for 'states' rights." In Robert Goldwin (ed.), *A Nation of States.* Chicago: Rand McNally.

Kirk, Russell (1962). "The prospects for territorial democracy in America." In Robert Goldwin (ed.), *A Nation of States.* Chicago: Rand McNally.

Larsen, J. A. O. (1968). *Greek Federal States.* Oxford: Clarendon Press.

Laski, Harold (1939). "The obsolescence of federalism." *New Republic* 98:367–69.

Leach, Richard H. (1970). *American Federalism.* New York: Norton.

LeFur, Louis (1896). *État Fédéral et Confédération d'Etats.* Paris: Marchal et Billard.

Livingston, William S. (1952). "A note on the nature of federalism." *Political Science Quarterly,* 67:81–95.

_____ (1956). *Federalism and Constitutional Change.* Oxford: Oxford University Press.

_____ (1963). *Federalism in the Commonwealth: A Bibliographical Commentary.* London: Cassel.

Lowenthal, David (1960). *The West Indies Federation.* New York: Columbia University Press.

Maass, Arthur (1959). *Area and Power: A Theory of Local Government.* Glencoe, Ill.: Free Press.

Mackintosh, John P. (1962). "Federalism in Nigeria." *Political Studies* 10:223–47.

MacMahon, Arthur, ed. (1955). *Federalism: Mature and Emergent.* Garden City: Doubleday.

Martin, P. C. (1938). "Federalism in Brazil." In Conyers Read (ed.), *The Constitution Reconsidered.* New York: Columbia University Press.

Martin, Roscoe (1965). *The Cities and the Federal System.* New York: Atherton.

Maxwell, James A. (1946). *The Fiscal Impact of Federalism in the United States.* Cambridge: Harvard University Press.

May, R. J. (1969). *Federalism and Fiscal Adjustment.* Oxford, Clarendon Press.

Mayer, Lawrence (1970). "Federalism and party behavior in Australia and Canada." *Western Political Quarterly* 23:795–807.

McKinnon, Victor S. (1964). *Comparative Federalism: A Study in Judicial Interpretation.* Hague: Nijhoff.

McWhinney, E. W. (1960). *Judicial Review in the English Speaking World.* 3d ed. Toronto: University of Toronto Press.

_____ (1962a). *Comparative Federalism: States' Rights and National Power.* Toronto: University of Toronto Press.

_____ (1962b). *Constitutionalism in Germany and the Federal Constitutional Court.* Leyden: Nijhoff.

Mecham, J. Lloyd (1938). "Origins of federalism in Mexico." In Conyers Read (ed.), *The Constitution Reconsidered.* New York: Columbia University Press.

Meekison, J. Peter, ed. (1968). *Canadian Federalism: Myth or Reality.* Toronto: Methuen.

Menon, V. P. (1956). *The Integration of the Indian States.* New York: Macmillan.

Mentschikoff, Soia (1964). "Federalism and economic growth." In David P. Currie (ed.), *Federalism and the New Nations of Africa.* Chicago: University of Chicago Press.

Merkl, Peter (1959). "Executive legislative federalism in West Germany." *American Political Science Review* 53:732–41.

_____ (1963). *The Origin of the West German Republic.* London: Oxford University Press.

Miller, J. D. B. (1954). *Australian Government and Politics.* London: Duckworth.

Mills, L. A. (1958). *Malaya: A Political and Economic Appraisal.* Minneapolis: University of Minnesota Press.

Mogi, Sobei (1931). *The Problem of Federalism: A Study in the History of Political Theory,* 2 vols. London: Allen and Unwin.

Morgan, Lewis Henry (1962). *The League of the Iroquois.* Reprint ed. (Originally published 1851). Introduction by William N. Fenton. New York: Corinth Books.

Morley, Felix (1959). *Freedom and Federalism.* Chicago: Henry Regnery.

Muller, Steven (1967). "Federalism and the party system in Canada." In Aaron Wildavsky (ed.), *American Federalism in Perspective.* Boston: Little, Brown.

Munger, F. J., and R. F. Fenno (1962). *National Politics and Federal Aid to Education.* Syracuse: Syracuse University Press.

Murphy, Jerome T. (1971). "Title I of ESEA: the politics of implementing federal education reform." *Harvard Educational Review* 41:35–63.

Musgrave, Richard A., ed. (1965). *Essays in Fiscal Federalism.* Washington: Brookings Institution.

Nathan, Richard P., Allen D. Manuel, and Susannah E. Calkins (1975). *Monitoring Revenue Sharing.* Washington, D.C.: Brookings Institution.

Neumann, Franz L. (1955). "Federalism and freedom: a critique." In Arthur W. MacMahon (ed.), *Federalism Mature and Emergent.* Garden City: Doubleday.

Neustadt, Richard E. (1960). *Presidential Power: The Politics of Leadership.* New York: Wiley.

Nye, Joseph (1965). *Pan-Africanism and East African Integration.* Cambridge, Mass.: Harvard University Press.

Oates, Wallace E. (1972). *Fiscal Federalism.* New York: Harcourt Brace Jovanovich.

Odumosu, O. I. (1963). *The Nigerian Constitution: History and Development.* London: Sweet and Maxwell.

Official Language Commission (1956). *Report.* New Delhi: Manager of Publications.

Olson, Mancur, Jr. (1969). "The principle of fiscal equivalence." *American Economic Review* 59:479–87.

Ostrom, Vincent (1969). "Operational federalism." *Public Choice* 6:1–17.

_____ (1971). *The Political Theory of a Compound Republic.* Blacksburg, Va. *Public Choice.* Virginia Polytechnic Institute.

Ostrom, Vincent, and Elinor Ostrom (1965). "A behavioral approach to the study of intergovernmental relations." *Annals of American Academy of Political and Social Sciences* 359:137–46.

Ostrom, Vincent, Charles M. Tiebout, and Robert Warren (1961). "The organization of government in metropolitan areas: a theoretical inquiry." *American Political Science Review* 55:831–42.

Patterson, James T. (1969). *The New Deal and the States: Federalism in Transition.* Princeton: Princeton University Press.

Pennock, J. Roland (1959). "Federal and unitary government—disharmony and frustration." *Behavioral Science* 4:147–57.

Peterson, Phyllis (1970). "Coalition formation in local elections in the state of São Paulo, Brazil." In Sven Groennings, E. W. Kelley, and Michael Leiserson (eds.), *The Study of Coalition Behavior.* New York: Holt, Rinehart and Winston.

Philip, Kjeld (1954). *Intergovernmental Fiscal Relations.* Copenhagen: Institute of Economics and History.

Pinney, Edward L. (1963). *Federalism, Bureaucracy, and Party Politics in Western Germany: The Role of the Bundesrat.* Chapel Hill: University of North Carolina Press.

Publius: The Journal of Federalism (1971–). Philadelphia: Center for the Study of Federalism, Temple University.

Pylee, M. V. (1960). *Constitutional Government in India.* New York: Asia Publishing House.

Rafuse, Robert W., Jr. (1965). "Cyclical behavior of state, local finances." In Richard A. Musgrave (ed.), *Essays in Fiscal Federalism.* Washington, D.C.: Brookings Institution.

Rappard, W. E. (1948). *La Constitution Fédérale de la Suisse, 1848–1948.* Neuchâtel, Suisse: Baconniere.

Ray, Amal (1966). *Intergovernmental Relations in India.* New York: Asia Publishing House.

Regan, Michael D. (1972). *The New Federalism.* New York: Oxford University Press.

Reuss, Henry (1970). *Revenue Sharing.* New York: Praeger.

Ridgeway, Marian E. (1970). *Interstate Compacts.* Carbondale: Southern Illinois University Press.

Riker, William H. (1955). "The Senate and American federalism." *American Political Science Review* 49:452–69.

——————— (1957). "Dutch and American federalism." *Journal of the History of Ideas* 18:495–521.

——————— (1958). *Soldiers of the States.* Washington: Public Affairs Press.

——————— (1964a). *Democracy in the United States.* Rev. ed. New York: Macmillan.

——————— (1964b). *Federalism: Origin, Operation, Significance.* Boston: Little, Brown.

——————— (1969). "Six books in search of a subject or does federalism exist and does it matter?" *Comparative Politics* 2:135–46.

Riker, William H., and William Bast (1969). "Presidential action on congressional nominations." In Aaron Wildavsky (ed.), *The Presidency*. Boston: Little, Brown.

Riker, William H., and Ronald Schaps (1957). "Disharmony in federal government." *Behavioral Science* 2:276–90.

Rockefeller, Nelson A. (1962). *The Future of Federalism*. Cambridge, Mass.: Harvard University Press.

Rossiter, Clinton (1966). *1787: The Grand Convention*. New York: Macmillan.

Rotberg, Robert I. (1965). *The Rise of Nationalism in Central Africa: The Making of Malawi and Zambia 1873–1964*. Cambridge, Mass.: Harvard University Press.

Rothchild, Donald S. (1960). *Toward Unity in Africa*. Washington, D.C.: Public Affairs Press.

Rothenberg, Jerome (1970). "Local decentralization and the theory of optimal government." In Julius Margolis (ed.), *The Analyses of Public Output*. New York: National Bureau of Economic Research.

Rowe, L. S. (1921). *The Federal System of the Argentine Republic*. Washington, D.C.: Carnegie Institution.

Roy, Naresh (1962). *Federalism and Linguistic States*. Calcutta: Mukhopodhyay.

Royal Commission on Bilingualism and Biculturalism (1967–69). *Report*, 3 vols. Ottawa: Queen's Printer.

Royal Commission on Dominion Provincial Relations (1940). *Report*. Ottawa: King's Printer.

Royal Commission on Taxation (1967). *Federal Provincial Relations*. Ottawa: Queen's Printer.

Samberg, Robert (1971). "Conceptualization and measurement of political system output." Ph.D. dissertation, University of Rochester.

Sanford, Terry (1967). *Storm Over the States*. New York: McGraw-Hill.

Sarmiento, D. F. (1961). *Life in the Argentine Republic in the Days of the Tyrants*. (Originally published 1845). Edited by Mary Mann. New York: Collier.

Sastri, K. V. S. (1966). *Federal-State Fiscal Relations in India: A Study of the Finance Commission and the Techniques of Fiscal Adjustment*. Bombay: Oxford University Press.

Sawer, Geoffrey (1969). *Modern Federalism*. London: Watts.

————, ed. (1952). *Federalism: An Australian Jubilee Study*. Melbourne.

Sawer, Geoffrey, et al. (1949). *Federalism in Australia*. Melbourne: F. W. Chesire.

Scheiber, Harry N. (1966). *The Condition of American Federalism: A Historian's View*. Subcommittee on Intergovernmental Relations of Committee on Government Operations, 89th Cong., 2d sess. Washington, D.C.: Government Printing Office.

Schiller, A. Arthur (1955). *The Formation of Federal Indonesia*. Hague: Van Hoeve.

Schlesinger, Rudolph (1945). *Federalism in Eastern and Central Europe*. London: Kegan Paul.

Schmidhauser, John R. (1958). *The Supreme Court as Final Arbiter in Federal-State Relations 1789–1957*. Chapel Hill: University of North Carolina Press.

Schuler, Edgar, and Kathryn Schuler (1967). *Public Opinion and Constitution Making in Pakistan*. East Lansing: Michigan State University Press.

Schwarz, Fredrick (1965). *Nigeria: The Tribes, the Nation, or the Race—the Politics of Independence*. Cambridge, Mass.: M.I.T. Press.

Shapley, L. S., and Martin Shubik (1954). "A method of evaluating the distribution of power in a committee system." *American Political Science Review* 48:787–92.

Sharan, Parmatma (1968). *Political System of Pakistan*. Meerut: Meenakshi Prakashan.

Sharma, B. U., and L. P. Choudhry (1967). *Federal Polity*. Bombay: Asia Publishing.

Shoup, Paul (1968). *Communism and the Yugoslav National Question*. New York: Columbia University Press.

Simandjuntak, B. (1969). *Malayan Federalism 1945–63*. Kuala Lumpur: Oxford University Press.

Simeon, Richard (1972). *Federal Provincial Diplomacy: The Making of Recent Policy in Canada*. Toronto: University of Toronto Press.

Smiley, Donald V. (1965). "The two themes of Canadian federalism." *Canadian Journal of Economics and Political Science* 31:80–97.

Spiro, Herbert J. (1968). "The federation of Rhodesia and Nyasaland." In Thomas M. Franch (ed.), *Why Federations Fail*. New York: New York University Press.

Stein, Michael (1968). "Federal political systems and federal societies." *World Politics* 20:721–37.

Stokes, William S. (1961). "The centralized federal republics of Latin America." In George C. S. Benson (ed.), *Essays in Federalism*. Claremont: Institute for Studies in Federalism.

Stolberg, Winton (1958). *The Federal Convention and the Formation of the Union of the American States*. New York: Liberal Arts Press.

Stolz, Otto G. (1974). *Revenue Sharing: Legal and Policy Analysis*. New York: Praeger.

Sundquist, James L., and David W. Davis (1969). *Making Federalism Work*. Washington, D.C.: Brookings Institution.

Tarlton, Charles D. (1965). "Symmetry and asymmetry as elements of federalism: a theoretical speculation." *The Journal of Politics* 27:861–74.

Temple, Sir William (1932). *Observations upon the United Provinces of the Netherlands*. Reprint from 3d ed., 1676. (Originally published 1672). Introduction by G. N. Clark. Cambridge: Cambridge University Press.

Tilman, R. O., and Taylor Cole, eds. (1962). *The Nigerian Political Scene*. Durham: Duke University Press.

Trager, Frank N. (1968). "The Federation of Malaysia." In Thomas M. Franch (ed.), *Why Federations Fail*. New York: New York University Press.

Triepel, Heinrich (1924). "Der Federalismus und die Revision der Weimaren Reichsvergossung." *Zeitschrift fur Politik* 14:28.

Trotter, R. G. (1924). "Some American influences upon the Canadian federation movement." *Canadian Historical Review* 5:213–28.

Trudeau, Pierre-Eliott (1968). *Federalism and the French Canadians.* Toronto: Macmillan.

Truman, David (1955). "Federalism and the party system." In Arthur MacMahon (ed.), *Federalism: Mature and Emergent.* Garden City: Doubleday.

Venkataraman, K. (1968). *States' Finances in India.* London: Allen and Unwin.

Vile, M. J. C. (1961). *The Structure of American Federalism.* London: Oxford University Press.

Wagner, Richard E. (1971). *The Fiscal Organization of American Federalism.* Chicago: Markham.

Wagner, W. J. (1959). *The Federal States and Their Judiciary.* Hague: Mouton.

Waite, P. B., ed. (1963). *The Confederation Debates.* Toronto: McClelland and Stewart.

Watts, R. L. (1966). *New Federations: Experiments in the Commonwealth.* Oxford: Clarendon Press.

Wechsler, Herbert (1955). "The political safeguards of federalism: the role of the states in the composition and selection of the national government." In Arthur MacMahon (ed.), *Federalism: Mature and Emergent.* New York: Doubleday.

Weiner, Myron (1967). *Party Building in a New Nation: The Indian National Congress.* Chicago: University of Chicago Press.

Welch, Claude E. (1966). *Dream of Unity: Pan Africanism and Political Unification in West Africa.* Ithaca: Cornell University Press.

_____ (1969). "Federalism and political attitudes in West Africa." In Kenneth Kirkwood (ed.), *African Affairs #3.* London: Oxford University Press.

Wells, Roger (1961). *The States in West German Federalism, 1949–60.* New York: Bookman Associates.

Wheare, K. D. (1956). *Federal Government.* 3d ed. London: Oxford University Press.

Whitelaw, W. Menzies (1938). "American influence on British federal systems." In Conyers Read (ed.), *The Constitution Reconsidered.* New York: Columbia University Press.

Wildavsky, Aaron (1961). "Party discipline under federalism." *Social Research* 28:437–58.

_____, ed. (1967). *American Federalism in Perspective.* Boston: Little, Brown.

_____, ed. (1969). *The Presidency.* Boston: Little, Brown.

Ylvisaker, Paul (1956). *Intergovernmental Relations at the Grass Roots.* Minneapolis: University of Minnesota Press.

_____ (1959). "Criteria for a 'Proper' areal division of governmental powers." In Arthur Maass (ed.), *Area and Power.* Glencoe, Ill.: Free Press.

Yurchenko, O. (1956). *The Nature and Function of Soviet Federative Forms.* Munich: Institute for the Study of the USSR.

3
EXECUTIVES

ANTHONY KING

INTRODUCTION: THE LIMITATIONS OF THE LITERATURE

Surprising as it may seem in view of the central role played by executives in all political systems, there is remarkably little academic literature on the subject. To be sure, there are any number of textbooks on the American presidency and a certain number of studies of the British cabinet. But there is hardly anything on the executives of most other countries and almost nothing by way of a genuinely comparative literature. Wildavsky (1969) has drawn attention to the irony of the situation: "The eminence of the institution ... is matched only by the extraordinary neglect shown to it by political scientists" (p. ix). Although made with specific reference to the United States, Wildavsky's remark is much more generally applicable.

Moreover, small though it is, the volume of literature on executives is not matched by an equal volume of what can reasonably be called research. Most of the available literature is based on secondary sources and is impressionistic and repetitive. Students of executives seem peculiarly prone to taking in one another's washing. To read most general studies of the United States presidency, for example, is to feel that one is reading not a number of different books but essentially the same book over and over again. The same sources are cited; the same points are made; even the same quotations ("bully pulpit," etc.) appear again and again. In addition, the existing literature is mainly descriptive and atheoretical: general hypotheses are almost never advanced and, when advanced, almost never tested. Largely for this reason, a subject that might be thought to bristle with difficulties has so far aroused remarkably little scholarly —as distinct from purely political—controversy, about either methodology or substantive research findings.

What explains this neglect? One factor is undoubtedly the problem of

173

access to information. For reasons that would themselves be interesting to go into, executives typically conduct their business in secret. They meet behind closed doors; they do not, Nixon apart, keep verbatim records of their proceedings; their papers are not published until after considerable lapses of time, if at all. Executives are not in the business of divulging information. Typically, they divulge it only when it suits their convenience or when they are forced to (see Rourke, 1961). The flow of information from executives is thus even more partial and distorted than from other branches of government. Moreover, even if this were not the case, it would still be true that men and women in executive positions are busy people—frequently, alas, too busy to answer the questions of importunate academics.

A second factor accounting for the neglect is that the actions and deliberations of executives tend to be difficult to analyze quantitatively. This is partly because the number of cases available for analysis is small—for example, there have been only thirteen American presidents in this century compared with more than four thousand members of Congress—and partly because, as Wildavsky points out, it is hard to know what one's units of analysis should be. In the case of legislatures (or at least in the case of some of them), the roll-call vote is readily available as a behavioral datum to which other kinds of data—attitudinal, situational, and so on—can be linked. But what is the comparable datum in the case of executives? The decision? The interaction? The initiative? The policy? All of these present formidable problems of conceptualization and operationalization.

Yet these two factors, taken by themselves, are not really enough. For one thing, although the problems of access and quantification/precision may be particularly acute in the executives field, they are hardly peculiar to it: they arise in many other fields—interest groups, for example—in which much of the work is of a high order nonetheless. For another, although there exist few outstanding pieces of executives research, enough are available to show what is possible. Intelligent inference can be a substitute for access; analysis can be rigorous without necessarily being quantitative. One suspects that executives have been neglected, not because research in this field is, in some sense, impossible, but rather because of the vagaries of academic fashion. In recent years intellectually ambitious researchers have tended to move into fields such as voting behavior mainly because relevant data' are available but also because in such fields it is not difficult to identify the intellectual challenges. Executives have been neglected because data are harder to come by, to be sure, but also because it has been less clear what the intellectual challenges are. What are the big questions in executives research? No one seems to know. One of the purposes of this chapter is to suggest some of them.

The paucity of executives research means that what follows is more restricted in scope than would have been ideal. A choice had to be made between trying to survey the whole of the literature and concentrating on certain limited portions of it. It seemed better to go for concentration: a survey of the whole literature would have been extraordinarily diffuse; also, by concentrating, one can determine which bits are missing from the overall picture and which specific questions need to be asked if they are to be filled in. The concentration in this chapter is along two dimensions. First, the bulk of it deals with the United States and Great Britain, though a number of points concerning other countries will be made. Second, the chapter deals with only four selected topics: the recruitment of executives, the internal dynamics of executive institutions, the relations between executives and legislatures, and psychological approaches to the study of executives. Other topics are touched on, but only in passing.

It would be good at this stage to be able to plunge straight in: questions of substance are always more interesting than questions of definition. The trouble is that, if one were to plunge straight in, it would not be at all clear what one was plunging into. The term "executive" is so familiar that probably most people assume they know what it means. And in a vague sort of way they undoubtedly do. But in fact the various attempts that have been made to spell out its implications suggest that we should not take too much for granted: there are almost as many views about what executives are as there are writers on the subject. Accordingly, the next two sections deal with problems of definition— the greater one of trying to understand what an executive is and the lesser one of deciding which of all of the possible definitions of executives we should try to work with.

THE GREATER PROBLEM OF DEFINITION: WHAT IS AN "EXECUTIVE"?

It is of course the case that there exist in the real world institutions and clusters of institutions to which men attach the labels "the legislature," "the executive," and the "judiciary." Sometimes the labelling is formal and has firm legal foundations, as in the United States; sometimes it is largely informal, as in Britain. The practice of labelling institutions in this way is remarkably widespread. Even in the Soviet Union the constitution contains references to "the legislative power of the USSR" and to "the highest executive and administrative organ of the state power." But, as we have already suggested, the use of these labels— and in particular the use of the label "executives"—has to be explained. It is by no means obvious why, for example, institutions as dissimilar as the American presidency and the British cabinet should both be thought of as executives, or why agencies as diverse as (say) the Secret Service, the Employees Compensation Appeals Board, and the Bonneville Power Administration should all, legally, form part of the executive branch in the United States.

What accounts for this conventional labelling? Three different sorts of explanation have been advanced: one in terms of the functions of the various institutions, another in terms of their operating procedures, a third in terms of what one might call (inelegantly) their "historical/normative" development. The three types of explanation do not logically preclude one another; they could all be true at the same time. But, as we shall see, one of them—the one in terms of historical/normative development—is almost certainly closer to the truth than the other two. We shall consider each in turn.

The Answer in Terms of Functions

The first of the three explanations posits that the three familiar structures of government—the legislature, the executive, and the judiciary—correspond to three functions of government—the legislative, the executive, and the judicial. The fullest discussions of this explanation are to be found in Finer (1949), Gwyn (1965) and Vile (1967). Vile, in his study of the doctrine of the separation of powers, points out that those who hold to this doctrine maintain that the three functions exist and, moreover, that they exist to be performed in all governmental situations without exception—"whether or not they are in fact all performed by one person or group, or whether there is a division of these functions among two or more agencies of government" (p. 16). In other words, according to the holders of the doctrine the existence of the functions is in effect a sociological truth or law. Vile notes that this particular conception of the functions of government is highly abstract and is to be distinguished from the more mundane listings of governmental functions that include such items as keeping the peace, providing for defense, building roads, and so on.

The modern idea of the three functions took a long time to develop. Men at first conceived of two functions only: the legislative and the executive. The legislative function was conceived of as the law-making function, the executive function as the law-enforcement function; thus, the executive function at first encompassed what was later thought of as the separate judicial function. By the middle of the seventeenth century the judicial function was beginning to be separated out from the executive ("And why," asked one writer, "may not the Sacred Trinity be shaddowed out in Bodies Politick, as well as in Naturall?" [Vile, p. 15]), but the executive function was at this time thought of as being limited to carrying out the will of the courts. In other words, the executive function, which was once thought of as encompassing the judicial function, was now considered merely ancillary to it. The modern conception emerged between 1650 and 1750. Lawson, Locke, and—with especial clarity—Montesquieu asserted the view that (as Vile puts it, p. 90) "to legislate is to make the law; to execute is to put it into effect; the judicial power is the announcing of what the law is by the settlement of disputes." These functions, it was widely believed, exhausted the "powers" of government: there were three functions and no more. It was also widely believed that the three functions could clearly be distinguished from one another.

Recent writers, notably Almond (1960), have taken up much the same position. Indeed Almond, conscious that he is merely adapting well-established categories, does not redefine the three traditional functions. Instead, referring to them as "output functions" or as the "authoritative governmental functions," he simply gives them new names. The legislative function becomes "rule-making," the executive function "rule application," and the judicial function "rule adjudication." Although Friedrich (1963) uses slightly different categories—rule-making, measure-taking, and dispute-settling—and others have used other terminologies, the only recent writer to break completely with the legislative/executive/judicial division is Loewenstein (1965), who suggests a new tripartite classification, consisting of policy determination, policy execution, and policy control. Loewenstein's classification has not caught on, however, and it is the Montesquieu classification that most people still use.

The question is: Can the Montesquieu classification be used to explain our customary three-part labelling of institutions? One might suppose that it can. On a naive view, executives are institutions that execute; legislatures are institutions that legislate; judiciaries are institutions that judge. Just like that.

But in fact the Montesquieu classification, as a rationale for the labelling of institutions, is open to at least three serious objections. One of them is familiar; the other two are less so. The familiar objection has been advanced by Finer, Almond, and many others. These writers begin by accepting the Montesquieu classification itself; that is, they agree with Montesquieu that there are three functions of government and that these three functions can be distinguished from one another. But they then go on to point out that, although one may be able to distinguish among the functions, it is not the case that each branch of government performs one of them and only one. On the contrary, all governmental structures perform, and always have performed, several of them at once. All structures are multifunctional. There is no neat fit between structures and functions.

Legislatures do not monopolize rule making; executives do not monopolize rule application; judges do not monopolize rule adjudication. More than that, legislatures do not only make rules, executives do not only apply rules, judges do not only adjudicate. Congress intervenes in administration, the Supreme Court makes new law in the guise of interpreting old, the president initiates much legislation—and so on. All of this is true, and Finer is undoubtedly right to refer, with this in mind, to "the fall of the triad of powers" (p. 108).

The other objections, although less familiar, are at least as damaging—if anything, more so. The first denies what the other critics accept, namely, the Montesquieu classification itself. According to this objection, not only can one not assign each function neatly to each structure: one cannot even distinguish among the functions. In this view it may just be possible to distinguish conceptually—in some very abstract way—among acts of rule making, rule application, and rule adjudication; but in practice it is almost impossible to do so. The person who makes a new rule is almost invariably applying at least one old rule and adjudicating in terms of another. The application of existing rules practically always involves the working out of new ones. Acts of rule application are exceedingly hard to distinguish, even conceptually, from acts of rule adjudication. All of these points are apparent if one looks even briefly at any major decision of the United States Supreme Court; the Montesquieu classification simply breaks down. If it does, then the familiar Finer/Almond objection to the identification of structures with functions ceases to be an important empirical observation and becomes merely a truism. Obviously one cannot identify the structures with the functions if one cannot identify the functions in the first place.

The other less familiar objection is, if anything, even more damaging (since conceivably definitions of the functions of government that would meet the point just made could be produced). The Montesquieu classification, in Almond's version of it, asserts that each and every act of government can be construed as an act of rule making and/or rule application and/or rule adjudication. The business of government, in this view, has to do with rules and nothing else. This view, however, is contrary to all experience. Locke himself in the *Second Treatise* recognized that in the conduct of external relations governments were not to be thought of as putting the law into effect or as applying rules. He divided the executive function into two parts: one the law-applying function proper, the other a "federative" function. The federative function was conceived of as containing the "Power of War and Peace, Leagues and Alliances, and all the Transactions, with all Persons and Communities without the Commonwealth." Locke noted that the federative function was not capable of being directed by "antecedent, standing, positive laws" (Laslett, 1967, pp. 383–84). Vile, the only recent writer on the subject, takes Locke's point and is inclined, especially in connection with foreign affairs, to separate out a "discretionary" or "prerogative" function.

It is important to see, however, that this discretionary area of government does not relate only to foreign affairs. It also takes in such matters as the settlement of industrial disputes, the attempt to influence various forms of economic activity without resort to the law (for example, the establishment in the 1960s of "wage-price guidelines" in the United States), the conduct of enquiries and investigations, and the exercise or attempted exercise of moral leadership (for example, de Gaulle's attempts to restore the national pride of Frenchmen, or Churchill after Dunkirk). These kinds of activities are important; on occasion they may be all-important. Yet none of them has to do with "laws" or "rules" in any ordinary understanding of those terms. In other words, to perceive governmental action solely in terms of laws or rules is to misperceive it. That this simple fact is usually overlooked is a tribute to the hold that the Montesquieu formula still has on people's minds.

One other point should be noted in passing. It happens that in modern states most governmental activities that are not law-related or rule-related fall within the sphere of the institutions that we call the executive. Thus, if "rule making" will not do as a shorthand term for what legislatures do, "rule application" certainly will not do as a shorthand term for what executives do.

The Answer in Terms of Procedures

It follows from all this that the usual three-part division of governmental structures cannot be explained in terms of these structures performing discrete functions—or at least not the traditional ones. We must seek alternative explanations.

A possible alternative is one not in terms of functions but in terms of procedures. Jennings (1959b, p. 25) writes: "It is necessary to have at least three classes of authorities, but they are distinguished rather by their composition and their methods than by characteristics of their functions." Although Jennings does not spell the point out at any length, it is fairly clear what he has in mind. The point is that the different branches of government typically carry out their duties in different ways. Legislatures go in for public debate. They usually discuss a bill or motion with a view to arriving at some collective decision. Their elaborate rules are designed both to ensure orderly debate and to specify the means by which the final decisions shall be taken; similar rules ("parliamentary procedure") tend to be adopted by any body wishing to function in a debate/decision mode. Courts, by contrast, are not concerned with debate in the formal sense. Their procedures call for the examination and cross-examination of witnesses, the production of evidence, and the expounding of legal doctrine. Because legal doctrine is to be expounded, the personnel of courts—the judges—are normally expected to be learned in the law, whereas legislators are not normally expected to have any special qualifications. Executives operate differently again. They seldom debate in public; they often lack formal decision rules; their personnel may or may not be qualified; they deal in papers, files, minutes, telephone calls, and committee meetings. We take these different modes of procedure so much for granted that, if we were invited in a strange country first to listen to a formal debate, then to observe men in black robes listening to argument, then to attend an informal meeting in someone's private office, most of us would know without having to be told that we had visited in turn a legislative assembly, a court, and the office of some kind of executive.

All the same, any sustained attempt to account for the traditional three-part division in terms of these distinctive modes of procedure would be bound to fail. In the real world, none of the three branches of government employs one mode of procedure exclusively; nor, in the real world, is one mode of procedure employed exclusively by any one branch of government. On the contrary, each branch of government is "multiprocedural" and each mode of procedure is employed, at least on occasion, by more than one branch. Supreme Court justices in open court function in a judicial mode, but when they deliberate in private their discussions may be just as "executive" in style as those of (say) a meeting of the National Security Council. Legislatures not only debate, they also hold hearings and consider the details of legislation in committee. They may also behave like courts. The private bills procedure of the British Parliament, for instance, is highly judicial in form, and American legislatures function as courts in impeaching public officials. Executive agencies, for their part, seldom hold formal debates in public (though they do occasionally), but they frequently function in a judicial or quasi-judicial mode, as witness the hearings before a United States regulatory agency or the various administrative tribunals in Britain. The "fit" between procedures and institutions is thus very loose, far too loose to allow the one to be defined or explained completely in terms of the other.

And there is a further difficulty. It is fairly easy to characterize a legislative mode of procedure: the holding of debates, the moving of resolutions, etc. It is also fairly easy to characterize a judicial mode: the hearing of witnesses, etc. But it is virtually impossible to characterize an executive mode of procedure except by exclusion, that is, by saying that executive procedure is what legislative and judicial procedures are not. It was said above that executives typically "deal in papers, files, minutes, telephone calls and committee meetings." But so do legislatures and courts, and so do all sorts of other bodies—businesses and trade unions, for instance—that are not legislatures or courts or executives in the sense in which we are using these terms. This puzzling indeterminacy of executive procedures is related to the fact, noted earlier, that "rule application" will not do as a way of characterizing executive functions. The significance of these two points will become further apparent in a moment.

Historical/Normative Development

It seems, then, that there is no one-to-one relationship between the three branches of government and three types of governmental function. It also seems that there is no one-to-one relationship between the three branches and three different modes of procedure. Yet the three branches do exist, or at least we customarily think of them as existing. If neither a functional nor a procedural explanation will do, what are we left with?

The best answer is probably Finer's. To label it "historical/normative" is simply to draw attention to the fact that the modern idea of the tripartite division emerged in two related ways. In the first place, it emerged because in early modern times all governmental structures did—as a matter of historical fact—become increasingly differentiated into the now-familiar three branches. Second, it emerged because, also in early modern times, it was believed—normatively—that separate legislative, judicial, and executive institutions were a good thing: they were likely to promote liberty, justice, and so on. Independent legislatures and judicatures did not merely evolve from the sixteenth century onwards; they were often consciously created. Institutional developments gave rise to ideas; ideas gave rise to institutional developments. Not surprisingly, theories of the separation of powers, although they emerged partly in response to empirical circumstances, were, and are, more normative than empirical in content. As Vile puts it (1967, pp. 316–17), "The emergence of the idea of legislative and executive powers, or functions, had in itself little to do with an analysis of the essential nature of government: it was concerned more with the desire, by delimiting certain functional areas, to be able to restrict a ruler to a particular aspect of government and so to exercise limits on his power."

Finer would agree. What he says, in effect, is this. In the early stages of most political societies, power was exercised by an undivided government (or sovereign power or state). Whether this government or sovereign power was in the hands of a single ruler or a collectivity of some kind mattered less than the fact that there existed no institutionalized rivals to its authority. The state was a monolith. Inevitably, however, other centers of power, social and economic, emerged. These other centers of power usually lacked the strength to take over the state completely or else, recognizing the state's legitimacy, did not wish to do so. But they did want to limit the sovereign power and believed that the way to do this was either to create new institutions or to take over existing institutions with a view to converting them to their own purposes. The institutions so created or taken over were of two types. First, there were assemblies, or parliaments, which claimed to speak for those ruled by the sovereign and in time won the power to raise monies and make laws. Second, there were courts, which maintained the right to interpret the law irrespective of the wishes of the sovereign power and claimed that, whether the state liked it or not, the law was binding on both sovereign and subjects. The successful enforcing of these claims, where it occurred, transformed the state from a monolith into a trialith. It is with such trialiths that most of us in the West are still living.

This explanation of the modern division of governmental structure seems the most plausible. It also has an important corollary. The functional explanation sought to show that for each branch of government there was a function. The procedural explanation sought to show that for each branch of government there was a procedure. But the historical/normative explanation shows only that with the passage of time legislative and judicial institutions broke off, so to speak, from the central core of government. It says nothing about the emergence of executives precisely because executives did not emerge: being the central core of government, they were already there. The executive alone, on this account, does not need to be explained: it is neither more nor less than what is left of government (the greater part, as it happens) when legislatures and courts are removed.

If this view is accepted, it follows that there is little point empirically in trying to identify either functions or procedures that are uniquely the executive's: the executive is simply whatever the legislature and the judicature are not. In Finer's words, the executive has remained "the residuary legatee in government after other claimants like Parliament and the law courts have taken their share" (p. 575; see also Corwin, 1957, p. 3). It is this fact about executives which explains why "rule application" (or indeed "execution") is a peculiarly inadequate term for the activities of executives. It also explains why, whatever executives do, they do not do it in a single, characteristically "executive" way. To quote Finer again: "The executive comprises an assortment of functions which cannot be accurately inferred from the name, but can be known only by historic explanation and enumerative description" (p. 575).

This residuary-legatee view of executives has an additional advantage. It explains why the institutions we customarily bundle together under the heading "the executive" are so various. The legislative branch of government consists of the legislature. The judicial branch consists of the judiciary. But the executive branch, not being of the same type as the other two, consists not of a single structure or class of structures but of a wide variety of structures, including, in modern industrial states, monarchs, presidents, cabinets, central staffs, operating agencies, regulatory commissions, administrative tribunals, armed forces, investigatory commissions, advisory bodies, and publicly owned enterprises. Legislatures and judicatures are, so to speak, firms that specialize. Executives are conglomerates.

THE LESSER PROBLEM OF DEFINITION: WHICH "EXECUTIVES" TO STUDY?

The conglomerate nature of executives is reflected in the academic literature about them. Indeed most of the literature about executives is normally not thought of as being about executives at all. It is thought of as being about more or less separate entities within executive branches. There is a literature about bureaucracies, a literature about regulatory commissions and administrative tribunals, a literature about public enterprise, and so on. As a subject for study, in other words, the executive branch has been parcelled out among scholars with a wide variety of interests. It follows that, when we speak of "executives" in the discipline of political science, we usually have something more precise in mind. We are referring not to executive branches as a whole but to what the Marxists would call their "leading elements": to the people who run them, to top management.

Even so, a minor problem of definition remains, since it is not quite clear who we should regard as comprising top management. Some writers use the term executives to include both politicians and higher civil servants. Others (Meynaud, 1967; Curtis, 1968) use it to refer only to politicians (in other words, to what we generally call "the government" or "the administration," in the sense of "the Wilson government" or "the Kennedy administration"). Others (Dorsey, 1966; Fried, 1966) use it still more precisely to refer not to the whole of a government or administration but to the presumed locus of power within it: the president, cabinet, or whatever. Other writers, of course, are concerned only with heads of government, or so-called chief executives.

The rest of this chapter will take something of a middle way, more for reasons of convenience than anything else. It will deal with heads of government and also with the very top echelons of political administration, that is, with cabinets and leading staff personnel. It will not deal either with civil servants or with political executives of below cabinet rank. Civil servants have been excluded partly because they are dealt with elsewhere in this volume. Sub-cabinet political executives have been excluded solely because, apart from the Brookings studies in the United States (Mann and Doig, 1965; Stanley, Mann, and Doig, 1967; David and Pollock, 1967) almost nothing has been written about them. The focus of this chapter, in short, is on the top one or two dozen men and women who take—or are supposed to take—the top policy decisions.

EXECUTIVE RECRUITMENT

There are a number of reasons why one might be interested in executive recruitment. First, one might want to know what the recruitment process in a country tells one about the country's overall social structure: for example, if the pattern of recruitment is elitist, is the society also elitist? Second, one might be interested in what the recruitment process reveals about the organizations doing the recruiting—usually, in Western democracies, the political parties. Third, one might be interested in executive recruitment because one is actually interested in executives; that is, one might want to know what effects different recruitment processes have on the functioning of different executive institutions. What difference does it make that British party leaders are chosen by their parliamentary colleagues while American presidential nominees are chosen by national conventions? What difference does it make that British prime ministers choose their own cabinet colleagues while in Australia the members of Labor cabinets are elected by the Labor caucus? And so on.

There is a considerable volume of research on the relationship between recruitment and social structure (on the United States, see Warner *et al.*, 1963; Mann and Doig, 1965; Stanley, Mann, and Doig, 1967; Henry, 1969; on Britain, Bonnor, 1958; Guttsman, 1963; on Canada, Porter, 1965; on Australia, Encel, 1961, 1970; on the Netherlands, Dogan and Scheffer-Van der Veen, 1957). There is also a considerable volume of research dealing either with political parties or with recruitment processes for their own sake (on the United States, David, Moos, and Goldman, 1954; David, Goldman, and Bain, 1960; Tillett, 1962; Pomper, 1966; Davis, 1967; Polsby and Wildavsky, 1973; Matthews, 1973; Barber, 1974; on Britain, Carter, 1956; Willson, 1959; Buck, 1963a, 1963b;

Heasman, 1963; McKenzie, 1963; King, 1966b; on Canada, Punnett, 1969, 1970; Santos, 1970; LeDuc, 1971; Baar and Baar, 1973; on France, Melnik and Leites, 1958). But almost nothing has been written which seeks in a sustained way to relate executive recruitment to executive functioning. In the words of Heclo (1973): "Probably the greatest lack at present in the study of executive recruitment is the failure to establish any reliable connection between different selection processes and the winners' subsequent behavior in office" (p. 44). Indeed almost the only efforts to establish this connection are those of Bryce (1893), Rose (1971), Heclo, and Headey (1974a, 1974b).

The existing literature has another unfortunate characteristic: almost all of it is about the United States. Very little, if anything, has been written about executive recruitment in most other countries. Table 1 has the effect of indicating what the gaps are. Only reasonably thorough pieces of work have been cited; the more substantial is set in boldface type. In view of the number of gaps—more will become apparent as we proceed—the two parts of this section will each conclude with a brief summary of research that might usefully be done.

TABLE 1   Academic literature on executive recruitment in a number of countries other than the United States

	Head of government	Cabinet officers, ministers
Comparative	**Matthews (1973)**	—
Great Britain	—	Jones (1965)
France	Kaminsky (1973)	—
West Germany	—	Loewenberg (1967)
Canada	Baar and Baar (1973)	—
Australia	—	—
New Zealand	—	—
Italy	—	—

Heads of Government

In most countries the procedures for choosing the head of government differ sharply from those for selecting other executive personnel. The head of government is usually seen as by far the most important individual in the government. Moreover, because in most countries he chooses the ministers who will serve under him, the method used for selecting him obviously cannot also be used for selecting them. We shall therefore treat heads of government and other ministers separately.

One further point must be borne in mind. Almost all countries make a distinction between the process of selection or nomination, which is usually a party process, and the process of election proper, which is usually a mass-electoral process. Most, though not all, of the important differences between countries lie in the area of selection, not in the area of election. It is therefore mainly selection that will be considered below.

Selection Processes

It is possible analytically to make a distinction between the body of those who do the choosing, whether of a chief executive or anything else, and the methods by which they make their choice. The electoral system can change while the electorate remains the same; the electorate can change without changes being made in the electoral system. We will take these two matters together, however, because almost all of the countries that we know about exhibit both distinctive bodies of choosers and distinctive methods of choice.

For most countries there is no problem in finding out who the choosers are and how, at least formally, the choices are made. The only major country about which there is something of a mystery is France, in which, by 1975, only three elections for the presidency had been held since the introduction of direct elections—only two since the retirement of de Gaulle. It is clear that in France the choosers now include the mass electorate; but, as Kaminsky (1973) has shown, it is not clear who the other choosers are or what methods of choice will eventually be adopted. On the one hand, anyone is entitled to run for the office who can obtain the signatures of a hundred "eligible sponsors." On the other hand, no nominating agencies exist in France equivalent to the American conventions, and certainly there are no primaries.

The main points concerning methods of chief-executive recruitment in a number of other countries are set out in the five columns of Table 2. The headings at the top of the columns should be largely self-explanatory. "Election direct or indirect" refers not to the American distinction between the voters and the electoral college (United States presidential elections are taken to be direct) but to the distinction between elections in which the head of government is elected independently of parliament (e.g., in the United States and France) and those in which his election is the consequence of the success of his party in parliament (e.g., in Britain and West Germany). "Selection related to election timing?" refers to whether or not the nominee or leader is selected immediately prior to his standing for election, as in the United States, or at some more or less random time, as in parliamentary countries.

Table 2 suggests a number of questions. One, arising out of column 2, concerns the consequences of the fact that nominees and party leaders in some countries are chosen exclusively by members of the national legislature, while in other countries the choice is made by bodies in which members of the legislature play little part. To take two extreme examples, in Britain members of

TABLE 2   Features of head-of-government selection in various countries

	Chosen by members of national legislature?	Selection related to election timing?	Primary elections?	Election direct or indirect?	Choice usually result of interparty bargaining?
United States	No	Yes	Yes	Direct	No
Great Britain	Yes	No	No	Indirect	No
France (Fourth Republic)	Yes	No	No	Indirect	Yes
France (Fifth Republic)	No	Yes	No	Direct	No
West Germany	Yes	No	No	Indirect	No(?)
Canada	Yes	No	No	Indirect	No
Australia	Yes	No	No	Indirect	No
New Zealand	Yes	No	No	Indirect	No
Italy	Yes	No	No	Indirect	Yes

Parliament elect party leaders entirely on their own, while in 1972 in the United States members of Congress constituted only 1.8 percent and 5.3 percent of the delegates to the two parties' national conventions (the Democratic and Republican respectively). In Canada the figure is larger than in the United States but much smaller than in Britain—in the order of 15 percent (Baar and Baar, 1973). The proportion of members of national legislatures might not matter greatly if it were the case that, however small their numbers, they dominated the selection process nonetheless. But they do not do so in the United States and Canada, and there is no reason to believe that they do elsewhere.

What follows? Two sorts of things might be expected to. First, one might expect differently constituted bodies of choosers to consider different sorts of persons as being eligible to be chosen. This possibility will be discussed below when we consider eligibility (or, as the Americans say, "availability"). Second, one might expect differently constituted bodies of choosers to employ different criteria of choice. On the face of it, it would be surprising if bodies as differently constituted as parliamentary parties and national conventions chose their leaders/nominees on exactly the same basis. It is of course extremely difficult in nonexperimental situations to be sure what criteria any body of choosers is employing. On the one hand, the survey method is not wholly adequate, since the responses of choosers to survey questions may conflict with what appears to be the logic of their actual choices. On the other, it is not enough to rely on drawing inferences from the choosers' behavior, since—apart from any difficulties there may be in discovering what their behavior was—the same behavior is usually consistent with more than one set of criteria. All the same, it is odd that very few writers have addressed themselves, except in passing, to the whole question of criteria, which one might have supposed was central.

The exceptions include Polsby and Wildavsky (1973, Chapter 2) on the United States, King (1966a) on Britain, and Heclo (1973) on both. One has only to set the Polsby/Wildavsky and the King criteria side by side (Heclo does not differ substantially from the other two) to see that if these writers are correct, the United States and Britain differ strikingly (Table 3). Moreover, even the criteria that are the same in the two systems are likely to be ranked differently. For example, British M.P.s choosing a new party leader in (as is usual) a nonelection year might be expected to give less weight to electoral considerations than American convention delegates choosing a presidential candidate only a few weeks before polling day. Although no evidence is available on multiparty systems, one might suppose that in them party leaders would be chosen, in addition, on the basis of their ability to do business with other party leaders, especially with potential coalition partners.

TABLE 3   Selection criteria employed by American convention delegates, British M.P.s

United States	Great Britain
Ability to help party win election(s), e.g., by making good personal impression, winning uncommitted, holding party together for electoral purposes	Same
Acceptability in terms of policy, ideology	Same
Capacity to be successful president	Capacity to be successful prime minister
—	Ability to lead party in legislature
—	Ability to hold party together in long term
—	Effect of personality on members of legislature, who must "live with" leader on day-to-day basis for long period
Likelihood of head of government's granting favors to individuals, regions, localities	—
Likelihood of head of government's strengthening local party organization	—

If different selection criteria are in fact employed in different systems, this could be of considerable significance for the way executive institutions function. Bryce (1893) maintained that great men were not chosen as presidential candidates partly because of the way American convention delegates ranked the first two criteria listed in the table: "To [an American] party it is more important that its nominee should be a good candidate than that he should turn out a good President" (p. 79). It is not clear, incidentally, that Bryce was wrong. If the quality of presidential candidates has improved since he wrote (an arguable point), it may be not so much because convention delegates have come to rank the criteria differently as because they have revised "upwards," as it were, their notion of what makes a good president and, more important, have altered their conception of what constitutes "a good candidate" in the electorate's eyes.

More recently, Heclo has drawn attention to two possible consequences of these Anglo-American differences. First, the heavy emphasis laid in the British system on a leader's ability to preserve party unity frequently leads to the election of compromise candidates and, more generally, "suggests a concern for more cooperative and less openly combative qualities" (p. 33). It is evident, although Heclo does not say so, that a cooperative leader lacking in combative qualities might make quite a different prime minister from someone more combative and less cooperative. Heclo points out in the same vein that in the British system an extremely intimate and pervasive attention is likely to be paid to nuances of personality. Second, Heclo maintains that, although perceived public opinion probably plays as large a part in British leadership selection as in American, the greater emphasis placed in the United States on "palpable public appeal," together with the wider range of possible candidates considered, results in a greater unpredictability in the behavioral characteristics of presidents as compared with prime ministers: "Selection by the American process seems more likely than [by] the British to result in the election of unknown quantities" (p. 45). One need not accept Heclo's conclusions to see that he is raising important issues.

Of the other questions suggested by Table 2, one, dealing with timing (column 2) has already been touched on: it seems probable that the more closely related the selection of candidates and party leaders is to the holding of popular elections, the more likely it is that the selectors will have electoral criteria in mind. With regard to whether or not a country holds primary elections (column 3), it also seems highly probable—whether or not convention delegates are mandated by the primaries—that the salience of electoral criteria will be increased (see Davis, Chapers 4, 10). More important—although it is hard to be sure, since only the United States has experimented with national primaries—it seems probable that primaries, were they to be introduced elsewhere, would have the effect of extending the range and increasing the number of potential leadership candidates. Parliamentary parties would not be able, in effect, to preselect potential leaders. Even in convention systems such as the Canadian there would always be an incentive for would-be leaders, especially those unsure of their standing in the convention, to try their luck in the primaries. That primaries have, for better or worse, extended the range of choice in the United States is suggested, though not proved, by Pomper (1966, Chapter 5).

The effects of directly electing heads of government (column 4) are especially difficult to disentangle from the effects of other constitutional provisions, since, while all presidential systems provide for direct elections, no parliamentary system does. Heclo, in the paper already cited, suggests that there are likely to be three effects. First, the experience of direct election is likely to produce leaders conditioned to paying a good deal of attention to public preferences in justifying their actions. Second, a directly elected head of government is likely, irrespective of formal constitutional provisions, to have an individualistic rather than a collegial perspective on his office: he is likely to be concerned less with teamwork and more with the exercise of individual leadership. Third, in Heclo's view, the directly elected leader, at least if he has had to rely largely on his own efforts for election, will probably have learned to seek assistance from fairly wide circles of political and social leadership and not only from the legislature and the civil service.

The experience of Fifth Republican France is relevant here, since direct election was introduced in 1962 without any other major constitutional change. From the point of view of testing Heclo's hypotheses, it is unfortunate that the same man, de Gaulle, was president both before and after the change to direct election: instead of the election method inducing a conception of the office, de Gaulle's conception of the office induced the election method (Williams and Harrison, 1971, Chapter 10). Most writers on France, however, (Avril, 1969; Blondel and Godfrey, 1968; Williams and Harrison, 1971; Charlot, 1971) incline to the view that direct elections in France have had, or will have, the effects, first, of enhancing the president's moral authority; second, of forcing him to act as leader of the majority and not merely as *arbiteur;* and third, of tipping the balance of the constitution decisively away from parliamentarianism towards presidentialism.

It goes without saying that whether or not a head of government is chosen as the result of interparty bargaining (column 5) is likely to have a profound impact on his subsequent conduct in office. It is also the case that the role of head of government is likely to be quite different in a political system characterized by coalition and minority governments than in systems in which the existence of a stable, single-party majority is the norm. Since, however, there is no academic literature bearing directly on these matters (though see MacRae, 1967), and since the observed effects are probably less the result of the method of selection than of the party system underlying it, the subject will not be pursued here.

Those Eligible for Selection and Those Selected

We come now to the question of eligibility (or "availability"). This question is, in principle, quite distinct from the questions about bodies of choosers and methods of choice that we have just been dealing with. In principle, any set of decision rules could be combined with any set of eligibility rules: American conventions could decide to nominate for the presidency only congressmen and senators; British parliamentary parties could decide to consider as eligible for selection as party leaders not only M.P.s but also business people and trade union leaders. In practice, however, as was suggested earlier, the body of choosers and the methods of choice in a given system might be expected to have considerable impact on who is considered eligible to be chosen in that system.

The obvious hypothesis is that the larger the part played in the selection process by members of the legislature, the more probable it is that only members of the legislature will be considered. Conversely, the larger the part played by nonmembers, the more probable it is that a wider range of candidates will be considered—and possibly also a larger absolute number. That this hypothesis is indeed correct is suggested not so much by the contrast between the United States and Britain, countries with quite different constitutional systems, as by the contrast between Canada and Britain. Both Canada and Britain have parliamentary systems. Whereas, however, in Britain party leaders are chosen only by M.P.s, in Canada they are chosen by national leadership conventions in which, as we saw, M.P.s and senators are in a small minority. In Britain, no non-M.P. (except Lords Home and Hailsham in the rather peculiar circumstances of 1963) has been seriously considered for the leadership of either major party since at least 1922. In Canada, by contrast, of the twenty contenders for the leadership at the 1967 and 1968 major party conventions, the Progressive-Conservative and the Liberal, no fewer than eight were not M.P.s at the time they stood; a non-M.P., the premier of Nova Scotia, was in fact elected on the Conservative side.

The two Canadian conventions, moreover, not merely considered non-M.P. contenders: they also considered a larger number of M.P.s than either British party probably would have under comparable circumstances. One cannot be categorical about this, since the British Conservatives introduced a fully elective method for choosing their leader only in 1965, but it is probably fair to say that in this century no major British party has seriously considered more than four candidates for its leadership at any one time. By contrast, there were five M.P. contenders at the 1967 Conservative convention in Canada, seven at the Liberal convention in the following year. The difference is probably explained by the fact that, within the compass of a relatively small legislative party, a consensus is likely to develop about who are—and are not—potential leaders; developing over a number of years, the consensus is likely to exclude all but a handful of possibles. No such consensus is likely to develop under a convention system. Even if it did, aspiring leaders might well not have any way of knowing what it was.

In a country like Australia or New Zealand, where party leaders are selected in much the same way as in Britain, there is no particular problem about determining who is eligible for selection at any given moment. The eligibles comprise all of each party's M.P.s, or at least the half dozen or so leading M.P.s about whom a consensus has developed. In other countries, however, where the net is cast wider, it may be impossible to be sure: a Wendell Willkie or a Jean Lecanuet may suddenly come from nowhere. Eligibility should thus be thought of not as a dichotomy (eligibility/noneligibility) but as a continuum (more or less eligibility). Some potential heads of government will occupy the center of the political stage at any given moment; some will be in the wings; some will be waiting to be called on.

If the idea of a continuum is accepted, it follows that one can think in terms of assigning to every individual legally eligible to become head of government in a given political system a probability, politically determined, that he or she will make it to the top within a specified time. The probabilities will range from near zero in the case of the great mass of the population, through somewhere between (say) 0.001 to 0.01 in the case of the holders of minor political offices, to something approaching 1.0 in the case of a majority-party leader running for office in an electorally good year for his party (for example, Roosevelt in 1936). Clearly, despite these examples, it is not possible to think in terms of an interval scale, that is, to assign precise probabilities numerically expressed. But, equally clearly, it is possible to think in terms of a rough ordinal scale, with some individuals having a better chance of becoming head of government than others: Nixon in 1972 a better chance than McGovern, McGovern a better chance than Wallace, and so on. Each individual's probability is likely to change through time. It is likely to be greater when he is middle-aged than when he is young or old; it will probably be greater if he already holds elective political office than if he does not.

From the point of view of the political scientist interested in executive recruitment, the value of assigning probabilities in this way lies not in the possibility of assigning them to individuals within a given system (which would be a very doubtful exercise at the margin) but rather in the possibility of identifying classes of political actors that have higher probabilities than other classes of actors within the same system—or, alternatively, higher probabilities than similarly placed actors in other systems. For instance, although one might be hard put to it to decide which of two prominent state governors in the United States had the better chance of becoming president, one can be quite sure that a randomly chosen American governor has a much better chance of becoming head of government in his country than any British politician not in the national legislature does in his; American governors are "available" in a way that British non-M.P.s are not. As in the case of individuals, the probabilities of classes of actors can change through time. For example, in the eighteenth and nineteenth centuries, members of the British House of Lords had a much better chance of becoming British prime minister than they do today.

To sum up, one can think of there existing for each political system at each point in time a frequency distribution of probabilities relating to individuals' chances of becoming head of government—or, more realistically, to the chances of whole classes of individuals (members of cabinets, members of legislatures, local government leaders, and so on). These distributions vary from system to system and from time to time. One might hypothesize that the distributions for the United States and Britain in the mid-1970s look something like Fig. 1. (The figure is meant only to convey the general idea and is not based on actual data.) What one wants to know is what the frequency distributions are in reality, how they vary, and, more to the point, what the consequences are of such distributions and such variations for the actual conduct of chief executives in office.

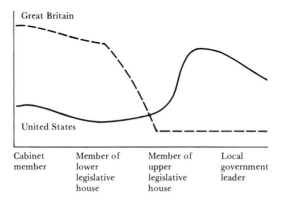

Fig. 1. Probabilities of individuals becoming head of government in United States, Great Britain (national data)

The sort of calculus outlined here underlies much of the writing about the recruitment of American presidents—for example, the well-known Hyman (1954) and Rossiter (1960) lists of qualifying and disqualifying attributes—but, rather surprisingly, only two efforts have been made to go into the subject in any detail: David, Goldman, and Bain (1960) and Pomper (1966). Pomper, exhibiting a commendable desire to test assertions and not merely make them, applied Hyman's nine criteria of eligibility to both the adopted candidates and the runners-up in the major parties in the period 1840–1960. He found that from 1928 onward "less available" candidates had in fact been adopted more often than "more available" ones and that (incumbent presidents apart) the less available candidate had more often won the election. To revert to the language used earlier, it seems that there may have occurred in the United States since 1928 a change in the distribution of probabilities (but cf. Elazar, 1965; see also Matthews, 1974).

Since no comparable work has been done on other systems—and in consequence no comparisons made between the eligibles in those systems and the individuals who actually succeeded in being selected—the rest of this section will deal only with those who succeeded, that is, with party leaders and nominees. Moreover, since data are not available for most countries, even on party leaders and nominees, it will deal exclusively with Britain and the United States.

British party leaders and American presidential candidates differ quite strikingly in their personal backgrounds, as might be expected given the different processes of recruitment in the two countries (on the United States, see David, Goldman, and Bain, 1960; Elazar, 1965; on Britain, Carter, 1956; on both, Heclo, 1973). All British leaders in the period 1900–1972 had served a long apprenticeship in the House of Commons, whereas only a minority of United States presidential nominees had served in Congress. All British leaders except Ramsay MacDonald had served in national cabinet-level office before their selection; at least fourteen United States nominees had not. Many more of the Americans than the British, by contrast, had served in government posts outside the national legislature and the politically appointed echelons of national government: in state and local government, in administration, even in the judiciary (Heclo, pp. 29–33). Moreover, although no detailed comparison has been made, it is clear that, whereas all of the British party leaders had been career politicians from an early age, at least a few of the American presidential candidates (e.g., Wilson, Willkie, Eisenhower) had not.

These findings are familiar, but their significance may be overlooked. The point is not (cf. Laski, 1940) that British prime ministers have had more previous administrative experience, as such, than American presidents. Indeed Heclo has shown that American presidential candidates have had, if anything, more such experience than British party leaders. The point is rather that more British prime ministers than American presidents have had previous experience directly relevant to the job of being head of government. First, almost all British prime ministers, because they have served in previous administrations, have observed at first hand the performance in office of at least one of their predecessors. The comparable figure for American presidents in this century is not more than 50 percent. Second, most British prime ministers have not only served in previous administrations but have served as head of one or more major departments. They know what it is like to run a major department; they are also likely to know a lot about at least one substantive field of government policy. Almost every British prime minister, in short, is familiar with both sides of the head of government/head of department (or bureau or agency) relationship. The only American presidents in the 1900–1972 period with comparable experience were Hoover and Franklin Roosevelt.

It is hard to believe that important consequences do not follow. It is equally hard to know what they are. The likelihood that American presidents will make more use than British prime ministers of assistance from outside the legislature and the civil service has already been referred to. It might also be expected that, other things being equal, presidents would be more inclined than prime ministers to think about the nature of their office (King, 1969, p. x) and to be innovative in exercising its functions. Whether or not this is part of the reason, it is certainly the case that the institutions surrounding the presidency have changed more radically over the past seventy years than those surrounding the prime ministership. (The last major institutional change affecting the workings of the British prime ministership, the introduction of the Cabinet Secretariat, took place in 1916; see Mosley, 1969.) The experience of sitting in cabinet, however, although it may make prime ministers less innovative institutionally, may also make them less heavily reliant on the advice of subordinates. At the very least, the problems of the transition from one administration to another are likely to be less acute (on the United States, see Henry, 1960, 1961; on Britain, there is nothing).

Data on leaders' and candidates' personal characteristics are much harder to come by than data on their backgrounds. We know whether heads of government and potential heads of government in any given period went to Harvard or Oxford and whether or not they served in the cabinet; we do not know in any systematic way whether they were intelligent or stupid, industrious or idle, introverted or extroverted, compulsive or able to tolerate a high level of ambiguity. By the same token, we do not know whether different recruitment processes have a systematic tendency to select out different types of personality. Some work has, however, been done on the personality characteristics of (mainly) American presidents and this work will be considered below.

Tenure

Much more has been written on the circumstances of chief executives' acquiring power than—assassinations apart—on the circumstances of their surrendering it. Yet one might have thought that how heads of government lose power, or run the risk of losing it, was of considerable interest. Some heads of government, like American presidents, have their period of office limited by law; some, like most prime ministers in parliamentary systems, can be deposed.

Leaving aside some of the countries of Latin America, the United States is the only Western democracy in which legal restrictions on chief executives' tenure of office are common: there are restrictions at the national level, as the result of the Twenty-Second Amendment, and in twenty-five of the fifty states. Since only two presidents have served a second term since the ratifying of the Twenty-Second Amendment (Eisenhower and Nixon), it is hardly surprising that no research has been done into its consequences. But it is a little surprising that nothing has been done with respect to the states. On the face of it, a one- or two-term limitation might be expected to have widespread repercussions. A lame-duck president or governor would probably find his authority declining. He would probably find it hard to recruit officials to his administration. More important, he would not be in a position to make long-term commitments requiring future action by him: everyone would know that he would not be around to fulfill his part of any bargain. A lame-duck chief executive would still be able to deal with short-term crises, but one suspects that in most other respects his administration would cease to be effective.

An American president may have limited tenure, but at least his tenure is, between elections, secure (or at least seemed so until the 1970s). A British prime minister's tenure is, by contrast, legally unlimited, but under the constitution he can be removed from office at any moment. There has been some discussion about how vulnerable British prime ministers are in practice. McKenzie (1963) maintains that they are highly vulnerable, citing Asquith, Lloyd George, Chamberlain, Eden, and Macmillan as examples of prime ministers who have been deposed in this century. King (1966a) and Mackintosh (1968) maintain, to the contrary, that they are virtually invulnerable, that under anything like normal circumstances a prime minister determined to defend his position is almost impossible to depose.

From the point of view of the functioning of executive institutions, however, what matters is not whether a head of government can be deposed but whether he thinks he can. And it is clear that most British prime ministers do believe themselves to be vulnerable (see Jones, 1965). For this reason alone, quite apart from the other differences between the two systems, British prime ministers are likely, other things being equal, to be weaker within their administrations than American presidents are in theirs. They will be disposed to weigh more heavily the views of their senior colleagues, who may also be their potential rivals (or potential supporters of their potential rivals); they will be tempted to try to prevent senior colleagues from building up power and prestige; they will be circumspect in seeking to exercise leadership, since initiatives that fail may be taken as evidence of prime ministerial weakness and therefore also of vulnerability. In extreme circumstances a British prime minister, while still in office, may find himself in a less commanding position within his own cabinet than one or more of his senior colleagues (see Mackintosh, 1968; Jenkins, 1970).

If all this is true of Britain, it will be true of other similar systems. Unfortunately almost nothing has been written about the question of tenure in countries apart from Britain, though much about the position of French prime ministers in the Fourth Republic can be inferred from Williams (1964) and MacRae (1967). The shift in the Fifth Republic from parliamentarianism to presidentialism is attested to by the ease with which both de Gaulle and Pompidou dismissed prime ministers who no longer had their confidence, even though their position in the cabinet and the National Assembly was still intact (Avril, 1969; Charlot, 1971; Williams and Harrison, 1971). That West German chancellors have even more reason than British prime ministers to believe that they can be deposed is suggested by the fact that two of the four in the postwar period—Adenauer and Erhard—actually were. Merkl (1962) suggests that Adenauer's authority as chancellor became progressively weaker as his retirement approached.

Research

It will already be apparent to most readers that much more research needs to be done before we can even begin to test most of the hypotheses set out above. What specific pieces of research are needed will also be apparent. Nevertheless, it seems worthwhile to list the main ones. The following list is, of course, meant to be illustrative rather than exhaustive.

Research is needed into:

1. the methods used for recruiting party leaders and head-of-government nominees;
2. the criteria used by the recruiters in different parties and in different countries;
3. the consequences for the functioning of executive institutions of the fact that different leaders/nominees have been selected in different ways;
4. the different patterns of eligibility at different times and in different countries;
5. the consequences of these different patterns;
6. the tenure of office of heads of governments; and
7. the consequences of the fact that tenure is sometimes limited, sometimes unlimited, sometimes secure, sometimes insecure.

Ministers

Apart from the office of head of government, the range of other offices to be filled "politically"—that is, by other than civil service means—varies considerably from country to country. An incoming American president has more than 500 executive posts to fill (Henry, 1969), a British prime minister about 100 (Rose, 1971), a German chancellor between 30 and 100, depending on the circumstances (Sontheimer, 1972). Not only does the number of posts to be filled vary, so does their type. The appointing power of an American president reaches well down into each line department; it also extends outwards to his own staff and to agencies like the National Security Council and the Office of Management and Budget. A British prime minister, by contrast, is largely confined to filling the top few political posts in each line department. A German chancellor, by contrast again, although he makes a smaller absolute number of appointments than a British prime minister, can, unlike a prime minister, fill senior civil service posts on political grounds.

The potential significance of such differences is apparent. Other things being equal, the greater the number of political appointees in a government, the easier it will be, one might suppose, for the political echelons to control the nonpolitical. Equally, other things being equal, the larger the number of political appointments made directly by a head of government, the greater will be, one might suppose, that head of government's capacity to control his administration. Unfortunately neither of these matters is more than touched on in the literature. No comparative work has been done, and very little on any individual country. David and Pollock (1957) considered whether a clear line should be drawn in the United States between political and nonpolitical appointments and, if so, where the line should be drawn; and Fenno (1959), Mann (1964), and Henry (1960, 1961, 1969) have written about various aspects of appointments by American presidents. But neither they nor anybody else has made a detailed comparison between the United States and other countries, and the writings about other countries, insofar as they exist at all, are mainly impressionistic; they also deal largely with the appointment of cabinet ministers in the old-fashioned sense and not with the appointment of subcabinet ministers, civil servants, and chief executives' personal staffs. Our discussion as a result has to be very restricted in scope.

Selection Processes

In some countries, Britain and West Germany for instance, appointments to ministerial office are made formally by the head of state. In almost all countries, however, the real decisions are made by the head of government. The head of government may be required to make his appointments from among a specific category of persons (e.g., members of Parliament in Britain); he may be required to have his appointments confirmed by some other body (e.g., the Senate in the United States). But otherwise his choices are usually constrained only by the exigencies of politics.

The major exception is the position of Labor prime ministers in Australia and New Zealand. Since 1908 the Australian Labor party has required all cabinet ministers to be elected by the party's parliamentary caucus; the prime minister merely allocates portfolios (Encel, 1961, 1962; Crisp, 1955, 1965). The New Zealand Labour party has had a similar requirement since 1940. The election of ministers in this fashion might be expected to lead, first, to the choice of ministers whom the prime minister would not himself have chosen (possibly ministers of lower caliber); second, to a weakening of the prime minister's position with respect to other cabinet ministers; third, to an eroding of the British practice of collective ministerial responsibility, since ministers defeated in cabinet might be tempted to appeal to the parliamentary caucus against the cabinet; and fourth, for the same reason, to a strengthening of caucus's position vis-à-vis the cabinet. The writers cited above allude to these possibilities but do not deal with any of them in detail.

In systems in which heads of governments choose their own ministers, the details of the selection processes can vary from the intimate and face to face to the fairly highly bureaucratized. British prime ministers normally know personally all those they are likely to appoint. In the nineteenth century it was usual for incoming prime ministers to consult four or five senior colleagues before deciding on the composition of their cabinets (Mackintosh, 1968). Since about 1900, although detailed evidence is lacking, it seems there has been much less consultation (Mackintosh, 1968; Gordon Walker, 1972). Incoming American presidents, by contrast, because they have more posts to fill and because their range of choice is not restricted in the way a British prime minister's is, are likely not to know many of their potential appointees personally and therefore have to rely heavily on their advisers (Fenno, 1959; Henry, 1960, 1969). To the extent that this is so, American cabinet officers might be expected to regard themselves less as "president's men"—in office to do the president's bidding—than one might suppose in the light of their formal relationship of dependency on the president.

A perhaps more important distinction is between selection processes that have a "by fiat" character and those in which consultation merges into negotiation. In Britain and the United States, and in most countries in which single-party majority governments are the norm, the head of government has to weigh the political consequences of his choices but does not normally have to enter into bargaining relationships with others. In minority government and coalition situations, however, the selection of ministers becomes largely a bargaining exercise (in which the smaller coalition partners may successfully claim a disproportionate share of the posts; see Browne and Franklin, 1973). The best-documented cases are those of the Fourth French Republic (Williams, 1964) and West Germany (Loewenberg, 1967). The consequences of this mode of selection, as with the selection of heads of government, are hard to distinguish from the consequences of the minority government or coalition situation generally. In West Germany chancellors have consulted not merely potential coalition partners but also parliamentary leaders of their own party (Loewenberg, 1967) and even on occasion interest group leaders (Braunthal, 1965). It is not clear, however, why they have done so or what the consequences have been.

Those Eligible

Different heads of government not only have different numbers and kinds of offices to fill; they also have different numbers and kinds of eligible persons to draw on. American presidents are not formally restricted in any way, provided only that members of Congress appointed to cabinet office must resign their seats. British prime ministers are not formally restricted either, but seats must be found for appointees who are not members of Parliament, and most appointees in practice are M.P.s already (though see Willson, 1959). In France under the Fifth Republic the president and prime minister are not restricted, but, as in the United States, members of parliament who are made ministers must resign their seats. In the early days of the new Republic, most important

French ministers had not previously been members of parliament; by the late 1960s, however, almost all of the ministers were former deputies or senators, and only a handful of nonpolitical "technicians" remained (Pickles, 1972). The West German practice has evolved in a way similar to the British. The first Adenauer government, in 1949, contained a number of ministers who were not members of the Bundestag; but nonparliamentarian ministers have now virtually disappeared (Loewenberg, 1967). France apart, in parliamentary systems it is quite general for ministers to be required to be members of the legislature. One of the few exceptions is the Netherlands, where an incompatibility rule operates as in France and where in practice only a minority of ministers have had parliamentary experience (Dogan and Scheffer-Van der Veen, 1957; Lijphart, 1968).

The consequences of differing eligibility rules are likely to be important (Headey, 1974a). Rose (1971) has considered some of them with regard to Britain. First, since all British ministers apart from a few peers must be majority-party M.P.s and since some M.P.s will inevitably be ruled out on grounds of age or other incapacity, the total number of persons effectively eligible to be ministers is very small. As a result, the prime minister's range of choice is strictly limited and he may be forced to offer positions to persons he would not otherwise consider suitable. Second, there is no reason to suppose that the work of an M.P.—or even of a junior minister—provides the most suitable training for cabinet office. Third, the desire for office on the part of M.P.s may lead them to be more loyal to the prime minister than they would be otherwise. Headey (1974a, 1974b) develops a number of the same points. The main thrust of his argument is that, because most British ministers are members of Parliament without extensive nonparliamentary experience, they typically lack a variety of the skills appropriate to executive office, notably the capacity to innovate in complex situations. These scholars' conclusions must, of course, be somewhat speculative given the prevailing uncertainty about what makes a "good" minister and the lack of objective measures of ministerial performance; but the points they raise are important.

Another possible consequence of the differing eligibility rules in different systems has apparently not been considered in the literature, namely, the effect of the pattern of eligibility in a given political system on the political career structure in that system. In most parliamentary systems—certainly in Britain, where the parliamentary career structure and the ministerial career structure are linked indissolubly—almost everyone seeking a political career of any kind seeks to become an M.P.; the level of aspiration for ministerial office is high. There is, so to speak, a single political ladder and a high proportion of those on it would like to climb to the top. In the United States, by contrast, quite different kinds of political careers are possible, and there are very few would-be national leaders who aspire specifically to cabinet office, or even to other leading posts in the administration. On the one hand, posts in the executive branch are not uniquely valued in the United States as they are in Britain; an important congressional committee chairman is likely to believe he is doing as important a job as he would be in the executive. On the other hand, so many persons are potentially eligible for executive posts that it would be unrealistic for any individual to organize his career around the hope of obtaining one. Under the circumstances, it is not surprising that American presidents sometimes find it difficult to fill all the posts in their administrations, whereas British prime ministers never do. Four of Hoover's first choices for cabinet office refused (Fenno, 1959, p. 59); by contrast, Ramsay MacDonald complained that far too many M.P.s were all too keen to accept: "I have had people in here weeping and even fainting" (Mackintosh, 1968, p. 443). Schlesinger (1966) has considered aspects of the American political career structure, but no one has written on the subject comparatively.

Criteria

The question of eligibility shades imperceptibly into the question of the criteria that heads of government employ, consciously or unconsciously, in choosing their ministers. In one sense a British Labour M.P. is "eligible" to serve in a Conservative administration; in another sense he clearly is not. In many respects it is up to each head of government to decide who is eligible and who is not. The same sorts of distributions of probabilities could be worked out for cabinet ministers as for heads of government.

It was suggested above that in the case of the selection of heads of government the criteria employed would be influenced by the composition of the selecting body and also by the timing of the selection. In the case of the selection of cabinet ministers, the question of the composition of the selecting body does not arise, since in all countries (Australia and New Zealand always excepted) the selector is the same: the head of government. The selection criteria will therefore be determined by the head of government's personality, values, and political situation and, more generally, by the norms of his country's political system.

Rather more has been written about ministerial selection criteria than about criteria relating to chief executives (on the United States, Fenno, 1959, 1964; on Britain, Carter, 1956; Richards, 1963; Mackintosh, 1968; Rose, 1971; on Germany, Loewenberg, 1967; on Australia, Encel, 1962). Most of the writers make the distinction, rightly, between criteria relating to the selection of individual ministers and criteria relating to the composition of an administration overall.

That the criteria can differ widely as between two systems is suggested by Table 4, which compares those employed in Britain and in the United States. The table chiefly reflects the fact that, whereas American cabinet officers are mainly important simply as the heads of executive departments, ministers in Britain play a wider range of politically significant roles. The British cabinet

TABLE 4   Selection criteria employed by American presidents, British prime ministers

United States	Great Britain
Membership of head of government's party (with occasional exceptions)	Same (but with very rare exceptions)
General administrative competence (often)	— (unless contrary proven, not always even then)
Specific policy competence (often)	— (except occasionally)
Client-group connections (especially for some offices)	—
Region of origin (for some offices, also with regard to overall composition of cabinet)	— (except for secretary of state for Scotland)
Presumed loyalty to head of government	— (except at margins)
— (except occasionally)	Political weight (especially in governing party)
—	Debating ability (especially in legislature)
—	Previous governmental experience (usually in subcabinet office)

in some meaningful sense constitutes the country's political directorate in a way that the American cabinet does not. The criteria used in Britain therefore include a number that relate to what Rose (1971) calls the "solidary" aspects of government; as compared with the United States, "instrumental" criteria in Britain are at a discount.

Nevertheless, although the differences in the two sets of criteria to a large extent simply reflect the well-known structural differences between the two systems, they might also be expected to have consequences of their own. For example, quite apart from anything else, relations between political executives and career officials in two otherwise similar political systems might be expected to differ substantially if in one system the executives were chosen on the basis of specific policy competence whereas in the other they were chosen on the basis of, for instance, their appeal to the party faithful and their ability to make speeches. It would be interesting to know more about the consequences of the fact that in the Netherlands ministers are chosen very largely on the basis of their specific policy competence and indeed are often former career civil servants (see Dogan and Scheffer-Van der Veen, 1957).

To take another example, region of origin is a moderately important criterion in the United States and in Australia (Encel, 1961, 1970) and a very important criterion in Canada, where each province is expected to have at least one representative in the federal cabinet and where racial, religious, and other sectional criteria are also taken into account in a thoroughgoing way (Dawson and Ward, 1963). Given the particular character of the Canadian federation, the federal cabinet could in any case be expected to function to some degree as a sort of "council of the provinces"; but one supposes that the selection criteria used by heads of government reinforce this tendency and that these criteria might go on being used even if the objective "need" for them were to disappear (see Porter, 1965).

Those Selected

We pointed out earlier that the bulk of the literature on executive recruitment is concerned with the relationship between recruitment and social structure, with the part played by political parties, and/or with recruitment more or less for its own sake. Most of the literature specifically on ministerial recruitment also falls into one or another of these categories. Data on the social and educational backgrounds of cabinet-level executives are provided for the United States by Stanley, Mann, and Doig (1967); for Britain by Bonnor (1958), Guttsman (1963), and Buck (1963a); for Canada by Porter (1965); for Australia by Encel (1961, 1970); and for the Netherlands by Dogan and Scheffer-Van der Veen (1957). Data on ministers' previous experience of government are provided for the United States by Schlesinger (1966) and Stanley, Mann, and Doig (1967); for Britain by Buck (1963a, 1963b), Heasman (1963), and Willson (1959, 1970); for Canada by Porter (1965); and for the Netherlands by Dogan and Scheffer-Van der Veen (1957). Most of the socioeconomic background data are roughly comparable on a cross-national basis. Unfortunately most of the experience-of-government data are not; neither American study, for example, is as detailed with respect to cabinet-level personnel as are the corresponding British studies. More important, few writers are concerned with linking these background variables to actual ministerial behavior.

One exception is Mann and Doig (1965), whose findings are suggestive even though they relate only to subcabinet personnel. Mann and Doig obtained from 29 political executives and 14 career officials ratings on 317 subcabinet officers who had served in the Truman and Eisenhower administrations. The ratings suggested that government officials as a group were more successful as executives than were people who lacked governmental experience, but in general the ratings raised "serious doubts [about] whether there is any important causal relationship between occupational background and performance" (p. 247). The Mann-Doig findings suggest that the caliber and style of British and American executives may differ less than one might suppose from the fact that, at most, about two-thirds of American cabinet officers have had previous subcabinet administrative experience compared with nearly all cabinet ministers in Britain (Stanley, Mann, and Doig, 1967; Willson, 1959).

Another exception to the general rule that political scientists fail to link background variables to actual behavior is the paper of Edinger and Searing

(1967). Edinger and Searing were not in a position to measure behavior directly, and their data, drawn from France and West Germany, relate to a variety of political and quasi-political elites and not just to cabinet ministers. Their techniques are, however, relevant to the study of cabinet-level elites, and their principal findings—that different background variables predict different attitudes in different countries and that some commonly used background variables (e.g., education) scarcely predict attitudes at all—suggest that the accumulation of background data on political executives does not have much to be said for it unless the data can be shown explicitly to be related to other factors, themselves politically important.

A comment that should, however, be made about research of the Mann-Doig and Edinger-Searing types is that for some purposes its categories are too gross. For example, even if it were the case that executives with business backgrounds were in general no more successful than executives with governmental backgrounds, and even if it were the case that the possession of a business background by no means guaranteed the possession of particular attitudes over a wide range of issues, it might still be true that specific kinds of business experience—say, in banking or commerce—might be related in some important way to a minister's ability to execute policy in specific areas and to his conception of what his policies in those areas should be. One is told that, in choosing cabinet ministers, Clement Attlee spoke of "horses for courses." It would not be easy to produce operationally realizable typologies of horses and courses—that is, of ministers or potential ministers and of the specific posts to which they were or might be assigned—but, without such typologies, it is not at all clear how one proceeds in this field (cf. Rose, 1971).

Tenure and Turnover

It stands to reason that the functioning of executive institutions will be influenced not merely by the mode of selection of ministers and by their background characteristics but also by how long they remain in office and the ways in which they move, if they do move, from one office to another. A John Foster Dulles (tenure six years, two months) might be expected to make a greater impact than a Christian Herter (tenure one year, eight months); a system like the British, in which ministers are moved frequently from department to department, might be expected to differ from systems like the German or Dutch, in which a minister, once appointed to a particular department, usually remains in that department for the rest of his ministerial career. The question of ministerial dismissals and resignations is dealt with in the next section. Here we are concerned with tenure and turnover in their more routine, though no less important, aspects.

Data on duration of tenure and rates of turnover are provided for the United States by Stanley, Mann, and Doig (1967), for Britain by Rose (1971) and Headey (1974a), and for the Netherlands by Dogan and Scheffer-Van der Veen

(1957). Much fuller comparative data are provided by Herman (1975), though Herman unaccountably omits consideration of the United States. Herman shows not only that governments in the 1945–1971 period lasted much longer in some countries than in others (the West German average was 33.4 months, the Italian 6.1 months) but that individual ministers, on the average, held the same office for much longer periods in some countries than in others (the average tenure of seven senior ministerial posts in Sweden was 70.8 months, in West Germany 46.2, in Britain 27.5, in the French Fourth Republic a mere 12.9) and that the rate of both within-government and across-government ministerial turnover was enormously higher in some countries than in others (low in Sweden and the French Fifth Republic, much higher in Britain and Italy, highest in Finland and the French Fourth Republic).

It has long been assumed that ministerial instability in the French Fourth Republic conferred effective policymaking power on the bureaucracy in France (see Williams, 1964), and King (1966b, 1968, 1970) has speculated about the consequences of the high rate of ministerial turnover in Britain. He suggests, first, that the high rate of turnover means that a large proportion of Britain's ministers are at any given moment unfamiliar with the matters they are dealing with; second, that in consequence the influence of civil servants is almost certainly greater than it would be otherwise; and third, that, because British ministers know in advance that they will probably not remain in their current post for any substantial period of time, they are likely to be tempted on the one hand to try to make their reputations in fields that do not involve long-term policymaking and on the other hand not to devote too much time and energy to mastering their department's subject matter. These suggestions remain speculative, however, and King produces no hard evidence.

Research

As in the case of heads of government, it is probably worth listing at this point research that might usefully be done into the recruitment of ministers. Research is needed into:

1. the extent of the head of government's appointing power in different countries and the different ways in which the power is exercised;

2. more generally, the extent to which government posts in different countries are filled politically or by the civil service;

3. the practice of the Australian Labor and New Zealand Labour parties in electing cabinet ministers;

4. the different eligibility rules/norms for government posts in different countries and the consequences of these different rules/norms;

5. the relationships, if any, between different countries' different eligibility rules/norms and their political career structures;

6. the different criteria employed by different heads of government in different political systems and the consequences of such differences;

7. the different backgrounds of ministers in different systems and the consequences of these;

8. the varieties of ministerial posts needing to be filled in different systems and the varieties of men and women available to fill them ("courses" and "horses"); and finally

9. the causes and consequences of different rates of ministerial turnover in different countries.

INTERNAL DYNAMICS

There is no need to justify at length the study of executives' internal dynamics —the ways in which executives influence one another in the taking of decisions. One cannot avoid studying executive dynamics if one wishes to understand governmental dynamics, and the study of government is, in one way or another, what political science is all about.

Unfortunately, we run into the same difficulties here as we did in connection with executive recruitment—if anything, in an even more acute form, since the problem of access referred to at the outset is particularly serious in this field. The academic literature is patchy; it is heavily skewed in both volume and quality towards the United States (which has the advantage of having an unusually open political system); there is very little comparative literature. It is also the case that, since executive processes can be looked at from so many different points of view, the literature on them is, perfectly understandably, a somewhat untidy literature. Some scholars ask one kind of question, some another; some do not ask questions at all but string facts together like beads. Because the literature is untidy, we shall organize our discussion of it under general headings, some derived from the approaches in the literature, some related to the ways in which executives might be, and have been, viewed. We shall again be concerned with identifying gaps in the literature. We shall again conclude with a summary of some of the areas in which more research is needed.

Historical Studies

In one sense all studies of executive institutions are historical, since they all make use of examples and since all of the examples are, in the nature of the case, drawn from the past, however recent. Some studies are, however, strictly historical in the sense of being concerned with tracing the development of institutions over time. The most important examples are, on the United States presidency, Binkley, 1964, and Cunliffe, 1968, and, on the British cabinet, Mackintosh, 1968. There is no full history of the American cabinet (though see Hinsdale, 1911, and Learned, 1912) or the British prime ministership (though

see Jones, 1974), nor are there histories of the executives of most other democratic countries.

To what extent a knowledge of how institutions developed in the past is
essential to an understanding of how they work in the present is an open question. Clearly the past is, from a legal or quasi-legal point of view, important as
a yielder of precedents. It is also important for anyone interested in reforming
an institution to know whether the reforms proposed were introduced in the
past and, if so, with what results (see Milne, 1955, and Daalder, 1964, on reform
of the British cabinet). But in general it is probably fair to say that the political
scientist need not be overly concerned with the detailed historical development
of the institution under study: the past matters chiefly as a source of data and
cases.

Legal and Constitutional Studies

The position is different with regard to a country's laws and constitution: the
workings of a country's executive institutions obviously cannot be understood
except against a background of knowledge of the legal requirements and constraints affecting both individual heads of government and ministers, and executives, especially cabinets, in their collective capacity. Fortunately, this is one
of the few areas in which the gaps in the literature are neither numerous nor
particularly serious. The major studies are, on the United States presidency,
Corwin (1957), on the British cabinet, Jennings (1959a), on France, Arne (1962)
and many articles in the *Revue du Droit Public,* on the German chancellorship,
Amphoux (1962) and Ulrich (1965).

Institutional Descriptions

Not only is a knowledge of the law and the constitution essential, so is a knowledge of the structure of institutions. Political scientists are concerned, rightly,
with developing empirical theory; they believe, rightly, that there is a sense in
which all descriptions of the world are predicated, explicitly or implicitly, on
theories about the world. But they are inclined to infer from this, wrongly,
that the task of institutional description is either intellectually unworthy and/
or impossible in the absence of theoretical knowledge. In fact, in the messy
business of scientific discovery new theories are at least as likely to arise out of
more or less randomly collected "facts" as "facts" are to be collected as the
result of theory. The study of executive dynamics has suffered greatly from a
lack of theorizing but also from a lack of empirical data collecting. There are
few facts because there are few theories; but there are also few theories because
there are few facts.

It is not difficult to produce an agenda of what one would like to know
about the executive institutions of any given country (or state or province).
First, what are the main institutional structures? Second, how are the main
structures composed? Who are the members? How are they chosen? Who are

the chairmen? Third, how are the main structures linked to one another, at least formally but preferably also informally? Fourth, what are the structures responsible for? What are they supposed to do? Fifth (a question easily overlooked), how are the main structures physically organized? In particular, where are they located geographically in relation to one another? It does not take much imagination to see that a presidential aide whose office is next door to the president's is likely to have more influence than one whose office is halfway across town. (Someone some day should produce a "political geography" of the world's main capitals; see Young, 1966).

Of course all these questions of political statics, so to speak, are closely related to questions of political dynamics. On the one hand, one may not be able to produce even simple static descriptions of structures without some knowledge of how they actually work in practice; on the other, it may turn out that a particular static description, accurate within its limits, is nonetheless false to reality because, for example, the structure to which it relates does not actually do what it is formally charged with doing. Nevertheless, such static descriptive information is clearly required even if one subsequently intends to go beyond it. What is striking in the executives field is its absence, especially with regard to countries other than the United States.

Table 5 indicates how little institutional description has been completed (or even undertaken) by political scientists. The main executive structures in the various countries have been identified, and works are cited which deal with one or more of the questions that can be asked about them. As in the case of Table 1 above (p. 184), only reasonably thorough pieces of work are listed; the more substantial are set in boldface type. Three other works on the American presidency are germane but do not appear because they do not fall neatly into one or more of the institutional categories; they are Seligman, 1956; Cronin and Greenberg, 1969; and Thomas and Baade, 1970. The American coverage, it should be added, is less complete than it seems, since much of the work is out of date and some does not deal with every aspect of the institution in question. It goes without saying that if the table covered more countries the number of gaps would be even greater.

Executive Processes

A knowledge of the law and the constitution is essential; a knowledge of institutional structures is essential. But political scientists interested in these matters obviously want to go further—to study how executive institutions work in practice. The literature even on this subject is patchy in both coverage and quality, but a number of major studies do exist and the importance of the subject is at least recognized. The chief problem about the literature is the one that emerges from Table 5: the United States and Britain are almost the only countries that have been written about. Our discussion will largely center on them for this reason.

TABLE 5   Descriptive literature on executive structures in four countries

United States		Great Britain	
White House staff	Neustadt (1963) Anderson (1968)	Prime Minister's Private Office	—
Cabinet	**Fenno (1959)**	Cabinet	Mackintosh (1968)
Office of Management and budget	—		**Gordon Walker (1972)**
National Security Council	Jackson (1965)	Cabinet committees	—
		Cabinet Office	—
	Clark and Legere (1969)	Central Policy Review Staff	Heclo and Wildavsky (1974)
Council of Economic Advisers	**Flash (1965)**		
Domestic Council	—		

France		West Germany	
Cabinet	—	Cabinet	—
General Secretariat of the Government	—	Chancellor's Department	—
Prime Minister's *Cabinet*	—		
Elysée Office	—		

Although the literature is, as we said, somewhat untidy, most of it can be seen as attempting to answer either or both of two questions: first, How are decisions arrived at within a given country's executive branch? and second, How great is (or can be, or should be) the power of the chief executive? With regard to the second question, we shall observe in passing that a very high proportion of the literature is chief-executive-centered; there are a number of reasons for thinking that this is not altogether a good thing.

Decision Processes

Let us suppose that we wish to know how executive decisions are taken in a given country, who participates in the taking of these decisions, and also which executives within the country are the most influential. If we wish to know all of these things, our investigation might proceed roughly as follows.

First, we would find out something about the country's executive decision rules, in the formal sense. We would want to know that in Britain the locus of decision-making authority resides in the cabinet, whereas in the United States it resides, for most purposes, in the president. We would want to know that a prime minister can be outvoted by his cabinet but that a president cannot be outvoted by his. And so on.

Second, we would go on to identify those offices within each country's executive which, by law, custom, accident, or whatever, enable those who hold them to wield influence. In Britain our list would undoubtedly include the prime minister, the cabinet, and possibly some of the other ministers not in the cabinet. (It would also include a range of senior civil service positions.) For the United States our list would include the president, leading members of his staff, most members of the cabinet, and probably also the heads of certain other agencies like (say) the Council of Economic Advisers and the Federal Reserve Board. (The American list, like the British, would also include offices not within the political executive echelon as we defined it earlier—for example, bureau chiefs and leading figures in Congress.) Even this simple listing exercise, if it were done comparatively and with any degree of political sensitivity, would yield useful information (see the excellent essay by Neustadt in this genre, 1969).

But it is a commonplace that even where decision-making authority is assigned to a collective body, as in the case of the British cabinet, not all members of the collective play an equal part in the taking of all decisions. The secretary for Scotland is unlikely to have much to do, in practice, with the taking of defense decisions; the defense minister is not likely to take a great interest in the welfare of the Highlands and Islands. This being so, we would want to have in our minds, third, a list of the particular decisions that a government was taking or, more generally, of a country's major policy areas: defense, foreign affairs, taxation, welfare, civil rights, and so on.

Taken together, our lists of offices and policy areas could be thought of as forming a simple matrix, as in Fig. 2. One can imagine the cells of the matrix being filled simply by (say) check marks to indicate whether the holder of a particular office could be expected to participate in some active way in the taking of decisions in a particular policy area. Alternatively, one can imagine the cells being filled by numbers corresponding either, on the one hand, to the probability that a particular officeholder will participate actively in a particular area or, on the other, more interestingly, to the "weight" within each policy area that he might be expected to have. The matrix can be read horizontally, if one is interested in the part that the same officeholder is likely to play in different policy areas, or vertically, if one is interested in the different officeholders who are likely to play major parts in the same area.

Our fourth step would follow naturally from the preceding two. Since there is clearly variation not only among offices but among the individuals who hold offices—even among the individuals who hold the same office—we would want to go on to construct an additional matrix (or set of matrices) resembling the first but with the rows composed of persons (Nixon, Johnson, Kennedy) instead of offices (president, vice-president, etc.). (See Fig. 3.) This matrix would be likely

Policy areas

Offices	Relations with major ally	Fiscal policy	Crime	Regional policy	Labor law	Pensions	Technical education
Head of government	✓	✓		✓	?		
Foreign minister	✓	✓					
Finance minister	✓	✓		✓		✓	✓
Interior minister		✓	✓	✓	✓		
Welfare minister		✓		✓		✓	✓
Industry minister		✓		✓	✓		✓
Housing minister		✓		✓			
Education minister		✓	✓	✓			✓
Labor minister		✓		✓	✓		✓

Fig. 2. Matrix relating offices to policy areas (national examples)

to differ from the previous one at any given moment in time; it would also be likely to change over time. For example, the attorney general of the United States normally participates in the taking of only a fairly narrow range of decisions; he is not normally a man of much influence outside his own field. Thus, in terms of Fig. 2, there would be few check marks next to his name; by the same token, the weights assigned to him in most policy areas would be small. Most attorney generals probably approximate this norm. Robert Kennedy and John Mitchell, by contrast, were almost certainly somewhat more influential than most of the others within the Justice Department's own field and were undoubtedly far more influential outside.

All this should not be taken too literally. As in the case of the head-of-government probabilities discussed in an earlier section, the filling in of the cells would be a matter for individual judgment; it would be misleading to suppose that one could assign absolutely precise weights to particular individuals; one would be dealing in ordinal rather than interval scales. All the same, a considerable proportion of the literature on executives can reasonably be read as falling in one way or another under this sort of general rubric. The legal and constitutional studies cited on p. 206 and the institutional descriptions cited on pp. 206–7 contain between them accounts of many of the most im-

Policy areas

Officeholders	Relations with major ally	Fiscal policy	Crime	Regional policy	Labor law	Pensions	Technical education
Smith	✓	✓	✓	✓			
Jones	✓	✓		✓			
Barker	✓	✓	✓	✓		✓	
Wilson	✓		✓		✓		
McKay		✓					
Kennedy	✓	✓		✓	✓		✓
Stewart		✓		✓			✓
Walters		✓					✓
Anderson	✓	✓		✓	✓		✓

Fig. 3. Matrix relating officeholders to policy areas (national examples)

portant decision rules, at least as regards the United States and Britain. Almost any work on the United States presidency or the British cabinet can be made to yield some sort of list—more or less impressionistic, more or less traditional —of the major decision-making offices (see for example, for the United States, Rossiter, 1960, Koenig, 1964; for Britain, Heasman, 1962, Morrison, 1964, Mackintosh, 1968). There is also a substantial body of literature—unfortunately relating almost exclusively to chief executives—on the varying ways in which different men have conducted themselves in the same office (see especially, on the United States, Neustadt, 1960, Rossiter, 1960, Cunliffe, 1968; on Britain, Mackintosh, 1968).

These various elements have not, however, been combined in any systematic way, even for one country, much less for several. Indeed only three writers seem to have moved in this direction. Neustadt (1969) argues that the functional equivalent of the British cabinet in the United States is not the American cabinet but "an informal, shifting aggregation of key individuals, the influentials at both ends of Pennsylvania Avenue" (p. 144); in other words, he indicates how greatly the lists of major decision makers in the two countries differ and how much the American list is likely to vary from moment to moment. Mackintosh (1968), offering a series of examples of the British cabinet at work, shows how greatly the composition of the effective cabinet, even in Britain, varies from issue to issue. Similarly, Rossiter (1960) advocated the creation of a series of "functional cabinets" in the United States, noting that one such functional cabinet, the National Security Council, had already been formally established. The idea of a series of overlapping functional cabinets is, of course, implicit in the layout of our two matrices, especially if they are read vertically.

It goes without saying that the four steps we have been outlining do not in themselves constitute knowledge or theory, but they are—or would seem to be—means towards knowledge and theory. Two examples will illustrate the kind of thing that might emerge. A detailed examination of the functional cabinet relating to foreign and defense policy in the United States would probably show that these matters are largely in the hands, within the executive branch, of a fairly self-contained policy community consisting of the president, his chief foreign affairs adviser, the leading figures in the State and Defense departments and the Central Intelligence Agency, and the chairman of the Joint Chiefs of Staff. The only members of this functional cabinet with continuing responsibilities in fields apart from foreign affairs and defense would probably turn out to be the president himself and possibly one or two others on his staff (Sapin, 1966). By contrast, a detailed examination of the comparable British foreign affairs "cabinet" would probably show that it consisted of the same sorts of foreign policy specialists but also that it contained a number of senior cabinet ministers—notably the chancellor of the exchequer—who have continuing responsibilities in a variety of other fields, indeed, who have an office-related stake, if not a personal one, in encouraging some kinds of foreign policies and discouraging others (see Boardman and Groom, 1973). It would be instructive against this background to compare the executive politics of (say) the British withdrawal from east of Suez and the American withdrawal from Vietnam (on east of Suez, see Gordon Walker, 1972; on Vietnam, see Hoopes, 1969). It might turn out that these two cases would suggest that the two countries' different decision rules and the differing composition of their effective decision-making bodies could be expected to lead the two countries' governments to behave in dissimilar ways in not dissimilar situations.

A second, more general hypothesis that suggests itself arises out of the fact—if it is a fact—that the various British functional cabinets overlap to a considerably greater degree than do their American counterparts: because of the British cabinet system, they have a considerably larger common membership. It follows that more members of any given British than of any given American functional cabinet are likely to have perspectives, interests, and stakes in addition to those specific to the functional cabinet in question. This simple fact could have a variety of consequences. It could lead to decisions in Britain being taken with a greater awareness of their possible ramifications in other fields of policy, to British public policy being, in some sense, more "coherent" than American. Equally, it could lead, precisely because of this greater awareness, to there being greater resistance, at least within the executive branch, to innovation in Britain than in the United States. The British cabinet system, with its emphasis on collective responsibility, means that up to a point every winning executive coalition has to be the same coalition. To the extent that this is so and to the extent that there are differences of opinion among leading members of British cabinets, no change becomes a much more probable outcome than change. That stalemate and deadlock may be more pronounced characteristics of the British executive than of the American is at least suggested by Neustadt (1969). Whether or not he is right, it is this sort of possibility that can be investigated in terms of the rubric outlined above.

The emphasis in each of our four steps is on variation: variation in decision rules between countries, in the composition of different countries' decision-making echelons at the same moment of time and in the same country's decision-making echelons at different moments of time, in the decision-making personnel likely to be found in different policy areas, and in the way the same offices are filled by different men. We have indicated what some of the consequences of such variation might be with respect to the United States and Britain. But we must also consider what the sources of such variation might be. If the main decision rules (presidential authority versus cabinet authority, etc.) are taken as given, the chief sources of variation will be found in the attributes of offices and of individuals and their political situations. We shall consider a number of these. Our discussion will inevitably touch on the position of the chief executive, though the bulk of our consideration of chief executives comes in the next section.

The following are among the factors that will determine the influence of executives, both as holders of offices and as individuals, in the taking of decisions and the making of policies.

1. The powers and obligations of their offices. Most cabinet-level executives other than "staffers" in the narrow sense are charged with a range of legal and quasi-legal responsibilities: to enforce certain laws, to make certain appointments, and so on. As a result, most cabinet-level executives have their own timetables and their own prerogatives—areas in which it is difficult for others to tell them what to do. It follows that anyone wishing to analyze specific situations and relationships needs to know what the relevant laws and customs are. This is not a factor that has been studied systematically, but it is one to which students of the American presidency, in particular, are alert (see especially Corwin, 1957; Neustadt, 1960).

2. Their propinquity to particular decision or policy areas. All this means is that someone with a recognized, continuing responsibility in or near a particular field is likely to have greater influence in that field than someone who does not. On the one hand the executive's colleagues will expect him to play a larger role; on the other the executive is likely to have greater resources with which to play the role. Propinquity in most cases is determined by an officeholder's formal responsibilities (e.g., an American secretary of the interior's responsibility for the national parks, a British chancellor of the exchequer's responsibility for taxation), but it may be determined by the head of government (as in the case, admittedly an extreme one, of Kennedy's "executive committee" at the time of the Cuban missile crisis) and by a country's formal decision rules (e.g., a British foreign secretary, simply by virtue of being a member of the British cabinet, is closer to decisions in the field of, say, housing than an American secretary of state, though how much closer is a matter for empirical enquiry). This, too, is not a matter that has been considered systematically in the literature (though on British cabinet committees, which to a considerable extent institutionalize the principle of propinquity, see Morrison, 1964; Mackintosh, 1968; and Gordon Walker, 1972).

3. The expectations that others have of them. People behave in the ways they do partly because other people expect them to behave in those ways; if they are able to exert influence, it is partly because others expect them to (on the relevance of role theory to politics, see McFarland, 1969). The expectations that others have of the holders of offices will usually be a function of the legal responsibilities of those offices and of propinquity. The status of a particular office may, however, lead others to have certain expectations of the holder of that office, irrespective of who he or she is. Equally, particular individuals may have certain things expected of them as individuals irrespective of the offices they hold. In the United States, the presidency apart, the fit between the legal responsibilities and the propinquity of a given office on the one hand and its ability to confer influence on its holder on the other is generally probably fairly close; the secretary of the treasury *qua* secretary of the treasury is not normally expected to intervene in the field of (say) penal policy and can therefore not normally exercise much influence in that field. In Britain, by contrast, the fit is less close; the holders of certain offices (chancellor of the exchequer, foreign secretary, home secretary) are, simply by virtue of holding those offices, expected to intervene and to exercise influence across a wide policy range (Heasman, 1962). The incidence of individuals who are accorded influence irrespective of their offices is probably about the same in the two countries and in both is probably fairly random. With regard to the expectations factor generally, the existing literature on executives contains an abundance of material. It is not, however, organized along these lines.

4. Their command of staff resources. Propinquity accords influence partly because of staff: those close to a particular policy area will usually have staff—and therefore expertise and information—in that area. But not all of those who find themselves close to an area (e.g., some of the individual members of Kennedy's Cuban executive committee) will have staff, and some not close to a particular area will nevertheless occasionally find themselves in possession of staff resources relevant to that area (which in itself may be enough to impel them towards the area). In the United States, presidents not in possession of staff resources in an area that they have moved into or wish to move into (e.g., economic management after World War II) will normally seek to acquire staff in that area (as it turned out, the Council of Economic Advisers). With regard to Britain, it is worth noting that despite the doctrine of collective cabinet responsibility (which formally requires all ministers to regard themselves as being in a relationship of propinquity to all policy areas), cabinet ministers do not possess staff specifically in connection with their cabinet responsibilities: the secretary of state for the environment, for example, is required, formally, to take decisions about foreign affairs but has no foreign affairs staff.

5. *Their conceptions of their own offices.* Expectations are what others expect of officeholders; conceptions are what officeholders expect of themselves. For the moment, as usual, the bulk of the literature on executives' conceptions of their offices is concerned with the United States in general and presidents of the United States in particular. This is a pity because the conceptions of other executives might be expected to have a considerable impact on their conduct in office. With regard to the United States, it would be interesting to know to what extent cabinet officers in particular regard themselves as "president's men" and to what extent they see themselves as department heads, spokesmen for interest groups, their own men, or whatever. The statement that most do not regard themselves as president's men is frequently made in the literature (Bailey, 1956; Fenno, 1959; Neustadt, 1960); but presumably not all cabinet officers conceive of their roles in the same way, and it would be interesting to know more about the extent of variation and its causes and consequences. With regard to Britain, there is at least a latent role conflict between cabinet ministers *qua* department heads and cabinet ministers *qua* members of the cabinet. Gordon Walker (1972, pp. 31–32) has recalled how shocked some of his cabinet colleagues were when, on two separate occasions, he seemed prepared to put the collective interests of the cabinet ahead of the interests of his own department. Headey (1974a) discusses the role perceptions of British ministers, but not in this connection.

6. *Their standing in the eyes of the head of government.* Other things being equal, it seems probable that a minister's (or adviser's) influence will vary directly with his or her standing in the eyes of the head of government. If a minister (or adviser) is in good standing with the head of government, the head of government himself will accord the minister greater influence; and if he is in good standing with the head of government, others will probably, although by no means certainly, accord him greater influence for the same reason. This is another matter which is often touched on in the literature (see Heclo and Wildavsky, 1974, and especially Neustadt, 1970) but is not usually gone into in any detail.

7. *Their professional reputations.* Neustadt in *Presidential Power* (1960) drew attention to the importance of the reputation factor in politics. "Their judgment of him," he wrote with respect to the relations between an American pres-

ident and the Washington political community, "is a factor of his influence
with them" (p. 58). Neustadt defined professional reputation somewhat narrowly, with specific reference to an individual's skill in identifying and exploiting bargaining advantages; but the term could be defined more broadly to refer also to the individual's intelligence, judgment, and skills in various other
directions, as these are seen in the eyes of others. However the term is defined,
there is every reason to suppose that reputation is as important for other chief
executives and for executives at other levels as for American presidents. It is
clear that reputations are made in different ways in different systems. A British
cabinet minister's standing, even in the eyes of his cabinet colleagues, would
appear to depend far more than an American cabinet officer's on the quality of
his appearances before the legislature (Headey, 1974a). Partly for this reason it
would seem that a British minister's reputation depends more than does an
American's on his ability to think on his feet—that is, on rhetorical skills.
These are no more than suppositions, however. Neustadt's lead has never been
followed up.

8. *Their public prestige*. Professional reputation has to do with an individual's
standing in the eyes of those who have some claim to be his peers or at least
who participate with him in some way in the business of government. Public
prestige has to do with an individual's standing in the eyes of the noninvolved
mass public. Neustadt suggests that this is a factor "operating mostly in the
background as a conditioner, not [a] determinant" (1960, p. 87) of others' responses to executive requests. Neustadt is writing specifically of American presidents, but the general hypothesis would be that, other things being equal, a
minister's influence with his colleagues varies directly with his public prestige.
This proposition is almost certainly true of American presidents; it may well
be true of American cabinet officers; but it is not at all clear that it is true of
British ministers or of ministers in other cabinet systems. Ministers in such systems are likely to be rivals in a personal as well as a political sense; their
rivalry may be intensified rather than the reverse by their continuing face-to-
face interaction. If so, the public prestige of one minister might be perceived
by others as a threat. Far from according him greater influence, they might be
tempted to cut him down to size. They would be peculiarly sensitive to any dis-
crepancy between his public prestige and his professional reputation. They
might in some cases suspect that a minister with great public prestige was court-
ing public favor and neglecting his policymaking and administrative roles.
Again, however, Neustadt's lead has not been followed up and these are only
suppositions. In any case, public prestige probably matters less at the ministerial than at the head-of-government level.

9. *Their political standing*. Political standing is something different from professional reputation and public prestige, though obviously the three factors in-

teract. Political standing refers to a person's perceived capacity to influence others—in his or her own party, in the legislature, with interest groups, or wherever. A minister might have a high professional reputation and considerable public prestige yet lack political standing if, for example, his own party regarded him with suspicion. The political standing of Douglas MacArthur posed problems for President Truman; George Marshall's political standing greatly assisted him (see Neustadt, 1960). The literature is replete with references to political standing (see especially, on the United States, Fenno, 1959, Neustadt, 1960; on Britain, Jones, 1965, Mackintosh, 1967–68); but, as is so often the case, there has been little sustained discussion. In comparative perspective the factor of political standing is of particular interest, since those with such standing are so differently distributed in different systems. In Britain almost all of those with standing, at least in the majority party, are brought together in the cabinet; in the United States, as Neustadt has pointed out (1969), the "set of influentials" in Washington has no single institutional locus. The effect of the congregating of influentials in Britain in the cabinet is almost certainly to reinforce the political authority of cabinet decisions, in the sense that if most of the influentials are inside the cabinet, decisions made in the cabinet are more likely to prevail outside than would otherwise be the case. A British cabinet in a minority government situation (Labour 1924, 1929, 1974) still possesses all of a normal cabinet's prerogatives; but since it does not, by definition, contain some of the influentials on which its continued existence depends, its real situation is quite different. It would be interesting to know more about the determinants of political standing in different systems and about how far those possessed of it are able to use it as a political resource.

10. Their skills and other personal qualities. An individual's political skills and other personal qualities—his or her ability, for example, to inspire trust or loyalty—will partly determine his or her professional reputation, public prestige, and political standing. Even given professional reputation, public prestige, and political standing, however, such personality variables will still help to determine an individual's influence in a particular situation. A consciousness of the importance of personality factors informs the literature on the American presidency (see especially Neustadt, 1960; Hargrove, 1966; Barber, 1972), and Headey (1974a) has discussed the skills required of cabinet ministers in Britain. In general, however, it is probably fair to say that, at least as far as the literature on executives is concerned, personality variables are treated as something of a residual category, to be called in aid when others have failed.

So much for possible sources of variation in individual executives' capacity to influence decisions. There are undoubtedly others, but these are the main ones. We shall pursue the subject further when we deal with heads of government.

One other question should be asked, however, which to some extent cuts across the categories we have been using. In terms of internal executive dynamics, what difference does it make that the United States has a system that is presidential and therefore, in some sense, unified, whereas Britain has a cabinet system and therefore a system that is, in some sense, collegial? Oddly enough, this question is almost never asked. Most discussions of differences between the two countries' systems deal not with this question but with the separate question of the nature of executive-legislative relations in the two countries. The question is separate since one could conceive of an executive that consisted of a number of persons, like the British cabinet, but that was nevertheless, like the American president, not responsible to the legislature. Indeed, the collegiality of the British cabinet owes at least as much to its collective dependence on the mass electorate as to its much more widely advertised collective responsibility to Parliament.

The unified/collegial distinction, considered apart from the question of an executive's relations with the legislature, would seem to have a number of possible consequences. One has been alluded to already: the possibility that a collective executive will find it hard to reconcile its differences and reach agreement and that there will therefore be greater resistances to innovation in a collective executive than in a unified one. This was clearly what Hamilton had in mind in No. 70 of *The Federalist* when he wrote: "Decision, activity, secrecy, and despatch will generally characterize the proceedings of one man in a much more eminent degree than the proceedings of any greater number." Unity, unlike collectivity, Hamilton maintained, is conducive to energy in government. The difficulty with this formulation is that the implicit "other things being equal" clause covers so many "other things." It is quite possible, as we also remarked earlier, that political divisions that manifest themselves inside the executive in one system may simply manifest themselves outside in another; many differences that are or are not reconciled inside British cabinets are or are not reconciled in the United States between executive and legislature. The divisions are the same; the arenas differ.

What does seem to follow from the existence of a collective executive—at least if it is based on a single-party majority in the legislature—is a consciousness among the members of the executive that collective stakes are also personal stakes, that what is in the common interest may also be in the interest of each member individually. Members of British cabinets, like cabinet-level executives in the United States, have their own perspectives, preoccupations, spheres of authority, and so on; but, unlike their American counterparts, they are also conscious that anything that damages any one member of the group is likely to damage them all (Gordon Walker, 1972). This consciousness is normally reinforced by the fact that they are all members of the same party, but it also reinforces their sense of belonging to the same party. It probably leads, for better or worse, to a more consensual style of decision making than in the United States. It undoubtedly leads, contrary to Hamilton's expectation, to government's being conducted amid greater secrecy than in the United States, since to reveal what goes on in government is to risk revealing information or differences of opinion that would damage the government (Gordon Walker, 1972; cf. the conventional view in Morrison, 1964).

This consciousness in British cabinets of common interests may have another corollary. Neustadt (1960), Sorensen (1963), and others have emphasized that in the American system the only one in a position to protect the president's political stakes is the president. Given the collegial character of the British system, it would seem to follow that in Britain the only institution capable of defending the cabinet's political stakes is the cabinet. Little is known about what sorts of issues, apart from the settling of interdepartmental differences, are discussed in detail in cabinet in Britain. But it would be surprising on the face of it if issues of importance to the cabinet politically were not especially likely to be decided by the cabinet collectively—in fact as well as in form (Boyle and Crosland, 1971, pp. 161–62).

If this is so, then it is a considerable anomaly in Britain that the timing of general elections—a matter of great importance to all cabinet ministers—is left in the hands of the prime minister (Carter, 1956; Jennings, 1959a; Mackintosh, 1968; Gordon Walker, 1972). It would take us out of our way to explain the anomaly here, but three considerations are probably important. First, although the judgments of the prime minister and other ministers may differ with regard to election timing, their interests seldom do; if the ministers lose their offices as the result of the prime minister's mistiming of an election, then so does he. Second, prime ministers typically have an even greater stake in election timing than do their cabinet colleagues, since, whereas other ministers stand to lose only their government positions if the government is defeated, the prime minister may stand to lose both his government position and his position as party leader (see Butler and King, 1966). Third, prime ministers in practice, whatever the constitutional convention, do frequently consult at least a few of their colleagues informally about the timing of an election; sometimes they consult virtually the whole cabinet, though individually rather than as a body (Butler and King, 1965).

There are other consequences of the differences between unified and collegial executives. But, since most of them are concerned with the role of chief executives, we will deal with them in the next section.

The Power of Heads of Government

If the question "How are decisions arrived at in the executive branch?" is often asked by scholars, the question "How great is (or can be, or should be) the power of the chief executive?" is asked even more often. Indeed it is hardly too strong to say that the bulk of the executives literature, certainly on the American presidency, has been concerned in one way or another with this question. The analytic paradigm is a simple one. The goals or aims of heads of government are assumed, and it is asked how, given these goals or aims, heads of government go about, or could go about, or ought to go about, achieving them. The analytic focus is also simple. It is on chief executives rather than other executives, on the offices of chief executives, as institutions, rather than on chief executives as participants in decision-making and policymaking processes.

These are sweeping statements and we will want to qualify them as we go along, but they are near enough the truth to invite a number of critical observations. (The reader should bear in mind that we are concerned for the moment solely with the internal dynamics of executive institutions; "external relations" are the subject of the next section.)

To begin with, it is not clear that the goals and aims of heads of government should simply be taken as given. On the one hand it is of considerable intrinsic interest to know how heads of government acquire their goals and aims; on the other there is every reason to suppose that they acquire them at least partly in the course of their dealings with their fellow executives. Goal acquisition, since it is something that goes on within executive branches (as well as elsewhere), should not be slighted in executives research.

There is, secondly, implicit in the "how heads of government get their way" paradigm the assumption that heads of government are invariably, or almost invariably, dealing with fellow executives who are hesitant, recalcitrant, or even antagonistic. "The members of the Cabinet are a President's natural enemies" is a remark often quoted (for example, by Neustadt, 1960, p. 39). The remark undoubtedly contains a good deal of truth, not just with regard to American presidents. Nonetheless, it seems unwise to cast one's entire analysis in a mold that assumes that conflict rather than collaboration is the *métier* of executive politics. For one thing, in every political system such a mold is false to some portion of reality. For another, it is false to larger proportions of reality in some systems than in others. We already have reason to expect, on the basis of our discussion of the collegiality of British cabinets, that the position of British prime ministers is subtly different in this respect from that of American presidents.

Third, it seems reasonable to argue that if we want to know what the job of a chief executive consists of (or might consist of), we should concern ourselves not merely with investigating institutional structures but with trying to find out, in detail, what chief executives actually do: how they spend their time, who they see, which fields of policy they participate in most actively, and so on. There is a body of literature dealing with chief executives in connection with the taking of particular decisions (e.g., McConnell, 1963) or with policymaking in particular fields (e.g., Flash, 1965); there is a larger body of literature on decisions and policies, which, although not primarily concerned with chief executives, can be made to yield a good deal of relevant information (e.g., Sundquist, 1968). But neither has so far made much of a contribution to the construction of detailed job descriptions for chief executives. Thus, the dominance of the "how they get their way" paradigm has not really been offset by an alternative paradigm centered on processes.

Fourth—and this is perhaps the most important point—the analytic focus on heads of government to the virtual exclusion of other executives has meant that our understanding of heads of government itself has suffered, given the fact that the office of head of government in any country is bound to some extent to be defined by its relationship to other offices. The office of the head of government may be the most important office, but it cannot be understood in isolation. Moreover, although the position of the head of government is in some ways unique, it is nevertheless a position that can, for many purposes, be analyzed in much the same ways as the positions of other ministers. The same questions can be asked of them as of him; they and he are both, in their different ways, in the business of exercising influence. It follows that the similarities as well as the differences between them should be remarked. Most of the analysis in Neustadt's *Presidential Power,* for example, could be applied without too many modifications to the position of (say) an American secretary of state or British home secretary—or indeed to the position of a senior executive in almost any field.

Since heads of governments are special kinds of executives but are executives all the same, we shall begin by discussing their power and influence in terms of much the same sources-of-variation variables as we used in connection with executives in general. Only then will we go on to examine the features of heads of government that are unique. For the reasons given earlier, we shall focus almost exclusively on the United States presidency and the British prime ministership, even though our style of analysis could, if data were available, be extended to comparable offices in other countries.

The following are among the factors that will determine the power and influence of chief executives.

1. The powers and obligations of their offices. The literature on the "powers" (in all senses) of American presidents is immense (see especially Corwin, 1957; Hirschfield, 1968); the literature on the powers (in any sense) of British prime ministers is minuscule. The reason is partly that a British prime minister has very few formal powers. He hires and fires ministers, determines the cabinet's agenda, determines the organization of cabinet committees, creates peers, and has a considerable influence over promotions in the upper echelons of the civil service (Crossman, 1972). Otherwise he has virtually no legally delimited sphere of authority. Almost all of the powers that in the United States are in the hands of the president in Britain are in the hands either of individual ministers or of the cabinet as a whole. There is no British equivalent to the United States president's "clerkship" (Neustadt, 1960, Chapter 1); or, rather, in Britain the clerical duties are parcelled out among a wide variety of persons and institutions. Indeed it is just possible to imagine the British system functioning for short periods without a prime minister at all; Neustadt (1969, p. 140) suggests that something very like this happened during the prime ministership of Home (on the American presidency *sans* president, see Neustadt, 1956). All modern American presidents find themselves forced to be activists; in the British system there is no such compulsion.

2. *Their propinquity to particular decisions or policy areas.* For most ministers propinquity is largely a function of office. Secretaries of defense cannot escape involvement in defense decisions; chancellors of the exchequer are inevitably close to tax decisions. For heads of government, however, propinquity is largely a function of choice. Neustadt (1956) has noted that on some matters law or custom requires heads of government to act, that on others a head of government's colleagues will seek his support for actions within their own spheres of authority, but that on still others a head of government may choose to say (when he might have chosen not to say) "count me in." Since, as we have seen, British prime ministers have few formal powers and obligations, they are probably freer than American presidents to decide when they want to be counted in—and out. No one has plotted in detail the incidence of head-of-government involvement in different policy areas either in different countries or over time; but there is general agreement that British prime ministers have always taken a particular interest in foreign and defense matters (Carter, 1956; Jennings, 1959a; Brown, 1968b; King, 1969; Bishop, 1973) and that American presidents' concern—sometimes preoccupation—with these matters has grown steadily during this century (Laski, 1940; Rossiter, 1960; Koenig, 1964; Warren, 1964; Sapin, 1966; Wildavsky, 1966; Waltz, 1967).

Wildavsky (1966) suggests that foreign affairs have absorbed an increasing proportion of American presidents' time, first, because of America's greater involvement with the outside world; second, because at a time of global confrontation small causes may have large effects; and third, because foreign policy decisions, unlike most domestic policy decisions, may have dangerous and irreversible consequences. For all these reasons presidents since 1945 have consistently given higher priority to foreign than to domestic affairs. Most of the same arguments also apply to Britain. If they are correct, one might predict that a period of detente and reduced danger would lead to a diminution of head-of-government involvement in foreign affairs, especially if other problems, notably economic ones, appeared relatively more serious. One should not make such a prediction overconfidently, however. For one thing, heads of government are likely to choose to participate actively in "generalist" issues rather than highly specialized and technical ones, and most foreign affairs issues—unlike, say, international monetary issues—still fall into this category. For another, many heads of government appear to be powerfully attracted by the glamorous, "climb to the top and see the world" aspects of their job (e.g., see Wilson, 1971).

3. The expectations others have of them. The literature on the United States presidency contains a good deal of material on expectations of presidents, most of the expectations in question being the mass public's (Brownlow, 1949; Heller, 1960; Seligman and Baer, 1969). Brownlow and Heller discuss expectations in very general terms, without adducing evidence; they note that the American people appear to expect presidents to be the guarantors of such disparate values as the dignity of the government and national prosperity. Seligman and Baer show, on the basis of sample survey data, that a substantial majority of the mass public, at least in 1962–63, expected presidents to choose moral ends and courses of action rather than purely expediential ones. Comparative evidence is not available for Britain, but it seems almost certain that many popular expectations, which in the United States attach themselves to the president, in Britain attach themselves not to the prime minister, who is a largely demythologized figure, but to either "the government" or the monarch (see Greenstein *et al.*, 1974).

Although the contours of both presidency and prime ministership are undoubtedly determined in part by popular expectations—more in the American case than the British—they are at least equally determined by the expectations of others closer to them in government: cabinet ministers and officers, senior civil servants, their own staffs, legislators, possibly the press, and so on. In the British case, given the prime ministership's lack of formal powers, it seems plausible to argue that the prime ministerial role is determined very largely by the expectations of others. In the absence of guidance from an authoritative text like the United States Constitution, and in the absence of a body of theorizing about the prime ministerial office comparable to much of the literature on the American presidency, a British prime minister might be expected to derive almost all of his ideas about his role either from direct observation of previous prime ministers or from cues emanating from those around him. Unfortunately, in neither the American nor the British case is much known in detail about this possibility.

4. Their command of staff resources. No difference between the presidency and the prime ministership is more striking than their differential command of staff resources. If command of staff resources were taken as an indicator of the ability of heads of government to exert influence, British prime ministers would seem feeble indeed as compared with American presidents. In the early 1970s the White House Office employed some 580 persons, at least 45 or 50 of them personal aides to the president; the Private Office at 10 Downing Street numbered some 20 persons, of whom no more than 4 or 5, apart from stenographers, worked directly to the prime minister. The academic literature on presidential staffing is large (Price, 1946; Hobbs, 1954; May, 1955; Seligman, 1956; Fenno, 1959; Neustadt, 1963, 1965a, 1965c; Falk, 1964; Flash, 1965; Jackson, 1965; Sapin, 1966; Lacy, 1967; Anderson, 1968; Clark and Legere, 1969;

Cronin and Greenberg, 1969; Carey, 1969; Wildavsky, 1969; Cronin, 1970) and can be supplemented by an extensive biographical and memoir literature. The literature on prime ministerial staffing is as meager as the staff itself, the major contributions, apart from two short descriptive accounts of the Cabinet Secretariat (Hewison, 1952; Mosley, 1969), being Neustadt (1966) and Jones (1973). The memoir literature also yields little (though see Petrie, 1958; Egremont, 1968; Williams, 1972).

Neustadt (1966) notes, first, that the prime minister's Private Office, because it is manned mainly by career civil servants, cannot serve the prime minister's personal interests in the way the White House staff serves the president's; second, that the Cabinet Secretariat, although it is controlled administratively by the prime minister, owes its allegiance not to him but to the cabinet collectively; and third, that any efforts by prime ministers to try to enhance the role of the Private Office or to change the role of the Cabinet Office would almost certainly encounter the hostility of both ministers and senior civil servants. Success, even if it were achieved, would be bought at a high price. But neither Neustadt nor anyone else has explored in detail the functioning of either the Private Office or the Cabinet Secretariat. Until someone has, it will be impossible to say whether the consequences of this Anglo-American difference are in fact as great as would appear on the surface.

5. *Their conceptions of the office.* Perhaps because the American constitution is written, perhaps because of the separation of powers, perhaps because the American presidency is such a visible institution, presidents themselves, presidential candidates, and political scientists have thought a good deal about the presidency, about the scope of its formal powers and about what leadership styles are appropriate to it. Presidents' views have varied from Taft's "There is no undefined residuum of power which [a president] can exercise because it seems to him to be in the public interest" (Taft, 1916, p. 140) to Kennedy's "He must be prepared to exercise the fullest powers of his office—all that are specified and some that are not" (Hirschfield, 1968, p. 130). Extensive materials on conceptions of the presidential office can be found in Taft's book and in Tourtellot (1964), Johnson and Walker (1964), Haight and Johnston (1965), Warren (1967), and Hirschfield (1968). No particular effort has been made to link conceptions to performance, since it seems fairly clear that, for example, activist-in-conception presidents have also been activists in execution.

As in the case of staffing, the Anglo-American contrast could not, on the face of it, be more complete. There have been more or less activist prime ministers (contrast Macmillan and Home) just as there have been more or less activist presidents; but prime ministers, by contrast with presidents, have had little to say, either in or out of office, about how they have conceived of the office. Wilson (see King, 1969) is a rare exception. This means that prime ministers' conceptions, if one wanted to know them, would have to be inferred from their behavior in office—a task that has not been undertaken. It also means that British prime ministers, not having thought much about the possibilities inherent in the prime ministerial office, may have overlooked some of the possibilities. Unselfconsciousness may make for institutional conservatism.

6. *Their standing in the eyes of their colleagues.* In the case of ministers, it was useful to distinguish between their standing in the eyes of the head of government and their professional reputations. A minister or cabinet officer might be a personal favorite of the head of government without having much of a reputation. A head of government, by contrast, could be thought well of in the upper echelons of the executive branch without having a high professional reputation in other branches of government. But it seems unlikely, and in any case it is convenient analytically to treat a head of government's standing in the eyes of his colleagues as simply one case of his general professional reputation —or lack of it.

7. *Their professional reputations.* The different reputations of different heads of government will have a bearing on their influence. The reputations of individual heads of government are likely to fluctuate through time; .in the 1960s and 1970s the fluctuations were often violent (Johnson and Nixon in the United States, Wilson in Britain). It would be interesting to know more about the sources of reputation, how reputations are disseminated, and how they can be—and have been—changed. One suspects that "professional reputation" is too inclusive a term and that heads of government, like other people, are apt to be reputed to be good at some things, less good at others. But, as we remarked earlier, Neustadt's lead has not been followed up. Chapter 4 of *Presidential Power*, like so many other parts of the book, has been regarded more as a useful source of quotations than as an agenda for enquiry.

8. *Their public prestige.* If little has been written about professional reputation, much more has been written about public prestige. Few ministers or cabinet officers can reasonably aspire to it; fewer still achieve it. All heads of government aspire to it; most feel they need it. Unfortunately, as is so often the case, almost all of the academic literature is concerned with the United States.

The literature divides itself into three categories. The first consists of work concerned with the content of public attitudes towards the presidency and individual incumbents and with the determinants of those attitudes. Important examples are Converse and Dupeux (1966), Sigel and Butler (1964), Greenstein (1965, 1974), Sigel (1966) and Mueller (1973). The second consists of work on how presidents seek to acquire prestige and to influence public opinion generally. The chief study here is Cornwell (1965), which is essentially a history of presidential public relations in this century together with an attempt to assess the impact of radio and television (see also Koenig, 1964, Chapter 8; the extracts reprinted in Haight and Johnston, 1965; Johnson and Walker, 1964; cf., on Britain, Carter, 1956, Chapter 3). The third category is concerned partly with the acquiring of public prestige but mainly with the bearing that the possession (or nonpossession) of prestige has on presidential performance, in particular on presidents' ability to get their way. Neustadt's chapter has already been cited (1960, Chapter 5); there is a more extended treatment in Brown (1966) and a less extended one in McConnell (1967, Chapter 5). Whereas Neustadt is chiefly concerned with prestige as a "conditioner" of presidential influence, McConnell discusses the circumstances in which prestige can be used to achieve specific ends, as in Kennedy's conduct of the 1962 steel crisis.

The case of public prestige is a good one for demonstrating the utility of enquiry conducted on a systematic comparative basis (even if one is mainly interested in the politics of a single country), because the neglect of public prestige as a factor in British prime ministerial politics has led in turn to the neglect of a major source of variation in prime ministerial power—and also to scholars' failure to notice one of the most important differences between the positions of presidents and prime ministers.

It was remarked in an earlier section that, other things being equal, a prime minister can be expected to be weaker inside his administration than a president inside his, if only because prime ministers, unlike presidents (impeachment apart), can be deposed. We can now see that the factor of public prestige is directly relevant to this point. A British prime minister whose public prestige sharply declines suffers the same sort of diminution in effectiveness as would an American president in comparable circumstances. But in addition he is almost certain to suffer an extra diminution, since the lower his prestige, the more likely it is that he will believe himself to be in danger—and that others will also believe him to be in danger—of being turned out. And the belief that he may be turned out is likely to gain credence from the fact that in a majority-party, collegial-cabinet system like the British the fates of prime minister, cabinet and party are bound up together. If a prime minister's unpopularity seems likely to lead not only to his downfall at the next election but also to the cabinet's and the party's, they will have—and will be believed by him to have—ample incentive to get rid of him. The prime minister's ability to exert influence will accordingly be impaired. Even if the chances of his actually being deposed are not high, he will be in no position to take risks. Examples of fluctuations in prime ministerial influence, which were caused in part by fluctuations in prime ministerial prestige, are given in Mackintosh (1968, Chapter 20). It will be seen that the amplitude of such prestige-induced fluctuations is likely to be considerably greater for the British head of government than for the American. Apart from Mackintosh's brief passage, however, this factor in British executive politics has not been studied.

9. Their political standing. The remarks just made apply with even greater force to the factor of political standing, except that this factor has been neglected—apart from a few comments in Neustadt (1956)—almost as much in studies of the presidency as of the prime ministership. Political standing, as we saw earlier, may often covary with professional reputation and public prestige; but they are not the same thing. Franklin Roosevelt, for example, during the Court packing controversy still enjoyed a high professional reputation (certainly in Neustadt's sense) and a good deal of public prestige, but his political standing fell dramatically, in that he could no longer get his way with groups that mattered to him, notably in Congress. In terms of internal executive dynamics, political standing, like public prestige, is a factor likely to be more important in Britain than in the United States. Whereas an American president seldom has to deal within the executive branch with men of standing comparable to himself, British prime ministers frequently have to, given that British cabinets contain most of the influentials from the majority party. Even if a prime minister's public prestige does not decline sharply, his influence vis-à-vis his cabinet colleagues may diminish if his political standing—especially within his own party (Carter, 1956, Chapter 4; Brown, 1968b)—is declining while theirs is rising. The fact that a prime minister can be deposed is always there in the background. Mackintosh (1968, p. 452) asserts that after the 1967 devaluation of the pound and the appointment of Roy Jenkins as chancellor of the exchequer, it is doubtful whether Jenkins could have been removed: "The Prime Minister (Harold Wilson) was, at least for a time, dependent on him." Such a situation is virtually inconceivable in the United States.

10. Their skills and other personal qualities. When we discussed personality factors in connection with executives in general, we pointed out that they tend to form something of a residual category—a group of variables to be called in aid when others had failed to perform some explanatory task. The reason is that while there is a substantial literature on personality and leadership, it has not been integrated with the literature on executives. Students of executives have little to say, except implicitly, about personality; students of political psychology have a good deal to say about executives, but largely in terms of psychological rather than institutional categories. It is striking, for example, that not a single textbook on the American presidency—with the exception of Wildavsky's reader (1969)—contains a sustained treatment of personality variables; Hargrove's *Presidential Leadership: Personality and Political Style,* which appeared in 1966, is not mentioned in books published much later. Similarly, the personality literature does not address itself to questions that students of executives would assume are important. This is too important a subject, however, to be dealt with in passing here. We shall return to it below.

The ten variables we have considered so far can—and should—all be considered in relation to both heads of governments and other leading executives.

But in addition there are a number of factors that pertain only to heads of government. We shall consider three of them, which, in addition to those already mentioned, may be thought to determine in part the power and influence of chief executives.

Their power, or lack of it, to dissolve the legislature. It used to be believed that British prime ministers were at an advantage compared with American presidents in having the power to dissolve the legislature (e.g., Laski, 1940). Not only, it was argued, did the prime minister's power to dissolve confer an electoral advantage on him and his party, it also conferred a special advantage on him as prime minister, since by threatening a dissolution he could at any time bring to heel rebels in his own ranks. It was supposed that this power in the hands of prime ministers accounted in large part for the discipline of the British parties. To be sure, the fact that a government losing the confidence of its party supporters may no longer be able to govern and may be forced to go to the country does undoubtedly contribute to the high level of partisan cohesion in the British House of Commons. But this is not a fact that confers any special advantage on the prime minister. A threat by a prime minister to dissolve Parliament would, under anything like normal circumstances, be hollow, since an election that eliminated those rebelling against the prime minister would almost certainly eliminate the prime minister as well (Andrews, 1960; Jones, 1965; Mackintosh, 1968; Jackson, 1968). The right to request the monarch to dissolve Parliament, often listed as one of a British prime minister's "powers," should rather be cited as one of his duties or responsibilities. If it is a "power," it is not one that is useful for anything.

The "moral" authority they possess arising directly out of their position as head of government or head of state. This factor needs to be distinguished from that of public prestige. A head of government's prestige may vary considerably during his term of office. Moral authority, by contrast, refers to whatever authority is, in some sense, inherent in the office, irrespective of who holds it or what his formal powers are. A certain amount of moral authority undoubtedly inheres in the office of prime minister in Britain, although the fact that almost no authors refer to it suggests that the amount is not very great. Certainly British prime ministers are not accorded the same deference as American presidents; no bands strike up when they appear, no one sings "Hail to the Prime Minister." The literature on the American presidency contains a large number of references to the authority inherent in the office. McConnell (1967, p. 70) writes of "the sheer mystique of the office": "The moment the successful candidate has been elected, he becomes a man set apart. His friends cease to address him by his first name and he walks in an atmosphere of deference and awe." Such deference and awe are undoubtedly in part the consequence of America's lacking a separate ceremonial institution like the British monarchy.

In the absence of an alternative, the presidency comes to serve a variety of largely symbolic functions (Greenstein, 1965; Vinyard, 1971). What is less clear is whether presidential authority, in this sense, can be made to serve presidential purposes. It seems probable that the authority that inheres in a president in his role of head of state (i.e., as monarch) cannot easily be transferred to him in his role of head of government (i.e., as prime minister) and that efforts to transfer such authority from one sphere to the other will be likely to fail or at least to succeed only very occasionally (see McConnell, 1967, pp. 70–73).

Their power to hire and fire. This power of chief executives could have been subsumed under (1) above (*powers and obligations*), but since this is a power common to all chief executives and one that is central to their office, it seems better to consider it separately. We must also look at the other side of the coin —the influence that can be brought to bear on chief executives by threats of resignation made by other executives. Ministerial recruitment was dealt with in a general way above; the question here is how the power of heads of government to hire and fire bears specifically on their power and influence.

We noted above that some heads of government have a larger number and a wider variety of posts to fill than others. We also noted that eligibility rules and the selection criteria that heads of government employ differ from country to country. Only in Australia and New Zealand, however—and even there only in the case of Labor administrations—do heads of government not make the final determination of who shall be appointed to and dismissed from ministerial office.

A chief executive within any given political system might be expected to concern himself, above all, with two things in choosing ministers (or dismissing them, or making other ministerial changes): the probable effects on his personal political position and capacity to survive and on his ability to achieve his policy objectives (if any). A chief executive's stakes are never higher than when he makes appointments; his choices protect, or fail to protect, his power (see Neustadt, 1960, p. 56).

This being so, it is surprising that so little has been written about the politics of hiring and firing (and, especially in the British case, reshuffling). General discussions abound (Carter, 1956; Fenno, 1959), but there has been no detailed investigation of how hiring and firing practices differ from country to country or even of the hiring and firing practices of heads of government within individual countries. There exists, for example, no detailed case study of the formation of an incoming administration in any country, seeking to show why the head of government made the appointments he did—and did not make some of the ones he might have. Admittedly, such a study would not be easy to do, since most heads of government are not about to reveal their innermost thoughts to enquiring political scientists (and in some cases are probably none too sure themselves what their motives were). But it ought to be possible to reconstruct tolerably accurately what particular heads of government had in mind, especially given the enormous volume of journalistic, historical, and biographical material available. By means of such studies, one could begin to understand the operational codes characteristic of different heads of government and different systems.

The Anglo-American contrast is instructive in this, as in so much else. Appointments usually matter rather more to British prime ministers than to American presidents, for three reasons. The first is that prime ministers normally have more control than presidents over the composition of the body of "influentials" (to use Neustadt's term) with whom they must deal. American presidents, to be sure, can appoint cabinet officers at will, but they have little or no say in the selection of, for example, congressional leaders. A British prime minister, by contrast, although he is bound on first coming into power to appoint to cabinet office most of the leading figures in his party, can determine which of them to appoint to which office. Moreover, over the lifetime of his government he can, by means of promotions, demotions, and dismissals, strengthen the position of some ministers and weaken that of others. In the British system the influence that other ministers have over the prime minister they have partly because he gave it to them.

The second reason why appointments matter more in Britain than in the United States is related to the first. In the United States, given the independence of Congress and the existence of both the Supreme Court and the independent regulatory agencies, the connection between specific head-of-government appointments and the attainment—or nonattainment—of specific policy objectives is inevitably somewhat tenuous. In Britain the connection is close. No prime minister concerned with Britain's relations with the European Economic Community, for example, would overlook the fact that some patterns of appointments would be likely to further his own purposes with regard to Europe while others would not. According to Camps (1964), Harold Macmillan during the original Britain/EEC negotiations took great care, from his own point of view, "to see that the right ministers were in the right positions" (p. 374).

The third reason is also related. If cabinet ministers in Britain have influence over the prime minister partly because he gave it to them, they also have influence in their own right—as cabinet ministers. The cabinet, not the prime minister, is the ultimate authority. It therefore matters enormously to the prime minister who his ministers are and what positions they hold. It matters to him not least because almost every cabinet contains the prime minister's future successors and therefore, probably, his present rivals.

Many of the considerations that apply to appointments also apply to dismissals. A British prime minister's needs are greater than a president's, but the constraints on him may also be more imperative. On the one hand, he may wish to dismiss a minister because the minister is thwarting his purposes or is a rival to his authority; on the other, he may on occasion (more often than in the case of an American president) not be able to dismiss a minister if the minister's standing, especially with the party, is high. However, if the dismissal weapon in the hands of a British prime minister is sometimes a dangerous weapon, it is also a peculiarly potent one. For most prominent Americans, being a cabinet officer or other political executive is only one of a number of possible occupations and not necessarily the most desirable; presidents often have to try to dissuade political appointees from resigning on personal grounds (Fenno, 1959). For a high proportion of British politicians, by contrast, cabinet office is the whole aim of the exercise; it is what being in politics is all about. To be dismissed from the cabinet—even from junior ministerial office—is to have suffered a major, perhaps fatal career setback. For this reason the powers to hire and fire, however circumscribed, are in Britain formidable. As a serving minister put it (Crossman, 1972): "I am aware I am there at the Prime Minister's discretion. The Prime Minister can withdraw that discretion on any day he likes without stating a reason. And there's nothing much I can do about it" (p. 63).

Just as there is little literature on appointments and dismissals (though on dismissals in Britain see Jones, 1965; Mackintosh, 1967–68; Brown, 1968a), so there is little on resignations and threats of resignation. There is no American study. Two relate to Britain, Madgwick (1966–67) and Alderman and Cross (1967). Threats of resignation matter more to British prime ministers than to American presidents for much the same reasons that appointments and dismissals matter more. Few British ministers are so important that if they threatened to resign the prime minister would be seriously worried. But some are. A British cabinet is the assembly of those who are, at any given moment, the country's political "influentials"; they take collective responsibility for their decisions. If a senior minister threatens to resign, the prime minister has to calculate how much of the minister's influence is personal and would therefore be retained outside the cabinet. He also has to calculate how much damage the resignation would do to the government generally and to his own position within it. No one has produced an estimate, but most British cabinets—unlike the majority of American administrations—probably contain at least two or three ministers whose resignations no prime minister could contemplate with equanimity. Resignations in Britain, moreover, are not only liable to be more serious than in the United States, they are also far more frequent. An American White House staffer or cabinet officer who dissents from general government policy need not resign; he is in no sense responsible for it. The same is true in West Germany, where the sense of collective responsibility for overall government policy is weak (Johnson, 1973, pp. 60–61). In Britain, however, to remain in a cabinet is to indicate support for its policies. In almost every administration there are some ministers who, for whatever reason, would rather resign than support policies with which they disagree.

It remains to say a word about two debates about the roles of chief executives which to some extent cut across the categories used in this section.

One debate concerns the role that presidents of the United States ought to play in the American system of government. The two opposing views can be labelled with the names of their chief protagonists: Burns (1963, 1965) on the one hand, Corwin (1941) and de Grazia (1965, 1967; de Grazia and Schlesinger, 1967) on the other. The Burns view is broadly that the problems of American society demand the intervention of government and that the presidency is the only agency of government capable of organizing such intervention. The Burns view further maintains that the presidency as it is now organized is not strong enough for the purpose of intervention and that therefore it ought to be strengthened (for example, by the granting to the president of full powers over executive branch organization). The Corwin/de Grazia view does not dissent (at least not explicitly) from the view that America needs strong government. It questions, rather, whether president-centered government will necessarily be good government. It points out that strong presidents are apt to be insensitive to some of the minority interests represented in Congress, that strong presidents are apt to ignore dissent even when they do not try to suppress it, and that when presidents are not only strong but wrong, as in the case of Vietnam, the costs to the nation may be incalculable. Nothing much need be said about this debate (for recent contributions on the Corwin/de Grazia side, see Schlesinger, 1974; Tugwell and Cronin, 1974) except that, largely because its presuppositions are more normative than empirical, it has not inspired research. Because of the debate we may think more about the presidency; we do not know more about it.

The other debate revolves round the question of whether British government has become "prime ministerial" government. One school (Crossman, 1964, 1972; Mackintosh, 1968, 1967–68; Berkeley, 1968) holds that the cabinet is no longer of major importance in the British system and that in modern circumstances the prime minister, largely because of his position as party leader and his control of appointments, in effect governs the country. The other (Chester, 1962; Jones, 1965; Brown, 1968a, 1968b; Gordon Walker, 1972) holds that the position of the cabinet, in practice as well as constitutionally, is as strong as it ever was, that prime ministers are frequently defeated in cabinet, and that most of a prime minister's powers are far from absolute. Unlike the debate about the president's proper role, the debate on the power of the prime minister could, in principle, be settled empirically. At least it ought to be able to be. Unfortunately, neither side has ever specified in any detail what it takes the term "prime ministerial government" to mean and therefore what its empirical referents are; both sides, instead of analyzing the available evidence systematically, have resorted to proof by illustration ("On this occasion, the prime minister did so and so;" "ah yes, but on another occasion, he did such and such"). As a result, most of the debate has been conducted at the level of a barroom brawl. Some good points have been made, just as at least a few good punches are landed in most barroom brawls. But remarkably little new evidence has been forthcoming, and the terms of the debate in the 1970s are almost exactly what they were in the early 1960s. The curious can follow the proceedings, in outline if not in detail, in King (1969).

Research

The amount of work that needs to be done in the whole field of executives' internal dynamics is enormous, but, since most of the areas that need to be studied have already been referred to, at least in passing, in this section, they can be summarized briefly here. More research is needed into:

1. the structures, formal and informal, of the executive institutions of almost every country except possibly the United States (see Table 5, p. 208);
2. the composition of the bodies of "influentials" at different times and in different countries;
3. the extent to which policymaking and decision making are, in effect, parcelled out to formal and informal functional cabinets in different countries;
4. the composition of these functional cabinets under different circumstances and how they interact;
5. the sources of cabinet-level executives' influence at different times and in different systems;
6. the sources of chief executives' influence at different times and in different systems; and finally
7. the jobs that executives, including chief executives, actually do.

EXTERNAL RELATIONS: EXECUTIVES AND LEGISLATURES

To the extent that, as was claimed in an earlier section, executives are not merely a part of government but are, in some meaningful sense, government itself, they impinge on—and are impinged on by—the whole of the societies of which they form part and by other societies as well. It would be possible to write at length about executives' relationships with the civil service, the armed services, interest groups, courts, the executives of other countries, "the people," and so on almost indefinitely. Some of these relationships deserve more study than they have had; the relationships between politicians and civil servants, for example, are among the great gaps in all political science. By contrast, the whole question of leadership—inevitably, mainly executive leadership—has been studied much more in recent years than for a long time past (see especially Edinger, 1967).

The relationship that has most interested political scientists, however, is the one between executives and the institutions known, sometimes rather misleadingly, as legislatures. Our discussion of the executive/legislative relationship cannot be as full as our discussion of executives' internal dynamics. All the same, there are several points worth making. They can perhaps best be organized under three headings, corresponding to the three modes of executive/legislative relationships most commonly found in Western democracies: the separation of powers mode, the majority government mode, and the minority government/coalition mode.

The Separation of Powers Mode

The separation of powers mode ought perhaps to be called the "separation of institutions" mode, since, while the institutions are always separate, the powers are usually shared. The defining features of this mode are the existence of separate executive and legislative institutions, normally with nonoverlapping memberships, the separate election of the two institutions, the nondependence of the two institutions on one another (the executive is not "responsible" to the legislature), and the assigning to the two institutions, normally by a written constitution, of independent spheres of authority. It is really only in this mode, as we shall see, that it makes sense to speak *tout simple* of the relationship between "the executive" and "the legislature."

The best example of this mode—indeed, almost the only example outside Latin America—is the United States. The United States is also, as we have come to expect by now, almost the only country about which there is a substantial literature. It is a literature in which there are not really any major gaps. Several studies, notably Herring (1940) and Polsby (1964), discuss in general terms how in the United States legislation is a joint legislature-executive enterprise. Binkley (1962) approaches the same subject historically; Fisher (1972) is concerned with its formal, legal aspects. The relationships between Congress and the bureaucracy are discussed, also in general terms, by Harris (1964), Freeman (1965), and Neustadt (1965b). In addition there are more specific studies, either of the passage of particular pieces of legislation (Bailey, 1950; Berman, 1962) or of particular policy areas (Dahl, 1950; Huntington, 1961; Sapin, 1966; Sundquist, 1968; Manley, 1970). Most of these studies approach the subject mainly from Congress's point of view, but several writers approach it from the executive's (Chamberlain, 1946a, 1946b; Neustadt, 1954, 1955; Holtzman, 1970). If there is a gap in the literature, albeit (relatively speaking) a minor one, it is that no one has explored to what extent congressmen and senators adopt, consciously or subconsciously, a proexecutive or antiexecutive posture, that is, to what extent members of Congress see themselves —or behave as though they see themselves—as defenders of Congress's prerogatives per se against executive encroachments. This possibility is often mentioned in the literature but has never been systematically investigated.

The Majority Government Mode

The majority government mode differs from the separation of powers mode in every material respect. The institutions are not separate; most leading figures in the executive are also members of the legislature. They are elected at the same time. The executive is dependent on the legislature. The two institutions do not have independent, clearly delineated spheres of authority. Indeed, in a system like the British—on occasions when a single party has an overall majority in the House of Commons—it is not clear that Parliament is properly described as a legislature at all. Its part in the legislative process is usually small (see Walkland, 1968); the important things it does are not usually legislative in character.

Not only is it misleading to speak of Parliament as a legislature, it is equally misleading to speak of Parliament influencing or not influencing "the executive," as though the two bodies could be distinguished in the way that Congress and the presidency can be distinguished. They cannot be. And any analysis of executive/legislative relations in countries with political systems like Britain's should begin by jettisoning the Montesquieu formula. In systems like the British, the relationships that matter are not those between "the legislature" and "the executive" but those, first, between governments and their own backbench supporters, second, between governments and the opposition, and third, between governments and backbenchers of all parties on those occasions when backbenchers of opposing parties feel that what unites them as backbenchers (or advocates of particular policies, or whatever) is more important than what divides them as partisans. This last relationship is the only one that corresponds even remotely to the traditional executive/legislature paradigm. It is also the least common and least important relationship of the three. The failure to grasp this point has meant that much writing about Parliament is woollier than it need be and that a wide range of possible research topics has been neglected. (For a critical review of the literature on the British Parliament generally, see Patterson, 1973.)

The volume of writing on the British Parliament is prodigious, and most of it inevitably touches on M.P.s' relations with the government. Walkland (1968) discusses Parliament's role in legislation, Reid (1966) Parliament and financial control, Richards (1967) Parliament and foreign affairs. Bradshaw and Pring (1972) compare Parliament with the United States Congress. Wiseman (1966) collates almost everything said or written up to that point about Parliament's influence on the executive. Richards (1972) and King (1974) explore in general terms the role of the backbencher. Hanson and Crick (1970) present papers on recent changes in parliamentary procedures. Barnett (1969) presents a rare case study of the passage of an act of Parliament, indicating what a peripheral role the House of Commons and the Labour opposition played. Granada (1973) consists of the transcripts of three long television programs on

Parliament and includes a case study of the passage of a bill, assigning rather more importance than does Barnett to the role of the House of Commons.

None of these volumes, however, seeks to explore in detail the relations between governments and backbenchers or governments and opposition. Few of them—Barnett and Granada are important exceptions—are based on field research as distinct from a reading of published materials. Almost the only study providing a detailed account of the relations between governments and their own parliamentary supporters is Butt (1969), and Butt's study is more historical than systematic; it deals in detail neither with what governments and backbenchers need from one another and what resources they can bring to bear in their relations with one another, nor with the circumstances in which backbench influence is likely to be at a maximum. British ministers are fond of saying, apropos of giving their backbench supporters an advance indication of impending legislation, "You have to let them see the cat before you let it out of the bag;" but there is no study of how British governments seek to anticipate the reactions of their own party in Parliament. Nor is there any study of the influence of the opposition parties on governments, though Butt, Herman (1972), and Punnett (1973) provide some information.

Most of the detailed scholarly work has gone into the relationship that, in practice, matters least, namely, that between governments and backbenchers *qua* backbenchers. Richards (1970) investigated "free votes" in the House of Commons, which occur when the whips are off and members are allowed to vote as they like. Coombes (1966), Johnson (1966), and Morris (1970) deal with various select committees—the point being that select committees in the British House of Commons can function only when both the members of the committee and the party whips agree that the subjects to be discussed by the committee are of a nonpartisan nature and are unlikely seriously to embarrass the government. Even in this connection, no serious effort has been made to discover what conditions have to be fulfilled before a subject is deemed nonpartisan for this purpose or under what conditions M.P.s play pure backbench roles instead of government-supporter or opposition-supporter roles. If all these subjects have been neglected with regard to Britain, they have been even more completely neglected with regard to other countries with British-type systems, notably Canada, Australia, and New Zealand. One can cite no major study.

The classic majority government regimes have been in Anglo-Saxon countries. But the Fifth Republic in France, as it has operated since 1958, probably deserves to be assimilated to this type. Although legislature and executive have been separated in a variety of ways (a directly elected president, a clearly delineated *domaine de la loi*), it remains true that the survival of a French government depends on its ability to secure a majority in the National Assembly and that every French government since 1958 has been in a majority or near-majority position. Under these circumstances one would expect the government/backbench and government/opposition relationships in France to resemble quite closely those in Britain. That this is indeed the case is suggested by the few available studies of the subject (notably Charlot, 1971; Williams, 1968, pp. 102–13; Williams, 1971), though the opposition in the French parliament seems, if anything, to have even less influence than in the British. It is not clear to what extent and under what circumstances nonpartisan backbench roles have developed in France.

The Minority Government/Coalition Mode

The minority government/coalition mode is the predominant mode on the continent of Europe (Herman and Pope, 1973). It resembles the majority government mode in every respect save that the government is dependent on the support in parliament not of a single party but of two or more parties. These parties may form a coalition government, or one or more of them may remain outside, supporting the resulting minority government with their votes. This mode would seem on the face of it to give great power to the legislature, since the legislature can not only, like Congress, refuse to enact legislation but can also, unlike Congress, topple the government. Again, however, the term "the legislature" is misleading. The relationships that matter are those among the leaders of all the parties forming the coalition or supporting the minority government, and among all of these leaders and their followers. Executive/legislative relations largely take the form of, and are best described as, inter- and intraparty relations. The procedures of the legislature become the means through which these relationships express themselves. Fortunately for the political scientist, whereas backbench pressure on majority governments tends to occur behind closed doors, the party maneuvering that attends minority and coalition governments tends to take place more in public. Partly for this reason, executive/legislative relations in the *locus classicus* of the minority government/coalition mode—the French Fourth Republic—have been explored in considerable detail, notably in Williams (1964) and MacRae (1967).

Executive/legislative relations in West Germany are an interesting hybrid. They conform broadly to the norms of the minority government/coalition mode, but the number of parties is much smaller in West Germany than in most Western European countries and, despite the West German cabinet's dependence on the Bundestag, a "separation of powers mentality" seems to have survived into the post-1949 period from an earlier period when German parliaments were separate from the executive and indeed were meant to act primarily as a check on the executive (Loewenberg, 1967; Sontheimer, 1972; see also Ridley, 1966). The continued existence of this mentality would seem to explain why parliament, especially its committees, plays a considerably larger part in the legislative process in West Germany than in Britain, even though party discipline is almost equally stringent in the two countries. It probably also explains why, to a much greater extent than in Britain, the parliamentary leadership of the parties making up the majority in West Germany is organizationally distinct from the leadership of the cabinet. In Britain there is one center of power within each parliamentary party; in Germany, at least among the government parties, there are two.

Perhaps because the West German system is a relatively new one, the literature on executive/legislative relations in West Germany, although less voluminous than the comparable British literature, is more sensitive to the nuances of the political substructures underlying the constitutional superstructure. Loewenberg (1967) deals in detail with the interactions between cabinet and Bundestag; so, more briefly, does Johnson (1973). There are, moreover, two full-length case studies of the passage, or nonpassage, of legislation in West Germany: Safran (1967) on health insurance reform and Braunthal (1972) on transport finance. In both cases, opposition in the Bundestag thwarted the cabinet, or at least deflected it from its original purpose. Unfortunately, the research on France and West Germany cannot be matched for other Western European countries.

THE EXECUTIVE PSYCHE

This chapter of the *Handbook* is concerned with executive institutions—with the dynamics and interplay of more or less permanent structures and processes. It follows that it is not concerned with "random events"—events that, however important *sub specie aeternitatis,* do not form part of some continuing institutional pattern. The assassination of President Kennedy, for instance, does not fall within our terms of reference (though it certainly would if assassinations of American presidents became so frequent as to have a major impact on the functioning of the presidency); neither does the megalomania, if such it was, of President de Gaulle.

It is against this background that we must consider the relevance to executive studies of a body of literature discussed elsewhere in the *Handbook*—the literature on personality and politics. Obviously the personalities of executives matter; no one denies that. The question for us is whether anything has been said, or could be said, about the personalities of executives which would, in a systematic way, increase our understanding of the functioning of executive institutions.

Greenstein, in his chapter in Volume 4 and more fully in an earlier study (1969), suggests that most politically relevant studies of personality fall into one of three categories. The first consists of psychological analyses of single political actors, the most obvious examples being psychological biographies like the George and George study (1956) of Woodrow Wilson. The second consists of psychological analyses of types of political actors, such as those with "authoritarian personalities." The third consists of studies of the aggregate effects of personality characteristics on political systems, examples being studies of national character and some studies of voting behavior. Greenstein discusses these categories at considerable length in both places, and there is no need to go over the same ground here.

What is clear is that almost none of the psychological work has an institutional focus, in the sense that the author(s) set out to explore the workings of (say) a legislature or an executive using psychological evidence. More than that, it is virtually impossible even to make inferences about the workings of institutions from the great bulk of the psychological work, whatever its focus. Most of the single-actor studies, as one would expect, are concerned exclusively with a single man and a single set of events; the George and George study tells us a great deal about Woodrow Wilson and early twentieth-century American history but very little, even by implication, about the presidency. The typological studies have not typically been concerned with ascertaining whether certain psychological types are to be found in disproportionate numbers in certain institutions—still less with assessing the influence of the various types on those institutions. The aggregative studies have been concerned mainly with very large aggregations like "the nation" or "voters."

There is, however, a small number of studies that do focus on institutions, and they are worth noting, partly because of their intrinsic importance, partly because they give an indication of the sorts of things that are possible. Moreover, some of the studies that say little about institutions could, without the authors altering their techniques in any way, have said more.

Single-Actor Studies

The central point about single-actor studies is a simple one. Very few political biographies take the trouble to place their subject in his or her institutional setting. We are told what the views of the book's subject were, how he fought his battles, whom he liked and disliked, what he said in his speeches; we are seldom told what his operating style was, who he saw (and refused to see), how much or how little he consulted his colleagues, how he allocated his time, what his relations with civil servants were like—and so on. The rare exceptions to this rule, such as Schlesinger's trilogy on Franklin Roosevelt (1957, 1959, 1960), are widely quoted in political science textbooks precisely because they are exceptions.

The same is true of the psychological biographies. Their mode of explanation is peculiar to themselves; but what they seek to explain is what all biographies seek to explain. Rogow's life of James Forrestal (1963; see also Edinger, 1965), for example, is chiefly a study of an interesting individual in politics and is only tangentially a study of a department head and cabinet officer functioning within the American system. The George and George study of Wilson, as we said, tells us little about the presidency as an institution. But it could easily have done so; indeed, three of the chapters—"Wilson and Congress,"

"The 'Break,'" and "Battle with the Senate"—could still provide the growth points for a major study, not just of Wilson, the man, but of Wilson, man-in-office. Few things are as central to people, and as revealing about them, as the way they do their job. Few jobs are unaffected by the personalities of the men and women who do them. The psychological approach ought to be—but has not so far been—peculiarly valuable in illuminating the interplay between individuals and institutions.

Studies of Types of Actors

Happily, a few of the typological studies constitute partial exceptions to this general rule. Several of them do seek to relate the psychological characteristics of officeholders to these same officerholders' behavior in office. The most ambitious of them suggest lines of enquiry that students of executives might well pursue.

Barber in *The Presidential Character* (1972; see also Barber, 1968) proposes that American presidents be divided into four psychological types, depending on whether their personalities are "active" or "passive" and whether they display a "positive" or "negative" affect towards political activity. Franklin Roosevelt, Truman, and Kennedy were active-positive presidents; they achieved much as presidents and enjoyed achieving it. Nixon was an active-negative president; he felt impelled towards political action but derived few emotional rewards from it. Having defined the four types, Barber is concerned with the phenomenology, dynamics, and genesis (to use Greenstein's terms) of each of them, but he is also concerned with using presidential personality to predict presidential performance—with relating psychological characteristics to behavior in office. In the case of Nixon, for example, he relates his need for power ("a core need") to his tendency to take decisions on his own and to isolate himself even from his own aides.

Barber's analysis bristles with difficulties (see also George, 1974). Why should activity/passivity and positive/negative affect be conceived of as dichotomies instead of as continua? Why two "baselines" defining four psychological types instead of (say) three defining eight? Even though he allows for only four psychological types, Barber's definition of them is a good deal more precise than his definition of the types of behavior to which they are supposed to relate. Perhaps most important, it is never made clear whether the four types are types only of American presidents or whether others can be categorized in the same way. If they can, which others? The entire human race? (At one point, p. 12, Barber speaks of his two dimensions as standing for "two central features of anyone's orientation toward life.") Or simply all politicians? Or all heads of government? In practice, it is disconcerting to discover that it is impossible to assign most modern British prime ministers to one or other of the four categories without stretching the definitions of the categories to the point where they are meaningless. Nevertheless, despite all this, if psychological knowledge is to throw light on the functioning of institutions, it must almost certainly be by means of the discovery and application of such typologies. Barber's work deserves to be followed up.

An even more problematical, but equally suggestive, study is Iremonger's *The Fiery Chariot* (1970). Iremonger's point of departure was the discovery that fully 62.5 percent of all British prime ministers between Spencer Perceval and Neville Chamberlain were either illegitimate or else suffered the loss of one or other parent before the age of fifteen. She went on to suggest that not only these prime ministers but also almost all of the others exhibited certain common psychological characteristics—conformed, in effect, to a single psychological type. This type she dubbed "Phaeton" after the Greek demigod Phaeton, who, seeking proofs of his father's affection, asked to be allowed to drive his father's fiery chariot, the sun, for a day. The Phaeton type, according to Iremonger, is characterized by abnormal sensitivity, isolation and reserve, aggression combined in many cases with marked natural timidity, a propensity to depression, often by a touch of recklessness.

Like Barber, Iremonger is concerned with the phenomenology, dynamics, and genesis (to use Greenstein's terms again) of her single type; she sees the origins of the Phaeton complex in the deprivation of parental affection. She is also concerned with the bearing of her psychological discoveries on politics. But here her analysis trails off. It is never quite clear whether the Phaeton complex is supposed to explain British prime ministers' ambition, or their success in attaining their ambition, or (as Iremonger sometimes seems to argue) their ultimate failure in office. Some of Iremonger's figures are inaccurate, as Berrington (1974) has shown, and some recent prime ministers (Attlee, Wilson) appear not to conform to her type. Moreover, Iremonger's single type accommodates American presidents no better than Barber's four types accommodate British prime ministers. Both theories, like certain wines, do not travel well. It would be interesting to know why not.

Probably the best-known typological study, apart from *The Authoritarian Personality* by Adorno *et al.* (1950), is Barber's *The Lawmakers* (1965). Barber discerned among first-term members of the Connecticut state legislature four psychological types, resembling closely the four types of president he was to describe later in *The Presidential Character*. The activity/passivity dimension is common to the two studies; in the later work, willingness or unwillingness to return to the legislature is generalized into positive or negative affect. Barber's descriptions of the four types are well known. What is generally overlooked, however, is that his analysis includes a discussion of the contribution that each type makes—or fails to make—to the work of the legislature. The "lawmaker" infuses energy and reason into an all too often sluggish and irrational system; the "spectator" reduces interpersonal tensions; the "reluctant" helps ensure that the legislative rules of the game are obeyed; only the "advertiser" probably contributes nothing, although just conceivably his or her presence encourages rational debate.

Barber has not developed this aspect of his research, but the broad lines he has laid down are clear enough. One begins with an institution or set of institutions and asks what kinds of psychological actors the institution attracts, what the frequency is of different psychological types within the institution, how the different types interact, and what the impact of each type is on the institution's functioning. Different institutions could, of course, be compared along these dimensions. The institutions studied could as well be executives as legislatures.

Aggregative Studies

Aggregative studies are concerned with the aggregate effects of personality characteristics on political systems. Greenstein suggests that four complementary research strategies are appropriate in this connection: first, "building up" from direct observation of small-scale political processes (e.g., Barber's *Power in Committees,* 1966, a study of decision making by town boards of finance, and Browning and Jacob's, 1964, and Browning's, 1968, work on the links between personality and involvement in specific types of political activity); second, using surveys to estimate the frequency of psychological attributes in populations and relating the frequencies to system characteristics (e.g., Converse and Dupeux's investigation, 1966, of the relationship between the incidence of party identification in France and the phenomenon of the "flash" political party); third, modifying such frequency analyses to take account of "nonadditivity," that is, of the fact that not all actors and roles are of equal weight; and fourth, "working back" to data from theoretical analyses of systems and from the hypothetical psychological requirements for their functioning, a strategy suggested by Lasswell's speculations (1951) on democracy and "the democratic character."

It will not have escaped the reader's notice that for the student of executives and other institutions the distinction between typological studies and aggregative studies is a distinction without a difference: typologies are developed not for their own sake but precisely to explore their aggregate effects on some larger system or systems. From this point of view Barber's *The Presidential Character* and *The Lawmakers* are just as much aggregative studies as is his *Power in Committees.* Of the strategies proposed by Greenstein, the one most appropriate to executives research is probably "building up." The work of both Barber and Browning/Jacob could easily, with a little imagination, be adapted to the study of (say) White House staffs or British, French, or German cabinets.

CONCLUDING REMARKS

We conclude where we began, with the assertion that executives are important institutions of government—probably the most important—and that their neglect by recent generations of political scientists cannot be justified. There are gaps in our knowledge of individual countries. A genuinely comparative literature scarcely exists. The problem in the mid-1970s is not to decide what the right questions are; they are evident. The problem is to answer them.

It remains only to set out a number of observations, in no particular order, about some of the characteristics that the best future research will probably display.

1. It will be based on detailed investigation. A large proportion of the existing work, as we said at the beginning, is impressionistic and repetitive, based on a mixture of bland constitutional description and accounts of recent historical incidents chosen (one is sometimes forced to conclude) more or less at random. Executives deserve to be studied with just as much of an eye for detail as (say) committees of the United States Congress.

2. It will be comparative. There are two reasons for studying institutions comparatively, which, taken singly or together, strongly suggest that single-instance studies are almost bound to be defective. The first is that observing several instances almost invariably leads one to ask questions of each single instance that one would not have asked otherwise. To take a simple example, a student of the British cabinet is unlikely to pay close attention to the planning of the government's legislative program and to the mechanisms for effecting liaison between the government and its own backbench supporters unless he or she has observed the elaborate ways in which these matters are organized in Washington. The second reason for studying institutions comparatively is that unless one does, one has no "control," in the scientific sense. One does not know what is peculiar to a specific country, what general to a number of countries; one has no means of discovering which correlations among phenomena are accidental or spurious, which are genuinely causal. Does, for example, the explanation for the secrecy surrounding the deliberations of British cabinets lie in aspects of British political culture or in features common to all single-party majority governments in parliamentary systems? There is no way of answering this question if Britain alone is studied.

3. Most of the comparisons that the best future research will make will be among countries with political systems that are broadly similar. Most of what little comparative work exists at the moment is concerned with the United States and Great Britain, and in at least one instance, Neustadt (1969), it is brilliantly successful. But most of it is flawed, because the two entities being compared are too unalike. They differ in almost every respect, and it is therefore virtually impossible to isolate those specific factors that account for the particular differences that one is interested in. It is as though a biologist were to compare the behavior not of two different bird species but of one bird species and one fish species. Gross differences could be detected, and gross explanations offered for the differences; but the finer points would be lost. The com-

parisons that suggest themselves in the present state of the art are among the countries of the old white Commonwealth, almost all of which have similar British-type parliamentary systems, and among the coalition-based parliamentary systems of continental Europe.

4. Finally, it will seek to answer specific, answerable questions (some of which have been indicated elsewhere in this chapter). Although it is impossible to prove the point, it is almost certain that the best way forward lies in attempting to answer specific questions and to solve specific intellectual puzzles. Problems of concepts and methodology will arise in the course of such attempts. They should be tackled as they arise. Some concepts and some notions about methodology are, of course, a precondition of conducting research at all. But attempts to solve in advance all problems of concepts and all problems of methodology will tend in practice to be substitutes for research, not preludes to it. They are anyway doomed to failure since the most intractable problems of concepts and methods almost never manifest themselves until research is actually under way. As Medawar puts it (1957, p. 87):

> No scientist is admired for failing in the attempt to solve problems that lie beyond his competence. The most he can hope for is the kindly contempt earned by the Utopian politician. If politics is the art of the possible, research is surely the art of the soluble. Both are immensely practical-minded affairs.

REFERENCES

Adorno, Theodore W., Else Frenkel-Brunswik, Daniel J. Levinson, and R. Nevitt Sanford (1950). *The Authoritarian Personality.* New York: Harper.

Alderman, R. K., and J. A. Cross (1967). *The Tactics of Resignation: A Study in British Cabinet Government.* London: Routledge & Kegan Paul.

Almond, Gabriel A. (1960). "Introduction." In Gabriel A. Almond and James S. Coleman (eds.), *The Politics of Developing Areas.* Princeton: Princeton University Press.

Amphoux, Jean (1962). *Le Chancelier Fédéral dans la Régime Constitutionnel de la République Fédéral d'Allemagne.* Paris: Librairie Générale de Droit et de Jurisprudence.

Anderson, Patrick (1968). *The President's Men.* Garden City, N.Y.: Doubleday.

Andrews, William G. (1960). "Some thoughts on the power of dissolution." *Parliamentary Affairs* 13:286–96.

Arne, S. (1962). *Le Président du Conseil des Ministres sous la IVme République.* Paris: Librairie Générale de Droit et de Jurisprudence.

Avril, Pierre (1969). *Politics in France.* Translated by John Ross. Harmondsworth, Middlesex: Penguin Books.

Baar, Carl, and Ellen Baar (1973). "Party and convention organization and leadership selection in Canada and the United States." In Donald R. Matthews (ed.), *Perspectives on Presidential Selection*. Washington, D.C.: Brookings Institution.

Bailey, Stephen Kemp (1950). *Congress Makes a Law: The Story behind the Employment Act of 1946*. New York: Columbia University Press.

——————— (1956). "The president and his political executives." In Sidney Hyman (ed.), *The Office of the American Presidency. Annals of the American Academy of Political and Social Science* 307:24–36.

Barber, James David (1965). *The Lawmakers: Recruitment and Adaptation to Legislative Life*. New Haven: Yale University Press.

——————— (1966). *Power in Committees: An Experiment in the Governmental Process*. Chicago: Rand McNally.

——————— (1968). "Classifying and predicting presidential style: two 'weak' presidents." *Journal of Social Issues* 24:51–80.

——————— (1972). *The Presidential Character: Predicting Performance in the White House*. Englewood Cliffs, N.J.: Prentice-Hall.

———————, ed. (1974). *Choosing the President*. Englewood Cliffs, N.J.: Prentice-Hall.

Barnett, Malcolm Joel (1969). *The Politics of Legislation: The Rent Act 1957*. London: Weidenfeld and Nicolson.

Berkeley, Humphry (1968). *The Power of the Prime Minister*. London: George Allen & Unwin.

Berman, Daniel M. (1962). *A Bill Becomes a Law: The Civil Rights Act of 1960*. New York: Macmillan.

Berrington, Hugh (1974). "Review article: *The Fiery Chariot: British Prime Ministers and the Search for Love*" by Lucille Iremonger. *British Journal of Political Science* 4: 345–69.

Binkley, Wilfred E. (1962). *President and Congress*. New York: Vintage Books.

——————— (1964). *The Man in the White House: His Powers and Duties*. New York: Harper & Row.

Bishop, Donald G. (1973). "The cabinet and foreign policy." In Robert Boardman and A. J. R. Groom (eds.), *The Management of Britain's External Relations*. London: Macmillan.

Blondel, Jean, and E. Drexel Godfrey, Jr. (1968). *The Government of France*. New York: Crowell.

Boardman, Robert, and A. J. R. Groom, eds. (1973). *The Management of Britain's External Relations*. London: Macmillan.

Bonnor, Jean (1958). "The four Labour cabinets." *Sociological Review* 6:37–48.

Boyle, Edward, and Anthony Crosland in conversation with Maurice Kogan (1971). *The Politics of Education*. Harmondsworth, Middlesex: Penguin Books.

Bradshaw, Kenneth, and David Pring (1972). *Parliament and Congress*. London: Constable.

Braunthal, Gerard (1965). *The Federation of German Industry in Politics.* Ithaca, N.Y.: Cornell University Press.

_____ (1972). *The West German Legislative Process: A Case Study of Two Transportation Bills.* Ithaca, N.Y.: Cornell University Press.

Brown, A. H. (1968a). "Prime ministerial power (part I)." *Public Law* Spring 1968:28–51.

_____ (1968b). "Prime ministerial power (part II)." *Public Law* Summer 1968: 96–118.

Brown, Stuart Gerry (1966). *The American Presidency: Leadership, Partisanship, and Popularity.* New York: Macmillan.

Browne, Eric C., and Mark N. Franklin (1973). "Aspects of coalition payoffs in European parliamentary democracies." *American Political Science Review* 67:453–69.

Browning, Rufus P. (1968). "The interaction of personality and political system in decisions to run for office: some data and a simulation technique." *Journal of Social Issues* 24:93–109.

Browning, Rufus P., and Herbert Jacob (1964). "Power motivation and the political personality." *Public Opinion Quarterly* 28:75–90.

Brownlow, Louis (1949). *The President and the Presidency.* Chicago: University of Chicago Press.

Bryce, Lord (James Bryce) (1893). *The American Commonwealth.* London: Macmillan.

Buck, Philip W. (1963a). *Amateurs and Professionals in British Politics 1918–1959.* Chicago: University of Chicago Press.

_____ (1963b). "The early start toward cabinet office, 1918–55." *Western Political Quarterly* 16:624–32.

Burns, James MacGregor (1955). *Roosevelt: The Lion and the Fox.* New York: Harcourt, Brace.

_____ (1963). *The Deadlock of Democracy: Four-Party Politics.* Englewood Cliffs, N.J.: Prentice-Hall.

_____ (1965). *Presidential Government: The Crucible of Leadership.* Boston: Houghton Mifflin.

Butler, D. E., and Anthony King (1965). *The British General Election of 1964.* London: Macmillan.

_____ (1966). *The British General Election of 1966.* London: Macmillan.

Butt, Ronald (1969). *The Power of Parliament.* London: Constable.

Camps, Miriam (1964). *Britain and the European Community 1955–1963.* Princeton: Princeton University Press.

Carey, William D. (1969). "Presidential staffing in the sixties and seventies." *Public Administration Review* 29:450–58.

Carter, Byrum E. (1956). *The Office of Prime Minister.* London: Faber and Faber.

Chamberlain, Lawrence H. (1946a). *The President, Congress and Legislation.* New York: Columbia University Press.

_____ (1946b). "The president, Congress, and legislation." *Political Science Quarterly* 61:42–60.

Charlot, Jean (1971). *The Gaullist Phenomenon: The Gaullist Movement in the Fifth Republic.* Translated by Monica Charlot and Marianne Neighbour. London: George Allen & Unwin.

Chester, D. N. (1962). "Who governs Britain?" *Parliamentary Affairs* 15:519–27.

Clark, Keith C., and Laurence J. Legere, eds. (1969). *The President and the Management of National Security: A Report by the Institute for Defense Analyses.* New York: Praeger.

Converse, Philip E., and Georges Dupeux (1966). "De Gaulle and Eisenhower: the public image of the victorious general." In Angus Campbell, Philip E. Converse, Warren E. Miller, and Donald E. Stokes, *Elections and the Political Order.* New York: Wiley.

Coombes, David (1966). *The Member of Parliament and the Administration: The Case of the Select Committee on Nationalized Industries.* London: George Allen & Unwin.

Cornwell, Elmer E., Jr. (1965). *Presidential Leadership of Public Opinion.* Bloomington: Indiana University Press.

Corwin, Edward S. (1941). "Some aspects of the presidency." *Annals of the American Academy of Political and Social Sciences* 218:122–31.

_____ (1957). *The President: Office and Powers 1787–1957.* New York: New York University Press.

Crisp, L. F. (1955). *The Australian Federal Labour Party 1901–1951.* London: Longmans, Green.

_____ (1965). *Australian National Government.* Croydon, Victoria: Longmans.

Cronin, Thomas E. (1970). " 'Everybody believes in democracy until he gets to the White House . . .': an examination of White House-departmental relations." *Law and Contemporary Problems: The Institutionalized Presidency* 35:573–625.

Cronin, Thomas E., and Sanford D. Greenberg, eds. (1969). *The Presidential Advisory System.* New York: Harper & Row.

Crossman, Richard (1964). "Introduction." In Walter Bagehot, *The English Constitution.* London: C. A. Watts.

_____ (1972). *Inside View: Three Lectures on Prime Ministerial Government.* London: Jonathan Cape.

Cunliffe, Marcus (1968). *American Presidents and the Presidency.* New York: American Heritage.

Curtis, Michael (1968). *Comparative Government and Politics.* New York: Harper & Row.

Daalder, Hans (1964). *Cabinet Reform in Britain 1914–1963.* Stanford: Stanford University Press.

Dahl, Robert A. (1950). *Congress and Foreign Policy.* New York: Harcourt, Brace.

David, Paul T., ed. (1961). *Presidential Election and Transition, 1960–61.* Washington, D.C.: Brookings Institution.

David, Paul T., Malcolm Moos, and Ralph M. Goldman, eds. (1954). *Presidential Nominating Politics in 1952*. Baltimore: Johns Hopkins University Press.

David, Paul T., Ralph M. Goldman, and Richard C. Bain (1960). *The Politics of National Party Conventions*. Washington, D.C.: Brookings Institution.

David, Paul T., and Ross Pollock (1957). *Executives for Government: Central Issues of Federal Personnel Administration*. Washington, D.C.: Brookings Institution.

Davis, James W. (1967). *Presidential Primaries: Road to the White House*. New York: Crowell.

Dawson, R. MacGregor, revised by Norman Ward (1963). *The Government of Canada*. Toronto: University of Toronto Press.

de Grazia, Alfred (1965). *Republic in Crisis: Congress Against the Executive Force*. New York: Federal Legal Publications.

——————, ed. (1967). *Congress: The First Branch of Government*. Washington, D.C.: American Enterprise Institute for Public Policy Research.

de Grazia, Alfred, and Arthur M. Schlesinger, Jr. (1967). *Congress and the Presidency: Their Role in Modern Times*. Washington, D.C.: American Enterprise Institute for Public Policy Research.

Dogan, Mattei, and Maria Scheffer-Van der Veen (1957). "Le personnel ministériel Hollandais (1848–1958)." *L'Année sociologique* 8:95–125.

Dorsey, John T., Jr. (1966). "Political executives." In Alex N. Dragnich and John C. Wahlke (eds.), *Government and Politics: An Introduction to Political Science*. New York: Random House.

Edinger, Lewis J. (1965). *Kurt Schumacher: A Study in Personality and Political Behavior*. Stanford: Stanford University Press.

——————, ed. (1967). *Political Leadership in Industrialized Societies: Studies in Comparative Analysis*. New York: Wiley.

Edinger, Lewis J., and Donald D. Searing (1967). "Social background in elite analysis: a methodological inquiry." *American Political Science Review* 61:428–45.

Egremont, Lord (John Wyndham) (1968). *Wyndham and Children First*. London: Macmillan.

Elazar, Daniel J. (1965). "Which road to the presidency?" *Southwestern Social Science Quarterly* 46:37–46.

Encel, S. (1961). "The political *élite* in Australia." *Political Studies* 9:16–36.

—————— (1962). *Cabinet Government in Australia*. Melbourne: Melbourne University Press.

—————— (1970). *Equality and Authority: A Study of Class, Status and Power in Australia*. London: Tavistock Publications.

Falk, Stanley L. (1964). "The National Security Council under Truman, Eisenhower, and Kennedy." *Political Science Quarterly*. 79:403–34.

Fenno, Richard F., Jr. (1959). *The President's Cabinet: An Analysis in the Period from Wilson to Eisenhower*. Cambridge, Mass.: Harvard University Press.

_____ (1964). "Now is the time for cabinet makers." In Donald Bruce Johnson and Jack L. Walker (eds.), *The Dynamics of the American Presidency*. New York: Wiley.

Finer, Herman (1949). *The Theory and Practice of Modern Government*. New York: Holt.

Fisher, Louis (1972). *President and Congress: Power and Policy*. New York: Free Press.

Flash, Edward S., Jr. (1965). *Economic Advice and Presidential Leadership: The Council of Economic Advisers*. New York: Columbia University Press.

Freeman, J. Lieper (1965). *The Political Process: Executive Bureau-Legislative Committee Relations*. New York: Random House.

Fried, Robert C. (1966). *Comparative Political Institutions*. New York: Macmillan.

Friedrich, Carl Joachim (1963). *Man and His Government: An Empirical Theory of Politics*. New York: McGraw-Hill.

George, Alexander L. (1974). "Assessing presidential character." *World Politics* 26:234–82.

George, Alexander L., and Juliette L. George (1956). *Woodrow Wilson and Colonel House: A Personality Study*. New York: John Day.

Gordon Walker, Patrick (1972). *The Cabinet*. London: Jonathan Cape.

Granada Television (1973). *The State of the Nation: Parliament*. London: Granada Television.

Greenstein, Fred I. (1965). "Popular images of the president." *American Journal of Psychiatry*. 122:523–29.

_____ (1969). *Personality and Politics: Problems of Evidence, Inference, and Conceptualization*. Chicago: Markham.

_____ (1974). "What the president means to Americans: presidential 'choice' between elections." In James David Barber (ed.), *Choosing the President*. Englewood Cliffs, N.J.: Prentice-Hall.

Greenstein, Fred I., Valentine Herman, Robert N. Stradling, and Elia Zureik (1974). "The child's conception of the queen and the prime minister." *British Journal of Political Science* 4:257–87.

Guttsman, W. L. (1963). *The British Political Elite*. London: MacGibbon & Kee.

Gwyn, W. B. (1965). *The Meaning of the Separation of Powers: An Analysis of the Doctrine from its Origin to the Adoption of the United States Constitution*. Tulane Studies in Political Science, Vol. 9. New Orleans: Tulane University; The Hague: Martinus Nijhoff.

Haight, David E., and Larry D. Johnston, eds. (1965). *The President: Roles and Powers*. Chicago: Rand McNally.

Hanson, A. H., and Bernard Crick, eds. (1970). *The Commons in Transition*. London: Fontana/Collins.

Hargrove, Erwin L. (1966). *Presidential Leadership: Personality and Political Style*. New York: Macmillan.

Harris, Joseph P. (1964). *Congressional Control of Administration.* Washington, D.C.: Brookings Institution.

Headey, B. W. (1974a). *British Cabinet Ministers: The Roles of Politicians in Elective Office.* London: George Allen & Unwin.

——————— (1974b). "The role skills of cabinet ministers: a cross-national view." *Political Studies* 22:66–85.

Heasman, D. J. (1962). "The prime minister and the cabinet." *Parliamentary Affairs* 15: 461–84.

——————— (1963). "Parliamentary paths to high office." *Parliamentary Affairs* 16:315–30.

Heclo, Hugh (1973). "Presidential and prime ministerial selection." In Donald R. Matthews (ed.), *Perspectives on Presidential Selection.* Washington, D.C.: Brookings Institution.

Heclo, Hugh, and Aaron Wildavsky (1974). *The Private Government of Public Money: Community and Policy inside British Politics.* London: Macmillan.

Heller, Francis H. (1960). *The Presidency: A Modern Perspective.* New York: Random House.

Henry, Laurin L. (1960). *Presidential Transitions.* Washington, D.C.: Brookings Institution.

——————— (1961). "The transition: transfer of presidential responsibility." In Paul T. David (ed.), *The Presidential Election and Transition 1960–1961.* Washington, D.C.: Brookings Institution.

——————— (1969). "The presidency, executive staffing, and the federal bureaucracy." In Aaron Wildavsky (ed.), *The Presidency.* Boston: Little, Brown.

Herman, Valentine (1972). "Backbench and opposition amendments to government legislation." In Valentine Herman and Dick Leonard (eds.), *The Backbencher and Parliament: A Reader.* London: Macmillan.

——————— (forthcoming). "Comparative perspectives on ministerial stability in Britain." *British Journal of Political Science* 5.

Herman, Valentine, and John Pope (1973). "Minority governments in Western democracies." *British Journal of Political Science* 3:191–212.

Herring, Pendleton (1940). *Presidential Leadership: The Political Relations of Congress and the Chief Executive.* New York: Rinehart.

Hewison, R. J. P. (1952). "The organisation of the cabinet secretariat." *Public Administration* 30:221–25.

Hinsdale, Mary (1911). *A History of the President's Cabinet.* Ann Arbor: University of Michigan Press.

Hirschfield, Robert S., ed. (1968). *The Power of the Presidency: Concepts and Controversy.* New York: Atherton.

Hobbs, Edward H. (1954). *Behind the President: A Study of Executive Office Agencies.* Washington, D.C.: Public Affairs Press.

Holtzman, Abraham (1970). *Legislative Liaison: Executive Leadership in Congress.* Chicago: Rand McNally.

Hoopes, Townsend (1969). *The Limits of Intervention: An Inside Account of How the Johnson Policy of Escalation in Vietnam Was Reversed.* New York: McKay.

Huntington, Samuel P. (1961). *The Common Defense: Strategic Programs in National Politics.* New York: Columbia University Press.

Hyman, Sidney (1954). *The American President.* London: Odhams Press.

Iremonger, Lucille (1970). *The Fiery Chariot: A Study of British Prime Ministers and the Search for Love.* London: Secker & Warburg.

Jackson, Henry M. (1965). *The National Security Council: Jackson Subcommittee Papers on Policy-Making at the Presidential Level.* New York: Praeger.

Jackson, Robert J. (1968). *Rebels and Whips: An Analysis of Dissension, Discipline and Cohesion in British Political Parties.* London: Macmillan.

Jenkins, Peter (1970). *The Battle of Downing Street.* London: Charles Knight.

Jennings, Ivor (1959a). *Cabinet Government.* Cambridge: Cambridge University Press.

——————— (1959b). *The Law and the Constitution.* London: University of London Press.

Johnson, Donald Bruce, and Jack L. Walker, eds. (1964). *The Dynamics of the American Presidency.* New York: Wiley.

Johnson, Nevil (1966). *Parliament and Administration: The Estimates Committee 1945–65.* London: George Allen & Unwin.

——————— (1973). *Government in the Federal Republic of Germany: The Executive at Work.* Oxford: Pergamon Press.

Jones, G. W. (1965). "The prime minister's power." *Parliamentary Affairs* 18:167–85.

——————— (1973). "The prime minister's advisers." *Political Studies* 21:363–75.

——————— (1974). "The office of prime minister." In Herbert van Thal (ed.), *The Prime Ministers: From Sir Robert Walpole to Sir Robert Peel.* London: George Allen & Unwin.

Kaminsky, Elijah Ben-Zion (1973). "The selection of French presidents." In Donald R. Matthews (ed.), *Perspectives on Presidential Selection.* Washington, D.C.: Brookings Institution.

King, Anthony (1966a). "Britain's ministerial turnover." *New Society* 8:257–58.

——————— (1966b). "Britain: the search for leadership." In William G. Andrews (ed.), *European Politics I: The Restless Search.* Princeton: Van Nostrand.

——————— (1968). "Too many reshuffles." *Spectator* 220:476–77.

——————— (1970). "Who cares about policy?" *Spectator* 224:38–39.

——————— (1974). *British Members of Parliament: A Self-Portrait.* London: Macmillan in association with Granada Television.

———————, ed. (1969). *The British Prime Minister: A Reader.* London: Macmillan.

Koenig, Louis W. (1964). *The Chief Executive.* New York: Harcourt, Brace & World.

Lacy, Alex B., Jr. (1967). "The development of the White House office." Unpublished paper delivered at the 1967 annual meeting of the American Political Science Association.

Laski, Harold J. (1940). *The American Presidency: An Interpretation.* New York: Harper.

Laslett, P. (1967). *John Locke, Two Treatises of Government: A Critical Edition with an Introduction and Apparatus Criticus.* Cambridge: Cambridge University Press.

Lasswell, Harold D. (1951). "Democratic character." In *Political Writings of Harold D. Lasswell.* New York: Free Press.

Learned, Henry B. (1912). *The President's Cabinet.* New Haven: Yale University Press.

LeDuc, Lawrence, Jr. (1971). "Party decision-making: some empirical observations on the leadership selection process." *Canadian Journal of Political Science* 4:97–118.

Lijphart, Arend (1968). *The Politics of Accommodation: Pluralism and Democracy in the Netherlands.* Berkeley: University of California Press.

Loewenberg, Gerhard (1967). *Parliament in the German Political System.* Ithaca, N.Y.: Cornell University Press.

Loewenstein, Karl (1965). *Political Power and the Governmental Process.* Chicago: University of Chicago Press.

Mackintosh, John P. (1967–68). "A rejoinder." *Parliamentary Affairs* 21:53–68.

——————— (1968). *The British Cabinet.* London: Methuen.

MacRae, Duncan, Jr. (1967). *Parliament, Parties, and Society in France 1946–1958.* New York: St. Martin's Press.

Madgwick, P. J. (1966–67). "Resignations." *Parliamentary Affairs* 20:59–76.

Manley, John F. (1970). *The Politics of Finance: The House Committee on Ways and Means.* Boston: Little, Brown.

Mann, Dean E. (1964). "The selection of federal political executives." *American Political Science Review* 58:81–99.

Mann, Dean E., with Jameson W. Doig (1965). *The Assistant Secretaries: Problems and Processes of Appointment.* Washington, D.C.: Brookings Institution.

Matthews, Donald R., ed. (1973). *Perspectives on Presidential Selection.* Washington, D.C.: Brookings Institution.

——————— (1974). "Presidential nominations: process and outcomes." In James David Barber (ed.), *Choosing the President.* Englewood Cliffs, N.J.: Prentice-Hall.

May, Ernest R. (1955). "The development of political-military consultation in the United States." *Political Science Quarterly* 70:161–80.

McConnell, Grant (1963). *Steel and the Presidency, 1962.* New York: Norton.

——————— (1967). *The Modern Presidency.* New York: St. Martin's Press.

McFarland, Andrew S. (1969). *Power and Leadership in Pluralist Systems.* Stanford: Stanford University Press.

McKenzie, R. T. (1963). *British Political Parties: The Distribution of Power within the Conservative and Labour Parties.* London: Heinemann.

Medawar, P. B. (1957). *The Art of the Soluble: Creativity and Originality in Science.* London: Methuen.

Melnik, Constantin, and Nathan Leites (1958). *The House Without Windows: France Selects a President.* Translated by Ralph Manheim. Evanston, Ill.: Row, Peterson.

Merkl, Peter H. (1962). "Equilibrium, structure of interests and leadership: Adenauer's survival as chancellor." *American Political Science Review* 56:634–50.

Meynaud, J. (1967). "Introduction." In UNESCO, *Decisions and Decision-Makers in the Modern State.* Paris: UNESCO.

Milne, R. S. (1955). "The experiment with co-ordinating ministers in the British cabinet, 1951–1953." *Canadian Journal of Economics and Political Science* 21:365–69.

Morris, Alfred, ed. (1970). *The Growth of Parliamentary Scrutiny by Committee: A Symposium.* Oxford: Pergamon Press.

Morrison of Lambeth, Lord (Herbert Morrison) (1964). *Government and Parliament: A Survey from the Inside.* London: Oxford University Press.

Mosley, R. K. (1969). *The Story of the Cabinet Office.* London: Routledge & Kegan Paul.

Mueller, John E. (1973). *War, Presidents and Public Opinion.* New York: Wiley.

Neustadt, Richard E. (1954). "Presidency and legislation: the growth of central clearance." *American Political Science Review* 48:641–71.

——————— (1955). "Presidency and legislation: planning the president's program." *American Political Science Review* 49:980–1021.

——————— (1956). "The presidency at mid-century." *Law and Contemporary Problems: The Presidential Office* 21:609–45.

——————— (1960). *Presidential Power: The Politics of Leadership.* New York: Wiley.

——————— (1963). "Approaches to staffing the presidency: notes on FDR and JFK." *American Political Science Review* 57:855–62.

——————— (1965a). "Staffing the presidency." In Henry M. Jackson (ed.), *The National Security Council: Jackson Subcommittee Papers on Policy-Making at the Presidential Level.* New York: Praeger.

——————— (1965b). "Politicians and bureaucrats." In David B. Truman (ed.), *The Congress and America's Future.* Englewood Cliffs, N.J.: Prentice-Hall.

——————— (1965c). "Testimony." In *Administration of National Security: Inquiry of the Subcommittee on National Security Staffing and Operations: Staff Reports and Hearings.* Washington, D.C.: United States Government Printing Office.

——————— (1966). "10 Downing Street." In Henry Brandon, *Conversations with Henry Brandon.* London: Andre Deutsch.

——————— (1969). "White House and Whitehall." In Anthony King (ed.), *The British Prime Minister: A Reader.* London: Macmillan.

——————— (1970). *Alliance Politics.* New York: Columbia University Press.

Patterson, Samuel C. (1973). "Review article: the British House of Commons as a focus for political research." *British Journal of Political Science* 3:363–81.

Petrie, Charles (1958). *The Powers behind the Prime Ministers.* London: MacGibbon & Kee.

Pickles, Dorothy (1972). *The Government and Politics of France.* Volume 1, *Institutions and Parties.* London: Methuen.

Polsby, Nelson W. (1964). *Congress and the Presidency.* Englewood Cliffs, N.J.: Prentice-Hall.

Polsby, Nelson W., and Aaron B. Wildavsky (1973). *Presidential Elections: Strategies of American Electoral Politics.* New York: Scribner's.

Pomper, Gerald (1966). *Nominating the President: The Politics of Convention Choice.* Evanston, Ill.: Northwestern University Press.

Porter, John (1965). *The Vertical Mosaic: An Analysis of Social Class and Power in Canada.* Toronto: University of Toronto Press.

Price, Don K. (1946). "Staffing the presidency." *American Political Science Review* 40:1154–68.

Punnett, R. M. (1970). "Selection of party leaders: a Canadian example." *Journal of Commonwealth Political Studies* 8:54–69.

——————— (1971). "Leadership selection in opposition: the case of the Progressive-Conservative party of Canada." *Australian Journal of Politics and History* 17:188–201.

——————— (1973). *Front-Bench Opposition: The Role of the Leader of the Opposition, the Shadow Cabinet and Shadow Government in British Politics.* London: Heinemann.

Reid, Gordon (1966). *The Politics of Financial Control: The Role of the House of Commons.* London: Hutchinson University Library.

Richards, Peter G. (1963). *Patronage in British Government.* London: George Allen & Unwin.

——————— (1967). *Parliament and Foreign Affairs.* London: George Allen & Unwin.

——————— (1970). *Parliament and Conscience.* London: George Allen & Unwin.

——————— (1972). *The Backbenchers.* London: Faber and Faber.

Ridley, F. F. (1966). "Chancellor government as a political system and the German constitution." *Parliamentary Affairs* 19:446–61.

Rogow, Arnold A. (1963). *James Forrestal: A Study of Personality, Politics, and Policy.* New York: Macmillan.

Rose, Richard (1971). "The making of cabinet ministers." *British Journal of Political Science* 1:393–414.

Rossiter, Clinton (1960). *The American Presidency.* New York: Harcourt, Brace.

Rourke, Francis E. (1961). *Secrecy and Publicity.* Baltimore: Johns Hopkins University Press.

Safran, William (1967). *Veto-Group Politics: The Case of Health-Insurance Reform in West Germany.* San Francisco: Chandler.

Santos, C. R. (1970). "Some collective characteristics of the delegates to the 1968 Liberal party leadership convention." *Canadian Journal of Political Science* 3:299–308.

Sapin, Burton M. (1966). *The Making of United States Foreign Policy*. New York: Praeger.

Schlesinger, Arthur M., Jr. (1957). *The Age of Roosevelt: The Crisis of the Old Order 1919–1933*. Boston: Houghton Mifflin.

——————— (1959). *The Age of Roosevelt: The Coming of the New Deal*. Boston: Houghton Mifflin.

——————— (1960). *The Age of Roosevelt: The Politics of Upheaval*. Boston: Houghton Mifflin.

——————— (1974). *The Imperial Presidency*. Boston: Houghton Mifflin.

Schlesinger, Arthur M., Jr., and Alfred de Grazia (1967). *Congress and the Presidency: Their Role in Modern Times*. Washington, D.C.: American Enterprise Institute for Public Policy Research.

Schlesinger, Joseph A. (1966). *Ambition and Politics: Political Careers in the United States*. Chicago: Rand McNally.

Seligman, Lester G. (1956). "Presidential leadership: the inner circle and institutionalization." *Journal of Politics* 18:410–26.

Seligman, Lester G., and Michael A. Baer (1969). "Expectations of presidential leadership in decision-making." In Aaron Wildavsky (ed.), *The Presidency*. Boston: Little, Brown.

Sigel, Roberta S. (1966). "Image of the American presidency: Part II of an exploration into popular views of presidential power." *Midwest Journal of Political Science* 10:123–37.

Sigel, Roberta S., and David J. Butler (1964). "The public and the no third term tradition: inquiry into attitudes toward power." *Midwest Journal of Political Science* 8:43–44.

Sontheimer, Kurt (1972). *The Government and Politics of West Germany*. Translated by Fleur Donecker. London: Hutchinson University Library.

Sorensen, Theodore C. (1963). *Decision-Making in the White House: The Olive Branch or the Arrows*. New York: Columbia University Press.

Stanley, David T., Dean E. Mann, and Jameson E. Doig (1967). *Men Who Govern: A Biographical Profile of Federal Political Executives*. Washington, D.C.: Brookings Institution.

Sundquist, James L. (1968). *Politics and Policy: The Eisenhower, Kennedy, and Johnson Years*. Washington, D.C.: Brookings Institution.

Taft, William Howard (1916). *Our Chief Magistrate and His Powers*. New York: Columbia University Press.

Thomas, Norman C., and Hans W. Baade (1970). *Law and Contemporary Problems: The Institutionalized Presidency*. Durham, N.C.: Duke University School of Law.

Tillett, Paul, ed. (1962). *Inside Politics: The National Conventions, 1960*. Dobbs Ferry, N.Y.: Oceana.

Tourtellot, Arthur Bernon, ed. (1964). *The Presidents on the Presidency.* New York: Russell & Russell.

Tugwell, Rexford G., and Thomas E. Cronin, eds. (1974). *The Presidency Reappraised.* New York: Praeger.

Ulrich, Junker (1965). *Die Richtlinien Kompetenz des Bundeskanzler.* Tübingen: Mohr.

Vile, M. J. C. (1967). *Constitutionalism and the Separation of Powers.* Oxford: Clarendon Press.

Vinyard, Dale (1971). *The Presidency.* New York: Scribner's.

Walkland, S. A. (1968). *The Legislative Process in Great Britain.* London: George Allen & Unwin.

Waltz, Kenneth N. (1967). *Foreign Policy and Democratic Politics: The American and British Experience.* Boston: Little, Brown.

Warner, W. Lloyd, Paul P. Van Riper, Norman H. Martin, and Orvis F. Collins (1963). *The American Federal Executive: A Study of the Social and Personal Characteristics of the Civil and Military Leaders of the United States Federal Government.* New Haven: Yale University Press.

Warren, Sidney (1964). *The President as World Leader.* Philadelphia: Lippincott.

──────, ed. (1967). *The American President.* Englewood Cliffs, N.J.: Prentice-Hall.

Wildavsky, Aaron (1966). "The two presidencies." *Trans-Action,* no. 4:7–14.

──────, ed. (1969). *The Presidency.* Boston: Little, Brown.

Williams, Marcia (1972). *Inside Number 10.* London: Weidenfeld and Nicolson.

Williams, Philip M. (1964). *Crisis and Compromise: Politics in the Fourth Republic.* London: Longmans.

────── (1968). *The French Parliament 1958–1967.* London: George Allen & Unwin.

────── (1971). "Parliament under the Fifth French Republic: patterns of executive domination." In Gerhard Loewenberg (ed.), *Modern Parliaments: Change or Decline?* Chicago: Aldine, Atherton.

Williams, Philip M., and Martin Harrison (1971). *Politics and Society in de Gaulle's Republic.* London: Longmans.

Willson, F. M. G. (1959). "The routes of entry of new members of the British cabinet, 1868–1958." *Political Studies* 7:222–32.

────── (1970). "Entry to the cabinet, 1959–68." *Political Studies* 18:236–38.

Wilson, Harold (1971). *The Labour Government 1964–1970: A Personal Record.* London: Weidenfeld and Nicolson and Michael Joseph.

Wiseman, H. V. (1966). *Parliament and the Executive: An Analysis with Readings.* London: Routledge & Kegan Paul.

Young, James Sterling (1966). *The Washington Community: 1800–1828.* New York: Columbia University Press.

4

LEGISLATURES

NELSON W. POLSBY

The purpose of this essay is to offer a few preliminary observations about legislatures: their similarities and differences, their origins and activities, and their varying roles and uses in political systems. It asks how a peculiar organizational form, the legislature, embeds itself in a variety of environmental settings, and it explores the consequent contributions that legislatures bring to each of a number of types of political settings in which they are found, along with some problems associated with each setting. This is a far more modest undertaking than a comprehensive survey of the world's legislatures would be. And necessarily so; the literature, both scholarly and popular, on legislatures has in recent years grown to such an extent that it would take an encyclopedia fully as large as this *Handbook* to do complete justice to its mysteries.[1] There is, moreover, the awkward fact that talking about the literature is not necessarily talking about the thing itself—or, more accurately, the things themselves—

I have had the kind assistance of Steven Van Evera, Matthew Pinkus, Arthur Trueger, and especially Byron Shafer in writing this essay. Their time was paid for by the Institute of International Studies and the Committee on Research of the University of California, Berkeley. Typing assistance was granted by the Institute of Governmental Studies, Berkeley. A first draft was circulated to a few friends and I am grateful for the comments of Aaron Wildavsky, Carolyn Webber, Martin Trow, Giuseppe DiPalma, Leon D. Epstein, Harry Eckstein, Austin Ranney, Robert D. Putnam, Robert C. Fried, Rufus Davis, Lewis Anthony Dexter, Robert Packenham, Samuel C. Patterson, Emanuel Gutmann, Richard Fenno, Charles O. Jones, Richard Sisson, Richard Gunther, Joseph LaPalombara, Duane Lockard, Ernst B. Haas, Karl Jackson, Robert Price, Gerhard Loewenberg, David Laitin, William Lunch, and of course my inexhaustibly creative colleague Fred Greenstein. Collectively, and in some cases individually, they know a great deal more about legislatures than I do, and where I have neglected their suggestions it has often been because of the limitations on my knowledge that the limitations on my time prevented me from overcoming. Copyright © 1975 Nelson W. Polsby.

since in virtually every political system known to mankind, past, present, or prospective, there is an entity or state of activity or function that an observer can identify as legislative in character. Indeed, it may be—if our words are to take their common usage—that there can by definition be no such thing as a political system without legislative activity.

SIMILARITIES: PROBLEMS OF DEFINITION AND CONCEPTUALIZATION

Legislative activity at its core refers to a process of lawmaking, to a pattern of actions which regularly results in the promulgation of general rules having application to some specified population. While this activity is undoubtedly at the heart of all political life and hence for most purposes is virtually a defining characteristic of government, wherever government is found, legislative activity is not precisely synonymous with legislatures, the ostensible subject of this essay. For as more than one observer has pointed out, laws—or at least regulations incorporating sanctions for noncompliance having a high probability of enforcement—are sometimes made through agencies not considered legislatures, and legislatures often find themselves engaged in activities other than lawmaking. K. C. Wheare observes:

> . . . a large part of the time of these bodies is not devoted to law making at all. One of their most important functions is to criticize the executive. In some countries they make or unmake governments. They debate great issues of public concern. They constitute "a grand inquest of the nation." (Wheare, 1963, p. 1)

This reflects the opinion of John Stuart Mill:

> . . . the proper office of a representative assembly is to watch and control the government: to throw the light of publicity on its acts, to compel a full exposition and justification of all of them which any one considers questionable; to censure them if found condemnable. . . . In addition to this, the Parliament has an office . . . to be at once the nation's Committee of Grievances, and its Congress of Opinions. . . . (Mill, 1962, p. 111)

There occasionally arises a natural confusion among scholars because sometimes lawmaking is done outside legislatures, and sometimes legislatures do things other than lawmaking. A functionalist orientation toward this mildly schizoid condition sends students scurrying into the woods looking for agencies through which and occasions on which lawmaking is performed. Frequently enough we must conclude that executives are legislatures, courts are legislatures, armies and parties are legislatures, but legislatures are not legislatures, functionally speaking.

An intellectual cousin to this approach would be a structuralist solution, which follows the legislature rather than the legislative function and asks, If legislatures do not legislate, what do they do? Scholars then commonly find —and enumerate—other functions that legislatures actually account for: the granting of legitimacy, let us say, or the maintenance of a pool of potential recruits for future political leadership, to take the two most important examples.[2]

Since it is occasionally unclear whether a given scholar is pursuing a functionalist or a structuralist strategy, it is possible for an observer to interpret as contradictory propositions that actually refer to different things—that is, to lawmaking versus legislatures—and that may well turn out to be perfectly compatible. The statement, for example, "The twentieth century . . . has been hard on legislatures" (Truman, 1965, p. 1), does not necessarily say that the sphere of legal regulation has shrunk or that the amount or extent of lawmaking has declined. Rather, it says something about a special institutional form and how this form has fared in competition with other agencies of governance.

Keeping this small distinction in mind helps in scanning common definitions of the term legislature itself. Some are structuralist in character:

> A body of persons having the power to legislate; specifically: an organized body having the authority to make laws for a political unit. . . . *(Webster's Third New International Dictionary)*

> The department, assembly, or body of men that make the laws for a state or nation. *(Black's Law Dictionary)*

And some are functionalist:

> Properly speaking, the legislative function is simply that of law-making. (W. F. Willoughby, 1934, p. 20)

There is a certain redundancy, at least for students who remember their Latin, in associating the term legislature with an agency that makes laws. As we have seen, though lawmaking supplies a core to the meaning of the term legislature, a rather sizeable penumbra of connotations, associations, and functions has come in practice to surround the term. And two questions arise: (1) How are we to discuss a legislature that is relatively uninfluential in the making of laws in a given political system? (2) What distinguishes a *legislature* that engages in lawmaking—as well as all the other varied activities that may be attributed to it—from other sorts of institutions that, in greater or lesser measure, do likewise?

We can stipulate, to begin with, that legislatures are official bodies within their respective polities. This immediately distinguishes legislative debates, opinions, and grand inquests—and regulations—from those conducted or enacted in the private sector or outside whatever political system is at the focus of concern.[3] Not all acts of officials who are legislators are acts of the legislature. It is the acts of the legislature that presumably engage the power of the polity to sanction noncompliance and stamp as authoritative the acts that legislatures perform.

But since legislatures are not alone in performing official acts, we must look further for distinguishing characteristics. In some respects, legislatures are like elected executives, multimembered appellate courts, Anglo-Saxon juries, and bureaucracies in their official character (see Table 1). Like courts and juries, their official acts follow a formal process of deliberation. Like juries and elected executives, what they do receives its ultimate support because they are in some sense the embodiment of the people governed by their decisions. Like courts and juries, legislatures vote in order to work their will. Nevertheless they differ from these other official organizations in a number of ways. Unlike courts or bureaucracies, they receive their legitimacy by virtue of their direct links with the population governed. Unlike elected executives, legislatures are composed of numerous persons who meet as formal equals to do business. Unlike courts, legislatures need not give reasons or invoke principles other than those that empower the legislature itself to sit. And unlike juries, legislatures are, in principle, directly and subsequently accountable to the people from whom they arise.

This mélange of characteristics—officiality, a claim of legitimacy based on links with the people, multimemberedness, formal equality, collective decision making, deliberativeness—typifies and distinguishes legislatures in a wide variety of settings. This is what makes legislatures similar, and it provides a basis for identifying and classifying the organization with which we shall be concerned. That is, the term legislature, as I shall consider it here, refers to an organizational form. A legislature can be identified in the first instance by certain of its structural properties: it has more than one member and they meet, deliberate, and vote as equals as a way of doing their business. This structural form, as it happens, exactly describes the luncheon group of Art Buchwald, Benjamin Bradlee, and Edward Bennett Williams, who frequently meet at an expensive restaurant in Washington, D.C., to consider, and reject, the candidacies of other hungry Washingtonians to join them. In order to return this group, and others similarly situated, to their well-merited privacy, it seems to me desirable to stipulate a small number of associated characteristics that will identify the legislative organizations with which we shall be concerned, namely, that their formal enactments be officially binding on some meaningful population and that their legitimacy arise by virtue of their direct relationship to that population.

This formula is vague, and purposely so, since it must embrace several kinds of popular accountability. There is, first of all, accountability *prior* to decision making, which suggests that the means by which a decision-making body is constituted bears upon its entitlement subsequently to command the

TABLE 1 Properties of a legislature, compared with other official bodies

Official body	Is multimembered	Must deliberate formally before acting	Makes decisions by voting	Arises from the population subject to its rules	Is subsequently accountable to the people
Legislature	Yes	Yes	Yes	Yes	Yes
Jury	Yes	Yes	Yes	Yes	No
Multimember appellate court	Yes	Yes	Yes	Not necessarily	No
Bureaucracy	Yes	Not necessarily	No	Not necessarily	No
Elected executive	Rarely	Not necessarily	No	Yes	Yes

obedience of a subject population. Legislatures make a claim for this obedience, and hence rest their legitimacy, upon the notion that they are in some
meaningful sense like, or constituted from, or representative of the people
whom they govern.

A second sense in which legislatures can be accountable is *subsequent* to
decision making, in which members of a legislative body subject themselves to
popular election. I also wish to consider as legislatures official deliberative assemblies that do not rely on representativeness because they are extremely inclusive, such as town meetings. Likewise it seems to me desirable not to define
away the fact that for some official deliberative assemblies the relevant subject
population consists not of atomized individuals but of families or clans, and
each clan (not a representative number of them) is a part of the legislature.

I have adopted a structural definition of the term legislature in part because this seems to me to be most responsive to the classificatory scheme of the
Handbook, which assigns to others the discussion, for example, of executives and
courts. Beyond this, however, a definition stressing structural attributes possesses
the formidable virtue of providing an observer with criteria visible to the naked
eye which can readily establish whether a real-world instance is a case of the
thing being talked about, or not. This aids in the further task of framing and
testing empirical propositions by reference to concrete experience. Moreover
a structural definition of legislatures facilitates the direct empirical consideration of variation in the performance of functions. It focuses our attention on
the mixed, multifaceted character of legislatures and encourages us to attempt
to sort out explanations that account for observed regularities and differences in
their functioning.

DIFFERENCES: PROBLEMS OF CLASSIFICATION

I have made the claim that official, accountable, deliberative assemblies, which
I call in shorthand legislatures, arise in a variety of political settings. We can
distinguish these settings along two axes and identify the types of legislatures
that typically arise under each of four combinations of conditions.

Political systems may vary, first of all, in the degree to which the process
of legislating is formally conducted by a restricted part of the government, as
distinguished from government by an all-purpose agency or by the population
at large. This is the distinction between political systems having a division of
labor and those without, and yields for the purposes of crude comparison two
types of regimes, those in which legislative activity (as distinct from other governmental and communal activity) is devolved upon a specialized and specific
organization and those in which it is not. A second variation that can be observed among political systems has to do with the degree to which the relevant
population at large can influence or gain access to the process of government

for limited purposes, such as affecting specific governmental policies or changing the personnel who staff the government. The distinction here is the well-known contrast between open and closed regimes. The types of legislatures that occur under each variation are given in Table 2.

TABLE 2   Types of legislative forms

	When political system is	
	Closed	*Open*
When government activity is		
Unspecialized	1. No legislature: junta or clique makes laws	3. No specialized legislature: town meeting or folkmoot makes laws
Specialized	2. Corporate board of directors; rubber-stamp legislature	4. Parliamentary arena; transformative legislature

Readers will immediately note that virtually all legislatures that scholars have found worth their time—that is, those that are "modern," "advanced," and "democratic" in character—are clustered in the southeast (specialized, open) quadrant of the figure. Nevertheless there is something more at stake than logical completeness in beginning a discussion of legislatures by giving brief consideration to legislatures when they are not well differentiated from other institutions of government or when they occur in closed systems. These more confining circumstances provide a useful setting for the consideration of the varieties of services performed by legislative organizations in political systems and for the identification of alternative methods for the performance of legislative tasks.

CLOSED REGIME AND UNSPECIALIZED POLITY: ALTERNATE ROUTES TO REGIME LEGITIMACY

When the regime is closed and the polity is unspecialized, can we say that there is a legislature at all? The making of laws by proclamation, or fiat, is an extremely common form of legislative behavior, but it is less clear that this is common behavior by legislatures. Over most of human history one of the most frequent forms of government has been simple dictatorship by a relatively small group monopolizing control over the organized means of coercion in a society, a monopoly that gives a small group the means to enforce its will within the political system and hence grants it the power to make the laws.

In ancient Egypt and Mesopotamia, for example, there was government by

priests, and in the early Roman Republic as well as in the communes of northern Italy during the late Renaissance, by an oligarchy. In modern times the
existence of government by junta in such widely separated places as Greece,
Brazil, Egypt, and Indonesia has been frequently remarked. Consider Ghana
from 1966 to 1972. There, the affairs of the country were in the hands of a
seven-man National Liberation Council. "The Council, established immediately after the successful coup d'etat by the Ghana Armed Forces in cooperation with the Police Services . . . [was] empowered to rule, by decree, until true
democracy . . . has been restored to the country" (*Ghana Official Handbook,*
1968, p. 14).

Is a junta a legislature? It is uncommon for the internal workings of organizations like Ghana's National Liberation Council to become sufficiently well
known for observers to be able to describe their decision making as "deliberative" or their edicts as following upon the votes of equals. Moreover, revolutionary doctrine, by stressing the temporary character of the regime, acknowledges the prior unaccountability of junta rule.[4] The fact that dictators and
ruling juntas frequently establish rubber-stamp legislatures after they have
successfully seized control of government suggests that a principal task of legislatures is to confer legitimacy upon the acts of government. They do so by increasing the range of the population that formally endorses the edicts of the
regime.

In the end, government is possible only because people obey the rules and
keep the commitments that governments make. "Legitimacy" refers to a probability that obedience will in fact occur in a population.[5] It is possible for governments to obtain this obedience by a variety of means: by terrorizing the
populace, for example, by indoctrinating them, by receiving their acquiescence
through habit or custom, or by obtaining the freely granted consent of the
governed. All governments contain elements of each, and all promote ideologies that seek to justify the particular mixture prevailing within their own
society.

Moreover, each of those elements making for citizen acquiescence—coercion, indoctrination, custom, and consent—is in principle replaceable at the
margins by the others.[6] Thus it is for some purposes useful to think of legislatures as primarily embodying and symbolizing the giving of consent and consequently as substitutable for—and by—secret police, armies, the deference
characteristic of traditional stratification systems, and mass propaganda campaigns. Presumably when governments undertake marginal shifts from the use
of one of these instrumentalities to another they are responding to changes in
the relative costs of these alternatives. Since in most societies institutional inertia is likely to be great, it would be a mistake to assume that a lack of such
marginal shifts implies an equilibrium of societal costs. One of the great difficulties of complex governments is precisely their incapacity to register these
costs with great sensitivity. In consequence, it may well be that many ruling

groups buy more propaganda, and conceivably more surveillance and terror, than they need to maintain themselves in office.[7]

Relatively closed and undifferentiated polities rely more heavily on custom and coercion than on consent: this is implied in the definition of closed, which means low access to government by citizens. For primitive societies, the costs of coercion are fairly high on a per-capita basis, owing to the backwardness of technology available for the purposes of coercion. In general, the larger the population governed and the more advanced it is in terms of education, literacy, access to mass media and to capital goods, the more costly it becomes in absolute terms for ruling groups to rely on coercion as a regular method of obtaining citizen acquiescence. Thus it is not uncommon to observe within closed societies that give scant employment to legislatures energetic efforts to legitimize acts of the regime by massive campaigns of political indoctrination as the educational level of the populace (which is frequently a necessary condition of economic development) rises.

For short periods of time—measured in less than a generation—nearly total reliance on coercion and terrorism appears to be a feasible and even a reasonably inexpensive method of obtaining citizen acquiescence in nearly any society.[8] Strong and deep-rooted traditions of citizen noninvolvement in political decision making and social deference associated with near-feudal social stratification systems appear to be necessary for the maintenance of large-scale societies for any greater length of time without a significant movement toward legitimization processes that are more representative, explicitly consent-oriented, and hence more legislative in character.

Even in the more backward situation, it appears, legislatures frequently seem to be very much in evidence, for decoration if for nothing else. As we will see in our consideration of rubber-stamp legislatures, it is significant that the powerlessness of legislative bodies in closed societies evidently does not lessen the efforts of the regime to make them nominally representative of all recognized social groups.

Thus our argument is that instability occurs as the number of people encompassed by a closed, unspecialized regime increases and as such a polity modernizes. It is not necessarily the case, however, that such a regime will become more open: historical experience suggests an alternative possibility, namely, that control over basic policies will remain closely held but organizational specialization will take place. It is well understood by students of authoritarian regimes—and not just those of modern vintage, as our childhood memories of the Sheriff of Nottingham should remind us—that bureaucracies can be made to serve the ends of a closed polity.[9] As we will discover in the next section, much the same is true of legislatures. Legislatures may, because of their structural characteristics, potentially embody a strain toward openness. This potential, however, has under many circumstances been kept well under control.

CLOSED REGIME AND SPECIALIZED POLITY: REPRESENTATION FOR CO-OPTATION

Modern industrial societies contain within them many specialized legislatures. For example, the structure of the modern corporation commonly consists of a meticulously differentiated board of directors that acts as a sovereign legislature, set off from the owners of most stock, on one hand, and corporate management on the other.[10] Workers, subcontractors, competitors, customers, and suppliers (with the frequent exception of suppliers of large amounts of capital and of certain classes of legal advice) are also normally excluded from direct influence upon legislative deliberations, though not necessarily from influence upon certain aspects of corporate decision making. In this respect, however, they are analogous to the "interest groups" of national politics.

The modern corporation is, to be sure, an instance in which a relatively closed system is in important respects operated through a powerful, but narrowly representative, legislature. Another common pattern, especially at the level of the nation-state, is for legislatures in closed regimes to be less narrowly based, but powerless. Consider, for example, Merle Fainsod's description of the chief legislative body of the Soviet Union, the Supreme Soviet:

> ... the role of the Supreme Soviet appears largely ornamental and decorative. The matters which engage its attention are of transcendent importance. They embrace such weighty problems as the Five Year Plans, the enactment of the annual budget, and the organization of the government of the USSR. But the proceedings of the Supreme Soviet convey the impression of a well-rehearsed theatrical spectacle from which almost all elements of conflict have been eliminated. The slight budget modifications which are initiated by the Supreme Soviet and the occasional criticisms of the performance of lagging ministries give every evidence of being part of a prepared script. Like the elections, the meetings of the Supreme Soviet symbolize national unity. The proposals of the government are unanimously hailed and unanimously ratified. ...
>
> The task of the Supreme Soviet is not to question but to execute, to clothe the Party thesis in the garb of constitutional legality. The result is necessarily to minimize the authority of the whole apparatus of soviets. As long as the top Party command remains the real seat of power in Soviet society, the soviets and the constitutional structure built around them remain imposing facades rather than sovereign organs. (Fainsod, 1953, pp. 325–26)

This feature, at least, of the Soviet system, does not seem to have changed over the years. (See also McClosky and Turner, 1960, p. 322; Meyer, 1965, p. 245; and Wesson, 1972, p. 198.)

This is possibly the most famous example in world history of a rubber-stamp legislature, but it is assuredly not the only example. From other parts of the ideological spectrum one can easily find equally powerless legislatures: the Cortes of modern Spain, for example (see Anderson, 1970; Medhurst, 1973; Trythall, 1970, pp. 191, 266; Welles, 1965, pp. 37–38).[11]

What needs explaining about such organizations is the fact that they exist at all. If monopoly of legitimate sources of violence in a society is securely vested, and if lawmaking, the ostensible purpose of the assembly, is actually done elsewhere, why bother? John A. Ballard's account of four African legislatures (Central African Republic, Chad, Congo-Brazzaville, and Gabon) offers a clue:

> Each ethnic group and each region demand representation in [The National Assembly] roughly proportional to their numerical importance. This remains true despite the Assemblies' loss of real legislative power. Each deputy owes his nomination to a party controlled by the President, and renomination in case of dissolution of the Assembly is in the hands of the President. This gives members of the Assembly little incentive to criticize, much less oppose, the Government's legislative program. Thus political sanctions reinforce constitutional limitations on the Assembly's powers. In addition, the power of the government to override the deputies' immunity from prosecution—either by sudden arrest under emergency powers or by dictation of Assembly votes stripping individual deputies of their immunity during sessions—has been demonstrated in each of the four states.... (Ballard, 1966, p. 304)

Although legislatures such as these have little or nothing to do, they retain independent significance on two counts. First, the fact that they exist at all gives mute testimony to the relatively low cost of consent as a means of legitimizing the acts of government as compared with the alternatives available to dictatorial regimes. While it cannot be said that dictatorships tend over time to wither away, it is remarkable that they should come, in time, to value the appearance of legislative sanction in the conduct of their business.[12] Second, such figurehead legislatures may serve as personnel pools from which active members of the regime may be recruited. In more open systems this phenomenon of legislative service as a means to advancement in political parties, and ultimately in government, is well known. In an attenuated form this process may be observed in closed regimes as well.

Robert Packenham says, of the Brazilian Congress:

> Some politicians gain experience in the legislature which enables them to go on to other posts like governorships, national ministries, state ministries, and the like. They learn the norms of the elites, they learn political skills, and they acquire visibility and prestige resources which are useful to them in acquiring, maintaining, and utilizing these other roles. In this

sense, the activities of the Brazilian Congress constitute a training ground for Brazilian politicians. (Packenham, 1970, pp. 530–31)

It is apparent that closed regimes do not provide great scope for the flourishing of legislative institutions. That such regimes maintain legislatures at all is a fascinating, and somewhat puzzling, phenomenon. We cannot assert that legislatures are themselves the cause of the movement of regimes from closed to open or that the need to create legislatures moves political systems from unspecialized to specialized. It is not uncommon, after all, to observe legislatures powerless to prevent their own abolition; consider, for examples, the contemporary cases of the Philippines, Uruguay, and Ghana, or the greatly lamented Weimar Republic (see Loewenberg, 1971b; Hakes, 1973; and Stauffer, 1974).

The possible uses in a society of any size or complexity of a "representative" body that is highly visible but not necessarily a "lawmaking" body have been briefly explored. Our argument is that such bodies exist to aid closed regimes in gaining the obedience of their citizens and that their principal costs for the regime entail giving some corporate groups, ethnic or sectional groups, and ambitious politicians representing these groups a certain privileged entree to the policymaking process—an entree that stops short of current participation but which may eventually lead to co-optation into elite roles.

As Ballard describes the situation in his four equatorial states:

> The chief function of the Assembly . . . is to provide an organized and recognized body of loyal supporters of the regime who can claim to represent a national synthesis of particular interests and who therefore provide a semblance of parliamentary approval for the policy and program of the regime. . . . The government consults at least certain deputies concerning local opinion, and a few deputies are almost certain to be high in party councils or personally close to the President. (Ballard, p. 305)

Not all closed regimes can afford to pay this modest price, however. Where ethnic or religious or linguistic conflict is very pronounced, for example, it may be that even nominal representation of warring groups in a rubber-stamp assembly would threaten the capacity of the regime to maintain itself in power. But where these conflicts are less pervasive, or less murderous, the creation of rubber-stamp legislatures is evidently regarded as a sound and inexpensive investment tending to buttress the stability of closed regimes.

OPEN REGIME AND UNSPECIALIZED POLITY: COMMUNITY WITHOUT REPRESENTATION IN SMALL-SCALE, STATUS-RIDDEN SYSTEMS

Here government proceeds by folkmoot, tribal council, town meeting, or open forum, and all the varied activities of government are done within the framework of the same relatively accessible process of decision making. In such circumstances two questions that normally vex students of legislatures in open systems do not arise: the problems of subsequent accountability and representativeness. When the rules that govern a group are made by an institution embracing the group as a whole, there is by definition neither another body to call it to account nor a population that differs from and hence, under some theories of representation, must be mirrored or served by the lawmaking population. Thus our attention shifts to matters of internal structure, where we may take note of the possibility of short-run, de facto specialization—as contrasted with a formal division of labor—in the performance of legislative activity.

Consider, for example, the New England town meeting:

> For the first few years after the founding of the Massachusetts Bay Colony, the only organ of government in the towns within its limits was the town meeting or general assembly of all the male inhabitants of the town.... It was the only form of government in force in all towns until they grew so large that they found other organs of government necessary.... Any question of public interest could be brought before the meeting, any of the inhabitants being privileged to do this, and opportunity being given to all to discuss the questions presented. (Maclear, 1908, pp. 106–107, 112)

A certain romance has grown up around this legislative form. A mid-nineteenth century celebration (written in 1835)—not without its own shrewd insight—by Ralph Waldo Emerson discusses the institution as he found it in the record books of the town of Concord, Massachusetts:

> In a town-meeting, the roots of society were reached. Here the rich gave counsel, but the poor also; and moreover, the just and the unjust. He is ill informed who expects, on running down the Town Records for two hundred years, to find a church of saints, a metropolis of patriots, enacting wholesome and creditable laws. The constitution of the towns forbid it. In this open democracy, every opinion had utterance; every objection, every fact, every acre of land, every bushel of rye, its entire weight. The moderator was the passive mouth-piece, and the vote of the town, like the vane on the turret overhead, free for every wind to turn, and always turned by the last and strongest breath. In these assemblies, the public weal, the call of interest, duty, religion, were heard; and every local feeling, every private grudge, every suggestion of petulance and ignorance, were not less faithfully produced. Wrath and love came up to town-meeting in company. By the law of 1641, every man—freeman or not—inhabitant or not—might introduce any business into a public meeting. Not a complaint occurs in all the volumes of our Records, of any inhabitant being hindered from speaking, or suffering from any violence or usurpation of any class. The negative

ballot of a ten-shilling freeholder was as fatal as that of the honored owner of Blood's Farms or Willard's Purchase. . . . I shall be excused for confessing that I have set a value upon any symptom of meanness and private pique which I have met with in these antique books, as proof that justice was done; that if the results of our history are approved as wise and good, it was yet a free strife; if the good counsel prevailed, the sneaking counsel did not fail to be suggested; freedom and virtue, if they triumphed, triumphed in a fair field. And so be it an everlasting testimony for them, and so much ground of assurance of man's capacity for self-government.

It is the consequence of this institution that not a school-house, a public pew, a bridge, a pound, a mill-dam, hath been set up, or pulled down, or altered, or bought, or sold, without the whole population of this town having a voice in the affair. A general contentment is the result. And the people truly feel that they are lords of the soil. In every winding road, in every stone fence, in the smokes of the poorhouse chimney, in the clock on the church, they read their own power, and consider, at leisure, the wisdom and error of their judgments. (Emerson, 1904, pp. 47–49)

A century later, a citizen of Brunswick, Maine, wrote:

Town meeting is a collection of individualists. When a man arises and cries, "Mr. Moderator!" and is properly recognized, no man living is big enough to make him sit down. So long as he speaks on the subject, uses proper words, and obeys parliamentary procedure he can say what he pleases. And every listening citizen in the hall knows that the same privilege will be extended in turn. So long as anyone wishes to speak, the matter at hand is held open for discussion. Knowing this, the Yankee carries the Town Meeting privileges over into his private life, and likewise into his state and national politics. Town Meeting may have developed the Yankee frame of mind, or the Yankee may have developed Town Meeting, but they go together like pork and beans and one explains the other. Each voter brings his utter independence into the hall, and from the congregation results a majority decision in which unity is attained without anyone's losing the least bit of his own separate self. (Gould, 1940, p. 35)

Harder-eyed analysts, however, have looked beyond the formality of the highly inclusive membership of the town meeting:

When we speak of the government of the seventeenth century towns being carried on by a town meeting, we are apt to think that the form of government found there must have been as democratic as any that the world has seen; every inhabitant apparently having an equal voice in the making of orders, the appropriation and expenditure of money, and in the choice of officials. But this was far from being the case. On the contrary, com-

paratively few of the inhabitants of these towns had any share in its government. Only those inhabitants who were freemen—that is, members in good
and regular standing of a duly recognized church—were considered citizens of the colony and town and as such were allowed to vote. The other
inhabitants of the town—the non-freemen—could attend the meetings
called to settle town affairs, and could discuss all questions, but could not
vote except in certain specified instances. Hence, the towns were in the
habit of holding two different meetings, one composed of all the inhabitants of the town and the other of freemen only. The difference in the
nature and duties of these town meetings is shown by the call issued for a
meeting in Dorchester in 1669: "It is ordered that a warrant should be issued out to the constable to warn a meeting of the freemen to meet the
last week in March to bring in votes for nomination of magistrates and to
choose deputies and commissioners; and the rest of the inhabitants also
to choose constables and county Treasurer and other business that may be
done." (Maclear, pp. 114–15)

Even passing the issue of the inclusiveness of the town meeting's voting
(as contrasted with speaking) membership, some of those present surely had
stronger voices than others; some had the high regard of their fellows and
others did not; some were better informed, more articulate, and cared more
about some or all decisions; some were known to be wealthier, some holier,
some more vengeful. When these various attributes of individuals ran together
in some pattern that was widely discerned within a community, relatively stable, de facto differences in legislative power undoubtedly resulted, making
these assemblies what I shall call "status-ridden." And unequal power to make
the rules may lead to rules themselves that affect citizens unevenly and persistently.

Stephan Thernstrom illustrates the point in this account of the legislature
of colonial Newburyport, Massachusetts:

Democracy as practiced in the town meeting rarely provided significant
political choices because of the Federalist institutional framework within
which it operated. . . . To be sure, the journeyman carpenter with enough
property to vote was formally free to stand up in the town meeting to oppose a measure favored by the owner of the shipyard in which he worked,
by the minister of his church, and by the rest of the most powerful men in
the community. But the social system of Federalist Newburyport provided
persuasive sanctions against the exercise of this freedom.

Local pressures for conformity produced a pattern of *deference voting,*
in which the lower orders pliantly followed the lead of their superiors.
Only this habit of deference voting can account for the striking unanimity

with which the town meeting so often acted on the bitterly disputed issues of the day. (Thernstrom, 1964, pp. 40–41)

It must be conceded that the existence of unanimity in voting is evidence that can be read in more than one way; and the instance of the carpenter versus the shipyard owner poses rather starkly an influence relationship that in other —conceivably more frequently occurring—cases might well embrace more in the way of ambiguity and nuance.

Hence there is some question whether a town-meeting form of a legislature lends itself as readily as other forms to the stabilization of inequality among citizens over long periods of time. It is sufficient to grant that this form fails to preclude the development of short-run political inequalities based on status. But how constraining was this condition in fact? The central puzzle has to do with the problem of policy alternatives, as we shall presently see. Highly inclusive, nonrepresentative, status-ridden legislatures such as the town meeting are useful instruments for the confirmation of the status quo, for the application of already settled-on norms, for activities that require neither expertise nor innovation in problem solving and that have as their primary thrust the assertion of community, the drawing of social boundaries. In short, circumscription by the status structure of the community is more significantly a precondition than a result of policymaking by this sort of legislature.

New England before the coming of the Federal Highway Program is not the only locus of an open, unspecialized legislative form.[13] Intermittently in Athens between the sixth and the fourth centuries—that is, from the time of Solon to the time of Pericles—final political authority was vested in an assembly that consisted of free males over twenty. From this Assembly were chosen jurors; a council of 500, which served to convene the Assembly and arrange its business; officers of war; and a large number of other officials, frequently selected by lot and for short periods of time, such as a year.

In Periclean Athens, the Assembly

> ... had forty regular meetings a year.... The Council's presiding committee appointed its chairman by lot every day, and the chairman of the Assembly was the chairman appointed for the Council's presiding committee on the day when the Assembly met. The four regular meetings of the Assembly in each 35–36 day period dealt with different kinds of business. The first meeting considered whether the holders of offices were performing their work satisfactorily, problems of corn-supply and defence, proposals for political prosecutions, the list of property confiscated, the list of heiresses and (once a year only) the desirability of holding an ostracism. At the second regular meeting anyone might ask the Assembly to consider his motion on private or public affairs. At the third and fourth regular meetings, the Assembly debated three motions chosen by lot on religious affairs, three on foreign affairs, and three on secular affairs. (Webster, 1973, p. 106)

The frequent use of the lottery to fill subordinate offices, their short terms, the sheer size of the Assembly (upwards of twenty thousand members), and the practice of voting as a means of giving direction to the policy of the community all lend to the Athenian constitution of classical antiquity a remarkable character. It is difficult to contemplate the operation of such an unwieldy political order in the face of a protracted and complex series of decisions such as confront the rulers of modern societies. Homogeneity on those basic characteristics that most frequently and poisonously separate the peoples of mankind—race, ethnicity, religion, language—are clear prerequisites for the operation of such a system at all. Similarities along these dimensions are more likely to assure sentiments of consensus of sufficient breadth and depth to assuage the minor disagreements of ordinary policymaking.

It is significant in this connection to observe the note of discomfort that creeps into the celebration of the New England town meeting as its author contemplates threats to the social homogencity of the town:

> Many mill towns have received outlanders who speak different languages —and whose nationality and make-up is immediately at odds with Town Meeting traditions. French Canadians, for example, are fine people—but in politics they organize almost solidly. Organization and Town Meeting are, politically, North and South.
>
> Again: the summer people from urban areas . . . . (Gould, p. 60)

Policymaking itself is typically not terribly complex in open, undifferentiated political systems. Mostly, alternatives are sharply attenuated by customary practice. Deliberation is a process by which the proper customary solutions are invoked and legitimized, that is, found, not invented, and analogies between precedents and contemporary circumstances are discovered and certified. This reinforces the solidarity of the community, as wrangling over new alternatives or the importation of technical advice would not.

Scholars ordinarily trace the town meeting legislative form not to the Athenian Assembly, which greatly degenerated and failed to survive the Peloponnesian Wars (concluded 404 B.C.), but to the Anglo-Saxon folkmoot. W. J. Shepard says:

> These primitive European assemblies were composed of all the freemen of the tribe or, as the tribes were integrated into larger units, of the citizenry of the nation. Measures were proposed by chiefs or nobles, perhaps after previous discussion in a council of chiefs. . . . (Shepard, 1933, p. 355)

The Roman historian Tacitus, writing at the end of the first century on the customs of the German tribes, comments:

> On affairs of smaller moment, the chiefs consult; on those of greater importance, the whole community; yet with this circumstance, that what is

referred to the decision of the people is first maturely discussed by the chiefs. They assemble . . . on stated days, either at the new or full moon, which they account the most auspicious season for beginning any enterprise. . . . An inconvenience produced by their liberty is that they do not all assemble at a stated time, as if it were in obedience to a command; but two or three days are lost in the delays of convening. When they all think fit, they sit down armed. Silence is proclaimed by the priests who have on this occasion a coercive power. Then the king, or chief, and such others as are conspicuous for age, birth, military renown, or eloquence, are heard, and gain attention rather from their ability to persuade, than their authority to command. If a proposal displeases the assembly reject it by an inarticulate murmur; if it prove agreeable, they clash their javelins; for the most honourable expression of assent among them is the sound of arms.

Before this council, it is likewise allowed to exhibit accusations and to prosecute capital offences. (Tacitus, 1901, pp. 300–301)

This legislative form is clearly most suited to relatively small-scale political systems. A fundamental threat to the town meeting or folkmoot arrangement is an increase in the scale of the polity. Deliberation and consensus on the part of the whole community or some significant fraction thereof that is selected by custom and tied to the rest by bonds of kinship and unbreakable obligation is replaced in open systems as the polity grows by a system of "democratically" elected representatives and the development of what the authors of the *Federalist* referred to as "the mischiefs of faction." [14]

Underlying this drift is a change in the purpose and character of the deliberative process from the reaffirmation of norms in the service of group solidarity to the consideration of alternatives in the service of rational problem solving, from overarching community interest to mutual self-interest as the goal of deliberation, from meditation and the search for right principles to negotiation and compromise as the means by which policies are settled upon.

OPEN REGIME AND SPECIALIZED POLITY: CONSTITUTIONAL VARIATION IN MODERN DEMOCRATIC LEGISLATURES

Because of the relatively open character of the town meeting, in which all members of the community having standing as political persons might partake in deliberation and decision making, the problem of accountability, of trusteeship or responsibility to some population beyond itself, does not arise. This problem does arise, however, in all specialized regimes and especially those that are open in character.

These are the circumstances that give legislatures the most to do and provide the greatest scope for their development. Even in a relatively open political system containing specialized institutions, however, it does not necessarily fol-

low that legislatures are powerfully engaged in producing meaningful outcomes. In modern democracies, legislatures vary significantly in the ways in
which they are embedded in their respective political systems.

The most obvious difference is of course constitutional, the distinction between parliamentary regimes and those having a separation of powers. Jean
Blondel (1969, p. 319) has compiled a useful table which reveals that in the
contemporary world, in the 58 political systems having more than one active
political party (a reasonable provisional indication of "openness"), the constitution essentially provides for one system or the other, with only 4 nation-states
unaccounted for.[15]

TABLE 3   Constitutional systems in the contemporary world arising from systems of
more than one party

	Parliamentary or cabinet	Presidential	Other	Total
Atlantic	18	1	1	20
Eastern Europe and North Asia	—	—	—	0
Middle East	3	—	2	5
South and South-East Asia	6	1	—	7
Africa south of Sahara	6	2	1	9
Latin America	5	12	—	17
Total	38	16	4	58

What differentiates parliamentary and presidential regimes? The most significant difference is that in parliamentary systems the chief political leaders of
the administrative bureaucracies are chosen from the parliament itself and subsequently remain, in principle, directly accountable to parliamentary majorities, whereas in the separation of powers, or presidential, scheme, members of
the legislature are frequently strictly forbidden simultaneously to hold administrative responsibilities and in practice never do so (see Huitt, 1968). The consequences of this arrangement for governing coalitions and for political systems
as a whole have frequently been explored. Less often have the consequences
for legislatures of these varying arrangements been spelled out. Yet even in
superficial ways they are dramatic.

It is instructive, for example, for the student of the United States Congress
to visit the mother of parliaments at Westminster, or the Italian Chamber of
Deputies, or the Knesset in Jerusalem. In Washington, the Capitol building
teems with life, and the business of Congress overflows into five giant office

buildings nearby. Senators and representatives each have a suite of offices and a staff to help in their very individual relationships with the people back home who nominated and elected them.[16] Xerox and mimeograph machines hum. Committees and subcommittees abound, all with projects, personnel, budgets, press releases, hearings. Political careers are in such a system plainly a product of much entrepreneurial activity—as well as good fortune.

The contrast with life in Westminster or at the Montecitorio is striking: to someone accustomed to the hurly-burly of Capitol Hill, the leisurely pace, the absence of activity, the paucity of actual working facilities in and around a parliament is memorable. The visitor who takes the guided tours is reminded of the apocryphal query voiced by the American who is taken around the beautiful Moscow subway: Where are the trains?

Occasionally, complaints are heard in the House of Commons:

Remarks of **Honorable Paul Hawkins:** Every hon. Member, especially the back bencher, knows that conditions for work here are so incredibly inefficient that they would not be believed outside the House. . . .

I was given a key to a locker and after some difficulty I found that locker. It was on the floor outside the dining room in direct line with where the waitresses come out with loaded trays to go into the dining room. I am not built in a way that makes it easy to kneel down. I found that when I bent down to the locker I would trip up a waitress with a loaded tray. After six months I returned the key. I later found that some hon. Members had filing cabinets. On asking for one I was told that there was not one available, but after four or five months I got a key to a filing cabinet and I thought that I was making great progress but my filing cabinet, with some others, was in the cloisters. Now I find that where my cabinet is there is to be another Government Whips' office. . . .

Of course, I had to arrive there very early because the desk was not mine and if one got there between 9 o'clock and 9.30 one was swept up by the sweepers and they did not leave until getting on for 10 o'clock.

Despite this, I felt that I was fortunate after six months to have achieved a filing cabinet. Rejoicing, I went to tell my secretary. Then the blow fell for I found that no women are allowed in the cloisters, although the cleaners use it. So I had to learn a new job, filing, and I am extremely bad at it. This was not the end, because when I went down to dictate letters in the only place one could find, on the interview floor, I would get a letter from the file in the cabinet and then have to go up two flights in the lift, down the steps, along the corridor, down more flights of stairs, cross the cloakroom to the part of the cloisters to the filing cabinet. I then had to reverse the process to get the file back to my secretary.

This seemed to be rather wasting time. I found that it took me 10 minutes every time I wanted a letter from the file. (Hansard, October 1966, pp. 360–62)[17]

Office space for deputati in Rome consists of a large, dreary, uninhabited bullpen; such office space as there is in the building called the Montecitorio—and it is limited, though very gracious—is reserved for the small elite cadre of civil servants who staff the parliamentary secretariat. In Jerusalem, committee rooms are sparsely furnished with the bare minimum of tables and chairs; there appears to be virtually no provision for committee staff at all. Upstairs in the Knesset building there are unused offices for individual members of the Knesset and considerably better facilities for the parties represented there.

Such observations are instructive for the student who wishes to understand how legislatures can vary—and vary sharply—in the functions they perform even in open, specialized political systems. Legislatures may resemble one another in that they assemble, conduct business by means of spoken deliberation according to parliamentary rules, and vote in order to express their official will. But these acts, because they contribute to the outputs of organizations differently embedded in their respective systems, are arrived at in vastly different ways.

ARENAS VERSUS TRANSFORMATIVE LEGISLATURES

Upon what do these differences depend? The central distinction I shall propose describing these differences to some degree cuts across the simple constitutional distinction just noted and posits a continuum of legislative power which expresses variations in the legislature's independence from outside influences. At one end lie legislatures that possess the independent capacity, frequently exercised, to mold and transform proposals from whatever source into laws. The act of transformation is crucial because it postulates a significance to the internal structure of legislatures, to the internal division of labor, and to the policy preferences of various legislators. Accounting for legislative outputs means having to know not merely who proposed what to the legislature and how imperatively but also who processed what *within* the legislature, how enthusiastically —and how competently.

Such legislatures—which I shall call *transformative legislatures*—can be contrasted with their fellows at the other end of the continuum. These latter I think of as *arenas*. Arenas in specialized, open regimes serve as formalized settings for the interplay of significant political forces in the life of a political system; the more open the regime, the more varied and the more representative and accountable the forces that find a welcome in the arena. These forces may originate in the stratification system of society or even, as in medieval times, in estates of the realm. The crucial question we must ask of arenas is exemplified by Sir Lewis Namier's celebrated inquiry about eighteenth century Britain— why men *went into* Parliament—in short, the question of political recruitment, which significantly is not a study of the acquisition or exercise of power once they got there.[18]

The existence of legislative arenas leaves unanswered the question of where the power actually resides that expresses itself in legislative acts—whether (as is palpably the case in many modern democratic systems) in the party system, or the economic stratification system, the bureaucracy attached to the king, the barons and clergy, or wherever.

Two contrasting quotations may help to illustrate a salient difference between arenas and transformative legislatures. In principle, both may divide themselves into committees to pursue their work. In practice, an effective committee system may well be a prerequisite of independence for a legislative body, since by such means a legislative body can reap the benefits of a division of labor—e.g., continuity of interest, expertise—in placing its imprint upon public policy.

Consider in this light statements by Woodrow Wilson about the power of congressional committees. Although Wilson did not admire the situation, he clearly saw the relationship between strong committees and the independence of the legislative branch:

> There is no great minister or ministry to represent the will and being of Congress in the common thought. The Speaker of the House of Representatives stands as near to leadership as any one; but his will does not run as a formative and imperative power in legislation much beyond the appointment of the committees who are to lead the House and do its work for it, and it is, therefore, not entirely satisfactory to the public mind to trace all legislation to him. . . . He appoints the leaders of the House, but he is not himself its leader.
>
> The leaders of the House are the chairmen of the principal Standing Committees. Indeed, to be exactly accurate, the House has as many leaders as there are subjects of legislation; for there are as many Standing Committees as there are leading classes of legislation, and in the consideration of every topic of business the House is guided by a special leader in the person of the chairman of the Standing Committee, charged with the superintendence of measures of the particular class to which that topic belongs. It is this multiplicity of leaders, this many-headed leadership, which makes the organization of the House too complex to afford uninformed people and unskilled observers any easy clue to its methods of rule. For the chairmen of the Standing Committees do not constitute a cooperative body like a ministry. They do not consult and concur in the adoption of homogene-

ous and mutually helpful measures; there is no thought of acting in concert. Each Committee goes its own way at its own pace.

The privileges of the Standing Committees are the beginning and the end of the rules. Both the House of Representatives and the Senate conduct their business by what may figuratively, but not inaccurately, be called an odd device of *disintegration.*

Of course it goes without saying that the practical effect of this Committee organization of the House is to consign to each of the Standing Committees the entire direction of legislation upon those subjects which properly come to its consideration. As to those subjects it is entitled to the initiative, and all legislative action with regard to them is under its overruling guidance. It gives shape and course to the determinations of the House. (Wilson, 1956, pp. 58–59, 62, 64)

Although the existence of committees may be a necessary condition of legislative independence, it is clear that when committees exist they need not be strong or autonomous, and hence they are far from a sufficient condition. The point is well illustrated by a contemporary analysis that discusses committees in the British and the Canadian Houses of Commons:

The Canadian system of specialist standing committees is unusual among parliamentary legislatures which, generally speaking, have been slow to develop comprehensive committee systems. The rationale supporting the Westminster model postulates that the influence of parliament over the executive normally comes not so much through the approval, rejection, or alteration of bills by parliament as through the deterrent effect of bad publicity arising from parliamentary scrutiny and debate. Like a court in the British tradition, parliament relies on an adversary technique. Government and opposition sides, with the electorate as jury, put the arguments for and against proposals. The parliamentary system is based on competition not consensus. The argument against strong parliamentary committees is that they submerge the distinction between parties and give power to "irresponsible" legislative committees rather than a "responsible" government.

In contrast to British practice the Canadian House of Commons has had since Confederation a system of specialist standing committees paralleling the departmental structure. Occasionally they have been put to good use. . . . But the system as a whole has not been effective. . . . The Canadian House of Commons now has a system of active specialist committees, and most members of parliament spend as much time in committee sittings (frequently as many as five in a week) as they do in the House itself. . . . Delegation of government business to committees coupled with more stringent control of the time of parliament were obvious necessities. Since 1969 the activities of the standing committees have greatly reduced the pressure of business on the floor of the House. . . .

In many committees turnover during a session will exceed membership. When a member is away from parliament for several weeks, he will be replaced to keep up the party strength on the committee. The Progressive Conservatives try to have experienced members on all committees, which entails some juggling of membership. Frequently a member will be placed on a committee while it is considering a piece of business which affects his constituency or other interests. This high turnover works against the hope of the Select Committee on Procedure that members would specialize. Members of parliament, it appears, are not specialists, but are interested in a variety of issues which might come before any one of several committees.

The demands of committee work on MPs are large. Normally a member will sit on more than one committee, and a member will often have two meetings scheduled for the same time, or two or even more meetings in one day. This reduces the time and attention MPs can give to any single committee, and reduces as well the cohesion and group identity of committees. It is not unusual for a member, after a week of going from one meeting to another, to be uncertain of which of several committees held meetings or of what events occurred. Problems of getting a quorum, and of maintaining party representation on committees are frequent. The Parliamentary Secretary to the President of the Privy Council has complained "that members of this House do not show up at committee meetings and do not participate in the way they should."

In contrast, the opposition has objected that the work of committees reduces the attention members pay to the House itself, and that the government puts members on committees simply to maintain their majority. They claim there are "roving squads of [government] members whose chief ability is to sit on committees, read newspapers, sign letters and at the same time raise their right hands in approval of matters on which they have had no previous experience. These members have not participated in the committee discussions, and are merely present to fill a seat or fill out a quorum."

In Britain, where only about half the 630 members sit on standing committees and a much smaller number on select committees, lack of willing members is one of the main obstacles to expansion of the committee system. (Franks, pp. 461, 462–63, 465–66)

The contrast between arenas and transformative legislatures, as we have seen, captures many of the differences that scholars customarily note in their discussions of the two great legislatures on which legislatures in most of the rest of the world are modeled—the British and the American. Because legislatures elsewhere are more often adaptations than carbon copies, I find it useful to contemplate these two classic cases as tending toward the ends of a continuum rather than as halves of a dichotomy, as is often proposed.

Britain, at any rate, is customarily, and understandably, identified as the home of an arenalike legislature. The truncated character of parliamentary committees, already mentioned, is one indication of this condition. Another is the long-standing preoccupation of observers of Parliament with the social composition of the membership.

It is entirely unnecessary for our purposes to enter into the dispute that has raged among historians of early modern England about how much weight to place upon the selfish, or class-oriented, as contrasted with altruistic, or state-oriented, impulses of the principal actors in English politics during the formation of the modern parliament.[19] For our purposes it suffices to note that none argue the view that a man's position or role within the parliamentary structure had a significant impact upon his attitudes or his influence. A politician's bearing, his "personality, eloquence, debating power, prestige" (Namier, 1963, p. 7) might weigh heavily, but these are personal, not organizational, attributes and further suggest the basic permeability of the parliamentary arena.

Consider also the concern students of Parliament have shown with the process and content of debate, including the well-known English obsession with the shape of the legislative chamber and its alleged effects upon oral exchange (see Wheare, 1963; Jennings, 1940; and Taylor, 1951). Debate means the ventilation of opinion for the education of the country at large. It also functions to mobilize interest groups and to proclaim loyalties not only within the chamber but also between those inside Parliament and their allies outside. As an aid to deliberation, debate is especially useful when the alliances that are most salient to politicians lie beyond the four walls of the chamber from which words are launched. And debate may be contrasted, as Woodrow Wilson did so favorably, with forms of deliberation that are more consultative or negotiatory in spirit and hence more suited to the private politicking of the committee room, the cloakroom, or even the smoke-filled room.

John Stuart Mill's view was that Parliament not only was but should be

> an arena in which not only the general opinion of the nation, but that of every section of it, and as far as possible of every eminent individual whom it contains, can produce itself in full light and challenge discussion; where every person in the country may count upon finding somebody who speaks his mind, as well or better than he could speak it himself—not to friends and partisans exclusively, but in the face of opponents, to be tested by adverse controversy; where those whose opinion is overruled, feel satisfied that it is heard, and set aside not by a mere act of will, but for what are thought superior reasons, and commend themselves as such to the representatives of the majority of the nation; where every party or opinion in the country can muster its strength, and be cured of any illusion concerning the number

or power of its adherents; where the opinion which prevails in the nation makes itself manifest as prevailing, and marshals its hosts in the presence of the government, which is thus enabled and compelled to give way to it on the mere manifestation, without the actual employment, of its strength; where statesmen can assure themselves, far more certainly than by any other signs, what elements of opinion and power are growing, and what declining, and are enabled to shape their measures with some regard not solely to present exigencies, but to tendencies in progress. . . . I know not how a representative assembly can more usefully employ itself than in talk. (Mill, 1962, pp. 111–12)

The British Parliament came by its oral style, which persists to this day, in a historically explicable fashion. The traditional role of Parliament was from the beginning less to forge the details of legislation than to assert certain rights against the sovereign—early in the name of the people as organized into estates (economic-status groupings), later as organized into parties. This is characteristic of many Parliaments. "The standard pattern," says Peter Gerlich, "especially in the central European countries, was one of Crown plus bureaucracy against loosely organized representatives of the main societal classes or groups (nobility, bourgeoisie, peasantry)" (1973, p. 96).

The historical fulcrum around which centralized government—both bureaucracy and legislature—pivoted was the issue of taxation. Kings needed to devise means to raise the money to protect themselves, to go on crusades and other foreign adventures, to build public works and pay armies. In return they offered to the domestic populace a measure of protection: recourse for the enforcement of obligations, a means of mobilizing against foreign invaders, the rudiments of law and order in public places. A legislature was a useful tool of central government because it served as an arena for the establishment of tax obligations and legitimized the raising of money. In return, legislatures set constraints on the central government.[20]

What determined the balance of power between the legislature and the sovereign, once both were in place? Essentially, the balance of power was determined by who controlled the greater armed force—king or barons, king or militia. Many of the armed conflicts of European history come down to a test of this question, and the agreements that followed upon these conflicts were arms control agreements and agreements about levels and distributions of taxation.[21]

Thus the prerequisites of a central legislature, glimpsed in historical perspective, are (1) the spread of prosperity sufficient to make widespread taxation feasible as a method of supporting central government; (2) the spread of arms sufficient to make it necessary for the central government to bargain over, rather than unilaterally impose, tax burdens; and (3) some readiness to bargain about the rational restriction of arms and the supply of services to the populace.

The British Parliament did not develop an internal structure that took significant legislative prerogatives unto itself. Rather, such meager internal differentiation as it has developed has been imposed for the convenience of the political parties in operating Parliament as a necessary tool of the government of the day. And insofar as internal differentiation and structure has been resisted it has been likewise because of the resistance of the leaders of the government, who saw that to empower Parliament as a transformative body was to empower their party opposition. The growth of the parties has provided one element in the superimposition of modern British democracy (in the form of a legislative Parliament) on the institutions of English feudalism; the other crucial element was the growth of the civil service, the modern technocratic successor to the centralized, executive monarchy.[22]

More than a word should be spent on the significance of British parliamentary parties in the workings of Parliament. These parties' central role is to provide a talent pool of decision makers from which the government of the day is staffed; but little is known about how the parliamentary party operates as a collective entity so as to aid in the selection and winnowing of governmental leaders and in constraining their policy options by carrying and amplifying public and elite opinion. The suspicion persists that while the influence of the parliamentary party is far from negligible, the expression of that influence is to be found not in structural features of Parliament but in extraparliamentary forces and in the characters and the connections of individual members. Nevertheless, it is true that careers in future governments of the day are made and broken in the parliamentary party. Thus, because the reputations individuals make for themselves in the House are highly significant for their careers, there is a sense in which the real constituents of Cabinet officials are their own backbenchers. As informed parliamentary opinion influences careers, so also does it frequently constrain the options of public policy.[23] But here, again, it is difficult to pierce the veil and determine how much of this opinion arises within Parliament alone and how much is the product of the broader elite subculture of British governing circles.

Students of the Parliament urge on us the proposition that "the true function of the House is to question and debate the policy of the government" (Jennings, 1940, p. 8) and that consequently to understand the policymaking of Parliament one must look elsewhere—to the social origins of members, especially in an earlier day, to the interests they represented, to the strength in society of interest groups themselves, to the plans of the government and civil service, and to the strategies and the institutions of the party system. Students of the United States Congress have likewise looked to these very same influences and have often enough found ample evidence of their importance in explaining the emergence of policy.

Yet these factors, powerful as they have been, have time and again fallen short of satisfying students of American policymaking processes. For time and again a crucial transformation has occurred between "inputs" from the rest of the political system and the final results of the legislative process. This transformation is not universally admired. For years on end, proponents of various progressive measures, for example, were convinced that they could enact new and useful laws by substantial majorities if they could only bring their proposals to a vote on the floor of both chambers of Congress. In the Senate their hopes were occasionally frustrated by skillful exploitation by minorities of an item of internal structure—a rule ordaining that debate could be terminated only by an extraordinary majority. In the House of Representatives the cards were stacked in even more complex ways: no bill can reach the floor save by a number of alternative clearance systems, each a yellow brick road strewn with pitfalls and tended by trolls. The main route is through the Committee on Rules, for years controlled by a bipartisan conservative coalition. Short of structural reform, to revamp this—or any—committee meant waiting until the years took their toll of senior members, who otherwise served by a custom of reappointment ranked by party in order of committee service. When committee vacancies occur, a complex process of musical chairs takes place, moving newer members into coveted positions. This process of committee assignment engages the efforts of party leaders within the House and frequently entails competition among state delegations and bargaining within the party committees on committees.

In fact, something drastic has more than once had to be done to the Committee on Rules. Most recently, in 1961 the Democratic leadership of the House conducted a successful knock-down-drag-out fight to change the committee's size in order to break what would otherwise have been a conservative coalition stranglehold on the legislative program of the incoming Kennedy administration. By 1961 House Democrats had suffered for more than thirty years at the hands of the Committee on Rules. One recent memory in particular rankled. In 1958 the voters produced a Democratic landslide and sent an overwhelming number of liberals to Congress. Nevertheless, in that same Congress, the Rules Committee actually became more conservative. Speaker Rayburn had had a long-standing arrangement with Republican leader Joe Martin that provided a modicum of Republican cooperation in the committee on bills especially important to the Speaker. In 1959, when House Republicans replaced Joe Martin with the much less compliant Charles Halleck, the Republican accommodation with Rayburn went out the window, and the conservatives tightened their grip on the Rules Committee at a time when there was a large and restless liberal majority in the House as a whole.

Late or soon, structural considerations take their toll: the simple and straightforward desire to pass this or that item of legislation through Congress must give way to a more cunning calculation of strategy based on detailed knowledge of structure.

This realization did not come early or often to political observers, however. Rather, over the years two strands wove themselves into the literature on Congress—and both come to much the same thing. On the one hand there are the nostalgic and mostly favorable reminiscences of Capitol Hill old-timers, sometimes rich in anecdote but more often not, and the bland biographies of congressional notables. On the other there are the denunciations of Congress, congressmen, and all their works, accompanied by trumpet blasts for constitutional reform.[24] In both these modes what is communicated is not information about how things work, but rather information about whether the author approves or disapproves of what he has seen. There is no disputing the value of such information in principle; in practice, however, the knowledge that writers approve or disapprove of Congress has rarely proven valuable much beyond the immediate context of original publication. A cry for constitutional reform rarely echoes resonantly across the generations, and possibly not even over a few years.

The tiny trickle of resolutely empirical studies on Congress, however, has all the staying power of good brandy.[25] All grasp the central significance in understanding Congress of internal structure. It is worth dwelling for a moment on these studies and their successors. If the identification of a legislature as an arena points the scholar away from the detailed examination of the legislature per se and toward the study of outside institutions such as party or stratification systems, the reverse holds for transformative legislatures, the most significant example of which is the Congress.[26]

In the last fifteen years it is generally observed that the study of Congress has taken major strides. In part this phenomenon can be accounted for by calling it a scholarly reaction to the developing tension in the polity at large between increasingly importunate liberal—and mostly Democratic—electoral majorities and a long-standing conservative cross-party majority coalition that for thirty years dominated Congress.[27]

Political science is an awkward hybrid discipline that takes its agenda from the world of actual politics as well as from the work of political science theorizing. Allowing for the normal rhythms of cultural lag and academic gestation, it seems somehow appropriate that Franklin Roosevelt's inability to continue the New Deal past 1936, the failure in Congress of Harry Truman's domestic program, and the long, uncomfortable hibernation of these proposals in the fields of civil rights and social welfare during the era of McCarthy and Eisenhower all would after a while seem intellectually anomalous and not merely personally distasteful to observers of national politics in the Academy. Intellectual anomaly means seeing Congress not merely as a nuisance or a bottleneck. Rather, one begins to ask if liberal academic principles are really so self-evident and political institutions simply perverse in failing to enact them into law, or whether something meaningful and worthy of study is going on within Congress which will better serve than the perversity of institutions to explain the tardy arrival of the millennium.

Most researchers would undoubtedly concede to Ralph Huitt of the University of Wisconsin the principal intellectual paternity of this new mood among political scientists who study Congress. In a series of articles that were persuasively written, thoroughly grounded in empirical research, and theoretically sophisticated, Huitt brought the internal structure and culture of Congress to the top of the academic agenda. (These are collected in Huitt and Peabody, 1969.)

It is clear from his more general, theoretical efforts that Huitt's appreciation of Congress as a political subculture is the product of a larger vision of human nature and human interaction under specified structural constraints. What gave Huitt's view its special interest, however, was his demonstration of its utility in the explication of empirical events. An early article (Huitt and Peabody, pp. 77–112), showing how the record of committee hearings could be read to reveal the operation of congressional norms, was a kind of finger exercise. Then came three important case studies: one on the ways in which internal Senate norms limited the application of sanctions to Wayne Morse when he changed his party affiliation, one on the ways in which Lyndon Johnson gathered up and deployed the resources available to party leadership within the highly structured confines of the Senate, and one on the ways in which boundaries of acceptable senatorial behavior were tested by William Proxmire and Proxmire's adaptation to these boundaries was assimilated by the social system of the Senate.

Huitt's concern with boundaries was itself an intellectual adaptation to the insight, already available in the literature, that the Senate was a formidably encapsulated social entity, a citadel, in the plangent words of William S. White, a very knowledgeable, admiring journalist (1956). One difficulty with White's formula—and there were others (see, e.g., Polsby, 1964 and 1971a)—was that the elaborately formal and stilted norms of behavior it enshrined were at best ideal prescriptions rather than adequate descriptions of actual interaction. The reality, as Huitt saw, contained many elements of White's description but other things in addition, and what emerges from Huitt's account is a picture of a social organization capable of containing diversity, conflict, and even change, while maintaining a core of values and expectations.

Huitt's influence was not confined to the written word but also extended to the graduate program at the University of Wisconsin, which in a few years' time produced several gifted scholars who joined their mentor in helping to reshape the face of congressional studies. In consequence, knowledge began to accumulate on such matters as the means by which interest groups adapted to congressional committee structure (Jones, 1969) (Ph.D., Wisconsin, 1960), the detailed political maneuvers surrounding the House of Representatives committee assignment process (Masters, 1969) (Ph.D., Wisconsin, 1955), and the scope, influence, and quality of congressional staffs (Patterson, 1970), (Ph.D., Wisconsin, 1959).[28]

Other scholars, though trained in different places, soon picked up and elaborated the central message; some, had arrived independently in the late 1950s and early 1960s at similar conclusions about the character of Congress and the most productive strategies for studying it. In particular, Lewis Anthony Dexter, an imaginative social science generalist, whose intellectual roots were in communications theory and the transactional sociology of Arthur Bentley, argued as early as 1954 that it was foolish to contemplate "pressures" on Congress until it could be discovered by empirical study how congressmen perceived, stimulated, and regulated the stimuli to which they were subjected. "Pressure is how you see it," Dexter declared. In his own work, Dexter demonstrated that there were great variations among congressional responses even when external stimuli seemed to be similar (see Bauer, Pool, and Dexter, 1963; Dexter, 1954, 1966a and b).

What accounted for these differences? In part, surely, differences in the placement of various congressmen in the social structure at large. This provided a potential link, mediated, for example, by variations in the contingencies of the nomination and election process from district to district, between the career aspirations and perceptions of individual congressmen and external demands upon them (see Snowiss, 1966). What turned out to be crucial in Dexter's study, however, as far as legislative results were concerned, was the internal structure of Congress. "Pressure," no matter how fierce, when applied to congressmen who didn't sit on the right committee or to the right committee two weeks after it had considered the bill, was bound to be wasted. Scholars who considered only the noise that pressure groups made or marveled at the size of their budgets and neglected the structural problems of reception and compliance were studying the fall of unheard trees in the forest.

If, as Wilson long ago insisted, the committees of Congress were where the action (as well as the inaction) really was, it followed that ultimately scholars would have to learn in detail about committees and their work. One of the first committees to engage the sustained scrutiny of scholars was the House Rules Committee, which had long been the most troublesome one to liberal presidents and to the majority of the majority party (Robinson, 1963; Peabody, 1969). Other committee studies soon followed: Richard Fenno's compendious examination of the Appropriations Committees (1966) made the explicit argument that the pattern of committee activity—how the division of labor was arranged and what expectations and constraints members felt in the conduct of their work—was directly related to the nature of the committee's tasks and to its status in the congressional system. In a follow-up comparative study of six congressional committees (1973), Fenno elaborated upon this central insight, showing how different committees gratify different ambitions of congressmen and tend over time to do their work in different ways.[29]

Nowhere is the significance of internal standards more apparent in the United States Congress than in the ways in which the congressional parties select their leaders. Since 1960, half a dozen opportunities have arisen to watch the process of leadership selection in action. In the first of these, a battle for the majority leadership of the House in 1962, a candidate employing what was called an "inside" strategy of campaigning for the office—stressing personal relations, friendship, the legitimacy of established internal arrangements—was thrown up against a candidate employing an "outside" strategy—stressing ideology, party programs, and constituency pressures. The inside candidate won handily (Polsby, 1969).

In general, "outside" criteria enter only intermittently into the congressional leadership-selection process of either party; this is one secure conclusion that can be derived from Robert Peabody's meticulous reconstructions of leadership contests since 1962. It is noteworthy, moreover, that to do these studies, Peabody reversed the research procedure of Woodrow Wilson, that admirer of the legislature as arena. Where Wilson prided himself on never leaving the Baltimore campus of The Johns Hopkins University to study Capitol Hill at first hand, Peabody, a Hopkins professor, has virtually camped out in the halls of Congress for over a decade.[30]

The strength of the internal structure of Congress and the significance of its imprint on legislative outcomes have led students to ask how long this has been going on. For different purposes, different answers are possible. Some might argue, for example, that James Sterling Young's demonstration (1966) that at the dawn of the nineteenth century, boardinghouse cliques had a significant impact on voting in Congress shows that internal congressional groupings have always dominated the affairs of Congress. Young's larger argument, however, is that the national government did not matter very much in those days, that national parties had not yet truly come into being, and that Congress was insignificant both as arena and as legislature.

A more intriguing case, first—and not too successfully—argued about the United States Senate by David Rothman in his Harvard doctoral dissertation (1964) and shortly thereafter suggestively elaborated for the House by H. Douglas Price (1971), places the probable turning point at some place between 1870 and 1910. Although there is a growing tendency in political science to assign responsibility for nearly everything—including congressional modernization—to the party realignment that took place in the national election of 1896, careful inspection of at least some congressional empirical indicators in time series does not appear to support this proposal (Polsby, 1968). It is much too soon, however, to rule out the suggestion that significant changes in Congress were indeed the product of the "System of 1896" (see Schattschneider, 1956; Shannon, 1968; Burnham, 1970; Brady, 1973; and Ray, 1974). For the time being, evidence does at a minimum suggest that in the last decade of the nineteenth century something like "institutionalization" was taking place in the House of Representatives: a strengthening of boundaries, a growth of internal complexity and a marked shift from discretionary to universalistic norms of decision making in the conduct of internal business.

One of the things that unobtrusive measures such as were employed in the institutionalization study are unsuccessful in elucidating is how actors feel about structural changes that go on around them. It is possible, by looking backward at the end of a long span of time, to see that some congressmen were beginning at the very end of the nineteenth century to embark on careers as representatives that would stretch far into the twentieth century. This was much less common a generation before. And so it is worthwhile to ask how aware congressmen were of the changed opportunity structures that governed their life chances and how these patterns of awareness affected their behavior within the institution. If it is plausible to argue that some congressmen became aware fairly early in the game that their careers would be tied to Congress in ways unimaginable to their predecessors, then it is also plausible to guess that changes in congressional behavior appropriate to the new set of expectations (e.g., drives toward professionalization and subject matter specialization) might have appeared in Congress well in advance of the evidence of structural changes that are capable of being registered by aggregate measures of such things as mean terms of service, which tend to build up into impressively high numbers only after a substantial portion of incumbent congressmen have served out the bulk of their careers. So the fact that measures currently in hand do not support the "System of 1896" hypothesis (or for that matter a hypothesis tracing the responsibility for the transformation of this sector of American politics back to the Depression of 1893) cannot yet be taken as conclusive evidence that these hypotheses are incorrect.

Similar patterns of institutionalization have been observed by American historians of other institutions during the same period. Thus organizations as disparate as the modern medical school (Fleming, 1954), the Ph.D.-granting university (Veysey, 1965), and the business corporation (Chandler, 1962) emerged in the same period. Significant modernization of institutional structures and standardization of practices took place, as well, in agriculture, transportation, and finance (Wiebe, 1967). But to observe these similarities is not to account for them. It nevertheless seems reasonable to suppose that when the historical accidents responsible for the modern institutional structure of Congress are uncovered, what is attributed to them will not be inconsistent with whatever is asserted of historical causes that are ultimately assigned for the modernization of these other American institutions.

Students have argued that institutionalization is both a good thing and a bad thing, an indication of high social development and of institutional "integrity" on the one hand and of organizational retrogression, insulation, and lack of initiative on the other.

> During the twentieth century [says one writer] Congress has insulated itself from the new political forces which social change has generated. . . . Hence the leadership of Congress has lacked the incentive to take the legislative initiative in handling emerging national problems. . . . The members of Congress are "isolated" from other national leaders. At gatherings of national leaders, "members of Congress seem more conspicuous by their absence than by their presence." One piece of evidence is fairly conclusive: of 623 national opinion-makers who attended ten American Assembly sessions between 1956 and 1960, only nine (1.4 percent) were members of Congress! . . . On Capitol Hill the nineteenth-century ethos of the small-town, the independent farmer, and the small business man is still entrenched behind the institutional defenses which have developed in this century to insulate Congress from the new America. (Huntington, 1965a, pp. 8, 15, 16)

And yet:

> In a highly developed political system, political organizations have an integrity which they lack in less developed systems. In some measure, they are insulated from the impact of non-political groups and procedures. In less developed political systems, they are highly vulnerable to outside influences.
>
> At its most concrete level, autonomy involves the relations between social forces, on the one hand, and political organizations, on the other. . . . Political institutionalization, in the sense of autonomy, means the development of political organizations and procedures which are not simply expressions of the interests of particular social groups. . . . A judiciary is independent to the extent that it adheres to distinctly judicial norms and to the extent that its perspectives and behavior are independent of those of other political institutions and social groupings. . . . So also with legislatures. . . . (Huntington, 1965b, p. 401)

It would no doubt be presumptuous for an outsider to join this debate. The contradictions it discloses may in any event be resolvable—or if not resolvable, at least ignorable—through the adoption of more adequate and operational indices of the underlying phenomena.[31] Some of these have in fact been provided in the case of the United States House of Representatives (see Polsby, 1968) and for other institutions the possibilities seem promising.

It is certainly not the case that institutionalization is an inevitable process, nor is it irreversible, unidirectional, or monotonic. When it occurs it may do so in a variety of patterns. Nevertheless, when we look for the causes and effects of institutionalization in any one sector, it seems reasonable to ask whether the explanations we formulate are compatible with what we know of circumstances elsewhere. It seems most implausible that there should be one set of laws governing human behavior in business corporations, another set for legislatures, still another set for institutions of higher education, another for the legal profession, and another for the military. Underlying all sectors there should be, if not uniformity, at least kinship in the propositions that purport to explain growth and change. When this kinship is made explicit, examples from one sector may strengthen or weaken propositions asserted of another. When it is not, propositions are unlikely to possess sufficient generality to arouse much interest.

It is possible to summarize characteristic problems of studying arenas and to contrast them with characteristic problems of studying transformative legislatures. For arenas the impact of external forces is decisive in accounting for legislative outcomes. For transformative legislatures, what is decisive are variables depicting internal structure and subcultural norms. The student of arenas is perforce the student of social backgrounds of legislators,[32] of legislative recruitment, of "pressure" groups, of extraparliamentary party politics, of the organization of parliamentary parties, and of debate. The student of transformative legislatures must consider committee structure and appointment processes, institutional socialization processes, the perception and regulation of interests by legislators, the dispositions of informal legislative groups such as state delegations in the case of the American Congress (Fiellen, 1969; Kessell, 1964; Clapp, 1963; Deckard, 1972, 1973), the operations of rules of internal procedure, and customs such as seniority (see Polsby, Gallaher, and Rundquist, 1969; Abram and Cooper, 1968).

Between the pure cases of arenas and transformative legislatures there stretches a continuum whose breadth and main features are not well understood. In part this understanding is hampered by the occasional impurity of even the supposedly pure types as, for example, when Congress obeys clear and urgent signals from its electorate on such issues as busing or when British MPs stir in the ranks as, for example, a few did on Suez, thus giving the legislative body for at least a short time an independent life of its own although this is not frozen into structural features of the system (see Epstein, 1964; Mackintosh, 1972).

Despite these problems, can we find some reasonably clear-cut intermediate cases? One hypothesis that has some plausibility proceeds from the observation that the main influence on the independence and hence the transformative capacity of the legislature in modern democratic political systems lies in the character of parliamentary parties. And this in turn refers to a number of separate variables. It is easiest simply to state, in bald propositional form, the influence these variables are hypothesized to have.

1. The broader the coalition embraced by the dominant parliamentary group that organizes the legislature, the more transformative the legislature. (The independent variable is indexed, e.g., by homogeneity of class and group composition of party electorates.[33])

2. The less centralized and hierarchical the management of legislative parties, the more transformative the legislative. (The independent variable is indexed, e.g., by locus of control over the nomination process.)

3. The less fixed and assured the composition of legislative majorities on successive specific issues, the more transformative the legislature. (The independent variable is indexed, e.g., by bloc structure analysis for successive votes and by the congruence of blocs with party labels.)

Not all of these independent variables run together along the same set of tracks, although at the extremes their influence is fairly plain. American legislative parties are extremely coalitional, decentralized, and flexible; British legislative parties are somewhat less coalitional, hierarchical, and fixed. Systems that lie between the two in their transformativeness show a variety of patterns.

Netherlands. The Dutch political system provides for a modified separation of powers between the executive branch and the parliament, the States General. Cabinet members may speak in the States General but are not members and do not vote there, and most are not recruited from the parliament. Parliamentary service is not a full-time occupation, and since the Netherlands is a small country, members of parliament commonly live at home and commute to the Hague. Members are elected not from their hometowns but at large, in one of eighteen electoral districts, and they belong to well organized but not well disciplined parliamentary parties. Legislative initiative is in the hands of cabinet ministers, who work in collaboration with the large and powerful civil service, but the States General retains significant rights of amendment. The more powerful second chamber has in the last twenty years developed a specialized committee system, and there is also a parliamentary privilege to question individual ministers on specific subjects. In addition the parliament occasionally undertakes inquiries analogous to congressional investigations.

Dutch parliamentary parties are small and must form coalitions to govern. They are somewhat decentralized and moderately flexible in their creation of successive parliamentary majorities. Lijphart (1968, pp. 136–37) says, "Major pieces of legislation are often passed with the help of some 'opposition' parties and with a 'government' party voting against." This results in a less transformative legislature than the American case but a more transformative legislature than in most parliamentary democracies (see Weil, 1970).

Sweden. Policymaking in the Riksdag of Sweden is dominated by three inter-acting forces: the cabinet and civil service, which provide much of the agenda and staff work of the Riksdag and hence are powerful external influences on outcomes; the parliamentary parties; and the Riksdag's own committee system. Parliamentary parties caucus, provide background research material on specific issues to their members, select leaders, who are important figures in the bar-gaining process that goes on for all major questions, and work out parliamen-tary strategy. But they do not deliver the votes of their members en bloc. Joseph Board (1970, p. 137) says, "There are forces other than party membership which may tug at the loyalties of an individual Riksdagsman. Among these are the sense of the Riksdag as a whole, the integrity of a particular committee, membership in a particular interest organization, or the demands of the na-tional party and different factions within it." All legislation of any significance is routed through committees. Although their powers of initiative are sharply limited, they meet privately and hammer out the details of legislation that is set before them from the government (principally) or private members. Com-mittee members tend to specialize in their committee service and build up seniority. Committee leadership is far less significant than in the American Congress, owing to the influence of staff work by the government and civil service and the weakness of independent committee staffs. Floor debate is far less significant than in pure arenas. "Decisions on important issues are likely to have been made in committee or by inter-party agreement, and thus debate is more or less superfluous" (Board, p. 140). Thus the Swedish parliament ap-pears to satisfy perfectly the legendary tropism of the Swedish national char-acter toward moderation, producing a moderately transformative legislature, out of moderately coalitional parliamentary parties, with moderately cen-tralized party management, and moderate differences in the composition of successive legislative majorities.

Germany. In Germany there has been a slow increase in the power and signifi-cance of parliamentary committees, more or less concomitant with the increase in the coalitional character of the major parties, especially the Socialists (see Loewenberg, 1967, pp. 151–52). Party discipline remains relatively high, al-though more so for the Socialists (SPD) than for the Christian Democrats (CDU/CSU). Christian Democratic deputies do defect in some numbers, al-though not on matters that would "embarrass" the government of the day. The trend is clearly toward increased influence for specialized committees of the Bundestag and increased logrolling among subgroup representatives within the parliamentary parties (who are aided by any trend toward committee in-dependence). Scholars increasingly note the trappings usually associated with transformative legislatures—for example, private offices and staffs for legisla-tors, a decline in the significance of floor debate, and more and more cases of cross-party voting within committees.[34]

Italy. In Italy the dominant party—which organizes parliament—is highly coalitional, the other parties much less so. Italy falls somewhere in the middle on all three of the scales proposed here. All parties strive to maintain a strong discipline over their members, and party leaders do succeed in fixing legislative majorities on a few major policy issues once they assemble the government —although the ability to do so is conditioned by the party balance in parliament and is often in danger of evaporating as the concrete details of policy must be hammered out. In matters of lesser importance, however, party control is continually threatened by the existence of a full slate of committees in both houses (fourteen in the Chamber of Deputies, twelve in the Senate) and the constitutional provision that allows these committees to *adopt* laws independently under some conditions. These structural features, plus the highly fragmented party system, plus the factional, comparatively undisciplined nature of the largest party, sometimes combine to give the legislature important transformative opportunities even when the legislature is not directly threatening to the government of the day (see Manzella, n.d.).

France. Fourth Republic France must be classed as a modified arena. It did develop narrowly focused, occasionally powerful committees (and hence some transformative capability) owing to the instability of governments. With the exception of the Communists, parliamentary parties were strongly decentralized and nonhierarchical, and this became more true as one moved toward the center of the ideological spectrum—where all governmental coalitions had to be built. The combination of this instability in internal party cohesion with the large number of parties and the large size of the antisystem parties (which were always available to help break up legislative majorities) meant that there were few fixed majorities for dealing with successive major issues.

Such a situation might, in other circumstances, favor the evolution of a transformative legislature. However, because of the coexistence of undisciplined parties, few fixed legislative majorities, and a third element running in the opposite direction—that is, because of the lack of one or two broadbased, dominant parliamentary parties capable of organizing parliament—the only transformative characteristic that emerged was the legislature's continuing ability to bring down the government. In an indirect way, the exercise of this power gives the legislature independent opportunities to influence policy, since the government is the body that originates policy. But in the sense that the parliament itself alters the details of specific policies to suit imperatives internal to its own operation, there is little transformative effect.

This mild departure from the pure arena model—the ability to alter the identities of those who make policy without the ability to alter the details of policy itself—is what students of Fourth Republic France apparently mean when they assert that internal legislative politics was important, that structural factors in the legislature (e.g., committees) had impact, but that parliament was at the same time impotent.[35]

To deal with this dilemma (among others), the Constitution of Fifth Republic France proposed to make the legislature an arena mainly for the use of the separately elected president of the Republic and secondarily for his party. The possibility that the legislature would retain any transformative characteristics was, the framers hoped, crushed out through constitutional engineering.[36] The parliamentary agenda was turned over entirely to the government, as was the ability to determine the form of the vote. Only the government can initiate appropriations measures, and parliament can neither cut taxes nor raise expenditures. Each chamber is limited to a maximum of six standing committees, which guarantees that they will be too large to make independent legislative inputs. The government is free to make any piece of legislation a question of "confidence," but parliament cannot "dissolve" the president by voting "no confidence"; all that will happen is that *parliament* will be dissolved.[37]

Belgium. In Belgium the three main parliamentary parties are centrally disciplined, and voting in parliament is, on most issues, highly predictable. Moreover, parliamentary parties, never broadly based, have become less coalitional as the language question has increased in salience. This is the classic recipe for a nontransformative legislature, and indeed we find that the formula that creates the cabinet dominates the legislative process. The cabinet initiates virtually all proposals considered by the parliament, and deviation from party expectations in voting on particular measures jeopardizes the governing coalition. Although committees exist, the real work of negotiating among interest groups and party leaders goes on elsewhere. "If the Cabinet, majority parties, and interest groups can come to terms," says Gordon Weil (1970, p. 170), "there is little doubt that the proposed legislation will pass Parliament." (See also Lorwin, 1966.)

Table 4 summarizes the results of this brief European travelogue. It suggests that the legislatures surveyed fall into four main clusters, varying in their transformativeness more or less in accord with the three propositions earlier suggested. These "findings" are, of course, to be taken with more than a grain of salt, and not only because they are based on rough-and-ready classification and superficial knowledge of the politics of the individual countries.[38] At best, this exercise can serve as an illustration of the sort of variables that ultimately may explain variations in the independent capacities of legislatures to affect outcomes. (For other attempts see Kornberg, 1973; Mezey, 1974; Grumm, 1973; and Shaw and Lees, 1973.)

TABLE 4 Determinants of transformativeness in legislatures

Independence of legislature	Example	Parliamentary organizing majorities	Parliamentary party management	Successive policy majorities
Highly transformative	United States	Highly coalitional	Very decentralized	Very flexible
Modified transformative	Netherlands	Coalitional	Decentralized	Flexible
	Sweden	Moderately coalitional	Moderately decentralized	Moderately flexible
Modified arena	Germany	Coalitional	Moderately decentralized	Moderately flexible
	Italy	Coalitional	Moderately centralized	Moderately fixed
	France IV	Unstable	Decentralized	Flexible
Arena	United Kingdom	Moderately coalitional	Centralized	Fixed
	Belgium	Narrowly based	Centralized	Fixed
	France V	Narrowly based	Centralized	Fixed

LEGISLATIVE REFORM: TOWARD TRANSFORMATIVENESS?

Only a little scholarly attention has been paid to the issue of the reform of legislatures, looking toward the enhancement of their independent powers. One favored place to begin has been for reformers quite consciously to adopt as their model the United States Congress. In American state legislatures this has meant a movement toward the establishment of a respectable pay scale, provision for independent staff services, and increases in the time allowed for legislatures to sit (Citizens' Conference on State Legislatures, 1971; Rosenthal, 1974; Herzberg and Rosenthal, 1971). What has been at stake for these legislatures has been a movement toward professionalization of the legislatures' capacity to deliberate, oversee, and legislate. This has meant a shift of emphasis away from the representational values of legislators as amateur citizens embedded in their local communities. It has more and more demanded their frequent attendance at the state capital, and while decreasing the salience of local preference, it has increased the significance of legislative structure. This has for some state legislatures followed by a few decades a pathway very much like the road trod by Congress.

But what about similar reformist yearnings in parliamentary arenas? To empower the select committees of the House of Commons, for example, from the standpoint of government and ministries alike would be suicidal, since such a move would place significant weapons in the hands of the party opposition (Royal Commission on the Constitution, 1973; Hill and Whichelow, 1964; Walkland, 1968, pp. 99–104; Crick, 1965). The British must operate without a constitutional system that legitimizes the separating of powers and without a political history of fragmentation in party structure and policymaking. Consequently, the idea, although seriously advocated, seems alien to the genius of the British Constitution. It is as though British reformers had bravely set out in a small boat into the raging Atlantic, hoping to bump in mid-ocean into Anglophile American party reformers, who years ago started rowing madly out from Eastport.

The German parliament has meanwhile been moving slowly in recent years toward emulation of the American model, and this has led to complaints similar to those heard in America: not enough party responsibility, not enough public accountability, not enough debate (see Hennis, 1971). Evidently there is no perfect solution to the ongoing legislative problem of providing, on the one hand, for competence and hence capacity to respond to the internal promptings of expertise and specialization versus the needs for representativeness and accountability and hence capacity to respond to external demands.

Observers who deplored the incapacity of the American political system easily to rid itself of a Watergate-tainted administration pointed to the speedy efficiency with which parliamentary governments could be overthrown for lack of confidence. But these same observers then had somehow to confront the massive difficulties encountered by parliamentary regimes in forming stable governing majorities in country after country, thus effectively devolving governing power on politically unresponsive bureaucracies. It is possible, under the circumstances, for students to develop powerful and meaningful preferences for one or another organizational design and therefore for one or another reform that moves a political system toward the preferred state of affairs. It is not possible, however, to escape the fact that under some circumstances *all* alternatives are costly and inefficient.

REPRESENTATION IN SPECIALIZED, OPEN REGIMES

Our argument thus far is that it is possible to discern a characteristic range of decision-making structures in legislatures that occur in open, specialized regimes. In dealing with the ways in which legislatures organize and make contributions to outcomes, we have thus far only touched on a central problem— that of representation. Only for legislatures in open, specialized regimes is representation a problem. In closed regimes, as we have seen, the purpose of a legislature is essentially cosmetic, although it may also be an agency of co-optation, which increases in effectiveness as significant groups in the society are represented there. In open, unspecialized regimes there is no clear or permanent line between governors and governed or between the act of legislating and the ceremonial invocation of agreed-on customary norms, and the polity is in important respects coextensive with the legislature.

For open and specialized regimes, however, there is a problem of finding a formula that adequately relates "openness" to "specialization." Insofar as a regime is open, anyone may have access to authoritative decision making. Insofar as it is specialized, only certain people in practice do so. This dilemma is reflected in two complementary strands in theories of representation. One of these defines representation as action by an agent *as if* the agent were the people represented in all relevant respects. The other proposes a rule of representation which states that a representative acts *for* those represented and in their behalf. Under one theory the task of the representative is solely to ascertain the wishes of the represented; under the other the task is to act in accord with the representative's own view of the best interests of the represented. Thus contradictory imperatives are, at least in theory, enshrined at the heart of a central legislative task (Pitkin, 1967).

In practice, it is normally quite impossible to follow either of these imperatives. Over the broad range of legislative matters, representatives commonly find that their constituents are mute, their demands confused or contradictory. Where none of these conditions obtains, and where there is no party discipline, it is a rare representative who fails to discern the fact and act accordingly. Likewise over the broad range of legislation, it is exceedingly difficult to be sure of the best interests of one's constituents. Where the signals are clear, legislators rarely miss their chances to act. Here again, the problem of party discipline introduces a complicating factor. But even when it plays no part in guiding the behavior of legislators, it is more common by far for the interests of one set of constituents to be confounded with those of another set, for legislative proposals to be ambiguously related to special interests and tenuously, but arguably, related to more general interests. These commonly end up prevailing in the rationalizations for action given by most legislators most of the time.

Because in its pure state the dilemma of representation appears to be insoluble, thoughtful observers have proposed alternative means of determining whether or not representatives are representing their constituents. One popular alternative substitutes for the idea of representation the idea of subsqent accountability. A legislature is accountable insofar as its members are subject to frequent, fair, contested elections and hence can be turned out of office if they displease the represented.

This formula is not without its own problems. Consider the problem of fair elections. These are not possible, according to an authority as august as the United States Supreme Court, if the votes of voters located differently on the map are weighted differently. And different weights occur if the populations of single-member districts supplying different members to the same legislature are greatly different in population.[39] Electorates are made more equal in population by redrawing the boundaries of districts. Typically, in the course of this highly sensitive political activity, districts do indeed become more equal in population but less competitive between the major political parties. This depresses the "contestedness" of elections in the very act of enhancing their "fairness."

The foregoing discussion deals with the most straightforward case, namely, the single-member district of relatively small size, and without the complicating pressures of party discipline. We know, however, that party discipline counts for a great deal in many ostensibly representative democracies and that in order fairly to provide an accountable national party program it is sometimes necessary for party whips to require that individual legislators vote against the strong wishes of their local constituents. Some theorists consider that in so doing legislators are providing a greater measure of representation, because of the contribution of their vote to the overall coherence of the party program and hence to the party's delivery on its nationwide electoral promises. There is clearly another point of view on this matter, which holds that the important covenant that a legislator's voting behavior should uphold is the promise made as an individual to his or her individual constituents.

I do not see any way to avoid arbitrariness in settling this disagreement; one believes either that the locus of accountability is at the individual and district level or that it is at the collective and party level. Political systems frequently resolve the issue by means of their constitutional rules. Thus the single-member district and the decentralized nomination processes of the American Congress broadcast an entirely different theory of representation than the theory it is possible to contemplate under the Israeli system of a single, nation-wide constituency and proportional representation, with the probability of actual legislative service based on a candidate's ranking in the party list.

There are still other problems that increase the ambiguities in the linkage between legislatures and voters. We have established that in even the best of circumstances representatives cannot mirror the relevant characteristics or preferences of their constituents. In most respects neither can they deliberate over the broad range of issues and thus vote in the legislature according to their independent calculation of the best interests of their constituency. In the House of Commons this is the case because so little such activity is permitted to back-benchers, and so much of the real work of shaping proposals goes on elsewhere. In Congress the division of labor means that no one legislator actually deliberates over more than a fraction of the issues. The arena of Commons is an electoral college for the Cabinet in a sense even weaker than described by Bagehot (1963). The transformative Congress is internally structured to channel deliberation along fairly narrow lines, which perforce excludes most legislators from the process most of the time.

Thus even if the diagnostic capacities of voters were up to the job of identifying where and how to vote to maximize their policy preferences, there appears to be for most voters no surgically precise way, overall, to do so. There are, of course, trivial exceptions: a voter who cares passionately about taxes and who lives in eastern Oregon can vote for or against Al Ullman and thereby make strict accountability work—for him. Presumably voters in the British electoral districts in which party leaders of the House of Commons are running have similar opportunities, although only in rare cases is a major figure overturned, or when overturned, by virtue of that permanently excluded from a crack at the next open safe seat and a return to parliamentary leadership.

Thus we must conclude that representation is a will-o'-the-wisp, and strict accountability likewise. Yet both ideas retain a significant core of meaning and inform the actual mechanisms that modern legislatures employ in seeking to represent.

There is no wholly satisfactory description of these substitute mechanisms in the literature, but perhaps a first approximation of the representation process would be something like this: "representation" takes place in the legislatures of open, specialized regimes by means of changes in the alliances among elites which are the result of elite perceptions of changes in public opinion and interest-group activity. Perhaps this is easiest to see in the reformations of British cabinets that issue indirectly from the results of by-elections and public opinion polls. "Greater love hath no man," said one wag after a particularly comprehensive bloodletting by Harold Macmillan, "than to give up his friends for his life."

Other fully institutionalized examples of this pattern occur in arenas having multiple parties but with one party dominant. Thus as Etzioni (1963) argues for Israel, it is possible—and on occasion necessary—for the dominant party to change its alliances with minor parties in accord with its reading of public opinion.

Even in the notoriously impervious United States Congress, representation of the kind we have described does take place. Party leaders attempt—and frequently succeed—in packing committees to accord with their interest-group alliances. Small and medium sized caucuses of like-minded Congressmen have sprung up in response to changes in the climate of opinion outside Congress, and one of these, the Democratic Study Group, has been singularly successful in pressing for changes in the rules and other structural barriers to the pursuit of what it conceives to be its mandate. In consequence, the House Democratic caucus has grown in significance, a party steering committee has been established and given the power to appoint Democrats to committees, subcommittee chairmanships have been spread among a wider range of members, and committee chairmen have been restricted in some of their managerial prerogatives and in addition are now subject to a less than assured election by mandatory secret ballots in caucuses at the beginning of each Congress.

Activity of this kind, prompted and abetted by interest-group agitation, and newspaper stories, constitutes a modern, practical substitute for representation and for strict subsequent accountability by legislatures as collective entities. As individuals, legislators do what they can—or will—to represent. Sometimes this is a lot, sometimes a little. Whether these processes, taken all together, are good enough, or democratic enough, or result in enough genuine representation, can of course be determined only as observers consult their own preferences.

IN CONCLUSION: LEGISLATURES AS MULTIPURPOSE ORGANIZATIONS

At some point in the historical development of legislative institutions it becomes possible to see legislatures as focusing a sufficient portion of the resources of a society to give them standing as an independent link between the populace and the government. It is at this juncture, somewhere in the late eighteenth or early nineteenth century, that the romantic doctrine of revolution as the only feasible source of popular expression in government became outmoded. Thomas Jefferson's welcoming response to Shay's rebellion, his notion of occasionally watering the tree of liberty with the blood of patriots as a necessary check upon the arbitrariness of government, was one such statement of this doctrine. The growth of legislatures, and the substitution of the saliva of patriots for patriotic gore, provides a much better device in open societies for the episodic transmission of popular sentiments to political leaders, through the medium of popular election, through exercise of the right of petition, through lobbying and party and interest-group influence on legislative policy-making.

Even where finely calibrated lobbying, inserting detailed plans for the redress of grievances into the policymaking process, is not possible, legislative elections and demands for symbolic representation in rubber-stamp legislatures (as well as in more effective ones) offer outlets for political dissatisfaction that may forestall, if not entirely preempt, revolutionary activity. Just as the good is frequently the enemy of the best, amelioration by the creation of a popular branch of government has become the enemy of popular revolt.

I do not know of an extended period of time when representative assemblies attached to large and complex political systems did not find life difficult. In any such assembly tensions must continuously press internally between forces of stability and coherence and those of change and responsiveness. Diversity of interests must somehow be cabined so that legislative power can be exercised. The routines of government, perforce vested in other places, provide a constant base for the expansion of nonlegislative power. The exercise of oversight over these routines entails a division of labor and a loss of collective coherence, or else reliance—and ultimately, dependence—on a rival bureaucracy, or else domination of the legislature by a superior organizing force, such as extraparliamentary party leaders. Where division of labor is the solution, individual legislators are unable to satisfy their appetites for general expertise; where party leadership is the solution, individual legislators are ineffective and passive.

Thus modern legislatures are bound to share one fundamental institutional difficulty even when they adopt opposite solutions to the problem of legislative power. This difficulty has to do with recruiting able persons to careers of legislative work. Although it is a problem infrequently faced, it goes to important questions relating to the ways in which incentives are embedded in organizational structures. Without adequate incentives for participation and persistence, organizations wither. Since no organizations seem to do precisely what legislatures do in their political systems, one assumes that over the long run the prospects are good for the survival of at least some of the legislative forms we have been discussing. However, whether these legislatures will operate as effective and independent forces in decision making remains uncertain and problematic.

For what in the end seems most intriguing about legislatures is their all-purpose flexibility. They are not so efficient as a secret police in gaining for a ruling clique the short-run popular obedience that is necessary for them to govern. Yet in many systems they do the job of gaining legitimacy for government tolerably well and in addition serve as training grounds for future elites.

Undoubtedly an experienced corps of experts can explore policy alternatives and select solutions to problems more expeditiously and more intelligently than a legislature, but legislatures have learned to do this, too, tolerably well and in addition can test alternatives against the demanding criterion of political acceptability in ways not readily available to experts. A modern, well-equipped army can generally stave off a revolt, but so may a legislature, by providing a regular forum for the hearing and, occasionally, the redress of grievances.

It is the fact that legislatures in different times and circumstances do all these things, and sometimes all of them at once, that makes them so baffling to the analyst. It also makes them fascinating and instructive organizations and commends them to the student of man's long and difficult struggle for self-government.

NOTES

1.   A recent, useful bibliography is available in the journal *Scienze Sociali* 2 (August, 1972). Fairly recent summaries of pertinent American literature are contained in Manley (1974), Eulau and Hinckley (1966), and Huitt and Peabody (1969). Von Beyme (1970) has a 951-item bibliography organized by topic and country. In addition, three broad overviews, by Walter Shepard (1933), Robert Fried (1966), and Robert Packenham (1970), have been especially useful in the preparation of this essay.

2.   For examples of these alternative strategies see Wahlke *et al.* (1962) (functionalist) and Packenham (1970) and Loewenberg (1967, 1971) (structuralist).

3.   This purposely leaves open the question whether nation-states, as conventionally defined, or their subdivisions, are the only political systems for which the discussion that follows holds. My view is that other sorts of political systems or polities can usefully be identified. In principle, any corporate entity capable of making and enforcing laws can be so considered: a business corporation, as a later example illustrates, or a labor union, or a university can be analyzed as a political system in much the same way as a more conventionally recognized polity. This point, while not universally accepted, has more than a few adherents. One imaginative application of this viewpoint is Cyert and March (1963).

4.   Robert Fried (1966, p. 82) describes the undifferentiated quality of many such groups when they exist in mass societies: "Parties, especially extremist parties, have tended to organize as military forces, with weapons, uniforms, military discipline, social isolation, elaborate organization and violent tactics. Armies, on the other hand, have tended to take on the roles and trappings of political parties; competing for control of government, making nominations, electing candidates, organizing paracivilian auxiliaries, adopting and furthering programs of reform. What is an army? A kind of political party. What is a party? A kind of army."

5.   The organization theorists Chester Barnard (1938, pp. 163ff.) and Herbert Simon (1957, pp. 11–12) have suggested operationalizing the concept of legitimacy as a "zone of acceptance" or "zone of indifference" within which subordinates will more or less automatically agree to the behavioral prescriptions of leaders.

6.   It is no casual tribute to the insight of Max Weber (1947) that so much of what he wrote about the development of political systems in general resonates through what purports to be a modern discussion of the different forms of an institution about which

he had very little to say. Our discussion of "custom" is of course entirely compatible with Weber's notion of traditional forms of legitimation, and "consent" sounds very like "rational-legal" legitimation. "Indoctrination" I regard as a slight adaptation to modern mass conditions of "charismatic legitimation." It would take this discussion far afield to defend this usage in detail, but I hope there is some prima facie plausibility to the claim, since indoctrination in modern communities often constitutes an attempt by means of the manipulation of symbols to establish a linkage between masses and elites which attributes special qualities to members of the elite group.

"Coercion," as a separate category, may need a word of further explanation. To Weber, the defining characteristic of government was the monopoly of the legitimate use of force, and so his classical constructs describing alternative forms of legitimacy all go to the question of the different circumstances in which a population will acquiesce to the lodgement of this monopoly with particular leaders. But Weber is relatively silent on the use of this capacity as a further resource. Thus some readers may question whether the repeated and systematic employment of coercion on a domestic population leads to a grant of legitimacy in Weber's sense.

My view is that it does; that is, it is a frequently employed resource and it unquestionably leads to acquiescence, which I take to be an acceptable core meaning of legitimacy. Certainly for the purpose of making predictions about the stability of regimes, information about internal uses of coercion is quite useful and in many cases essential. Moreover it is by no means a certainty whether coercion systematically applied is a wholly ineffective means for generating other forms of loyalty to a regime over the long run. Consider, for example, the "cult of personality" that provided, in the latter parts of the Stalin era, an instance of the routinization of charisma generated in part by indoctrination but in part—and especially at the elite level—by violence.

7.   One blatant example of this is the domestic intelligence-gathering plan evidently approved by President Nixon in 1970. See Submission of Recorded Presidential Conversations (1974). A theoretical argument to this point, embedded in a most useful discussion of the costs of hierarchy, is contained in Dahl and Lindblom (1953). One is also reminded of the remark once allegedly made to Nikita Khrushchev that it was a pity there were no free elections in his country, since if there were he would undoubtedly win.

8.   See Pryor (1968, pp. 239–52).

9.   Indeed, Fred Riggs (1974) argues that the prior existence of a powerful, highly differentiated, or active bureaucracy discourages the formation of legislatures. His examples are drawn mostly from the politics of Asian nations. See Keen (1973, pp. 5–6) for a brief discussion of the role of the sheriff in the English medieval bureaucracy.

10.   The classic statement of this theme, which thoroughly explores the metaphor of a modern corporation as a political system, is Berle and Means (1932).

11.   Here is another example: Persons who desire to sit in the Iranian Majlis must first pay a substantial fee to the government in order to get on a list of candidates, then survive a thorough investigation by the secret police, and finally avoid being struck off the list by the shah. Those who pass all three hurdles can rest secure in the knowledge that the slate backed by the shah has never lost an election. If, by some strange chance, such a legislature should not prove absolutely malleable, the shah also has constitutional authority to call a new constitutional convention and appoint its members (Bill, 1971).

12.   As Bill (p. 364) says of Iran, "The Pahlavi monarchs and political elites have consciously struggled to protect and preserve the existence of the Majlis in Iranian society. The public presence of this institution strongly suggests limited monarchy and popular

political participation. As such, the Majlis stands as a conspicuous symbol that is strategically available to confront those who would challenge the legitimacy of the system."

13. As Freeman (1883, Vol. 1, p. 6) says: "A New England town-meeting is essentially the same thing as the Homerica ἀγορή, the Athenian ἐχχλησία, the Roman *comitia*, the Swiss *Landesgemeinde*, the English folk-moot. The circumstances of New England called the primitive assembly again into being when in the older England it was well nigh forgotten. What in Switzerland is a *sur*vival was in New England rather a *revival*."

14. The anthropologist Ralph Nicholas (1966, pp. 54–55) has studied this transition in Canadian Indian tribes. He comments:

> One characteristic that has been noted repeatedly by anthropological observers of small-scale political arenas is the "consensus procedure" for making public decisions. Many societies, from American Indian tribes to Indian peasant villages, either do not know about, or they reject, voting and majority rule. Debates and discussions are prolonged and issues are redefined until the decision-makers achieve unanimity. A major change that has been sought by modern governments—in North America and India, as in many other areas—is the "democratization" of politics in small-scale political arenas. When the Canadian government in 1924 installed a "democratically elected" council on the Grand River Iroquois Reserve in Ontario, it initiated a sharp factional conflict which continues to the present.... In many parts of rural India, the attempt of the Congress government to have village councils elected by universal adult franchise has sharpened already existing factional conflicts and has made some local systems, whose factions were previously peripheral, into segmentary factional political systems.
>
> In situations of rapid social change, factions frequently arise—or become more clearly defined—because factional organization is better adapted to competition in changing situations than are the political groups that are characteristic of stable societies. Traditional Iroquois matrilineages could function only under the rule that government was by the council of chiefs. Factions, on the other hand, are not necessarily bound by only one set of rules, either traditional or modern. Thus it is possible for the Mohawk Worker faction on the Six Nations Reserve to oppose the tribal council, which is elected under the modern set of rules, by supporting the re-installation of government by the chiefs, who are chosen under the traditional rules of adelphic succession. When universal adult franchise elections were introduced in rural India, factional organization proved to be the most successful way of bringing in votes, although votes had never before been essential for obtaining political rewards. When the indenture system was ended in Fiji, the settlements of Indian laborers were set free, and, with virtually no internal authority systems, they formed themselves into political communities. Factions arose "automatically," as a way of organizing people in political conflicts.

15. There may be some legitimate disagreement as to whether all the systems classified by Blondel in this table would survive scrutiny as "open, specialized" political systems in the sense implied by our classification scheme. There are some difficulties, for example, in the listing of as many as 17 Latin American nations as "open": Martin Needler (1963, pp. 156–57) lists 20 Latin American nations, and in 14 of them the normal political role of the military is held to be highly significant. Most of these 14 are nevertheless classified by Needler as having multiparty systems. The 6 nations where the military was considered as of 1963 to be relatively weak were Uruguay, Mexico, Colombia, Chile, Bolivia, and Costa Rica. For alternative classifications of polities see Dahl (1971, Appendices A and B) and Rustow (1967, Appendix 5).

16. David B. Truman (1955) has a notably succinct and intelligent account of the consequences for the American party system of the decentralization of the process of congressional nomination and election. For the contrasting story in parliamentary regimes see Epstein (1967).

17. Here is a rough comparison of emoluments available to members of the British Parliament and those available to members of Congress.

Parliament		*Congress*
Annual salary:	$7,800	$42,500
Staff pay	$1,200	ca. $125,000 for up to 12 employees
Office equipment:	None	$5,500 worth, new or used
Other:	$48 stationery allowance; free travel to the constituency; can ask for a desk, filing cabinet, and telephone extension, though they all will not necessarily be in the same place; free telephone calls from the House of Commons, but only within the London area.	$4,500 stationery allowance; 35,000 minutes of long-distance telephone time per two-year term; 480,000 heavy-duty brown envelopes per year; $700 worth of stamps per year; $2,400 per year for rental of office space in the district; $2,400 per year for district office supplies, equipment, and telephone expense; free and unlimited franked first-class postage; free office space (usually a three-room suite) in a House office building; one free round trip per month to the home district plus three additional trips, one for the congressman, two for staff members.

For more on the life of the individual member of Parliament see A. P. Herbert (1937, 1951), Richards (1959), and Barker and Rush (1970). Corroborative comments contrasting facilities at Westminster with those on Capitol Hill can be found in Hanson and Walles (1970, pp. 79–82).

18. See Namier (1963). "Why Men Went into Parliament" is the title of the first chapter, which sets the theme for the entire inquiry.

A sympathetic biographical sketch of the historian (Price and Weinberg, 1968, p. 5) comments:

> The problem Namier set himself was to explain how the eighteenth century parliaments, in trying to meet imperial problems, lost the empire. But his documentary evidence revealed that the House of Commons was not, in fact, trying to meet imperial problems. It lacked a comprehensive collective identity or policy; instead it was a collection of factions, of local and family interests. . . .
>
> Namier's greatest success came in structural analysis. He related Parliament to its social context. He considered elections a register of social weight and analyzed the House of Commons that resulted from the electoral process for its economic and social composition, for geographic and family connections, and even for the less obvious ties of friendship or dependence that brought one man under the influence of another. Finally, he showed that the traditional labels of Whig and Tory were relatively meaningless, compared with the stronger bonds of the family-based "connection."

A strategy similar to Namier's is followed by Neale (1963) in his study of the House of Commons in the late sixteenth and early seventeenth centuries and by Namier's student John Brooke in his *The House of Commons 1754–1790, Introductory Survey* (1964). Neale's key questions are: "Who were these members of Parliament? To what classes of society did they belong? How did they come to be elected? How were elections conducted? . . . In addition to a study of the membership of Parliament, the book aims at conveying a picture of the House of Commons at work; of its officials, its ceremonies, its procedure, its manners and conventions, even the style of speaking there" (p. 14).

19. See, for example, the controversy as described by Hexter (1963, pp. 136–39, 187–93).

20. See Keen (1973, pp. 8ff. and 98ff.): "Because the king had no automatic right to a stipulated contribution by way of tax, he had to bargain with his taxpayers as to what they should pay, and in order to do so he needed to assemble them, or their accredited representatives" (p. 8).

21. Magna Charta, for example, of 1215, pretty clearly resulted from a taxpayers' revolt. Its immediate precursor was a baronial uprising over the prospect of a third Norman campaign by King John. Much of its text concerns the regularization of taxes and fees and the stabilization of law concerning the rights of heirs and debtors. In Chapter Fourteen King John says:

> And for obtaining the common counsel of the kingdom anent the assessing of an aid (except in the three cases aforesaid) or of a scutage, we will cause to be summoned the archbishops, bishops, abbots, earls, and greater barons, severally by our letters; and we will moreover cause to be summoned generally, through our sheriffs and bailiffs, all others who hold of us in chief, for a fixed date, namely, after the expiry of at least forty days, and at a fixed place; and in all letters of such summons we will specify the reason of the summons. And when the summons has thus been made, the business shall proceed on the day appointed, according to the counsel of such as are present, although not all who were summoned have come.

22. See S. A. Walkland's helpful book (1968, especially pp. 12–20), which my account generally follows.

23. This is the highly plausible conclusion of several of the articles in Leonard and Herman (1972).

24. The best of this old style of congressional study is undoubtedly Galloway (1946).

25. Students of the speakership still read and cite Mary Parker Follett (1909) and Chang-wei Chiu (1928). Likewise DeAlva Alexander (1916), Robert Luce (1926), Paul Hasbrouck (1927), George Rothwell Brown (1922), Lindsay Rogers (1968, first published 1926) and Lawrence Chamberlain (1946) repay investigation, even today.

26. This should suggest one sort of prior judgment of intellectual strategy that the student of the "institutionalization" of a political organization should make. Both transformative and nontransformative organizations may be "institutionalized"; but only the study of the internal structure of the former will yield significant increments to knowledge about the disposition of important political outcomes. This is a point worth underscoring, because it has some considerable implications for research. The reason why studying congressional institutionalization is important is because Congress evolved into a highly transformative legislature, and these transformations account for a significant share of political outcomes in American national politics. But this does not imply that the House of Commons, though far less transformative, did not also institutionalize. Indeed it did. See, e.g., Zaller (1971, pp. 1–2):

> Parliament had, by the time of the Stuarts, [early seventeenth century] acquired a powerful sense of corporate consciousness. Its members no longer conceived of

themselves as a body sporadically assembled at the king's pleasure, and existing, like the Cheshire cat, only when the sovereign's eye was upon it, but as an ongoing and permanent function of state, a "continuous performance," in Professor Notestein's phrase. This sense of continuity was evidenced in a number of ways. The end of one Parliament had developed the habit of carefully preparing unfinished business against the beginning of the next. The two houses began to keep records of their proceedings, and employed antiquarians to search the yellowed records in the Tower for older accounts. New orders and procedural innovations were scrupulously preserved, and from session to session the manner of transacting business, of reading bills and investigating grievances, became more fixed, exact, and efficient.

In the thirteenth century, says R. F. Treharne (1970, p. 81):

> Parliament is not yet either an institution or a body: it is an occasion. That being so, it is ... premature to talk of its "functions"; we should rather say that we can observe certain things being done at, in, or during the time of parliament.

I should like readers to entertain the notion of an arena as a "continuous performance" or an institutionalized "occasion." See also Notestein (1924, esp. pp. 41, 49, 53).

27. The workings of this set of arrangements and its effects on congressional strategy and structure were vividly portrayed in the 1950s by Roland Young (1943, 1958), David Truman (1959), Bertram Gross (1953), and Stephen K. Bailey (1950).

28. See also the work of John Bibby (Bibby and Davidson, 1967) (Ph.D., Wisconsin, 1963), John Kingdon (1968, 1974) (Ph.D., Wisconsin, 1965) and Dale Vinyard (1968) (Ph.D., Wisconsin, 1964).

29. A number of other committee studies also deserve special mention: for example, John Manley's depiction, in his doctoral dissertation (1970) of the inner politics of the House Ways and Means Committee earned him a niche as a leading student of Congress as soon as it was published. See also Holbert N. Carroll (1966), Green and Rosenthal (1963), Goodman (1968), and David Price (1972).

30. See Wilson's letter to Ellen Louise Axson of January 22, 1865 (in Link, 1967, pp. 630–31): "... if I wrote 'Cong. Govt' without visiting Washington, much more can I write upon the science of administration without doing so!" For Peabody's work see Peabody (1976).

31. For a similar sentiment see Loewenberg (1973, pp. 142–43).

32. A counterexample—but one that proves the rule—is contained in some of Donald Matthews' work on the U.S. Congress. Matthews' doctoral dissertation (1954), which is about social backgrounds, is inconclusive and unrevealing about Congress. In his book on the U.S. Senate (1960) Matthews attempts a typology in an early chapter that seeks to divide senators in part according to their social backgrounds; nothing is accounted for by this classification scheme, however, and Matthews essentially drops it in later chapters from further consideration. More significant by far—and more widely reprinted—is the chapter in this same book outlining "Folkways of the Senate."

33. It may be worthwhile to expand briefly on the notion of the "organizing coalition." This is meant to summarize a number of states of affairs that are, for present purposes, interchangeable. (1) If there is a single dominant political party in the legislature, but this party is made up of disparate parts and diverse interests and must pursue the politics of compromise within its own councils, I count this party as broadly "coalitional" rather than "narrowly based." Likewise, (2) if there is a dominant party, but it falls short of a majority and must coalesce with splinter parties, or (3) if the orga-

nizing coalition is an alliance of two or more parties without a single consistently dominant party, I consider the organizing group as "coalitional." What counts as "disparate" rather than "similar" parts? One index is suggested in the text: the purity and tendency to segregation by class and group of those voting for the party. The problem is easily solved in political systems in which there are opposed and allied linguistic and confessional parties. In political systems in which truth in labeling has not proceeded so far, one can easily foresee methodological difficulties, but these do not seem to me utterly insuperable.

34. Rothman (1972, p. 546) reports that "committees are beginning to develop a sense of corporate unity centered around a common command of the subject matter and identification with particular interests. This is aided by the fact that the privacy of committee meetings permits voting across party lines. On many occasions, committee members have agreed to rewrite bills and have brought their parties around to the committee's position." See also Loewenberg (1971, pp. 8–10) and Hennis (1971).

35. This strange combination of characteristics is one way that assertions about parliamentary power, e.g.:

> In the Fourth Republic as in the Third, the balance of power lay fundamentally with the legislature and its committees, not with the government. (Rothman, 1972, p. 505)

can be reconciled with assertions about parliamentary impotence, e.g.:

> When after the First World War and especially during the depression of the Thirties a more active role was thrust upon the state, a parliament which lacked stable majorities proved unable to provide the needed legislation. In order to avoid chaos, it periodically abandoned its legislative authority to the government. During the interwar years, eleven governments obtained special powers from parliament to override existing laws and to enact new legislation by so-called decree-laws.... The constitution of the Fourth Republic sought to forestall such practices and their political consequences by addressing a stern prohibition to the National Assembly against delegating its legislative authority. But since the reasons for political disorder had not been removed and no disciplined majority emerged in parliament, constitutional provisions were flouted. Using only slightly different techniques than before the war, parliament found ways to surrender its sovereign powers as the law-making authority to the executive. Yet as if to compensate for such weakness, it continuously shortened the life span of succeeding governments. (Ehrmann, 1968, pp. 278–79; see also Melnick and Leites, 1958)

36. "Debre's acknowledged model was the political system of Great Britain where the place of parliament in policy-making is as well defined (though by custom rather than by law) as it is strictly limited. Whether Debre fully understood that such limitations are primarily an outcome of the party discipline which permits the Cabinet to control the majority in the House of Commons, is a moot question. He simply started with the assumption that the French voter could never be expected to send coherent majorities to the National Assembly" (Ehrmann, 1968, p. 279).

37. "The Framers of the Constitution of the Fifth Republic wanted to maintain the ultimate control of the National Assembly over the Government without permitting either the National Assembly or the Senate to become policy-making agencies" (Pierce, 1973, p. 108).

38. In principle, other legislatures could have been included in this world tour, some easily, some not so easily. Here are a few examples, to begin with, from the arena end of the spectrum:

Irish parties in the Oireachtas are not coalitional in any meaningful sense, and one of two tightly disciplined parties has dominated Irish government since independence. Committees play even less a role than in Britain. Where the British at least refer bills to ad hoc "standing committees," the Irish do not ordinarily bother to appoint such bodies. Where the British allow several "select committees" to look into governmental activities in a limited way, the Irish have only two such committees, and both are "mainly concerned with form and trivia" (Chubb, 1970, p. 198).

Dawson (1962, p. 207) says "the best that can be said of the Canadian committee system is that when it is given legislation to consider, it does the work reasonably well. Little important legislation is dealt with this way." The Canadian Senate, whose main power consists of the right to reject bills passed in the Commons, last exercised this power on a major bill in 1926.

Of Japan, a committee of the Social Science Research Council recently concluded (*Items*, 1973) that there is "a prevailing notion that the Diet has been powerless to influence policy-making. However ... while the Diet does not meet the abstract 19th century ideal of a ruling legislature, it is comparable in structure and function with the legislatures of other advanced nations."

Latin American legislatures in general present a puzzle. Many of them are or recently have been involved in policymaking. They frequently have resisted presidents and refused assent to presidential policies. Frequently, also, presidents have declared states of emergency or the military has intervened, and normal political processes under the constitution have ceased. Colombia provides a case in point. Prior to 1968 the Congress often withheld the two-thirds majority necessary to pass legislation. Rather than bargain with Congress, however, a common presidential tactic was to suspend the two-thirds rule or, by declaring a "state of siege," suspend Congress (see Duff, 1971).

Such suspensions have by all accounts been least common in Latin America in Chile until the coup of 1973. Prior to that a strong presidential form of government was operative, although the Congress retained significant (largely veto) powers. Congressmen were elected for fixed terms, a frequent precondition for transformative behavior, yet a few parties succeeded in maintaining strong central discipline through their control of the party label—subject to the disarming Latin American pattern under which a party member who was liable to receive "discipline" simply switched parties. Each chamber had more than a dozen standing committees with sharply drawn subject-matter foci, and committee decisions were rarely overturned on the floor of either House of Congress. On the other hand, major legislation never even got committee consideration if party leaders had not reached agreement on the need for it in advance and if a majority vote in the chamber were not available to affirm "the idea of legislating on the question" (Gil, 1966, p. 116). During the short-lived Allende regime, the Congress did make severe alterations in many presidential initiatives. Consequently, Allende often resorted to legislation by decree. Obviously, in such circumstances, the Chilean Congress was permitted the role only of rubber stamp.

39. For a thorough review and critique of decisions on this point and related problems see the essays in Polsby (1971b).

REFERENCES

Abram, Michael E., and Joseph Cooper (1968). "The rise of seniority in the House of Representatives." *Polity* 1:52–85.

Agor, Weston H., ed. (1971). *Latin American Legislatures: Their Role and Influence.* New York: Praeger.

Alexander, DeAlva Stanwood (1916). *History and Procedures of the House of Representatives.* Boston: Houghton Mifflin.

Anderson, Charles W. (1970). *The Political Economy of Modern Spain.* Madison: University of Wisconsin Press.

Bagehot, Walter (1963). *The English Constitution.* (1st ed. 1867.) London: Cox and Wyman.

Bailey, Stephen K. (1950). *Congress Makes a Law.* New York: Columbia University Press.

Ballard, John A. (1966). "Four equatorial states." In Gwendolyn Carter (ed.), *National Unity and Regionalism in Eight African States.* Ithaca, N.Y.: Cornell University Press.

Barker, Anthony, and Michael Rush (1970). *The British Member of Parliament and His Information.* Toronto: University of Toronto Press.

Barnard, Chester (1938). *The Functions of the Executive.* Cambridge, Mass.: Harvard University Press.

Bauer, Raymond, Ithiel de Sola Pool, and Lewis Anthony Dexter (1963). *American Business and Public Policy.* New York: Atherton Press.

Berle, Adolph A., and Gardiner C. Means (1932). *The Modern Corporation and Private Property.* New York: Macmillan.

Bibby, John F., and Roger H. Davidson (1967). *On Capitol Hill.* New York: Holt, Rinehart and Winston.

Bill, James A. (1971). "The politics of legislative monarchy: the Iranian Majlis." In Herbert Hirsch and M. Donald Hancock (eds.), *Comparative Legislative Systems.* New York: Free Press.

Blondel, Jean (1969). *An Introduction to Comparative Government.* New York: Praeger.

Board, Joseph B., Jr. (1970). *The Government and Politics of Sweden.* Boston: Houghton Mifflin.

Brady, David (1973). *Congressional Voting in a Partisan Era.* Lawrence: University of Kansas Press.

Brooke, John (1964). *The House of Commons 1754–1790, Introductory Survey.* London: Oxford University Press.

Brown, George Rothwell (1922). *The Leadership of Congress.* Indianapolis: Bobbs-Merrill.

Burnham, Walter Dean (1970). *Critical Elections and the Mainsprings of American Politics.* New York: Norton.

Carr, Robert K. (1952). *The House Committee on Un-American Activities.* Ithaca, N.Y.: Cornell University Press.

Carroll, Holbert (1966). *The House of Representatives in Foreign Affairs.* Boston: Little, Brown.

Chamberlain, Lawrence H. (1946). *The President, Congress and Legislation*. New York: Columbia University Press.

Chandler, Alfred D. (1962). *Strategy and Structure: Chapters in the History of the American Industrial Enterprise*. Cambridge, Mass.: M.I.T. Press.

Chiu Chang-wei (1928). *The Speaker of the House of Representatives Since 1896*. New York: Columbia University Press.

Chubb, Basil (1970). *The Government and Politics of Ireland*. Stanford: Stanford University Press.

Citizens' Conference on State Legislatures (1971). *State Legislatures: An Evaluation of Their Effectiveness*. New York: Praeger.

Clapp, Charles L. (1963). *The Congressman: His Work as He Sees It*. Washington, D.C.: Brookings Institution.

Crick, Bernard (1965). *The Reform of Parliament*. Garden City, N.Y.: Doubleday.

Cummings, Milton C., and Robert L. Peabody (1969). "The decision to enlarge the Committee on Rules: an analysis of the 1961 vote." In Robert L. Peabody and Nelson W. Polsby (eds.), *New Perspectives on the House of Representatives*. 2d ed. Chicago: Rand McNally.

Cyert, Richard M., and James G. March (1963). *A Behavioral Theory of the Firm*. Englewood Cliffs, N.J.: Prentice-Hall.

Dahl, Robert A. (1971). *Polyarchy*. New Haven: Yale University Press.

Dahl, Robert A., and Charles E. Lindblom (1953). *Politics, Economics and Welfare*. New York: Harpers.

Dawson, W. F. (1962). *Procedure in the Canadian House of Commons*. Toronto: University of Toronto Press.

Deckard, Barbara (1972). "State party delegations in the U.S. House of Representatives: a comparative study of group cohesion." *Journal of Politics* 34:199–223.

_____ (1973). "State party delegations in the U.S. House of Representatives: an analysis of group action." *Polity* 5:311–34.

Dexter, Lewis Anthony (1954). "Congressmen and the people they listen to." Mimeographed. Cambridge, Mass.: Cenis, M.I.T. Much of this material later published in Bauer, Pool, and Dexter (1963).

_____ (1966). *The Sociology and Politics of Congress*. Chicago: Rand McNally.

_____ (1969). "The representative and his district." (Originally published as a paper, 1957.) In Robert L. Peabody and Nelson W. Polsby (eds.), *New Perspectives on the House of Representatives*. 2d ed. Chicago: Rand McNally.

Duff, Ernest A. (1971). "The Role of Congress in the Colombian political system." In Weston H. Agor (ed.), *Latin American Legislatures: Their Role and Influence*. New York: Praeger.

Ehrmann, Henry W. (1968). *Politics in France*. Boston: Little, Brown.

Emerson, Ralph Waldo (1904). "Historical discourse at Concord, on the second centennial anniversary of the incorporation of the town, September 12, 1835." In *Miscellanies*. Boston: Houghton Mifflin.

Epstein, Leon (1964). *British Politics in The Suez Crisis*. Urbana: University of Illinois Press.

──────── (1967). *Political Parties in Western Democracies*. New York: Praeger.

Etzioni, Amitai (1963). "Alternative ways to democracy: the example of Israel." In Nelson W. Polsby, Robert A. Dentler, and Paul A. Smith (eds.), *Politics and Social Life*. Boston: Houghton Mifflin.

Eulau, Heinz, and Katherine Hinckley (1966). "Legislative institutions and processes." In *Political Science Annual 1966*, Vol. 1. Indianapolis: Bobbs-Merrill.

Fainsod, Merle (1953). *How Russia is Ruled*. Cambridge, Mass.: Harvard University Press.

Fenno, Richard F., Jr. (1966). *The Power of the Purse*. Boston: Little, Brown.

──────── (1973). *Congressmen in Committees*. Boston: Little, Brown.

Fiellen, Alan (1969). "The functions of informal groups: a state delegation." In Nelson W. Polsby and Robert L. Peabody (eds.), *New Perspectives on the House of Representatives*. 2d ed. Chicago: Rand McNally.

Fleming, Donald (1954). *William H. Welch and the Rise of Modern Medicine*. Boston: Little, Brown.

Follett, Mary Parker (1909). *The Speaker of the House of Representatives*. New York: Longmans, Green.

Franks, C. E. S. (1971). "The dilemma of the standing committees of the Canadian House of Commons." *Canadian Journal of Political Science* 4:461–76.

Freeman, Edward A. (1883). "An introduction to American institutional history." In Herbert B. Adams (ed.), *Johns Hopkins University Studies in Historical and Political Science*. Vol. 1, *Local Institutions*. Baltimore: The Johns Hopkins University.

Fried, Robert C. (1966). *Comparative Political Institutions*. New York: Macmillan.

Galloway, George (1946). *Congress at the Crossroads*. New York: Crowell.

Gerlich, Peter (1973). "The institutionalization of European parliaments." In Allan Kornberg (ed.), *Legislatures in Comparative Perspective*. New York: McKay.

Ghana Official Handbook (1968). Accra-Tema: Ghana Information Services.

Gil, Federico (1966). *The Political System of Chile*. Boston: Houghton Mifflin.

Goodman, Walter (1968). *The Committee*. New York: Farrar, Straus & Giroux.

Goodwin, George (1970). *The Little Legislatures*. Amherst: University of Massachusetts Press.

Gould, John (1940). *New England Town Meeting: Safeguard of Democracy*. Brattleboro, Vt.: Stephen Daye Press.

Green, Harold P., and Alan Rosenthal (1963). *Government of the Atom*. New York: Atherton.

Gross, Bertram (1953). *The Legislative Struggle*. New York: McGraw-Hill.

Grumm, John G. (1973). *A Paradigm for the Comparative Analysis of Legislative Systems*. Beverly Hills: Sage.

Hakes, Jay E. (1973). *Weak Parliaments and Military Coups in Africa*. Beverly Hills: Sage.

Hansard (1966). *Parliamentary Debates*. 5th Series, Vol. 734, House of Commons Official Report 18th–28th October. London: Her Majesty's Stationery Office.

Hanson, A. H., and Malcolm Walles (1970). *Governing Britain*. London: Fontana-Collins.

Hasbrouck, Paul DeWitt (1927). *Party Government in the House of Representatives*. New York: Macmillan.

Hennis, Wilhelm (1971). "Reform of the Bundestag." In Gerhard Loewenberg (ed.), *Modern Parliaments: Change or Decline?* Chicago: Aldine.

Herbert, Alan Patrick (1937). *The Ayes Have It*. London: Methuen.

——— (1951). *Independent Member*. Garden City, N.Y.: Doubleday.

Herzberg, Donald, and Alan Rosenthal (1971). *Strengthening the States: Essays on Legislative Reform*. Garden City, N.Y.: Doubleday.

Hexter, Jack H. (1963). *Reappraisals in History*. New York: Harper.

Hill, Andrew, and Anthony Whichelow (1964). *What's Wrong With Parliament?* Harmondsworth, Middlesex: Penguin.

Huitt, Ralph K. (1968). "Legislatures." In *International Encyclopedia of the Social Sciences,* Vol. 9. New York: Macmillan and the Free Press.

Huitt, Ralph K., and Robert L. Peabody (1969). *Congress: Two Decades of Analysis*. New York: Harpers.

Huntington, Samuel P. (1965a). "Congressional responses to the twentieth century." In David B. Truman (ed.), *The Congress and America's Future*. Englewood Cliffs, N.J.: Prentice-Hall.

——— (1965b). "Political development and political decay." *World Politics* 17: 386–430. Copyright © 1965 by Princeton University Press. Excerpt reprinted by permission of Princeton University Press.

Items (1973). "Japanese studies." New York: Social Science Research Council, March 1973, p. 7.

Jennings, W. Ivor (1940). *Parliament*. New York: Macmillan.

Jewell, Malcolm E., and Samuel C. Patterson (1966). *The Legislative Process in the United States*. New York: Random House.

Jones, Charles O. (1964). *Party and Policy Making*. New Brunswick, N.J.: Rutgers University Press.

——— (1967). *Every Second Year*. Washington, D.C.: Brookings Institution.

——— (1969). "The Agriculture Committee and the problem of representation." In Robert L. Peabody and Nelson W. Polsby (eds.), *New Perspectives on the House of Representatives*. 2d ed. Chicago: Rand McNally.

——— (1970). *The Minority Party in Congress*. Boston: Little, Brown.

Keen, M. H. (1973). *England in the Later Middle Ages*. London: Methuen.

Kessell, John H. (1964). "The Washington congressional delegation." *Midwest Journal of Political Science* 8:1–21.

Kingdon, John W. (1968). *Candidates for Office: Beliefs and Strategies.* New York: Random House.

—————— (1974). *Congressmen's Voting Decisions.* New York: Harper & Row.

Kornberg, Allen, ed. (1973). *Legislatures in Comparative Perspective.* New York: McKay.

LaPalombara, Joseph (1974). *Politics Within Nations.* Englewood Cliffs, N.J.: Prentice-Hall.

Leonard, Dick, and Valentine Herman (1972). *The Backbencher in Parliament.* London: Macmillan.

Lijphart, Arend (1968). *The Politics of Accommodation.* Berkeley: University of California Press.

Link, Arthur S., ed. (1967). *Papers of Woodrow Wilson.* Vol. 3, *1884–5.* Princeton: Princeton University Press.

Loewenberg, Gerhard (1967). *Parliament in the German Political System.* Ithaca, New York: Cornell University Press.

—————— (1971a). "The role of parliaments in modern political systems." In Gerhard Loewenberg (ed.), *Modern Parliaments: Change or Decline?* Chicago: Aldine.

—————— (1971b). "The influence of parliamentary behavior in regime stability." *Comparative Politics* 3:177–200.

—————— (1973). "The institutionalization of parliament and public orientation to the political system." In Allan Kornberg (ed.), *Legislatures in Comparative Perspective.* New York: McKay.

Lorwin, Val. R. (1966). "Belgium: religion, class and language in national politics." In Robert A. Dahl (ed.), *Political Oppositions in Western Democracies.* New Haven: Yale University Press.

Luce, Robert (1926). *Congress.* Cambridge, Mass.: Harvard University Press.

Mackintosh, John P. (1972). "Parliament now and a hundred years ago." In Dick Leonard and Valentine Herman (eds.), *The Backbencher in Parliament.* London: Macmillan.

Maclear, Anne Bush (1908). "Early New England towns: a comparative study of their development." Ph.D. dissertation, Columbia University.

Manley, John (1970). *The Politics of Finance.* Boston: Little, Brown.

—————— (1974). "The presidency, Congress and national policy-making." *Political Science Annual, 1974.* Indianapolis: Bobbs-Merrill.

Manzella, Andrea (n.d.). "The role of parliament in Italy." Mimeographed. Prepared for the European Parliament Symposium on European Integration and the Future of Parliaments in Europe.

Masters, Nicholas A. (1969). "Committee assignments." In Robert L. Peabody and Nelson W. Polsby (eds.), *New Perspectives on the House of Representatives.* 2d ed. Chicago: Rand McNally.

Matthews, Donald R. (1954). *The Social Backgrounds of Political Decision Makers.* Garden City, N.Y.: Doubleday.

_____ (1960). *U.S. Senators and Their World.* Chapel Hill: University of North Carolina Press.

McClosky, Herbert, and John E. Turner (1960). *The Soviet Dictatorship.* N.Y.: Mc-Graw-Hill.

Medhurst, Kenneth N. (1973). *Government in Spain.* Oxford: Pergamon Press.

Melnik, Constantin, and Nathan Leites (1958). *The House Without Windows.* Evanston, Ill.: Row, Peterson.

Meyer, Alfred, G. (1965). *The Soviet Political System: An Interpretation.* N. Y.: Random House.

Mezey, Michael (1974). "A framework for the comparative analysis of legislatures." Mimeographed. University of Hawaii.

Mill, John Stuart (1962). *Considerations on Representative Government.* (1st ed. 1861.) Chicago: Regnery.

Namier, Lewis (1963). *The Structure of Politics at the Accession of George III.* (1st ed. 1929.) London: Macmillan.

Neale, J. E. (1963). *The Elizabethan House of Commons.* London: Peregrine.

Needler, Martin (1963). *Latin American Politics in Perspective.* New York: Van Nostrand.

Nicholas, Ralph W. (1966). "Segmentary factional political systems." In Marc J. Swartz, Victor W. Turner, and Arthur Tuden (eds.), *Political Anthropology.* Chicago: Aldine. Quoted by permission.

Notestein, Wallace (1924). *The Winning of the Initiative by the House of Commons.* Raleigh Lecture on History from the Proceedings of the British Academy. London: Oxford University Press.

Packenham, Robert A. (1970). "Legislatures and political development." In Allan Kornberg and Lloyd D. Musolf (eds.), *Legislatures in Developmental Perspective.* Durham, N.C.: Duke University Press.

Patterson, Samuel C. (1970). "Congressional committee staffing: capabilities and constraints." In Allan Kornberg and Lloyd D. Musolf (eds.), *Legislatures in Developmental Perspective.* Durham, N.C.: Duke University Press.

Peabody, Robert L. (1969). "Party leadership change in the United States House of Representatives." In Robert L. Peabody and Nelson W. Polsby (eds.), *New Perspectives on the House of Representatives.* 2d ed. Chicago: Rand McNally.

_____ (1976). *Leadership in Congress: Stability, Succession and Change.* Boston: Little, Brown.

Pierce, Roy (1973). *French Politics and Political Institutions.* New York: Harper & Row.

Pitkin, Hanna Fenichel (1967). *The Concept of Representation.* Berkeley: University of California Press.

Pollard, A. F. (1964). *The Evolution of Parliament.* (1st ed. 1920.) New York: Russell and Russell.

Polsby, Nelson W. (1964). *Congress and the Presidency.* Englewood Cliffs, N.J.: Prentice-Hall.

_____ (1968). "The institutionalization of the U.S. House of Representatives." *American Political Science Review* 62:144–68.

_____ (1969). "Two strategies of influence: choosing a majority leader, 1962." In Robert L. Peabody and Nelson W. Polsby (eds.), *New Perspectives on the House of Representatives.* 2d ed. Chicago: Rand McNally.

_____, ed. (1971a). *Congressional Behavior.* New York: Random House.

_____, ed. (1971b). *Reapportionment in the 1970's.* Berkeley and Los Angeles: University of California Press.

Polsby, Nelson W., Miriam Gallaher, and Barry Spencer Rundquist (1969). "The growth of the seniority system in the U.S. House of Representatives." *American Political Science Review* 63:787–807.

Price, David (1972). *Who Makes the Laws?* Cambridge, Mass: Schenkman.

Price, H. Douglas (1971). "The congressional career: risks and rewards." In Nelson W. Polsby (ed.), *Congressional Behavior.* New York: Random House.

Price, Jacob M., and Gerhard L. Weinberg (1968). "Namier, L. B." In *International Encyclopedia of the Social Sciences,* Vol. 11. New York: Macmillan and Free Press.

Pryor, Frederic L. (1968). *Public Expenditures in Communist and Capitalist Nations.* Homewood, Ill.: Richard D. Irwin.

Ray, David (1974). "Membership stability in three state legislatures: 1893–1969." *American Political Science Review* 68:106–12.

Richards, Peter G. (1959). *Honourable Members: A Study of the British Backbencher.* London: Taber and Taber.

Riggs, Fred W. (1974). "Legislative origins: a contextual approach." Mimeographed. Social Science Research Institute, Honolulu.

Robinson, James A. (1963). *The House Rules Committee.* Indianapolis: Bobbs-Merrill.

Rogers, Lindsay (1968). *The American Senate.* (1st ed. 1926.) New York: Johnson Reprint Corporation.

Rosenthal, Alan (1974). *Legislative Performance in the States.* New York: Free Press.

Rothman, David (1964). "Party, power and the U.S. Senate 1869–1901." Ph.D. dissertation, Harvard University. Subsequently published as *Politics and Power: The U.S. Senate 1869–1901* (1966). Cambridge, Mass.: Harvard University Press.

Rothman, Stanley (1972). *European Society and Politics.* New York: Bobbs-Merrill.

Royal Commission on the Constitution (1969–73). Vol. 2 (1973), *Memorandum of Dissent.* London: Her Majesty's Stationery Office.

Rustow, Dankwart (1967). *A World of Nations.* Washington: Brookings Institution.

Schattschneider, E. E. (1956). "United States: the functional approach to party government." In Sigmund Neumann (ed.), *Modern Political Parties*. Chicago: University of Chicago Press.

Scienze Sociali 2 (August, 1972). Bologna, Italy: Il Mulino.

Shannon, Wayne (1968). *Party, Constituency, and Congressional Voting*. Baton Rouge: University of Louisiana Press.

Shaw, Malcolm, and John D. Lees (1973). "Committees in legislatures and the political system." Paper prepared for presentation at the Ninth World Congress of The International Political Science Association, Montreal.

Shepard, W. J. (1933). "Legislative assemblies: history and theory." *Encyclopedia of the Social Sciences,* Vol. 9. New York: Macmillan.

Simon, Herbert A. (1957). *Administrative Behavior*. New York: Macmillan.

Snowiss, Leo M. (1966). "Congressional recruitment and representation." *The American Political Science Review* 40:627–39.

Stauffer, Robert B. (1974). "The Philippine Congress: a retrospective on the causes of structural change." Mimeographed. University of Hawaii.

Submission of Recorded Presidential Conversations (1974). "To the Committee on The Judiciary of the House of Representatives by President Richard Nixon." Washington, D.C.: Government Printing Office.

Tacitus (1901). "A treatise on the manners of the Germans." In *Works*, Vol. 2. The Oxford Translation, revised. London: George Bell.

Taylor, Eric (1951). *The House of Commons at Work*. Baltimore: Penguin.

Thernstrom, Stephan (1964). *Poverty and Progress*. Cambridge, Mass.: Harvard University.

Treharne, R. F. (1970). "The nature of Parliament in the reign of Henry III." In E. B. Fryde and Edward Miller (eds.), *Historical Studies of the English Parliament*. Vol. 1, *Origins to 1399*. Cambridge: Cambridge University Press.

Truman, David B. (1955). "Federalism and the party system." In Arthur W. Macmahon (ed.), *Federalism Mature and Emergent*. Garden City, N.Y.: Doubleday.

_____ (1959). *The Congressional Party*. New York: Wiley.

_____, ed. (1965). *The Congress and America's Future*. Englewood Cliffs, N.J.: Prentice-Hall.

Trythall, J. W. D. (1970). *El Caudillo*. New York: McGraw-Hill.

Veysey, Laurence R. (1965). *The Emergence of the American University*. Chicago: University of Chicago Press.

Vinyard, Dale (1968). *Congress*. New York: Scribner.

_____ (1969). "Congressional committees on small business." *Midwest Journal of Political Science* 10:364–77.

Von Beyme, Klaus (1970). *Die Parlamentarischen Regierungssysteme in Europa*. München: Piper.

Wahlke, John C., Heinz Eulau, William Buchanan, and Leroy Ferguson (1962). *The Legislative System: Explorations in Legislative Behavior*. New York: Wiley.

Walkland, S. A. (1968). *The Legislative Process in Great Britain*. London: Allan & Unwin.

Weber, Max (1947). *The Theory of Social and Economic Organization*. New York: Oxford University Press.

Webster, T. B. L. (1973). *Athenian Culture and Society*. Berkeley: University of California Press.

Weil, Gordon L. (1970). *The Benelux Nations*. New York: Holt, Rinehart and Winston.

Welles, Benjamin (1965). *Spain: The Gentle Anarchy*. New York: Praeger.

Wesson, Robert G. (1972). *The Soviet Russian State*. New York: Wiley.

Wheare, K. C. (1963). *Legislatures*. New York: Oxford University Press.

White, William S. (1956). *Citadel*. New York: Harpers.

Wiebe, Robert H. (1967). *The Search for Order 1877–1920*. New York: Hill & Wang.

Willoughby, W. F. (1934). *Principles of Legislative Organization and Administration*. Washington, D.C.: Brookings Institution.

Wilson, Woodrow (1956). *Congressional Government*. (1st ed. 1885.) New York: Meridian.

Young, James Sterling (1966). *The Washington Community 1800–1828*. New York: Columbia University Press.

Young, Roland (1943). *This Is Congress*. New York: Knopf.

_____ (1958). *The American Congress*. New York: Harpers.

Zaller, Robert (1971). *The Parliament of 1621*. Berkeley: University of California Press.

5

COURTS

MARTIN SHAPIRO

THE PROTOTYPE OF COURT

Political scientists have generally employed an ideal type, or really a prototype, of courts involving (1) an independent judge (2) applying preexisting legal norms (3) after adversary proceedings in order to achieve (4) a dichotomous decision in which one of the parties was assigned the legal right and the other found wrong. The growth of political jurisprudence (Shapiro, 1964; Murphy and Tanenhaus, 1972) has been characterized largely by the discovery and emphasis of deviations from the prototype found in the behavior of particular courts, showing how uncourtlike courts are or how much they are like other political actors. While some political scientists and many lawyers have continued to protest against this approach, they have done so largely by reasserting the prototype (Becker, 1970). Such a tactic is unconvincing because, if we examine what we generally call courts across the full range of contemporary and historical societies, the prototype fits almost none of them. Defense of the prototype thus seems fruitless. A study of courts that is essentially the measurement of deviance from a type that is rarely approximated in the real world would appear to be equally fruitless.

THE LOGIC OF THE TRIAD IN CONFLICT RESOLUTION

Perhaps it would be wise to begin over, employing a root concept of courtness but more freely accepting the vast variety of actual social institutions and behaviors loosely related to that concept without worrying about where "true courtness" ends and something else begins. For in reality there are few if any societies in which courts are so clearly delineated as to create absolute boundaries between them and other aspects of the political system.

The root concept employed here is a simple one of conflict and its structuring into triads. Cutting quite across cultural lines, it appears that where two persons come into a conflict that they cannot resolve themselves, one solution appealing to common sense is to call upon a third for assistance in achieving a resolution. So universal across both time and space is this simple social invention of triads that we can discover almost no society that fails to employ it. And from its overwhelming appeal to common sense stems the basic political legitimacy of courts everywhere. In short, the triad for purposes of conflict resolution is the basic social logic of courts, a logic so compelling that courts become a universal political phenomenon.

The triad, however, involves a basic instability, paradox, or dialectic that accounts for a large proportion of the scholarly quarrels over the nature of courts and the political difficulties that courts encounter in the real world. At the moment the two conflictors find their third, the social logic of the court device is preeminent. A moment later, when the third decides in favor of one of the two conflictors, a shift occurs from the triad to a structure that is perceived by the loser as two against one. To the loser there is no social logic in two against one. There is only the brute fact of being outnumbered. A substantial portion of the total behavior of courts in all societies can be analyzed in terms of attempts to prevent the triad from breaking down into two against one. (Thus courts may be seen as a special case of the dyadic-triadic relationships of Simmel, 1950.)

Consent

The most fundamental device for maintaining the triad is consent. Early Roman-law procedures provide a convenient example (Wolff, 1951). The two parties at issue first met to decide under what norm their dispute would be settled. Unless they could agree on a norm, the dispute could not go forward in juridical channels. Having agreed on the norm, they next had to agree on a judge, a third person who would find the facts and apply the preagreed norm in order to decide their dispute. The eventual loser was placed in the position of having, himself, chosen both the law and the judge and thus having consented to the judgment rather than having had it imposed on him.

The almost universal reluctance of courts to proceed in the absence of one of the two parties is less a testimony to the appeal of adversary processes than it is a remnant of this emphasis on consent, of both parties themselves choosing the triad as the appropriate device for conflict resolution. At the early stages of English law, courts were frequently stymied by the absence of one of the parties, and medieval procedure is full of elaborate devices for enticing or compelling the unwilling party into court rather than proceeding without him (Allen, 1958). Modern British and American practice still prefers extended delay to the absence of one of the parties, and in many tribal societies the anthropologist encounters the same reluctance to proceed without all three members of the triad and comparable devices to cajole or coerce attendance (Pospisil, 1958).

All of this can, of course, be put in the form of the classic political question: Why should I obey? The loser is told that he should obey the third man because he has consented in advance to obey. He has chosen the norm of decision. He has chosen the decider. He has then chosen to obey the decision.

The Mediating Continuum

Nearly every triadic conflict resolver adds another device to consent in order to avoid the breakdown into two against one. This device is the avoidance of the dichotomous, imposed solution. In examining triadic conflict resolution as a universal phenomenon, we discover that the judge of European or Anglo-American courts, determining that the legal right lies with one and against the other of the parties, is not an appropriate central type against which deviance can be conveniently measured. Instead he lies at one end of a continuum. The continuum runs: go-between, mediator, arbitrator, judge. And placement on the continuum is determined by the intersection of the devices of consent and nondichotomous, or mediate, solution.

The go-between is encountered in many forms. In tribal or village societies he may be any person, fortuitously present and not connected with either of the households, villages, or clans in a dispute, who shuttles back and forth between them as a vehicle of negotiation (Hoebel, 1954). He provides communication without the dangerous physical contact of the disputants that would otherwise be required. In more modern guise we find him as the sovereign offering "good offices" in an international dispute or the real-estate broker shuttling between seller and prospective buyer and carefully keeping them apart at the negotiation stage. The go-between seems to operate in a pure consent, pure mediate-solution situation. He cannot function at all unless both parties consent to his offices and the solution reached is the product of free negotiation between the parties and is mutually satisfactory. And in theory, all resolutions offered and accepted are purely those of the parties themselves.

In reality, however, the go-between is not an inert communicator. He exerts influence by "rephrasing" the messages he delivers. He may manage to slip in a fair number of proposals of his own. And by his characterization of the adamance or flexibility of each side to the other, he may firm up or weaken the bargaining position of one or the other.

The mediator is somewhat more open in his participation in the triad. He can operate only with the consent of both parties. He may not impose solutions. But he is employed both as a buffer between the parties and as an inventor of mediate solutions. By dealing with successive proposals and counter-proposals he may actively and openly assist in constructing a solution meeting the interests of both parties (Cohen, 1966; Henderson, 1965).

The distinction between mediation and arbitration in any particular society is a matter of legal nuance and often the subject of bitter controversy, particularly in such areas as labor arbitration. Often too the distinction is made between voluntary and binding arbitration. For our purposes we may treat arbitration generically and speak of it as involving less consent by the parties and less mediate solutions than mediation. Persons are not normally compelled to consent to arbitration. In this sense the arbitrator, like the mediator and the go-between, cannot function without the consent of both parties. In modern societies, however, arbitration clauses frequently appear in contracts so that the consent is somewhat attenuated. It is not consent of the moment to the arbitration of the moment but advance consent to future arbitrations in general. Yet even such contracts almost invariably specify that the two parties must in each instance agree on who the arbitrator shall be.

The key distinction between the moderator and arbitrator, however, is that the arbitrator is expected to fashion his own resolution to the conflict rather than simply assisting the parties in shaping one of their own. And his solutions are not purely mediate in a number of senses. First, arbitrators, unlike mediators and go-betweens, usually work with a relatively fixed set of legal norms, either statutes or more typically contracts. The arbitrator then is in a position analogous to that of the early Roman judge. The parties have consented to or themselves constructed in advance the norms to which they will now be subject. If in a given dispute one party has violated these norms more than the other it is not expected that the arbitrator arrive at a compromise solution purely on the basis of the interests of the parties and quite apart from their obedience to the preexisting norms. Moreover, arbitration is frequently "binding" either by statute or under the terms of the contract, that is, the arbitrator has the legal authority to impose his solution on both parties even if one or both do not voluntarily consent to the solution (Fuller, 1963).

Nevertheless societies tend to turn to arbitration in situations in which, although overarching legal norms may exist, the most salient concerns are the interests of the two parties, neither of which is assigned greater legitimacy than the other. Mediate solutions acceptable to both parties are the goal, and as a practical matter, few arbitrators would find much employment if they did not develop a record of providing such solutions. Of course this is all the more true in "nonbinding" arbitration, in which the parties need not accept the arbitrator's resolution.

Where arbitration is in no sense binding it merges with mediation. Where arbitration is binding both in the sense that the two parties must go to arbitration on the demand of either and must then abide by the arbitrator's holdings, it tends to merge into judicial judgment. Indeed in many societies the arbitrator is one form of lay judge, or judge without the full panoply of judicial procedures, a category we shall return to later.

The Substitution of Law and Office for Consent

In turning now to judges we return to the problem of consent and to our Roman example. As societies become more complex they tend to substitute law for the particular consent of the parties to a particular norm for their particular dispute and office for their free choice of a particular third man to aid in the resolution of their dispute. The earliest Romans might seek the aid of anyone in formulating a norm. They came more and more to turn to city officials for this assistance. The Praetorian Edict, which was the closest thing to a civil code that Rome as a city attained, long took the form of a series of norms that such an official announced he would supply to contending parties at their request. It was initially not a body of preexisting law but a catalogue of "ready-made" goods that replaced the still earlier practice of "tailor making" a norm for each pair of disputants. As the practice grows of each of the new praetors reenacting the edict of his predecessors, we can literally see what begins as a system of free legal advice to mutually consenting parties becoming a set of preexisting compulsory legal rules. A parallel development can be seen in the writings of the jurisconsults, which begin as professional legal advice to the praetors and litigants and end as operative parts of the Code of Justinian (Merryman, 1969).

The key factor in the shift from consent to law is specificity. Ethnographic and sociological materials make clear that in only a very limited number of special situations do litigants literally make their own rule of decision free of all preexisting norms (Fallers, 1969). At the very minimum there is a social sense of appropriateness or natural justice, of how we always do things or what we never do, of the sort suggested by the Tiv informant who says of what we would call a lawbreaker that he "spoils the tjar" (Bohannan, 1967). Whether we express this consensus in terms of custom or fundamental principles of ordered liberty or, as the Tiv does, as a psychic harmony of men and nature, it no doubt creates the constraints under which prospective litigants shape a norm for themselves. Indeed much of judicial ritual, particularly in the holding of public trials, consists of reminding the litigants that as good men they must consent to the overarching norms of their society. Yet the more nebulous these norms, the greater the element of immediate and real consent in achieving a precise working rule for a particular case. At one extreme we find two disputing villagers working with an elder to settle the ownership of a pig according to the ways of the ancestors. If any rule of decision is actually formulated it is likely to arise out of the adeptness of the elder in eliciting the face-to-face consent of the parties. At the other extreme we find litigants in a modern industrial state who discover at trial that their earlier behavior was governed by a detailed preexisting rule, even the existence of which was unknown to them at the time and which they consent to only in the generalized, abstract sense that all citizens agree to live under the laws of the state. The judge, then, unlike the mediator, imposes "his" rule on the parties rather than eliciting a consensual one.

Moreover the parties may not specifically consent even to who shall impose his rule or decide under it. The most purely consensual situation is one in which the conflictors choose who shall assist them in formulating a rule and who shall decide the case under it, as the Romans initially did. In most societies, however, there seems to be instances in which it pays to choose a big man to do these tasks, whether a government official like the urban praetor or, as among the Papuans, the owner of many pigs (Pospisil, 1958). The disputants may turn to the big man because he knows more of the law and custom, because he has the economic, political or social power to enforce his judgment, or because his success or high position is taken as a symptom of his skill and intelligence at resolving disputes. Beyond and perhaps out of this tendency to consent to judging by big men, many societies develop the office of judge so that the parties do not choose their judge. If they choose to go to court at all, they must accept the official judge. The ultimate step, of course, is in those instances in which a legal system not only imposes the law and the officer of the law but also compels one or both parties to resort to legal processes, as in a criminal trial or civil suit. The judge, then, unlike the mediator, imposes himself on the parties rather than being chosen by them.

He also may impose his resolution of their conflict. It is possible to envision a system in which the parties were compelled to accept the rule of decision and the person of the judge but were not compelled to accept his decision. Compulsory nonbinding arbitration sometimes comes down to this. That is, the parties may be compelled by statute or a contract provision to go to arbitration where a contract provision is in dispute, but the same statute and/or contract may not compel them to accept the arbitrator's word. In some societies the losing party to one litigation might refuse the decision and resort to another forum or accept banishment. Appeal and pardon processes sometimes exhibit this feature, as for instance in "de novo" appeals, in which the dissatisfied party may get an entirely new trial from a higher court.

Nevertheless, in general, judges may impose a final resolution independent of the consent of the parties. Even where the third man must gain the consent of the parties to his resolution, as for instance the mediator must, it is possible for him to propose a dichotomous solution—one in which party A wins all and B loses all. But for obvious reasons he is unlikely to do so. Where the specific consent of the parties is not required, such resolutions are more feasible. Moreover, where the judge is administering a detailed body of law whose building blocks are concepts of legal right and obligation, such resolutions are at least partially dictated by the rules of decision he has imposed on the parties.

Curiously enough it is precisely the need to elicit the consent of the loser to a decisional process that has been largely imposed on him that may lead to a decision stripping him of everything. To the extent that he believes that a third person whom he has not chosen is exercising discretion in behalf of his opponent, he may deny the legitimacy of the whole judicial system. Mediate solutions that split the difference between the two parties in various ways are likely to most clearly expose judicial discretion. Thus judges may find it preferable to issue dichotomous solutions, denying their discretion by arguing that under the preexisting law one party was clearly right and the other clearly wrong. The losing party may be unhappy with the resolution, but so long as he accepts the legitimacy of the "law," he may not perceive the judge as acting with his opponent.

The substitution of law and office for consent entails very major destabilizing pressures on the triadic structure. For it was essentially his consent at every preliminary stage that enabled the losing disputant to continue seeing the triad as a triad rather than as two against one. Where the loser does not specifically consent in advance to the norm, he must be convinced that the legal rule imposed on him did not favor his opponent. Thus the yearning for neutral principles of law found among contemporary lawyers (Stone, 1968). And if he did not consent to the judge, he must be convinced that judicial office itself ensures that the judge is not an ally of his opponent. Thus the yearning for a professional and independent judiciary (Dawson, 1968).

Yet it is frequently difficult or impossible to convince the loser of these very things. First of all, many disputants are in a position to know or suspect that the law to be applied in this case does favor their opponents. Most laws in most societies favor some classes of persons and disfavor others. Secondly, where the judge is a governmental or religious officer, then a third set of interests quite independent of those of the two disputants is interjected. One or both prospective litigants may perceive that the interests of the government or the church is contrary to his own. It is for these reasons that the judges and their professional defenders in most advanced societies spend such a large proportion of their dialectic and ritual talents promulgating and defending the prototype noted at the beginning of this study. Contemporary courts are involved in a permanent crisis because they have moved so far along the routes of law and office from the basic consensual triad that provides their essential social logic.

In describing a spectrum from go-between to judge we have so far been dealing essentially with two dimensions. The first is the degree to which the third man is an independent source of the rule of decision. The second is the degree to which he is the source of the decision. A third element might be added—that of enforcement. The go-between has little or no enforcement power. The mediator may do somewhat better by bringing to bear general social sentiment in favor of resolution. We often distinguish the arbitrator from the mediator on the basis that the arbitrator's decisions are subsequently enforcable by court action. Judges are furthest along the spectrum toward complete enforcement, typically having means to tap the organized forces of coercion in the society.

Courts in the Mediatory Continuum

Having said all these things, if we could now focus exclusively on judging in any further discussion of courts, the path would be fairly clear. However, if we turn to the work of those men and institutions to which we normally award the titles judges and courts, we shall see that in reality they are simply at one end of a spectrum rather than constituting an absolutely distinct entity. It is because elements of mediation and remnants of consent are so integral to most court systems that the conventional prototype of courts is often misleading.

At least one of the world's major judicial cultures has been essentially mediatory. Although classical Chinese law experienced a running debate between proponents of mediation and "legalists," who wished to impose dichotomous judgments according to preexisting rules, mediation clearly remained dominant in the imperial courts. The judicial ideal was a mediate solution that restored comity between the parties (Bodde and Norris, 1967).

Mediate solutions are most possible where the disputed matter is divisible or can be converted into something divisible. At first glance it would seem to be injury or trespass that would be least amenable to mediation and most subject to the rule of "an eye for an eye." The common-law system has often been taken as the model of dichotomous resolution, since it is a "strict" law system seeking to assign legal right to one of the parties and legal wrong to the other (Allen, 1958). Yet the insistence of the common law that the central and usually sole remedy is money damages and that no resolution is possible unless one party can show he has been damaged in a compensable way reveals another dimension. The common law consistently converts indivisible disputes into divisible disputes, that is, disputes over injury to person and property and disputes over the fulfillment and nonfulfillment of obligations into disputes over sums of money. Moreover, where the Anglo-American law has developed equity as a means of resolving conflicts through remedies other than money damages, that is, through equitable decrees ordering someone to do something or not to do something, it invokes the doctrine of "balancing of equities." That doctrine requires an equity court to shape remedies so as not to impose costs on one of the parties that far outweigh benefits to the other. In short, below the facade of dichotomous solution presented by Anglo-American courts lies the potential for mediation.

That potential is frequently realized in the courtroom itself, for instance when judge or jury reduces the amount of a damage award because the plaintiff, while legally right, was himself partly at fault. More fundamentally, money damages are mediatory because they allow the loser to substitute a money payment for the performance of some action to which he is strongly adverse or for the acceptance of some distasteful retribution like suffering the loss of an arm because he has taken off someone else's.

However, in modern Anglo-American law systems, and for that matter in Continental ones, the area of mediation often moves outside the courtroom. The bulk of conflict resolution through legal channels occurs by negotiation between the parties and their attorneys under the compulsion of eventual court proceedings should negotiations fail. To dismiss the vast bulk of conflict resolution by law in modern societies as somehow extrajudicial would both direct the student of courts away from the central phenomenon and lead to fundamental distortions of reality. For previously announced judicial rules and the anticipation by the disputants of the costs and benefits of eventually going to trial are key parameters in such negotiations. They are not free bargaining based solely on the wills and immediate resources of the parties, but legalized bargaining under the shadow supervision of an available court. Such negotiation is not purely mediatory, because the bargain struck will depend in part on the "legal" strength of the parties, that is, predictions of how each would fare in court. Yet such negotiations aim at, and in most instances achieve, a solution sufficiently satisfactory to both parties to avoid litigation. Failed negotiations may end up in court, where their judicial resolution sets the parameters for further negotiations. Thus the principal arena of modern legalized dispute settlement intimately intermixes elements of mediation and dichotomous solution, consent and judicial imposition (Blumberg, 1967; Davis *et al.*, 1962).

Judicial striving for consent can be found everywhere in court procedures and proceedings. In criminal law, plea bargaining is the mediation of the interests of prosecution and defendant. Ethnographic materials, including those on American trial courts, give us numerous examples of judges proposing one solution after another and, by threat, persuasion, and the application of the social pressure brought by the audience, moving both parties to at least profess satisfaction with one of them (Gluckman, 1967; Hoebel, 1954; Jacob, 1973). The reluctance of English and American courts to proceed in the absence of one of the parties, symptomized by their willingness to grant endless delays, obviously stems from this consensual base. Indeed most of the conventional attachment to adversary proceedings is based not on the desire to heighten the level of conflict in judicial proceedings but quite the opposite, on the need to have both parties present before the judge if he is to have any chance of creating a resolution to which both parties will consent. Every effort is made to preserve the appearance that the parties voluntarily come before the court. A striking feature of European and Anglo-American court systems in general is the extent to which the complaining party in civil suits must shoulder the burden of getting the other side into court with relatively little assistance from the court itself.

Perhaps more fundamental than these remnants of mutual consent to trial is the almost universal phenomenon that at least one of the disputants must choose to go to court. Only in isolated instances, such as the authority of the

Soviet procurator to intervene in civil disputes (Berman, 1963), are judicial services imposed on disputants neither one of whom wants them. In this sense while the parties no longer choose their particular law and their particular judge, at least one of them must choose the law and the courts.

In a substantial proportion of civil proceedings courts are used to settle contractual disputes in which the parties have in fact created the detailed rules of decision for themselves when they initially wrote the contract. Here again the partial phenomenon suggests the more general one. It is not only in contract disputes after all that the parties in consultation with the judge make the law. More often than not what we would label adversary proceedings are rituals in which three law speakers, the judge and the two parties or their attorneys, speak on until arriving at some verbal formulation of the law synthesized from their various versions. This can be seen at the simple level of a debate among tribal litigants about what the customs of the people truly are (Barton, 1949) and at the elaborate level of appellate opinions constructed out of bits and pieces of the opposing briefs (Shapiro, 1972). Most courts make some law as they go along, and when they do so it is usually with the assistance of the parties.

Along the dimension of enforcement too we find the judge less far from the mediator than one might expect. In most societies courts have had only the most rudimentary enforcement mechanisms, often only a mélange of voluntary compliance and self-help. Courts typically do not monitor compliance, and they reintervene to exact compliance only at the request of one of the parties. The reintervention often takes the form of a simple repetition of the previous order. The successful suitor even in a modern industrial society frequently finds that the decree is only the first in a long series of painful, expensive, and often inconclusive steps aimed at getting his remedy. Courts, we are repeatedly and rightly told, have neither the purse nor the sword. Perhaps more important, they rarely have the administrative resources to follow up on their resolutions. Most court systems seem to operate on the assumptions that both parties consent sufficiently to voluntarily comply at least as long as some vague threat of further judicial action is maintained.

It is hardly surprising that most judges spend a good deal of time as mediators. It might once have been argued that the emphasis on mediation in oriental courts was wholly or largely a result of Confucianism or the like, so that the oriental judge as mediator was a peculiar and culturally determined phenomenon. Structural rather than cultural factors, however, seem to be at the root of the matter. Even where law and courts are accorded a high level of legitimacy, true adversary proceedings culminating in a dichotomous verdict are an optimal mode of conflict resolution only for parties who in the future need have no relations or only arms-length relations with one another. For those who must maintain close economic or social relations, proceedings according to the prototype of courts are unlikely to be satisfactory. Given the substitution of law and office for consent, the loser will rarely feel sufficiently satisfied with the most extreme form of the judicial process to fully reenter those relations with the winner. And the less legitimacy is accorded the regime of which the court is a part, the less capable it will be at restoring a working relationship.

Although there are some societies where even those in close and continuing relationships are willing to accept dichotomous solutions with good grace, we generally find highly mediatory styles of judging in agrarian villages, with a strong tendency on the part of the villagers to avoid the more courtlike courts of the central regime and frequently an adoption of mediatory styles even by the courts of the regime. The classic Chinese situation may represent an extreme upward percolation of mediatory styles (Cohen, 1966). The medieval English arrangement may be more typical. There the large landowners, who were not only at arm's length but often at sword's point, resorted to the king's common-law courts for strict law judgments of disputes with one another. However, where conflicts arose between lord and tenant or between tenants in the context of communal or partially communal agricultural production, they were generally resolved either in the lord's own or the communal (hundreds) courts by a bailiff or group of elders working in more mediatory style (Allen, 1958). On the other hand, in seventeenth century England and colonial and nineteenth century America where there were large numbers of individually owned and operated agricultural units producing for a cash market, there seemed to be specially high levels of litigatiousness (Haskins, 1960).

The tendency toward mediation even by formally structured courts is not limited to communal agricultural settings. In modern Japan, for instance, which imported a highly adversary and dichotomous judicial style along with the German Civil Code, mediation continued as the basic judicial mode in the villages. Adversary litigation became more prevalent with urbanization and most prevalent in auto accident cases in which the parties had no continuity of relationships. Yet the major Japanese industrial cartels engage in relatively little litigation with one another or their subcontractors (von Mehren, 1957).

In Western societies as well, firms that must maintain continuous business relationships are not prone to litigation. Continuous business relation is usually expressed legally by contracts, and it is precisely in contract relations that formal instruments of mediation and arbitration have exhibited tremendous growth in modern industrial states. Perhaps more important, as we noted earlier, negotiation under the umbrella of and within the restraints imposed by potential adversary proceedings with dichotomous solutions has become the principal mode of legalized conflict resolution in industrialized societies. And out-of-court settlement has become a major mode of resolution of even those conflicts that reach the stage of law suits. In criminal law, too, where the prosecutor has come to perceive his relation with criminals as a continuous one, plea bargaining has become the dominant mode of resolution in at least one highly urbanized, industrialized society, the United States (Jacob, 1973). Indeed many observers trained to the prototype of courts are shocked by the informal, familial, conciliatory, and mediatory style of most American criminal proceedings.

Another clear example of the relation of mutual interdependency to the choice of mediatory rather than strict judicial proceedings is, of course, the endless proliferation of mediation and arbitration arrangements throughout the Western world for the resolution of labor-management conflicts.

In short, if one were to review all societies, or even to confine oneself to modern industrial and commercial states where one would most expect to find the prototypic court, one discovers that legal processes are not necessarily or entirely court processes if we confine our definition of court to the prototype. For we frequently find intermediate rather than dichotomous resolution, aimed at the mutual satisfaction of the parties, conducted by their chosen representatives and often by a chosen third, through procedures·emphasizing mutual conciliation rather than adversary confrontation.

To put the matter another way, judges tend to share the same means of conflict resolution with other triadic figures, and most of those we would label judges engage in a great deal of mediation. Moreover the substitution of law and office for consent has not been total even for those judges who act most independently of the wills of the parties in acquiring and resolving conflicts. As a result, even from the perspective of conflict resolution, where the prototype of court would seem to be most clear, we encounter grave difficulties. Either we must accept all triadic conflict resolvers as judges, or we must admit that most of those we call judges do a lot of nonjudging, *or* we must confine the area of judicial studies to a very thin slice of the real world and one so arbitrarily sliced that it would appear senseless to most of the participants.

Nevertheless, so long as we remain strictly in the area of conflict resolution, the prototype can be saved by making it broader and more vague. Even a judge thrust on the parties rather than chosen by them may be independent in the sense of favoring neither of them. The substitution of office for consent may simply be the substitution of one means for another in achieving judicial neutrality. Something parallel can be said to the substitution of legislation for the creation of norms by the parties. And indeed the strong remnants of consent found even in legal systems formally based on office and law further ensure the neutrality of the third man and the rules of decision. A greater appreciation of the ties between judges and mediators leads up to modify the notion of adversary proceedings. It is enough that both parties present their views to one another and a third or with the option of going to a third. The style of the interchange may be cooperative, benevolent, even familial rather than one of ritualized trial by battle. Similarly the judicial resolution may be one shaped to the perceived interests of both parties. The decision must reflect the fact that two parties are in conflict, but it need not assign victory entirely to one and defeat to the other.

The basic tension to be found in courts as conflict resolvers lies not in their deviation from the basic prototype of courts but rather in their need to persuade the parties that judges and laws they have not chosen nonetheless constitute a genuine, neutral third. Most of the ties courts maintain to the mediator, and many of the hiatuses of coercive power that we observe in the procedures of courts for acquiring the parties and imposing and enforcing verdicts, stem from this tension.

SOCIAL CONTROL

More serious tensions arise when we consider courts as social controllers as well as conflict resolvers. While an analytical distinction can be drawn between these two activities of courts, in practice they are almost inevitably intertwined. Particularly in dealing with go-betweens and mediators or with judges chosen by the parties and employing a rule formulated by the parties, one may encounter a resolution based solely on the interests of the parties and unconstrained by overreaching social norms, customs, or laws. But even where mutual consent of the parties is the dominating concern, what the two parties will usually find themselves able to mutually consent to is that their conflict should be governed by some general norm of the society to which they belong. While our two early Romans may have occasionally invented a wholly new legal rule for themselves, most of their energies were no doubt directed at achieving an agreed verbal formulation of a Roman tribal usage or custom, and it was to gain assistance in this task that they later turned to a praetor.

Thus even absent the imposition of law and office, the resolution of disputes through reference to a third is likely to entail the enforcement of broader norms on the parties either directly or as bounding constraints. Only the go-between shuttling between parties embedded in two quite different societies is likely to be acting without exerting any social control over the parties.

It is of course in the substitution of office and law for consent that the social-control aspects of courts become most evident and most clearly create tensions with conflict resolution. Where the two parties must go to a third who is an officer, it is as evident to them as to the observer that they are no longer going to a disinterested third. Instead they are introducing a third interest: that of the government, the church, the landowner, or whoever else appoints the official. To be sure, even the Papuans who mutually choose a "big man" to settle their disputes do not expect him to be neutral in the sense of having no interests of his own. Indeed the bigger he is, the broader is likely to be the web of his interlocking social and economic interests among the various genetic, economic, and social units to which the disputants belong. But the requirement of mutual consent allows the Papuans, like modern corporations in search of an arbitrator, to settle on a third who will not see his interests, whatever they may be, as parallel to those of one but not the other of the parties.

Where litigants do not freely choose their judges a number of alternatives arise. First, where both parties perceive the interests of the regime to be hostile to their own, the parties will not go to the official court. Indeed, considering the whole of human experience, this avoidance of courts because they represent the interests of others or outsiders is more the norm than the exception. Secondly, where both parties perceive the interests of the regime to be complementary or irrelevant to their own, they may go to court. Thus the bailiff of an exploitive, foreign, and hated feudal lord may be the perfect judge for two serfs in conflict over the rightful possession of a cow precisely because the lord doesn't care which of them milks it so long as he gets half the milk.

Thirdly, where one of the parties perceives the interests represented by the judge as hostile to his own and favorable to his opponent, litigation may occur if the other party or the court has sufficient coercive resources to bring the reluctant party in, but the basic social logic of the court will disappear. Should the self-perceived underdog actually lose, he will see the situation as two against one and the role of the court not as conflict resolver but as coercer.

It is for this reason, of course, that the prototype stresses the "independence" of the judge. In the most basic and usually the least important sense, independence would mean that the judge had not been bribed or was not in some other way a dependent of one of the parties. But where we ensure this kind of independence by creating the office of judge within some governmental structure, in a far more important sense he is not independent, for he is a dependent of those for whom he holds office. Thus explicators of the prototype have come to define independence not so much as independence from the contending parties as independence from those to whom the judge owes his office. They stress the institutional separation of courts from the remainder of the political system (Abraham, 1968; Becker, 1970; Eckhoff, 1965). To make independence in this sense the touchstone of courtness is to measure from the most deviant case. Looking at all known societies we find a number of typical locations within the political structure for judging. One is the whole body of the tribe, the folkmoot, in which, far from having separate judges, the entire polity does the judging (Gibbs, 1963). In tribal societies organized under strong chiefs, the chiefs judge with or without the assistance of the elders and the body of tribesmen (Gluckman, 1965). In village societies the elders do much of the judging. Heads of families and other genetic units do much of their own judging (Pospisil, 1971). In feudal societies the feudal magnates do much of the judging. In empires almost invariably the administrator of the geographic unit is the judge in those matters not delegated to or retained by the conquered peoples. In short, the universal pattern is that judging runs as an integral part of the mainstream of political authority rather than as a separate entity. In those societies in which sovereignty can be located the sovereign judges. In those in which political authority is not clearly concentrated, those who hold the dispersed authority judge.

Judging and Administration

The congruence of administrating and judging must be specially noted. Indeed the observer who did not so firmly believe in the independence of judging might take judging for a special facet of administering. Both the judge and administrator apply general rules to particular situations on a case-by-case basis. Both tend to rely heavily on precedent, fixed decisional procedures, written records, and legalized defense of their decisions. Both are supplementary lawmakers engaged in filling in the details of more general rules. Both are front-line social controllers for more distant governing authorities. And in a startling number of instances both are the same person, and a person who draws little or no distinction between administering and judging.

The most striking example is the imperial administrator. The all-purpose geographic officer is the mainstay of empire, whether he be British district officer or Chinese mandarin. Such officers are there to keep the peace and collect the taxes—not unrelated functions. And for better or worse, in practice the imperial prefects are also the imperial judges. While in very wealthy empires, and at the highest levels of geographic subdivision, one may sometimes catch even substantial judicial subspecialization among the immediate subordinates of a governor, the norm is the all-purpose officer serving in the field.

The connection between tax gathering and judging is not confined to purely imperial situations. Much the same phenomenon is to be found in feudal monarchies. The English Exchequer is an obvious example, but in Tokugawa, Japan, as well, a good rule of thumb is that whoever is responsible for supervising the tax rice is also a judge (Wigmore, 1970). Feudal systems like empires make liberal use of the all-purpose local administrator. And far more important than the fact that feudal magnates enjoyed the rights of the high justice and the low was that their bailiffs, who were primarily local agricultural administrators and tax collectors, also presided over the local baronial court.

English common-law judges begin as royal administrators who dispensed the king's justice in the course of doing the rest of the king's business. And that great rival of the common-law courts, the courts of equity, are the courts of the chief administrative official and tax collector of the realm, the chancellor. The justices of the peace were simultaneously judicial and administrative officers (Dawson, 1960).

We also encounter this affinity between judging and administration in the town magistrates, who are in many ways the equivalent of the general-purpose administrators of the countryside. From imperial Japan to colonial Massachusetts and medieval France, wherever a body of local notables has been vested with the authority to direct municipal affairs, it will be found with authority to do local judging. Indeed the title "magistrate" has become an almost purely judicial one in the United States, although clearly the magistrates of colonial America, like those of medieval Europe, were all-purpose urban authorities

(Haskins, 1960). Indeed, precisely because judging is traditionally an integral part of the local governor's tasks, in England and America we sometimes get the reversal of titles, as in those midwestern American states where county administrators bear the title "judge."

We can attribute this congruence of judging and administration to a number of factors. First of all, to return to our triad, it is as natural for two disputing parties to turn to a government official in places where there is a government as it is for two tribesmen to turn to the owner of many pigs where there is not. The local governor is a big man and thus "available" for judging. Like the owner of many pigs, he may impart interests of his own into the resolution of the dispute, but also like him, this drawback may be counterbalanced by his greater resources for eliciting the consent of or coercing the reluctant party. Secondly, endless disputes about the whole web of obligations owed by the locals to their lords, churches, sovereigns, and chiefs inevitably arise in the course of bringing the demands of the higher to the lower, which is the core of feudal and imperial administration. Moreover, as the growth of the Exchequer Courts shows, these disputes grow outward from conflicts between man and distant master to conflicts between local man and local man. "I cannot pay my taxes because I loaned my neighbor money which he refuses to pay back. Get my money back and I will pay my tax." In these instances the administrator will find the settlement of disputes a routine part of his job. There is usually no one else to do the judging chores, and if he doesn't do them, he cannot get his job done.

Thirdly, the mandarin or district officer is there to exert a certain measure of social control. Because the imposition of norms as a means of settling a dispute between two individuals is one mode of exercising social control, he will seize on it along with all the others.

Courts and the Regime

Perhaps the most important factor in explaining the historical congruence of judging and administering is to be found in a far broader aspect of the administrator's responsibility for social control. The origin of judicial systems in many parts of the world is to be found in conquest. This is obviously true for imperial judicial systems such as those of Rome, China, and the black empires of central Africa such as the Barotse. It is also clearly true for the common-law courts imposed over the old moot and hundred folk courts by the Norman conquerors, and for the British courts of colonial India and Africa as well as many other colonial court systems. It is true for the Supreme Court of the United States and the lower federal courts insofar as they operate on the old Confederacy. Even where courts are not directly imposed by force of arms, they will often be identified with the political regime or with distant rather than local authority.

Conquerors use courts as one of their many instruments for holding and controlling conquered territories. And more generally, governing authorities seek to maintain or increase their legitimacy through the courts. Thus a major function of courts in many societies is a particular form of social control, the recruiting of support for the regime.

Where conquerors impose courts, often we discover a form of "extraterritoriality." The new courts serve to resolve conflicts between one conquering cadre and another or between a conqueror and a native where the native courts cannot be trusted to do the job. The claim to Roman citizenship was in part a claim to Roman courts and Roman procedure even in those portions of the empire where indigenous courts functioned. At their inception English common-law courts were resorted to on the civil side almost entirely by Norman overlords in their relations with one another. The King's Peace enforced by those courts was largely a body of rules designed to protect Normans from Saxons. The clerical courts of the Roman Catholic Church, which are so important in the whole development of Continental judicial systems, are one of the foremost examples of such extraterritorial courts.

Aside from this extraterritorial value of newly imposed courts, the conqueror is soon likely to discover a number of other advantages they may yield. A scattered population living largely by customary and localized law may be governed more efficiently by central authorities if a unified body of law is introduced. Moreover the conqueror often finds that rule is facilitated by reaching some working relationship with the indigenous notables and delegating considerable authority to them in exchange for their support. As a result of the interaction of these two considerations, an imposed body of law is typically the set of particular laws and customs that have previously governed the notables transformed into a body of uniform law designated to govern everyone. In short, the conqueror melds his own and indigenous upper-class law, universalizes it, and imposes it over the local and particular rules that have previously been the body of law of the peasantry and small holders. The Normans combine their own law with that evolved by Saxon notables in their relations with one another to create a body of law that is essentially landowners' law. They impose that law over the existing plethora of local customary law and make it common to all of England. Some centuries later their descendants combine their own law with Brahmin law and impose it over local custom and caste rules to make it the law common to all of India (Rudolph and Rudolph, 1967).

Thus a major function of courts in many societies is to assist in holding the countryside by providing not only an extraterritorial court to adjust relations among the occupying cadres according to their own rules but also a uniform body of national law in order to facilitate central administration and a body of law designed to cement the alliance between conquerors and local notables and further their joint interests.

There is yet another strand to this development. One mode of cementing the legitimacy of an imposed regime is providing more and better government services than its predecessor. Newly imposed courts might provide not only the advantages just indicated but speedier, fairer, more just resolutions of conflicts within the indigenous population. New courts might compete with indigenous modes of conflict resolution. To the extent that they won the competition, they would aid the central authorities in breaking into the cake of local custom and bringing government influence down into the villages. Judicial services, like medical services, are a way into the countryside. Such new courts would provide a body of more specific, uniform, and flexible law that would appeal to those locals inhibited by the old customary law (Hutchison *et al.,* 1968; Kuper and Kuper, 1965). They would also provide an "independent" judge freer of local dominant interests than the village elders or the folk courts. Thus what we often mean by an independent judiciary is one that serves a set of upper class and nationalizing interests rather than dominant local interests and thus one more satisfactory to persons trying to break through the web of local interests (Gluckman, 1963).

Given these considerations the congruence between administering and judging is hardly surprising, for judging, like administering, may be principally designed to hold and exploit the countryside for the central regime.

Social Control, Legislation, and Conflict Resolution

The relation of the social-control function to the prototype of courts must be seen, however, in a far broader context than the special case of the newly imposed courts of conquering regimes, even though the special case accounts for a large proportion of court systems. To do so it is convenient to move from the substitution of office for consent to the substitution of legislation for disputant-originated rules of decision.

The substitution of law for the immediate consent of the parties to a particular rule is to be widely found in the dispute settlement as well as the social-control aspect of judicial work. Indeed, while it would be overly ambitious to propose a general evolutionary hypothesis, laws of social control seem frequently to arise out of recurrent dispute-settlement situations. Criminal law is the most obvious form of social control through law. Yet simple societies rarely distinguish private from criminal law. The moot and more generally the popular witnessing of and participation in judicial proceedings often seem to express the understanding of communal societies that, where social units are small, any dispute between two members has immediate consequences for the whole. The whole therefore judges, and judges not only with an eye to conflict resolution but to its own more general well-being. This understanding may also be expressed in the conception of the crime of witchcraft, which is often seen as the carrying of an interpersonal dispute to a level of intensity dangerous to the community (Currie, 1968; Evans-Pritchard, 1937). Banishment, a popular form of remedy in relatively simple societies, is obviously a simple mode of conflict resolution through the physical separation of the parties. But it is also a simple mode of social control by getting rid of a troublemaker. And more deeply, its rationale is frequently the fear that harboring a wrongdoer will bring the wrath of the gods on the community as a whole (Llewellyn and Hoebel, 1961).

At English common law, criminal law is not clearly separated from tort until the seventeenth century. Tort law represented the extension of judicial conflict-resolution services by the crown to individual disputants where one man had injured another. Yet throughout the medieval period, many of these same personal injuries, such as assault, were recognized as "crimes" against the King's Peace. A single judicial proceeding might result in the levy of money damages to be paid to the injured party and a fine to be paid to the crown. Of course even today, in both common and Roman law systems, a single act may give rise to both criminal and civil proceedings (David and Brierly, 1968). In the earliest Roman law, all of the offenses that we would today label criminal were treated as civil injuries subject to private conflict resolution by judges selected by the parties. Roman criminal courts with preselected juries were first created for the peculiarly political crime of malfeasance in public office and only gradually acquired general criminal jurisdiction (Gruen, 1968).

Even when we look at property and tort—the central pillars of interpersonal conflict resolution—we discover important impositions of social control through bodies of law apparently designed essentially to serve only the private interests of the parties. In tort law the "reasonable man," and his equivalent in the civil law of delict, is a vehicle for importing into personal disputes general social standards of how men should act. If one does not act in accord with the general social norms defining reasonable conduct, the court will award damages to one's opponent. Anglo-American property law is essentially feudal in origin and thus is marked by the intimate mixture of rights reserved against one's equals and inferiors and obligations owed one's superiors which characterizes feudal law. Even to the extent that modern Continental property law claims to be purified of its own feudal experience, it harks back to a classic Roman law of property that specifically subjects the personal use of property to the interests of the state (Cappelletti *et al.*, 1967).

Let us leave aside for the moment those instances in which the rulers independently decide that certain conduct is undesirable and forbid it by law. At the point at which the judge is expected to apply general preexisting law in the settlement of disputes, that law becomes an element of social control. That law must come from somewhere. Whether its origin is in custom, or in the systematizing of earlier judgments, or in the fiat of the rulers, or in some legitimated process of legislation, its very nature as a general rule applicable to future situations imports some element of social concern beyond the particular concerns of the particular disputants. The Marxists tell us that laws always embody the interests of the ruling classes. Certainly even those rules consciously designed to meet only the interests of prospective disputants cannot be totally neutral in the sense of embodying no general social vision of right and wrong or appropriate and inappropriate conduct. Even societies that profess no conscious desire to impose general social norms in the process of resolving interpersonal disputes, in the sense of conscious social regulation, will in fact resolve those disputes on the basis of whether the parties have acted "as we always do things" or, alternatively, have "bloodied the arrows" or "spoiled the tjar."

Thus so long as a judge acts to impose preexisting rules on the disputants, he is importing an element of social control. Or to put the matter differently, he is importing a third set of interests, whatever interests are embodied in those rules, to be adjudicated along with the interests of the two parties.

Public Regulation

When we reach the criminal law itself, and the other bodies of law that openly purport to impose the interests of the regime on individuals and groups, the vision of the triad becomes even more difficult to maintain, particularly where judicial office exists. Where the judge is himself an officer of the crown, and the dispute is in the from of the *Crown* v. *Doe,* in what sense do we have a triad as opposed to a simple inquisition? We have noted that judging is a concomitant of sovereignty or at least political authority. Where the whole tribe, or its representative jury, or the village elders meet to judge a transgression against the people or the community, in what sense do we have a folkmoot or a village "court"? Yet over the whole range of our experience we observe acts that are defined as offenses against the collectivity judged by the collectivity itself or by "judges" who are supposed to be the representatives of the collectivity.

Thus even if we could preserve the notion of the completely independent third in the realm of "pure" conflict resolution, assuming such a realm existed, we could not do so in the realm of social control because of the very nature of judicial office and proceedings in that realm. Moreover, in that realm the legal rules applied to a litigation that in form is a dispute between one party —the community—and a second party—the alleged transgressor—are rules that consciously and openly were created by and for one of the parties. Thus to return to our prototype, the very facts that (3) the proceedings are adversary and (2) apply preexisting legal norms ensure that we will *not* have (1) an independent judge. For even in those few societies that seek to insulate the judge from the rest of government, he is expected to administer the criminal law, that is, to impose the will of the regime on a party being prosecuted by the regime. With extremely great care to the various rituals of independence and impartiality, some criminal courts may succeed in maintaining the appearance of thirdness. However, few of the defendants in contemporary Western criminal courts are likely to perceive their judges as anything other than officers of the regime seeking to control them (Casper, 1972). So to put the matter somewhat differently, where the government or the people are one of the parties to a dispute, the triadic structure is necessarily weakened when the judge is either an officer of the government or is the people themselves.

While this weakening of the triad is clearest in criminal law, it is also fairly evident in all bodies of "public" law, that is, law setting out the relations between governor and governed. Those societies that engage in the greatest separation of powers or specialization of judicial function approach nearest to a perception of judicial independence. At least the private party engaged in a dispute with one segment of government is judged by an officer of another segment. But, as we have already seen, it is a far more typical governing arrangement to subsume judicial under administrative tasks than to create a judicial specialization. Moreover it is typical of Continental legal systems and their offspring to handle a substantial proportion of public law litigation in "administrative courts," which are less clearly differentiated from the administrative agencies than are the regular courts of the same systems (Friedman, 1967). Even in the United States and Commonwealth countries, where constitutional separation of powers is most complete, a curious paradox arises because of the very inclination to separate. We encounter a common pattern in which the courts of the central government are relatively independent of the rest of that government, a federal system exists, and the highest court of the central government referees constitutional disputes between the central government and the federal units. In this situation the central court is frequently and often rightly perceived not as an independent third but as an arm of the central government imposing central control on the federal units. Particularly where the central court is imposing the will of a national majority over that of a local majority, as in many of the United States Supreme Court's race and religion decisions, the local majority sees the court not as an independent adjudicator but rather as the imposer of national uniformity over local diversity.

We have now argued that the substitution of office and law for consent gravely impairs the basic triadic logic of courts in the sphere of conflict resolution and even more particularly when courts are primarily engaged in social control. Another way of putting this is that precisely because we vest social control as well as conflict resolution in courts, their triadic position is impaired. For in most legal systems the litigants are aware that the judge is concerned not only with refereeing their two sets of interests but with imposing a third set of interests on them both. Whether the triad is maintained will then depend in large part on whether either or both parties perceive the law as neutral in relation to them or alternatively as clearly favoring the interests of the other. Indeed one of the many factors contributing to the court avoidance phenomenon found in most societies is that either one or both disputants perceive the law as inimical or irrelevant to their interests, so that a court of law is an inappropriate instrument for the particular conflict resolution task. Aid in resolution is sought elsewhere.

COURTS AS LAWMAKERS

When we move from the conflict-resolution and social-control tasks of courts to their lawmaking tasks, the triad may be even further weakened. Nearly all contemporary students of courts agree that courts do engage in at least supplementary and interstitial lawmaking, filling in the details of the statutory or customary law (Shapiro, 1968). In several major legal systems courts go far beyond interstitial lawmaking. The common law of the Anglo-American legal system is largely judge made. Whether we should speak of the *jus gentium* and other praetorian law of imperial Rome as judge made depends on whether we choose to call the praetors judges or administrators. Similarly, Jewish and Islamic law contain large components of judge-made law if we choose to call judicial the legal pronouncements of religious officials who frequently performed in triadic contexts (Chigier, 1967; Lev, 1972). Moreover, the affinities and overlappings between judicial lawmaking and administrative rule making are so great that they can be only artificially separated. Where administrators do judging, it is often impossible to distinguish between "case law" and administrative law, as for instance in the mass of *harigami,* which formed an important portion of traditional Japanese law (Wigmore, 1970). Even in modern Roman-law systems, where theoretically the lawmaking power of courts is severely limited, substantial and systematically articulated bodies of law have been judicially constructed from very slight statutory foundations (Friedman, 1967; von Mehren, 1957).

Much of the thrust of the judicial behavior literature (see Schubert, 1963 and 1972) has been toward showing that there has been a high correlation between judges' political attitudes and their decisions for and against certain categories of litigants. This literature further suggests that these judicial attitudes fall into the same relatively coherent ideological patterns found in the national political culture. While considerably less success has been encountered in linking these patterns of political attitudes to the personal backgrounds of the judges, their modes of appointment, or the social and political structures in which they operate, the brute fact of judicial discretion, even within systems of highly articulated statutory and constitutional law, has been more than sufficiently demonstrated. In short, while the development of a political psychology of judging may be still at an early stage, the behavioral literature has fairly convincingly demonstrated that many judges are not entirely "neutral" thirds but instead bring to the triad distinct public policy preferences, which they seek to implement through their decisions.

Aside from actual empirical discovery of widespread judicial lawmaking, it is clear that such lawmaking is logically required wherever law is substituted for consent in the triadic resolution of conflict. For if the third man must resolve conflict, and if he must do so by preexisting law, then he must "discover" the preexisting law. Because no human society has ever sought to set down an absolutely complete and particularized body of preexisting law designed to exactly meet every potential conflict, judicial "discovery" must often of necessity be judicial lawmaking.

In addition to the simple fact and logical necessity of judicial lawmaking, it is clear that many societies, including even those that seek to separate judicial from administrative and legislative office, quite deliberately vest major lawmaking functions in courts. In common-law countries numerous instances may be found in which legislatures have given courts new jurisdictions without giving them new substantive statutory law for those jurisdictions. Alternatively they may have written statutes whose key operative words are common-law terms of art that incorporate past and invite future judicial lawmaking. In the United States the statutory creation of a federal labor contract jurisdiction without the provision of any substantive federal law of contracts and the Sherman Anti-Trust Act's condemnation of "conspiracies in restraint of trade" are obvious examples. In France the creation of an elaborate hierarchy of administrative courts with extensive jurisdiction combined with a singularly cryptic body of statutory administrative law was surely an invitation to administrative judges to make their own law—an invitation that they have accepted (Abraham, 1968; David, 1972).

Two basic judicial lawmaking situations exist. The judges may make law in the sense that a generalized political authority does triadic conflict resolution, administers and enforces various social norms, and announces new norms without clearly differentiating among the three. Thus in Llewellyn's and Hoebel's famous example of Cheyenne lawmaking, the "soldiers," a group whose principal task is to supervise the tribe's collective buffalo-hunting operation, are confronted by an incidental task of conflict resolution and in this context announce that from now on no one should borrow another's horse without asking permission. In short, frequently when we speak of judicial lawmaking, we are really observing the phenomenon of merged judicial, administrative, and lawmaking powers in a single political authority, which we have already noted is far more common than judicial separation.

The second basic judicial lawmaking situation is one in which a separated and specialized judiciary nevertheless makes law. We have just noted that in theory, in fact, and in the consensus of scholarly observers, all such courts do engage in lawmaking.

Both of these lawmaking situations arise from political economy in the most fundamental sense of that term. Most societies cannot afford or do not choose to allocate sufficient resources to provide three men or three institutions to do the job of governing that can be done by one. The general governor, whether he be king, chief, popular assembly, or district officer, will do the lawmaking and the judging because he has enough resources to do all the governing.

On the other hand, where a society chooses to nourish a number of governing bodies, including one or more primarily devoted to triadic conflict resolution, two other interlocking elements of political economy come to the fore. Separate courts are a very expensive commodity. Once in existence there will be strong and continuous pressure to pile additional tasks on them, to get one's money's worth out of them, so to speak. In the United States a strong constitutional tradition of separation of powers has allowed the Supreme Court to fend off some unwanted additional tasks. But that very same tradition has served as a basis for the court acquiring enormous lawmaking powers. In the United States today federal and state courts are drawing school district lines, administering prisons, supervising railroads, prescribing personnel procedures for police departments, altering the time schedules and design features of vast construction projects, determining patterns of urban development, and preserving the seacoasts. And one basic reason they are doing these things is that where there are tasks to be done, it will frequently appear quicker and cheaper to assign them to an existing government agency than to create a new one. Thus even in the context of a strong ideological commitment to separation of powers, courts will pick up many lawmaking and administrative tasks simply because they are there.

Because there is a general tendency to economize by piling tasks on existing institutions, any expensive institution of government can be expected to have multiple functions. This phenomenon appears in preliterate, feudal, mercantile, and industrial societies. Multiple-function government institutions also have a second political economic advantage. Sometimes consciously and sometimes not, they create governmental redundancies that have significant survival value for the political system. In no society is politics marked by totally rational sequences or even certainty of outcome. In all governing systems, key links intermittently fail. Thus the existence of many alternative channels for accomplishing any given task of government may be an important guarantee of even minimal political efficiency. If the police cannot quell the riot, perhaps the army can. If the city government cannot provide vocational education, perhaps the state can. If the legislature will not respond to the needs of racial minorities, perhaps the executive will.

The earlier enthusiasm of students of organization for rationalizing administration through an extreme form of the division of labor, in which each unit did do and could do only one thing, has faded. The messiness of most governments, with their multiple overlapping and competing agencies, has certain advantages after all (Landau, 1969). Governmental redundancy is not only an advantage in the sense that a new agency can be found to take over from a failing one. As proponents of mixed government and the division of powers have argued from ancient times, multiple government agencies may also serve as a salutory check on one another. But what has often been less clear is that agencies cannot check one another unless each is capable of performing at least some of the vital functions of the other. If each agency of government is so specialized that it cannot do anything but one preset operation in the total process of government, the assembly line that results will give each agency an absolute veto over the operations of government. For if any one withdraws, the product cannot be completed. In theory, perhaps, skillful bargaining with elaborate side payments among the veto wielders could produce both internal checks and a functioning government. In practice, the more each participant can meet other participants' threats of absolute veto by moving to perform the tasks of the threatener, the more likely we are to achieve the functioning moderation that seems to be the aim of the proponents of mixed government.

Thus it is precisely in those governments in which the independence of the judiciary is stressed, because of a desire to check and balance, that the judiciary is likely to acquire substantial lawmaking and administering capabilities. In such governments the existence of checks and balances means numerous roadblocks along any policy-making avenue, so that a great premium is placed on exploring alternative avenues or detours. In those same governments, agencies pushed to watch and check one another necessarily learn to acquire one another's capabilities. Thus the ultimate strategy for anyone wishing to get something out of government is to treat all agencies as multiple purpose, shopping among them until any one or any combination of them will yield what is desired (Shapiro, 1964). Americans, for instance, have learned that if the Congress won't give them what they want, the president may, and if he will not, perhaps the Supreme Court will.

Judicial Independence and Judicial Lawmaking

In a great many nations judicial independence is conceived not in terms of a tripartite constitution with checks and balances but simply in terms of a professional judiciary sufficiently insulated from other governmental influences to operate within its own sphere under the rule of law. The courts of Great Britain and Czarist Russia would show the range of this sort of independence, which may be found all the way from liberal constitutional systems emphasizing responsible but centralized political authority to pure autocracies. Obviously some political systems that seek to concentrate political authority will find that the triad is an extremely useful tool of conflict resolution. Such systems will then encounter the dynamics of the triad that we have already encountered. But they may be willing to pay the costs to centralization of creating a relatively independent judicial authority in order to reap the benefits of increased capacity for conflict resolution.

Precisely because they want such triads for routine conflict resolution among private citizens while seeking to keep political power away from the judges, such regimes necessarily encounter difficulties with their judiciaries. For we have already seen that in the course of doing conflict resolution, either under preexisting legal rules or otherwise, courts will make law, or, to express the same thing differently, exercise political power. When this inevitable phenomenon is encountered, both autocratic and constitutional regimes of centralized political authority can respond in one of four ways. First, they can yield and in the process become less centralized. Secondly, they can systematically withdraw from the legally defined competence of the judiciary all matters of political interest to themselves. Thirdly, they may intervene at will to pull particular cases out of the courts and into their own hands. Fourthly, they can create systems of judicial recruitment, training, organization, and promotion that ensure that the judge will be relatively neutral as between two purely private parties but will be the absolutely faithful servant of the regime on all legal matters touching its interests.

Various mixes of all four of these solutions are to be found in Western legal systems. Both England and most Continental countries have deviated sufficiently from theories of parliamentary sovereignty to allow considerable autonomy to their courts (Abraham, 1968; Merryman, 1969). Nevertheless the intersection of courts and the powerful bureaucracies in these countries is particularly instructive and illustrative of tactic two. Let us suppose that courts actually sought to serve as triadic conflict resolvers between administrative agencies and aggrieved individuals and that they sought to do so according to the prototype set out at the beginning of this discussion. That is, let us suppose that an independent judge, applying the preexisting law, sought, in an adversary setting, to decide whether the bureaucracy or the individual citizen should triumph in their dispute. Such court proceedings would inevitably operate to substitute judicial fact-finding and lawmaking for administrative fact-finding and lawmaking. For bureaucracies typically operate under rather broad and vague statutory mandates and either uncertain or changing fact situations. Thus they are inevitably themselves supplementary lawmakers. Just as inevitably, then, where courts seek to resolve conflicts by the application of "preexisting" legal rules where an administrative agency is one of the parties, they must either accept the agency's supplementary lawmaking or do their own. But the agency's own lawmaking is likely to be highly particularized and deeply embedded in the very decision being disputed by the other litigant. Thus if the court accepts the agency's lawmaking in many instances it will also automatically be finding for it and against the other litigant. It is rather as if, in the ancient Roman situation, instead of the two disputants having to agree on the legal rule to govern their dispute, one disputant was authorized to impose a rule of his choosing on the other. On the other hand, if the court does its own supplementary lawmaking, it has become willy nilly a sharer in the political power of the regime.

The British solution to this paradox has essentially been tactic two, that is, to selectively but systematically withdraw large areas of conflict from judicial resolution. British administrative law is principally a series of doctrines that command courts to defer to bureaucratic lawmaking and thus to render themselves incapable of providing a neutral and independent resolution of most conflicts that might arise between government and citizens. The French solution has essentially been tactic four, the creation of a corps of administrative judges who form an integral part of the bureaucracy itself. At the Revolution of 1905, the Czarist regime, apparently embarrassed by the highly independent and professional judiciary it had been nurturing for many years, adopted tactic three. It promptly set up special courts to bring revolutionaries to Siberia and the scaffold. These courts plucked what cases they liked from the regular criminal processes. Tactic four is also a favorite of military juntas that impose themselves atop going civil regimes, one of whose features is a relatively independent judiciary. While the regular courts function, courts martial take those few cases of special concern to the regime.

Read in one way, the prevalence of these four tactics is testimony to the real independence of judiciaries. In many nations at many times judges have been sufficiently their own masters to require even highly centralized regimes to adopt special tactics to avoid sharing power with them. Even in highly centralized regimes, judicial lawmaking is a reality that must be dealt with, just as it is in regimes that deliberately assign substantial lawmaking authority to the judiciary.

If judges then are inevitably lawmakers, what happens to our prototype of independence, preexisting legal rules, adversary proceedings, and dichotomous solutions, and more particularly, what happens to the substitution of legislation for legal rules consented to by the parties? In the first place, lawmaking and judicial independence are fundamentally incompatible. No regime is likely to allow significant political power to be wielded by an isolated judicial corps free of political restraints. To the extent that courts make law, judges will be incorporated into the governing coalition, the ruling elite, the responsible representatives of the people, or however else the political regime may be expressed. In most societies this presents no problem at all because judging is only one of the many tasks of the governing cadre. In societies that seek to create independent judiciaries, however, this reintegration will nonetheless occur, even at substantial costs to the proclaimed goal of judicial independence. Thus in the United States there has been a long debate over elected versus appointed judiciaries, with the key question being the extent to which judges ought to be subordinated to the democratic political regime. This debate is ultimately unresolvable because it involves two conflicting goals: one, that triadic conflict resolvers be independent; two, that lawmakers be responsible to the people. Indeed it is because judging inevitably involves lawmaking and social control as well as conflict resolution that the tendency of judging to be closely associated with sovereignty or ultimate political authority, noted early in this discussion, is to be found in all societies.

Clearly, where judicial lawmaking occurs, adversary proceedings are something of a facade. If the judge is consciously seeking to formulate general rules for future application, his considerations must range far beyond the immediate clash of interests of the two parties. The whole development of the "Brandeis brief," with its parade of "legislative" facts, that is, facts about general social conditions as opposed to the immediate facts of the dispute, is an open acknowledgment by bench and bar that the parties are essentially an example or sample of the social reality to be legislated upon rather than disputants whose conflict is to be resolved. Even where judicial lawmaking is less conscious or more surreptitious, the creation of general rules necessarily involves looking well beyond the two parties typically by the vehicle of appealing to custom, reasonableness, common sense, business necessity, fairness, or some other similar cover for considerations of general social utility.

Case-by-Case Lawmaking and the Prototype

Most obviously, case-by-case judicial lawmaking violates the prototype's demand for preexisting legal rules. There has recently been considerable interest in prospective overruling (Mishkin and Morris, 1965; Friedman, 1966). This interest has been coupled with calls for more rule making and less case-by-case lawmaking by administrative agencies. At the base of both movements has been the feeling that a party should not be told that his past actions have been legally incorrect because of a legal rule that has been discovered subsequent to his actions. Indeed, the legal rule is typically discovered in the very process of deciding whether his past actions were correct or not. This uneasiness has arisen primarily in constitutional and regulatory agency adjudication. It is in these areas of American law that case-by-case lawmaking is most dramatically evident and thus where the prototype of courts is most clearly challenged. Yet the basic tension between lawmaking and the prototype exists in many other areas of law as well.

Indeed it is difficult to understand why the prototype has been so popular among Anglo-American commentators. For the common-law system openly proclaims that its principal virtue is lawmaking through case-by-case adjudication. Then the resolution of conflict proceeds, not by preexisting rules, but by rules discovered in the very course of resolving the conflict. Thus there is an important element of retroactivity in common-law-style lawmaking. The individual disputant does not know what rule will govern his actions until after he has acted. The rule is announced in the course of the litigation subsequent to his act.

Generally, common-law systems tend to cover their deviation from the prototype of preexisting norms by two rationales. The first is the familiar one, that common law is essentially the ordinances of right reason indwelling in the race, or at least in the legal profession, and that new legal decisions only discover or draw forth the principle that has existed all along. Although a yearning for such principles still permeates the common-law ideology, no one any longer believes that judicial lawmakers simply discover and apply the ancient legal principle. The second, or "gray area," rationale is more realistic. In effect it admits that judges make new law for current cases but stresses the incremental nature of such decision making. There is a large body of well-settled statutory and case law. There are also some gray areas in which the law is not yet clearly settled and in which new case law is reasonably to be expected. The individual enters the gray area at his own risk. That is, where he commits acts that are at the edges of preexisting law, he consciously takes the chance that when the new law is announced it will run against him. This rationale is most likely to arise in precisely those cases in which new legal rules are announced that could not have been easily anticipated and that turn out to be highly unfavorable to one of the parties. Indeed, quite typically such a new rule is announced precisely because the judge wishes to extend the law to discourage future conduct of the sort engaged in by one of the parties. In the course of doing so, however, the initial conduct is penalized just as if there had been a law against it before it occurred.

Common-law judicial lawmaking is only the most dramatic example of the more general phenomenon, however. So long as societies entrust courts with case-by-case lawmaking powers, and nearly all societies do, then conflict resolution cannot proceed solely by reference to preexisting legal rules. And where conflict resolution does not proceed by preexisting rules or, alternatively, by rules mutually consented to by the parties, then the loser of a case may well perceive himself to have been legislated against rather than impartially resolved. This fundamental deviation from the prototype is unavoidable. Judicial lawmaking necessarily creates a fundamental tension between courts and their basic social logic.

THE LOGIC OF COURTS

To briefly summarize then. The basic social logic, or perceived legitimacy, of courts rests on the mutual consent of two persons in conflict to refer that conflict to a third for resolution. This basic logic is threatened by the substitution of office and law for mutual consent, both because one of the two parties may perceive the third as the ally of his enemy and because a third interest, that of the regime, is introduced. Even within the realm of judicial conflict resolutions, no rigid prototype of court is applicable to the real world. Along one dimension we find a continuum of go-between—moderator—arbitrator—judge, in which most of those officials we normally label judges engage in a great deal of moderation and arbitration. Along another dimension we discover that most triadic conflict resolvers are deeply embedded in the general political machinery of their regimes and that the administrator or general big man as judge is far more typical than the holder of a separable judicial office. When we move from courts as conflict resolvers to courts as social controllers, their social logic and their independence is even further undercut. For in this realm, while proceeding in the guise of triadic conflict resolver, courts clearly operate to impose outside interests on the parties. Finally, in the realm of judicial lawmaking, courts move furthest from their social logic and the conventional prototype because the rules they apply in the resolution of conflicts between two parties are neither directly consented to by the parties nor "preexisting" but instead are created by the third in the course of the conflict resolution itself. Thus, while the triadic mode of conflict resolution is nearly universal, courts remain problematical in the sense that considerable tension invariably exists between their fundamental claims to legitimacy and their actual operations.

TRIAL COURTS AND APPELLATE COURTS—FACT-FINDING

So far we have not differentiated between trial and appellate courts, but it is useful to do so for certain purposes. Both trial and appellate courts make law. Both trial and appellate courts find facts. This latter point requires some clarification, given the normal American practice, which is that appellate courts are to hear questions of law but not questions of fact, which are left to the trial court. A similar practice obtains in many other common-law jurisdictions and in most European legal systems. However, side by side with this appellate division of fact and law, we find many other legal systems that use or have used trial de novo as the standard mode of appeal. Where appeal is by trial de novo, the appellate court simply hears the whole case all over again. Trial de novo is found in most nonliterate societies, no doubt in large part because of the difficulty of preserving trial court findings of fact to serve as a basis for appellate decision. But it is also used in Great Britain and a number of other industrialized countries, and remnants of it are to be found in many American states. In advanced societies it frequently does not take the form of a complete rehearing of oral testimony but instead involves appellate court review of the trial court record and then its own independent findings of fact. In the United States, trial de novo is usually a device for bringing cases from minor courts of incomplete jurisdiction and incomplete juridical status into higher courts of general jurisdiction and completely judicialized procedures. For instance in Massachusetts, a defendant in minor felonies may choose to appear in the municipal courts, whose jurisdiction and sentencing powers are limited, whose judges need not be lawyers, and where prosecution is typically handled by the police rather than by a professional prosecutor. Should he be convicted, he may appeal for trial de novo to the Superior Court, which is a fully professionalized trial court of general criminal jurisdiction.

Trial de novo would therefore appear to be something more than a necessity forced on preliterate societies. This becomes even more clear when we note the extreme reluctance of non–de novo appellate courts to confine themselves to pure issues of law. In the United States the distinction between questions of fact and questions of law, which is supposed to be the key to the limits of appellate jurisdiction, is a notoriously slippery one. It is so slippery that a whole new category, "mixed questions of fact and law," has been invented. In reality that category defines the huge number of instances in which appellate courts have refused to accept trial court findings of fact and substituted their own fact-finding under the guise of law finding. The Supreme Court has long held that it will make its own findings of "constitutional fact," that is, of facts necessary to determine a basic constitutional question. But constitutional facts are often the same routine facts that the trial court has already decided. For instance, let us suppose a trial court has determined that a given speech did incite a riot and so convicts a speaker of incitement to riot. The Supreme Court will, under the constitutional fact doctrine, redetermine exactly the same factual question in determining on appeal the constitutional issue of whether the speech constituted such a clear and present danger of serious social evil that its repression might be justified in the face of the First Amendment's guarantees of free speech.

This pull of appellate courts toward the facts can also be seen in the endless proliferation in the United States, Great Britain, and on the Continent of statutes, rules, and practices about how much evidence a trial court or administrative agency must have to support its decisions. Typically there has been pressure from the legislature or the courts themselves to keep appellate courts from substituting their own fact-finding for that of the decision maker who hears the evidence in the first instance. Two basic rationales underlie this pressure. One is that the first instance trier actually sees and hears the witnesses, examines the physical evidence, and is simply closer in space and time to the disputed events than the appeals court that sees only a printed record. The second, particularly important where administrative agencies are the first-instance trier, is that the agencies are more competent to find facts in the highly specialized areas of their expertise than are appeals courts staffed by nonspecialist judges. This pressure manifests itself in various rules requiring appellate courts to pay various levels of deference to initial fact-finding by others. In the United States there are generally three grades of deference, although similar standards in different verbal formulations are to be found in other countries. Indeed the verbal formulations are far from uniform even in the United States. The strictest standard of deference is the "no evidence" rule used by the Supreme Court in review of state court fact-finding and the "some evidence" rule involved frequently where courts are reviewing agency fact-finding. The Supreme Court announces that it will reverse state courts on the facts in criminal cases only when the state record contains "no evidence" supporting conviction. While in theory this would mean that the presence of even a single bit of evidence tending to show guilt would be sufficient to obviate review, in practice the Court has sometimes found that what others would consider quite a bit of evidence turns out to be "no evidence." Similarly courts frequently say that they will not reverse on factual grounds an agency's decisions in areas of its peculiar expertise unless the record is totally devoid of agency fact-findings supporting its decision. In other words so long as the agency can show some evidence in support of its decision, the court will not make its own judgment as to where the preponderance of evidence lies.

The next lower standard of deference is the "substantial evidence" rule, which in various verbal formulations and degrees of severity has become the most typical rule of judicial review of agency fact-finding throughout the Western world. The court will look to see if an administrative agency has developed a substantial body of evidence in support of its decision, but it will not weigh the evidence of one side against that on the other and substitute its own judgment for that of the agency as to where the preponderance of evidence lies.

The lowest standard of deference is a "preponderance of evidence" rule. Under such a rule appellate courts generally purport to give great weight to first-instance fact-finding but nonetheless strike their own final balance of the weight of evidence on each side. Of course legislatures may seek to prevent court review of agency fact-finding altogether by providing that their decisions are final and unreviewable.

But why does this whole body of jurisprudence arise in legal systems that employ the general rule that appellate courts should not redetermine facts? Obviously because there is such a strong thrust in appellate courts toward fact-finding that it cannot be contained by the general rule. And that thrust occurs because while the principal job of appellate courts is lawmaking, they continuously seek to reiterate their connection with the basis of all judicial legitimacy, conflict resolution. So long as appellate courts do their lawmaking under the guise of doing substantial justice between man and man in particular cases—and they must do this if they are to be perceived as and supported as courts—they will keep clawing their way back toward the facts. For disputes about the facts are at the root of a large proportion of the conflicts to be resolved.

At the very opposite pole of appellate fact-finding lies the distinction between judicial and legislative fact. In theory courts are supposed to confine themselves to the particular facts of the particular case. And because they are supposed to follow adversary proceedings, they are supposed to limit themselves to consideration of the facts presented by the two parties rather than ranging broadly over social data in a way permissible to legislatures drafting new laws. These limitations, rooted as they are in the conflict-resolution aspect of judicial activity, work in a rough and ready way for trial courts. Where appellate court lawmaking is involved, they hardly work at all. Whether it be dressed in the language of American sociological jurisprudence, Continental free decision making, or a tribal chief's commonsense concern with preserving his authority, it is clear that where an appellate body seeks to formulate a legal rule, it must consider the fit of that rule to the society at large, not just to the two contending parties. In most societies the arguments presented to courts have either presumed or injected a great deal of general knowledge of the operation of the society. Courts usually hold that even the adversary model does not require them to be blind to what any fool can plainly see just because neither party got it into evidence. Doctrines like judicial notice have allowed either one of the parties or the judge himself to assume widely known social facts without proving them.

In the United States the "Brandeis brief," first invented for the special purpose of defending state regulatory statutes against constitutional attack, has now blossomed forth in nearly every instance in which an appellate court is in reality being asked to make new law. Today's brief on an environmental, desegregation, apportionment, or welfare issue frequently contains exactly the same data in exactly the same format as would a presentation to a congressional committee. The United States no doubt represents the extreme case. But on narrower fronts, for instance in the willingness of English and Continental courts to hear evidence on general commercial practices, most courts find some way of touching base with general social reality. Of course this is as true of trial as appellate courts, but the issue of just what range of facts a court may hear arises most dramatically at appellate levels because appeals court lawmaking in rivalry to legislatures is much clearer than that of trial courts.

Trial Courts as Fact Finders

In spite of all these obvious connections of appellate courts to facts, it is still possible to focus on the trial as one of society's basic devices for finding facts (Frank, 1949). Just how good trial proceedings are as a fact-finding device is a perennial question but also a misleading one if put too generally. It must always be remembered that the basic aim of a trial is to resolve a conflict or impose social controls, not to find the facts. Much of what may appear to be unsatisfactory as pure fact-finding, if we were applying general scientific canons for empirical inquiry, may be quite satisfactory in the specific context of trials.

The early stages of the English legal system and many tribal legal systems employed trial by ordeal, oath, combat, or divination. Explanation of these forms of trials in quasi-scientific terms is not totally incorrect. No doubt reference of factual issues to the Divinity, who was thought to be omnisciently willing to intervene in ordeals and combats in behalf of the person wronged, was a form of striving after accurate and complete fact-finding. And various physiological rationales for ordeal, such as that lying produces a dry mouth incapable of tolerating hot pebbles thrust in it, are also no doubt partially correct. Above all it is clear that reference of a factual dispute to the gods or to ordeal will lead many parties who believe in the efficacy of these modes of inquiry and who know they have misrepresented the facts to change their stories or withdraw from the litigation.

However, quite apart from these attempts to bring primitive modes of fact-finding into accord with modern notions of empirical inquiry, the oath and ordeals can be seen as serving the specific purposes of trials even where they were not the most reliable form of inquiry. In the context of conflict resolution, the major virtue of a trial is that it provides a definitive point of termination to the conflict. The conclusion of a trial allows the disputants to stop trying to get even with one another. In this sense it is more important that a termination be provided than that a just solution be reached. For the endless continuation of a dispute often creates psychological, social, and/or economic costs that neither the parties nor the society is prepared to bear. The oath or ordeal provided both a catharsis and a dramatic climax which assisted in providing termination. Instead of leaving factual issues dangling, they were decided once and for all.

Even legal systems that seem to rely heavily on supernatural modes of factual inquiry are likely to employ them only as the culmination of more commonplace methods of inquiry. In most such systems the litigants are permitted to first tell their own stories and/or bring witnesses. Members of the community may also be heard. Thus something like a trial in the sense of a factual inquiry typically takes place before the trial in the sense of the oath, ordeal, or combat. Not always, but typically, the real power of the court is its discretion in assigning the ultimate burden of proof to one or the other of the two parties. In some instances, for instance when the ultimate proof is a simple sworn oath, whoever gets the burden is very likely to win the case. In others, for instance when the ultimate proof is carrying live coals without being burned, whoever gets the burden almost surely loses. So long as the court assigns the burden, however, it can do so in such a way as to favor the party whom the weight of empirical evidence gathered at the preliminary stage seems to favor. That is why we may encounter one society in which a man is in the wrong if a hot rock burns his hand, and another in which he is in the wrong if it does not, and then also discover that trials seem to do substantial justice in both. Preliminary factual inquiry, plus the discretion to assign the supernatural burden of proof, plus the perceived definitiveness of such modes of truth may provide a mode of fact-finding roughly as accurate and far more likely to lead to the essential termination of conflict than would a simple factual inquiry alone.

The universal history of the rules of evidence is far too complex a subject to review here. As we emerge from dependence on supernatural assistance, the central problem of judicial fact-finding is the problem of certainty. Testimony under oath is often the transitional stage. For the oath is in one sense an ordeal inviting divine intervention and in another an attempt to ensure more reliable human testimony. The medieval English practice of oath helping is instructive. The oath helpers were not witnesses who supported a disputant's assertion of fact from their own knowledge of the facts but persons who testified to the general reputation for veracity of the witness by standing forth to share his oath and the risk of divine retribution, which was the lot of the false swearer. At the same time oath helpers were unlikely to be forthcoming if the disputant's story rang false to the community.

Once confidence of divine intervention in routine trials is reduced, problems of credibility and weight of evidence arise. Few human societies have found probabilistic treatment of evidence morally satisfying. This is one of the many reasons so many triadic conflict resolvers resort to mediation of one sort or another. For mediation obviates the need to establish an agreed version of the facts. Most trial courts, of course, pretend to a certainty that they know is not there. And, as in medieval Continental criminal litigation, if a real need for absolute certainty is felt by courts, the results may be untoward. It is probable that Continental reliance on torture of the accused in part derived from the reluctance of judges to convict on any other basis but confession, which was one of the few certain ways to establish the facts of a crime.

Where fact-finding is done in the context of conflict resolution, reliance is typically placed on the stories told by the two disputants. The use of witnesses and physical evidence comes late in the development of legal procedures and is usually sporadic and incomplete. In part this is because the gathering of such evidence is expensive and time consuming. Thus even in advanced industrial societies, small claims courts aimed at quick, cheap disposition will usually operate on little more than the disputants' testimony. In part the reluctance to hear "outside" evidence rests on the fear of manufactured or falsified evidence, which is understandable where courts must rely on evidence brought in by the parties rather than developed by their own investigations. At least the judge may directly observe the demeanor of the party giving testimony. The well-known contrast between English and French legal developments illustrates this point. Until at least the eighteenth century, English courts were so reluctant to accept anything other than direct parole (spoken) evidence that they were severely hampered in resolving many kinds of disputes, particularly commercial ones in which ledgers, bills of lading, etc., were often crucial. French courts on the other hand proceeded by Romanist procedure, which involved almost no parole evidence and relied almost exclusively on written interrogatories and responses and the examination of documents. But the Royal Courts of England consisted of a mere handful of judges, while medieval France developed a huge judicial bureaucracy to gather, digest, and evaluate evidence.

In the seventeenth century notions of probability or relative certainty seem to develop side by side in theology, science, and law (B. Shapiro, 1969). In Western societies a trial gradually comes to be seen as an empirical investigation designed to determine the weight of evidence on each side rather than as an attempt to discover the absolute truth. This progression from the search for absolute truth by divine intervention up to modern notions of balance of evidence should not be taken, however, as a necessary or universal phenomenon.

Ethnographic materials show us some tribal judges who seek to assert definitive fact-finding capacity while others openly admit to weighing or balancing the evidence and picking the more convincing story.

With notions of weighing evidence, however, Western law develops a new, policy-oriented discretion similar to the earlier discretion involved in assigning the "trial" or "proof" to one or another of the litigants. In civil cases, where conflict resolution is the dominant mode, most legal systems hold the burden of proof even, the victory going to the party with the preponderance of evidence. Where social control is the dominant mode, as in criminal law, all sorts of shifts in the balance of proof may be made for policy reasons. To an extent these shifts may even predate the development of notions of probabilistic proof. For instance in medieval England, where treason and certain other crimes that the regime particularly wished to crush were involved, the defendant was forbidden to make a statement under oath, thus cutting him off from the best mode of establishing the certainty of his story.

Presumptions, burdens of proof, and per se rules are the standard form for manipulating factual issues to achieve policy goals (Shapiro, 1964). The easiest example is the presumption of innocence and the burden to prove beyond a reasonable doubt in modern Anglo-American criminal law. Just as the medieval English law made it more difficult for certain defendants to prove their innocence, so modern law makes it more difficult for the state to prove their guilt. The presumption of innocence is not some fixed truth but a declaration of social policy. For various reasons we prefer to make it easier for the criminal accused than for the state.

Where social control is involved, however, there are numerous instances in which it appears preferable to shift the burden of proof in the other direction. The per se rules frequently encountered in American labor and antitrust law are good examples. When a court says that a tieing agreement is a conspiracy in restraint of trade per se, it is simply relieving the government of the burden of proving that the accused's actual conduct did in fact constitute such a conspiracy. Courts and legislatures can make very fine adjustments in burden of proof, for instance by making a presumption rebuttable or irrebuttable.

Behind this politics of fact-finding lies the fundamental reality that courts are far from perfect fact finders. Those who have contravened social controls are often in an excellent position to conceal the facts of their misdeeds from courts, particularly when they are themselves organizations of great resources like corporations or unions, or cabals of treasonous barons. On the other hand, many of those who fall afoul of social controls have so few resources that they can hardly be expected to develop the necessary facts for their own defense. Thus the adjustment of the fact-finding *incapacities* of courts to the relative power of those subjected to social controls is itself a significant aspect of social control and ultimately of political authority.

THE USES OF APPEAL

As we noted earlier, one of the principal virtues of a trial is that it provides an official termination to conflict, relieving the disputants of the necessity of further reciprocal assertions or retributions. But too much finality may be disturbing to the losing member of the triad. One of the major functions of a "right of appeal" is to provide a psychological outlet and a social cover for the loser at trial (Becker, 1970). For appeal allows the loser to continue to assert his rightness in the abstract without attacking the legitimacy of the legal system or refusing to obey the trial court. Indeed the loser's displeasure is funnelled into a further assertion of the legitimacy of the legal system because appealing to a higher court entails the acknowledgment of its legitimacy.

We also noted earlier that the principal problem of the triadic form of conflict resolution was keeping the loser from perceiving the final situation as "two against one." Appeals mechanisms are devices for telling the loser that if he believes that it did turn out two against one, he may try another triadic figure. Perhaps just as important, the availability of appeal allows the loser to accept his loss without having to publicly acknowledge it. The purpose of a trial is to effect a termination of conflict. But too abrupt a termination may be counterproductive of true conflict resolution. Appeal, whether actually exercised, threatened, or only held in reserve, avoids adding insult to injury. The loser can leave the courtroom with his head high talking of appeal and then accept his loss, slowly, privately, and passively by failing to actually make an appeal. Generally we concentrate on these aspects of appeal and look at it principally as a mode of ensuring against the venality, prejudice, and/or ignorance of trial court judges and of soothing the ruffled feelings of the loser. Appeal does indeed serve these functions, but it does so by the imposition of hierarchical controls on trial court behavior. A great deal of interest to political scientists lurks in that hierarchical element.

We have already noted that in a predominant share of the governing systems that have existed in the world, judging is either a facet of or closely aligned with administration, particularly administration in the field. It is a commonplace of administrative lore that no matter what the theory, Weberian hierarchies do not give the top or center adequate control over rank and file administrators in the field unless a number of alternative channels of information are available that can be cross-checked at or near the top. The best-known modern example is obviously the Soviet Union, with its trade union, government, party, control commission, and police hierarchies superimposed on one another. Where administrators hold courts, appeal becomes such a mechanism of control. A "right" of appeal is a mechanism providing an independent flow of information to the top on the field performance of administrative subordinates. Moreover, precisely because the form of appeal is a "case," appeal provides a partially random sample of highly concrete data on day-to-day performance which can be set against the typically general and summary performance data provided by administrative subordinates to their superiors.

Of course, where there is a separate judicial hierarchy, appeal is typically the central mode of supervision by higher courts over lower, and reversal on appeal a central form of administrative sanction. In such instances the need for multiple channels of information and control leads the top to demand other institutions in addition to appeal, such as judicial conferences, centralized personnel systems, and administrative reporting, to increase their contol over their subordinates.

The insistence, so frequently encountered, that the chain of appeal eventually arrive at the chief, the king, or the capitol, instead of stopping at some intermediate level, is difficult to explain except in terms of centralized political control. If the only function of appeal were to ensure against corruptness or arbitrariness on the part of the trial judge, then appeal to anyone even a single step higher in the scale of authority would be sufficient. The top insists on being the ultimate level of appeal because it serves its purposes, not those of a losing disputant.

Of course just as one of the functions of any appeal is to reduce the psychic shock to losers, so the right to "take the case all the way to the Supreme Court" provides even greater catharsis for the loser whether he employs it only rhetorically or actually does it. Yet even at this personal level, and quite apart from the question of hierarchical control, the top is likely to see advantages in preserving a right of ultimate appeal. Earlier we noted that the extension of judicial services outward and downward is a device for wedding the countryside to the regime. So the preservation of appeal to the chief-king-emperor-capitol is a device for keeping the strings of legitimacy tied directly between the ruled and the person of the ruler or the highest institutions of government. Conversely the ability to occasionally reach down into the most particular affairs of the countryside provides an important means of reminding the rank and file that the rulers are everywhere, that no one may use his insignificance or his embeddedness in the mass to hide from central authority. Thus the personal ruler, be he Zulu war chief or medieval monarch, rarely totally gives up his personal participation in appeals. Nor do modern central governments often provide that there be only a single appeal from trial court to regional appeals court without any opportunity to go on to a central appeals court.

Even if judges did nothing but conflict resolution, appeal would be an important political mechanism both for increasing the level of central control over administrative subordinates and ensuring the authority and legitimacy of rulers. When we enter the realms of social control and lawmaking, the multiple functions of appeal are even more apparent. Where trial courts or first-instance judging by administrators is used as a mode of social control, appeal is a mechanism for central coordination of local control. The "questions of law" passed on to the appeals courts are in reality requests for uniform rules of social conduct and indicators of what range of case-by-case deviation by first-line controllers from those rules is permissible.

A partial breakdown of this supervisory mechanism is largely responsible for the wave of discontent with American criminal courts. In most Western criminal law systems there can be no appeal after a plea of guilty. Something over 90 percent of American criminal cases are settled by a guilty plea or its equivalent, frequently as a result of specific or tacit plea bargaining. As we have noted, appeals courts do not normally consider questions of fact. In the United States "disposition," or sentencing, that is, the decision as to what to do with the person of the convicted criminal, is not normally reviewable by appellate courts.

These three factors combine to create a major anomaly, at least within the Western political and administrative tradition. The basic business of American criminal courts is not the triadic resolution of disputes cast in the form of the *People* v. *John Doe*. And this is quite apart from the point that casting criminal law enforcement in this ritual form of conflict between individual and the state is a transparent fiction. Most American trial courts rarely bother even with the ritual of trial. Their time is spent in disposing of the bodies of those who have pled guilty. Thus they are clearly administrators distributing the scarce sanctioning and rehabilitative resources of society among a mass of "applicants." In this sense trial courts have ceased to be courts.

This absorption of "courts" in administrative tasks is not particularly surprising or alarming in view of the natural affinities between judging and administration that we have repeatedly noted. The anomaly arises precisely because we persist in formally viewing these administrative tasks as judicial. As a result we get an enormous volume of particularized administrative discretion without any of the hierarchical supervision we normally exercise over low-level administrators. In short, what trial courts really do, sentence, is not subject to appellate court review. And because trial courts are *courts* in a political system that endorses judicial independence, they are not subject to any other form of hierarchical supervision. Thus they are one of the few agencies of government in which rank-and-file operators are subject to almost no supervision at all in the wielding of enormous discretion. Imagine the loss in legitimacy that any bureaucratic agency would suffer if the clients were told that the clerks at the windows had broad discretion and their decisions were not reviewable by their superiors.

This American situation is an example of the need to focus clearly on appeal as a mode of hierarchical political management, as well as a guarantee of fairness to the accused, if we are to understand the actual operation of real political systems.

In this context social control and lawmaking are usually intimately connected. Appeal is not simply a device for ensuring a certain uniformity in the operations of rank-and-file social controllers. It also ensures that they are following rules or laws or policies of social control acceptable to the regime. Indeed appeal is a key mechanism in injecting centralized social control into the conflict-resolution activities of courts as well. For appeal is the channel through which the central political authority assures itself that its rank-and-file conflict resolvers are applying legal rules that resolve conflicts in the desired directions. Earlier we noted that the substitution of legislated law for rules created by the mutual consent of the parties introduced a third set of interests into two-party litigation, whatever interests were embodied in the legislation. At least in large and complex societies, trial courts are too many and too localized to articulate this third set satisfactorily. Appellate courts are more suitable.

Tort serves as a good example. Where social policy is stationary, trial courts will finally dispose of most tort cases. The reasonable-man doctrine applied by juries will impose sanctions on those who deviate from commonly accepted standards of conduct. The parties will see their conflict as existing within fairly clearly preestablished rules, enunciated in the pattern of previous cases. It will be resolved by a judgment of their peers as to who was at fault or more at fault. However, where new social and economic policies are to be introduced, appellate courts will become active, enunciating new tort doctrines, or theories, and creating or plugging exceptions to existing rules. Thus during the rapid industrialization of the United States in the nineteenth century, when allocating the costs of industrial accidents became an important economic issue, the high courts of the states created or expanded the contributory negligence and fellow-servant rules and the doctrine of assumed risk. Trial courts still resolved conflicts between employer and injured worker and controlled deviations from accepted standards of proper industrial conduct. But they now did so within a set of overarching doctrines that injected the national interest in industrial growth as a counterweight to the interests of injured workers (Friedman, 1973).

In the United States, where the jury is usually the decider of both facts and law in civil cases, there is a special symptom of the incursion of central policies on local courts. Appeals courts cannot normally review trial court fact-finding. The only written record of trial court law finding is the judge's instructions to the jury. Appeals courts wishing to impose their policies will begin quashing trial court judgments on the basis of faulty jury instructions. Trial courts will then begin framing their instructions to meet the demands of the appeals courts. If the appeals courts remain dissatisfied with the substantive outcomes in trial courts—with which interests are favored—they will find fault with even the new and more careful instructions. As the process continues, jury instructions will become too technical and complex to really guide jurors. However they will serve as a battleground where no matter what he says to the jury, the trial judge is threatened with reversal if he does not achieve outcomes satisfactory to the central authorities (Shapiro, 1970).

On the broadest scale, of course, constitutional review by the highest appeals courts in federal systems has been a principal device of centralized policy-making, as for instance with school desegregation in the United States. And appeal has been used in highly centralized political systems such as that in France as one of numerous routine mechanisms for controlling and coordinating government agents in the field. Appeals courts can and do act in this capacity whether they are themselves doing a great deal of lawmaking or acting as enforcers of law made by others. An interesting variant is the sending of trial judges on "circuit" from the capitol or the insistence that suitors travel to the capitol for trial, both important tactics of the medieval English monarchs for centralizing political authority. It is because England had this special overlay of national trial courts, above the essentially local county and baronial courts, that a large proportion of English common law has been made by what are technically trial courts, while most of American judicial lawmaking occurs in appeals courts. Similarly, much of the Roman *jus gentium* was made in what was formally a trial court setting, but by the praetor peregrinus, an imperial judge sitting in Rome to hear disputes among the lesser people of the empire (Schlesinger, 1959). Far more typical are the arrangements of the nineteenth and twentieth century European-based empires, all of which provided for appeal either to a high court sitting in the metropolis or a territorial high court employing metropolitan law and/or staffed by judges trained as imperial servants. The British system of appeal to the Privy Council is the best-known example (Abraham, 1968).

Quite obviously, if there is any level of judicial lawmaking within a territorially dispersed system of courts, then a pyramid of appeal is necessary in order to assure that any central body of law is relatively uniformly administered throughout its domain. For instance, in spite of its onerous constitutional duties, the United States Supreme Court devotes about 40 percent of its opinions to creating uniform interpretations among the intermediate federal courts of appeal. In a unitary (as opposed to federal) non-common-law state, in which courts do not enjoy the power to declare laws unconstitutional and in which intermediate appellate courts exist, about the only rationale possible for the existence of a high court of appeal is the need for uniformity of statutory interpretation, and that indeed does seem to be the major task of most Continental high courts.

To emphasize this function, however, is to assert that most high courts of appeal are barely courts at all. That is, while in form they may be engaged in finally resolving one particular dispute between two particular litigants, their principal role may be to provide uniform rules of law. Naturally such rules must be based on considerations far broader than the concerns of the two litigants, essentially on considerations of public policy that may have little to do with the particular litigation. At worst the litigants are irrelevant—at best they are examples or samples of the general problem to be solved. Political science has tended to concentrate on appellate courts. Appellate courts are the furthest removed from the basic social logic of courts. As a result courts appear far more problematic to political science than they do to the citizenry. Nevertheless the study of appellate courts makes clear that courts always exist in a state of tension between their basic source of legitimacy as consensual triadic resolvers of conflict and their position as government agencies imposing law on the citizenry. To put this matter somewhat differently, the social legitimacy of courts as a universal social device for conflict resolution and the political legitimacy of courts as a particular segment of a particular political regime are sometimes additive and mutually supportive and sometimes quite the contrary.

POPULAR COURTS

Early in this discussion we noted a certain natural affinity between judging and administration, or that judging is normally one of the functions of ruling elites or simply "big men." The extended discussion of appeal tends to further emphasize the elite element. Therefore it might be well to conclude this discussion of courts with some discussion of popular elements in judging. It is doubtful, however, that very many societies experienced much pure popular judging. The Greek jury and its Roman derivative, chosen by lot under procedures that ensured the representation of all the genetic components of the society, probably came the closest in form to complete democracy. But these juries typically operated in highly politicized contexts, subject to constraints and manipulations that reflected a far from democratic basic political structure. They may have represented a popular element in Greek and Roman governance, but they are far from a pure form of judging by the people.

The folkmoot, in which judgment is theoretically rendered by the whole people, is encountered in a number of societies. Whatever patterns of social and political hierarchy existed in the society at large no doubt were reflected at the moot as well. Far more common than the moot as such is judging by the chief, or the chief and his advisors, or the elders, *surrounded by* a participant audience of the people. The audience may participate in a number of ways. First it may be an important channel of fact-finding. Either individually or collectively, and by specific testimony or general demeanor, the audience may convey to the judges information on specific facts, local customs and usages, and on the good character of litigants and witnesses. Secondly, they may provide important levels of judicial enforcement. Their presence may be a strong incentive to the litigants to behave properly before the court. They will remember its judgment when the losing litigant seeks to forget it. And they may provide social pressure toward obedience to the court's decree. Most importantly they are likely to provide strong pressure toward consensual behavior, superficial or real, on the part of the litigants. Even where judges cannot arrive at a mediatory settlement, truly satisfying both parties, the presence of the people may elicit a "good citizen" or "good sport" consent from the loser and subsequently may hold him to that consent on pain of loss of his moral reputation. Thirdly, the popular audience may serve as the receptacle for the received legal tradition or a sounding board for the invention of new legal rules. In practice no distinction is likely to be made between the two—the judges simply make trial enunciations of the "law" and see how they play to the audience. Finally, by its participation the audience attests to the legitimacy of the judges—that they are perceived as holding judicial office—and links the court to the affective and effective world of local affairs, a particularly important function if the judges are themselves envoys from a distant central regime.

Modern court systems reflect this popular, participatory role in many different ways. The grand and petit juries employed in common-law judicial systems are remnants of the employment of local citizens to provide the facts to judges on circuit from the capital. Later they came to be seen as popular checks on the administration of justice by professional elites (Kalven and Zeisel, 1966). In Roman-law countries, where the jury is largely foreign, mixed panels of lay and professional judges have sometimes been introduced for similar reasons. Imperial powers sometimes employ mixed panels of metropolitan and native judges, in part to provide some element of local participation in government and in part to provide expertise on native law. Whenever a central legal system is attempting to absorb or make use of local, idiosyncratic, or specialized bodies of laws, customs, usages, or technologies, it may add representatives of the specialized communities to the regular judicial staff. Thus medieval courts both in England and the Continent sometimes employed panels of merchants or craftsmen to assist in commercial and technological litigation. The privileged position of expert witnesses to offer the court opinion evidence is a similar device. The alternative is extraterritoriality or other forms of judicial enclaves, in which merchants, tribesmen, town dwellers, men of the sea, religious sects, etc., are allowed special courts partially or wholly divorced from the general judicial system.

In all these instances the need for special factual and/or legal expertise and the need to increase the legitimacy and penetrating power of the courts in resistant enclaves can be met simultaneously by provisions for community participation. Such participation, however, runs partially against the capacity of the court system to wed local elements to a central regime and so is often an intermediate stage that tends either to disappear as the national government becomes stronger or, to be transmitted into a general democratic safeguard as the jury has in England.

A similar set of dynamics is encountered in the use of lay as opposed to professional judges (Dawson, 1960). The distinction only superficially rests in the absence or presence of formal legal training. Its real significance is in the relative independence from or incorporation into a government personnel system with its capacity for disciplining subordinates. The English justice of the peace system, the American use of nonlawyers as local magistrates, and the encouragement or toleration of village elder courts by many governments ruling over peasant populations are major examples of lay judging. Such courts provide a cheap means of thrusting law down into the local communities. The countryside rather than the regime pays the lion's share of the costs of the administration of justice, usually in the form of unpaid or low-paid time devoted to judging by local, prominent men. As against the cheapness of this device must be balanced the reduced capacity of the regime to control such judges as opposed to professional local judges at the lowest step on a career ladder, who must look to the central authorities for promotion. Thus in some instances, most notably that of the English justices of the peace, the institutions of lay judging may be a successful device for exploiting the pool of judicial and administrative skills in the countryside, while in others it may be part of a deliberate refusal or failure of a central regime to push its legal controls and services down into that countryside.

As we noted earlier, the other side of the coin of the capacity to control professional judges by controlling their career patterns may be the resistance of a professional judicial corps to government policies contrary to its conception of law and justice. One variant of lay judging, the "people's courts" of communist regimes, seems specifically designed to deal with this problem. As with many other communist institutions, this one varies markedly between the revolutionary stage and the stage of consolidation of the new regime. During the revolution, people's courts are little more' than the borrowing of a familiar, legitimate form through which to identify local noncommunist populations with the destruction of the class enemy. By requiring the people, as an egalitarian mass under the leadership of communist cadres, to directly participate in the murders and expropriations of the landlords and capitalists and to share in the distribution of the spoils, the people's courts serve as an integral part of the revolutionary process itself. Their ritualized violence breaks old social structures and loyalties, brings to the fore the most violent, malicious, and alienated, and openly fastens responsibility for the revolutionary acts on the participants.

Once a communist regime is established, people's courts serve more court-like purposes, largely in the mediatory solution of minor disputes between fellow workers or fellow tenants who must maintain day to day relations with one another. For more serious or complex disputes and in criminal matters, the use of people's courts has varied with the "stage" of popular revolutionary participation the regime has been encouraging at a particular moment. In most communist states people's courts retain some minor criminal jurisdiction. But over the long haul they tend to coexist with strong procuracies, which combine investigative and judicial functions, and a formal criminal court system. The Chinese have used people's courts very prominently (Cohen, 1968), but in the Soviet Union and Eastern Europe a wide range of arbitration tribunals, administrative tribunals, professionally staffed courts, courts martial, and police tribunals has grown up to do most "regular" judicial business as well as administer the terror (Berman, 1963).

No doubt people's courts have certain ideological advantages and are particularly appropriate to the system of massive mutual surveillance encouraged by communist regimes. Modern noncommunist societies, however, have also proliferated small claims courts, domestic relations and juvenile tribunals, industrial and commercial arbitration panels, housing courts, counseling services, and administrative boards that handle a great deal of conflict resolution and social control through quasi-judicial proceedings but without professional judges or outside of the normal forms of litigation. People's courts, often in conjunction with people's "militia," can perform many similar functions.

If we ground our notion of courts in the triadic structure of conflict resolution, a wide range of social phenomena are courtlike, many of which are not specifically political unless we choose to label all situations of conflict political. However, once we encounter the substitution of judicial office and law for spontaneous consent, the intermix of conflict resolution, social control, and lawmaking in most courts, and the frequent integration of judging with administrative or general political authority, a substantial share of courts and judges seems to be engaging in politics. Like most other major political institutions, courts tend to be loaded with multiple political functions, ranging under various circumstances from bolstering the legitimacy of the political regime to allocating scarce economic resources or setting major social policies.

REFERENCES

Abel-Smith, Brian, and Robert Stevens (1967). *Lawyers and the Courts.* Cambridge, Mass.: Harvard University Press.

Abraham, Henry (1968). *The Judicial Process.* Rev. ed. New York: Oxford University Press.

Allen, C. K. (1958). *Law in the Making.* London: Oxford University Press.

Arens, Richard, and Harold Lasswell (1961). *In Defense of Public Order.* New York: Columbia University Press.

Auerbach, Carl A., Lloyd K. Garrison, Willard Hurst, and Samuel Mermin, eds. (1961). *The Legal Process.* New York: Chandler.

Bartholomew, Paul G. (1969). "The Irish judiciary." *Notre Dame Lawyer* 44:560–73.

Barton, R. F. (1919). "Ifugao law." *University of California Publications in American Archaeology and Ethnology* 15:1–186.

_____ (1949). *The Kalingas: Their Institutions and Custom Law.* Chicago: University of Chicago Press.

Becker, Theodore (1970). *Comparative Judicial Politics.* Chicago: Rand McNally.

Bentzon, Agnete Weis (1966). "The structure of the judicial system and its function in a developing society." *Acta Sociologica* 10:121–46.

Berman, Harold J. (1963). *Justice in the USSR.* Cambridge, Mass.: Harvard University Press.

Blumberg, Abraham S. (1967). "The practice of law as a confidence game: organizational cooptation of a profession." *Law and Society Review* 2:15–39.

Bodde, Derk, and Clarence Norris (1967). *Law in Imperial China.* Cambridge, Mass.: Harvard University Press.

Bohannan, Paul J. (1957). *Justice and Judgment Among the Tiv.* London: Oxford University Press.

——————— (1960). *African Homicide and Suicide.* Princeton, N.J.: Princeton University Press.

———————, ed. (1967). *Law and Warfare.* Garden City, N.Y.: Natural History Press.

Cappelletti, Mauro, John Henry Merryman, and Joseph M. Perillo (1967). *The Italian Legal System.* Stanford, Calif.: Stanford University Press.

Casper, Jonathan D. (1972). *American Criminal Justice: The Defendant's Perspective.* Englewood Cliffs, N.J.: Prentice-Hall.

Cavazan, John (1965). "The jurisdiction of the Supreme Court of Canada: its development and effect on the role of the court." *Osgoode Hall Law Journal* 3:431–44.

Chigier, M. (1967). "The rabbinical courts in the state of Israel." *Israel Law Review* 2:147–81.

Cohen, Jerome (1966). "Chinese mediation on the eve of modernization." *California Law Review* 54:1201–27.

——————— (1968). *The Criminal Process in the People's Republic of China 1949–1963.* Cambridge, Mass.: Harvard University Press.

Cohn, E. J. (1968). *Manual of German Law,* Vol. 1. Dobbs Ferry, N.Y.: Oceana Publications.

Cook, Beverly Blair (1967). *The Judicial Process in California.* Belmont, Calif.: Dickenson.

Crabb, John H. (1962). "The court of appeal of England and the Supreme Court of North Dakota: a psychological comparison." *North Dakota Law Review* 38:554–62.

Currie, Elliot P. (1968). "Crimes without criminals: witchcraft and its control in Renaissance Europe." *Law and Society Review* 37:7–32.

David, René (1972). *French Law.* Baton Rouge: Louisiana State University Press.

David, René, and John E. C. Brierly (1968). *Major Legal Systems in the World Today.* London: Stevens & Sons.

David, René, and Henry P. De Vries (1958). *The French Legal System: An Introduction to Civil Law Systems.* Dobbs Ferry, N.Y.: Oceana Publications.

Davis, F. James, Henry H. Foster, C. Ray Jeffery, and E. Eugene Davis (1962). *Society and the Law: New Meanings for an Old Profession.* New York: Free Press.

Dawson, John P. (1960). *A History of Lay Judges*. Cambridge, Mass.: Harvard University Press.

_____ (1968). *The Oracles of the Law*. Ann Arbor: University of Michigan Law School.

Dolbeare, Kenneth M. (1967). *Trial Courts in Urban Politics*. New York: Wiley.

Douglas, R. N. (1968). "Courts in the political system." *Melbourne Journal of Politics* 1:36–47.

Eckhoff, Torstein (1965). "Impartiality, separation of powers, and judicial independence." *Scandinavian Studies in Law* 9:9–48.

Evans-Pritchard, E. E. (1937). *Witchcraft, Oracles and Magic among the Azande*. Oxford: Clarendon Press.

_____ (1940). *The Nuer*. Oxford: Clarendon Press.

Fallers, Lloyd A. (1969). *Law Without Precedent*. Chicago: University of Chicago Press.

Fleming, Donald, and Bernard Bailyn (1971). *Law in American History*. Boston: Little, Brown.

Frank, Jerome (1949). *Courts on Trial*. Princeton, N.J.: Princeton University Press.

Friedman, Lawrence M. (1973). *A History of American Law*. New York: Simon & Schuster.

Friedman, Lawrence, and Stewart Macaulay, eds. (1969). *Law and the Behavioral Sciences*. Indianapolis: Bobbs-Merrill.

Friedman, Wolfgang (1966). "Limits of judicial lawmaking and prospective overruling." *Modern Law Review* 29:6–34.

_____ (1967). *Legal Theory*. 5th ed. New York: Columbia University Press.

Fuller, Lon (1963). "Collective bargaining and the arbitrator." *Wisconsin Law Review* 1963:3–27.

Garland, William (1966). "Wanji law and legal process." *Syracuse Law Review* 18:15–36.

Gibbs, Jack L., Jr. (1963). "The Kpelle moot: a therapeutic model for the informal settlement of disputes." *Africa* 33:1–11.

Glick, Henry Robert, and Kenneth Vines (1973). *State Court Systems*. Englewood Cliffs, N.J.: Prentice-Hall.

Gluckman, Max (1959). *Custom and Conflict in Africa*. (1st ed., 1956.) New York: Free Press.

_____ (1963). "Civil war and theories of power in Barotseland: African and medieval analogies." *Yale Law Journal* 72:1515–46.

_____ (1965). *Politics, Law and Ritual in Tribal Society*. Chicago: Aldine.

_____ (1967). *The Judicial Process among the Barotse of Northern Rhodesia*. (1st ed., 1955.) Manchester: Manchester University Press.

Goldman, Sheldon, and Thomas F. Jahnige (1971). *The Federal Courts as a Political System*. New York: Harper & Row.

Grossman, J., and J. Tanenhaus, eds. (1969). *Frontiers of Judicial Research*. New York: Wiley.

Gruen, Erich S. (1968). *Roman Politics and the Criminal Courts, 149–78 B.C.* Cambridge, Mass.: Harvard University Press.

Gulliver, P. H. (1963). *Social Control in an African Society*. Boston: Boston University Press.

Hahm, Pyong-Choon (1967). *The Korean Political Tradition and Law*. Seoul: Hollym Corporation.

Harvey, William Burnett (1966). *Law and Social Change in Ghana*. Princeton, N.J.: Princeton University Press.

Haskins, George L. (1960). *Law and Authority in Early Massachusetts*. Cambridge, Mass.: Harvard University Press.

Henderson, Dan Fenno (1965). *Conciliation and Japanese Law*. Seattle: University of Washington Press.

Herndon, James (1964). "The role of the judiciary in state political systems: some explorations." In G. Schubert (ed.), *Judicial Behavior: A Reader in Theory and Research*. Chicago: Rand McNally.

Higgins, Rosalyn (1968). "Policy considerations and the international judicial process." *International and Comparative Law Quarterly* 17:58–84.

Hoebel, E. Adamson (1954). *The Law of Primitive Man*. Cambridge, Mass.: Harvard University Press.

_____ (1961). "Three studies in African law." *Stanford University Law Review* 13:418–42.

Hogbin, H. Ian (1961). *Law and Order in Polynesia*. (1st ed., 1934.) Hamden, Conn.: Shoe String Press.

Howard, J. Woodford, Jr. (1968). "On the fluidity of judicial choice." *American Political Science Review* 62:43–56.

Howell, P. P. (1954). *A Manual of Nuer Law*. London: Oxford University Press.

Hurst, Willard (1950). *The Growth of American Law*. Boston: Little, Brown.

Hutchison, Thomas W., ed. (1968). *Africa and Law: Developing Legal Systems in African Commonwealth Nations*. Madison: University of Wisconsin Press.

Jacob, Herbert (1972). *Justice In America*. 2d ed. Boston: Little, Brown.

_____ (1973). *Urban Justice*. Englewood Cliffs, N.J.: Prentice-Hall.

Kalven, Harry, Jr., and Hans Zeisel (1966). *The American Jury*. Boston: Little, Brown.

Karst, Kenneth L. (1966). *Latin American Legal Institutions: Problems for Comparative Study*. Los Angeles: UCLA Latin American Center.

Kommers, Donald P. (1964). "The emergence of law and justice in pre-territorial Wisconsin." *American Journal of History* 8:20–33.

Kuper, Hilda, and Leo Kuper, eds. (1965). *African Law: Adaptation and Development*. Berkeley: University of California Press.

Landau, Martin (1969). "Redundancy, rationality, and the problem of duplication and overlap." *Public Administration Review* 29:346–58.

Lawson, F. H. (1953). *A Common Lawyer Looks at the Civil Law*. Ann Arbor: University of Michigan Law School.

Lawson, F. H., E. A. Anton, and L. Neville Brown, eds. (1963). *Amos & Walton's Introduction to French Law*. 2d ed. Oxford: Clarendon Press.

Lev, Daniel S. (1972). *Islamic Courts in Indonesia*. Berkeley: University of California Press.

Lingat, Robert (1973). *The Classical Law of India*. Berkeley: University of California Press.

Llewellyn, Karl N. (1960). *The Common Law Tradition: Deciding Appeals*. Boston: Little, Brown.

Llewellyn, Karl N., and E. Adamson Hoebel (1961). *The Cheyenne Way*. (1st ed., 1941.) Norman: University of Oklahoma Press.

Maine, Henry Sumner (1963). *Ancient Law*. Reprint of 1861 ed. Boston: Beacon Press.

Malinowski, Bronislaw (1959). *Crime and Custom in Savage Society*. (1st ed., 1932.) Paterson, N.J.: Littlefield, Adams.

Massell, Gregory J. (1968). "Law as an instrument of revolutionary change in a traditional milieu: the case of central Asia." *Law and Society Review* 2:178–228.

Merryman, John Henry (1969). *The Civil Law Tradition*. Stanford, Calif.: Stanford University Press.

Mishkin, Saul J., and Clarence Morris, eds. (1965). *On Law in Courts*. Brooklyn: Foundation Press.

Morris, H. F. (1967). "Two early surveys of native courts in Uganda." *Journal of African Law* 11:159–74.

Murphy, Walter F. (1964). *Elements of Judicial Strategy*. Chicago: University of Chicago Press.

Murphy, Walter F., and Joseph Tanenhaus (1972). *The Study of Public Law*. New York: Random House.

Nader, Laura (1964). "An analysis of Zapotec law cases." *Ethnology* 3:404–19.

——————, ed. (1969). *Law in Culture and Society*. Chicago: Aldine.

Nader, Laura, Klaus F. Koch, and Bruce Cox (1966). "The ethnography of law: a bibliographic survey." *Current Anthropology* 7:267–94.

Nader, Laura, and Duane Metzger (1963). "Conflict resolution in two Mexican communities." *American Anthropologist* 65:584–92.

Nonet, Philippe (1969). *Administrative Justice*. New York: Russell Sage.

Peltason, Jack W. (1953). "A political science of public law." *Southwestern Social Science Quarterly* 34:515–16.

——————— (1961). *58 Lonely Men*. New York: Harcourt, Brace.

Posner, Richard A. (1972). *Economic Analysis of Law*. Boston: Little, Brown.

Pospisil, Leopold (1958). *Kapaku Papuans and Their Law*. Yale University Publications in Anthropology, No. 54. New Haven: Yale University Department of Anthropology.

_____ (1964). "Law and societal structure among the Nunamiut eskimo." In Ward H. Goodenough (ed.), *Explorations in Cultural Anthropology: Essays in Honor of George Peter Murdock*. New York: McGraw-Hill.

_____ (1971). *Anthropology of Law*. New York: Harper & Row.

Reich, Donald R. (1963). "Court, comity and federalism in West Germany." *Midwest Journal of Political Science* 7:197–228.

Reid, John Phillip (1970). *A Law of Blood: The Primitive Law of the Cherokee Nation*. New York: New York University Press.

Riasanovsky, V. A. (1937). *Fundamental Principles of Mongol Law*. Tientsin, China: Telberg's International Bookstore.

Richardson, Richard J., and Kenneth Vines, eds. (1970). *The Politics of Federal Courts*. Boston: Little, Brown.

Rudolph, Lloyd, and Suzanne Rudolph (1967). *The Modernity of Tradition: Political Development in India*. Chicago: University of Chicago Press.

Schlesinger, Rudolph B. (1959). *Comparative Law: Cases-Text-Materials*. 2d ed. Brooklyn: Foundation Press.

Schubert, Glendon (1963). "Behavioral research in public law." *American Political Science Review* 57:433–45.

_____ (1967). "Judges and political leadership." In Lewis Edinger (ed.), *Political Leadership in Industrialized Societies: Studies in Comparative Analysis*. New York: Wiley.

_____ (1972). "Judicial process and behavior during the sixties." *Political Science* 5:6–15.

Schubert, G., and D. Danelski, eds. (1969). *Comparative Judicial Behavior*. New York: Oxford University Press.

Schur, Edwin M. (1968). *Law and Society: A Sociological View*. New York: Random House.

Schwartz, Richard D., and James C. Miller (1964). "Legal evolution and societal complexity." *American Journal of Sociology* 70:159–69.

Sedler, Robert Allen (1967). "The development of legal systems: the Ethiopian experience." *Iowa Law Review* 53:562–635.

Selznick, Philip (1963). "Legal institutions and social controls." *Vanderbilt Law Review* 17:79–90.

Shapiro, Barbara J. (1969). "Law and science in seventeenth-century England." *Stanford Law Review* 21:727–66.

Shapiro, Martin (1964). *Law and Politics in the Supreme Court*. New York: Free Press.

_____ (1968). *The Supreme Court and Administrative Agencies*. New York: Free Press.

_____ (1970). "Decentralized decision-making in the law of torts." In S. Sidney Ulmer (ed.), *Political Decision-Making*. New York: Van Nostrand.

_____ (1972). "Toward a theory of stare decisis." *Journal of Legal Studies* 1:125–34.

Shepardson, Mary (1965). "Problems of Navajo tribal courts in transition." *Human Organization* 24:250–53.

Shklar, Judith (1964). *Legalism*. Cambridge, Mass.: Harvard University Press.

Simmel, Georg (1950). *The Sociology of Georg Simmel*. Edited by Kurt H. Wolff. New York: Free Press.

Smith, David N. (1968). "Native courts of northern Nigeria: techniques for institutional development." *Boston University Law Review* 48:49–82.

Smith, Watson, and John M. Roberts (1954). *Zuni Law: A Field of Values*. Papers of the Peabody Museum of American Archaeology and Ethnology, Harvard University, Vol. 43, No. 1. Cambridge, Mass.: Peabody Museum.

Stone, Julius (1966). *Social Dimensions of Law and Justice*. Stanford, Calif.: Stanford University Press.

_____ (1968). *Legal Systems and Lawyers' Reasonings*. Stanford, Calif.: Stanford University Press.

Torgerson, Ulf (1963). "The role of the Supreme Court in the Norwegian political system." In G. Schubert (ed.), *Judicial Decision-Making*. New York: Free Press of Glencoe.

van de Sprenkel, Sybille (1967). *Legal Institutions in Manchu China*. New York: Humanities Press.

Vines, Kenneth N. (1965). "Courts as political and governmental agencies." In H. Jacob and Kenneth N. Vines (eds.), *Politics in American States*. Boston: Little, Brown.

Vinogradoff, Paul (1909). *Roman Law in Medieval Europe*. London: Harper & Row.

von Mehren, Arthur (1957). *The Civil Law System*. Boston: Little, Brown.

_____, ed. (1963). *Law in Japan*. Cambridge, Mass.: Harvard University Press.

Vose, Clement (1973). *Constitutional Change*. New York: Heath.

Wagner, W. J. (1959). *The Federal States and Their Judiciaries*. Mouton: The Hague.

Watson, Richard A., and Rondal G. Downing (1969). *The Politics of the Bench and the Bar*. New York: Wiley.

Weiler, Paul (1968). "Two models of judicial decision-making." *Canadian Bar Review* 46:406–71.

Wells, Richard J., and Joel B. Grossman (1967). "The concept of judicial policy-making: a critique." *Journal of Public Law* 15:286–310.

Wigmore, John Henry (1928). *A Panorama of the World's Legal Systems*. Washington, D.C.: Washington Law Book Company.

_____, ed. (1970). *Law and Justice in Tokugawa Japan*. Tokyo: University of Tokyo Press.

Wolff, Hans Julius (1951). *Roman Law: An Historical Introduction*. Norman: University of Oklahoma Press.

6

BUREAUCRACIES

MARK V. NADEL AND FRANCIS E. ROURKE

INTRODUCTION

There are many perspectives from which bureaucracy may be examined. This analysis focuses on the role of bureaucratic organizations in the political system—as instruments of power or as sources of policy. Much of the material on which it is based comes from the experience of the United States, where the political impact of bureaucracy has been extensively investigated. However, we have also tried to call attention to relevant data on bureaucratic politics in the expanding literature of comparative administration (Heady, 1966; Raphaeli, 1967; Riggs, 1964; Waldo, 1964; Heady and Stokes, 1960; 1962). In recent years much of this comparative research has focused on the developing nations— leading to what Alfred Diamant has called the "not-so-benign neglect" of Western European administrations (1973).

One aspect of our approach deserves special mention. We have put particular stress on the power exercised by private, especially corporate, bureaucracies in the framing of public policy. This phenomenon is primarily characteristic of Western industrialized societies, where a highly differentiated infrastructure of private organizations is intertwined with the bureaucratic apparatus of the state. But in the form of multinational corporations, corporate organizations are now beginning to play an increasingly important role in the politics of underdeveloped nations. The influence exerted by private bureaucracies is thus growing in all parts of the world—in developing as well as technologically advanced societies. It deserves far more attention than it has received in the literature of public policy, and the design of our analysis is meant to point up its importance.

This chapter begins with an examination of expertise as a source of bureaucratic power in all political systems and then turns to the special efforts of bureaucracies in advanced societies to mobilize political support from the adjacent socioeconomic structure. Attention then shifts to the role of private bureaucracies in politics and policymaking, and the analysis concludes with a review of the mechanisms and strategies through which modern democratic societies attempt to impose limits on bureaucratic organizations that threaten at times to acquire a monopoly of power over political and economic decision making.[1]

BUREAUCRATIC EXPERTISE

The influence bureaucrats exert in all political systems—whether democratic or nondemocratic—stems in large part from the expert skills they bring to the governing process. As career civil servants, bureaucrats acquire specialized knowledge by virtue of long tenure in office if they do not already have it as a result of education or professional training prior to appointment. With the advent of modern technology the gap between the professionalism of the bureaucrat and the amateur status of other governmental participants in the policy process has greatly widened. Technology and bureaucracy are closely linked in their simultaneous ascent to a preeminent position in modern society. (Ferkiss, 1969).

It is the technical expertise of bureaucrats that makes their role both most useful and most controversial in modern societies (Benveniste, 1972). The presence of bureaucrats in the governmental structure provides assurance that the decisions of political leaders will be guided by competent technical advice and carried out by skilled personnel. It is inconceivable that any modern state could operate effectively without highly trained bureaucracies. In the development of backward nations, modernization has meant bureaucratization, and where administrative skills have been deficient, social and economic development have inevitably lagged.

But the autonomy that these bureaucratic skills generate is a source of considerable anxiety in the political sphere, because of the possibility that administrative organizations will become "inner-directed"—responsive to cues and directions they give themselves rather than those they receive from political bodies that are the source of legitimate authority in the state. No fear has been more constant in modern politics—shared by revolutionaries and reactionaries alike—than the possibility that bureaucrats might become a power elite and dominate the governmental process in which they are meant to play a subordinate role. The basic dilemma, as Eisenstadt puts it, is "whether bureaucracy is master or servant, an independent body or a tool, and, if a tool, whose interests it can be made to serve" (1965, p. 179).

Expertise as a source of bureaucratic influence is manifested in three principal ways: (1) the ability of bureaucrats to give advice that often shapes the decisions of political officials; (2) the capacity of bureaucratic organizations to carry out the tasks that must be performed if policy goals are to be attained; and (3) the discretion with which bureaucracies are commonly vested when they participate in the implementation of public policy. Each of these avenues of bureaucratic power will be examined in the sections that follow.

Our knowledge of the role of bureaucratic expertise in the policy process has been greatly expanded by recent studies of the conduct of American foreign policy. Graham Allison led the way in this endeavor: first in a pioneering article (1969) and then in a full-scale study of the Cuban missile crisis (1971). Morton Halperin has also examined the subject in a very comprehensive manner (Halperin and Kanter, 1973; Halperin, 1974). Both Allison and Halperin tend to argue that the expertise of national security organizations permits them to channel American foreign policy in directions that fit the interests and self-serving goals of the bureaucracy itself.

There has been considerable criticism of this "bureaucratic politics" approach on the grounds that it exaggerates the importance of organizational interests in shaping the development of foreign policy and understates the significance of pressures from the international environment as perceived and interpreted by the president and other high policymaking officials (Krasner, 1972; Rourke, 1972; Art, 1973). But there can be little doubt that the work of Allison, Halperin, and others has greatly improved our understanding of the stakes bureaucratic organizations have in the resolution of policy issues, the strategies open to them for protecting or advancing their interests, and the impact this organization-centered activity may have on the outcome of policy itself. Recent studies of both British and American diplomacy have been enriched by analyses that draw on the bureaucratic politics paradigm (Neustadt, 1970; Neustadt and Allison, 1971).

It is also clear that the domination of policymaking in the United States since World War II by national security issues has created much more awareness of bureaucracy as a factor in the political process (Rourke, 1970, pp. 172–82). Prior to World War II, when domestic issues were paramount on the policy agenda, interest groups outside of government were customarily assigned the leading role in studies of policymaking. However, in the national security field as it has evolved since 1945, the structure of outside interests has been perceived as being either very weak, as in the case of the State Department (Cohen, 1973), or linked to bureaucracy in a relationship of dependency, as exemplified by the Defense Department's military-industrial complex (Melman, 1970, Yarmolinsky, 1971).[2] In a policy environment of this sort, bureaucratic actors come inevitably to be viewed as sitting at the center of decision.

Advice as Influence

In both domestic and foreign affairs a fundamental source of bureaucratic power is the ability of career officials to mold the views of other participants in the policy process. Bureaucracies are highly organized information and advisory systems, and the data they analyze and transmit cannot help but influence the way elected officials perceive political issues and events. Herbert Simon has emphasized (1957) the utility of being able to shape the value or factual premises of decision makers as a means of ensuring control over decisions themselves, and it is precisely in this way that bureaucratic information and advice often function in the policy process.

A notable illustration of the bureaucratic role in this respect was the influence exerted by George Kennan from his vantage point in the State Department in the years immediately following World War II. During this period, Kennan's arguments on the need to contain Soviet power and the methods by which this goal might be achieved did much to shape the assumptions on which American foreign policy was based in dealing with the communist powers around the world. The views he expressed in a widely read article on foreign policy, written under the pseudonym of "X" (1947), became the basic American text of the cold war for both government officials and attentive publics outside of government.

The influence that bureaucrats exert on the policy process through their power to give advice should not be exaggerated. The American experience during the cold war suggests that it is easiest for bureaucrats to appear powerful when their advice matches and reinforces the preexisting views of the political officials responsible for policy. As noted above, the advice of Kennan seemed highly influential in the early days of the cold war, when the doctrine of containment was eminently congenial to the goals of leading political elites in the country. Later on, however, when Kennan attempted to restrain policymakers from putting undue emphasis on military force in applying the principle of containment, his advice was largely ignored, and he found himself increasingly isolated from power, as he later revealed in his memoirs (1967).

But while the appearance and reality of bureaucratic power may not always coincide, it is clear that the ability to channel information into policy deliberations provides substantial leverage with which bureaucrats can affect the shape of decisions. If there are cases in which administrators appear only to be telling political officials what they want to hear (Halberstam, 1973), there are equally striking illustrations of situations in which staff members of executive agencies have substantially reshaped the attitudes of political leaders in both Congress and the executive. A notable example in this regard is the shift in the views of Clark Clifford on the Vietnam War following his appointment as secretary of defense in 1968—a change that occurred in good part as a result of briefings Clifford received from his civilian staff after he took over at the Pentagon (Hoopes, 1969). In an earlier role as an advisor to President Truman, Clifford was himself the source of enormous influence on presidential behavior (Anderson, 1968).

A group of agencies in which the power of advice can be seen in its clearest form in American administration are the staff agencies that surround the president in the United States (Cronin and Greenberg, 1969). These agencies have little operational authority of their own. They influence policy primarily by giving advice to the president. The economists who serve with the Bureau of the Budget and the Council of Economic Advisers can shape the president's perspective on fiscal policy and hence his recommendations to Congress on tax and expenditure measures. The natural scientists who give advice to the president are equally influential with the chief executive in the areas of their scientific and technical competence. Through their role as bureaucratic advisers, professionally trained economists and natural scientists obtain a degree of influence in the policy process they would never otherwise enjoy. The members of most professional groups have neither the time, inclination, nor the capacity to win political office, and involvement in bureaucracy is, therefore, the only avenue to political power open to them.

Apart from the expertise such highly skilled bureaucrats bring to the policy process, their participation in executive deliberations also adds to the legitimacy of a president's decisions. The wisdom of his policies is greatly enhanced in the eyes of the electorate when he is in a position to assert that these decisions rest on the best professional advice he has been able to obtain. As has been said, for example, of the Council of Economic Advisers: "The acceptance of the Council's expertise as the President's economists increases the acceptance of his authority in matters of economic policy, and where applicable it adds economic persuasion to his strategies of influence. In return, the president provides the principal market for the Council's expertise" (Flash, 1965, pp. 309–10). The same point has been made with respect to the role of natural scientists in government: "The scientist may find himself on the political firing line, placed there by a politician interested in using the scientist's prestige as an 'expert' to disarm the critics of his (the politician's) choices" (Schilling, 1964, p. 169).

There are risks as well as benefits for any political executive in his relationship with his advisers. It is, for example, highly important to a president that no one adviser be allowed to exercise monopolistic influence over his decisions. "An executive relying on a single information system became inevitably the prisoner of that system." So wrote Arthur Schlesinger, Jr., in describing the elaborate system of checks and balances which Franklin D. Roosevelt maintained to prevent any single adviser from becoming the Rasputin of his administration. "Roosevelt's persistent effort . . . was to check and balance information acquired through official channels by information acquired through a myriad of private, informal, and unorthodox channels and espionage networks" (Schlesinger, 1959, p. 523).

The danger to which Schlesinger was pointing became abundantly clear during World War II, when the Joint Chiefs of Staff began to exercise a high degree of influence over Roosevelt's decisions in the field of military affairs: "The mere fact of direct access to the President did not account for the authority of the Joint Chiefs in the conduct of the war. Their power was rather a product of their direct access combined with the exclusion of civilian advice. . . . Ironic as it was, Roosevelt, who normally skillfully played subordinates off against each other in order to maximize his own authority, allowed one set of advisers to preempt the field with respect to his most important decisions" (Huntington, 1957, p. 320).

One of the chief reasons why Roosevelt was not able to maintain the same balance with respect to military advice that he had earlier established in the domestic area was because military decisions had to be surrounded with so much more secrecy than domestic policy discussions. This requirement of secrecy prevented the use of an open system in which the president could draw advice from as many quarters as he chose: "Wartime . . . imposed secrecy and censorship. No longer could the President look anywhere and everywhere for scraps of information and advice on his preeminent concerns, his most compelling choices. No longer could he pick up any aide or friend he chose to spy out the terrain of his official advisers. His instinct for alternative sources, his avid curiosity, his reach for information and ideas, now had to be confined to men with a 'need to know' " (Neustadt, 1963, p. 859).

In domestic as well as military affairs, a president can overcome some of the disadvantages of dependence on a closed circle of advisers by relying for advice on committee structures within bureaucracy, which permits a broader canvassing of alternatives and even emergence of majority and minority points of view between which the president may choose. With a committee a president has some assurance that the advice he is getting reflects pure expertise rather than—as might be the case with a single adviser—professional prejudice or personal idiosyncrasy. C. P. Snow's account of the excessive influence exercised over British Prime Minister Winston Churchill by his scientific adviser, Lord Cherwell, points up this problem (Snow, 1961).

In American government many of the major advisory institutions in the executive branch—the Joint Chiefs of Staff, the National Security Council, and the Council of Economic Advisers, for example—are in fact committees. In the literature of public administration, committees are usually held in low esteem as management instruments, since they disperse rather than focus executive leadership and control. But as an advisory institution, the committee has a great deal of utility, and with administrative agencies moving increasingly into the development as well as the execution of policy, committees have become as indispensable for deliberative purposes in the administrative process as they have long been in legislative decision making. Janis, however, has called attention to the pathologies to which committee decision making is subject (1972).

From the perspective of the president or any agency head who uses an advisory committee, such a group is most valuable if it is under his jurisdiction and owes its primary administrative loyalty to him. Under this arrangement the executive has some assurance that advisers look at problems from his perspective rather than the vantage point of some institutional interest of their own. A model in this respect is the office of the special assistant for national security affairs in the White House. This office has no constituency other than the president himself. It has no allies in Congress and no bureaucratic interests or identity of its own to advance or protect.

Of course, an advisory group that is totally dependent on the chief executive for its own survival may be highly reluctant to tell him unpleasant truths he ought to hear. In time the advice a president gets from these experts may do little more than mirror his own opinions if advisers refrain from giving advice that goes against the presidential grain (Reedy, 1970). This is likely to be a particularly acute problem when the adviser is a career civil servant whose employment opportunities outside of government are limited. It contributes to candor in the advisory process if advisers are drawn from universities or other outside institutions to which they can return if need be—an option open to the members of the Council of Economic Advisers, for example (Flash, 1965; Hirschman, 1970).

Increasing attention has been given to the possibility of diversifying the advisory process surrounding presidents and other political executives so that they do not in fact become prisoners of their own bureaucratic information system. Alexander George, for example, has argued for a "multiple advocacy" system in the process by which presidents receive advice on foreign policy (1972). The need to break down information barriers that prevent bureaucrats from transmitting certain kinds of advice to political officials has also been stressed (Thomson, 1968; Destler, 1972). There is no area of bureaucracy more persistently linked with pathological or dysfunctional behavior patterns than the communications process (Wilensky, 1967).

The impact of bureaucratic advice on the policy process stands out very clearly not only in the activities of staff agencies that serve the presidency but also in the increasing tendency for the deliberations of Congress to be dominated by "agency bills"—legislation that has been initially drafted in the offices of executive agencies. Much of what ultimately comes to be regarded as the president's legislative program stems in the first instance from the advice of bureaucrats in the executive establishment (Fisher, 1972, pp. 42–54). Located as they are in intimate contact with the everyday processes of government, bureaucrats have an unexcelled vantage point from which to see the need for new legislation. Indeed, there has arisen a specialized segment of the federal bureaucracy primarily concerned with legislative liaison (Holtzman, 1970). The influence of bureaucratic advice thus manifests itself in the process of legislative as well as executive decision.

With regard to all the above sources of advice, a distinction can be drawn between *absolute* expertise and *relevant* expertise. Absolute expertise is a real monopoly of information that is vital to a policy decision. This form of expertise is especially prominent in military, scientific, and technical areas. The power of military bureaucracies, for example, is significantly enhanced by their undisputed possession of information regarding enemy capabilities. While other participants in the political process may dispute the evaluation of such information, none can seriously contest the factual data itself. The information, of course, may be incorrect, but no one else has rival information with which to establish a superior claim to expertise in giving advice.

Relevant expertise differs in that it is not control over factual information but advice on matters not definitely known by anyone. It is a matter of probabilities. Here the agency possessing expertise has political power because policymakers assume that the agency's particular body of expertise is most relevant to the decisions at hand. Not surprisingly, the advice stemming from bureaucracies holding relevant expertise usually coincides with the preferences of the policymakers seeking advice. For example, political decision makers have a choice of whether to accept police agencies as their primary source of advice on law enforcement or to listen to the claims of lawyers, jurists, sociologists, or other experts. However, once an agency has been accepted as having relevant expertise, it may then have great influence in defining policy options and formulating public policy.

Because greater and more stable power accrues to the holder of absolute expertise, a common strategy of bureaucracies is to claim the possession of such expertise of a specialized sort. This can be attempted through claims to "secret" information unavailable to others—a frequent device of American bureaucratic organizations during the war in Vietnam. However, not all bureaucracies can establish a credible claim to absolute expertise no matter how hard they try. It ultimately depends on having a body of knowledge or information inaccessible to others.

Organizational Capabilities

The expertise of bureaucratic organizations also takes the form of control over the capabilities through which policy is carried out and upon which its success eventually depends. While elected officials may have far-reaching ambitions for new programs or policies, it is the determination and skill of the bureaucratic apparatus that ultimately determine whether these objectives will be realized. In many situations the policy alternatives open to officials are confined to the courses of action their organizational machinery has the will and the means to carry out. Bureaucratic resistance or incapacity may spell the doom of even their most modest policy proposals.

Consider, for example, the case of an American president. There are many ways in which the executive apparatus over which he presides is an annoying burden to the president. It often drags its feet in carrying out his proposals or generates jurisdictional disputes he must settle—in this way consuming his time and exhausting his energy. But in the end the president is heavily dependent on the ability of bureaucratic organizations for his own success. Indeed, as

President Johnson discovered in the case of Vietnam, a president's orders may be disastrous for him if their execution is beyond the capabilities of his bureaucracy.

Graham Allison has given us an illuminating description of the degree to which the choices of political leaders are limited by the talents of the bureaucratic organizations under their jurisdiction. As Allison puts it:

> ... existing organizational routines for employing present physical capabilities constitute the range of effective choice open to government leaders confronted with any problem. . . . The fact that fixed programs (equipment, men and routines that exist at the particular time) exhaust the range of buttons that leaders can push is not always perceived by these leaders. But in every case it is critical for an understanding of what is actually done. (1971, p. 79)

Controlling policy options. While there is no iron law dictating that a bureaucratic capability once established will invariably be used, certain consequences usually follow when a bureaucratic organization is created to provide policymakers with a desired capability. For one thing, such an organization inevitably has a vested interest in its own survival. It will thus tend to search for missions in which its value to society can be demonstrated and the flow of resources into the organization encouraged. Ordinarily it becomes a staunch protagonist of policies that enable it to display its skills, and these policies acquire a weight in executive deliberations they would not otherwise possess.

Hence a policy option that is strongly supported by a bureaucratic organization is much more likely to be adopted than one that lacks such sponsorship. Predicting which of several possible alternatives will be followed in the development of public policy can in no small measure be based on an assessment of the relative strength of the organizations responsible for carrying out each of the options under consideration. Policymakers will always be under strong pressure to follow courses of action that serve strong organizational interests and to ignore those that do not. Indeed in some areas of policy, decisions are shaped primarily by the lobbying activity and pressures exerted by executive organizations rather than—as is commonly expected will occur in democratic societies —as a result of pressures from private groups outside of government (Huntington, 1961).

The ability of bureaucratic organizations to define the options open to policymakers presents the constant possibility that organizational interests will transcend national interests, and executive agencies may then force the adoption of policies that reflect, not the needs and interests of the country, but their own appetite for power, prestige, or security.

It is also possible for organizations performing similar roles in two adversary nations to develop a close identity of interests which transcends national boundaries. The military bureaucracies in the United States and the Soviet

Union have, in effect, been allied with each other during the cold war in the pursuit of complementary objectives, since the development of the armed forces in each country has depended on the health and vitality of the counterpart organization in the other.

The same is true of space agencies in the two countries, for whom the "space race" has been highly functional in terms of the financial support they have received from the public treasury. In a situation of such competitive inter-dependence between organizations in two hostile nations, it is useful for each of the agencies involved to heap praise on the performance and efficiency of the other, since its own continued support depends upon the other's apparent effectiveness. It is not, therefore, surprising that United States space officials have so consistently praised the achievements of their organizations' competitors in the Soviet bureaucracy. Anything less than lavish praise on their part would be clearly against their own organizational interests.

The implementation problem. Because bureaucratic organizations provide the capabilities through which policy decisions are executed, the actual shape of policy as it emerges from the machinery of bureaucracy reflects not only the intentions of decision makers at the head of government but also the characteristics of the organizations through which decisions are carried out. Policy outputs thus generate many surprises among political officials responsible for decisions, or what is often referred to as "unanticipated consequences." In extreme cases the original intentions of policymakers may hardly be visible in the outputs of the organization charged with putting decisions into effect.

Several characteristics of organizations help account for this tendency of organizational outcomes to differ from original policy decisions. It is common for executive agencies to execute decisions through what organization manuals describe as standard operating procedures—predetermined ways of handling specific problems as they arise. These routines are the set procedures through which an organization has carried out its responsibilities in the past, and they have been sanctified by tradition and usually by successful experience. Employees have been programmed to perform these procedures and they are often subject to sanctions if they deviate from them.

The ironic fact about such bureaucratic routines is that they are developed essentially to curb the ability of individual bureaucrats to influence policy through the exercise of personal discretion. Routines are designed to make the behavior of employees conform to organizational goals rather than their own personal inclinations. Organizations without routines place policy at the mercy of individual idiosyncrasies. But while intended to limit the power of executive officials, such routines may also have the effect of enormously increasing the power of bureaucratic organizations in the total governmental process.

These bureaucratic routines derive much of their impact on policy from the fact that they are very difficult to start and, once begun, no less difficult to stop. Thus the celebrated law of bureaucratic inertia: "Bureaucracies at rest tend to stay at rest, and bureaucracies in motion tend to stay in motion." The slowness with which bureaucratic organizations respond to presidential desires for action is legendary and a constant source of exasperation for chief executives. It was not until six weeks after President Kennedy's Vienna meeting with Khrushchev that the State Department finally prepared a response to the Russian leader's *aide memoire* on Berlin.

> Kennedy had expected a quick American response capable, among other things, of making some appeal to world opinion. Instead, week followed week with no word from the Department, and the President's exasperation grew. When a draft finally came over in mid-July, nearly six weeks after Vienna, it was a tired and turgid rehash of documents left over from the Berlin crisis of 1958–59. . . . By this time it was too late to do anything but put the paper out. . . . (Schlesinger, 1965, p. 384)

Similarly, at the time of the Cuban missile crisis in October of 1962, Kennedy discovered that the American missiles he had ordered removed from Turkey several months earlier were still in place—a highly vulnerable target for Soviet efforts to win American concessions in exchange for removing Russian missiles from Cuba. Exasperating as the inertia of bureaucratic organizations often is for American presidents, it is not altogether without value to them. The cumbersome routines through which bureaucratic organizations operate often save political officials from making an overly rapid or rash response in an emerging crisis.

If the slowness with which executive agencies act in emergency situations can be described as a function of the inertia that characterizes large organizations, the difficulty of stopping bureaucratic organizations once they are launched on a course of action reflects the momentum that bureaucratic routines acquire after being initiated. This momentum may take the form of carrying on procedures no longer needed simply because they have been built into an organization's repertoire and their discontinuance would bring a reduction in the scope of an agency's activities or perhaps require the release of personnel. It may also reflect the fact that bureaucratic services generate constituencies that oppose their liquidation.

In the cases just cited, bureaucratic momentum manifests itself in the ongoing performance of routines that are no longer required, since the problem to which they were addressed no longer exists. Such momentum may also take the form of a series of logically progressive short-term decisions that escalate into consequences far beyond those originally intended. Some observers have interpreted the American involvement in Vietnam in precisely this way, as the final product of a series of continuing steps by bureaucratic organizations that were never intended to lead, as they ultimately did, into a major conflict.

This tendency of bureaucratic momentum to transform small-scale commitments into large ones is highly visible in weapons development activities. Warner Schilling has shown (1961) that the original decision to initiate the development of the hydrogen bomb was intended to leave open the possibility of discontinuing the project. However, once the H-bomb project was started, it required such formidable investments of resources over long periods of time that policymakers found themselves committed to the eventual production of the bomb as soon as they had decided to launch a preliminary inquiry to see if it was feasible to construct such a weapon.

This kind of bureaucratic momentum tends to invalidate the argument of Braybrooke and Lindblom (1963; Lindblom, 1965) that policymaking in the United States is protected from irrationality by the fact that it moves incrementally in one sequential step after another from initial decision to final outcome, thus permitting a discontinuance of effort or the reversal of direction at any point at which either is considered desirable. In point of fact the momentum of the organizations charged with putting a decision into effect may make it very difficult to stop or reverse gears once the bureaucratic machinery has been set in motion. Irreversibility may thus become a major hazard of policy decisions carried out through large organizations.

A major factor contributing to such irreversibility is the fact that large bureaucracies arrive at policy positions only after an elaborate process of consultation and accommodation among diverse organizational interests. Agreements negotiated with such painstaking effort resist change, because such change would require reopening the whole bargaining process with no certainty that the trade-offs required might not yield a less effective policy outcome (Kissinger, 1969).

Of all the factors that give bureaucracy power over the execution of decisions, none perhaps is more important than the simple ability of executive agencies to do nothing. Inertia may be the most potent form of energy available to bureaucracies. It has certainly played a major role in policymaking in foreign affairs during recent years. A study of the way in which the United States became inadvertently committed to the defense of the islands held by the Chinese Nationalists off the mainland of China concludes that it constitutes a "sobering example in the realm of foreign policy of the general proposition that to make the bureaucracy change its position is much more difficult than allowing it to continue a given policy: the bureaucracy prefers the known dangers of an existing course to the uncertain costs and gains of change" (Halperin and Tsou, 1966).

This kind of bureaucratic veto by inaction is akin to what has been described as non-decision-making—the ability of some participants in the policy process to prevent certain kinds of decisions from even appearing on the agenda of choice (Bachrach and Baratz, 1970; Crenson, 1971). Where bureaucratic influence of this sort prevails, executive organizations exclude some policy alternatives from consideration in policy discussions altogether. The core of bureaucratic power becomes not the ability to make things happen but the ability to prevent them from happening.

Recent years have seen increasing attention focused on these problems of implementation—the difficulties that beset efforts to attain policy goals once they are decided on. It has become abundantly clear that no policy decision should be finalized before the ease or difficulty of carrying it out has been taken into account, at least where the use of large-scale organizational processes is essential for the achievement of program objectives. In the past the appraisal of policy alternatives has not always included the feasibility of implementation within the framework of analysis. This is what Allison calls the "analysis gap" —the failure to study the area lying "between preferred solutions and the actual behavior of the government" (Allison, 1971, p. 267).

This new interest in implementation contrasts sharply with the attention that was lavished in the United States during the 1960s on improved techniques for deciding on courses of action—systems analysis, cost-effectiveness ratios, and the other instruments of managerial science. It is now recognized that the most advanced techniques for making decisions are of little avail when the organizational procedures needed to translate these decisions into results are either nonexistent or ineffective. A study by Pressman and Wildavsky (1973) of the failure of a manpower training program in one American city provides the clearest study we have of this problem of administrative implementation. However, as their analysis reveals, it is not always easy to distinguish between difficulties that are peculiar to the implementation process itself and flaws in the original design of policy. As is often true in Soviet politics, bureaucracies can be blamed for a failure to carry out plans that were impractical from the outset.

The Power of Discretion

No aspect of the growth of bureaucratic power in this century has been more important than the steady expansion in the scope of the discretion vested in individual administrators (K. Davis, 1969). The term *discretion* here refers to the ability of an administrator to choose among alternatives—to decide, in effect, how the power of government should be used in specific cases. The range of situations in which bureaucrats exercise discretion today is virtually boundless. It includes the policeman deciding whether or not to make an arrest (Skolnick, 1966; Wilson, 1968), a regulatory agency deciding the level of a price increase (Redford, 1969), or a selective service board determining whether to draft or defer a particular individual (Davis and Dolbeare, 1968). These decisions may have a vital effect on the fortunes or even the survival of the individual concerned. Whether or not discretion is, as has been asserted, the "lifeblood" of administration, its exercise may well have a life-or-death effect for the individual citizen.

In the traditional theory of public administration in the United States, it was assumed that the administrator's discretion extended only to decisions on means, while the ends, or goals, of administrative action were fixed by statute or by the directives of a responsible political official. This was the celebrated distinction between politics and administration presented by such early pioneers in the field as Woodrow Wilson (1887) and Frank J. Goodnow (1900). This distinction was designed among other things to provide a rationale for insulating administrative agencies from exploitation by politicians bent on using administrative offices and powers as the "spoils" of victory at the polls. If bureaucrats did not shape policy, then there was no reason why administrative agencies could not be left in splendid isolation, free to make decisions on personnel or on administrative organization and procedure so as to attain maximum efficiency in carrying on the business of government. As Woodrow Wilson put it: "The broad plans of government action are not administrative; the detailed execution of such plans is administrative" (1887, p. 212). This was also the explicit professional ethos of career civil servants such as city managers.

This was a highly useful doctrine for bureaucracy during the late nineteenth century and early twentieth century in the United States, when public administration was an "infant industry" that needed a protective ideology behind which it could develop. It is no longer a valid doctrine today, when the center of power in policymaking has shifted from the legislative to the executive branch and when all bureaucratic decisions are recognized as having at least some implications for policy.

The scope of bureaucratic discretion in all societies is vast with respect to both the everyday routine decisions of government agencies and the major innovative or trend-setting decisions of public policy. These two broad types of administrative decision have been categorized by Herbert Simon as programmed and nonprogrammed decisions. In Simon's words: "Decisions are programmed to the extent that they are repetitive and routine, to the extent that a definite procedure has been worked out for handling them so that they don't have to be treated *de novo* each time they occur. . . . Decisions are nonprogrammed to the extent that they are novel, unstructured, and consequential" (1960, pp. 5–6). Philip Selznick draws a parallel distinction between "routine" and "critical" decisions (1957, pp. 29–64).

The policy impact of administrative discretion when it is exercised with respect to nonprogrammed decisions is clear and unmistakable. If the Federal Reserve Board abruptly changes the discount rate or alters the reserve requirements for member banks to control inflationary tendencies in a booming economy or to stimulate investment in the face of an impending economic recession, these are major policy decisions of obvious importance to the society at large. Or the Federal Communications Commission, when it sets forth criteria for determining how many television stations are to be allowed in each section of the country, is clearly taking the lead in designing a national communications policy through the exercise of its discretionary authority. The independent regulatory agencies as a group have been assigned major responsibilities by Congress for making nonprogrammed decisions that require "a high degree of expertness, a mastery of technical detail, and continuity and stability of policy" (Bernstein, 1955, p. 4).

What is perhaps not quite so clearly apparent is the power inherent in the capacity of bureaucrats to exercise discretion in the area of programmed, or routine, decision. The fact of the matter is, however, that decisions that may seem merely routine from the point of view of an administrative agency are often of critical importance to the parties affected by these administrative determinations. An individual denied the right to practice a profession as a result of a negative judgment on his qualifications by a licensing board has been grievously affected by the exercise of routine discretion in a situation in which the state controls entry into a profession. In a case of this sort the denial of a license is equivalent to what has been called "professional decapitation." During the time when the United States had large draft calls, the routine discretion exercised by the Selective Service local boards had very nonroutine consequences for registrants (Davis and Dolbeare, 1968). There can be no doubt that even the routine exercise of discretion can lead to widely varying policy outcomes among different bureaucratic agencies. Thus, in the area of routine discretion, Wilson (1968) found very large differences in traffic citation rates, related to variations in administrative norms, among eight communities he studied.

Furthermore, decisions that in one set of circumstances are routine may in another context take on crucial importance. For this reason a political executive may find it expedient to monitor the exercise of bureaucratic discretion in an area of critical importance to him. During the war in Vietnam, for example, President Johnson personally participated in the selection of targets for American aircraft bombing in the North—a kind of decision that in other wars was left to subordinate military officials.

Nonetheless, in both routine and nonroutine areas, a substantial range of policymaking activity resides with bureaucrats. While discretion is sometimes viewed as a necessary *evil,* this is not the case. The fact is that the exercise of discretionary authority by administrators plays a vital role in protecting and advancing human welfare. Illustrations of these beneficial effects of discretion abound in the daily life of every community, as public health officials inspect restaurants, fire departments enforce theater safety regulations, and the police attempt to control and prevent traffic accidents. Without administrative discretion, effective government would be impossible in the infinitely varied and rapidly changing environment of twentieth-century society. But the exercise of judgment involves choice, and choice means the formulation of policy.

Furthermore, recent scholars of administration, primarily those of the "new public administration" movement, not only accept the desirability of administrative discretion but even urge its expansion. Frederickson (1971, p. 314) noted that the "New Public Administration seeks not only to carry out legislative mandates as efficiently and economically as possible, but to both influence and execute policies which more generally improve the quality of life for all." In general, proponents of the "new public administration" thus advocate an expansion of discretionary policymaking by administrators guided by not only the traditional criteria of efficiency and economy but also the criterion of social equity.

Bureaucracy and Rationality

As the preceding discussion has shown, the ascendancy of bureaucracy in modern society is based in large part on a general acceptance of its superior efficiency—the belief that bureaucratic organizations can outperform alternative ways of mobilizing human efforts. This is what Max Weber (1946) long ago saw as the distinctive attribute that gave bureaucracy its enormous influence in modern society.

> The decisive reason for the advance of bureaucratic organization has always been its purely technical superiority over any other form of organization. The fully developed bureaucratic mechanism compares with other organizations exactly as does the machine with the nonmechanical modes of production. (Gerth and Mills, 1946, p. 214)

Bureaucratic organizations derive this efficiency from a variety of sources. For one thing a large bureaucratic organization is itself a mechanism for enhancing human competence. People joined together in complex organizational systems can achieve results that individuals alone could never hope to accomplish—the construction of an atom bomb, the launching of a space vehicle into orbit, or the establishment of an educational system capable of meeting the intellectual needs of all citizens from primary school to postdoctoral training.

Bureaucratic organizations achieve this level of competence by taking complex problems and breaking them down into smaller and hence more manageable tasks. Once problems have been subfactored in this way, each segment can be handled separately, and then by piecing the parts together an organization can provide solutions to what may have originally seemed to be insoluble problems. This division of labor within large-scale organizations also allows groups of employees to acquire specialized expertise, even though they may not themselves have unusual technical qualifications. It is for these reasons that an organization is itself a source of expertise, quite apart from the skills that its members initially bring to the job.

A second way in which bureaucracies acquire expertise is through the concentrated attention they give to specific problems. Dealing day in and day out with the same tasks gives public agencies an invaluable kind of practical knowledge that comes from experience. This knowledge in time becomes part of the memory of a public organization and is transmitted to new employees by training and indoctrination programs. The task an agency performs may not on the surface appear terribly complex—the cleaning of streets or the removal of snow, for example—but the agency is the institution in society which by experience has come to know the most about it.

The sustained attention that bureaucrats can devote to specific problems gives them a decided advantage in framing policy decisions over political officials, who deal with a wide variety of problems and confront each issue of public policy only at sporadic intervals. This advantage is characteristic of both democratic and nondemocratic societies. It is perhaps particularly important in the United States because American bureaucrats tend to specialize early and to remain in the service of a particular agency throughout their career. But in European as well as American bureaucracies, expertise reflects continuity in office as well as concentration of energy. Not only do bureaucrats focus their attention on specific problems but they also remain in office for longer periods of time than is customary for politicians.

The knowledge that agencies acquire by continuous attention to particular functions puts them in an especially advantageous position to influence policy when the facts they gather cannot be subject to independent verification or disproof. Intelligence units are especially well situated in this respect. A monopolistic or near-monopolistic control of the "facts" provides tremendous reinforcement to the power that bureaucrats possess from specialized and continuous attention to a particular set of responsibilities.

But while organizations have certain inherent assets that contribute greatly to their decision-making skills, it is not these organizaional characteristics alone that account for the expertise which is the hallmark of modern bureaucracy. In the modern state this expertise comes also from the fact that a variety of highly trained elites practice their trade in public organizations—physicists, economists, engineers. In the roster of professions in American society there is not a single skill that does not find extensive employment in one or more executive agencies. And there are several professions, such as the military, that are employed only in the public service. Moreover, the tendency for professionals to seek employment in public and private organizations is on the increase. Etzioni argues that as "the need for costly resources and auxiliary staff has grown, even the traditional professions face mounting pressures to transfer their work to organizational structures such as the hospital and the law firm" (1964, p. 71).

In view of this traditional deference to the superior efficiency of bureaucracy, one of the most striking developments in the past decade in the United States has been the growing tendency to question the competence of organizations—their ability to achieve the goals and satisfy the public needs for which they were created. The "bureaucracy problem," as James Wilson (1967) put it, has been in part that bureaucratic organizations do not do very well many of the things they are asked to do. As noted earlier, this may be because they are sometimes asked to do impossible things. But criticism of organizational performance—the failure to deliver expected services—is nonetheless widespread in Western society. It reflects a growing belief that rather than being a necessary and inevitable instrument of rationalization—as Weber so devoutly believed—bureaucracy can be a source of irrationality as well as rationality. Recent studies of public administration in the United States, for example, have focused increasing attention on the tendency of bureaucrats to tailor organizational goals and procedures to fit their own needs rather than those of their clients. In short, as Martin Albrow has noted: "Two incompatible concepts— bureaucracy as administrative efficiency and bureaucracy as administrative inefficiency—compete for space in twentieth-century theory" (1970, p. 31).

BUREAUCRACY AND ITS PUBLICS

In an open system of politics a vital source of power for administrative agencies is their ability to attract the support of outside groups. Strength in a constituency is no less an asset for an administrator than it is for a politician in such an environment, and some agencies succeed in building outside support as formidable as that of any political organization. The lack of such support severely circumscribes the ability of an agency to achieve its goals and may even threaten its survival as an organization. As Norton Long describes this problem in the United States: "The bureaucracy under the American political system has a large share of responsibility for the public promotion of policy and even more in organizing the political basis for its survival and growth" (1949, p. 259).

This entanglement of bureaucracy with politics is a product of certain distinctive characteristics of the American political system. Since American political parties do not function effectively as organizations for the development and support of policy objectives, administrative agencies are forced to develop their own basis of political support, negotiating alliances and building coalitions in and out of government with a variety of groups in order to advance bureaucratic objectives or to assist in fending off attack. The political neutralization of bureaucracy is impossible in a democracy when the political parties are incapable of performing the functions expected of them in the governmental structure of which they are a part. When the parties do not provide for program development and the mobilization of political support, executive agencies are required to perform these tasks for themselves. Additionally, legislative mandates are sometimes deliberately vague, passing on to the bureaucracy the responsibility for decisive policy action (Long, 1962).

Once an agency succeeds in building an infrastructure of public support, it can ordinarily expect to receive favorable treatment from representatives of the public in both the legislature and the executive branches of government. Power gives power, in administration as elsewhere, and an agency that has established a secure base with the public cannot easily be harassed by political officials in positions of authority.

Attentive and Mass Publics

There are essentially two ways in which agencies seek to achieve such popular support in the United States. The first is by creating a favorable attitude toward the agency in the public at large. The second is by building strength with "attentive" publics—groups that have a salient interest in the agency—because it has either the capacity to provide them with some significant benefit or the power to exercise regulatory authority in ways that have a critical impact on their welfare as they perceive it.

Of course these methods are not mutually exclusive. An agency can seek to create general public support while building alliances with interest groups that have a special stake in its work. This is in fact the strategy most agencies follow in the United States. Only a comparatively few agencies carry on functions that have a high degree of visibility for the general public. An agency like the FBI, which has been performing a dramatic role in law enforcement for several decades, does command a broad pattern of public support that stretches throughout all strata of society. Part of this public standing springs from skillful use of publicity—agencies like the FBI exploit every opportunity to catch the public eye with their achievements. But the power of publicity is not boundless, even in America, where good public relations are a first concern of every organization, and an agency whose activities do not match the FBI's in intrinsic dramatic appeal will not equal it in public esteem no matter how assiduously it carries on public relations activity in its own behalf (Cater, 1959; Rourke, 1961; Wilensky, 1967).

There may be occasions, of course, when any agency finds itself basking temporarily in the limelight of publicity. The Food and Drug Administration, for example, may languish out of sight as far as the general public is concerned until suddenly the injurious effects of a new drug arouse public concern, as was the case a few years ago with thalidomide, a tranquilizer whose use by pregnant women brought about the delivery of a large number of infants with birth deformities. Immediately the agency and its pronouncements became a matter of front-page interest. For a brief period at least, it was an organization with a very extensive public indeed.

Furthermore, periods of heightened public attention to broad issues, such as energy policy or the environment, provide many agencies with the opportunity (or threat) of a larger audience. Frequently there is a bandwagon response and a variety of agencies proclaim their commitment to the popular side of a policy issue. For example, in the late 1960s, when consumer protection was a salient and popular issue, a number of agencies appointed "consumer advisers" who actually had little influence or importance. Other agencies with only the most peripheral and loosely defined consumer responsibilities, such as the Department of Defense, also publicized their consumer activities (Nadel, 1971, pp. 46–59). It is not surprising that government agencies adopt a popular term, but it is significant that a wide variety of agencies can claim to represent the same interest. This shows that when an interest is shared by nearly all citizens, any agency may find it advantageous to proclaim it as one of the organization's goals.

In any case it is clear that many agencies have a potential public that far exceeds the size of their normal constituency. The existence of such a potential public reflects the fact that an agency carries on activities that affect the interests of a far larger group than the public that consistently identifies itself with its program. Both the food and drug and air pollution agencies are in the public health field, where agencies perform functions that are of vital importance to a general public that may not even be aware of their existence. However, if events arouse the attention of this latent public, the agency's power in the community and the legislature may suddenly swell in importance and the usual patterns of political power will change (Schattschneider, 1960). To the extent that it depends on a broad pattern of public support, administrative power may thus be extremely volatile—shifting, like a politician's, with changing tides of public opinion.

It should be noted, however, that a rapid expansion of public interest and support does not *automatically* result in increased agency power. As Charles Jones (1972, p. 508) notes: "Unless its capabilities are vastly and rapidly improved ... the agency will not be able to meet the expectations of those supporting the new authority. Thus, far from serving as a source of power, this type of public support may actually threaten the agency." Increased visibility may simply highlight an agency's weakness.

Hence it is useful to any agency to have the support of attentive groups whose attachment is grounded on an enduring tie of tangible interest. The groups an agency directly serves provide the most natural basis of such political support, and it is with these interest groups that executive organizations ordinarily establish the firmest alliances. Such groups have often been responsible for the establishment of the agency in the first place. Thereafter, the agency and the group are bound together by deeply rooted ties that may be economic, political, or social in character. From an economic perspective, the agency usually carries on activities that advance the material welfare of members of the group. The group in turn may supply private employment opportunities for employees of the agency. Also, in return for the political representation with which the agency provides the group in the executive apparatus, the group ordinarily supports the agency in a variety of undertakings, including its requests for financial support, its attempts to secure the passage of legislation expanding its powers, or its efforts to defend itself against legislative proposals that threaten its status and security as an administrative organization. Finally, frequent social contact between agency and group breeds ties of familiarity and friendship that help seal the alliance. In its most developed form, the relationship between an interest group and an administrative agency may be so close in the United States that it is sometimes difficult to know where the group leaves off and the agency begins.

This identity between an interest group and an executive agency is strongly reinforced by the practice, especially common at the state level, of having occupational or professional qualification as a requirement for appointment to administrative office. Under law, appointees to state licensing boards that control entry into a variety of professions—including law and medicine—must come from the profession under their jurisdiction. In this way, the state virtually turns over a regulatory agency to its professional constituency—to be used at the group's discretion for its own purposes. A profession like medicine may play a similarly dominant role in other agencies as well, such as a state health department.

The power thus vested in professions merely gives formal legal blessing to the common political practice of allowing all interest groups to have a major voice in, if not a veto power over, appointments to agencies that administer functions in which they have a vital stake. Legal support for interest-group involvement in the affairs of administrative agencies may also come from statutes requiring group representation on agency advisory committees stipulating, as is common, for example, in agricultural administration in the United States, that the agency secure the consent of interest-group members before exercising certain regulatory powers. There are also cases—the administration of grazing on public lands in the West, for example—in which individuals representing interest groups are given the power to enforce administrative regulations at the point of impact (Foss, 1960; McConnell, 1966, pp. 200–11).

Building a Constituency

Some agencies are able to manipulate the dispensation of their tangible rewards in order to weld together a politically powerful coalition of constituency groups and congressmen. Thus, in a time of lessening general public support, the National Aeronautics and Space Administration required bidders on its multibillion-dollar space-shuttle project to plan for geographically widespread subcontracting. In this way, the immediate economic benefits of the project would be spread throughout many congressional districts, thus greatly broadening the size of NASA's constituency.

Agencies that are not in a position to dispense important benefits or favors to any segment of the community are in a disadvantageous position with respect to their ability to attract organized group support. The State Department is commonly regarded as having no "natural constituency" in the sense of groups for which the department is able to do tangible and significant favors. Even though the fate of the entire population may depend on the effective conduct of foreign affairs, there is no strongly organized group structure in the outside community which regards the department as "its department" and stands ready to defend and assist it in attaining its goals.

Hence, in order to secure public backing on matters of major concern to it, the department has often had to resort to organizing outside group support itself. The organization by the department of a blue-ribbon committee of distinguished citizens to lead a campaign in behalf of the Marshall Plan in 1947 is an illustration of the department's success in establishing its own public support. A similar group was formed in 1967 to win support for the government's Vietnam policy.

Executive agencies like the State Department can in fact be extremely adroit in organizing pressures to which they seem to be responding but which they are in fact initiating. The organization of such apparent pressure-group activity thus provides a means by which these agencies can conceal their own central role in the policy process. The initiative appears to lie with outside organizations, but the activities of these external groups are actually instigated by the agency itself. Of course, an agency runs a risk when it pursues this strategy, since the mass opinion it is helping to create may eventually be a constraint on it if it decides to change the policies for which it is currently seeking public support.

Domestic agencies have been even more adept at organizing their own infrastructure of interest-group support. The Department of Agriculture played a principal role in the creation and development of the American Farm Bureau Federation—the largest and most powerful of the agricultural interest-group organizations (Truman, 1951). And very early in its history the Department of Labor became convinced that the only way in which it could reach the wage-earning clientele it was obligated to serve was by encouraging the development of trade unions. Labor organizations provided an avenue for the dissemination of the informational material that was, in the beginning, the department's chief contribution to improvement of the welfare of its wage-earner clientele. The department had to communicate with its constituency, and, as it was to point out itself: "Freely as conferences with unorganized wage earners are welcome, official intercourse with individuals as such has practical limits which organization alone can remove."

Not only did the department thus defend its close liaison with existing trade union organization; it also came, not illogically in view of the need to facilitate communication with its clientele, to support the extension of trade union organization among wage earners. The reason the department gave for this support was that the growth of labor union membership would facilitate collective bargaining and promote industrial peace. "The absence of organization," the department stated, "means the absence of a medium through which the workers *en masse* can discuss their problems with employers. The denial of this organization is the denial of the only means of peaceable settlement they have" (Rourke, 1954, pp. 661–62). Pragmatic considerations were also involved in the department's support of expanded trade unionism since the strengthening of wage-earner organizations would increase the size of the department's effective clientele and the weight of its political support.

One of the major advantages the support of interest groups has for an executive department is the fact that such groups can often do for a department things that it cannot very easily do for itself. Interest groups can take a position on policy questions that department officials secretly hold but cannot publicly advocate because it may put them in disfavor with the president. The outside groups that support each of the various branches of the armed forces in the Department of Defense have often given military officials assistance in precisely this way. As Huntington puts it:

> The allies and supporters of a service are at times more royalist than the king. They do not necessarily identify more intensely with service interests than do the members of the service, but they do have a greater freedom to articulate those interests and to promote them through a wider variety of political means. (1961, p. 397)

While deference to their commander in chief may not permit military officials to disagree with the president when he cuts their appropriation or gives jurisdiction over a weapons system they believe to be rightfully theirs to another branch of the armed forces, no such restrictions prevent defense industries with which they have contractual relations from springing to their defense, or keep a backstop association such as the Navy League and the Air Force Association from vociferous protest against these efforts to trim the appropriations or the jurisdiction of a military agency.

Outside organizations thus play a valuable role in enabling administrative agencies to oppose directives from the president. They are also useful in helping these agencies evade legislative controls. Congress has enacted statutes designed to prevent administrative agencies from propagandizing the public in their own behalf or lobbying in the legislature to secure the passage of bills they favor. These laws are difficult to enforce, since administrative agencies are also charged with responsibility for keeping the public informed on what they are doing and the line between unlawful propaganda and legitimate public information activity is as fine as any distinction that exists in the American political system. But agencies can often escape such restrictions by having outside organizations carry on public relations or lobbying activity for them. Senator Goldwater of Arizona once observed that "the aircraft industry has probably done more to promote the Air Force than the Air Force has done itself." This kind of claim could be made for a great variety of interest groups that identify and associate themselves with the fortunes of an executive agency.

There are other intermediaries that bureaucratic organizations can use in their efforts to shape public opinion. Agencies will often give information they want disclosed to a sympathetic congressman and rely on him to perform the task of disseminating it to the public at large. The transmission of information in this way represents a profitable exchange for both parties. The congressman attracts public attention to himself and enhances his own career by generating news. The executive organization gets its message across to the public and in the process ties a congressional supporter even more firmly to its own cause, since he has benefited from his role as intermediary for the organization. Members of the Armed Services Committee in both the House and Senate have often served their own and the Pentagon's purposes in precisely this fashion.

A friendly news media representative can perform the same function. An agency can "leak" information to a reporter or allow him to identify it as coming from "anonymous" or "highly placed" sources in the agency. Again the transaction is one that serves the interests of both the giver and the receiver of information. The agency succeeds in getting information disseminated to the public and the reporter or columnist obtains a highly prized exclusive story. Such relationships between the Pentagon and friendly newspaper columnists are not uncommon in the United States (Sigal, 1973).

Agencies in Captivity

The external support that administrative agencies receive from interest groups is not without its perils for them. The agency may come to lean so heavily on the political support of an outside group that the group in time acquires a veto power over many of the agency's major decisions. In extreme cases of this kind the agency becomes, in effect, a "captive" organization—unable to move in any direction except those permitted it by the group on which it is politically dependent.

Administrative units that are especially vulnerable to domination of this sort are clientele agencies—public organizations established to provide comprehensive services to a special segment of the population. On the American scene such clientele agencies include the Veterans Administration, the Department of Agriculture, the Children's Bureau, and the Department of Labor. Each of these agencies has a long history of close association with and subordination to outside organizations representative of its clientele.

As noted earlier, the Department of Labor has from its very beginning been closely identified with the trade union movement. When it was first set up in 1913 the department was intended to be—in Samuel Gompers' words—"labor's voice in the cabinet." While this relationship was helpful in many ways, it also tended to narrow the scope of the department's authority. For one thing, the trade unions were allowed to exercise a great deal of influence over major departmental decisions—including the selection of assistant secretaries of labor. In addition, this association with the union movement made the department suspect in the eyes of other groups—employers, for example—and for a long time its jurisdiction over labor activities was limited by the reluctance of business and agricultural groups to allow the department to administer functions in which its bias in favor of the trade unions might be disadvantageous to their interests. As this illustration makes clear, an agency makes enemies as well as friends when it identifies itself with a particular group, since it inherits hostilities directed at the group with which it has entered into an alliance.

But while clientele agencies are particularly prone to capture by the groups they serve, an agency established on the basis of any principle of organization can hardly avoid developing a very close relationship with the groups that benefit from the activities it carries on. In terms of classical organization theory, the principal alternatives to clientele as a basis for allocating tasks among administrative agencies are the criteria of function to be performed, process or skill to be carried on by agency personnel, or geographical area to be served (Gulick and Urwick, 1937). However, agencies organized on the basis of function, such as highway, welfare, or education departments, are also susceptible to domination by outside groups, as are agencies organized on the process or skill criterion—the Corps of Engineers, for example.

As far as organization in terms of area is concerned, Selznick's classic study of the interaction between a public agency and its environment—*TVA and the Grass Roots* (1949)—clearly revealed a pervasive pattern of outside control over the foremost agency of the national government organized on the basis of geographical area, the Tennessee Valley Authority. In return for the support it received from important groups in the Valley area, the TVA proceeded to modify many of the original objectives of its agricultural program which were offensive to this constituency.

Of course in its own defense, the agency could point out that the goals it modified were not of salient importance to it, that its real concern was with its public power program in the Tennessee Valley, and if support for this activity could be obtained only by "selling out," so to speak, on agricultural goals, then this was an exchange well worth making. Selznick himself later conceded the validity of such a strategy:

> ... the TVA purchased a considerable advantage with these concessions. It gained the support of important local interests and of a powerful national lobby. These defended not only the agricultural program but TVA as a whole. In this way, by modifying its agricultural program and certain broad social policies, the Authority was able to ward off threatened dismemberment and to gain time for the successful development of its key activity—the expansion of electric power facilities. (1957, p. 44)

Any public agency may thus find it necessary to yield control over a segment of its program to a significant interest group in order to buy the support of that group for more important policy goals. Some of an agency's activities may thus serve as "loss leaders"—activities that represent a loss or at least small profit from the point of view of an agency's major goals but that simultaneously widen the basis of political support for objectives that are of more significance to it. Of course, it is always possible that this kind of support will be purchased at the price of serious damage to major institutional goals. Activities that are initially designed to be merely supportive in character may in time grow so large as to have wide-ranging and debilitating effects on an institution's capacity to achieve its major goals. Some of the worst illustrations of this kind of goal distortion have occurred in the area of regulatory administration. At both the state and national levels of government, agencies established to regulate particular kinds of economic activity have always exhibited an extraordinary penchant for falling under the control of the groups placed under their jurisdiction. The regulatory agency thus becomes, in effect, the pawn of the regulated industry. This kind of relationship represents a radical inversion of organizational goals, as an agency enters into collusion with the very group whose behavior it is supposed to control (Bernstein, 1955; Kohlmeier, 1969).

While it is easy to censure this kind of collusion, a close relationship between a regulatory agency and the groups under its jurisdiction is often essential to an agency's achievement of its goals. In the case of an air pollution commission, for example, the effectiveness of the commission may be enormously enhanced by including in its membership representatives of some of the principal industries responsible for the discharge of waste materials into the atmosphere. These representatives can help secure the compliance of their firms with air pollution regulations—a consideration that is especially important when an agency has very little coercive authority and must rely largely on voluntary compliance to achieve its regulatory goals. In its inception, at least, cooperation with the groups it is trying to control may thus be functional for a regulatory agency. It becomes dysfunctional only when, at some further point in the relationship, an agency modifies or even abandons its goals in order to retain group support.

Generally speaking, the tendency for capture by an outside group to take place is greatest when an agency deals with a single-interest constituency. In a case of this kind, an agency has nowhere else to turn if the group on which it depends should threaten to withdraw its support. Diversification of support is as desirable for a government agency as product diversification is for a private business firm. Consider the case of grazing administration as described by Wildavsky:

> The Grazing Service suffered because of its rather complete dependence on stockmen and those who spoke for them in Congress. By merging the Service into an expanded Bureau of Land Management, an act accomplished with the aid of interests adversely affected under the previous arrangement, the new organization has reduced its dependence by being able to appeal to a broader constituency. (1964, p. 172)

The heterogeneity of an administrative agency's group support thus seems to be more important in determining its freedom of action than the question of whether it is organized on the basis of clientele, purpose, process, or area to be served. The design of its political system, rather than its organizational structure, is the critical consideration.

For all agencies it is highly important to keep abreast of changes in the structure of interests affected by the activities they carry on. Huntington traces the administrative decline of the Interstate Commerce Commission to the failure of the agency to develop support among the new groups that emerged in the twentieth century as major transportation interests—the truckers, the water carriers, and the airlines. Instead, the agency tied itself to the railroads—a declining industry it had been originally created to curb in the nineteenth century. "The ICC," Huntington says, "has not responded to the demands of the new forces in transportation. . . . Consequently, it is losing its leadership to those agencies which are more responsive to the needs and demands of the times" (1952, pp. 472–73). The establishment in 1966 of the Department of Transportation as the major transportation agency of the national government provides striking confirmation of this argument.

On the other hand, agencies that have been considered stagnant and frozen into a particular pattern of policymaking can become revitalized as a result of shifts in their constituency. One of the most important changes that has taken place in the environment of American bureaucracy in modern times has been the emergence of public-interest organizations—groups like Common Cause and the cluster of reform organizations sponsored by Ralph Nader. As a result of pressures exerted by these groups, many agencies—particularly in the field of economic regulation—have substantially altered their procedures, normative assumptions, or policy outputs. This is true even of agencies like the Corps of Engineers that were traditionally considered to be conservative and highly resistant to change (Mazmanian and Lee, 1975).

PUBLIC AND PRIVATE BUREAUCRACIES—RECIPROCAL IMPACT

The discussion of private organizations in the previous section might seem to suggest that they function in the policy process primarily as constituencies of public agencies. In point of fact, however, private organizations, particularly corporations, exert a great deal of independent influence of their own on the formulation of public policy. In many settings policy emerges from a broad range of reciprocal impacts between public and private bureaucracies in which it is not always easy to tell which organization is a constituent of the other.

The incentives for private organizations to turn public agencies into their constituents come essentially from the increasingly important role of the government in the creation and regulation of wealth.

In advanced industrial societies, governments have not only increasingly managed economic resources, they have also been instrumental in the transfer of these resources. As a result the government itself, particularly in the United States, has emerged as a major source of wealth. For example, free broadcast licenses are allocated to fortunate recipients by the Federal Communications Commission—awards that may be worth millions of dollars (B. Schwartz, 1959). Licenses and charters granted to liquor stores, bus lines, and national park concessionaires also rest on the utilization of government power to create value by limiting entry into a particular field of enterprise. Other forms of government-created wealth include subsidies, contracts, income and benefits, jobs, occupational licenses, government services, and the use of public resources (Reich, 1964). In virtually every instance it is a public bureaucracy that administers the transfer and creation of wealth, which increasingly takes the form of rights or status (e.g., a profession) rather than tangible real property. Moreover, this agency power is exercised with few legislative guidelines controlling the use of discretion (e.g., "public convenience and necessity"), and the holders of such wealth are less secure in their legal rights to this property than is the case with real property (Reich, 1964). Although it is infrequent, a television-license renewal application may be denied and the station owners thus deprived of property without compensation.

Government agencies have the power not only to create and maintain certain forms of property but also to regulate the use of all wealth whatever its source. Public bureaucracies administer both general and specific regulatory schemes. All private corporations regardless of product line face potential scrutiny in regard to particular aspects of their operations, such as antitrust regulation by the Federal Trade Commission and the Justice Department, labor relations regulation by the National Labor Relations Board, and securities regulation by the Securities and Exchange Commission. Beyond this general policing and enforcement of economywide rules, certain industries interact with agencies that regulate the bulk of their operations in areas in which rules are vague and agency discretion is broad. This includes industries whose wealth is based on government franchise, such as broadcasting and transportation, as well as those less dependent on the government, such as the pharmaceutical industry. Although the adequacy of its regulation has periodically been attacked (Mintz, 1967; Turner, 1970), the United States Food and Drug Administration is a good case in point. Its decisions to certify and to decertify prescription drugs for marketing have enormous economic consequences for particular drug firms. Even after market clearance, an FDA decision that a particular drug is not efficacious or is unreasonably hazardous may deprive a drug firm of a product accounting for a significant share of its total revenue. Although we can consider the drug industry a constituency of the FDA, it is also appropriate to view the FDA as a vital constituency of the pharmaceutical corporations.

Sources of Political Influence

As is the case with public bureaucracies, private organizations have a substantial need for stability and order in their environment. Given the dependence, as outlined above, of some private bureaucracies on public agencies, there are great incentives for private-sector representatives to reach a favorable accommodation with their major client—the government. Its success in reaching such a favorable accommodation reflects the political strength of a private bureaucracy. We have noted above that the political viability of a public bureaucracy rests in its relative constituency strength and in its skills. These same factors are of equal importance in determining the political viability of private bureaucracies.

Constituency strength. The constituency strength of private bureaucracies rests in their ability to influence relevant public bureaucracies directly or through other political entities. Some public bureaucracies such as the Departments of Labor and Commerce in the United States are set up explicitly to serve the needs of private bureaucracies and other private organizations. Even more significant is the process by which public bureaucracies gradually alter their orientations in line with the needs of their major constituents. This can be seen most strikingly in the case of the regulatory agencies in the United States. Huntington (1952) and Bernstein (1955) have chronicled the process by which such agencies voluntarily undergo goal displacement as they protect and promote the industries they were originally charged with regulating. While there have been doubts raised about the extent to which this is actually goal displacement (Stone, 1973; Kolko, 1963), there is little doubt about the responsiveness of agencies to the needs of those they regulate.

Several explanations have been offered for this phenomenon of excessive clientelism on the part of regulatory agencies. One, based on a biological metaphor, posits a "life cycle" of agencies in which they proceed from gestation and youth, when they vigorously pit themselves against hostile regulated groups, through maturity (devitalization), to the debility and decline of old age (Bernstein, 1955). At the root of this agency process is the change in the effective constituency of the agencies. Initially, agencies are responsive to the reform constituency responsible for their creation and reflect the adversary relationship between the "reformers" and the regulated industry. Generally, the reform constituency dissolves, its initial goals satisfied, and the agencies are left with the regulated industry as an attentive constituency. The goals of the agency gradually shift to stability and organizational maintenance (Downs, 1967). The only way to satisfy these goals of the "maturity" phase is to seek support from the regulated industries. These stability goals neatly coincide with similar goals on the part of the regulated private bureaucracies, and thus the agencies adapt a posture of protecting and promoting the regulated industries, which they then define as their primary constituency. It can also be seen that for the private bureaucracies their agency protectors become the industry's primary constituency.

Edelman (1964) offered a somewhat different view on the changing constituency relationship of regulatory agencies. He poses the question of why there is no continuation or resurgence of reform fervor in the face of regulatory agency failure to carry out reform goals—why there is instead political quiescence. He answers that, in effect, the widespread potential reform constituency has the wool pulled over its eyes, that it is satisfied with symbolic outputs. The existence of reform laws and agencies symbolically reassures the public that it is being protected against exploitation even though the reality may be completely different. Again, it should be noted that the ultimate reason for agency behavior rests in the difference between an attentive and an inattentive constituency. Only actual policy outputs by the agency can satisfy its attentive constituency of affected interests. Thus a relatively small group of private bureaucracies can dominate a public bureaucracy because they are more prescient than the public at large.

Another explanation of the dominance of private interests is more basic and implies a more indirect role to constituency factors. Lowi (1969) argues that it is the vague legislative mandate conferring excessive administrative discretion that allowed agencies to enter a partnership with private interests. For example, the original Interstate Commerce Act authorized the Interstate Commerce Commission to set maximum rates under specific legislative and judicial guidelines. However, the Transportation Act of 1920 gave the agency power to set *minimum* rates with only vague guidelines. Lowi argues that this type of change was responsible for what is now viewed as the dominance of private interests.

A different set of causes for private dominance is most commonly found in the journalistic literature on bureaucracy and posits corruption in various forms as the central factor (Cox, 1969; Fellmeth, 1970; Turner, 1970). In general, agency personnel are the root of the problem as they are overcome by the various political, financial, and social inducements of the private bureaucracies they deal with.

It should be noted that the explanations summarized above are by no means mutually exclusive. While they may indicate the chronological order of events (e.g., excessive discretion may lead to constituency realignment), their overall impact is probably simultaneous. Thus, operating in an area with few realistic legislative guidelines, administrators are more readily able to reach a series of accommodations with once hostile interests, and some administrators may exceed the bounds of ethics, law, or propriety in the process of accommodation.

Regardless of the ultimate roots of accommodation between public and private bureaucracies, its manifestation is well established in direct and indirect forms. Direct pressure on an agency may be brought by constituent groups simply by means of overwhelming presence and pressure. This takes a variety of informal and formal approaches. In addition to social and professional contacts, private constituent interests exert influence through institutionalized meetings with public bureaucracies. This is a more highly formalized process in Europe, where such organizations as the Confederation of British Industries (Blank, 1973) and the Netherlands Social and Economic Council (Lijphart, 1968) are expected to represent particular business interests in planning and regulatory bureaucracies. Even in the United States, however, trade associations and corporation representatives have regularly scheduled meetings with regulatory officials to present their views. Altogether, corporate bureaucracies in the United States have no less ability to forcefully press their claims than do their European counterparts. The main difference is that in the United States the process is perceived to be much less legitimate (Schonfield, 1965).

To supplement direct approaches, private bureaucracies are able to exert influence on public bureaucracies through other constituency connections. For example, in the United States private interests that are adversely affected by government agencies may sometimes obtain effective relief through the intercession of congressmen or congressional committees. In fact, the relationship between private interest, congressional committee, and agency can be conceptualized as a policy subsystem of interdependent constituencies (Freeman, 1965). A particularly potent form of constituency influence can be exercised through the top levels of the executive branch. This can be accomplished through the mechanisms of control of the Office of Management and Budget or through less formal means of influence by the president. Finally, private bureaucracies can use other elements of their constituency to join them in influencing government agencies. This can include generalized appeals to the public through advertising or the use of other clientele groups. For example, the American drug industry has been successful in harnessing practicing physicians to support industry goals in Congress and the Food and Drug Administration (U.S. Senate Select Committee on Small Business, 1969).

Expertise. As with public bureaucracies, constituency support is only one pillar of the overall political strength of private bureaucracies. The other major source of influence is expertise. The political power of expertise has often been noted in regard to professional groups, particularly the "scientific estate" (Price, 1965; Schilling, 1964). In a variety of scientific and technical areas, corporations as private bureaucracies also enjoy political power based on skills and expertise. The same distinction can be drawn between absolute expertise and relevant expertise in the private sector as was made earlier with regard to the public sector (pp. 379–80). As an example of *absolute* expertise, it was made dramatically clear in 1974 that information about crude oil reserves and the realities of the supply situation resided exclusively with the major oil companies. The energy situation, however, pointed out an important qualifying factor regarding private bureaucratic expertise—where it exists, it exists at the sufferance of the government. Under threats ranging all the way to virtual nationalization, American based oil companies became considerably more forthcoming with previously withheld information. Private bureaucracies more frequently possess *relevant* expertise. Thus in the areas of space and weapons-systems contracting, the space and defense bureaucracies and congressional committees have held that only the major contracting corporations were qualified to produce authoritative advice regarding feasibility, cost, and utility.

A primary arena for the utilization of nongovernmental expertise as a political resource is the network of private organizations advising governments in every Western industrial country. In the Netherlands, for example, the cabinet is required by law to seek the advice of the Social and Economic Council, composed equally of business and labor representatives, on all proposed social and economic measures. Lijphart (1968) asserts that it is this advisory role that gives the Council a political power and significance equal to that of the cabinet or parliament. Its power is enhanced by the frequent practice of secret deliberations and secret advice to the cabinet—practices not uncommon in other private advisory situations.

In the United States at last count there were 1,439 federal advisory committees attached to agencies of the federal government (United States Senate, Committee on Government Operations, 1973). While the majority of these committees were not composed of corporate or other private bureaucracies, business interests were particularly well placed to exert influence. For example, in the United States the Business Council on Federal Reports advises the Office of Management and Budget (OMB) on questionnaires that federal agencies plan to send out to business firms. Under a 1942 law, all questionnaires that federal agencies plan to send out to ten or more businesses or persons must be cleared by OMB. The Business Council has fully realized the power inherent in its advisory role—a role that goes considerably beyond the provision of technical advice. Thus, in 1963 the Federal Trade Commission proposed a survey to study interlocking ownership among the 1,000 largest corporations in the United States. At the OMB, business advisors objected vigorously to the purpose of the study. Nonetheless, it was approved. Knowing of the plans for the survey, the corporate representatives took their fight to Congress, which then refused to appropriate money for the survey and even forbade OMB from conducting it for the following three years (Nugent, 1968). Similar attempts by other agencies to survey pollution problems were also prevented or long delayed as a result of business pressure (Reinemer, 1970). Until corrective legislation was enacted in 1972, the advisory power of private bureaucracies was greatly bolstered by allowing them to give advice in secret. Many advisory committee meetings were closed to nonmembers, and no useful public accounting was given of their proceedings. Of course, advisory committees are not always dominated by the private sector. Pempel (1974), for example, found that in Japan educational advisory committees were dominated by the various educational bureaucracies themselves.

Influence on organizational forms. In the United States, the business firm has served not only as a source of influence on public bureaucracies but also as a model for their organization and operation. The cliché about bureaucrats who have "never met a payroll" is not simply a pejorative assessment; it is indicative of an underlying ideology that has strongly influenced public programs and organization. Various tenets of managerial theory that originated in the private sector have been applied to government on the assumption that public administration is a management, rather than a political, process. Thus the scientific-management movement in business was carried over into the public sector through organizational forms whose implicit assumption was that public administration was nonpartisan and even nonpolitical. Political choices were to be made by legislative bodies and the job of the bureaucrat was simply to apply "scientific" principles to implement those choices (Wilson, 1887; Goodnow, 1900).

A major manifestation of this private sector ideology was the development of the council-manager form of city government. This new form, which spread rapidly after being first introduced in 1915 in Dayton, Ohio, was a response to corruption and poor administration in American cities. It was spurred by the combined interest of civic and business leaders (White, 1927; Weinstein, 1968). Although there is evidence that the reformers were most interested in honest administration and optimal policy outputs, the plan was consciously promoted as a governmental analogy to the popular image of an efficiently run business corporation, with the city council to function as the community's "board of directors" (Price, 1941). Thus the plan was pegged to the notion of big business as the optimal model of governmental organization. As a reflection of their business origins, there is some evidence that taxes and expenditures are relatively lower in council-manager cities than in cities with an elected mayor as chief executive (Lineberry and Fowler, 1967).

Executive-reorganization plans usually have been proposed with preference for corporate organizational and control forms and for managerial efficiency over other social values. Thus we find a consistent preference for strong centralized executive leadership in the reports of the Brownlow Committee in 1937, both Hoover Commissions, in 1949 and 1955, and the Ash Council in 1971. It is not only the organizational framework of public bureaucracies that has been influenced by the private sector but also procedures within public agencies. Most recently, the federal government briefly utilized program budgeting in its most recent form, Planning, Programming Budgeting System (PPBS), with mixed results (Schick, 1969; Wildavsky, 1969). Extending from initial application to the Defense Department, the use of PPBS illustrated some of the problems that arise when management techniques designed for and appropriate to business firms are applied to public bureaucracies. Thus, in the area of health and welfare, interpersonal utility values must be assigned to human life, suffering, and the undesirability of various diseases in order to compare the cost effectiveness of alternative programs. This is clearly not the same as resolving production problems that arise in private industry.

Not surprisingly, the process by which reorganization plans have been formulated and new procedures advanced has itself been dominated by businessmen. Thus, four of the six members of the Ash Council on executive organization during the Nixon administration were businessmen. It was no accident that the systems-management techniques of Secretary of Defense Robert MacNamara during the Kennedy and Johnson administration were transplanted from their successful use by MacNamara during his earlier tenure as president of the Ford Motor Company.

In general, then, the organizational forms and procedures of public bureaucracies in the United States have been heavily influenced by the model of the business organization. It may be argued that this business orientation fails to distinguish between the values to be maximized by a business firm and by a public agency in a democracy. Thus, Wildavsky (1966) contends that it is futile to pursue pure economic rationality in the public policy process through such devices as systems analysis. He asserts that economic-efficiency maximizers view the political universe as if it were devoid of noneconomic cost and benefits. However, policies that appear to be optimal in economic cost-benefit terms may have unacceptable political costs. Political power, political flexibility, and political support are as much realities in the policy process as are the economic costs and benefits of a reclamation project, and Wildavsky warns against ignoring such components of political rationality.

The pursuit of economic rationality in executive organizations has been criticized on other grounds as well. A constant goal of governmental reorganization plans has been to avoid and remove duplication of services. Yet Landau (1969) argues that redundancy provides reliability in organizations, as it does in mechanical systems. Thus attempts to streamline and avoid duplication actually remove back-up and parallel systems and increase the probability of error. Unless redundancy is structured into bureaucracy, "when one bulb blows, everything goes" (p. 354). Particularly in public bureaucracies "rational" redundancy is important because it provides much greater assurance that a governmental function will be carried out than does a system in which a single agency is given sole responsibility for its performance.

Another major form of private sector influence on public bureaucracies is found in the initial creation of public bureaucracies, many of which were established to promote the interests of private organizations. Such large departments in the United States as the Department of Labor or the Department of Commerce were not "captured" by their constituencies; they were always expected to give primary allegiance to their clientele. Particularly in regulatory agencies is this phenomenon prevalent. Meat inspection agencies in the states and federal government were originally established at the behest of the large packing houses seeking government assurance of quality in order to promote meat exports (Kolko, 1963, pp. 98–100). The Federal Communications Commission (originally the Federal Radio Commission) was established in response to the needs of the fledgling broadcast industry, and the Civil Aeronautics Board emerged from the needs of the airline industry and from private-enterprise-oriented belief systems (Redford, 1969). Indeed, there is agreement among conservatives and liberal reformers that much of the regulatory apparatus in the United States currently serves to promote and protect the economic interests of regulated industries from competition and from intervention by other sectors of the government (Noll, 1971; Green and Nader, 1973; Winter, 1973).

Thus, it can be seen that the impact of the private sector on public bureaucracies stems from a complex web of factors. For some public bureaucracies there is no clear agency-constituency relationship. Rather, there is a series of interorganizational relationships with public and private bureaucracies having comparable political resources (Aldrich, 1972). Private bureaucracies themselves depend on constituency support and expertise as their prime resources. Private bureaucracies also impinge on the public sector in terms of the assumptions, organization, and procedures of public bureaucracies. The situation is made even more complex by the public role of private bureaucracies.

The Public Role of Private Bureaucracies

In the past, political scientists have often made a sharp distinction between governmental and nongovernmental organizations. Bureaucracies, however, do not always break down into such mutually exclusive categories. Indeed, the boundary between public and private organizations has long been questioned by a number of scholars. In an early discussion of the subject Charles Merriam (1944, p. 16) pointed out that the "lines between 'public' and 'private' are not absolutes, but . . . there are zones of cooperation and cohesion in the common cause and on a common basis in many fields of human action." In another early formulation John Dewey (1927) analyzed the distinction between public and private and argued that it was the externalities of transactions that gave them a public character.

In a more recent formulation of the problem, Robert A. Dahl and Charles E. Lindblom (1953) go further than Dewey and Merriam and dismiss the sharp public-private distinction as being too rigid, unrealistic, and unnecessarily limiting of the real choices at hand. They demonstrate that the situation is more accurately conceived as a continuum on which organizations display varying degrees of public and private function. On this continuum, which shows some of the choices available between government ownership and private enterprise, the possibilities run from "an enterprise operated as an ordinary government department such as the post office" to "a hypothetical small proprietorship subject only to common law" at the private end. They present additional continua showing the range of organizational choices with regard to control (direct and indirect), compulsion (voluntary and compulsory), and hierarchy (autonomy to prescription by hierarchical superior).

While there are clear differences in the legal standing of public and private bureaucracies, their differences in function are not so great. In addressing the question of the differences between a corporation and a government, Gordon Tullock (1970, p. 53) states: "The answer to this question is simply that we have grown accustomed to calling one particular type of collective organization a government. Characteristically, there is one collective apparatus in society that is more powerful than any other . . . . This apparatus we call the government. It should be emphasized, however, that the difference between this organization and a general contract is less than one might suppose."

For purposes of boundary setting and manageability of research, political scientists have handled the boundary problems simply by regarding as "public" all bureaucracies that are governmental. Thus in a bibliographic essay on public organization, Peabody and Rourke (1965, p. 803) explicitly equate "public" with "governmental" bureaucracies, while admitting that it is still necessary to decide whether a given institution is governmental or nongovernmental. Herein lies the crux of the problem. In some situations, even a reliance on formal legal status is insufficient to establish a clear distinction between governmental-public on the one hand and nongovernmental-private on the other. There are three aspects to this blurring of boundaries between public and private organizations. Beyond the various ways in which private bureaucracies influence government policy, there is such extensive cooperation between governmental and nongovernmental organizations that it is difficult to know where one ends and the other begins. For example, in the field of defense procurement, weapons systems have been developed through the coequal cooperation of the Pentagon and "private" industry, particularly in the 1960s (W. Kaufman, 1964). During the Johnson administration, private industry contracted to provide job training programs through the old Job Corps. The interconnectedness of public and private may be even greater at the local than at the national level. In many small localities private business and associations perform a variety of planning and service functions in cooperation with or instead of local government (Grodzins, 1963).

A prime example of bureaucratic organization that does not fit neatly into a governmental or nongovernmental category is the Communications Satellite Corporation (COMSAT). Had the result of legislative battle been otherwise, COMSAT might have been organized under complete government control—like the Tennessee Valley Authority. Instead, after much debate between proponents of government ownership and proponents of unfettered ownership by the communications common carriers, the solution was a modified form of private ownership dominated by the common carriers (Galloway, 1972, pp. 47–73). Although COMSAT acts primarily as "private" enterprise, it has two other roles. It is the quasi-governmental representative of the United States in the International Telecommunications Satellite Organization, and it is the manager and representative of this international organization. Furthermore, its enabling legislation explicitly designates COMSAT as the designated instrument of United States foreign policy—a role that sometimes conflicts with its role as a business corporation (Galloway, 1972, pp. 137–47). The boundary problems of COMSAT are also seen in the mixture of governmental and private representation on its board of directors (H. Schwartz, 1965).

A second aspect of the boundary problem is the direct policymaking role of completely nongovernmental organizations based on the explicit delegation of government functions to these private organizations (McConnell, 1966; Lowi, 1969). This process included direct participation in policymaking by business, labor, and farm groups and semiautonomous formulation of policy by such groups. Probably the most extensive instance of this phenomenon is government-sanctioned licensing by professional associations. Small bureaucracies in a variety of occupational areas limit occupational entry and, in effect, maintain legal cartels (Gilb, 1966).

The third feature of public-private boundary blurring is the impact and nature of actions taken by private bureaucracies at their own discretion. Probably because they are the largest and most pervasive entities that are popularly regarded as "private," much of the discussion of this question concerns business corporations. For example, Dahl (1972, p. 18) argues that large corporations are political entities and notes that by their decisions large corporations may "cause death, injury, disease, and severe physical pain . . . . Impose severe deprivations of income, well-being, and effective personal freedom . . . . Exercise influence, power, control, and even coercion over employees, customers, suppliers, and others . . . ."

Of course, corporations are not the only quasi-government political entities. Gilb (1966) points out the role of professional associations as being somewhere in the middle of a continuum between public and private activities. Nongovernmental foundations can also be viewed as political entities. The activities of the governmental National Institutes of Health or the National Science Foundation are often functionally equivalent to the nongovernmental Ford Foundation or the Social Science Research Council. Indeed, there has been considerable controversy and discussion over the public-private mix of American foundations, whose bureaucratic structure has, nevertheless, been little studied (Weaver, 1967).

Given both the impact of nongovernmental bureaucracies on government agencies and the uncertain boundaries of the political system, it is clear that in many respects nongovernmental bureaucracies are political entities. Thus, in discussing public policy we must take into account certain outputs of these major quasi-governmental or nongovernmental organizations. In a modification of Lowi's (1964; 1972) categorization, these outputs can be conceptualized in three categories: resource transfer, regulatory, and constituent policies (Nadel, 1975). Resource transfer includes such binding allocations of material resources as administered pricing structures of corporate bureaucracies in concentrated markets (Means, 1962; Galbraith, 1967) and large-scale investment policies by insurance companies (Orren, 1972). Regulatory policy involves the direct control of behavior and environmental conditions affecting health and welfare such as occupational safety (Heilbroner, 1972). Constituent policy involves direct control of political resources through such conditions as campaign financing and control over company towns (Phelan and Pozen, 1973). Corporations implement all three types of policy.

This view of the corporation as a political and public-policymaking entity is by no means universally accepted, and the resulting disagreement is reflected in the discussion of corporations as bureaucratic structures. At one end of the argument, Jacoby (1973) argues that the political power of the corporation is conditioned by market factors and motivated by a concern for profits. Barber (1970) and especially Galbraith (1967) give more weight to the unilateral decision-making discretion of corporations and stress their various linkages to government bureaucracies. So, as is the case with government bureaucracies, there is considerable disagreement over how much influence corporate organizations actually exert on public policy. A major difference between the two situations is that in the case of the corporation the alternative contributors to public policy are the broader factors of competitive conditions, consumer behavior, and the policies of various governmental entities. As with government bureaucracies, unilateral power and policymaking discretion can be overemphasized.

The resolution of this controversy may well rest in its restatement in terms analogous to governmental bureaucractic policymaking. For both governmental and nongovernmental bureaucracies the scope of policymaking is largely determined by the amount of discretion exercised by the bureaucracy. While the constraints on corporate bureaucratic discretion are of a different nature than those on governmental bureaucracies, nonetheless discretion is still the relevant concept in appraising the scope of corporate policymaking. Just as government agencies operate within broad parameters set by external political forces, so too do corporate bureaucracies, whose parameters consist of market forces in addition to political forces. The scope of corporate discretion is well illustrated in the context of administered prices by Means (1962, p. 43), who notes that market power does not mean that the corporation can set prices at *any* level it chooses but that "the price leader in steel operates within an area of pricing discretion such that within a significant range it can set one price rather than another."

There are also differences in the utilization of discretion within bureaucratic structures. The top levels of nongovernmental bureaucracies have more discretion in controlling internal behavior at lower levels because, unlike government bureaucracies, they can manipulate agreement from the top more readily than can executives in public bureaucracies who have to rely on bargaining (Gawthrop, 1969, pp. 21–36). Similarly, private organizations have a simplified decision-making task because their objectives are clearer and they are not subject to political fragmentation (Gawthrop, 1969, pp. 127–30).

Thus, in assessing the policy outputs of nongovernmental bureaucracies, the parameters and degree of discretion may differ. Nonetheless it is this central concept of discretion that highlights the policymaking role of bureaucracies. Both governmental and nongovernmental bureaucracies are the source of policy outputs. The limitations on private bureaucracy policymaking, far from indicating a fundamental difference from government bureaucracies, testify to the fact that both types of bureaucracies face constraints on their actions. The need for and the range of constraints on bureaucratic action are considered in the next section.

BUREAUCRATIC RESPONSIBILITY

The General Problem

Thus far we have examined the nature of bureaucracies as policymaking organizations and the sources of their power. While there may be questions about the inevitability of the bureaucratization of the state (Gouldner, 1955), there is a concensus that bureaucracies exercise a great deal of influence in nearly every type of political regime. Yet, a growing reliance on bureaucratic skills in the operation of the modern states has long been accompanied by a pervasive fear of bureaucratic power. Indeed, nineteenth century writers such as Bagehot and John Stuart Mill viewed bureaucracy as a distinct form of government and administration that was antithetical to democracy.[3] By the end of the nineteenth century and in the early years of the twentieth century, however, bureaucracy was increasingly seen as inevitable. Even before Weber's equation of bureaucracy with rational modern government, Mosca (1896) in *The Ruling Class* classified governments into only two types—feudal and bureaucratic—and in the latter form bureaucrats were a major element in the ruling class. Among early theorists it was Michels (1911) who most prominently linked the inevitability of bureaucracy to a pejorative concept of bureaucracy—the "iron law of oligarchy."

The fear and distrust of bureaucracy is found among conservatives and liberals alike. On the part of conservatives this has been primarily a fear of civilian bureaucrats taking over areas of social and economic decision making that they believe should be left in the hands of private business firms. On the liberal side, apprehension has focused on the power of the military bureaucracy. More recently there has also been dissatisfaction and disillusionment on the left with the performance of social welfare bureaucracies. As James Wilson (1967) points out, this general dissatisfaction with bureaucracy reflects several specific concerns over such matters as accountability to political superiors, equity (treating like cases in a like manner), efficiency, responsiveness to constituencies, and fiscal integrity. Yet we will subsume these problems into the broader concept of bureaucratic responsibility—the traditional task of keeping bureaucracies servants rather than masters. This orientation does not ignore the more specific components of the bureaucracy problem. Rather, it argues that the more basic problem is to assure that bureaucracies do pursue whatever more specific goals are given priority in a particular society—whether equity, responsiveness, or sheer efficiency.

Bureaucracy and Society

In countries as diverse as the United States, France, and the People's Republic of China there has been great concern with the problem of harnessing public bureaucracies to societal needs, goals, and prevailing social values. Although our discussion focuses primarily on bureaucracies in modern democratic states, the problem of responsibility is at least of equal significance in non-Western societies. Despite utopian Marxist visions of a nonbureaucratized state, Lenin and later Soviet leaders have had to grapple with the bureaucracy problem continuously—even when they pretended it did not exist. The paradox of a socialist bureaucracy that was autonomous and privileged was most conspicuously criticized as a "new class" by Djilas (1957). To a great extent, control of the bureaucracy has been a continuing theme in the politics of China. From the Hundred Flowers Campaign through the Cultural Revolution, a profoundly important element was control of the bureaucracy in accord with prevailing societal goals —in the Chinese case, reducing the "alienation" of the bureaucrats from the masses and preventing the bureaucracy from acquiring a privileged status in the society (Dittmer, 1974).[4]

In underdeveloped areas the problem of bureaucratic responsibility is somewhat different.[5] There is the familiar problem of assuring bureaucratic action in accord with previously determined social and political goals. While a correspondence between bureaucratic and social values may be taken for granted in stable societies, it sometimes takes a strenuous effort to harness bureaucratic activities to new social goals in times of change (Esman, 1966). In the transitional stages of nationhood, this is complicated by the presence of a holdover bureaucracy from the colonial era, whose own goals may seriously conflict with those of the new political leadership. At another stage of development, however, bureaucracies may themselves be modernizing agents consciously attempting to implant a new "rationalizing" orientation in the social and political system (Benveniste and Ilchman, 1969).

In stable modern societies the broad outlines of bureaucratic organization normally reflect the goals and ideological orientation of the societies of which they are a part. Leonard White's (1948, 1954, 1957) seminal studies of administration in the United States demonstrate the way in which bureaucracy has been intertwined in American political and social history. More concisely, Kaufman (1956) states that the administrative institutions of the United States have been organized and operated in pursuit of three values: representativeness, neutral competence, and executive leadership. These values, which have been overlapping modes of thought, were reflections of broader political preferences that were dominant in particular historical eras. Thus, a neutral and "scientifically" managed bureaucracy was a central premise of progressivism. Similarly, the quest for representativeness in administration was a key tenet of Jacksonian democracy, just as current drives toward decentralization and citizen participation are joined to larger goals of minority-group political power and community control.

Not just the administrative forms, but the power and utilization of bureaucracies are also deeply rooted in the political development of a state. Thus, Strauss (1961, p. 223) argues that bureaucratic rule in France is "the residuary product of the great social and political conflicts which mark the historical epochs of modern French society from the overthrow of the absolute monarchy by the Great Revolution to the overthrow of the Fourth Republic by General De Gaulle."

Bureaucratic organization is equally entwined in the social and cultural mores of a state. In the United States the Jacksonian stress on "amateurism" in public service surely owed as much to widely shared perceptions of the need for a classless society as it did to the needs of party organizations. Crozier (1964, p. 222) argues that in France the quirks of administration are a reflection of the French social system: ". . . the French bureaucratic system of organization is the perfect solution to the basic dilemma of Frenchmen about authority"— a tension between absolute authority and personal autonomy.

The search for the public interest. Quite apart from the desire to make bureaucracies correspond in their orientation to social goals and cultural mores, the more fundamental problems of bureaucratic responsibility on a routine basis present themselves. In the United States the problem of bureaucratic responsibility has been formulated as a search for the "public interest." Emmette Redford (1954, p. 1106) concisely restated the ancient and recurring problem:

"There is little chance that the immediate interests of organized groups will not receive adequate attention. The real danger is that the interests of the unorganized and weak, the shared interests of men generally, and the interests of men for tomorrow will not have proper weight in government councils." How then can these notions of the common good, or public interest, find expression in the administrative process—assuming for the moment that this is a proper focus?

In a useful discussion of public-interest theory, particularly as applied to the administrative realm, Schubert (1960) classified public-interest theorists into three categories: the rationalists, the idealists, and the realists. The rationalists postulate a common good "which reflects the presumed existence of various common—frequently majoritarian—interests." Bureaucratic responsibility is thus found in the context of institutions that allow expression of the majority will—especially greater centralization of the political executive. The independent regulatory commissions are thus an anathema to rationalist scholars and practitioners. Such rationalist views have dominated all reports and recommendations on executive organization in the United States.

The idealists view the public interest in terms of a true interest that may not be perceived by the public itself. The public interest thus reposes not in the positive law made by man but in higher law or higher good. Prominently included in this school are scholars like Marver Bernstein (1955) who urge an independent assessment of the public interest by administrators: "Whatever objectives and policies are set forth by Congress, the overriding task of policy formation in the independent commission is the search for the public interest, that is, the determination of the goal of public policy and the way in which the goal can be achieved" (pp. 154–55).

In his discussion of realists, Schubert is speaking mainly of the group theorists. Had he written a few years later he would probably have included the later pluralists such as Dahl, Polsby, and Lindblom among those with a realist conception. The realists deny the existence of an interest of the nation as a whole. Policy and the public interest can emerge only from a competitive struggle among organized interests. This concept of the public interest as it applied to administrators found early expression in the works of Herring (1936) and Truman (1951), both of whom conceived of the public interest as some inescapable combination of special group interests. The major substantive prescription of the realists is the admonition that the administration process allow a fair hearing for all affected interests.

Unfortunately, the concept of the public interest in all its varied forms is difficult to apply.[6] In the rationalist and idealist approaches, we are left with the problem of determining either the majority will or the public good respectively, and determining the mandate either of the voters or of heaven is no mean feat. The realists acknowledge the problem and simply sidestep any independent consideration of the public interest. Because of the difficulty of defining and operationalizing the concept, Schubert ultimately concludes by urging political scientists to disregard the public interest as an analytic concept since it offers no operational utility. Likewise, Sorauf (1957), after a similar analysis of the public interest, argues that its definitional problems rendered the public interest useless as a tool of analysis. To the extent that the concept survives, the public interest is today viewed mainly from a realist perspective. Thus, Sorauf argues that if there is a public interest, it can mean only an interest arrived at through a process of group accommodation. Harmon (1969) makes the process of political competition a more explicit criterion of the public interest, which he asserts is a process of activist policymaking by bureaucracies coupled with a maximum amount of responsiveness to affected groups.

Apart from its analytical weakness, a broad focus on the public interest offers little operational guidance in seeking bureaucratic responsibility. Thus, even if we accept the value of bringing as much competition and adjustment of interests as possible into bureaucratic policymaking, we still face two key questions: How can the bureaucracy be encouraged to pursue this (or any other) standard of the public interest? What remedies are available if a bureaucracy does not follow the prescribed view of the public interest? It is in response to such questions regarding political accountability that we can evaluate more specific devices designed to impose restraints on the power of bureaucracies.

The Forms of Control

Although a variety of solutions, old and new, have been offered to the problem of bureaucratic responsibility, most of them originate in two opposing positions stated a generation ago by Carl Friedrich and Herman Finer. While obtaining responsible administration is a necessity, Friedrich (1940) contended that administrative accountability could not be secured through the formal and legal institutions of control. Bureaucratic responsibility, he argued, is less formal and more internally based. It derives primarily from two internal norms: adherence to technical competence as gauged by the bureaucrat's professional peers, and anticipations by bureaucrats of reactions to their decisions by both the public and their political superiors. Policy thus follows the broad outlines of public desires as these can be discerned or anticipated.

In a vigorous rebuttal to Friedrich's position, Herman Finer (1941) argues for strict accountability to formal and external modes of control. Finer reasserts the distinction between making policy as an expression of popular will (the legislative function) and executing policy (the administrative function). The authority of the bureaucrat is only a "conditioned, derived authority" (p. 343). Finer characterized his chief disagreement with Friedrich as resting in his own "insistence upon distinguishing responsibility as an arrangement of correction and punishment even up to dismissal both of politicians and officials" (p. 335).

He further asserts that this formal, external standard of accountability is, contrary to Friedrich's argument, both workable and indispensable to democratic government.

Much of the later debate and reform proposals relating to bureaucratic responsibility are rooted in one of these two themes—reliance on informal, inner-directed controls or formal, externalized controls. Of course these categories are not mutually exclusive. Even Finer acknowledges that bureaucratic responsibility is aided by inner moral imperatives, although it ultimately must rest in "objective" subservience to political authority. Drawing largely on the distinction between the Friedrich and Finer positions, we can usefully conceptualize the varieties of controls on bureaucratic power along two dimensions —location of control and formality of control. The alternative methods of securing bureaucratic responsibility (actual or proposed) are presented in terms of this framework in Table 1. In order to have a more detailed and conceptually clear analysis, the examples we use are drawn primarily from American bureaucracies.

TABLE 1   Typology of controls for bureaucratic responsibility

	Formal	Informal
External	Directly or indirectly elected political chief executive: president, prime minister, governor, etc. Elected legislature: congress, parliament, city council, etc. Courts Ombudsman	Public opinion The press Public interest groups Constituencies Competing bureaucratic organizations
Internal	Representative bureaucracy where legally required Citizen participation where legally required Decentralization	Perception of public opinion (anticipated reaction) Professional standards Socialization in the norms of responsibility

Formal external controls. In the United States the dominant mode of assuring bureaucratic responsibility is through political control by an elected chief executive. At the national level this was recommended by various special commissions on the executive branch starting with the Brownlow Committee in 1937, and it has been sought through a variety of measures, particularly the creation of the Bureau of the Budget (now the Office of Management and Budget) and a succession of reorganization acts. A similar tendency has been present in the American states in which the executive budget has been a principal instrument of hierarchical control.

This centralizing tendency is, however, paradoxical. While centralization is sought in theory and practice, it is also widely recognized that bureaucratic accountability to the president or other political executives is as elusive as accountability to legislatures and the public generally. Thus while the president has a variety of formal sanctions, these are rarely applied except in extreme circumstances. Neustadt (1960) has argued that the use of these formal sanctions or commands actually represents failure of presidential leadership. In spite of his formal powers, the power of the president vis-à-vis the bureaucracy (as well as in relation to other institutions) is actually the "power to persuade." Indeed, the relationship between the president and the bureaucracy is one of reciprocal control, and the bureaucracy is commonly regarded as a restraint on presidential power (Rossiter, 1960).

The tenuous hold of the president on the bureaucracy can be seen in his relations with his own cabinet. Although the cabinet, as a collectivity, has been somewhat successful as a "sounding board" reflecting the views of diverse constituencies, presidents have seldom been able to utilize it to coordinate the activities of the various departmental bureaucracies (Fenno, 1959). The lack of coordination and control is due largely to the dual nature of the cabinet member's job. He is at once the president's chosen instrument of department leadership and the representative and champion of that department's interests. The cabinet member's loyalty to the department, essential if he is to be effective as an administrator, makes him much less suitable as an agent of presidential control. Partly in response to this problem, the task of coordination of the departmental bureaucracies has been given to interdepartmental bodies, especially the National Security Council (Hammond, 1960). But these groups serve primarily to advise and coordinate the broad outlines of policy and do not reach down to control policymaking at the lower levels of the bureaucracy.

In the United States, presidents have attempted to impose their will on the bureaucracy by a variety of other formal and informal means through increased institutionalization in the Executive Office of the President.[7] In large part the task has fallen to the Office of Management and Budget not only through the executive control of the budget but also through central clearance of agency legislative proposals to assure that they are in accord with the program of the president (Neustadt, 1954, 1955). In the last fifteen years presidents have attempted to centralize this process even further by directly involving themselves and their personal staffs in the clearance of high-priority legislation (Gilmour, 1971).

Presidential control has also been manifested in the budgetary process through the utilization of program budgeting (PPBS). Theoretically, this gives the president greater power to enforce bureaucratic responsibility by tying the executive agencies to long-range program goals and permitting the president more control over those programs. However, at least one scholar has argued that committing the president to such long-range programs greatly limits his flexibility of action and thus affords him less control over day-to-day bureaucratic policymaking (Wildavsky, 1966).

In attempting to control the bureaucracy the president is left with a fundamental dilemma. He must rely on his own staff to monitor those segments of the bureaucracy he deems most salient to his goals. As he seeks to expand his control of the bureaucracy, his staff must grow correspondingly. As his staff grows and is targeted in more comprehensively on the bureaucracy, the president then is confronted with the new problem of controlling his own staff. Thus, in attempting to enforce bureaucratic responsibility by centralizing power in the presidency, theory and practice depart significantly.

It should be noted that a fundamental corollary to bureaucratic accountability to a political chief executive is an organizational arrangement emphasizing hierarchical authority relationships. That is, officials within an agency must be subordinate and responsible to the head of the agency in the same formal sense that the agency head is himself accountable to the political executive. Such an arrangement is easier to achieve in theory than in practice, and there are substantial problems of information and control. For example, in a study of the ability of bureaucratic executives to gain useful information about the actions of subordinates, Kaufman (1973) found that such information feedback was generally adequate in federal agencies. The problem, however, was that for a variety of reasons superiors may not want to learn too precisely the details of action by subordinates. Thus a hierarchical organization may not produce the results, in terms of accountability, that are claimed in theory.

A second external device for enforcing bureaucratic responsibility is control through the legislature. In parliamentary regimes this is the primary device and the one stressed and preferred by Finer (1941). In Britain, parliamentary control is most strikingly and symbolically manifested by the question hour in the House of Commons, during which cabinet members submit to interrogation by Parliament.

In the United States, Congress has a number of avenues through which it can perform the function of legislative oversight in accord with its legal mandate. Traditionally, this control has been exercised through annual appropriations, the audit, investigation, and new legislation. The appropriations process is the most routinized and comprehensive form of congressional control. Appropriations subcommittee jurisdictions correspond to the organization of the executive branch, and subcommittee chairmen and staff thus have the opportunity to develop considerable expertise on the agencies under their control. Agencies are forced to justify new expenditures, and the legislative norm, particularly in the House Appropriations Committee, is to cut budget requests. Agencies do not enjoy equal standing in this process. Some are notably more successful than others due to their popular and noncontroversial functions, well-defined work load, and constituency-oriented clientele support (Fenno, 1966, pp. 366–81).

Recently, two additional techniques of legislative control have been utilized. The first is the requirement that agencies seek annual authorization for all their expenditures or for specific programs. Annual authorizations have been required in such policy areas as space exploration, foreign aid, and defense weapons systems, and the requirement now covers approximately 35 percent of the federal budget (Saloma, 1969, pp. 130–68). Second is the "legislative veto" —the requirement for the president and some agencies that certain agency decisions be reviewed by Congress or a particular committee before going into effect. Even more important and pervasive than these formal statutory requirements, however, is the de facto veto and control exercised by appropriations and substantive committees, which regularly convey instructions to agencies during hearings and at other times (Harris, 1964, pp. 204–48).[8]

Congress, however, is greatly limited (externally and internally) in its ability to be an instrument of legislative oversight. Most devices of legislative control tend to fractionalize administration and are directed at the periphery of policy. Every agency is confronted with at least three congressional committees in each house: the Government Operations Committee, an appropriations subcommittee, and a substantive area committee. Thus control is exercised by committees rather than Congress as a whole. Administrative intervention by high-seniority committee chairmen is a far cry from formal bureaucratic responsibility. Even in the appropriations process control is exercised at the margins, and each agency normally deals only with increments to existing budgets and programs (Wildavsky, 1964).

Ultimately, Congress is confronted with the same dilemma as the president. Congressional attempts to exert more control require larger staffs. But as congressional staffs get larger and more specialized they begin to constitute a legislative bureaucracy—one that itself presents problems of control and responsibility (Manley, 1968).

The courts are a third external check on bureaucracies. The importance of the courts has grown in response to the expansion of the discretionary power of bureaucracies in dealing with cases affecting the rights of individuals. Davis (1969) argues that control over the administration of justice by executive agencies has been the major change in the American legal system during the twentieth century. Since in these instances agencies such as the Social Security Administration and the Internal Revenue Service are de facto courts of original jurisdiction, the task of enforcing bureaucratic responsibility in specific cases often rests with the judiciary.

The importance of discretionary justice highlights another feature of the relationship between bureaucracies and courts—the degree to which the functions of the two institutions are similar. We have long since been accustomed to referring to certain of the independent regulatory commissions as quasi-judicial, and agencies such as the Federal Trade Commission have independent hearing examiners and highly structured judicial procedures. While agencies proceed judicially, it must also be stressed that courts participate in the making of administrative policy. Thus Shapiro notes that

> the distinctive characteristic of appellate courts is that they are supplemental law makers engaged in small-step incremental decision making constrained by the expectation of both the general public and certain of their key constituencies that each of their decisions involves only minimal, necessary change. Having said this, one must also add immediately that if these are indeed the distinctive characteristics of appellate courts, appellate courts are very difficult to distinguish from the administrative bureaucracy. (1968, p. 44)

Thus, while courts are certainly external to the agencies, both institutions are properly conceptualized as parallel bodies, neither of which can by itself determine policy with absolute finality.

Usually the courts do not substitute judicial determination for administrative discretion. From his study of the United States Supreme Court's review of the decision of ten executive agencies during the period 1947–56, Tanenhaus (1960) concluded that the Court upheld federal agencies more frequently than it opposed them by a statistically significant degree. Nonetheless, the courts do provide a pervasive system of accountability. They offer an institutionalized access point for the redress of alleged grievances against bureaucratic agencies. Increasingly in the United States, individuals and groups are turning to the courts to fight policy battles lost in the bureaucracy. In the 1930s reformers commonly looked to the bureaucracy for the achievement of their goals. In the 1970s, however, groups like the environmentalists have increasingly asked the courts to reverse bureaucratic decisions they regard as injurious to the public.

A technique of controlling bureaucracy that has gained increasing prominence in European administrations is the use of an ombudsman as an intermediary between the individual citizen and public officials. The ombudsman has become popular where the remedies available through the judiciary or legislature were thought to be sporadic, cumbersome, or expensive for citizens who have a grievance against a bureaucracy. The ombudsman is utilized on the national level in several industrial nations, especially Scandinavia, with varying degrees of institutionalization and success (Rowat, 1968, 1973). There are many varieties of ombudsmen and the data on their operations and effectiveness is somewhat sketchy. Nonetheless, some tentative generalizations can be made. The ombudsman's capacity to assist citizens ultimately rests on the power of persuasion rather than the exercise of legal sanctions. To be successful, the ombudsman and his staff must be perceived by the public to be highly competent and above reproach (Gellhorn, 1966). Finally, both as a means of making its presence known to the public and as a potential sanction, publicity is very important to the operation of an ombudsman's office (Gellhorn, 1966; Stephens, 1970).

Informal external controls. The press has long played an oversight role with respect to the government in general and executive agencies in particular. While the press cannot itself impose sanctions, it has a substantial capacity to mobilize the public and other political participants who can exert continuing pressure on the bureaucracies. There are two broad aspects of press-bureaucracy relationships. The first is the external oversight role of the press acting in behalf of the public. One of the favorite self-images of reporters is that of crusading public defender (Broder, 1969). This oversight role, although among the most dramatic devices for securing bureaucratic accountability, is also the most sporadic. It is aimed at gross improprieties and examples of official malfeasance and nonfeasance—a reportorial tradition going back to the original muckrakers and beyond (Regier, 1932). It is thus a *post hoc* method of enforcing responsibility by causing sanctions to be levied by others on culpable officials.

The press also has a more internal role with regard to bureaucratic responsibility through its participation in bureaucratic politics. Most of the relationships between agencies and the press consist of the routine transmission of news, and this process contributes to bureaucratic responsibility by conveying information about the activities of government to the public. A less routine but extremely significant portion of this activity, however, consists of unofficial and informal contacts between officials and reporters and is most dramatically symbolized by the "leak" from official to reporter. This utilization of the press is an important tactic in bureaucratic politics. Officials use the press not out of vague sentiments about the public's right to know but rather to achieve the governmental actions they desire (Cater, 1959; Sigal, 1973). Bureaucrats whose policy preferences are vetoed by their superiors can bypass these superiors and appeal directly to the public through the press.

In terms of bureaucratic accountability there are two relevant characteristics of this use of the press in bureaucratic politics. First is the "whistle blowing" aspect. Lower level officials who perceive policies being formulated by their superiors that violate the law, legislative intent, or presidential directive can "short-circuit" the normal hierarchical relationships and use the press to force a change in policy direction or at least publicize the actual direction of policy (Nadel, 1971, pp. 191–214). Secondly, it is possible for top-level officials to use the press to publicize a decision in order to assure compliance by subordinates. It is far more difficult for subordinates to resist policy directives that have been widely publicized in this way (Sigal, 1973, pp. 131–50).

The use of the press to assure bureaucratic responsibility poses a dilemma in that it directly contravenes more formal theories of responsibility. When subordinates pursue their own version of the public interest or proper policy and undermine their superiors by leaking to the press, their action is contrary to bureaucratic responsibility as expressed in formal authority relationships. It may involve accountability to "higher" standards, but to the extent that it fragments administration it undermines responsibility to superiors and ultimately to elected political authority. However, when the claims of political superiors conflict with bureaucrats' understanding of their own responsibility to the law, the press can be used to enforce the more crucial standard of legal responsibility all the way up the hierarchical ladder (Greenberg, 1969; Hershey, 1973).

A recent form of externally imposed administrative responsibility is the activity in the United States of "public-interest" groups, usually led by lawyers, which rely on aggressive monitoring and litigation to influence bureaucratic behavior in specific areas. In areas like consumer protection and environmental policy, such groups have assumed the role of advocating widely shared interests in an attempt to counteract the superior access and influence enjoyed by narrower special-interest groups. Because of their ultimate strategy of influence, public-interest groups are instruments of administrative accountability rather than lobbying organizations. While traditional constituency groups have relied on persuasion to achieve their goals, public-interest lawyers have gone to the courts in order to *compel* bureaucrats to take or to refrain from certain actions. Thus, with the help of the courts, public-interest lawyers act as (unwelcome) enforcers of bureaucratic responsibility in terms of legal standards.

Finally among the informal external controls that can be exerted over bureaucracy is the constituency. An attentive constituency can provide either support or opposition based on administrative performance. It is therefore in an agency's interest to be responsive to its constituency and to seek or maintain jurisdictional boundaries that will allow it to satisfy its constituency. Holden (1966) argues that "bureaucratic imperialism," in the form of an agency's search for public support, can make a bureaucracy more representative of the community and more dynamic. Holden sees in bureaucratic competition essentially the same virtues that are claimed for the economic market, and he states: "Agency initiative in a competitive political atmosphere permits the dissatisfied to 'shop around' until they find somewhere in the administrative system agencies responsive to their claims" (Holden, 1966, p. 950). An even more competitive market method of control is preferred by Niskanen (1971), who argues for competition not only between agencies but between public agencies and private organizations. This, he asserts, would assure not only bureaucratic accountability but also the optimal distribution of public goods.

It should be noted, however, that constituency control assures bureaucratic behavior in accord with the needs of only the best organized and most attentive groups in the environment. The bureaucratic structure does not mirror the claims of all groups in proportion to their numbers and their needs, and some groups have to struggle long and hard to win organization and recognition in the bureaucratic apparatus. Groups that have a low socioeconomic status are particularly disadvantaged (Sjoberg, Brymer, and Farris, 1966). Constituency interests are frequently defined by the larger and more powerful organized interest groups. Thus, the United States Department of Agriculture defines its agricultural constituency in terms remarkably coincident with the interests of large corporate farming, and the Planning Commission in France tries to coordinate individual commercial sectors through relations with the largest 20 percent of its constituent firms (Shonfield, 1965). While the more openly competitive model urged by Niskanen tends to relieve excessive clientelism by breaking bureaucratic monopolies, as long as individual bureaucracies have control over the distribution of public goods the problem remains. Thus, reliance on constituency control can be dysfunctional for bureaucratic responsibility by leading an agency toward excessive clientelism, which diminishes accountability to a broader public.

Formal internal controls. There are several closely interrelated strategies for combining formality of control with internal administration of control. Basically these are the movements for representation, decentralization, and citizen participation. These strategies are closely related to each other and are frequently combined in reform proposals. Thus, citizen participation usually implies decentralized administration, and these two techniques are often conceived of as remedies for inadequate representation. All these strategies seek to ensure responsibility to prevailing social values by making the bureaucracy internally closer (in terms of attributes and geography) to the public (Krislov, 1974). It is assumed that those who fulfill the proper criteria of representativeness (up to and including direct participation) will automatically be responsible to the interests of those they represent.

The term *representative bureaucracy* was given early currency by Donald Kingsley (1944). Kingsley traced the dominance of the middle class in Britain's higher civil service. While showing some concern for the need for more working-class representation, Kingsley asserted that the middle class nonetheless reflected the dominant forces in society and thus could exercise power responsibly.

Subramaniam (1967) pointed out that there are two modes of thought in discussing representative bureaucracy. One is the ascriptive mode, in which the bureaucracy is representative of every economic, racial/ethnic, and regional group in exact proportion to the numbers of such people in the population. The other is "performance oriented," in which the bureaucracy is drawn from all groups in society but on the basis of ability.

It is this second mode that is characteristic of American bureaucracies and is the more prevalent notion of representative bureaucracy today. Thus, Van

Riper (1958, pp. 549–59) posits as requirements of representative bureaucracy that it consists of a cross section of the citizenry in terms of economic status, geography, and other relevant factors and be in tune with the prevailing social norms. Subramaniam concludes that under these criteria the United States does indeed have a representative bureaucracy, but this is because it is a middle-class bureaucracy in a primarily middle-class country. In his survey of six countries (the United States, Denmark, Britain, France, Turkey, and India) he found that people with middle-class origins occupy most of the posts of all these countries regardless of their stage of development simply because the middle class possesses the skills and advantages relevant to bureaucratic service. If, as Subramaniam argues, the United States civil service is representative of the middle-class nature of society, its responsiveness flows from factors other than mere representativeness, such as shared value concensus, occupational mobility, etc. Thus representative bureaucracy outside the United States and similar societies is unlikely and its benefits are tenuous.

The quest for representativeness in bureaucracy goes beyond a concern for bureaucratic responsibility. American bureaucracy has been viewed as being more representative of the diverse interests of the citizenry than Congress (Long, 1952) and as being in good measure responsible for the success of American democracy (Van Riper, 1958). Indeed, the demands for a more representative bureaucracy form a recurrent theme and one that is closely linked to demands for greater representation generally (Kaufman, 1956).

A frequently occurring structural component of the move for greater representation is bureaucratic decentralization. As a specific mode of bureaucratic responsibility, decentralization has been championed by both radicals and conservatives. Radicals view decentralization as a means of increasing the power of disadvantaged groups, which can then dominate the decentralized decision-making arena in which bureaucracies function. Conservatives seek to break up the concentrated power of bureaucracy and, sometimes, to increase decision making in arenas that they dominate. Inherent in the desire for decentralization is the assumption that administration will be more representative as the decision-making center is brought geographically closer to the constituency.

Citizen participation is necessarily coupled with decentralization but relies less on assumptions of automatic representation due to proximity. Not only must decision-making centers be geographically close to constituents, but they must be close in terms of the salient characteristics of the constituency—particularly race and economic status. In practice, decentralization is thus combined with the "ascriptive" mode of representation, or the "descriptive" representation in the typology of Hanna Pitkin (1972).

Decentralization and participation are seen by their proponents not only in terms of bureaucratic responsibility but as a mode of administration possessing other administrative virtues as well. Smith (1971), for example, argues the Aristotelian notion that participation is a viable method for reducing citizen alienation, which tends to be particularly prevalent in constituencies of large-scale social service bureaucracies. On more traditional grounds it has been found that increased community participation is related to bureaucratic innovation (Gittell and Hollander, 1968; Eckland, 1969).

Greater decentralization and participation are not without their costs, however. One observer found that Office of Economic Opportunity Community Action Organizations had excessively high organizational costs and urged that participatory mechanisms be designed to reflect the freely expressed cost valuations of all the people affected by programs (Kafoglis, 1968). Beyond considerations of cost and efficiency, there are two additional difficulties with such direct-representative programs. First, although it is a popular American conception, it is not always clear that democratic values are maximized by small units. In small units, political and other minorities may be even more isolated, and a seemingly homogeneous amalgamation of interests may mask real differences (McConnell, 1966). Thus, community control of schools and other relevant institutions in black neighborhoods may appear to maximize the political power of all blacks in the constituency. Yet, if some blacks do not share the values and policy preferences of those identified as "community leaders," the dissenting group will be even more powerless than when they were confronted by a centralized bureaucracy. Decentralization combined with increased participation may also accelerate the privatization of public affairs, or "interest group liberalism" (Lowi, 1969), since in the most extreme versions of community control essentially private groups may control public funds and programs.

Citizen participation can also raise other problems for existing bureaucratic organizations. As innumerable conflicts in such volatile areas as school and police administration have shown, citizen participation is viewed by civil servants as highly threatening to their values of professionalism and freedom from "political interference." Indeed, Herbert Kaufman (1969) has predicted that just as it did in the past, the demand for neutral competence will increasingly collide with the movement for greater representativeness as the interests of citizens and bureaucrats increasingly diverge.

Informal internal controls. It was primarily on informal internal controls that Friedrich pinned his greatest hopes for bureaucratic responsibility. There are primarily two modes through which such responsibility can be achieved. First are the combined perceptions and anticipations of bureaucrats. That is, while public opinion may be viewed as a force external to the agency, perceptions of public opinion and demands also form an internalized set of beliefs on the part of bureaucrats. Moreover, bureaucrats' perceptions of the general political ethos of their community serve as a guide to organizational decision making (Wilson, 1968). Bureaucratic behavior is also very much affected by the anticipated reactions of the public and politicians to contemplated actions. Ordinarily, bureaucrats are unwilling to go beyond public expectations of the permissible bounds of their behavior.

A second internal mode of control consists of the internalized professional norms of career civil servants. These norms can relate either to the bureaucratic organization itself or to broader norms of professional groups such as city managers, accountants, or engineers. For example, in the case of the city managers, there is an explicit professional code setting forth the responsibilities of managers and the bounds of their behavior.

An administrative agency can itself go a long way toward controlling the decisions of its own employees through an effective program of professional training. As Herbert Kaufman (1960) has shown with respect to the United States Forest Service, subordinate officials can be so thoroughly indoctrinated with an agency's policy goals that the exercise of their discretion can be relied on to mirror faithfully the objectives of the organization. This process of socialization to agency norms is accomplished through a uniform educational background, in-service training, and an agency manual that clearly delineates the choices appropriate in particular situations.

While Friedrich may have been right in asserting that in practice we have little choice but to rely on internalized norms, such reliance presents many problems. First, it may be objected that "to rely on a man's conscience is to rely on his accomplice" (Finer, 1941). Second, conformity to professional norms, particularly informal norms, may be in the interest of the bureaucratic group but be quite dysfunctional in terms of a wider public constituency. Thus it has been argued that the formal and informal norms of such social service bureaucracies as teachers (Kozol, 1967) and social workers (Steiner, 1966; Piven and Cloward, 1971) may be antithetical to their clientele. This problem of the clash between norms and responsibility is particularly acute in police bureaucracies. Thus, as evidenced by the findings of the Knapp Commission in New York City, corruption may become part of an internally sanctioned code of behavior. Also, as Skolnick (1966) found, there is a considerable gap between the dominant ethic of police professionalism (the maintenance of order) and the rule of law (due process). Thus, while good faith, internalization of societal and professional norms. and anticipated reactions may assure a considerable degree of responsibility, they may also exact substantial costs.

Internalized norms may also be inadequate for bureaucratic responsibility in a democracy on a more general level. There is evidence of a substantial body of antidemocratic attitudes even at the highest levels of the American civil service. In a survey of federal executives utilizing McClosky's (1964) earlier questionnaire items on democratic ideology, Wynia (1974) found that about one-third of the respondents agreed with most or all of the "antidemocratic" statements concerning freedom of speech, equality, and democratic rules of the game. Contrary to finding that internal socialization inculcates democratic values, Wynia found that antidemocratic sentiment increased with the length of time that executives had been in the bureaucracy. While such beliefs may indeed be representative of the population as a whole, it can still be argued that the more formal external checks on public officials are needed precisely because of these attitudes.

Trends of Bureaucratic Responsibility

In assessing the trends of thought concerning bureaucratic responsibility, it should be noted that there has been an increasing tendency toward treating governmental and nongovernmental bureaucracies in the same manner. Many of the newer methods of controlling bureaucracy apply to private as well as public organizations. For example, private companies like General Motors have been as much subject to surveillance by public interest groups as have executive agencies. Parallel to the demands for citizen participation in public bureaucracies have been demands for public representatives on corporate boards of directors (Herman, 1972). To take a more extreme case, there have even been arguments that corporations whose existence depends largely on defense contracts should be nationalized to assure accountability to elected political authority (Galbraith, 1973). Federal chartering of large corporations has been advanced as another means of tying these public-affecting private bureaucracies into the formal accountability of the political process.

Moreover, the economic market is coming to be regarded as a formidable mechanism of control over public as well as private bureaucracies. Although the market may be highly imperfect in concentrated industries in the private sphere, nonetheless it still presents a more immediate and direct sanction than any to which public agencies are normally subject. Hence there is increasing interest in the possibility of forcing public agencies to respond to their clientele by threatening them with loss of consumer patronage—through, for example, an educational voucher system. Methods of control over public and private organizations may thus be converging, as both public and private organizations find themselves increasingly subject to similar kinds of sanctions.

This is a highly desirable development from the point of view of some analysts who feel that public agencies should be guided by the same goals as business firms, such as profit maximization. This is the approach currently being taken in the so-called public-choice literature, which attempts to use economic models to improve our understanding of administrative behavior and decisions. Public-choice analysis is clearly one of the most innovative areas of research today (Niskanen, 1971; Ostrom, 1973; Ostrom and Ostrom, 1971; Wamsley and Zald, 1973). One author has made fruitful use of concepts drawn from economic theory in the study of American foreign policy (D. Davis, 1972). A basic assumption of the public-choice school is that the closer a public agency approximates a business firm in its decision making, the more responsive it will be to its constituents.

From a quite different point of departure, another group of authors has begun to stress the need for a more "humane" orientation on the part of public agencies. They argue that the role of bureaucratic organizations in promoting or damaging human welfare tends to be neglected when concern is centered on organizational output or productivity (Dvorin and Simmons, 1972). A collection of essays by younger writers in the field (Marini, 1971) strongly reflects this view. Thus, the effort to make bureaucracy more responsive or responsible stirs continuing ferment and is the principal focus of several new schools of thought in the field.

CONCLUSION: POWER, EFFECTIVENESS, AND RESPONSIBILITY

Inherent in all the modes of bureaucratic responsibility that we have examined there is a common problem. It is the familiar dilemma of reconciling accountability and responsiveness on the one hand with effectiveness and expertise on the other. Some proponents of the "new public administration" have argued that this places too negative a coloration on the matter and that administrative freedom of action is actually congruent with democratic politics (Harmon, 1971). In fact, there have been notable attempts to define bureaucratic responsibility in terms of maximizing the values of effectiveness and rationality. Thus, Norton Long (1954) acknowledged the problem of bureaucratic power that stems from expertise but argued that true responsibility requires bureaucratic rationality—an active bureaucratic role in establishing factual premises for political policymakers. Long asserted that both effectiveness and responsibility could be maximized by structuring bureaucracies to provide alternative points of view to political policymakers even to the extent of maintaining a "loyal opposition" within bureaucracies. Although this seems to skirt the problem of any trade-off between effectiveness and responsibility, it should be noted that his prescription would nonetheless increase decision-making costs within bureaucracies.

The fundamental dilemma can also be seen in the analysis of Victor Thompson (1961). Thompson argues that defining responsibility in hierarchical terms is an artificial device for apportioning blame. The real problem of organizations is the gap between authority and specialization—between those who have the right to make decisions and those who have the ability. It is this gap that leads to "bureaupathic" behavior. While yielding more decision-making power in the direction of expertise, as Thompson advocates, may alleviate problems within organizations, the essential problem of social control of expertise still remains. We are long past the era of automatic acceptance of the wisdom of specialized experts.

As we have noted throughout this chapter, the benefits of specialized expertise create both the need for and the power of bureaucracies. But in dealing with bureaucracies, the application of expertise is only one of the values that societies seek to maximize—it is not the only value. Effectiveness and political accountability are not mutually exclusive, but it is nonetheless true that there has been a continuous history of tension between these two values.[9] As Kaufman (1956, 1969) points out, there is a cycle in the values that society seeks to maximize—recurring periods during which one type of value (e.g., representativeness) is dominant in administrative organization while others remain as secondary values. Thus, the modes of bureaucratic responsibility are very much reflections of a particular era, and a combination of modes which is reflective of society at one time is less reflective at another time. Both within a particular society and across societies, the power and needs accruing from expertise and constituency strength have encountered various attempts at control in accord with other and broader social values.

NOTES

1.   Two way comprehensive surveys of the literature of organizations—public and private—are Gross (1964) and March (1965). For an annotated bibliography see McCurdy (1972).

2.   However, some writers such as Kolko (1969) see the military bureaucracy as the servant rather than the master of the outside industrial interests with which it is closely associated.

3.   See Albrow (1970) for a concise analysis of early theories of democracy and an excellent analysis of the development of social theory regarding bureaucracy.

4.   For further discussion see also the *Journal of Comparative Administration* 5 (August 1973 and February 1974), both issues of which are devoted to "Bureaucracy and Administration in Socialist States."

5.   For a general discussion see Montgomery and Siffin (1966).

6.   For an excellent analysis of the varying concepts of the public interest on a more general level see Benditt (1973). Benditt examines the concept in terms of the philosophical traditions of Rousseau and Bentham and addresses himself to the question of which policies can be said to be in the public interest. See also, Brian Barry (1967) and Virginia Held (1970).

7.   See Thomas and Baade (1970) for a comprehensive anthology of original essays on the various facets of the "institutionalized presidency."

8.   See L. Fisher (1972) for a comprehensive analysis of the relative balance of control exercised by the president and Congress over tax, tariff, budget, and war policy.

9.   On a more specific level, Wilson (1967) points out that the solution to one bureaucracy problem may be incompatible with the solution to another problem. For example, being responsive to the demands and needs of a constituency may contradict accountability to political superiors.

REFERENCES

Albrow, Martin (1970). *Bureaucracy*. New York: Praeger.

Aldrich, Howard (1972). "An organization-environment perspective on cooperation and conflict between organizations in the manpower training system." In Anant R. Negandhi (ed.), *Conflict and Power in Complex Organizations*. Kent, Ohio: Kent State University Center for Business and Economic Research.

Allison, Graham T. (1969). "Conceptual models and the Cuban missile crisis." *The American Political Science Review* 63:689–718.

—————— (1971). *Essence of Decision: Explaining the Cuban Missile Crisis*. Boston: Little, Brown.

Anderson, Patrick (1968). *The Presidents' Men*. Garden City, N.Y.: Doubleday.

Art, Robert J. (1973). "Bureaucratic politics and American foreign policy." *Policy Sciences* 4:467–90.

Bachrach, Peter, and Morton S. Baratz (1970). *Power and Poverty*. New York: Oxford University Press.

Barber, Richard J. (1970). *The American Corporation: Its Power, Its Money, Its Politics*. New York: Dutton.

Barry, Brian (1967). *Political Argument*. New York: Humanities Press.

Benditt, Theodore M. (1973). "The public interest." *Philosophy and Public Affairs* 2:291–311.

Benveniste, Guy (1972). *The Politics of Expertise*. Berkeley: Glendessary Press.

Benveniste, Guy, and Warren F. Ilchman, eds. (1969). *Agents of Change: Professionals in Developing Countries*. New York: Praeger.

Bernstein, Marver H. (1955). *Regulating Business by Independent Commission*. Princeton: Princeton University Press.

Blank, Stephen (1973). *Government and Industry in Britain: The Federation of British Industries in Politics, 1945–1965*. Lexington, Mass.: Heath.

Braybrooke, David, and Charles E. Lindblom (1963). *A Strategy of Decision*. New York: Free Press of Glencoe.

Broder, David (1969). "Political reporters in presidential politics." *Washington Monthly*, February 1969:1:20–33.

Cater, Douglass (1959). *The Fourth Branch of Government*. Boston: Houghton Mifflin.

Chamberlain, Lawrence H. (1946). *The President, Congress, and Legislation*. New York: Columbia University Press.

Cohen, Bernard C. (1973). *The Public's Impact on Foreign Policy*. Boston: Little, Brown.

Cox, Edward, Robert Fellmeth, and John Schulz (1969). *The Nader Report on the Federal Trade Commission*. New York: R. W. Baron.

Crenson, Matthew A. (1971). *The Unpolitics of Air Pollution*. Baltimore: Johns Hopkins University Press.

Cronin, Thomas E., and Sanford D. Greenberg (1969). *The Presidential Advisory System*. New York: Harper & Row.

Crozier, Michel (1964). *The Bureaucratic Phenomenon*. Chicago: University of Chicago Press.

Dahl, Robert A. (1972). "A prelude to corporate reform." *Business and Society Review* 1:17–23.

Dahl, Robert A., and Charles Lindblom (1953). *Politics, Economics and Welfare*. New York: Harper and Brothers.

Davis, David H. (1972). *How the Bureaucracy Makes Foreign Policy: An Exchange Analysis*. Lexington, Mass.: Heath.

Davis, James W., Jr., and Kenneth Dolbeare (1968). *Little Groups of Neighbors: The Selective Service System*. Chicago: Markham.

Davis, Kenneth C. (1969). *Discretionary Justice*. Baton Rouge: Louisiana State University Press.

Destler, I. M. (1972). *Presidents, Bureaucrats, and Foreign Policy*. Princeton: Princeton University Press.

Dewey, John (1927). *The Public and Its Problems*. Denver: Alan Swallow.

Diamant, Alfred (1973). "Bureaucracy and administration in Western Europe: a case of not-so-benign neglect." *Policy Studies Journal* 1:133–38.

Dittmer, Lowell (1974). "Revolution and reconstruction in contemporary Chinese bureaucracy." *Journal of Comparative Administration* 5:443–86.

Djilas, Milovan (1957). *The New Class*. New York: Praeger.

Downs, Anthony (1967). *Inside Bureaucracy*. Boston: Little, Brown.

Dvorin, Eugene P., and Robert H. Simmons (1972). *From Amoral to Humane Bureaucracy*. San Francisco: Canfield Press.

Eckland, Bruce C. (1969). "Public participation, innovation, and school bureaucracies." *Public Administration Review* 29:218–25.

Edelman, Murray (1964). *The Symbolic Uses of Politics*. Urbana: University of Illinois Press.

Eisenstadt, S. N. (1965). *Essays on Comparative Institutions*. New York: Wiley.

Esman, Milton (1966). "The politics of development administration." In John Montgomery and William Siffin (eds.), *Approaches to Development: Politics, Administration, and Change*. New York: McGraw-Hill.

Etzioni, Amitai (1964). *Modern Organizations*. Englewood Cliffs, N.J.: Prentice-Hall.

Feit, Edward (1973). *The Armed Bureaucrats*. Boston: Houghton Mifflin.

Fellmeth, Robert C. (1970). *The Interstate Commerce Omission*. New York: Grossman.

Fenno, Richard F., Jr. (1959). *The President's Cabinet*. Cambridge, Mass.: Harvard University Press.

——————— (1966). *The Power of the Purse*. Boston: Little, Brown.

Ferkiss, Victor C. (1969). *Technological Man*. New York: George Braziller.

Finer, Herman (1941). "Administrative responsibility in democratic government" *Public Administration Review* 1:335–50.

Fisher, Louis (1972). *President and Congress*. New York: Free Press.

Flash, Edward S., Jr. (1965). *Economic Advice and Presidential Leadership*. New York: Columbia University Press.

Foss, Phillip O. (1960). *Politics and Grass*. Seattle: University of Washington Press.

Frederickson, H. George (1971). "Toward a new public administration." In Frank Marini (ed.), *Toward a New Public Administration: The Minnowbrook Perspective*. Scranton, Pa.: Intext Press, Chandler Publishing Co.

Freeman, J. Leiper (1965). *The Political Process: Executive Bureau-Legislative Committee Relations*. New York: Random House.

Friedman, Robert S. (1971). *Professionalism: Expertise and Policy Making*. New York: General Learning Press.

Friedrich, Carl J. (1940). "Public policy and the nature of administrative responsibility." *Public Policy* 1:3–24.

Galbraith, John Kenneth (1967). *The New Industrial State*. Boston: Houghton Mifflin.

——————— (1973). "On the economic image of corporate enterprise." In Ralph Nader and Mark J. Green (eds.), *Corporate Power in America*. New York: Grossman.

Galloway, Jonathan (1972). *The Politics and Technology of Satellite Communications*. Lexington, Mass.: Lexington Books.

Gawthrop, Louis C. (1969). *Bureaucratic Behavior in the Executive Branch*. New York: Free Press.

Gellhorn, Walter (1966). *Ombudsmen and Others: Citizens' Protectors in Nine Countries*. Cambridge, Mass.: Harvard University Press.

George, Alexander M. (1972). "The case for multiple advocacy in making foreign policy." *American Political Science Review* 66:751–85.

Gerth, H. H., and C. Wright Mills (1946). *From Max Weber: Essays in Sociology*. New York: Oxford University Press.

Gilb, Corinne Lathrop (1966). *Hidden Hierarchies: The Professions and Government*. New York: Harper & Row.

Gilmour, Robert (1971). "Central legislative clearance: a revised perspective." *Public Administration Review* 31:150–59.

Gittell, Marilyn, and T. Edward Hollander (1968). *Six Urban School Districts: A Comparative Study of Institutional Response*. New York: Praeger.

Goodnow, Frank (1900). *Politics and Administration*. New York: Macmillan.

Gouldner, Alvin W. (1955). "Metaphysical pathos and the theory of bureaucracy." *American Political Science Review* 49:496–507.

Green, Mark J., and Ralph Nader (1973). "Economic regulation vs. competition." *Yale Law Journal* 82:871–89.

Greenberg, Gary (1969). "Revolt at Justice." *Washington Monthly* 1:32–40.

Grodzins, Morton (1963). "Local strength in the American federal system: the mobilization of public-private influence." In Marion Irish (ed.), *Continuing Crises in American Politics.* Englewood Cliffs, N.J.: Prentice-Hall.

Gross, Bertram (1964). *The Managing of Organizations.* New York: Free Press.

Gulick, Luther, and L. Urwick (1937). *Papers on the Science of Administration.* New York: Institute of Public Administration.

Halberstam, David (1973). *The Best and the Brightest.* New York: Random House.

Halperin, Morton H. (1974). *Bureaucratic Politics and Foreign Policy.* Washington, D.C.: Brookings Institution.

Halperin, Morton H., and Tang Tsou (1966). "United States policy toward the off-shore islands." *Public Policy* 15:119–38.

Halperin, Morton H., and Arnold Kanter (1973). *Readings in American Foreign Policy: A Bureaucratic Perspective.* Boston: Little, Brown.

Hammond, Paul Y. (1960). "The National Security Council as a device for interdepartmental coordination: an interpretation and appraisal." *American Political Science Review* 54:890–910.

Harmon, Michael M. (1969). "Administrative policy formulation and the public interest." *Public Administration Review* 29:483–91.

_____ (1971). "Normative theory and public administration: some suggestions for a redefinition of administrative responsibility." In Frank Marini (ed.), *Toward a New Public Administration: The Minnowbrook Perspective.* Scranton, Pa.: Intext Press, Chandler Publishing Co.

Harris, Joseph P. (1964). *Congressional Control of Administration.* Washington, D.C.: Brookings Institution.

Heady, Ferrel (1966). *Public Administration: A Comparative Perspective.* Englewood Cliffs, N.J.: Prentice-Hall.

Heady, Ferrel, and Sybil L. Stokes (1960). *Comparative Public Administration: A Selective Annotated Bibliography.* 2d ed. Ann Arbor: Institute of Public Administration, University of Michigan.

_____ (1962). *Papers in Comparative Public Administration.* Ann Arbor: Institute of Public Administration, University of Michigan.

Heilbroner, Robert L. (1972). *In the Name of Profit.* Garden City, N.Y.: Doubleday.

Held, Virginia (1970). *The Public Interest and Individual Interests.* New York: Basic Books.

Herman, E. S. (1972). "The greening of the board of directors." *Quarterly Review of Economics and Business* 12:87–95.

Herring, E. Pendleton (1936). *Public Administration and the Public Interest.* New York: McGraw-Hill.

Hershey, Gary (1973). *Protest in the Public Service.* Lexington, Mass.: Heath.

Hirschman, Albert O. (1970). *Exit, Voice, and Loyalty.* Cambridge, Mass.: Harvard University Press.

Holden, Matthew (1966). "Imperialism in bureaucracy." *American Political Science Review* 60:943–51.

Holtzman, Abraham (1970). *Legislative Liaison: Executive Leadership in Congress*. Chicago: Rand McNally.

Hoopes, Townsend (1969). *The Limits of Intervention*. New York: McKay.

Huntington, Samuel P. (1952). "The marasmus of the I.C.C.: the commission, the railroads, and the public interest." *Yale Law Journal* 61:467–509.

─────────── (1957). *The Soldier and the State*. Cambridge, Mass.: Harvard University Press.

─────────── (1961). *The Common Defense*. New York: Columbia University Press.

Jacoby, Neil H. (1973). *Corporate Power and Social Responsibility*. New York: Macmillan.

Janis, Irving L. (1972). *Victims of Groupthink*. Boston: Houghton Mifflin.

Jones, Charles O. (1972). "The limits of public support: air pollution agency development." *Public Administration Review* 32:502–8.

Kafoglis, M. L. (1968). "Participatory democracy in the Community Action Program." *Public Choice* 5:73–85.

Kaufman, Herbert (1956). "Emerging conflicts in the doctrines of public administration." *American Political Science Review* 50:1057–73.

─────────── (1960). *The Forest Ranger*. Baltimore: Johns Hopkins University Press.

─────────── (1969). "Administrative decentralization and political power." *Public Administration Review* 29:3–15.

─────────── (1973). *Administrative Feedback*. Washington, D.C.: Brookings Institution.

Kaufman, William W. (1964). *The McNamara Strategy*. New York: Harper & Row.

Kennan, George F. (1947). "The sources of Soviet conduct." *Foreign Affairs* 25:566–82.

─────────── (1967). *Memoirs 1925–1950*. Boston: Little, Brown.

Kingsley, J. Donald (1944). *Representative Bureaucracy*. Yellow Springs, Ohio: Antioch Press.

Kissinger, Henry A. (1969). *American Foreign Policy*. New York: Norton.

Kohlmeier, Louis M. (1969). *The Regulators*. New York: Harper & Row.

Kolko, Gabriel (1963). *The Triumph of Conservatism: A Reinterpretation of American History, 1900–1916*. New York: Free Press.

─────────── (1969). *The Roots of American Foreign Policy*. Boston: Beacon Press.

Kozol, Jonathan (1967). *Death at an Early Age: The Destruction of the Hearts and Minds of Negro Children in the Boston Public Schools*. Boston: Houghton Mifflin.

Krasner, Stephen D. (1972). "Are bureaucracies important?" *Foreign Policy* 7:159–79.

Krislov, Samuel (1974). *Representative Bureaucracy*. Englewood Cliffs, N.J.: Prentice-Hall.

Landau, Martin (1969). "Redundancy, rationality, and the problem of duplication and overlap." *Public Administration* 29:346–58.

Lijphart, Arend (1968). *The Politics of Accommodation: Pluralism and Democracy in the Netherlands.* Berkeley: University of California Press.

Lindblom, Charles E. (1965). *The Intelligence of Democracy.* New York: Free Press.

Lineberry, Robert L., and Edmund P. Fowler (1967). "Reformism and public policies in American cities." *American Political Science Review* 61:701–16.

Long, Norton (1949). "Power and administration." *Public Administration Review* 9:257–64.

_____ (1952). "Bureaucracy and constitutionalism." *American Political Science Review* 46:808–18.

_____ (1954). "Public policy and administration: the goals of rationality and responsibility." *Public Administration Review* 14:22–31.

_____ (1962). *The Polity.* Chicago: Rand McNally.

Lowi, Theodore J. (1964). "American business, public policy, case studies and political theory." *World Politics* 16:677–715.

_____ (1969). *The End of Liberalism.* New York: Norton.

_____ (1972). "Four systems of policy, politics and choice." *Public Administration Review* 32:298–310.

Manley, John F. (1968). "Congressional staff and public policymaking: the Joint Committee on Internal Revenue Taxation." *The Journal of Politics* 30: 1046–67.

March, James G., ed. (1965). *Handbook of Organizations.* Chicago: Rand McNally.

Marini, Frank, ed. (1971). *Toward a New Public Administration: The Minnowbrook Perspective.* Scranton, Pa.: Intext Press, Chandler Publishing Co.

Mazmanian, Daniel A. and Mordecai Lee (1975). "Tradition be damned! the Army Corps of Engineers is changing." *Public Administration Review* 35:166–172.

McClosky, Herbert (1964). "Consensus and ideology in American politics." *American Political Science Review* 58:361–82.

McConnell, Grant (1966). *Private Power and American Democracy.* New York: Knopf.

McCurdy, Howard E. (1972). *Public Administration: A Bibliography.* Washington, D.C.: College of Public Affairs, American University.

Means, Gardiner C. (1962). *Pricing Power and the Public Interest: A Study Based on Steel.* New York: Harper and Brothers.

Melman, Seymour (1970). *Pentagon Capitalism.* New York: McGraw-Hill.

Merriam, Charles (1944). *Public and Private Government.* New Haven: Yale University Press.

Michels, Robert (1911). *Political Parties.* New York: Collier Books.

Mintz, Morton (1967). *By Prescription Only.* Boston: Beacon Press.

Montgomery, William D., and William J. Siffin (1966). *Approaches to Development: Politics, Administration, and Change.* New York: McGraw-Hill.

Mosca, Gaetano (1896). *The Ruling Class.* English translation by Hannah Kahn. New York: McGraw-Hill, 1939.

Nadel, Mark V. (1971). *The Politics of Consumer Protection*. Indianapolis: Bobbs-Merrill.

——— (1975). "The hidden dimension of public policy: private governments and the policy making process." *Journal of Politics* 37:2–34.

Neustadt, Richard E. (1954). "Presidency and legislation: the growth of central clearance." *American Political Science Review* 48:641–71.

——— (1955). "Presidency and legislation: planning the president's program." *American Political Science Review* 49:980–1021.

——— (1960). *Presidential Power: The Politics of Leadership*. New York: Wiley.

——— (1963). "Approaches to staffing the presidency: notes on FDR and JFK." *American Political Science Review* 57:855–64.

——— (1970). *Alliance Politics*. New York: Columbia University Press.

Neustadt, Richard E., and Graham T. Allison (1971). "Afterword." In Robert F. Kennedy, *Thirteen Days*. New York: Norton.

Niskanen, William A. (1971). *Bureaucracy and Representative Government*. Chicago: Aldine-Atherton.

Noll, Roger (1971). *Reforming Regulation: An Evaluation of the Ash Council Proposals*. Washington, D.C.: Brookings Institution.

Nugent, Jan (1968). "Unheralded committees molding statistics." *Journal of Commerce*, 26 November 1968, p. 3.

Orren, Karen (1972). *Corporate Power and Social Change: The Politics of the Life Insurance Industry*. Baltimore: Johns Hopkins University Press.

Ostrom, Vincent (1973). *The Intellectual Crisis in American Public Administration*. University, Ala.: University of Alabama Press.

Ostrom, Vincent, and Elinor Ostrom (1971). "Public choice: a different approach to the study of public administration." *Public Administration Review* 31:203–16.

Peabody, Robert L., and Francis E. Rourke (1965). "Public bureaucracies." In James G. March (ed.), *Handbook of Organizations*. Chicago: Rand McNally.

Pempel, T. J. (1974). "The bureaucratization of policy making in post-war Japan." *American Journal of Political Science* 18:647–64.

Phelan, James, and Robert Pozen (1973). *The Company State*. New York: Grossman.

Pitkin, Hannah (1972). *The Concept of Representation*. Berkeley: University of California Press.

Piven, Francis F., and Richard A. Cloward (1971). *Regulating the Poor: The Functions of Public Welfare*. New York: Random House.

Pressman, Jeffrey L., and Aaron Wildavsky (1973). *Implementation*. Berkeley: University of California Press.

Price, Don K. (1941). "The promotion of the city manager plan." *Public Opinion Quarterly* 5:563–78.

——— (1965). *The Scientific Estate*. Cambridge, Mass.: Harvard University Press.

Raphaeli, Nimrod, ed. (1967). *Readings in Comparative Public Administration*. Boston: Allyn & Bacon.

Redford, Emmette S. (1954). "The protection of the public interest with special reference to administrative regulation." *American Political Science Review* 48:1103–13.

—————— (1969). *The Regulatory Process: With Illustrations from Civil Aviation*. Austin: University of Texas Press.

Reedy, George (1970). *The Twilight of the Presidency*. New York: World Publishing.

Regier, C. C. (1932). *The Era of the Muckrakers*. Chapel Hill: University of North Carolina Press.

Reich, Charles (1964). "The new property." *Yale Law Journal* 73:733–87.

Reinemer, Vic (1970). "Budget Bureau: do advisory panels have an industry bias?" *Science* 169:36–39.

Riggs, Fred W. (1964). *Administration in Developing Countries*. Boston: Houghton Mifflin.

Rossiter, Clinton (1960). *The American Presidency*. New York: Harcourt Brace.

Rourke, Francis E. (1954). "The Department of Labor and the trade unions." *Western Political Quarterly* 7:656–72.

—————— (1961). *Secrecy and Publicity: Dilemmas of Democracy*. Baltimore: Johns Hopkins University Press.

—————— (1970). "The domestic scene." In Robert E. Osgood *et al.* (eds.), *America and the World*. Baltimore: Johns Hopkins University Press.

—————— (1972). *Bureaucracy and Foreign Policy*. Baltimore: Johns Hopkins University Press.

Rowat, Donald C. (1973). *The Ombudsman Plan: Essays on the Worldwide Spread of an Idea*. Toronto: McClelland and Stewart.

——————, ed., (1968). *The Ombudsman: Citizen's Defender*. London: Allen and Unwin.

Saloma, John S. III (1969). *Congress and The New Politics*. Boston: Little, Brown.

Schattschneider, Elmer E. (1960). *The Semisovereign People*. New York: Holt, Rinehart and Winston.

Schick, Allen (1969). "Systems politics and systems budgeting." *Public Administration Review* 29:137–51.

Schilling, Warner R. (1961). "The H-bomb decision: how to decide without actually choosing." *Political Science Quarterly* 76:24-46.

—————— (1964). "Scientists, foreign policy, and politics." In Robert Gilpin and Christopher Wright (eds.), *Scientists and National Policy Making*. New York: Columbia University Press.

Schlesinger, Arthur M., Jr. (1959). *The Coming of the New Deal*. Boston: Houghton Mifflin.

—————— (1965). *A Thousand Days*. Boston: Houghton Mifflin.

Schubert, Glendon (1960). *The Public Interest*. Glencoe: Free Press.

Schwartz, Bernard (1959). *The Professor and the Commissions*. New York: Knopf.

Schwartz, Herman (1965). "Governmentally appointed directors in a private corporation—the Communications Satellite Act of 1962." *Harvard Law Review* 79:350–64.

Scott, Andrew M. (1970). "Environmental change and organizational adaptation." *International Studies Quarterly* 14:85–94.

Selznick, Phillip (1949). *TVA and the Grass Roots*. Berkeley: University of California Press.

——————— (1957). *Leadership in Administration*. Evanston, Illinois: Row, Peterson.

Shapiro, Martin (1968). *The Supreme Court and Administrative Agencies*. New York: Free Press.

Shonfield, Andrew (1965). *Modern Capitalism: The Changing Balance of Public and Private Power*. New York: Oxford University Press.

Sigal, Leon V. (1973). *Reporters and Officials: The Organization and Politics of Newsmaking*. Lexington, Mass.: Heath.

Simon, Herbert (1957). *Administrative Behavior*. 2d ed. New York: Macmillan.

——————— (1960). *The New Science of Management Decision*. New York: Harper & Row.

Sjoberg, Gideon, Richard G. Brymer, and Buford Farris (1966). "Bureaucracy and the lower class." *Sociology and Social Research* 5:325–37.

Skolnick, Jerome H. (1966). *Justice without Trial*. New York: Wiley.

Smith, Michael P. (1971). "Alienation and bureaucracy: the role of participatory administration." *Public Administration Review* 31:658–64.

Snow, C. P. (1961). *Science and Government*. Cambridge, Mass.: Harvard University Press.

Sorauf, Frank (1957). "The public interest reconsidered." *Journal of Politics* 19:616–39.

Steiner, Gilbert Y. (1966). *Social Insecurity: The Politics of Welfare*. Chicago: Rand McNally.

Stephens, J. H. (1970). "Hawaii's ombudsmen." *National Civic Review* 59:81–84, 105.

Stone, Alan (1973). "The FTC and advertising regulation: an examination of agency failure." *Public Policy* 21:203–34.

Strauss, Eric (1961). *The Ruling Servants*. New York: Praeger.

Subramaniam, V. (1967). "Representative bureaucracy: a reassessment." *American Political Science Review* 61:1010–19.

Tanenhaus, Joseph (1960). "Supreme Court attitudes toward federal administrative agencies." *The Journal of Politics* 22:502–24.

Thomas, Norman C., and Hans W. Baade, eds. (1970). "The institutionalized presidency." *Law and Contemporary Problems* 35:427–665.

Thompson, Victor A. (1961). *Modern Organization*. New York: Knopf.

Thomson, James C., Jr. (1968). "How could Vietnam happen? an autopsy." *The Atlantic Monthly* 221:47–53.

Truman, David B. (1951). *The Governmental Process.* New York: Knopf.

Tullock, Gordon (1970). *Private Wants, Public Means.* New York: Basic Books.

Turner, James (1970). *The Chemical Feast.* New York: Grossman.

United States Senate, Committee on Government Operations (1973). *Federal Advisory Committees, First Annual Report of the President to Congress.* Washington, D.C.: U.S. Government Printing Office.

United States Senate, Select Committee on Small Business (1969). *Competitive Problems in the Drug Industry.* Hearings before the Subcommittee on Monopoly. 91st Cong., 1st sess.

Van Riper, Paul (1958). *History of the United States Civil Service.* Evanston: Row, Peterson.

Waldo, Dwight (1964). *Comparative Public Administration: Prologue, Problems, and Promise.* Chicago: Comparative Administration Group, American Society for Public Administration.

Wamsley, Gary L., and Mayer N. Zald (1973). *The Political Economy of Public Organizations.* Lexington, Mass.: Heath.

Weaver, Warren (1967). *U.S. Philanthropic Foundations.* New York: Harper & Row.

Weinstein, James (1968). *The Corporate Ideal in the Liberal State (1900–1918).* Boston: Beacon Press.

White, Leonard (1927). *The City Manager.* Chicago: University of Chicago Press.

_____ (1948). *The Federalists: A Study in Administrative History.* New York: Macmillan.

_____ (1954). *The Jacksonians (1829–61): A Study in Administrative History.* New York: Macmillan.

_____ (1957). *The Jeffersonians (1801–29): A Study in Administrative History.* New York: Macmillan.

Wildavsky, Aaron (1974). 2d ed. *The Politics of the Budgetary Process.* Boston: Little, Brown.

_____ (1966). "The political economy of efficiency." *Public Administrative Review* 26:292–310.

_____ (1969). "Rescuing policy analysis from PPBS." *Public Administration Review* 29: 189–202.

Wilensky, Harold (1967). *Organizational Intelligence.* New York: Basic Books.

Wilson, James (1967). "The bureaucracy problem." *The Public Interest* 6:3–9.

_____ (1968). *Varieties of Police Behavior.* Cambridge, Mass.: Harvard University Press.

Wilson, Woodrow (1887). "The study of administration." *Political Science Quarterly* 2:197–222.

Winter, Ralph K., Jr. (1973). "Economic regulation vs. competition: Ralph Nader and creeping capitalism." *Yale Law Journal* 82:890–902.

Wynia, Bob L. (1974). "Federal bureaucrats' attitudes toward a democratic ideology." *Public Administration Review* 34:156–62.

Yarmolinsky, Adam (1971). *The Military Establishment: Its Impact on American Society*. New York: Harper & Row.

INDEX